A Guide to Publications on the Book of Mormon

A Selected Annotated Bibliography

Edited by
Donald W. Parry
Jeanette W. Miller
Sandra A. Thorne

Foundation for Ancient Research and Mormon Studies
Provo, Utah

The Foundation for Ancient Research and Mormon Studies
P.O. Box 7113
University Station
Provo, Utah 84602

© 1996 The Foundation for Ancient Research and Mormon Studies
All rights reserved
Printed in the United States of America
02 01 00 99 98 97 96   10 9 8 7 6 5 4 3 2 1

ISBN: 0-934893-20-9

Contents

Introduction	v
Key to Abbreviations	vii
Key to Annotation Authors	vii
Annotations	1
Addendum: 1994–1995 Bibliography	363
Appendix: Book of Mormon Editions and Translations	373
Subject Index	377

Introduction

Since its original publication in 1830, the Book of Mormon has elicited intense curiosity and interest. Thousands of published articles and books have been written about the book's origins and its contents. Many of the book's responses have been passionate, both in praise and criticism.

Serving both as the keystone and as a foundational document for the restoration of the Church of Jesus Christ of Latter-day Saints, the volume has influenced the lives of a great many who accept it to be a revelation from God, and who shape their lives according to its contents. Many contemporaries of Joseph Smith, the book's translator, accepted the book to be a divine work and a record of ancient Americans who were visited by the resurrected Jesus Christ. One early convert, Parley P. Pratt, describes his first reaction to the book: "I opened it with eagerness.... I commenced to read its contents by course. I read all day; eating was a burden, I had no desire for food; sleep was a burden when the night came, for I preferred reading to sleep. As I read, the spirit of the Lord was upon me, and I knew and comprehended that the book was true." (Susan Easton Black, *Stories from the Early Saints: Converted by the Book of Mormon* [Salt Lake City, UT: Bookcraft, 1992], 64.) To members of the Church of Jesus Christ of Latter-day Saints (LDS), now numbering more than nine million adherents, the Book of Mormon stands with the Bible as canonized scripture. An LDS article of faith states, "We believe the Bible to be the word of God . . . we also believe the Book of Mormon to be the word of God."

Others do not share that same belief. On 29 June 1829, even before the book was published, a reporter for the *Wayne Sentinel* wrote: "[The book] is generally known as the 'Golden Bible.' Most people entertain an idea that the whole matter is the result of a gross imposition, and a grosser superstition." On 27 February 1830 the *Palmyra Reflector* announced that "the Book of Mormon has been placed in our hands. A viler imposition was never practiced. It is an evidence of fraud [and] blasphemy." Two months later the *Rochester Daily Advertiser,* dated 2 April 1830, featured this statement about the Book of Mormon: "It is frequently remarked that any scheme, however gross, will find more or less dupes."

The Book of Mormon has continued to arouse such intense interest and such passionate divisions for more than 160 years. Many individuals maintain that "the golden bible" is a fraudulant work while others believe or bear testimony that it is a record brought forth by the hand of God. Truly, as B. H. Roberts long ago stated, the Book of Mormon on the one hand remains to many "an enigma, a veritable literary sphinx" and to others it is "a revelation from God" that "will minister spiritual consolation" and draw individuals "into closer communion with God" (*New Witness for God,* 3:406).

Regardless of the many different approaches to the Book of Mormon, the book has seen heavy distribution since its publication. It has been translated into some ninety-six languages, including such languages as Bislam, Palauan, Chamorro, Urdu, Shona, Lingala, Braille, and Gilbertese (see the Appendix for a complete listing of translations) and it is presently being published and distributed in scores of languages.

The primary goal of the *Guide to Publications on the Book of Mormon* is to produce an extensive annotated listing of published items to help students in their study of this book of scripture. This work was created by selecting from the *Comprehensive Annotated Book of Mormon Bibliography* (also published by the Foundation) those items that were judged of most use to students of the scriptures who are not professional scholars. The chief categories not included in this selected bibliography are anti-Mormon literature, materials that have been outdated by more recent studies, and less substantive materials, such as pamphlets and news articles. What remains are more than 3000 entries that will guide the reader to worthwhile literature about the Book of Mormon.

Published items that have been annotated include articles and book reviews from journals, periodicals, books, full-length books and monographs, pamphlets, reports, dramatic plays, and a number of poetic pieces. Also included are a few substantive newspaper articles and selected unpublished pieces, such as theses and dissertations. The items fall into five categories: (1) General Studies—materials dealing with history, literature, linquistics, textual studies, political studies, archaeology, anthropology, philosophy, law, sociology, and geography; (2) Religion—materials dealing with theology, morality and ethics, practical religion, exhortation, doctrine, testimony, instructional aid, evangelism, devotional approaches, comparative religion, scriptural studies, and the Bible; (3) Polemics—a limited number of materials that are responses to critical publications; (4) Fiction—selected materials written for children and youth, theatrical productions and plays, poetry, novels, and similar writings; and (5) Book reviews.

Each entry includes (as appropriate) author's name, title, volume number, editor(s), facts of publication, page numbers, and a brief annotation. The annotation is designed to reflect a simple statement of the contents. It is not intended to be a critical review nor is it meant to be a complete summary or outline. The bibliography is arranged alphabetically by author. A subject index, located at the back of the volume, links a variety of Book of Mormon topics with bibliographic entries.

We have also included an Addendum and an Appendix in the volume. The Addendum comprises unannotated bibliographic entries of Book of Mormon materials published within the past several months, after our self-imposed cutoff date for the creation of annotations. This includes articles and books published in 1994 through the first half of 1995. The Appendix features a listing of Book of Mormon translations.

This is not an exhaustive bibliography. Complete indexes do not exist for a number of journals and periodicals, including the *Relief Society Magazine, Millennial Star, Saints Herald, Church News, Conference Report, Deseret News, LDS Messenger and Advocate, Wasp, Nauvoo Neighbor, Liahona, The Elders' Journal, Women's Exponent, Young Woman's Journal, Society for Early Historic Archaeology Newsletter, Times and Seasons,* and *University Archaeological Society Newsletter,* thereby making the task of collecting articles dealing with the Book of Mormon more difficult. Within these journals and periodicals the annotators manually sought items written about the Book of Mormon, no doubt missing a number of entries along the way.

We wish to extend our gratitude to those who made the publication of this work possible. We are grateful to John W. Welch, Gary Gillum, and DeeAnn Hofer for permitting us to use, as our starting point, their *Comprehensive Bibliography of the Book of Mormon: Arranged Alphabetically by Author* (Provo, UT: FARMS, 1987). We thank all of the annotators who physically reviewed every item in this bibliography and then created an annotation for that entry. Although this task was enormous, it was accomplished with skill and competence. Their voluntary service will be valued and appreciated by hundreds of students of the Book of Mormon for many years to come.

We also thank Melvin J. Thorne, executive editor, and others of the editorial staff of the Foundation for Ancient Research and Mormon Studies for their editorial work, fine-tuning, formatting, and copy editing. Finally, we are indebted to the Foundation for Ancient Research and Mormon Studies for providing various resources to enable us to complete this work.

It is our hope that the publication of this bibliography will foster further Book of Mormon research, and that it will facilitate quality studies. There are, no doubt, facets of the Book of Mormon yet unrecognized, understandings yet to be brought to light.

Key to Abbreviations

CN	Church News
CWHN	Nibley, Hugh. *The Collected Works of Hugh Nibley.* 13 vols. Salt Lake City: Deseret Book and FARMS, 1986-1994.
CR	Conference Report
DN	Deseret News
Dialogue	*Dialogue: Journal of Mormon Thought*
IE	*Improvement Era*
JD	*Journal of Discourses.* Liverpool, England: Albert Carrington, 1882. Lithographed by Gartner Printing, Los Angeles, California, 1956.
M&A	*LDS Messenger and Advocate*
Liahona	*Liahona, The Elders' Journal*
MS	*Millennial Star*
NE	*New Era*
SH	*Saints' Herald*
SEHA	*Society for Early Historic Archaeology Newsletter*
BYUSY	*BYU Speeches of the Year*
TS	*Times and Seasons*
UASN	*University Archaeological Society Newsletter*
Witness	*The Witness: Newsletter of the Foundation for Research on Ancient America*
ZR	*The Zarahemla Record*

Key to Annotation Authors

A.A.	Alan Ashton
A.A.L.	Amy Aurelie LaFranca
A.C.W.	Anita Cramer Wells
A.L.	Adam Lamoreaux
A.T.	Andrew Teasdale
B.D.	Brian Dickman
B.R.M.	Bruce R. Murdock
B.T.	Burke Theurer
B.W.J.	Bradley W. Jacobsen
C.C.	Cie J. Christian
C.F.C.	Carolyn F. Cannon
C.W.B.	Christina Welch Broberg
D.H.M.	Dan H. Matthews
D.L.L.	David L. Laughlin
D.M.	Daniel B. McKinlay
D.S.T.	David S. Taylor
D.W.P.	Donald W. Parry
E.G.	Erin Gilbert
G.A.	Gary Anderson
J.A.T.	John A. Tvedtnes
J.L.S	John L. Sorenson
J.W.M.	Jeanette W. Miller
J.W.W.	John W. Welch
K.M.	Kerry M. Muhlestein
L.D.	Lisa S. Dickman
L.M.	Laramie Merritt
M.D.P.	Matthew D. Parry
M.R.	Matthew Roper
N.K.Y.	N. Keith Young
P.H.	Paul Hoskisson
R.C.D.	Reed C. Durham Jr.
R.H.B.	Russell H. Ball
R.J.L.	Robert John Lefrandt
R.S.	Royal Skousen
S.P.S.	Scott P. Sharp
S.H.	Susan Hamilton

Annotations

A.

A.001 "Aaron Teaches Lamoni's Father." *Friend* 23 (March 1993): 32-33. Scenes from Aaron's conversion of King Lamoni's father illustrated in color for children. [S.H.]

A.002 Abdo, Michael J. "There's Room in My Chart Bag." *Ensign* 19 (September 1989): 67-68. While flying in an airplane from Brazil to Africa, the author tells of the joy of sharing a most priceless possession (the Book of Mormon) with someone who gave him aid. [J.W.M.]

A.003 "Abinadi and King Noah." *Friend* 12 (March 1982): 27-29. Cartoon for children presenting the story of Abinadi. [J.W.M.]

A.004 Adams, George J. *Joseph Smith Jr.'s Rare Reprints*. Burlington, WI: n.p., 1991. A copy of a "Lecture on the authenticity and scriptural character of the Book of Mormon," written by George J. Adams in 1844. Confirms that the Book of Mormon is not the only scripture accepted by the Church, the Mormons also believe the Bible "as far as it has been translated correctly." [L.D.]

A.005 Adams, L. LaMar. "I have a Question: Many non-LDS scholars claim that the second half of the book of Isaiah was written after the time Lehi left Jerusalem. Yet the Book of Mormon contains material from both halves. How do we explain this?" *Ensign* 14 (October 1984): 29. Disputes the claims of multiple and late authorship of the book of Isaiah and cites a literary style analysis claiming that "there is a unique authorship style throughout the various sections of Isaiah." [S.P.S.]

A.006 Adams, William James. "Some Ways in Which the 'Plain and Precious Parts' Became Lost." *SEHA* 159 (July 1985): 1-6. Finds that ancient scribes, both non-biblical and biblical, took many liberties in their translations. Suggests that up to 30 percent of the original text of the Old Testament may have been deleted as the angel told Nephi would occur (1 Nephi 13:23). [J.W.M.]

A.007 Affleck, Gordon Burt. "Testimonial Trustworthiness (Witnesses to the Book of Mormon)." *Instructor* 101 (December 1966): 490-92. In a credibility test for witnesses, the following standards must be met: honesty, ability, number and consistency, conformity of testimony with experience, and coincidence of their testimony with collateral circumstances. The Three and Eight Witnesses fulfill all of these requirements. [A.C.W.]

A.008 Alexander, Thomas G. "New Testament, Christianity and the Book of Mormon." *Sunstone* 12 (July 1988): 6-7. Argues that assisting people through "governmental measures" or "charity" is consistent with basic principles of Christianity, the Constitution, and free agency. [L.D.]

A.009 Allen, James B., and Glen M. Leonard. *The Story of the Latter-day Saints*. Salt Lake City: Deseret Book, 1976. Authors present (on pages 31-46) an "introductory overview" of Moroni's visit to Joseph Smith, and the subsequent translation and publication of the Book of Mormon. [D.W.P.]

A.010 Allen, Joseph L. "A Comparative Study of Quetzalcoatl, the Feathered-Serpent God of

Meso-America, with Jesus Christ, the God of the Nephites." M.A. thesis, Brigham Young University, 1970. A dissertation that draws on Spanish historical accounts, archaeological evidence, and the Book of Mormon scriptures. Draws parallels between Quetzalcoatl and Jesus Christ, suggesting that they may have been the same divine individual. Discusses the problems and possibilities of making the comparison. [J.W.M.]

A.011 Allen, Joseph L. *Exploring the Lands of the Book of Mormon.* Orem, UT: BYU Print Services, 1989. Describes the languages, history, geography, and culture of some of the peoples described within the Book of Mormon, and presents a number of possible sites where this ancient civilization actually lived. [L.D.]

A.012 "Alma Teaches About Faith." *Friend* 23 (November 1993): 15. Color illustrations for children of scenes from Alma's sermon on faith. [S.H.]

A.013 "American Antiquities." *TS* 3 (15 July 1842): 858-60. Presents a comparison of many of the metals, animals, and plants mentioned in the Book of Mormon with similar things found in the United States. [L.D.]

A.014 "American Antiquities: Corroborative of the Book of Mormon." *MS* 21-22 (1 January 1859–2 June 1860): 12-14, 28-30, 48-50, 64-66 161-63, 177-78, 193-94, 209-210, 226-27, 240-42, 258, 273-74, 306-7, 321-23, 370-71, 401-3, 433-34, 449-51, 467, 513-14, 546, 577-79, 593-95, 625-26, 657-58, 689-91, 706, 737-38, 786-87, 818-19, 835-36, 13-14, 30, 61-63, 77-78, 93-94, 124-27, 173-75, 158-59, 188-90, 206-7, 220-23, 237-39, 285-86, 300-301, 316-18, 349-50. Provides evidence to confirm the authenticity of the Book of Mormon. Describes the contents of the Book of Mormon and archaeological findings and discoveries, such as ancient cities, temples, and altars, tools, and wells. [J.W.M.]

A.015 "American Antiquities—More Proofs of the Book of Mormon." *TS* 2 (15 June 1841): 440-42. A report of two lectures on Central America by Mr. Catherwood who reports his findings at the sites of Copan, Santa Cruz del Quiche, Gueque Tenago, Ocosingo, Palenque, and Uamal. Sees proof that a nation skilled in the arts and sciences once resided in America. [B.D.]

A.016 "Ammon Meets King Lamoni's Father." *Friend* 23 (January 1993): 40-41. Scenes from Ammon's encounter with King Lamoni's father illustrated in color for children. [S.H.]

A.017 "Anachronisms and the Book of Mormon." *IE* 52 (October 1949): 644, 659-60. Discusses anachronisms or errors of time that would have occurred in the Book of Mormon had it been an uninspired book and shows that the Book of Mormon is the word of God because it lacks anachronisms. [L.D.]

A.018 Anderson, D. Brent, and Diane E. Wirth. "Book of Mormon Authorship." In *Encyclopedia of Mormonism*, edited by Daniel H. Ludlow, 166-67. New York: Macmillan, 1992. Critics claim that the Book of Mormon was an invention of Joseph Smith written from his own experiences. This claim has been proven false because of the book's complexity, harmony with ancient customs and languages, ancient poetic forms, and wordprinting [stylometry] studies. The time of composition of less than ninety days confirms translation as the only reasonable means to write the book. [N.K.Y.]

A.019 Anderson, Edward Henry. "Editors Table: How About It?" *IE* 30 (September 1927): 1050-51. Encourages Church members to read the Book of Mormon within the next sixty days and testifies that peaceful feelings will accompany the reading of it. [B.D.]

A.020 Anderson, Edward Henry. "Hagoth's Lost Ships and Hawaii." *IE* 27 (March 1924): 482-83. The episode about Hagoth and his sea-venturing ships is quoted from Alma 63 and the theory advanced that the Polynesians descended from Book of Mormon peoples who sailed to Hawaii. Compares rituals and customs of the ancient Hawaiians with the Israelites. [D.M.]

A.021 Anderson, Edward Henry. "How Are the American Indians Related to the Jews." *IE* 23 (March 1920): 453-54. The Book of Mormon points out that through marriages the Nephites united with the Mulekites who were of Jewish descent. Hence the tribe of Joseph (Nephites) mixed with the tribe of Judah (Mulekites) in a union that is presently found among the American Indians. [J.W.M.]

A.022 Andersen, H. Verlan. "Bring Up Your Children In Light and Truth." *Ensign* 21 (October 1991): 80-81. The Book of Mormon instructs parents to teach their children the gospel before the age when they can be tempted. They have a great ability to understand profound spiritual things. [J.W.M.]

A.023 Andersen, H. Verlan. *The Great and Abominable Church of the Devil*. Orem, UT: H. Verlan Andersen, 1972. Nephi and John the Revelator saw "the Great and Abominable Church of the Devil" that is operated by Satan, will eventually control every nation, and will make war on the Lord's church in the last days. A division will occur between the devil's church and the Lord's church that will cuminate in war. [J.W.M.]

A.024 Andersen, H. Verlan. *Many Are Called But Few Are Chosen*. Orem, UT: H. Verlan Andersen, 1967. The Book of Mormon foretells the rise of the United States of America and its divinely inspired constitution. In order for Latter-day Saints to exercise their freedom of religion the God-inspired government must be maintained. The Book of Mormon provides the pattern for maintaining the constitution and the freedom of governing oneself. [J.W.M.]

A.025 Anderson, Henry. *The First Americans: A Pictorial Version of the Book of Mormon*. Independence, MO: Herald House, 1947. A cartoon-style story of the Book of Mormon for children. [J.W.M.]

A.026 Anderson, Jack Northman. "Take It from a Famous Explorer." *IE* 47 (February 1944): 82, 118-20. Presents archaeological evidence of the Book of Mormon. Introduces the similarities between the religion of the Incas and Christianity, and a possible connection between the ancient Sumerians and the inhabitants of ancient America. [J.W.M.]

A.027 Anderson, James H. "Book of Mormon Promises and Promises," in Anderson's *God's Covenant Race—A Selection of Addresses*, 161-87. Salt Lake City: Deseret News, 1946. Teaches that the truthfulness of the Book of Mormon is proven through scientific, historical, doctrinal, and prophetic means. The Book of Mormon prophesies of the destiny of the United States. [J.W.M.]

A.028 Anderson, James H. "The Book of III Nephi." *IE* 27 (January 1924): 193-99. The teachings in the New Testament Gospels and 3 Nephi are harmonious, and events recorded in the New Testament have found some historical parallels with events listed in the Book of Mormon. Further, the great earthquakes and other upheavals of recent decades are comparable to the three days of darkness in America during the time of Jesus' crucifixion. [D.M.]

A.029 Anderson, James H. "The Book of III Nephi." *Young Woman's Journal* 35 (January 1924): 11-16. Discusses highlights in 3 Nephi regarding the birth of Jesus and his appearance to the Nephites. Shows historical instances outside of 3 Nephi that deal with thick darkness. [D.M.]

A.030 Anderson, James H. "Explanation For the Scriptural Word 'Stick.'" *DN* (20 February 1932): 6. The use of the term "stick" in Ezekiel 37 does not refer to books as some have suggested, but it has reference to nations, i.e., the stick of Judah is the Jewish nation and the stick of Ephraim is the Ephraimite nation. [A.T.]

A.031 Anderson, James H. "Fulfillment of Book of Mormon Prophecies." *MS* 91 (5 September 1929): 561-67. The Book of Mormon accepts the Bible to be a true record. Christ's teachings are similar in both because he visited America. Among the future events named in the Book of Mormon are the gathering of Israel, the awakening of Mexican Indians, and the removal of the "scales of Darkness" from the eyes of the Indians. [J.W.M.]

A.032 Anderson, James H. "Sariah, Mother of the American Remnant of Joseph." In Anderson's *The Present Time and Prophecy*, 592-603. Salt Lake City, UT: Deseret News, 1933. Sariah was the wife of Lehi, a member of a covenant family, the mother of the American Indians, and one of two "goodly parents" (1 Nephi 1:1). She played a vital role in the family's exodus from Jerusalem. [J.W.M.]

A.033 Anderson, Kenneth W. "What Parents Should Teach Their Children from the Book of Mosiah." In *The Book of Mormon: Mosiah, Salvation Only through Christ*, edited by Monte S. Nyman and Charles D. Tate Jr., 23-36. Provo, UT: Brigham Young University Religious Studies Center, 1991. Presents five simple, scriptural lessons from the book of Mosiah that parents can teach their children. [B.D.]

A.034 Andersen, Kent R. *The Glowing Stones*. Independence, MO: Herald House, 1977. An illustrated children's book describing the experiences of the brother of Jared. [D.W.P.]

A.035 Anderson, Lawrence O. "Joseph Smith: A Student of American Antiquities." *UASN* (30 January 1963): 1-7. Joseph Smith had a deep interest in archaeological discoveries and antiquities of ancient America as can be seen from his writings, sermons, and personal conversations. He seemed to show particular interest in the discoveries in Central America as proof of Nephite and Lamanite existence. The ruined city of Quirigua he believed was the same as the city of Zarahemla. [J.W.M.]

A.036 Anderson, Richard Lloyd. "Book of Mormon Witnesses." In *Encyclopedia of Mormonism*, edited by Daniel H. Ludlow, 214-16. New York: Macmillan, 1992. There were three primary witnesses to the Book of Mormon—Oliver Cowdery, David Whitmer, and Martin Harris—all of whom describe an angel showing them the records and a voice from heaven affirming the translation. The Three Witnesses were later excommunicated from the Church with two eventually rejoining, but none ever denied their testimony. Eight other witnesses testify that Joseph Smith showed them the gold plates. [N.K.Y.]

A.037 Anderson, Richard Lloyd. "By the Gift and Power of God." *Ensign* 7 (September 1977): 79-85. The translation of the Book of Mormon required the work of Joseph Smith in conjunction with the inspiration of the Holy Ghost. It was a work consisting of "considerable spiritual, intellectual, and physical labor." Those who desire to receive the benefits of the Book of Mormon must also set forth "considerable spiritual, intellectual, and physical labor." [J.W.M.]

A.038 Anderson, Richard Lloyd. "The Certainty of the Skeptical Witnesses." *IE* 72 (March 1969): 62-67. Martin Harris, a witness of the validity of the existence of the gold plates, stood firm in his testimony of the Book of Mormon and gave his report to all who would listen. [J.W.M.]

A.039 Anderson, Richard Lloyd. "Confirming Records of Moroni's Coming." *IE* 73 (September 1970): 4-8. Presents an analysis of the five published accounts of Moroni's visits with Joseph Smith on the night of September 21-22, 1823. These accounts were dictated to secretaries with known record-keeping skills. The article carefully examines eight elements of the vision to create a composite description. [J.W.M.]

A.040 Anderson, Richard Lloyd. "Cowdery, Oliver." In *Encyclopedia of Mormonism*, edited by Daniel H. Ludlow, 1:335-40. 5 vols. New York: Macmillan, 1992. Oliver Cowdery was second witness to many important events of the restoration, one of the Three Witnesses of the Book of Mormon, as well as scribe during the book's translation. [J.W.M.]

A.041 Anderson, Richard Lloyd. "The Credibility of the Book of Mormon Translators." In *Book of Mormon Authorship: New Light on Ancient Origins*, edited by Noel B. Reynolds, 213-37. Provo, UT: Brigham Young University Religious Studies Center, 1982. An examination of the historical evidence that gives credibility to Joseph Smith and Oliver Cowdery as they translated the Book of Mormon. Anderson argues through documentation that Joseph's and Oliver's private lives and activities were perfectly consistent with public statements they made. [L.D.]

A.042 Anderson, Richard Lloyd. "David Whitmer, The Independent Missouri Businessman." *IE* 72 (April 1969): 74-76, 78-81. Fifty years of the non-Mormon life of David Whitmer, one of the witnesses of the Book of Mormon, is discussed and his character explored. [J.W.M.]

A.043 Anderson, Richard Lloyd. "Did Oliver Cowdery, One of the Three Special Witnesses of the Book of Mormon, Express Doubt about His Testimony?" In *A Sure Foundation: Answers To Difficult Gospel Questions,* 39-45. Salt Lake City, UT: Deseret Book, 1988. Oliver Cowdery's "strong testimony of the Book of Mormon is well documented throughout his life." Both his wife Elizabeth Ann Whitmer and brother-in-law, David Whitmer, were witnesses of this fact. [J.W.M.]

A.044 Anderson, Richard Lloyd. "Five Who Handled the Plates." *IE* 72 (July 1969): 38-47. A review of five of the Eight Witnesses who handled the golden plates—the four Whitmer brothers and Hiram Page. The testimony of the five witnesses never failed. "In fellowship or alienation, youth or age, persecution, poverty or affluence, four Whitmer brothers and Hiram Page never altered their plain testimony that they handled the original metal record of the Book of Mormon." [B.W.J.]

A.045 Anderson, Richard Lloyd. "Gold Plates and Printer's Ink." *Ensign* 6 (September 1976): 71-76. Details the procedures and personalities behind the emergence of the Book of Mormon in New York and Pennsylvania, from the catalyst leading to the Moroni's vision to the time the book came off the press. [D.M.]

A.046 Anderson, Richard Lloyd. "I Have a Question: Did Oliver Cowdery, one of the three special Book of Mormon witnesses, express doubt about his testimony?" *Ensign* 17 (April 1987): 23-25. It is well documented that Oliver Cowdery's testimony as a Book of Mormon witness remained strong throughout his life. Some documents exist that purport to be records of Cowdery's denial of his testimony, but the author argues that these were fabricated after his death. [S.P.S.]

A.047 Anderson, Richard Lloyd. "Imitation Gospels and Christ's Book of Mormon Ministry." In *Apocryphal Writings and the Latter-day Saints,* edited by C. Wilfred Griggs, 53-107. Provo, UT: Brigham Young University Religious Study Center, 1986. Compares and contrasts apocryphal writings, Dead Sea Scrolls, Nag Hammadi library, and others with "Christ's Book of Mormon ministry." Discusses the resurrection, and the message and personality of Christ. [A.T.]

A.048 Anderson, Richard Lloyd. *Investigating the Book of Mormon Witnesses.* Salt Lake City: Deseret Book, 1980. An investigative historical summary of each of the Three Witnesses, Oliver Cowdery, David Whitmer, Martin Harris, and the Eight Witnesses. Provides a rebuttal to various arguments against the personal character of the witnesses. [A.T.]

A.049 Anderson, Richard Lloyd. "Martin Harris, The Honorable New York Farmer." *IE* 72 (February 1969): 18-21. The character of Martin Harris, one of the Three Witnesses of the Book of Mormon, is examined. The author examines accounts of the associates of Martin Harris in the three decades he lived in Palmyra, New York. [J.W.M.]

A.050 Anderson, Richard Lloyd. "The Mature Joseph Smith and Treasure Searching." *BYU Studies* 24 (Fall 1984): 489-546. Studies the later years of Joseph Smith's life and disproves the theory that the Prophet continued searching for treasure after 1827. Several primary documents are examined, including the letter from Joseph Smith to Josiah Stowell in 1825 and Martin Harris's letter in 1830 to William W. Phelps. [L.D.]

A.051 Anderson, Richard Lloyd. "Most Interviewed Witness." *IE* 72 (May 1969): 76-83. David Whitmer represents "the last surviving witness" of the Book of Mormon plates. This article presents a number of interviews with Whitmer by various figures who interrogated him at times throughout his life. [B.W.J.]

A.052 Anderson, Richard Lloyd. "Oliver Cowdery's Testimony." *Ensign* 17 (April 1987): 23-25. Anderson evaluates two documents—"A Confession of Oliver Overstreet" and "Defence in a Rehearsal of my Grounds for Separating Myself from the Latter Day Saints"—which claim to discredit Oliver Cowdery's testimony of the Book of Mormon, and argues that the documents were fabricated after the death of Cowdery. [D.L.L.]

A.053 Anderson, Richard Lloyd. "The Religious Dimension of Emma's Letters to Joseph." In *Joseph Smith: The Prophet, the Man,* edited by Susan Easton Black and Charles D. Tate Jr., 117-25. Provo, UT: Brigham Young University Religious Studies Center, 1993. Emma Smith shares many religious items in her letters to her husband Joseph Smith, including the fact that she touched the plates of the Book of Mormon as they lay wrapped in a linen cloth. Emma never doubted the divinity of the Book of Mormon. [J.W.M.]

A.054 Anderson, Richard Lloyd. "Religious Validity: The Sacramental Covenant in Third Nephi." In *By Study and Also by Faith,* edited by John M. Lundquist and Stephen D. Ricks, 2:1-51. Salt Lake City: Deseret Book and FARMS, 1990. Compares and contrasts the baptismal and sacramental covenants as presented in 3 Nephi to sacramental observances and beliefs as viewed by early and current Christians, from the New Testament setting to contemporary times. Similarities in New Testament and Book of Mormon teachings are shown, and differences in these views from current Christian practices are presented. Changes in the ordinances through history are documented. The personal nature of the sacramental covenant is discussed and the related principles of remembering the Savior and keeping his commandments are emphasized in relation to receiving his Spirit. [A.A.]

A.055 Anderson, Richard Lloyd. "Reuben Miller: Recorder of Oliver Cowdery's Reaffirmations." *BYU Studies* 8 (Spring 1968): 277-93. When Oliver Cowdery rejoined the LDS Saints, he gave a speech in 1848 at Council Bluffs, in which he discounted the Spaulding theory and testified that he transcribed the Book of Mormon as Joseph Smith dictated it and that an angel showed to him the plates and the interpreters. Reuben Miller recorded and published Cowdery's speech. Anderson looks at the background and integrity of Miller and determines that the recording of Cowdery's speech by Miller was accurate and correct. [L.D.]

A.056 Anderson, Richard Lloyd. "The Scribe as a Witness." *IE* 72 (January 1969): 53-59. An in-depth review of sources regarding Oliver Cowdery's testimony of the Book of Mormon. Gives details of the translation of the Book of Mormon and the disaffection and rebaptism of Cowdery. [B.W.J.]

A.057 Anderson, Richard Lloyd. "The Second Witness of Priesthood Restoration." *IE* 71 (September 1968): 15, 16, 18, 20-22, 24. In addition to Oliver Cowdery's testimony of the Book of Mormon, his testimony of the restoration of the two priesthoods is of great value. As newly-appointed editor of the Church newspaper he wrote an account in installments of the translation of the Book of Mormon. As a part of this series he told of John the Baptist's visit to restore the Aaronic priesthood. [J.W.M.]

A.058 Anderson, Richard Lloyd. "Smiths Who Handled the Plates." *IE* 72 (August 1969): 28-32. Many of the Smiths were witnesses of the gold plates, including Emma Smith, Lucy Mack Smith, William Smith, Joseph Smith, Sr., Hyrum Smith, and Samuel Harrison Smith. [J.W.M.]

A.059 Anderson, Ronald D. "*Leitworter* in Helaman and 3 Nephi." In *The Book of Mormon: Helaman through 3 Nephi 8, According to Thy Word,* edited by Monte S. Nyman and Charles D. Tate Jr., 241-49. Provo, UT: Brigham Young University Religious Studies Center, 1992. As in the Bible, a common literary device in the Book of Mormon is the repetition of a single word or brief phrase that acts as guiding theme words (*Leitworter*). Some words used in this way are: *remember, pondering, O Lord, Saith the Lord, a curse, riches,* and *your destruction is made sure.* [J.W.M.]

A.060 Andrus, Hyrum L. "The Call of a Modern Prophet—New Witness For Christ and Founding the New Dispensation." In Andrus's *God, Man, and the Universe,* 33-93. Salt Lake City: Bookcraft, 1968. Provides history of the early life and call of Joseph Smith, Moroni's visit, the Book of Mormon's fulfillment of biblical prophecy, its coming forth, translation and publication, the Anthon transcript and loss of the 116 pages, and the restoration of the priesthood. [J.W.M.]

A.061 Andrus, Hyrum L. *God, Man, and the Universe*. Salt Lake City: Bookcraft, 1968. Chapters two through four relate the history of the coming forth of the Book of Mormon. Contains excerpts from Joseph Smith's *History of the Church, History of Wayne County,* Lucy Mack Smith and various other historical sources. [J.W.M.]

A.062 "Another Witness." *MS* 100 (24 February 1938): 120-21. Stresses that the Book of Mormon, which has come through the house of Joseph, stands as a second witness of Jesus Christ. [R.H.B.]

A.063 "Answers to Interesting Questions." *IE* 2 (April 1899): 467-72. Discusses why parts of Moroni 7 and 10 are similar to sections of I Corinthians 12 and 13. Also answers why the Book of Mormon is called the stick of Ephraim, given the fact that Lehi was a descendant of Manasseh. [D.M.]

A.064 "An Apostate—But a Friend to the Book of Mormon." *Ensign* 16 (February 1986): 76-77. Discusses a letter written by Mormon apostate William E. McLellin in 1880 verifying his testimony of the Book of Mormon by stating that the Book of Mormon is "one of the truest, purest books on earth." [L.D.]

A.065 Archaeological Research Committee. "Archaeology Alert." *Witness* 67 (Winter 1989): 15. Reports a Maya codex that was discovered in a typical home, suggesting that common people were literate. This reportedly confirms the Book of Mormon indication that many people could read. Also reported is the discovery of Ponta de Chimino, "one of the most heavily fortified sites in the ancient Maya world." This and other sites "call to mind a way of defense designed by Chief Captain Moroni." [B.D.]

A.066 Archaeological Research Committee. "La Mojarra: A Voice from the Past." *Witness* 64 (February 1989): 4-6. The La Mojarra stela, a monument found November 1986 in the Acula River southeast of Veracruz, Mexico, is said to exhibit characteristics of Egyptian art and the "Hebrew literary device," chiasmus. [B.D.]

A.067 "Archaeological Testimony of the Book of Mormon." *Relief Society Magazine* 7 (November 1920): 665-71. Draws parallels between Book of Mormon peoples and ancient civilizations in Central and South America. Twelve reasons are given why Catlin, in the work entitled *North American Indians*, thought that the American Indians were descendants of the Hebrews. [J.W.M.]

A.068 *Archaeology and the Book of Mormon*. Provo, UT: Department of Seminaries and Institutes of Religion, LDS Church, 1966. The Book of Mormon explains ancient civilizations of the New World. It is a history of three early migrations from the Old World to the New. Testing the Book of Mormon on archaeological and historical terms corroborates the Book of Mormon and elucidates archaeological and historical finds. [J.W.M.]

A.069 Arnold, Marilyn. "Book of Enos." In *Encyclopedia of Mormonism*, edited by Daniel H. Ludlow, 1:148. 5 vols. New York: Macmillan, 1992. Enos, the son of Jacob, grandson of Lehi, recorded his own touching testimony and the promises that the Lord made to him concerning the Nephite records and his Nephite and Lamanite brothers. His mighty efforts to pray brought him a remission of his own sins. [J.W.M.]

A.070 Arnold, Marilyn. "Book of Jarom." In *Encyclopedia of Mormonism*, edited by Daniel H. Ludlow, 1:148. 5 vols. New York: Macmillan, 1992. The Book of Jarom was written by Jarom, son of Enos, who excuses his brevity by calling attention to limited space and lack of new doctrine. [J.W.M.]

A.071 Arnold, Marilyn. "Book of Omni." In *Encyclopedia of Mormonism*, edited by Daniel H. Ludlow, 1:148. 5 vols. New York: Macmillan, 1992. The Book of Omni records the brief writings of several authors, Omni, Amaron, Chemish, Abinadom, and Amaleki, who were not spiritual leaders, but were descendants of Jacob. [J.W.M.]

A.072 Arnold, Marilyn. "The Nephi We Tend to Forget." *Ensign* 8 (January 1978): 69-71. Nephi, the grandson of Helaman, led the church at the time of Christ's birth and appearance to the Nephites (3 Nephi 1:2). Mormon's abridgment of Nephi's record reveals that Nephi was a man of great faith, an overpowering preacher, and a courageous, effective leader of the church at a climactic time in the earth's history. [D.H.M.]

A.073 Arnoldson, A. J. *Book of Mormon Guide: With References Given so Plainly That a Child Could Understand Them.* Salt Lake City: n.p., 1931?. Presents an anthology of scriptural references from the Book of Mormon that pertain to the various doctrines, including the plan of redemption, baptism, law of Moses, and the coming of Christ. [D.W.P.]

A.074 Arnoldson, Larry M. "Making the Book of Mormon Study Irresistible." In *A Symposium on the Book of Mormon*, 24-25. Salt Lake City: Church of Jesus Christ of Latter-day Saints, 1979. Proposes a method to involve and interest students in Book of Mormon study that includes problem solving and finding answers to questions in the book. [N.K.Y.]

A.075 Arrington, Leonard J., and Joann Jolley. "The Faithful Young Family." *Ensign* 10 (August 1980): 52-57. After purchasing a Book of Mormon from Samuel Smith, brother of Joseph Smith, Phinehas Young thought it his duty to prove the book a fraud. He thought Joseph must have been deceived and read the book to discover the errors and save the people from the deception. He was soon convinced otherwise and recommended the book to his devoutly religious family, including Brigham Young, who joined the Church. [J.W.M.]

A.076 "Article." *M&A* 1 (February 1835): 77. Praises Orson Pratt's skills in explaining and defending the Book of Mormon. [D.M.]

A.077 "As I View the Thing, Mormonism and the Book of Mormon in the American Schoolroom." *IE* 44 (September 1941): 539, 65. Discusses and quotes at length Sam Tucker, a columnist of the *Decative Herald* in Illinois, who suggests that the Book of Mormon and Mormonism be taught in courses of religious instruction in the public schools. Tucker argues that (1) the Book of Mormon is the American Bible, and (2) the stories of the Book of Mormon and Mormon history are very exciting. [L.D.]

A.078 Asay, Carlos E. "Opposition to the Work of God." *Ensign* 11 (November 1981): 67-69. Three accounts of anti-Christs recorded in the Book of Mormon suggest ways to prevent individuals from being drawn in by Satan and his servants. The accounts instruct individuals to keep the commandments, avoid those who tear down faith, follow the living prophets, refrain from contending over doctrine, search the scriptures, stay true to the mission of the Church, pray for one's enemies, practice pure religion, and remember that some things must be taken on faith. Opposition to the Church has a refining influence, indicates that the work is divine, and is bound to fail because the cause of the Church is just. [J.W.M.]

A.079 Asay, Carlos E. "Words of Christ: A Liahona." *CR* (October 1978): 77-81. The words of Christ that are revealed in the scriptures must become, for each individual, a personal compass or liahona, giving light and guidance to the path of eternal life. Similarly, each individual must heed the words of the living prophet, for his words are the words of Christ. [R.C.D.]

A.080 Ashment, Edward H. "The Book of Mormon and the Anthon Transcript: An Interim Report." *Sunstone* 5 (May-June 1980): 29-31. Points out that the reformed Egyptian language in which the Book of Mormon was written was not new but was following a tradition. The Egyptian language of the brass plates was changed according to the manner of speech prevalent in the days of Nephi. Contains a comparison between the Anthon transcript and Micmac Indian script. [J.W.M.]

A.081 Ashment, Edward H. "The Book of Mormon—A Literal Translation?" *Sunstone* 5 (March-April 1980): 10-14. Examines the method of the translation of the Book of Mormon and provides second-hand statements made after the book's publication describing the method by which Joseph Smith accomplished the translation. Concludes that the translation was conceptual, not literal word for word. [J.W.M.]

A.082 Ashton, Marvin J. "Murmur Not." In *BYUSY* (9 December 1969). Provo, UT: BYU Press. The destructive influence of murmuring is explored. One principal difference between Laman and Lemuel and their brother Nephi was that the two older brothers possessed the habit of murmuring and finding fault. [J.W.M.]

A.083 Ashton, Marvin J. " 'Neither Boast of Faith Nor of Mighty Works.' " *Ensign* 20 (May 1990): 65-67. Also *CR* (March/April 1990): 82-85. Helaman told his sons, Lehi and Nephi, to refrain from boasting. Similarly, Church members should not proclaim their own achievements, but give honor to Heavenly Father and Jesus who have made accomplishment possible. Humble, quiet, compassionate service provides its own soul-satisfying rewards. [J.W.M.]

A.084 Ashton, Wendell J. " 'That Which I Have Written Is True.' " *MS* 97 (8 August 1935): 506-8. Ambrose R. Winch, through reading and manually copying a borrowed copy of the Book of Mormon, was converted to the Church. [R.H.B.]

A.085 Aston, Warren P., and Michaela J. Aston. "And We Called the Place Bountiful." Provo, UT: FARMS, 1991. Through an employment of historical and scriptural evidences, "this study concludes that an objective and precise identification of [the Book of Mormon] Bountiful with a present-day location is now feasible and introduces data on physical traces revealing very early human involvement at the site." [A.T.]

A.086 Aston, Warren P., and Michaela J. Aston. "The Place Which Was Called Nahom." Provo, UT: FARMS, 1991. A place in Yemen called Nehem, called such from the pre-Islamic era, may be the location of Nahom mentioned in the Book of Mormon. [A.T.]

A.087 Aston, Warren P., and Michaela J. Aston. "The Search for Nahom and Lehi's Trail." Provo, UT: FARMS, 1989. "Examines historical, geographical, and archaeological evidence which helps specify the location of Nahom and thus also of Bountiful." Determines that Nahom was most likely close to the wadi Jave in the present day Yemen Arab Republic. Argues against Dhofar as the location of Bountiful, as has been proposed by the Hiltons. The probable location for Bountiful is along the Hadramaut coast. [A.T.]

A.088 Aston, Warren P., Michaela Aston, Stephen D. Ricks, and John W. Welch. "Lehi's Trail and Nahom Revisited." In *Reexploring the Book of Mormon*, edited by John W. Welch, 47-52. Salt Lake City: Deseret Book and FARMS, 1992. Speculates on different possible sites for Nahom in Lehi's route to the Americas. [D.M.]

A.089 Avery, W. B. E. "A Letter on the Book of Mormon." *MS* 98 (17 September 1936): 605. A letter by a non-member of the Church who was impressed by the Book of Mormon and after reading it understood more fully what Mormons believe. [M.D.P.]

Axelgard, Frederick W. "1 and 2 Nephi: An Inspiring Whole." *BYU Studies* 26 (Fall 1986): 53-65. With so much emphasis on studying single words, phrases, verses, and short scriptural pericopes by scriptural commentators and scholars, "the holistic approach to the study of scriptural texts" is often ignored. Doctrinal/historical/literary themes are brought forward with greater force and are better understood when whole chapters or entire sections of scripture are considered by the student of the scriptures. To prove the point of his thesis, the author proposes that 1 and 2 Nephi should be seen as "an inspiring whole" by examining the recurring themes, evident correlations, and obvious connections, which unify all the segments and parts that make up these two books. [D.W.P.]

B.

B.001 Bachman, Danel W. "Anthon Transcript." In *Encyclopedia of Mormonism*, edited by Daniel H. Ludlow, 1:43-44. 5 vols. New York: Macmillan, 1992. The Anthon Transcript was a piece of paper that Martin Harris took to Professor Charles Anthon, professor of classical languages at Columbia College in 1828. It contained a sample of characters transcribed from the gold plates by Joseph Smith; it also contained a translation thereof. Martin Harris desired a scholarly opinion before investing time and money in the translation of the plates. [J.W.M.]

B.002 Backman, Milton V., Jr. *Eyewitness Accounts of the Restoration.* Orem, UT: Grandin Book, 1983. A narrative of the first vision, the coming forth of the Book of Mormon, visits of Moroni and other heavenly messengers assigned to instruct Joseph during the period 1823-1827 are presented using Joseph Smith's four written histories in conjunction with other accounts written by Lucy Smith, Orson Pratt, Oliver Cowdery, and others. Also provides observations and recollections concerning Joseph Smith during the period of the translation and publication of the Book of Mormon. [J.W.M.]

B.003 Backman, Milton V. Jr. "Joseph Smith and the Restitution of All Things." In *Joseph Smith: The Prophet, the Man*, edited by Susan Easton Black and Charles D. Tate Jr., 89-99. Provo, UT: Brigham Young University Religious Studies Center, 1993. The Book of Mormon was a great tool in restoring a religion that welded Old and New Testament doctrines, bringing about a restitution of all things. It contained the practices, doctrine, power, and authority of the primitive church. [J.W.M.]

B.004 Badlam, A. "A Cunning Device Detected." *TS* 1 (January 1840): 47. Contains an interview with Solomon Spaulding's widow, Matilda Davidson, and daughter, Mrs. McKinistry, concerning the Spaulding manuscript's connection with the Book of Mormon. The wife and daughter saw little resemblance between the two documents, thinking there may have been a similarity in some names. [D.M.]

B.005 Baer, James L. "The Third Nephi Disaster: A Geological View." *Dialogue* 19 (Spring 1986): 127-32. A scientific, geological answer to the question, "Could the disastrous events described in 3 Nephi 8 have really taken place?" The author concludes that the entire scene could indeed be explained by "a gigantic earthquake with attendant storms and volcanic activity" that would accompany such a catastrophic event in nature. [J.W.M.]

B.006 Bagley, C. Stuart. "A New Approach to the Geography of the Book of Mormon." In *14th Symposium on Archaeology of the Scriptures*, 70-86. Provo, UT: Brigham Young University, 1963. Book of Mormon lands are located in Mesoamerica. Many Book of Mormon sites are discussed, one of which, the city of Nephi, is located in the peninsula of Yucatan. A map is also provided. [B.D.]

B.007 Bagley, Pat. *If You Were a Boy in the Time of the Nephites.* Salt Lake City: Deseret Book, 1989. An imaginative children's activity book designed for boys, suggesting possible Nephite culture from a modern American point of view. [D.M.]

B.008 Bagley, Pat. *If You Were a Girl in the Time of the Nephites.* Salt Lake City: Deseret Book, 1989. An entertaining children's activity book geared to LDS girls, showing what life may have been like for their Nephite counterparts. Contains mazes, word games, and various puzzles. [D.M.]

B.009 Bahlinger, Heidi. "A German Girl's Prayer Answered." *NE* 5 (April 1975): 10-12. A story of a German girl who was converted to the Gospel by the Book of Mormon after praying to find out if it was true. [M.D.P.]

B.010 Bailey, George H. "What the Book of Mormon Means to Me." *MS* 90 (3 May 1928): 286-88. A testimonial of the truthfulness of the Book of Mormon. Provides a very brief account of the contents of the Book of Mormon and shares the lessons learned and the spiritual strength received by the author from the Book of Mormon. [A.T.]

B.011 Bailey, H. Deloyd, comp. *The Standard Works Digest* (Index to General Authority comments on scriptural verses). U.S.A.: H. D. Bailey, 1986. A collection of scriptural references from more than 225 books, magazines, and commentaries that reviews how the General Authorities of the Church of Jesus Christ of Latter-day Saints have used given scriptures. Includes references to scriptures in the Book of Mormon. [B.D.]

B.012 Baird, J. Edwin. *Selected Scriptural References Concerning Lamanites from the Book of Mormon.* Salt Lake City: Department of Education Church of Jesus Christ of Latter-day Saints, 1959. A sequential list of scriptures that deal with the Lamanites. [J.W.M.]

B.013 Baker, Christine Purves. "Helaman$_3$." In *Encyclopedia of Mormonism*, edited by Daniel H. Ludlow, 2:585. 5 vols. New York: Macmillan, 1992. Helaman, the son of Helaman, was the chief judge and keeper of the Nephite records for fourteen years. The book of Helaman takes its name from him; he received the records from Shiblon and left them to his son Nephi$_2$. [J.W.M.]

B.014 Baker, Christine Purves. "Ishmael." In *Encyclopedia of Mormonism*, edited by Daniel H. Ludlow, 2:704-5. 5 vols. New York: Macmillan, 1992. Ishmael was of the house of Ephraim and was summoned by Nephi to leave Jerusalem to join Lehi in the wilderness with his two sons and five daughters about 600 B.C. Zoram and the children of Lehi married Ishmael's children. [J.W.M.]

B.015 Baker, DeVere. *The Raft Lehi IV: 69 Days Adrift on the Pacific Ocean*. Long Beach: Whitehorn, 1959. Provides day-by-day descriptions of a voyage conducted by the author and three others from San Pedro harbor, California, to Hawaii. The voyage comprised a 69-day trip on an 18 X 24 foot raft. The purpose for the excursion was to demonstrate that Lehi's transoceanic crossing was possible. [A.T.]

B.016 Ball, Isaac B. "Additional Internal Evidence for the Authenticity of the Book of Mormon." *IE* 34 (May-June 1931): 387-89, 428-29, 457-59, 494-95. Defends the reality of the natural catastrophes described in 3 Nephi 8-10. Quotes descriptions of more recent hurricanes and earthquakes to show how similar the details are and how accurate the Book of Mormon account is. The account in 3 Nephi 8-10 is so accurate that neither Joseph Smith nor Oliver Cowdery could have had sufficient knowledge of the facts of natural disasters to have invented this description. [B.D.]

B.017 Ball, Russell H. "An Hypothesis Concerning the Three Days of Darkness Among the Nephites." *Journal of Book of Mormon Studies* 2 (Spring 1993): 107-23. Provides a list of the "mechanisms of destruction described in 3 Nephi 8 and 9," and notes that throughout the destructions, no rain was mentioned and yet the inhabitants of the land were unable to kindle a fire. Concludes that a tremendous earthquake with a local cloud of volcanic ash was the cause of the effects listed in 3 Nephi 8 and 9, including the three days of darkness. Also examines the phrase "whole earth" as it relates to the destructions. [A.T.]

B.018 Ball, Terry B. "Second Book of Nephi." In *Encyclopedia of Mormonism*, edited by Victor Ludlow, 1:146-47. New York, NY: Macmillan, 1992. Provides a summary description of 2 Nephi in sections: Lehi's admonitions and testament to his posterity before his death (1:1-4:11); Lehi pronounces blessings on all his children and Nephi writes a small historical segment (4:12-5:34); a sermon by Jacob (chapters 6-10), and a lengthy written discourse from Nephi (chapters 11-33) in which he quotes large portions of Isaiah. [B.D.]

B.019 Ballard, Melvin J. "Ancient Ruins of South America: Some External Evidences Supporting the Story of the Book of Mormon." *IE* 30 (September 1927): 960-73. This piece is largely an account (accompanied by photographs) of a trip by the author to ancient ruins in the Andes Plateau. Monoliths and the ruins of temples in the sites of three ancient cities are described. The workmanship of the ruins is marvelous, states the author, and comparable to ancient Egyptian buildings. [D.M.]

B.020 Ballard, Melvin J. "Book of Mormon Evidences." In *Sermons and Missionary Services of Melvin Joseph Ballard*, edited by Bryant S. Hinkley, 191-203. Salt Lake City, UT: Deseret Book, 1949. Also found in *Crusader for Righteousness*, edited by Melvin J. Ballard, 163-73. Salt Lake City: Bookcraft, 1966. Offers "tangible evidence" of the authenticity of the Book of Mormon, including archaeological ruins in Mexico, the Egyptian influence on ancient Book of Mormon culture, the temples built after the manner of Solomon's temple, the ancient Mayan calendar stone, traditions of the Great White God who visited ancient inhabitants, and others. [J.W.M.]

B.021 Ballard, Melvin J. "Book of Mormon Evidences." *MS* 94 (16 June 1932): 369-75, 378-80. The discovery of pyramids and other archaeological ruins, the usage of steel among the ancient peoples of America, the connections between Egyptian and Mayan alphabets, and the traditions of Quetzalcoatl are evidences for the Book of Mormon. [A.C.W.]

B.022 Ballard, Melvin J. "The Divine Purpose in the Bringing Forth of the Book of Mormon." *Liahona* 21 (29 January 1924): 297-300. The Book of Mormon came forth to bring redemption to the Lamanites, to benefit the world, to bring men to repentance, and to provide a sign of the nearness of the Second Coming. Exhorts members of the Church to be obedient to the teachings contained in the Book of Mormon. [A.T.]

B.023 Ballard, Melvin J. "The Mission of the Book of Mormon." *IE* 37 (March 1934): 160-61. Declares that the mission of the Book of Mormon, which is to show the great things that the Lord has done to the remnant of the House of Israel (including the Lamanites) and to convince them that Jesus is the Christ, has not been fulfilled. [B.D.]

B.024 Ballard, Melvin J. "New Witness for Christ." *IE* 39 (December 1936): 746-47. Also in *Handbook of the Restoration*, 487-91. Independence, MO: Zions Printing and Publishing, 1944. The sacred mission of the Church and the Book of Mormon is to bring all nations to Christ. The book gives an account of Jesus' visit on the American continent and provides a new witness for him. [J.W.M.]

B.025 Ballard, Melvin J. "Our Duty as Custodians of the Book of Mormon." *IE* 31 (December 1927): 103-8. Members of the Church are expected to obtain a spiritual testimony of the Book of Mormon and then help move it toward its divine destiny. The mission of the book is described on the title page. The book is to be taken to the descendants of Lehi and the time will come when substantial numbers of them will respond. [D.M.]

B.026 Ballard, Melvin J. Untitled talk. *CR* (October 1923): 28-33. The purpose of the Book of Mormon is to bring to pass the redemption of the Lamanites and to bring salvation to the people of the world. The elders of the Church need to work with God to bring about this end. [B.D.]

B.027 Bankhead, Reid E. "America's Decision About Christ." In *Sidney B. Sperry Symposium: The Book of Mormon*, edited by A. Gary Anderson, 1-10. Provo, UT: Brigham Young University Religious Studies Center, 1981. Those who reject the Book of Mormon will be brought into captivity, spiritually and temporally. The early Latter-day Saints left the inhabited areas of America because of the rejection of the Book of Mormon and of Christ by the American people. [J.W.M.]

B.028 Bankhead, Reid E. *The Bible and the Book of Mormon*. Salt Lake City: Church of Jesus Christ of Latter-day Saints, 1955. Reasons that if God is indeed no respecter of persons, then it is logical that Christ would make himself known to nations other than the Jews. The descendants of Joseph in America were in every way qualified to have Christ minister to them. The Bible and the Book of Mormon are both witnesses of the same God. [A.L. & P.H.]

B.029 Bankhead, Reid E. *Concluding Messages of the Book of Mormon*. Provo, UT: Brigham Young University, 1956. A transcript of a series of talks, wherein the author teaches various messages of the Book of Mormon including the atonement, sacrament, continuing revelation, Christian creeds, and Nephite destructions. His purpose is to encourage listeners to study the Book of Mormon as a means to becoming more effective teachers. [A.T.]

B.030 Bankhead, Reid E., and Glenn L. Pearson. *A Doctrinal Approach to the Book of Mormon*. Salt Lake City: Bookcraft, 1962. A study aid intended to demonstrate the many rich doctrinal topics contained in the Book of Mormon. One doctrinal topic discussed, for instance, is the divine birth of Jesus. Aids the reader with cross referencing and scripture marking. [A.T.]

B.031 Bankhead, Reid E., and Glenn L. Pearson. *The Word and the Witness: The Unique Mission of the Book of Mormon*. Salt Lake City:

Bookcraft, 1970. Instructional aid to assist LDS missionaries in using the Book of Mormon. The majority of the work contains sample dialogues between a missionary and investigator. [A.T.]

B.032 Bantista, M. "A Faith-Promoting Experience." *IE* 23 (September 1920): 978-84. A testimonial from Old Mexico, wherein the author explains the role of the Book of Mormon in his conversion to the Church of Jesus Christ of Latter-day Saints. [J.W.M.]

B.033 Barker, James L. "The Language of the Book of Mormon." *IE* 63 (June 1960): 388-89, 444, 446, 450-54. English, the language of translation employed by Joseph Smith, retains the original thought, personal writing styles, distinctive patterns, and unique phraseology belonging to each of the ancient writers and prophets of the Book of Mormon. Barker also discusses the language of the gold plates, which has been described as being a combination of the "learning of the Jews and the language of the Egyptians" (1 Nephi 12), and as "reformed Egyptian" (Mormon 9:32). Too little is known about the characters of reformed Egyptian, which had been "altered" by the Nephites (Mormon 9:32). [D.W.P.]

B.034 Barlow, Philip L. *Mormons and the Bible: The Place of the Latter-day Saints in American Religion.* New York: Oxford University Press, 1991. Deals with the use of the Bible in the LDS church. Compares the Book of Mormon with the Bible, showing similarities and differences. [A.C.W.]

B.035 Barnes, C. Douglas. "Lehi's Route to America." *IE* 42 (January 1939): 26-28, 49. Traces Lehi's possible migration route following ocean currents from the Arabian Peninsula across the Pacific Ocean to Central America. Includes a discussion of the theory surrounding the origin of the Polynesian people. [J.W.M.]

B.036 Barnett, Henry W. "The Aborigines of America." *MS* 22 (April 1860): 258-60. Old Testament and Book of Mormon prophecies provide answers to questions concerning the origins of the American Indians who are of the House of Israel. The record called the stick of Joseph came forth as the Book of Mormon. [J.W.M.]

B.037 Barrett, Ivan J. "A Nation Aroused: Alma 46." *Instructor* 104 (June 1969): 198-99. Reviews the story of Captain Moroni (Alma 46) as an example of a righteous leader, student of the scriptures, man of faith, and a "champion of human liberty." [A.T.]

B.038 Barrett, Robert T. "The Jaredites Leave Babel." *Friend* 20 (April 1990): 20-21. An illustrated story for children that tells of the Jaredites leaving Babel in order to find the promised land. [M.D.P.]

B.039 Barrett, Robert T. "The Lord Leads the Jaredites to a Promised Land." *Friend* 20 (May 1990): 19-22. An illustrated story for children that tells of the Jaredites traveling to the promised land through the Lord's guidance. [M.D.P.]

B.040 Barton, Marie Musig. *Our Promised Land: Book of Mormon Stories for Boys and Girls.* Salt Lake City, UT: Salt Lake Times, 1949. Consists of moral lessons from the Book of Mormon written for children. Emphasizes that the ancient Book of Mormon peoples were taught that they must serve God or perish. [J.W.M.]

B.041 Bassett, Arthur R. "Alma the Elder." *Ensign* 7 (February 1977): 5-10. Alma the Elder became the father of nine generations of prophets. His faith was so great that it brought him to repentance, sustained him for over twenty years in the wilderness, brought him to his knees over a rebellious son, and gave him compassion as a chief judge. [J.W.M.]

B.042 Bassett, Arthur R. "Floods, Winds and The Gates of Hell." *Ensign* 21 (June 1991): 6-11. Christ's visit to America was concluded when he taught four principles designed to protect individuals against "spiritual erosion": avoid unrighteous judgment, negative criticism, and embrace charity; remember that membership in the Savior's church requires responsible actions; look to Christ as a role model; come to know the Savior before seeking for the mysteries. [J.W.M.]

B.043 Bassett, Arthur R. "It Begins with a Family: Some Major Teachings in the First Half of the Book of Mormon." *Ensign* 6 (September 1976): 13-18. One may gain more from reading the Book of Mormon by placing one's self in the situation of some person in the book. For example, fathers might personally relate to the patriarch Lehi by reading the history of his life as presented in the Book of Mormon. Mothers may gain much by demonstrating empathy with mother Sarah, and righteous sons can identify with Nephi. In this manner one might better understand some of the principles illustrated by the various stories in the Book of Mormon. [B.T.]

B.044 Bassett, Arthur R. "Jesus' Sermon to the Nephites." *Ensign* 8 (February 1978): 58-62. Discusses the five major segments in Jesus' first sermon to the Nephites contained in 3 Nephi 11-14. The Savior invites all to come to him and focuses on how to gain the spiritual strength to become his true disciple. [D.H.M.]

B.045 Bassett, Arthur R. "Now Abideth These Three: Faith, Hope and Charity." *Ensign* 7 (September 1977): 7-11. A discussion of faith, hope, and charity as found in the last half of the Book of Mormon. [J.W.M.]

B.046 Bassett, Arthur R. "The Shepherd and His Other Sheep." *Ensign* 8 (February 1978): 53-57. Using the text of the Jesus Christ's visit to the American continent, as recorded in 3 Nephi 11-30, the author emphasizes the need to know the Savior, which knowledge leads to eternal life. Knowing the Savior leads one to become like him. [J.W.M.]

B.047 Bassett, K. Douglas. "Four Faces of Pride in the Book of Mormon." In *Doctrines of the Book of Mormon, 1991 Sperry Symposium*, edited by Bruce A. Van Orden and Brent L. Top, 16-28. Salt Lake City: Deseret Book, 1992. The four faces of pride are the wearing of costly apparel (which may have reference to conspicuous consumption in our day), class distinctions, contention, and anti-enemy attitudes. Those who possess an anti-enemy posture may have no time for the pro-kingdom of God. Pride can be overcome by humility. [B.D.]

B.048 Bassett, K. Douglas. "Nephi's Freedom Thesis and the Sons of Helaman." In *The Book of Mormon: Alma, The Testimony of the Word*, edited by Monte S. Nyman and Charles D. Tate Jr., 191-304. Provo, UT: Brigham Young University Religious Studies Center, 1992. Christ preserves freedom for the inhabitants of the land of America who live righteously. The account of Helaman's stripling warriors is representative of this theme. If the stripling warriors did not doubt the Lord's promise of protection and freedom, God would deliver them. Their obedience to leadership under trying circumstances has a message for Church membership today. [N.K.Y.]

B.049 Bates, Kathryn Ricks. "Scripture Sketches." *Ensign* 21 (June 1991): 67. Sunday evenings in the Bates family home are spent drawing pictures of Book of Mormon characters and stories in compliance with President Benson's challenge to display Book of Mormon pictures in the home. [J.W.M.]

B.050 Bayne, Elbert. "A Time Appointed." In *Recent Book of Mormon Developments; Articles From the Zarahemla Record*, 2:185-86. Independence, MO: Zarahemla Research Foundation, 1992. Argues using Alma 19:33-34 (RLDS versification), that there is an appointed time for the establishment of Zion that is not dependent upon the righteousness of Christ's followers. [B.D.]

B.051 Bean, Willard. *A.B.C. History of Palmyra and the Beginning of "Mormonism."* Palmyra, N.Y.: Palmyra Courier Co., 1938. Writes concerning the early history of Palmyra, the arrival and history of the Smith family, Joseph Smith's interest in the religious revival, the details of the First Vision, and the coming forth of the Book of Mormon. [J.W.M.]

B.052 Beardall, C. Douglas, and Jewel N. Beardall. *About the Three Nephites*. Provo, UT: LDS Book Publications, 1992. A discussion of the Three Nephites (3 Nephi 28:1-9). Presents a collection of some sixty different Three Nephites stories. [B.D.]

B.053 Bechler, C. F. J. "The Book of Mormon and I." *IE* 26 (March 1923): 405-8. A first person narrative testimonial of a man in Germany who found a friend in the Book of Mormon on a cold, lonely, and hopeless night. Following World War I, the man first found himself in despair, then found that the Book of Mormon offered him hope and comfort. [J.W.M.]

B.054 Beckert, Charles B. "What I Have Learned about Family Relations from the Book of Mormon." In *The Sixth Annual Church Educational System Religious Educators' Symposium on the Book of Mormon*, 1-4. Salt Lake City: Church of Jesus Christ of Latter-day Saints, CES, 1982. Draws upon the writings of Nephi, Jacob, Benjamin, as well as the story of Lamoni and his wife to learn about family relationships. The points emphasized include: all behavior has consequences, family unity is an important goal, worship is a family affair, and one can gain tremendous strength from a spouse. [A.T.]

B.055 Beecher, Maureen Ursenbach. "The 'Golden Bible.'" *Friend* 5 (December 1975): 11-13. Conversion story of Mary Elizabeth Rollins Lightner, taken from her autobiography and adapted for children. As a child she read the Book of Mormon and knew it was true. [A.C.W.]

B.056 Bell, James. "John W. Welch: Taking the Stand." *This People* 8-9 (February 1987): 48-50, 61, 63. Features the Foundation for Ancient Research and Mormon Studies (FARMS) and its founder, John W. Welch. One goal of FARMS is to better understand the ancient foundations and cultural background of the Book of Mormon, which will then strengthen an individual's testimony of the book. [J.W.M.]

B.057 Benard, David R., John W. Welch, and Daniel C. Peterson. "Secret Combinations." In *Reexploring The Book of Mormon*, edited by John W. Welch, 227-29. Salt Lake City, UT: Deseret Book and FARMS, 1992. Alexander Campbell was the first to suggest that the references to secret combinations in the Book of Mormon were merely Joseph Smith's anti-Masonic sentiments. Sometime later, even Campbell later dropped this flawed argument. The authors show several contemporaneous uses of the phrase "secret combinations" and demonstrate that the term was widely used and referred to by many organizations that sought to illegally get gain. [B.D.]

B.058 Bennett, Archibald F. "For a Wise Purpose." *MS* 100 (31 March 1938): 194-96, 203. Stresses that keeping genealogical records by all branches of the House of Israel is of great import. Outlines the sequence of prophets who prepared the sacred record that we have as the Book of Mormon. [R.H.B.]

B.059 Bennett, Archibald F. "Nine Generations of Spiritual Leaders." *IE* 48 (March-June 1945): 144, 160, 200, 284, 286, 352. Also in *A Book of Mormon Treasury*, 99-113. Salt Lake City: Bookcraft, 1959, [R]1976. Identifies a number of well-known Book of Mormon spiritual leaders, many of whom consisted of fathers and their sons (i.e., Alma/Alma the Younger, Mormon/Moroni). [A.T.]

B.060 Bennett, Joshua M. *The Gospel of the Great Spirit*. Salt Lake City: Morning Star, 1990. The sacred stories of the Indians from North, Central, and South America have many affinities and parallels with the stories featured in the Bible and Book of Mormon. [D.M.]

B.061 Bennett, Michael J. "The Book of Mormon and a World of Changing Beliefs." *MS* 112 (April 1950): 108-9. In an unbelieving world it is easier to prove a man to be a fraud than a prophet. The proof of a prophet lies in the witness of the Holy Ghost. The witness of the Spirit is more important than external evidences. The enlightened nature of the Book of Mormon startled the Christian world of the nineteenth century by answering numerous concerns. During the century that followed, religions modified their perspectives because of the Book of Mormon. [J.W.M.]

B.062 Bennett, William A. "Some Traditions of the American Indians." *MS* 68 (August 1906): 510-11. Compares Apache Indian traditions to the Three Nephites of the Book of Mormon (3 Nephi 28). Apache Indians celebrate a rite that appears to recall the power and ministerial actions of the Three Nephites. Further, Apache Indians do not eat pork, a practice that may have handed down to them from Lehi who carried the law of Moses to the American continent. [B.D.]

B.063 Bennett, William S. "My Struggle With the Book of Mormon." *Restoration Witness* (May 1973): 4-6. Recalls accepting the Book of Mormon in six stages—he first ignored the book, then opposed it, then tolerated it, followed by convicting it, and finally accepting it and using it as a "sword of the spirit." Bears testimony of the spiritual nature of the book. [J.W.M.]

B.064 Bennion, Francine. "Encounter in Ammonihah." *Ensign* 7 (April 1977): 24-29. Using the text of Alma 8-15 (the Ammonihah pericope), the author examines the motives and immoral tactics of those who seek for gain by twisting the laws of the land. [J.W.M.]

B.065 Bennion, Francine. "Women and the Book of Mormon." In *Women of Wisdom and Knowledge, Talks Selected from the BYU Women's Conferences,* edited by Marie Cornwall and Susan Howe, 169-78. Salt Lake City: Deseret Book, 1990. Why were women of the Book of Mormon seemingly placed in subsidiary roles, often not presented in the record by name, and not portrayed as significant individuals? Author concludes that the Book of Mormon speaks concerning the importance of both men and women. [A.T.]

B.066 Bennion, John W. "Book of Mormon Perspectives on Prosperity." *IE* 73 (May 1970): 14-17. Points out that "prosperity can become a curse and lead to moral and spiritual decay." Several scriptures are quoted and discussed to help teach the correct use of material wealth. "Prosperity in and of itself does not improve a man's character." [B.W.J.]

B.067 Bennion, Kenneth S. "What Plates Came from Cumorah?" *Instructor* 89 (January 1954): 64-65. Provides a description of the various sets of plates from which the Book of Mormon was translated and includes a serviceable diagram of the plates. [R.H.B]

B.068 Bennion, Lowell L. *The Book of Mormon: A Guide to Christian Living.* Salt Lake City: Deseret Book, 1985. Encourages students of the Book of Mormon to earnestly "look for religious ideas and feelings" in the Book of Mormon. Author's book is divided into three parts—"Wisdom in Everyday Living," "Principles and Ordinances of the Gospel," and "Some Universal Concepts." [A.T.]

B.069 Bennion, Lowell L. "The Book of Mormon—A Guide to Religious Living" (Series). *Instructor* 83 (January 1948–December 1948): 16, 54, 112, 165, 219, 273, 318, 357, 406, 461, 507, 567. The Book of Mormon teaches practical works and doctrinal truths: government by law brings blessings; all are precious in God's sight; faith, baptism, repentance bring mercy and satisfy justice, etc. [R.H.B.]

B.070 Bennion, Lowell L. *Understanding The Scriptures.* Salt Lake City, UT: Deseret Book, 1981. Gives keys on how to study and understand the scriptures. Claims that the Book of Mormon is not a book of great literary acclaim, nor is it a historical record, a geographical or archaeological guidebook. The Book of Mormon, however, is a "profoundly religious record." that is "enriched, like much of the Bible, by its authors' deep religious convictions." The Book of Mormon teaches us concerning the attributes of God and clearly adds to our "understanding of the gospel and church of Jesus Christ." [J.W.M.]

B.071 Bennion, Milton Lynn, and J. A. Washburn. *Our Standard Works.* Salt Lake City: Deseret Sunday School Union, 1946. Chapters 15-28 deal with the Book of Mormon. Explains why the Book of Mormon is needed, describes the history of its peoples, relates its coming forth and translation, and discusses its message of the divinity of Christ. [B.D.]

B.072 Bennion, Samuel O. Untitled talk. *DN* (6 April 1918): 42-45. Testifies of the promise to receive a testimony of the Book of Mormon by praying as Moroni 10:2-5 exhorts and encourages the Latter-day Saints to read the Book of Mormon regularly. [B.D.]

B.073 Benson, Alvin K. "Some Key Ingredients for Finding and Understanding the Truth in Science and Religion." In *The Book of Mormon: Second Nephi, The Doctrinal Structure*, edited by Monte S. Nyman and Charles D. Tate Jr., 341-54. Provo, UT: Brigham Young University Religious Studies Center, 1989. Citing 2 Nephi 9:31-32 and other sources, the author demonstrates God's prescribed way to find the truth of all things in both science and religion. [B.D.]

B.074 Benson, Ezra Taft. "America: Land of the Blessed." *IE* 51 (May 1948): 283, 342-43. Book of Mormon prophets proclaimed the Lord's intent to protect the blessed land of America. The brother of Jared, Nephi, Joseph Smith and others spoke concerning America's great destiny. Man-made governments often threaten the foundation of liberty. Though the Constitution will "hang by a thread," the promise guarantees that the thread will not break. [J.W.M.]

B.075 Benson, Ezra Taft. "Beware of Pride." *Ensign* 19 (May 1989): 4-6. Also in *CR* (April 1989): 3-7. The main message of the Book of Mormon, as defined in the Doctrine and Covenants, is directed to our day, "Beware of pride, lest ye become as the Nephites of old" (D&C 38:39). President Benson defines pride as enmity with God and our fellow men. It is basically competitive, rebellious, and selfish. [J.W.M.]

B.076 Benson, Ezra Taft. "The Book of Mormon and the Doctrine and Covenants." *Ensign* 17 (May 1987): 83-85. Also in *CR* (April 1987): 104-8. Speaks of the mission of the Book of Mormon and the Doctrine and Covenants. The Book of Mormon is the keystone and the Doctrine and Covenants is the capstone of the LDS religion. Each book testifies of the other, and the Doctrine and Covenants serves as the greatest external witness of the Book of Mormon, excluding the Three Witnesses. "The Book of Mormon brings men to Christ. The Doctrine and Covenants brings men to Christ's kingdom." [S.P.S.]

B.077 Benson, Ezra Taft. "Book of Mormon is a 'Standard for the Church' President Benson tells Priesthood Leaders." *Ensign* 16 (May 1986): 105. Reports of President Benson's address to Church leaders, April 4, 1986. The prophet explains the great mission of the Book of Mormon. [J.W.M.]

B.078 Benson, Ezra Taft. "The Book of Mormon Is the Word of God." *Ensign* 5 (May 1975): 63-65. Also in *CR* (April 1975): 93-97. Forcefully declares the Book of Mormon to be the word of God. God inspired the writing, compilation, and translation of the Book of Mormon. Bears personal testimony of the Book of Mormon and provides examples of how it should be used in everyday life. [B.T.]

B.079 Benson, Ezra Taft. "The Book of Mormon—Keystone of Our Religion." *Ensign* 16 (November 1986): 4-7. Also in *CR* (4-5 October 1986): 3-7. Also in *Studies In Scripture: 1 Nephi–Alma 29*, edited by Kent P. Jackson, 7:1-9. Salt Lake City, UT: Deseret Book, 1987. Outlines the careful preparation that went into the introduction of the Book of Mormon to the world at the proper time. The sequence of events that followed bear witness that this book is the keystone of the Church of Jesus Christ of Latter-day Saints. There are three ways that it is the keystone: It is a witness of Christ, it was meant for this day, and it helps people draw nearer to God. [J.W.M.]

B.080 Benson, Ezra Taft. "The Book of Mormon: Our Heritage of Freedom." *CR* (October 1961): 69-75. Warns of the threat of communism, likening it to a continuation of the war in heaven and the Gadianton robbers of Book of Mormon times. The warning is clear in the Book of Mormon, the threat comes from within in the form of socialism. Lists several steps to ensure freedom. [J.W.M.]

B.081 Benson, Ezra Taft. "Book of Mormon Outlines Our Duty to America." *CR* (April 1962): 103-6. Ancient Book of Mormon prophets foresaw the entire history and destiny of America and predicted continual freedom on the basis of righteousness. However, those same prophets warned of dire judgments and captivity if America fails to maintain its "spiritual integrity." [R.C.D.]

B.082 Benson, Ezra Taft. "The Book of Mormon Overcomes Deception." *CR* (October 1963): 15-19. Suggests three tests to assist individuals in avoiding deception: (1) Know what the scriptures say, especially the Book of Mormon, about a particular circumstance; (2) know what the Latter-day prophets say; and (3) the Holy Ghost. [J.W.M.]

B.083 Benson, Ezra Taft. "The Book of Mormon Warns America." In *BYUSY* (21 May 1968). Provo, UT: BYU Press. Testifies of the value of the Book of Mormon as a warning voice to America. Determines that communism is a great threat to society and is a secret combination. Warns concerning civil war in the United States. Raises the plea for people to listen to the warning voice of the Book of Mormon. [J.W.M.]

B.084 Benson, Ezra Taft. "Born of God." *Ensign* 15 (November 1985): 5-7. Also in *CR* (October 1985): 46-49. Commentary on Mosiah 1:7—"the Lord works from the inside out." Those who sincerely seek the Lord will experience an indescribable feeling of change, a transformation, fundamental and permanent. Those changed by Christ will be swallowed up in his will (John 5:30), they will desire to please the Lord. They are witnesses of Christ, losing themselves in him but finding eternal life. [J.W.M.]

B.085 Benson, Ezra Taft. "Civic Standards for the Faithful Saints. Four Guidelines to Help Saints Carry Out Their Civic Responsibilities." *Ensign* 2 (July 1972): 59-61. Also in *CR* (April 1972): 48-53. Benson calls the Book of Mormon the "greatest handbook for freedom in this fight against evil." Tells of the godless secret conspiracies that caused the downfall of two American civilizations and offers a warning against upholding the evils of the adversary. [J.W.M.]

B.086 Benson, Ezra Taft. "Cleansing the Inner Vessel." *CR* (5-6 April 1986): 3-6. Also in *Ensign* 16 (May 1986): 4-7. Unless members of the Church read and give heed to the teachings of the Book of Mormon, the whole Church will be under condemnation. Church members need not speak more of the Book of Mormon, but now is the time that they must "do more with it" by placing it in "the center of our personal study, family teaching, preaching, and missionary work." [J.W.M.]

B.087 Benson, Ezra Taft. "Come unto Christ." *Ensign* 17 (Nov. 1987): 63-65. Also in *CR* (October 1987): 101-4. Honest seekers of truth can gain a testimony of Jesus Christ through the prayerful study of the Book of Mormon. Individuals are invited to "come unto Christ" by learning the precepts taught in the Book of Mormon. [S.P.S.]

B.088 Benson, Ezra Taft. "Flooding the Earth with the Book of Mormon." *Ensign* 18 (November 1988): 4-6. Also in *CR* (1-2 October 1989): 3-5. The earth must be flooded with the Book of Mormon. Author presents many ways that he envisions the book being used, so that the condemnation that is upon the Church will be lifted. Saints are to use the book when teaching the gospel and are encouraged to participate in the family-to-family Book of Mormon program. The power of the Book of Mormon is beyond the understanding of man. [J.W.M.]

B.089 Benson, Ezra Taft. "Flooding the Earth with the Book of Mormon." *Friend* 19 (August 1989): inside front cover. A message to the children of the Church. Commends faithful members who read the Book of Mormon and take its message into all the world. [J.W.M.]

B.090 Benson, Ezra Taft. "Founding of America: Its Decline." *CR* (October 1944): 128-34. Quoting Ether 2:10, 12, President Benson admonishes America to beware of its growing spiritual decay. [R.C.D.]

B.091 Benson, Ezra Taft. "The Gift of Modern Revelation." *Ensign* 16 (November 1986): 78-80. Also in *CR* (October 1986): 100-3. The purpose of the Book of Mormon and the Doctrine and Covenants is to bless lives and help mankind to resist the powers of Satan. The Book of Mormon does not detract from the value of the Bible, but supports and sustains its truthfulness. The Book of Mormon is the keystone of the Church and has the power to reveal false doctrines, help people overcome temptations, and bring individuals closer to God than any other book. [J.W.M.]

B.092 Benson, Ezra Taft. "Godly Characteristics of the Master." *Ensign* 16 (November 1986): 45-48. Also in *CR* (October 1986): 59-64. Using the Savior's challenge in the Book of Mormon, "What manner of men ought ye to be? Verily I say unto you, even as I am" (3 Nephi 27-27), encouragement is given to the priesthood holders of the Church to obtain the divine attributes of the Savior. Each man can develop Christlike faith, virtue, knowledge, temperance, patience, brotherly kindness, and charity. [A.C.W.]

B.093 Benson, Ezra Taft. "In His Steps." *Ensign* 18 (September 1988): 2-6. By carefully reading the Book of Mormon and following Moroni's promise (Moroni 10:3-5), one will gain knowledge that the Church of Jesus Christ of Latter-day Saints is the Lord's Church. This knowledge will strengthen the individuals that they may become like Jesus Christ. [J.W.M.]

B.094 Benson, Ezra Taft. "Jesus Christ—Gifts and Expectations." *Ensign* 18 (December 1988): 2-6. Christ both lived and died for mankind. He has provided many great gifts, among which include the Book of Mormon. It was written for those of the present era and will help to dispel the false theories and philosophies of men of the present age. [J.W.M.]

B.095 Benson, Ezra Taft. "Joy in Christ." *Ensign* 16 (March 1986): 3-5. Also in *Ensign* 23 (December 1993): 2-5. The chief mission of the Book of Mormon is to convince the world that Jesus is the Christ. Using Book of Mormon scriptures, the author outlines the role and character of Jesus Christ—he is the creator, he is distinguished by his excellent character, he does not change, he cannot lie, he is no respecter of persons, he is a God of love, he is the Redeemer and Savior. [J.W.M.]

B.096 Benson, Ezra Taft. "The Keystone of Our Religion." *Ensign* 22 (January 1992): 2-7. Reprint from Benson's *A Witness and a Warning*. Salt Lake City: Deseret Book, 1988. The Book of Mormon is a greater gift than any modern invention. Its great worth was testified of by God himself. It is the keystone, stands as witness of Christ, it was written for our day, and it is the most correct book and will bring one closer to God than any other book. [J.W.M.]

B.097 Benson, Ezra Taft. "Last Days and Book of Mormon Promises." In *Proceedings of the Mexico Area Conference*, 127-32. Salt Lake City: Church of Jesus Christ of Latter-day Saints, August 1972. Book of Mormon prophets saw our day and provided a message for the world of this era. The great promises of the Book of Mormon give comfort and assurance to the faithful. The American hemisphere shall be protected so long as its inhabitants serve God. [J.W.M.]

B.098 Benson, Ezra Taft. "A Mighty Change of Heart." *Ensign* 19 (October 1989): 2-5. To truly come to repentance individuals must : (1) realize that the gospel plan is the plan of happiness; (2) understand that repentance must be preceded by faith in Jesus Christ; (3) have a change of heart as well as of actions; (4) have a "godly sorrow;" (5) know that the Lord is anxious to see a change of heart; and (6) do not lose hope. The author uses Book of Mormon to support these six principles. [J.W.M.]

B.099 Benson, Ezra Taft. "Moroni and the Communist Threat to America." *CR* (October 1962): 14-19. Uses the example of Moroni's "Title of Liberty" in a modern context to discuss God, religion, freedom, peace, family, and country. Communism is an enemy to freedom and liberty, and Americans must rise and fight (as Moroni did) or lose the freedoms of the land. [R.C.D.]

B.100 Benson, Ezra Taft. "A New Witness for Christ." *Ensign* 14 (November 1984): 6-8. The Church is under condemnation because its members are not "using the Book of Mormon as God intends." The Book of Mormon is of great value in drawing men closer to God. Its purpose is to "bring men to Christ and to be reconciled to him, and then to join his Church—in that order." The people of the world are on trial as to what they will do with the Book of Mormon. [S.P.S.]

B.101 Benson, Ezra Taft. "Of the Most Worth." *NE* 19 (June 1989): 4-7. Declares the Book of Mormon to be a missionary tool of greatest value. Coupled with the Spirit, the Book of Mormon will do more to bring the souls of men to the Lord than anything else. It is the great standard of the Church. [J.W.M.]

B.102 Benson, Ezra Taft. "The Power of the World." *Ensign* 16 (May 1986): 79. Daily scripture study, with special attention paid to the Book of Mormon, will produce more spiritual rewards than any of the important Church programs to increase the level of church activity. Testimonies will increase, families will be stronger, commitment greater, and personal revelation will flow as a result of meaningful study of the scriptures. [J.W.M.]

B.103 Benson, Ezra Taft. "Pray Always." *Ensign* 20 (February 1990): 2-5. Provides commentary on Alma 34:26, which gives the exhortation to "pray always." There are five ways to improve communication with Heavenly Father: pray frequently, find an appropriate place to meditate and pray, prepare for prayer, make prayer meaningful and pertinent, and take the responsibility to assist in making the request be granted. The Lord is always mindful and ready to respond. [J.W.M.]

B.104 Benson, Ezra Taft. "A Sacred Responsibility." *CR* (5-6 April 1986): 98-100. Also in *Ensign* 16 (May 1986): 77-78. In relating the threefold mission of the Church, President Benson stated that the second mission of the Church is to strengthen the membership of the Church. The most valuable way to do this is to learn the will of the Lord and then do it. There is a need to study the Book of Mormon as individuals and as families. Studying the Book of Mormon one-half hour daily was his recommendation. [J.W.M.]

B.105 Benson, Ezra Taft. "The Savior's Visit to America." *Ensign* 17 (May 1987): 4-7. Also in *CR* (4-5 April 1987): 3-7. Recounts the events leading up to and including the visit of Jesus Christ to the Nephites (3 Nephi), President Benson shows "parallels to our own day as we anticipate the Savior's second coming," and calls the book of 3 Nephi a "testimony of the resurrected Christ in America." [S.P.S.]

B.106 Benson, Ezra Taft. "To the Children of the Church." *Ensign* 19 (May 1989): 81-83. Also in *CR* (1-2 April 1989): 102-5. President Benson congratulates young people who were learning about the Book of Mormon, who have read it, and have sung songs about it. He calls the Book of Mormon "Heavenly Father's special gift." [J.W.M.]

B.107 Benson, Ezra Taft. "To the Young Women of the Church." *Ensign* 16 (November 1986): 81-85. Counsels young women to stay close to family members, to read the Book of Mormon, to ponder and apply its teachings. He gives a promise that the young woman who knows and loves the Book of Mormon will stand against evil and will be a tool in the hands of the Lord. [J.W.M.]

B.108 Benson, Ezra Taft. "To the 'Youth of the Noble Birthright.' " *CR* 56 (5-6 April 1986): 55-60. Also in *Ensign* 16 (May 1986): 43-46. Calling attention to the Book of Helaman and the relationship of the stripling warriors to their mothers, President Benson counsels young men to draw close to their mothers and other family members, to read again and again the Book of Mormon, and to prepare for missionary service by being chaste and clean. [J.W.M.]

B.109 Benson, Ezra Taft. "Trust Not the Arm of Flesh." *IE* 70 (December 1967): 55-58. The precepts of men are in conflict with the principles of God. Those who choose to follow the revelations of God are not deceived (2 Nephi 4:34; 28:14). The Lord does not give reasons for every commandment, some things need to be taken on faith. Only by loving God first can we best love and serve our fellowmen. [J.W.M.]

B.110 Benson, Ezra Taft. Untitled talk. *CR* (5-6 October 1985): 4-7. President Benson discusses the importance of the Book of Mormon and addresses the fact that the Church is under condemnation for neglecting this keystone of the Church. [A.L.]

B.111 Benson, Ezra Taft. "Using the Book of Mormon." *CR* (October 1984): 4-7. Raises five critical questions about the Book of Mormon and then provides answers to his questions. The questions posed are: Is the Book of Mormon the Word of God? For whom was it written? How important it is? What is its major purpose? And how are we to use it? [R.C.D.]

B.112 Benson, Ezra Taft. *A Witness and a Warning: A Modern-day Prophet Testifies of the Book of Mormon*. Salt Lake City: Deseret Book, 1988. Defines the many purposes of the Book of

Mormon and the method by which one may come closer to Christ. This book represents the testimony and attitude of the Prophet and President of the Church of Jesus Christ of Latter-day Saints, concerning the value of the Book of Mormon to men and women living in modern times. The book contains both a warning and a divine promise dependant upon the use of the Book of Mormon. [J.W.M.]

B.113 Benson, Ezra Taft, Gordon B. Hinckley, Thomas S. Monson, Howard W. Hunter, Boyd K. Packer, Marvin J. Ashton, L. Tom Perry, David B. Haight, James Faust, Neal A. Maxwell, Russell M. Nelson, Dallin H. Oaks, M. Russell Ballard, Joseph B. Wirthlin, and Richard G. Scott. "We Add Our Witness: Living Prophets Share Their Feelings About the Book of Mormon." *Ensign* 19 (March 1989): 5-9. The First Presidency and Quorum of the Twelve share their personal testimonies and experiences concerning the Book of Mormon. This in answer to the request of President Benson to "flood the earth with the Book of Mormon." This article is filled with heart-warming experiences, strong testimonies, and wonderful insights as prophets of God reveal inner thoughts about the Book of Mormon. [J.W.M.]

B.114 Benson, Ezra Taft. "Worthy Fathers, Worthy Sons." *Ensign* 15 (November 1985): 35-7. Provides examples of close relationships between fathers and sons in the Book of Mormon and shows that they are appropriate models for families today. [D.M.]

B.115 Benson, Reed A. "Sword of Laban." In *Encyclopedia of Mormonism*, edited by Daniel H. Ludlow, 3:1427-28. 5 vols. New York: Macmillan, 1992. The sword of Laban was taken from Laban's dead body by Nephi, following the Lord's command to kill him in order to obtain the brass plates. This sword was used as a model for weapons of war and was part of those items found with the gold plates by Joseph Smith. The witnesses were allowed to view this sword. [J.W.M.]

B.116 Benyola, Joseph. *Pocket Reference Book of the Bible and the Book of Mormon.* Monongahela City, PA: Church of Jesus Christ, 1956. A topical reference work containing a list of the books from the Book of Mormon and the Bible with their corresponding contents by chapter and verse. Topics include falling away, Restoration, baptism, and laying on of hands. [J.W.M.]

B.117 Bergin, Allen E. "Nephi: A Universal Man." *Ensign* 6 (September 1976): 65-70. Nephi possessed a multitude of talents and positive characteristics. He was a "prophet, teacher, ruler, colonizer, builder, craftsman, intellect, writer, poet, military leader, father of nations, son, husband and physical powerhouse." Certainly "he belongs . . . in the company of the greatest men of every age." [B.T.]

B.118 Berrett, LaMar C. "The So-Called Lehi Cave." Provo, UT: FARMS, 1982. Describes the cave found on the side of Khirbet Beit Lei (Southwest of Jerusalem) and attempts to determine if it was the cave used by Nephi and his brothers when fleeing Laban. Concludes that this was not the cave used by Nephi. [A.T.]

B.119 Berrett, Lyman C. "What I Like to Teach About the Book of Mormon." *IE* 67 (February 1964): 92-93, 116. Nephi warned future readers that the Book of Mormon was not a history (2 Nephi 5:32-33). Rather, the book is an instrument to bring people to Christ. Nephi, Lehi, Abinadi, Jacob, Alma, and other prophets knew the mission of Christ and taught it. [J.W.M.]

B.120 Berrett, William Edwin. "Great Teachings from the Book of Mormon." In *Know Your Religion Series*, 1:1-60. Provo, UT: Brigham Young University, 1953. Five lectures on the Book of Mormon (presented October 21—November 18, 1953) discussing such topics as the purpose of the Book of Mormon, the nature of man and God, the manner in which the Book of Mormon contributes to an understanding of the Bible, the relationship of spirituality to political and economic life, and a warning to the nations. [L.D.]

B.121 Berrett, William Edwin. "How to Teach the Book of Mormon." *IE* 63 (November 1960): 804-5, 856. Teachers of the Book of Mormon may teach the historical, geographical, literary, or archaeological aspects of the book, but they should emphasize the doctrines and teachings of Jesus Christ and demonstrate in what manner the book assists individuals in our present day world conditions. [R.C.D.]

B.122 Berrett, William Edwin. *The Latter-day Saints: A Contemporary History of the Church of Jesus Christ*. Salt Lake City: Deseret Book, 1985. Pages 35-76 contain Joseph Smith's account of the coming forth of the Book of Mormon, visitations of heavenly beings, obtaining the gold plates, the mode of translation of the plates, and related historical items. [J.W.M.]

B.123 Berrett, William Edwin. "The Relationship of Spirituality to National Prosperity." *IE* 55 (March 1952): 160-61, 176-78. Also published as "The Book of Mormon and National Prosperity." In *A Book of Mormon Treasury*, 251-59. Salt Lake City: Bookcraft, 1959, [R]1976. The Book of Mormon makes it clear that the economic welfare of any nation is inevitably linked with the level of spirituality among the people. Nations become prosperous when their spiritual level remains high or they sink into social decay with continual disregard for the word of God. [R.C.D.]

B.124 Berrett, William Edwin. *The Restored Church*. Salt Lake City: Deseret Book, 1974. Chapters 5-8 deal with the coming forth of the Book of Mormon, the Urim and Thummim, the facsimile taken to Professor Anthon, Grandin's Press, the publication and distribution of the Book, and the witnesses of the Book of Mormon. Analyzes the effect of the book since its publication and the world's opposition to it. [J.W.M.]

B.125 Berrett, William Edwin. "The Scriptures and Literature of the Church." In Berrett's *Doctrines of the Restored Church*, 324-32. Salt Lake City: Deseret Book, 1941. Moroni confirmed the Bible as an important book of scripture when he announced the coming forth of the Book of Mormon. Joseph was made aware of errors contained in the Bible and the need for further revelation to support the Bible and to rectify its errors. Those who abridged the Book of Mormon chose specific theological ideas to make the it the foundation of the new Church, thus creating a difference between the Restored Gospel and other Christian religious systems. [J.W.M.]

B.126 Berrett, William Edwin. "Spirituality and Armed Conflict." *IE* 55 (April 1952): 242-44, 271-73. Also published as "The Book of Mormon Speaks on War." In *A Book of Mormon Treasury*, 275-84. Salt Lake City: Bookcraft, 1959, [R]1976. The position of the Church concerning war and armed conflicts is dictated by the teachings in the Book of Mormon. War is condemned by God and peace is always valiantly sought. However, at times that wars must be fought by the righteous in order to safeguard liberty. Although God aids the righteous in war, the righteous may suffer or be slain. [R.C.D.]

B.127 Berrett, William Edwin. "Spirituality and Political Reform." *IE* 55 (February 1952): 86-88. Also published as "The Book of Mormon and World Government." In *A Book of Mormon Treasury*, 260-67. Salt Lake City: Bookcraft, 1959, [R]1976. On the subject of national political reform, the Book of Mormon speaks out with unwavering conciseness. It states that no form of government will succeed unless the people maintain a high spiritual level; national ills cannot be cured by any amount of legislation if the spirituality of the people remains neglected. [R.C.D.]

B.128 Berrett, William E., and Alma P. Burton. "The Coming Forth of the Book of Mormon." In Berrett and Burton's *Readings in LDS Church History: From Original Manuscripts,* 1:19-41. Salt Lake City, UT: Deseret Book, 1953. A compilation of early church historical accounts and commentaries that tell the story of the coming forth of the Book of Mormon, including accounts written by Oliver Cowdery, Joseph Smith, Brigham Young, Edward Stevenson, and Lucy Mack Smith. They tell of Moroni's visits, describe the Hill Cumorah, and write concerning the stone box, the gold plates, the breastplate, and Urim and Thummim. [J.W.M.]

B.129 Berrett, William E., and Alma P. Burton. "The Translation and Publication of the Book of Mormon." In Berrett and Burton's *Readings in LDS Church History: From Original Manuscripts*, 1:43-56. Salt Lake City, UT: Deseret

Book, 1953. Uses early church historical accounts and commentaries that tell the story of the translation and publication of the Book of Mormon, including the role of Joseph Smith, Martin Harris, Anthon, and those involved with the printing of the book. [J.W.M.]

B.130 Berrett, William E., and Alma P. Burton. "Witnesses to the Book of Mormon." In Berrett and Burton's *Readings in LDS Church History: From Original Manuscripts*, 1:57-63. Salt Lake City, UT: Deseret Book, 1953. Includes Joseph Smith's written account of the events that occurred when the Three Witnesses, Oliver Cowdery, Martin Harris, and David Whitmer viewed the gold plates. Subsequent testimonies from the Three Witnesses affirm the fact that they saw the plates, the angel, and heard the voice of God. [J.W.M.]

B.131 Berrett, William Edwin, Milton R. Hunter, Roy A. Welker, and H. Alvah Fitzgerald. *A Guide to the Study of the Book of Mormon*. Salt Lake City: Church of Jesus Christ of Latter-day Saints, Department of Education, 1938. An introduction to the Book of Mormon, featuring external evidences, teachings about God and Christ, immortality, and ethical and social teachings of the Book of Mormon. [D.W.P.]

B.132 Best, Brian. "Nephi, Lehi and Samuel the Lamanite." *Ensign* 7 (December 1977): 44-51. An intimate look into the lives and human characteristics of the prophets in the Book of Helaman—Nephi, Lehi, and Samuel. At a time when their nation was ripe in iniquity shortly before the coming of the Savior to the Nephites, these great men stood firm in defending the truth. [J.W.M.]

B.133 Beth. "The Deluge." *Juvenile Instructor* 13 (1 March 1878): 55. Relates the Book of Mormon and Indian legends to the flood at the time of Noah. Also speaks of stone and wood tablets found in Iowa, Illinois, and Ohio, some of which possess Egyptian-like characters. [D.M.]

B.134 Bickerstaff, George. *Book of Mormon Stories for Children*. Salt Lake City: Bookcraft, 1971. Book of Mormon stories told on a child's level of understanding. The stories tell of Joseph Smith, the brother of Jared and the shining stones, Lehi's vision, and Nephi and the brass plates. [L.D.]

B.135 Bickerstaff, George. *The Church Story: From Sacred Grove to Land of Zion*. Salt Lake City, UT: Bookcraft, 1974. An illustrated book for children that retells church history concerning the coming forth of the Book of Mormon from the angel Moroni's visit to its publication. [J.W.M.]

B.136 Bickerstaff, George. "Great Teachers in the Book of Mormon." *Instructor* 96 (May 1961): 179-81. Lehi, Jacob, King Benjamin, mothers, and other characters are honored as being great Book of Mormon teachers. [B.W.J.]

B.137 Bickerstaff, George. "The Nephite Wars." *Instructor* 102 (July 1967): 295-97. A discussion of war in the Book of Mormon. Reasons for Nephite successes and failures in war are cited. [B.W.J.]

B.138 Bigelow, Sabina H., and Sabina Susan Bytheway. *Book of Mormon Companion: Dictionary and More*. Sandy, UT: Bright Impressions, 1988. A reading guide for children. Contains a Book of Mormon chronology, drawings, games, and a dictionary. [D.M.]

B.139 Bingman, Margaret. *Encyclopedia of the Book of Mormon*. Independence, MO: Reorganized Church of Jesus Christ of Latter Day Saints, 1978. An encyclopedic work attending to a number of Book of Mormon topics. Entries deal with biography, history, and doctrine. [L.D.]

B.140 Bird, Randall C. "How to Make the Book of Mormon Exciting in the Lives of Students." In *Sixth Annual Church Education System Religious Educator's Symposium on the Book of Mormon*, edited by the Church Education System, 5-8. Salt Lake City: LDS Church 1982. Introduces a new principle for teaching called the me-here-now principle: the ability to inspire each individual to liken the scriptures to themselves in their own circumstances as a son or daughter of God. Urges teachers to use the principle in teaching the Book of Mormon. [B.D.]

B.141 Birrell, Verla L. *The Book of Mormon Guidebook*. Salt Lake City: Stevens and Wallis, 1948. A guidebook that treats such Book of

Mormon topics as prophecy, ancient records, topography, major and minor migrations of the people, government, political and social customs, military, language and writing, science, animal and plant life, archaeology, and a number of religious traditions and doctrines. [L.D.]

B.142 Bishop, Francis G. *A Proclamation from the Lord to His People Scattered throughout All the Earth.* Kirtland, OH: n.p., 1851. A proclamation written to the inhabitants of the world regarding the coming forth of the Book of Mormon and the restoration of the gospel. Provides a description of the golden plates, the Urim and Thummim, the breast plate, and the sword of Laban. [D.W.P.]

B.143 Bishop, Gary Lyman. "The Tradition of Isaiah in the Book of Mormon." M.A. thesis, Brigham Young University, 1974. "A textual and grammatical analysis of 52 passages of Isaiah as they are found in cave IV of the Dead Sea Scrolls, the Masoretic Text, the Septuagint, the King James Version, and the Book of Mormon. The objective was to determine the relationship, if any, of those verses in the Book of Mormon with the other textual traditions. Based on the differences between the Book of Mormon text and the King James Version, and upon the confirmation of those Book of Mormon differences by the other traditions, it was concluded that the Book of Mormon follows its own tradition." [A.T.]

B.144 Bishop, Lynn L., and Steven L. Bishop. "Book of Mormon Examples of Priesthood–Kingdom–Church Relationship." In *The Keys of the Priesthood Illustrated,* written and compiled by Lynn L. Bishop and Steven L. Bishop, 79-83. Draper, UT: Review and Preview Publishers, 1971. The books of Omni and Mosiah suggest that Nephite kings, Mosiah I, Benjamin, and Mosiah II, held roles of priesthood leadership over the people. Later when Alma became the head of the Church, he ultimately answered to Mosiah II who held a greater role of spiritual leadership. [J.W.M.]

B.145 Black, Don J. "Could I Touch This Holy Book?" *Ensign* 7 (September 1977): 76-77. The power of the Book of Mormon to change lives is evident in the stories of conversion set forth in this article. In presenting the Book of Mormon to investigators, the author was impressed by the humility of the young husband who, awestruck by the holiness of the book, asked in meekness if he could touch it. [J.W.M.]

B.146 Black, Susan Easton. "Behold, I Have Dreamed a Dream." In *The Book of Mormon: First Nephi, The Doctrinal Foundation*, edited by Monte S. Nyman and Charles D. Tate Jr., 113-24. Provo, UT: Brigham Young University Religious Studies Center, 1988. The significance and setting of Lehi's tree of life dream is set forth. Demonstrates the manner in which the family of Lehi was affected by the dreams of Lehi. [A.T.]

B.147 Black, Susan Easton. "The Book of Mormon Bears Witness of the Father Through the Son." In *A Symposium on the Book of Mormon*, 20-23. Salt Lake City: Church of Jesus Christ of Latter-day Saints, 1982. The Book of Mormon teaches that God the Father has a body, parts, and passions and that he is literally the Father of us, his mortal children. Statistical evidence is given for references to the nature of God in the Book of Mormon and names for Jesus Christ found in the Book of Mormon. [B.D.]

B.148 Black, Susan Easton. *Finding Christ through the Book of Mormon.* Salt Lake City: Deseret Book, 1987. Jesus Christ is the central figure in the Book of Mormon. He is referred to about every 1.7 verses and is called by 101 different names. The Book of Mormon explains how to know about Christ and be like him and how to be an example of him. Author includes helpful charts listing the names of Christ and the average number of references to Christ per book in the Book of Mormon. [B.D.]

B.149 Black, Susan Easton. "I Am Not Any Longer to Be Alone." *Ensign* 19 (January 1989): 50-56. Many individuals became fellow witnesses with Joseph Smith as they suffered persecution with him, received divine manifestations, and testified of the divine origin of the Book of Mormon. [J.W.M.]

B.150 Black, Susan Easton. "King Benjamin: In the Service of Your God." In *The Book of Mormon: Mosiah, Salvation Only through Christ*, edited by Monte S. Nyman and Charles D. Tate Jr., 37-48. Provo, UT: Brigham Young University Religious Studies Center, 1991. King Benjamin emphasized the importance of service and knowing the mysteries of God, two concepts that are interrelated. [B.D.]

B.151 Black, Susan Easton. "Lest Ye Become As the Nephites of Old." In *The Book of Mormon: The Keystone Scripture*, edited by Paul R. Cheesman, S. Kent Brown, and Charles D. Tate Jr., 256-68. Provo, UT: Brigham Young University Religious Studies Center, 1988. Discusses the righteous reasons to want to have the blessings of prosperity and the pitfalls associated with wealth, such as pride. [B.D.]

B.152 Black, Susan Easton. "Names of Christ in the Book of Mormon." *Ensign* 8 (July 1978): 60-1. The main purpose of the Book of Mormon is to testify of Christ. There exists in the book one-hundred different names and titles of Jesus, appearing an average of once every 1.7 verses in the Book of Mormon. Author includes a chart showing the average number of references to Christ per book in the Book of Mormon, and a second chart listing the one hundred different names and titles of Jesus in the book. [B.D.]

B.153 Black, Susan Easton. *Stories from the Early Saints: Converted by the Book of Mormon*. Salt Lake City, UT: Bookcraft, 1992. Presents a collection of conversion stories of early saints who relate in their own words how they received testimonies of Christ and his gospel through reading the Book of Mormon. Conversion stories are provided by Lucy Mack Smith, Wilford Woodruff, Orson Hyde, and others. [B.D.]

B.154 Blair, William W. "Harmony of the Bible, Book of Mormon, and Doctrine and Covenants." *True LDS Herald* 10 (1 September 1866): 69-73. The use of the terms "endless," "forever," and "everlasting" is consistent in the Book of Mormon, the Bible, and the Doctrine and Covenants. [B.D.]

B.155 Blake, Vira H. "A Mother's Dream." *Ensign* 16 (March 1986): 52-54. Having lost two children previously, faithful parents struggle to save the life of their fifth child. The mother dreams of the tree of life and two young men who were sent from God to save her child. LDS missionaries came a week later and were inspired to underline the passages concerning Lehi's dream in the Book of Mormon, which led to events that saved the child's life. [J.W.M.]

B.156 Blanch, Mae. "Challenges to the Reign of the Judges." In *Studies in Scripture: 1 Nephi–Alma 29*, edited by Kent P. Jackson, 7:283-93. Salt Lake City, UT: Deseret Book, 1987. The type of government existing under the reign of the judges was established by Mosiah as inspired law, given by covenant, and founded upon the law of Moses. This rule of law was ultimately undermined by class distinction, pride, and unrighteousness. [J.W.M.]

B.157 Blanch, Mae. "Samuel the Lamanite (Helaman 13-16)." In *Studies in Scripture: Alma 30–Moroni*, edited by Kent P. Jackson, 8:116-24. Salt Lake City, UT: Deseret Book, 1987. Expounds upon Samuel and the example of righteous Lamanites to the proud, iniquitous Nephites. Samuel's prophecies of Christ and his powerful sermon brought a number of Nephites to repentance, but most rejected his warning. Samuel's words were verified shortly thereafter, proving that he was a true prophet. [A.C.W.]

B.158 Blankmeyer, Helen Van Cleave. *David Whitmer*. N.p.: by the author, 1955. A history of David Whitmer written for his descendants, but also includes a history of Joseph Smith, the coming forth of the Book of Mormon, and the apostasy of the "Mormon Church." Also provides a historical sketch of Solomon Spaulding, calling attention to the fact that David Whitmer never denied his testimony of the Book of Mormon. [J.W.M.]

B.159 Blossom, Rose B. *The Four Standard Works of the Church of Jesus Christ of Latter-day Saints*. Los Angeles: Triple S., 1939. Provides a chart reviewing the different editions of the

Book of Mormon and their dates, an outline of the Book of Mormon, and a parallel outline of the Book of Mormon and the Bible, presenting a "bird's eye view." [B.D.]

B.160 Blumell, Bruce D. "Was the Book of Mormon Based on the Spaulding Manuscript or Ethan Smith's *View of the Hebrews*?" In *A Sure Foundation: Answers to Difficult Gospel Questions*, 54-60. Salt Lake City: Deseret Book, 1988. Also found in *Ensign* 6 (September 1976): 84-87. Provides a brief history of both the Spaulding Manuscript and Smith's *View of the Hebrews* and concludes that neither work bears relationship to the Book of Mormon in style or content. [J.W.M]

B.161 Bluth, J. V. "More Book of Mormon Evidence." *MS* 56 (8 October 1894): 648-50. While archaeologists search for the secrets to the origin of the early inhabitants of America, members of the Church believe the keys to understanding such things are contained in the Book of Mormon. [J.W.M.]

B.162 Bolitho, A. D., response by Elder B. H. Roberts. "Book of Mormon Controversy." *MS* 50 (20 February 1888): 113-17. An interchange of correspondences between Bolitho, who endeavors to prove the Book of Mormon false through a discussion of the dates of Christ's birth and death, and Roberts who explains the possible differences between the Nephite and Jewish calendrical systems. [A.C.W.]

B.163 "The Book of Ether." *Evening and Morning Star* 1 (August 1832): n.p. Brief outline of the contents of the book of Ether. [M.D.P.]

B.164 "The Book of Jacob." *Evening and Morning Star* 1 (September 1832): n.p. Summarizes the book of Jacob. [M.D.P.]

B.165 "The Book of Mormon." *DN* 27 (9 October 1878): 569. Reprint of an article from the *Richmond* (Missouri) *Conservater*. Concerns David Whitmer and his tenacious testimony of the Book of Mormon. Whitmer claimed to be in possession of the original manuscript. [D.M.]

B.166 "The Book of Mormon." *Deseret Weekly* 45 (10 December 1892): 779-80. Quotes excerpts from an article entitled "Criticism of the Old Testament" published in the *Edinburgh Review*. The same objections and methods applied to the Book of Mormon may be applied to the Bible. Both must stand or fall together. The LDS realize that the Book of Mormon "invite[s] investigation and maintain that if this record must be rejected, the Bible must be rejected, too, since every objection that can be raised against the Book of Mormon finds its true counterpart among the objections raised against the Bible." [J.W.M. & D.M.]

B.167 "The Book of Mormon." *IE* 26 (December 1922): 155-56. Consists of a compilation of quotes about the Book of Mormon from the *Journal of Discourses*. All quotes are from former leaders of the Church of Jesus Christ of Latter-day Saints. [L.D.]

B.168 "The Book of Mormon." *IE* 64 (March 1961): 189, 199. The Book of Mormon was important in the restoration of the priesthood and the Church. It has survived a century and a quarter of anti-Mormon criticism. [M.D.P.]

B.169 "The Book of Mormon." *MS* 48 (22 November 1886): 739-41. Testifies of Book of Mormon's truthfulness, exhorting all to read for "joy and solace." The Book of Mormon restores plain and precious things removed from Bible and does not depend on external evidences for its proof of divine origin. [A.C.W.]

B.170 "Book of Mormon Activity." *Friend* 16 (February 1986): 37. An activity for children. Cut out the pieces and make a replica of the Book of Mormon. [J.W.M.]

B.171 "The Book of Mormon and the Stranger." *IE* 67 (April 1964): 308. The Book of Mormon is a witness of Jesus Christ and a valuable tool in teaching the gospel. Discusses a program of placing copies of the Book of Mormon in hotel rooms. [L.D.]

B.172 "The Book of Mormon as a Literary Product." *Relief Society Magazine* 10 (September 1923): 432-35. The Book of Mormon is a standard work of American literature and its essentials are in harmony with the Bible. [J.W.M.]

B.173 "The Book of Mormon . . . Can It Add to Your Life?" *Readers Digest* (May 1981): 83-86. An advertisement insert in a popular magazine intended as a missionary vehicle. Explains what the Book of Mormon has done in a positive way for some people, and what it can do for the reader. [D.M.]

B.174 "Book of Mormon Chronology Chart." *Ensign* 6 (September 1976): 55-57. Provides three color pages listing Book of Mormon events according to their chronological order with a chart showing their order and scriptural passages where they are discussed. [J.W.M.]

B.175 "A Book of Mormon Claim Substantiated." *MS* 91 (24 January 1929): 61. Helaman 3:7-11 speaks of the use of cement. A recent article in Bulletin No. 145, Bureau of Plant Industry (Washington, D.C.), 1909 confirms that pyramids and ruins found in Mexico, Central, and South America contained cement. [J.W.M.]

B.176 "The Book of Mormon Confirmed." *MS* 60 (13 January 1898–10 February 1898): 24-28, 33-39, 56-63, 72-77, 81-87. Five-part series sets forth external evidences of the Book of Mormon, including the archaeological findings that "point to successive periods of occupation" in ancient America, evidence of Hebrew origin/descent for the American Indians, and the idea that there was an advanced civilization in ancient America. Also discusses metal plates and provides geological proof of the great destruction recorded in 3 Nephi 8. [A.C.W.]

B.177 *Book of Mormon Course of Study: Inservice Insert Sheets for Released Time Seminary Teacher.* N.p., 1974-75. Helpful teaching aids for teachers of the Book of Mormon. Includes a list of course objectives, course outline, methods of teaching the students, scripture chase items, and other teaching tools. [D.W.P.]

B.178 "A Book of Mormon Christmas." *NE* 23 (December 1993): 20-23. A list of verses from the Book of Mormon prophesying of the birth of Christ. [S.H.]

B.179 "Book of Mormon is Special Witness." *IE* 68 (July 1965): 634. Members bearing testimony of the Book of Mormon as inspired by the Holy Ghost are able to touch the hearts of those who listen. More witnesses to the Book of Mormon are needed. [J.W.M.]

B.180 *The Book of Mormon: It Begins with a Family.* Salt Lake City: Deseret Book, 1983. Contains twenty-three reprints of articles previously published in the *Ensign*. See under individual entries throughout this bibliography. [J.W.M.]

B.181 "Book of Mormon Light On a Profound Christian Truth." *Instructor* 85 (March 1950): 68, 79. Discusses the manner in which Jesus Christ is the Savior of mankind. [R.H.B.]

B.182 *The Book of Mormon: My Personal Study Guide.* Provo, UT: BYU, 1966. Provides a checklist that may be marked as study of certain Book of Mormon passages is completed. Claims that the Book of Mormon itself is the best study guide. [J.W.M.]

B.183 "Book of Mormon Names." *MS* 63 (21 March 1901): 177-80. Refutes a polemical claim that Book of Mormon proper names are not translatable, only transferable from one language to another. The fact that no Book of Mormon names appear in Central America does not prove the Book of Mormon to be false. Cites Book of Mormon names that have Hebrew origins and shows Mayan similarities to Book of Mormon names. [A.C.W.]

B.184 *The Book of Mormon: 1 Nephi–Alma 29. Historical and Doctrinal Exam Questions.* Provo, UT: Brigham Young University, 1973. A study aid that covers the first one-half of the Book of Mormon. Comprises approximately 206 historical questions, with scriptural references and approximately 167 doctrinal questions, also with scriptural references. [D.W.P.]

B.185 *Book of Mormon New World 1991: How to Get to Heaven.* Texas: New World Press, 1991. Cites a number of Book of Mormon scriptures dealing with selected topics including prayer, fasting, false prophets, baptism, and ancient America. Concludes that the Book of Mormon teaches humanity the way to heaven. [J.W.M.]

B.186 "Book of Mormon Personalities." In *Encyclopedia of Mormonism*, edited by Daniel H. Ludlow, 1:195. 5 vols. New York: Macmillan, 1992. Briefly identifies the primary personalities of the Book of Mormon, including the chief leaders, kings, statesmen, prophets, and historians. Jesus Christ is the most important personality of the Book of Mormon. [N.K.Y.]

B.187 *The Book of Mormon Picture Packet.* Salt Lake City: Bookcraft, 1976. A set of twelve Book of Mormon pictures by artist Arnold Friberg printed in color. The reverse side of each picture contains a description of the picture. [D.W.P.]

B.188 *The Book of Mormon Portfolio of Paintings.* Salt Lake City: Deseret Book, 1961. Paintings by Arnold Friberg of ten Book of Mormon events. Contains scriptural text to accompany the prints. [J.W.M.]

B.189 "Book of Mormon Studies." *MS* 90 (12, 19, 26 January; 2, 16, 23 February; 22, 29 March; 19, 26 April; 24, 30 May; 21, 28 June; 19, 26 July; 23, 30 August; 20, 27 September; 25 October; 1, 22, 29 November 1928): 22-23, 46-47, 62-64, 77-80, 109-11, 123-25, 181-83, 204-6, 251-54, 267-68, 332-33, 350-52, 396-98, 413-16, 459-62, 477-78, 542-43, 558-59, 606, 623, 683-84, 702-3, 750-51, 764-65. Series of articles intended for Relief Society course study. Discusses importance of the Book of Mormon, its coming forth (i.e., the translation, the witnesses, the publication, Joseph Smith), brief overview of its contents, and explains the text from 1 Nephi 1 through Alma 58. Each article features several questions that are helpful in synthesizing and applying the Book of Mormon to daily life. [A.C.W.]

B.190 "Book of Mormon Studies." *MS* 91 (January–November 1929): 14, 41-42, 102, 179-80, 244, 325-26, 387-88, 453-54, 517-18, 581-82, 660-61, 740-41. A series of articles that takes a story, message, or verses out of the Book of Mormon and relates it to everyday life. [M.D.P.]

B.191 "A Book of Mormon Year." *Instructor* 72 (December 1937): 526-27. Encourages Church members to read the Book of Mormon, and tells faith promoting stories of those who have read the book and have experienced a "spiritual revival" in their lives. [J.W.M.]

B.192 "Books." *TS* 3 (1 September 1842): 908-9. Speaks of the methods in which ancient books were bound. Books consisting of tablets, plates, metal, or wood were made of leaves bound with rings at the back. Flexible materials were sewn in long sheets and rolled around a stick, like a scroll. That the Book of Mormon was similarly bound is evidence of its authenticity. [J.W.M.]

B.193 Booth, A. L. "A Divine Record." *MS* 57 (August 1895): 488-90. A brief summary of David Whitmer's life and testimony of the Book of Mormon. [B.D.]

B.194 Booth, A. L. "An Objection Answered." *MS* 57 (14 March 1895): 168-69. Defends criticisms that the Book of Mormon contains bad grammar by stating that any errors of the book are the errors of man. Mentions the errors of the Bible. [B.D.]

B.195 Bousquet, George H. "Another Scholar Speaks! The Rigdon-Spaulding Theory Re-examined." *MS* 96 (October 1934): 626-30. A non-Mormon scholar states that the Spaulding theory is false and that Joseph Smith is not a fraud, arguing that the Book of Mormon witnesses who left the Church would have exposed the Book of Mormon story if it truly were fraudulent. [B.D.]

B.196 Bowen, Donna Lee, and Camille S. Williams. "Women in the Book of Mormon." In *Encyclopedia of Mormonism*, edited by Daniel H. Ludlow, 4:1577-80. 5 vols. New York: Macmillan, 1992. There is little information about women in the Book of Mormon, but some general conclusions may be reached. Men had the prominent roles in political, military, and religious institutions. As in the Near East, marriage and childbearing carried religious significance and great honor. Monogamy was expected unless otherwise commanded of the Lord. Husbands and wives were expected to be loyal and faithful to one another. Only six women are named in the book. [J.W.M.]

B.197 Boyce, Robert D. "Realism of Truth and the Anti-Christ." In *A Symposium on the Book of Mormon*, 1-4. Salt Lake City: Church of Jesus Christ of Latter-day Saints, CES, August 1986. The scientific method is too limited for the understanding of spiritual truth, as is shown in the case of two Anti-Christs, Sherem and Korihor, in the Book of Mormon. Alma and Jacob are examples of people who used man's reasoning supplemented with spiritual revelation to know truth. [B.D.]

B.198 Boyd, George. "The Traditional Mormon Doctrine of Man." In *Line Upon Line: Essays on Mormon Doctrine*, edited by Gary James Bergera, 145-57. Salt Lake City, UT: Signature Books, 1989. The concept of the nature of man in Mormon theology is influenced greatly by the optimistic view of the Book of Mormon. It teaches that men are to have joy, that the fall was a part of God's plan, that this earth was created for man, and that human beings are capable of perfection. [J.W.M.]

B.199 Bradford, William R. "How Do You Know?" *Ensign* 13 (November 1983): 68-69. The Book of Mormon is the record of a fallen people, and contains the solution to overcoming the fallen nature of mankind. It "outlines . . . what has been done for us and what we must do ourselves to overcome our fallen condition and return to the presence of God." [S.P.S.]

B.200 Bradley, Ruth Olive. *Great Themes from the Book of Mormon for Family Activities*. Independence, MO: Herald House, 1974. The goal of this work is "to increase family interest and skill in using the Book of Mormon" with the hope that all will better understand "the influence of Jesus Christ upon all people." Includes a series of activities designed to open the way to better communication within family groups. Activities include planting a Book of Mormon garden, planning a family reunion, and making a family autograph book. [A.T.]

B.201 Brady, Rodney H. *Book of Mormon Outline*. Tucson, AZ: Brady, 1961. An outline that intends to aid students of the Book of Mormon to understand how each part of the Book of Mormon relates to the whole. Author identifies various Book of Mormon writers according to book name and chapter, chronology and locale, and general and specific events surrounding the individual. [J.W.M.]

B.202 Bramwell, E. Craig. "Hebrew Idioms in the Small Plates of Nephi." M.A. thesis, Brigham Young University, 1960. An examination is made of the influence of biblical English literature prevalent in Joseph Smith's day upon the translation of the Book of Mormon. Also a scholarly inquiry into the verbal and syntactical structure in the small plates compared with Hebrew grammatical structures. [J.W.M.]

B.203 Bramwell, E. Craig. "Hebrew Idioms in the Small Plates of Nephi." *IE* 64 (July 1961): 496-97, 517. Inasmuch as the Book of Mormon is a literal translation from a Hebrew record, one would expect to find the frequent use of Hebraic idiomatic expressions in it. Bramwell provides examples of a number of Hebraisms, such as compound subjects, frequent usage of the conjunction "and," a limited number of vocabulary words, and the repetitive use of possessive pronouns. [R.C.D.]

B.204 Brandt, Edward J. "I Have a Question: Why are the words *adieu*, *bible*, and *baptize* in the Book of Mormon? These words weren't known in Book of Mormon times." *Ensign* 15 (October 1985): 17-18. Also in *A Sure Foundation: Answers to Difficult Gospel Questions*, 16-18. Salt Lake City: Deseret Book, 1988. Answers allegations that the words "adieu," "bible," and "baptize" in the Book of Mormon are anachronisms. [D.M.]

B.205 Brandt, Edward J. "The Law of Moses and the Law of Christ." In *A Witness of Jesus Christ*, edited by Richard P. Draper, 18-36. Salt Lake City: Deseret Book, 1990. Refers frequently to the Book of Mormon (and other sources) to explain the role of the law of Moses and the law of Christ in salvific history. [D.M.]

B.206 Brandt, Edward J. "The Name 'Jesus Christ' Revealed to the Nephites." In *The Book of Mormon: Second Nephi, The Doctrinal Structure*, edited by Monte S. Nyman and Charles D. Tate Jr., 201-6. Provo, UT: Brigham Young University Religious Studies Center, 1989. The name "Jesus Christ" is of Greek derivation. It appears, however, in the Book of Mormon because Book of Mormon prophets received revelation telling them the name by which Jesus would be known in the future. [B.D.]

B.207 Brannan, Samuel. "Another Evidence of the Book of Mormon." *The Prophet* Vol. "L" (8 March 1845): 1. Compares the story of the brother of Jared and his family with a Scythian/Phoenician historical account that possesses similar elements, i.e., building a tower, the confusion of tongues, and a family whose language was preserved. [J.W.M.]

B.208 Brannan, Samuel. "The Journey of Lehi and His Family from Jerusalem to the Continent of America" in Five Parts. In *The Prophet* Vol. "L" (1, 8, 15, 22, 29 March 1845): 1 (note: each of the five parts begins on page 1 and is one page long). Part 1 contains an Aztec map preserved among the Mexican natives, depicting the journey of their forefathers to America that recalls the Nephites journey to America; part 2 presents an old facsimile depicting four persons traveling toward a tree with a rod leading toward it, recalling the tree of life story of the Book of Mormon; parts 3 and 4 relate the Zion's Camp march and a report of finding a burial mound with stone altars, which resulted in the discovery of Zelph, who had fallen in the final battle among the Lamanites; part 5 does not deal directly with the Book of Mormon. [J.W.M.]

B.209 "The Brass Plates." *Friend* 19 (July 1989): 16-20. Cartoon depiction for children of the story of the brass plates. [J.W.M.]

B.210 Briggs, Kay, comp. *Most Quoted Scriptures of the Standard Works of the Church of Jesus Christ of Latter-day Saints*. Orem, UT: Randall Publishers, 1980. Lists scriptural passages from the Book of Mormon and other standard works under a comprehensive list of gospel topics. [J.W.M.]

B.211 Brigham, Johnson. "The Original Manuscript of the Book of Mormon." *World Today* 9 (October 1905): 1101-6. Recounts what happened to both the original manuscript of the Book of Mormon and a second manuscript deposited in the cornerstone of the Nauvoo House. Inserts a detailed account of the coming forth of the Book of Mormon, using Joseph Smith's own account as the main source. [D.M.]

B.212 Brigham Young University College of Religious Instruction. *A Catalogue of Theses and Dissertations Concerning the Church of Jesus Christ of Latter-day Saints, Mormonism and Utah*. Provo, UT: Brigham Young University, 1971. The theses and dissertations are listed according to authors and titles. Subjects such as "Lamanites and Polynesians," "Book of Mormon History," and "Book of Mormon" can be found in the subject index. [B.D.]

B.213 Brimhall, Dennis C. "The Eight-Year Book of Mormon." *Ensign* 19 (February 1989): 32-33. A family received many rewards from reading the Book of Mormon together every day until they finished it eight years later. [B.D.]

B.214 Brimhall, George H. "The Book of Mormon an Evidence in Itself of Its Divinity." *IE* 26 (September 1923): 981-82. The author notes that the Book of Mormon can be considered a classic work, since interest in it endures. Some people vouch for the valuable principles contained in it, but cannot accept the miraculousness of it. Its harmony with the Bible makes it a genuine new witness for the life, teachings, and divinity of Jesus Christ. [D.M.]

B.215 Brinley, Douglas E. "The First Families of the Book of Mormon." In *Doctrines of the Book of Mormon, 1991 Sperry Symposium*, edited by Bruce A. Van Orden and Brent L. Top, 29-41. Salt Lake City: Deseret Book, 1992. The Book of Mormon provides excellent guidance regarding family relationships. For instance, Lehi showed how to avoid family arguments, Sariah demonstrated qualities of motherhood, and a number of positive and negative familial attitudes appeared in the brothers of Nephi, Laman, and Lemuel. [B.D.]

B.216 Brinley, Douglas E. "The Promised Land and Its Covenant Peoples." In *The Book of Mormon: Helaman through 3 Nephi 8, According to Thy Word*, edited by Monte S. Nyman and Charles D. Tate Jr., 39-63. Provo, UT: Brigham Young University Religious Studies Center, 1992. Shows the covenantal relationship between God and the ancient inhabitants of the Americas—the antediluvian patriarchs, the Jaredites, the Lehites, and Mulekites. Includes a discussion of the gentiles. Enumerates ten stages that exist between righteousness and wickedness. [D.M.]

B.217 Brinley, Geri. "The Book of Mormon as a Guide for Parents." *Ensign* 18 (July 1988): 38-41. Finding solutions to parenting problems while studying the Book of Mormon was an answer to fervent prayer. This article contains a full-page chart of principles, scriptural references, and application to daily life. [J.W.M.]

B.218 Broadbank, Thomas W. "The Book of Mormon Plates." *MS* 68 (9 August 1906, 16 August 1906): 499-502, 524-27. An exhibition of the gold plates would not convert nonbelievers to the truthfulness of the Book of Mormon. Few people would have access to, or would be able to read the plates. The testimonies of the witnesses were never revoked. [A.C.W.]

B.219 Brockbank, Bernard P. "Book of Mormon on Prayer." *CR* (October 1979): 83-86. Book of Mormon teachings on prayer instruct individuals that repentance coupled with prayer purifies and leads to greater perfection, meaningful prayer leads to salvation, and sincere prayer brings answers and blessings. [J.W.M.]

B.220 Brockbank, Bernard P. "Seek and Ye Shall Find." *IE* 71 (December 1968): 61-63. The Book of Mormon is a missionary tool that teaches the true character of Jesus Christ. The proper approach to obtaining a testimony of the Book of Mormon is outlined. [B.W.J.]

B.221 Brookbank, T. W. "A Book of Mormon Consistency." *IE* 13 (September 1910): 997-98. The author notes that Jesus did not mention the Scribes and Pharisees in his 3 Nephi discourses, even in the parallel passages from the Sermon on the Mount. [D.M.]

B.222 Brookbank, T. W. "The Book of Mormon Needed." *MS* 72 (March 17, 24, 1910): 161-66, 177-80. The moral and religious principles contained in the Book of Mormon are akin to those in the Bible. The Book of Mormon does, however, contain new teachings. It specifies the proper mode of baptism, rejects infant baptism, rejects the doctrine of predestination, is a second witness of the Savior, stresses the terrible consequences of disobedience to gospel laws, and demonstrates the principle of modern revelation. [R.H.B.]

B.223 Brookbank, T. W. "The Book of Mormon Originally Written in Hieroglyphics." *IE* 14 (March 1911-September 1911): 395-99; 500-505; 703-10; 983-88. Offers some evidence from worldwide sources to corroborate Mormon's statement in the Book of Mormon that the text was written in reformed Egyptian characters. [L.D.]

B.224 Brookbank, T. W. "Concerning the Book of Mormon." *MS* 76 (February 1914): 88-92. Argues that the idea that Joseph Smith actually wrote the Book of Mormon is ridiculous and such an accomplishment would be similar to someone writing a 10 year historical work in a few weeks. [B.D.]

B.225 Brookbank, T. W. "Concerning the Book of Mormon Plates." *MS* 75 (July 1913): 424-28, 440-45. Argues that it would be useless to show the Book of Mormon plates to the public, for a display of the gold plates would not build faith in Jesus Christ. The Lord has already sent a multitude of witnesses to testify of the Book of Mormon. [B.D.]

B.226 Brookbank, T. W. "Concerning the Brass Plates." *MS* 83 (July-August 1921): 433-36, 449-53, 465-68, 481-84, 497-501. In response to the objection that Israelites could not have engraved a record on brass plates, Brookbank shows examples in the Old Testament that indicate that they did in fact use brass in creating records (Isaiah 8:1-2 and Habakkuk 2:2). The brass plates used by Isaiah and Habakkuk are what became the brass plates that Lehi took to the America. [B.D.]

B.227 Brookbank, T. W. "Concerning the Charge of Copying." *MS* 76 (3 September 1914): 568-73. Answers the charge that Joseph Smith copied passages from the Bible into the Book of Mormon by arguing that often the Lord does not repeat laws and prophecies to men verbatim. This is clearly seen in the Hebrew Bible where it is observed that men who lived in the same land and in corresponding time periods recorded events differently as a comparison between passages of the Bible shows. [J.W.M.]

B.228 Brookbank, T. W. "Concerning the Urim and Thummim." *MS* 76 (August 1914): 552-7. Argues that the Urim and Thummim used by Joseph Smith was the same employed by the Israelites as mentioned in the Bible. The Mulekites brought it to the American continent and it was handed down through the generations and finally buried with the plates that Moroni gave to Joseph Smith. [B.D.]

B.229 Brookbank, T. W. "A Defence [sic] of the Book of Mormon." *MS* 86 (17 January 1924): 36-39, 52-55, 59-60. Presents evidences of the Book of Mormon, including: the Book of Mormon omits the letters *q, x,* or *w* from proper names, does not use contractions, indicative of a Hebrew language; omits from the book of Ether references to the priesthood, the law of Moses, stories of Abraham, Isaac, Jacob, Joseph, Moses, and other references that are Israelite, except for commentary inserted by Moroni. Also argues that Joseph Smith did not use the published writings of Del Rio, who visited ruins in America in 1767, as he translated the Book of Mormon. [J.W.M.]

B.230 Brookbank, T. W. "Easily Caught." *MS* 75 (July 1913): 488-93. Responds to the objection that the Book of Mormon was originally inscribed on metal plates. Numerous examples in the Old Testament demonstrate the working of metal from early ages, including Tubal-Cain's work with brass and iron (Genesis 4:22), the brass gates of Babylon (Isaiah 45:1-2), the use of steel in Job's day (Job 20:24), the golden calf made in the wilderness, and all the gold of Moses' tabernacle (Exodus 25:17-36). [B.D.]

B.231 Brookbank, T. W. "Hebrew Idioms and Analogies in the Book of Mormon" (series). *IE* 13 (December 1909, January 1910, February 1910, March 1910, April 1910): 117-21, 234-39, 336-42, 418-20, 538-43. Vol. 17, 18 (January 1914, February 1914, March 1914, May 1914, July 1914, August 1914, September 1914, October 1914, December 1915): 189-92, 366-70, 471-75, 623-27, 881-84, 972-75, 1061-63, 1147-51, 136-43. A series that produces evidence that the Book of Mormon is an ancient Hebrew work, containing Hebraisms. Emphasizes: (1) The Book of Mormon contains peculiar grammatical structures that are similarly found in the Bible, (2) many of the proper names in the Book of Mormon possess a notable Jewish character, and (3) many of the Jaredite proper names contain Hebraic similarities that date back to the period predating the Tower of Babel. [D.M.]

B.232 Brookbank, T W. "Nephite—Christian Experience." *MS* 72 (10 February 1910): 81-85. There is no greater Christian experience than that of Nephi as recorded in 2 Nephi 4. Nephi traverses from the agony of spiritual battle with the hosts of darkness through various levels of assurance, obtaining relief, gratitude, then victory. Nephi's conflict provides an example to missionaries who must look to God. [J.W.M.]

B.233 Brookbank, T W. "Parentage of Ancient American Art and Religion." *MS* 72 (2 September–24 November 1910): 609-14, 628-31, 644-47, 661-63, 684-86, 692-95, 708-11, 730-33, 740-43, 747. A series that discusses the Babylonian and Israelite people who established Book of Mormon civilizations. Suggests that the Jaredites were Semites. The ancient ruins left in America have distinct Babylonian and Assyrian influence. The Nephite-Israelite people of the Book of Mormon have also left their mark upon civilization. [J.W.M.]

B.234 Brookbank, T W. "Pitfalls Avoided by the Translator of the Book of Mormon." *MS* 71 (6 May 1909): 273-79, 289-93. Describes many mistakes that Joseph Smith could have made if he were a fraud who wrote the Book of Mormon. For instance, Joseph Smith did not incorporate modern geographical names, punctuation, chapter and verse markings, modern terms for clothing, alcoholic beverages, military terms, days of the week, names of months, nor titles such as mister or doctor. [B.D.]

B.235 Brookbank, T. W. "Reply to a Recent Critic." *MS* 75 (9, 16 July 1914): 440-45, 456-61. Defends the Book of Mormon against the charge that it cannot be God-inspired since its literary merits are so poor. Believes that its poor literary style supports its claim even more since good style cannot be had from translating Egyptian hieroglyphics. [B.D.]

B.236 Brookbank, T W. "A Study in American Hebraic Names." *IE* 20-21 (December 1916; January, February, June 1917): 166-70; 224-36, 328-35, 669-76. Cites many words and names found in the Americas that coincide and correspond with Hebrew names and words. [L.D.]

B.237 Brookbank, T W. "Were the Brass Plates Written in Egyptian?" *Young Woman's Journal* 32 (April, May, June 1921): 204-8, 292-95, 368-

70. Looking at a variety of cultural and linguistic aspects to support his point of view, the author defends the Mormon belief that the brass plates were written in Egyptian. [L.D.]

B.238 Brooks, Melvin R. "Book of Mormon." In Brooks's *LDS Reference Encyclopedia*, 51-54. Salt Lake City: Bookcraft, 1960. A brief narration of the coming forth and publication of the Book of Mormon precedes a list and discussion of 28 "Peculiarities of the Book of Mormon," including: the Book of Mormon does not use surnames, nor names for modern fabric or articles of clothing. Typical of the Hebrew language, contractions are not used nor are the letters *q, x*, or *w* used in proper names. [J.W.M.]

B.239 Brooks, Melvin R. "Parables of the Book of Mormon." In Brooks's *Parables of the Kingdom,* 155-57. Salt Lake City: Deseret Book, 1965. A brief historical account of the Book of Mormon is given recognizing that the teachings of the Lord existed in the Book of Mormon before the Savior's ministry. However, the parables were absent. During his visit, he taught parables in America paralleling those in the Bible. [J.W.M.]

B.240 "The Brother of Jared." *Friend* 18 (January 1988): 16-17. A short summary of the story of the brother of Jared designed for children. [M. D. P.]

B.241 Brough, Janet N. *Book of Mormon Activity Book.* Salt Lake City: Acorn, 1983. Contains crossword puzzles, matching games, and other activities for children. [D.W.P.]

B.242 Brown, Amanda J. "A Design Study in Costume for Projected Dramatic Productions Prescribing a Book of Mormon Setting Identified Herein as Late Preclassic Mesoamerican Culture." M.A. thesis, Brigham Young University, 1968. Creates drawings of costumes that attempt to be historically accurate to the Late Preclassic period (500 B.C.–200 A.D.) of Mesoamerica and are dramatically effective. [B.D.]

B.243 Brown, Bruce L. "The Stick of Joseph and the Stick of Judah." In *BYU 1986-1986 Devotional and Fireside Speeches*, edited by Karen Seely, 172-179. Provo, UT: BYU Press, 1986. When studied in conjunction with each other, the Hebrew Bible and the Book of Mormon provide the reader with greater insights into scriptural studies. Author shares personal learning experiences. [J.W.M.]

B.244 Brown, Cheryl. "Book of Alma." In *Encyclopedia of Mormonism*, edited by Daniel H. Ludlow, 1:150-52. 5 vols. New York: Macmillan, 1992. An overall view of the longest book in the Book of Mormon, the book of Alma, which covers thirty-nine years of Nephite history (91-52 B.C.). The theme of the entire book is that the pure testimony of Christ is mightier than politics or the sword in establishing peace and goodness. [J.W.M.]

B.245 Brown, Cheryl. " 'I Speak Somewhat Concerning That Which I Have Written.' " In *The Book of Mormon: Jacob through Words of Mormon, To Learn with Joy*, edited by Monte S. Nyman and Charles D. Tate, 55-72. Provo, UT: Brigham Young University Religious Studies Center, 1990. Gives reasons why the Book of Mormon writers excluded some materials from the Book of Mormon and yet included other items. Knowing what was included and why permits members of the Church to know what the Lord wants them to learn from the Book of Mormon and how he wants them to approach the book. [B.D.]

B.246 Brown, Gayle O. "Love in the Book of Mormon." In *The Book of Mormon: The Keystone Scripture*, edited by Paul R. Cheesman, S. Kent Brown, and Charles D. Tate Jr., 151-63. Provo, UT: Brigham Young University Religious Studies Center, 1988. There are many ways that the Book of Mormon teaches about love. It instructs readers what to love and what not to love. It also demonstrates how individuals can increase their ability to love. [B.D.]

B.247 Brown, Hugh B. "Book of Mormon Testimony." In Brown's *Continuing the Quest,* 95-111. Salt Lake City: Deseret Book, 1961. Tells what the Book of Mormon says about Christ. [D.M.]

B.248 Brown, Hugh B. "A Book You Should Read—And Why." In *Eternal Quest,* edited by Charles Manley Brown, 140-43. Salt Lake City: Bookcraft, 1956. Presents an overview of the

Book of Mormon and its message. Bears his testimony and exhorts his readers to test Moroni's promise. [J.W.M.]

B.249 Brown, Hugh B. "We Affirm Our Faith." *IE* 61 (December 1958): 944-45. After one hundred thirty years the influence of the Book of Mormon continues to steadily increase. It is the word of God, a sacred record of ancient inhabitants of America, translated by the power of God. Though many have tried to discredit it, the Book of Mormon is probably the most influential and most widely discussed book in America. It is a witness of Christ. [J.W.M.]

B.250 Brown, Robert L., and Rosemary Brown. *They Lie in Wait to Deceive*. Vol. 2. Mesa, AZ: Brownsworth, 1984. A rebuttal and refutation of the claims made by the authors of *Who Really Wrote the Book of Mormon?* Shows that the authors apparently falsified statements made by handwriting analysts. Also shows why most today reject the Spaulding origin for the Book of Mormon. [M.R.]

B.251 Brown, S. Kent. "Alma's Conversion: Reminiscences in His Sermons." In *The Book of Mormon: Alma, The Testimony of the Word*, edited by Monte S. Nyman and Charles D. Tate Jr., 141-56. Provo, UT: Brigham Young University Religious Studies Center, 1992. Recalls Alma's conversion and the profound change it made upon the Nephite church. Allusions to his experience are given in most of Alma's recorded sermons (see Alma 5, 7, 9-13, 29, 30, 32, 33, 36, and 38-42). Alma saw himself racked with eternal torment for three days and finally received indescribable joy knowing of the atonement of Jesus, and was born again. [N.K.Y.]

B.252 Brown, S. Kent "The Exodus: Seeing It As a Test, a Testimony, and a Type." *Ensign* 20 (February 1990): 54-57. The Israelite exodus of the Old Testament parallels certain Book of Mormon passages and demonstrates that God can and will deliver his people from bondage. Several Book of Mormon characters recalled the Israelite exodus—Nephi, to provide encouragement for his brothers; Helaman, to members of the Gadianton robbers; Alma the Elder, when he fled from King Noah; and the people of King Limhi used it as a pattern. [J.W.M.]

B.253 Brown, S. Kent. "The Exodus Pattern in the Book of Mormon." *BYU Studies* 30 (Summer 1991): 111-26. An expansion of an article written for the *Ensign*, February 1990. Similarities between the exodus of the children of Israel and Lehi's departure are listed. The exodus motif is used throughout the Book of Mormon. [J.W.M.]

B.254 Brown, S. Kent. "Lehi's Personal Record: Quest for a Missing Source." *BYU Studies* 24 (1984): 19-42. An argument that the brothers Nephi and Jacob employed the personal record of Lehi their father as a primary source in writing their records. In developing their scriptural records, Nephi and Jacob would have had access to their father's writings or may have recalled his teachings and exhortations. This can be demonstrated by the fact that in many instances the brothers quoted their father directly and at other times they paraphrased what was said or written by him. Through detailed study of the writings of Nephi and Jacob much can be learned about the record of Lehi. In fact, "three easily discernible categories" pertaining to the nature and content of the record of Lehi come to view. These are his "prophecies, visions, and teachings." [D.W.P.]

B.255 Brown, S. Kent. "Nephi's Use Of Lehi's Record." In *Rediscovering The Book of Mormon*, edited by John L. Sorenson and Melvin J. Thorne, 3-14. Salt Lake City: Deseret Book and FARMS, 1991. Explores the references to Lehi's record as found in 1 & 2 Nephi and Jacob, and discusses Nephi's use of that record. Lehi's dreams and prophecies hold instructions on a variety of subjects including the marriage relationship, Adam and Eve, the fall, choices, the role of the Savior, and the house of Israel. [J.W.M.]

B.256 Brown, S. Kent. "The Prophetic Laments of Samuel the Lamanite." *Journal of Book of Mormon Studies* 1 (Fall 1992): 163-80. The sermon of Samuel the Lamanite comprises poetic forms that bear similarities to laments found in the Bible and the Dead Sea Scroll *Thanksgiving Hymns*. The prophetic laments of Samuel exhibit a set of prophecies that find fulfillment in later periods, including during the days of Mormon, the compiler and editor of the Book of Mormon. [R.H.B.]

B.257 Brown, S. Kent, and John Tvedtnes. "When did Jesus Appear to the Nephites in Bountiful?" Provo, UT: FARMS, 1989. Brown concludes that "the cumulative evidence weighs in the direction of the Savior's having come to the Nephites only after a substantial period of time. That period must have assuredly extended into the latter half of the year—presumably between October and April—if we trust Mormon's chronological notions concerning the timing of both the destruction (3 Nephi 8:5) and the manifestation of the Savior (3 Nephi 10:18)." See also under John Tvedtnes. [B.D.]

B.258 Brown, S. Kent, and Terrance L. Szink. "Lehi." In *Encyclopedia of Mormonism*, edited by Daniel H. Ludlow, 2:827-28. 5 vols. New York: Macmillan, 1992. Lehi, the patriarch of the Book of Mormon people, led his family from Jerusalem about 600 B.C. His descendants split into two groups following his death. He was a prophet whose words are partially retained in the Book of Mormon. Many of his prophecies are yet to be fulfilled. [J.W.M.]

B.259 Brown, Wade. *The God-Inspired Language of the Book of Mormon: Structuring and Commentary.* Clackamas, OR: Rainbow, 1988. Arranges the entire text of the Book of Mormon according to parallelistic patterns. Presents explanations on the different forms of parallelisms and poetic patterns and shows how they relate to the interpretation of the text. [B.D.]

B.260 Bucci, Timothy D. *Jew and the American Indian.* 3rd edition. Monongahela, PA: Church of Jesus Christ (Bickertonites), 1968. Gives a brief history of the Jewish people and biblical references concerning their future, then lists Book of Mormon prophecies relating to the future of the American Indian. [A.T.]

B.261 Budge, W. "A Marvelous Work." *MS* 41 (20 January 1879): 40-43. The promises and prophecies of the Book of Mormon made to the descendants of the ancient American inhabitants are being fulfilled. The descendants have accepted and rejoiced in the Book of Mormon, as was foretold in the book. The gathering of Israel is based upon faith, repentance, baptism, and the reception of the Holy Ghost. [J.W.M.]

B.262 "Building a Ship." *Friend* 11 (March 1981): 20-21. A two-page full-color cartoon depiction that recalls Nephi building the ship to carry the family to the promised land (1 Nephi 17-18). [J.W.M.]

B.263 "Building the Ship." *Friend* 17 (October 1989): 40-41. Children's illustrated story about Nephi building the ship. [M.R.]

B.264 Bunker, William E. "Promises of Old—Yet New." *IE* 47 (December 1944): 741. A collection of Book of Mormon scriptures that reiterate the promises of the Lord concerning the coming forth of the Book of Mormon. [J.W.M.]

B.265 Bunker, William E. "Some Facts Concerning America's Witness for Christ." *IE* 48 (September 1945): 500. A list of the fifteen books of the Book of Mormon and a chronological order of the Book of Mormon scribes, from Nephi to Moroni. [J.W.M.]

B.266 Burgess, Allan K. *Living the Book of Mormon.* Salt Lake City: Bookcraft, 1991. Sixty-one brief chapters discuss various sections of the Book of Mormon. Gospel application is the goal of the author. The author states, "When we immerse ourselves in the scriptures with the desire to apply what we learn, we receive a much deeper understanding and witness of the eternal truths found there than when we merely read to learn facts" (preface). [D.W.P.]

B.267 Burgess, Allan K., and Max H. Molgard. *Fun For Family Night: Book of Mormon Edition.* Salt Lake City: Bookcraft, 1990. Lessons and activities geared to the needs of children for family home evening. There are twenty lessons on Book of Mormon subjects and people. [J.W.M.]

B.268 Burgess, Allan, Max Jean, and Bette Molgard. *A Child's Book of Mormon Activity Book.* 3 vols. Salt Lake City: Bookcraft, 1987. A clever activity book for children in three volumes. A Book of Mormon story is retold, then games and puzzles follow to reinforce the story. [J.W.M.]

B.269 Burgon, Glade L. "The Book of Mormon and the Charge: 'The Product of One Man of Mediocre Ability.' " *IE* 65 (January-February 1962): 44-48 108-9, 134-35. An apologetic work responding to claims that the Book of Mormon is the product of one man of mediocre ability. The author reports the finds of an analysis comparing the styles of different Book of Mormon writers and concludes that the different writers each have different styles, which supports Joseph Smith's claim that he translated the work. [B.D.]

B.270 Burgon, Glade L. *The Tree of Life As a World Symbol of Divine Origin.* Provo, UT: n.p., August 1959. Writes concerning the symbolical nature of the tree of life in Old and New World cultures. The Book of Mormon treatment of the tree of life (1 Nephi 11-15) clarifies and adds greater significance to the subject than does the Bible. [J.W.M.]

B.271 Burgon, Heber J. "Internal Evidences of the Book of Mormon." *MS* 67 (11 May 1905): 292-93. Cites the promise made in Moroni 10:4 that honest seekers may receive a spiritual witness of the truthfulness of the Book of Mormon. The testimonies of many thousands of converts bears witness to this truth. [R.H.B.]

B.272 Burr, Brenda Hulse. "Home Evening Scripture Parties." *Ensign* 20 (April 1990): 73. One enjoyable way to approach Book of Mormon scripture reading with the family is given. [B.D.]

B.273 Burton, Alma P. "Book of Mormon." In Burton's *Doctrines From The Prophets: Choice Selections from Latter-day Leaders*, 56-62. Salt Lake City: n.p., 1970. A compilation of quotes that shares the testimonies of Joseph Smith, Brigham Young, Heber J. Grant, and George Q. Cannon concerning the coming forth of the Book of Mormon, its purpose and power, its contents, and the heritage of America. Also contains Joseph Smith's own testimony concerning the literal translation of the title page. [J.W.M.]

B.274 Burton, Alma P. "The Natural Man . . . An Enemy to God?" *IE* 68 (December 1965): 1094-95, 1182-83. King Benjamin stated that "the natural man is an enemy to God, and has been since the fall of Adam" (Mosiah 3: 19). Brigham Young declared mankind God's noblest work, but when Adam and Eve fell from the presence of God they were brought into an unnatural state, in contact with influences of an evil nature. The "natural man" spoken of by King Benjamin is equivalent to President Young's "unnatural man." Both refer to mankind that has been estranged from God. [J.W.M.]

B.275 Burton, Theodore M. Untitled talk. *CR* 155 (October 1985): 80-83. Uses Alma 41:9-10 and 3 Nephi 18 to exhort the Saints to love and help a person who has transgressed come back into the Church. [B.D.]

B.276 Burton, Theodore M. "Wisdom and Learning of the World." *CR* (April 1961): 126-29. Describes the pitfalls of scholarship without righteousness and obedience. Utilizes the Book of Mormon teaching, "to be learned is good if they hearken unto the counsels of God." [R.C.D.]

B.277 Bush, Edna K. "The Book of Mormon and My Conversion." *Ensign* 2 (June 1972): 28-31. A personal conversion account. Through the reading of the Book of Mormon, the author tells of the Spirit testifying of the truth of the book. [B.T.]

B.278 Bush, Edna K. *Dissecting the Book of Mormon: A Fresh Approach to the Book of Mormon.* St. Petersburg, FL: Edna K. Bush, 1968. A Book of Mormon classroom or Family Home Evening study aid, designed to help students reach a better understanding of the contents of the Book of Mormon. [L.D.]

B.279 Bush, Edna K. "Magnificent Messages." *Instructor* 102 (November 1967): 460. Gives references for several "choice passages" in the Book of Mormon, which include sermons, father-to-son talks, letters, missionary experiences, and visits of Jesus Christ. Accompanying chart details compilation of records that made up the plates given to Joseph Smith. [A.C.W.]

B.280 Bush, Lester E., Jr. "The Spaulding Theory Then and Now." *Dialogue* 10 (Autumn 1977):

40-69. A scholarly review of the Spaulding theory and its importance today. The author concludes that due to imprecise evidence, the Spaulding theory is not conclusive. Included are extensive notes and references on the subject. [B.D.]

B.281 Bushman, Richard L. "The Book of Mormon and the American Revolution." *BYU Studies* 16 (Autumn 1976): 3-20. Also in *Book of Mormon Authorship: New Light on Ancient Origins*, edited by Noel B. Reynolds, 189-212. Provo, UT: Brigham Young University Religious Studies Center, 1982. Analyzes the statement that "the Book of Mormon can best be explained by [Joseph Smith's] responsiveness to the [political] provincial opinions of [his] time." Bushman looks at the political milieu of Joseph Smith's New York, the attitude of heroic resistance or divine deliverance, enlightenment and popular opposition to monarchy, the reign of the judges and American constitutional government. Bushman concludes that Book of Mormon politics are biblical and American politics are not; the Book of Mormon does not reflect American political attitudes of Joseph Smith's time. [B.D.]

B.282 Bushman, Richard L. "The Book of Mormon in Early Mormon History." In *New Views of Mormon History: A Collection of Essays in Honor of Leonard J. Arrington,* edited by Davis Bitton and Maureen Ursenbach Beecher, 3-18. Salt Lake City, UT: University of Utah Press, 1987. Many scholars have concluded that magic "lay at the heart of nineteenth-century Mormonism," but they overlook the role that the Book of Mormon played in the attitudes of the early Church. Bushman proposes to analyze broad themes in the Book of Mormon and consider how they affected the early Church. Also explains how prominent the theme of record keeping is in the Book of Mormon, and the manner in which whole societies lived, perished, and were restored based on record keeping. The importance of records and their translation greatly affected the Church, especially Joseph Smith who was constantly occupied with translating records. [B.D.]

B.283 Bushman, Richard L. "Faithful History." In *Faithful History: Essays on Writing Mormon History*, edited by George D. Smith, 1-17. Salt Lake City: Signature Books, 1992. Written histories change as historical methods and new evidence is uncovered; Mormon history is consistent with this. Mormon historians may obtain insights into the nature of history from the Book of Mormon. It offers clues of what are appropriate concerns for Mormon historians—the tension between humanity and God, the Church and the world, and economic forces. The eyes of those who love God see the effects of revelation, providential direction, and inspiration on history. [J.W.M.]

B.284 Bushman, Richard L. *Joseph Smith and the Beginnings of Mormonism.* Chicago, IL: University of Illinois Press, 1984. Explains the history of Joseph Smith's family, the first vision, and the translation of the Book of Mormon. Provides details about the restoration of the gospel and early Mormon teachings relating to revivalist churches, such as the Cambellites. [L.D.]

B.285 Bushman, Richard L. "Joseph Smith in the Current Age." In *Joseph Smith: The Prophet, the Man,* edited by Susan Easton Black and Charles D. Tate Jr., 33-48. Provo, UT: Brigham Young University Religious Studies Center, BYU, 1993. The writings of the Book of Mormon prophets were concerned deeply with the rise and fall of nations as well as public and private morality. Such ideas from the book and subsequent revelations aided Joseph Smith in outlining a new organizational pattern that ultimately led to the desire to build Zion. It is the vision of Moroni, the concept of a miraculous translation of the Book of Mormon, and continuing revelation that makes it so hard for rational, educated people of our day to accept the gospel. [J.W.M.]

B.286 Bushman, Richard L. "The Lamanite View of Book of Mormon History." In *By Study and Also by Faith,* edited by John M. Lundquist and Stephen D. Ricks, 2:52-72. Salt Lake City: Deseret Book and FARMS, 1990. Considers the Book of Mormon story from the standpoint of the Lamanites and other people who dissented from the Nephites. The continual Lamanite complaints, beginning with Laman and Lemuel, were that the government power and rule belonged to them. The angry Lamanites and Nephite dissenters were consistently at war with the Nephites to subject them, to enslave them, to force them away from their belief in Christ and his gospel, and to destroy them. This militant, complaining, and forceful manner that led to deprivation is contrasted with the submissive, righteous, and faithful response of the Nephites that led them to prosperity and happiness. [A.A.]

B.287 Butler, Margot J. "Women in the Book of Mormon." In *The Sixth Annual Church Educational System Religious Educators' Symposium on the Book of Mormon*, 9-12. Salt Lake City: Church of Jesus Christ of Latter-day Saints, CES, 1982. Lists every woman mentioned in the Book of Mormon and provides a thought or note that might assist instructors when teaching about each woman. [A.T.]

B.288 Butterworth, F. E. *How to Mark the Book of Mormon, a Packet of Missionary Insert Materials with Instructions*. Independence, MO: Herald House, 1973. Presents a method of marking the Book of Mormon by linking certain subjects together. Includes missionary inserts to be glued to the pages of the Book of Mormon where the subject is marked. [B.D.]

B.289 Butterworth, F. E. *Pilgrims of the Pacific*. Independence, MO: Herald House, 1974. Discusses relations between the Jaredites and Polynesians, the story of Hagoth, and the route of Lehi out of Jerusalem. [B.D.]

C.

C.001 C., J. E. "Dr. Duncan and the Book of Mormon." *MS* 52 (1 September 1890): 552-56. A defense of the Book of Mormon against the criticism of Dr. Duncan in the *Islington Gazette* of August 18th. Dr. Duncan, evidently a literary critic, concluded that the Book of Mormon was either a clumsy or barefaced forgery or a pious fraud. The author writes that the Book of Mormon makes clear many doctrines that are difficult to understand in the Bible. Also, the history and gospel taught by the Bible and the Book of Mormon are similar because both were inspired of God. [B. D.]

C.002 Cadman, Sadie B., and Sara Cadman Vancik. *A Concordance of the Book of Mormon*. Monongahela, PA: Church of Jesus Christ, 1986. A complete but not exhaustive concordance, listing words alphabetically. Contains also a historical chronology of the events in the Book of Mormon. [D.W.P.]

C.003 Caldwell, C. Max. "A Mighty Change." In *The Book of Mormon: Alma, The Testimony of the Word*, edited by Monte S. Nyman and Charles D. Tate Jr., 27-46. Provo, UT: Brigham Young University Religious Studies Center, 1992. Alma reminds the people of Zarahemla of their recent physical and spiritual captivity and reviews how the devil is able to forge the chains of hell and make them captive. Truth, which brings freedom and a "mighty change" in the hearts of individuals, is available through scripture, living prophets, and the Holy Ghost. [N.K.Y.]

C.004 Call, Gail. "Antenantiosis in the Book of Mormon." In *Reexploring the Book of Mormon*, edited by John W. Welch, 96-97. Salt Lake City: Deseret Book and FARMS, 1992. Antenantiosis states a proposition in terms of its opposite. The figure of speech is used in Jacob 4:8 as "despise not the revelations of God," and Mormon 9:29, "if ye do this and endure to the end, ye will in nowise be cast out," and in several other places. The technique, used also in the Old Testament, is an effective teaching tool. [N.K.Y.]

C.005 Callis, Charles A. *Fundamentals of Religion: A Series of Radio Addresses*. Independence, MO: Zion's Printing and Publishing, 1945. Includes two addresses about the Book of Mormon: "Book of Mormon Prophecies Fulfilled," pages 102-13, sets forth many prophecies of the Book of Mormon that have been fulfilled; and "The Coming Forth of the Book of Mormon," pages 155-70, shows that the Book of Mormon came forth at a time of spiritual unrest and higher criticism of the Bible. Includes a short narrative of the angel Moroni's visit, the delivering of the gold plates to Joseph Smith, and provides six purposes for which the Book of Mormon was written. [J.W.M.]

C.006 Callis, Charles A. "Testimony from the Book of Mormon." *IE* 49 (November 1946): 700, 717. Presents his testimony of the truthfulness of the Book of Mormon. [L.D.]

C.007 Callis, Charles A. Untitled talk. *CR* (October 1911): 87-89. The Book of Mormon came forth to establish the truthfulness of the Bible and to declare the divinity of Jesus Christ. Joseph Smith brought forth the Book of Mormon and subsequently suffered persecution similar to the manner in which Wycliffe and Tyndall were persecuted as they made the Bible available. [J.W.M.]

C.008 Callis, Charles A. Untitled talk. *CR* (October 1916): 93-96. Burial mounds in the Southern United States prompt questions concerning the identity of the people who are buried there. The Book of Mormon may shed light on such questions. The warning issued by the Lord to the ancients and to those of the present day are to follow Jesus, experience a spiritual rebirth, and practice faith, repentance, and humility as recorded in Alma 32. [J.W.M.]

C.009 Callis, Charles A. Untitled talk. *CR* (October 1937): 120-23. The richest hills on earth have not brought forth gold and silver in great amounts, but have brought forth the greatest spiritual wealth. They are Calvary in Jerusalem where the Savior wrought the atonement and the Hill Cumorah, which brought forth the truth of the Savior's marvelous ministry to his people in America. Like the Bible, the Book of Mormon testifies of Christ and reveals the great destiny of America. [J.W.M.]

C.010 Campbell, Lester E. *Scripture Index of FARMS Reprints and Preliminary Reports*. Provo, UT: FARMS, 1987. "This index lists scriptures used in FARMS papers up to early 1987. It is organized according to the subject categories in the FARMS catalog" as follows: (1) The Book of Mormon and the Ancient Near East, (2) The Book of Mormon and Ancient Mesoamerica, (3) The Book of Mormon—commentary, (4) other scriptural studies and materials. [B.D.]

C.011 Cannon, Abraham H. *Book of Mormon Catechism: Questions and Answers on the Book of Mormon*. Salt Lake City: Juvenile Instructor Office, 1886. The work was created to "induce the young people of Zion to search with greater diligence for the valuable truths contained in the revelation so ancient and modern times." Contains 62 pages of basic questions and answers about the Book of Mormon. [A.T.]

C.012 Cannon, George Q. "The Abundant Testimonies to the Work of God." *JD* 22:252-59. Liverpool, England: Church of Jesus Christ of Latter-day Saints, 18 September, 1881. God has sent a number of witnesses who have testified concerning the truthfulness of the Book of Mormon, including the Three Witnesses, the Eight Witnesses, and Joseph Smith. The convincibility of the book also lies in its prophecies. For instance, the Book of Mormon prophesies concerning the persecution of the saints and others and also prophesies that the Indians will "become an enlightened people and be redeemed from their present condition." [B.D.]

C.013 Cannon, George Q. "Book of Mormon Geography." *Instructor* 73 (April 1938): 159-60. Voices strong objection to the introduction and circulation of maps that attempt to depict the geography of the Book of Mormon. Cannon raises doubts as to the authenticity of a piece entitled the "Route Traveled by Lehi and His Company" that places the landing site of Lehi's party in Chili. [R.H.B.]

C.014 Cannon, George Q. "The Book of Mormon Geography." *Juvenile Instructor* 25 (1 January 1890): 18-19. Contention over Book of Mormon geography is detrimental to the cause of truth. The reason for this contention is due to the fact that the Book of Mormon is not a geographical primer meant to teach geographical truths. The drawing of Book of Mormon maps is discouraged. [J.W.M.]

C.015 Cannon, George Q. "Book of Mormon Prophecies Fulfilled." *JD* 25:119-29. Liverpool, England: Church of Jesus Christ of Latter-day Saints, 6 April 1884. Analyzes Book of Mormon prophecies found in 2 Nephi 29, 30, and 3 Nephi 16 that had been fulfilled and emphasizes the divine origin of the book, the purity of its translation, and the great effect it would have on many nations and peoples. Also teaches that the gospel would be carried to the remnant of Lehi and that the Bible and the Book of Mormon would be united to confound false doctrine. [J.W.M.]

C.016 Cannon, George Q. *Book of Mormon Stories, Adapted to the Capacity of Young Children and Designed for Use in Sabbath Schools, Primary Association, and for Home Readings*. Salt Lake City: George Q. Cannon and Sons Co., 1892-99. "Written for the purpose of presenting the Book of Mormon narrative in language that can be understood by small children." Contains illustrations. [B.D.]

C.017 Cannon, George Q. "The Book of Mormon Witnesses—Answers to Questions." *Juvenile Instructor* 26 (1 September 1891): 534. Offers an explanation why eight of the eleven witnesses were members of two families. [J.W.M.]

C.018 Cannon, George Q. "Discourse by President George Q. Cannon." *JD* 25:119-29. Liverpool, England: Church of Jesus Christ of Latter-day Saints, 16 April 1884. Discusses the predictions of the Book of Mormon, some evidences of its divinity, and points out the plainness of its teachings. [L.D.]

C.019 Cannon, George Q. "Editorial Thoughts." *Juvenile Instructor* 3 (1 January 1868): 4. A didactic editorial lauding Nephi's obedience and recommending imitation by the youth of the Church. [D.M.]

C.020 Cannon, George Q. "Editorial Thoughts." *Juvenile Instructor* 3 (1 June 1868): 84. Asserts that the inhabitants discovered by the Europeans in America are descendants of Laman and Lemuel. The Book of Mormon peoples lived principally in Central and South America. LDS church members should recognize the important role of the Indians among the Gentiles. [D.M.]

C.021 Cannon, George Q. "Editorial Thoughts." *Juvenile Instructor* 7 (23 November 1872): 188. Describes a disease called epizootic, which killed many horses in the Eastern states. The Book of Mormon (3 Nephi 21:14) "foretells a time when, if the people would not repent, the Lord would destroy their horses." Author the asks "who can say that the epizootic has no connection with that threat of divine displeasure?" [B.D.]

C.022 Cannon, George Q. "Editorial Thoughts." *Juvenile Instructor* 10 (11 December 1875): 294-95. Discusses Korihor and refutes his anti-Christ methods and doctrines. Relates and compares anti-Christ teachings to American popular opinion, concluding that Satan has not changed his tactics through the centuries. [A.C.W.]

C.023 Cannon, George Q. "Editorial Thoughts." *Juvenile Instructor* 11 (1 February 1876): 30. Didactic essay, showing how the Ammonite striplings or sons of Helaman are examples of childhood training that might well be exemplified in LDS homes. [D.M.]

C.024 Cannon, George Q. "Editorial Thoughts." *Juvenile Instructor* 11 (1 March 1876): 54-55. Editorial reflections on the Book of Mormon concepts of America as the choicest of lands and the necessity for righteousness for its inhabitants. Discusses secret combinations. [D.M.]

C.025 Cannon, George Q. "Editorial Thoughts." *Juvenile Instructor* 11 (15 August 1876): 186. The hostile attitude of the Americans towards the Indians is a remarkable fulfillment of Book of Mormon prophecy. LDS chruch members should consider the glorious future of the Lamanites. [D.M.]

C.026 Cannon, George Q. "Editorial Thoughts." *Juvenile Instructor* 13 (1 July 1878): 150. Refers to the dangerous and unstable secret societies that are located throughout Europe and America and relates them to the secret combinations spoken of by Moroni. [D.M.]

C.027 Cannon, George Q. "Editorial Thoughts." *Juvenile Instructor* 14 (October 1879): 222.

Cannon reports that a German scholar, Professor Rudolph, noted striking resemblances between the leading Semitic languages (Arabic and Hebrew) and the Aymara language, belonging to the Incas in Peru. Cannon suggests that a reading of the Book of Mormon would enlighten the professor. [D.M.]

C.028 Cannon, George Q. "Editorial Thoughts." *Juvenile Instructor* 16 (1 May 1881): 102. Civilized manners were not taught to the Lamanaites by Laman and Lemuel, and the Lamanites existed in a degenerate condition. On the other hand, due to the instructions of Nephi, the Nephites existed in a more civilized condition. [D.M.]

C.029 Cannon, George Q. "Editorial Thoughts." *Juvenile Instructor* 17 (1 April 1882): 104. All churches except the Church of Jesus Christ of Latter-day Saints are part of the great and abominable church that was prophesied by Nephi. They will fight against the true church and will fall into the pit that they prepared for the people of the Lord. [B.D.]

C.030 Cannon, George Q. "Editorial Thoughts." *Juvenile Instructor* 18 (1 February 1883): 40. When the Book of Mormon was published it was assumed that the American Indians were headed for extinction, but the Book of Mormon predicted that they would become a mighty people. This prophecy will yet be fulfilled. [D.M.]

C.031 Cannon, George Q. "The Future Fate of the Red Man." In Cannon's *Writings From The "Western Standard,"* 269-73. Liverpool: George Q. Cannon, 1864. While most of the original inhabitants of America were destroyed in warfare, the Book of Mormon contains promises made to them that will be fulfilled with their descendants, the American Indians. The Indians will not always be treated as an inferior people nor will God allow them to be exterminated. It would be of benefit for nations today to embrace the American Indians and care for their needs. [J.W.M.]

C.032 Cannon, George Q. "The Indians: Death of Lehi." *Juvenile Instructor* 1 (1 June 1866): 43. Recounts sundry aspects of the Book of Mormon, including an evaluation of the disposition of the Lamanites as opposed to the Nephites. [D.M.]

C.033 Cannon, George Q. *The Life of Nephi, Son of Lehi, Who Emigrated from Jerusalem, in Judea to the Land Which is Now Known as South America, about Six Centuries before the Coming of the Savior.* Salt Lake City: Juvenile Instructor Office, 1883. A biography of Nephi, in which the author narrates Nephi's story by adding personal insights and scholarly insights. [A.T.]

C.034 Cannon, George Q. "A Marvelous Work." In Cannon's *Writings From The "Western Standard."* Liverpool: George Q. Cannon, 1864: 117-119. The Book of Mormon is a great and marvelous work that was brought forth by an angel and translated by Joseph Smith. Left without excuse, this generation will know that the Book of Mormon is an inspired record. [J.W.M.]

C.035 Cannon, George Q. "Nephi's Character." *Contributor* 13 (April 1892): 289-90. The character of Nephi is exemplified by his many accomplishments, skills, and relationships. He was a leader, son, and brother who possessed great love and inspired others. He was a craftsman and hunter who showed ingenuity, industry, and good sense. [J.W.M.]

C.036 Cannon, George Q. "Prophecies and Truth of the Book of Mormon." *Juvenile Instructor* 10 (23 January 1875): 16-17. Points out that plain and precious truths lost from the Bible are included in the Book of Mormon, specifically truths concerning the mortal ministry of Jesus Christ. Quotes the teachings of Nephi and King Benjamin regarding the Messiah's earthly advent. [A.C.W.]

C.037 Cannon, George Q. "A Remarkable Coincidence." *MS* 52 (13 October 1890): 641-42. Lehi, in his final farewell to his family, stated that he "must soon lay down in the cold and silent grave, from whence no traveler can return" (2 Nephi 1:14). Inasmuch as similar words appear in the writings of William Shakespeare, Church critics believe that Joseph Smith borrowed the Book of Mormon statement from Shakespeare. However, in the ruins of Mexico similar words have been found to have been used in an ancient funeral speech. [J.W.M.]

C.038 Cannon, George Q. "Secret Combinations." In *Collected Discourses Delivered by President Wilford Woodruff, His Two Counselors, the Twelve Apostles, and Others (1894-1896),* edited by Brian H. Stuy, 4:18-25. Burbank, CA: B. H. S. Publishing, 1991. The Book of Mormon warns against secret combinations (Ether 8:19-26). Such a warning is relevant in an era of communism, nihilism, and anarchism. Therefore, Church members are advised to avoid all secret societies. [J.W.M.]

C.039 Cannon, George Q. "The Standard Works. Our Scriptures." In *Gospel Truth: Discourses and Writings of President George Q. Cannon,* vol. 2, edited by Jerald L. Newquist, 246-62. Salt Lake City: Deseret Book, 1974. The Book of Mormon contains much internal evidence coupled with the power and Spirit of God so that readers may know of its divine authenticity. Those who reject the book will find that neither external evidences nor the testimonies of witnesses will satisfy them. [J.W.M.]

C.040 Cannon, George Q. "Topics of the Times." *Juvenile Instructor* 19 (1 April 1884): 106-8. Speaks concerning Martin Harris's visit with Professor Anthon and David Whitmer as one of the witnesses of the gold plates. [A.C.W.]

C.041 Cannon, George Q. "Visit to the Land and Hill of Cumorah." *Juvenile Instructor* 8 (5 July 1873): 108-9. After making a visit to the Hill Cumorah, located near Palmyra, the author presents a description of the hill, and considers the destruction of two Book of Mormon peoples at the site. [D.M.]

C.042 Cannon, George Q. "Who Are the Indians?" *Juvenile Instructor* 1 (1, 15 January, 1, 15 February, 1 April, 1 June 1866): 1, 2, 12, 15, 28, 43. Believes that "all the Indians in North and South America, and the inhabitants of some of the islands in the Pacific Ocean, are descendants of [the Lehite] family, who came away from Jerusalem about 2,400 years" ago. [D.M.]

C.043 Cannon, Lucy Grant. "You, Too, Have Freedom of Choice." *Instructor* 98 (June 1963): 225. President Heber J. Grant, hoping to help his wayward brother Brigham, prayed, then opened the Book of Mormon hoping for the answer to his brother's plight. The book fell open to Alma 36, a chapter of hope. When Brigham read the words of consolation and faith, his life was changed. [J.W.M.]

C.044 Card, Orson Scott. "The Book of Mormon—Artifact or Artifice?" In Card's *A Storyteller in Zion,* 13-48. Bookcraft: Salt Lake City, 1993. The translator's influence is apparent in a text because of his/her choice of words. The Book of Mormon is no different. Compares Joseph Smith to fiction writer James Macpherson who fraudulently claimed to have translated ancient Celtic poetry. The fraudulent author will inadvertently give himself away by his cultural perspectives that cannot be viewed out of context. Joseph Smith was not the author of the book but merely the translator. [J.W.M.]

C.045 Card, Orson Scott. "Dissent and Treason." *Ensign* 7 (September 1977): 53-58. Examines nine accounts of dissent in the Book of Mormon and determines why they failed. He shows that unrighteous, selfish desires for gain were the chief motivating factors among the dissenters. The unselfish desire to protect freedom and God was always successful in defending against the dissenters. [B.D.]

C.046 Card, Orson Scott. "Three Kings and a Captain: Nephite Leaders in the Land of Nephi." *Ensign* 7 (January 1977): 76-82. The land of Nephi produced many notable leaders including Alma, Abinadi, Zeniff, Noah, Limhi, and Gideon as recorded in the books of Omni and Mosiah. Righteous Zeniff stood in antithesis to the evil king Noah. Gideon was a righteous defender of the faith throughout his life, finally dying by the sword in defending the gospel against Nehor. [B.D.]

C.047 Cardall, Duane V. *The Day of the Lamanite.* Salt Lake City: University of Utah Institute of Religion, 1 April 1977. Shows how Book of Mormon prophecies concerning the Lamanites are beginning to be fulfilled. [D.M.]

C.048 Cardon, Joseph E., and Samuel O. Bennion, comps. *Testimonies of the Divinity of the Church of Jesus Christ of Latter-day Saints by*

Its Leaders. Independence, MO: Zion's Printing and Publishing, 1930. Contains testimonies of leaders of the LDS Church concerning the Book of Mormon as well as other topics. Included are Joseph Smith and his family members and close associates, the witnesses to the Book of Mormon, and those involved in the translation and publication of the Book of Mormon. [J.W.M.]

C.049 Carlisle, J. E. "Corroborating the Book of Mormon." *MS* 52 (17 May 1890): 312-14. Argues that archaeological evidences that predate Columbus indicate that two distinct races once inhabited the Americas. This and other findings corroborate the truthfulness of the Book of Mormon. [J.W.M.]

C.050 Carlisle, J. E. "A Modern Miracle." *MS* 52 (September 1890): 584-85. Author believes that it is as foolish to try to disprove the Book of Mormon as it is the Bible, for both works are built upon revelation. There are, however, many who refuse to accept the teachings of both scriptures. [J.W.M.]

C.051 Carlsen, Earl W. *Christ's Answer to the Atheist, to the Jew: Who Wrote It?* Amherst, WI: Palmer, 1987. The Bible and its followers do not provide adequate proof that God exists or that Christ is his Son. The Book of Mormon does provides that proof and testifies of the divinity of Christ. The author presents 52 evidences that support the authenticity of the Book of Mormon, including the use of chiasmus, engraved metal plates, cultural similarities between the ancient Near East and ancient Mesoamerican culture, and word-print analyses. [B.D.]

C.052 Carlson, A. Edward, Jr. "Isn't the Bible Enough?" *Ensign* 16 (March 1986): 54-55. Recounts the conversion story of an individual who believed that the Bible was the only scripture needed by mankind. He read and prayed about the Book of Mormon, and after reading 2 Nephi 29:6-8, he was convinced that the Book of Mormon represented an additional scripture that came from God. [J.W.M.]

C.053 Carmack, John K. *The Book of Mormon Witnesses.* Salt Lake City: University of Utah Institute of Religion, 24 October 1986. Chronicles the experiences of the Book of Mormon witnesses and reviews their tenacious testimonies. [D.M.]

C.054 Carter, Charles W. *Organization of the Church of Jesus Christ of Latter-day Saints and Their Belief. Also the Life and History of Their Prophet, Seer and Revelator, Joseph Smith, During His Brief Life of 38 1/2 Years.* Salt Lake City: Utah Lithography, n.d. Chapters 2 through 7 pertain to the Book of Mormon. Sets forth the coming forth of the Book of Mormon, including angel Moroni's visit, its translation and publication. Contains a description of the gold plates and testimonies of Church leaders. Rejects the Spaulding story. Writes concerning the room inside of the Hill Cumorah that was filled with plates and writings. [J.W.M.]

C.055 Carter, George F. "Before Columbus." In *The Book of Mormon: The Keystone Scripture*, edited by Paul R. Cheesman, S. Kent Brown, and Charles D. Tate Jr., 164-86. Provo, UT: Brigham Young University Religious Studies Center, 1988. The origins of New World plants and chickens prove the diffusionist theory of pre-Columbian transoceanic contacts. [B.D.]

C.056 Carter, Kate B., ed. *Mormondom's First Woman Missionary Louisa Barnes Pratt: Life Story and Travels Told in Her Own Words.* Vol. 8 Salt Lake City: Daughters of the Utah Pioneers, 1974. The Book of Mormon was introduced to Louisa Barnes Pratt and her husband by Louisa's sister. Both were eventually converted, and Louisa became the first woman missionary in the Church. [J.W.M.]

C.057 "A Catacomb of Mummies Found in Kentucky." *TS* 3 (2 May 1842): 781-82. The discovery of mummies in Kentucky recalls the Hebrew practice of embalming. Author suggests that this practice was brought to ancient America by the Hebrews because, according to the Book of Mormon, the native Americans are descendants of Hebrews. [L.D.]

C.058 Caywood, Charles Sr. *I was a Protestant Minister.* Independence, MO: Herald Publishing House, n.d. Caywood, a Baptist minister, was offered a Book of Mormon to read while visiting the home of his brother. Doubt was replaced with intense interest and conversion came through reading the book. [J.W.M.]

C.059 Cazier, Donald A. "I Have A Question: We Learn in Mosiah 25:6 that the account of Alma's group covered the time they left Zarahemla until they 'returned again.' Since Alma and his followers were presumably born in the land of Nephi and had never been to Zarahemla, how is this matter reconciled?" *Ensign* 22 (August 1992): 60-1. Cazier gives a brief summary of Nephite history, and then suggests two possible explanations to the question posed in the title. (1) "Alma and his brethren" includes ancestors involved in the original colonization effort. (2) Perhaps a different time frame is involved and it is possible that Alma came from Zarahemla to colonize. [A.C.W.]

C.060 Cazier, Donald A. "Mormon's Message to Modern Militants—Or, Why Is There So Much about War in the Book of Mormon?" In *A Symposium on the Book of Mormon*, 5-11. Salt Lake City: Church of Jesus Christ of Latter-day Saints, CES, August 1986. Explores possible reasons for Mormon's inclusion of so much material relating to war and analyzes the teachings of Book of Mormon concerning the following four questions: (1) When is war justified? (2) What rules govern the righteous conduct of war? (3) What must a nation do in order to win a war? (4) What effects, good or bad, can a righteous people expect from war?" [A.T.]

C.061 Cazier, Donald A. "Nephite and Israelite Governmental Institutions and Policies." In *A Symposium on the Book of Mormon*, 26-32. Salt Lake City: Church of Jesus Christ of Latter-day Saints, 1979. Reviews the patriarchal origins of Nephite government, the theocratic ideal government, and how it was developed by biblical and Nephite civilizations. Other topics discussed include government by popular consent, protection of personal liberty from government, crime and punishment, morality and public welfare, and the resolution of disputes with other nations. [N.K.Y.]

C.062 Cazier, Donald A. *A Study of Nephite, Lamanite, and Jaredite Governmental Institutions and Policies as Portrayed in the Book of Mormon*. M.A. thesis, Brigham Young University, 1972. Analyzes the Book of Mormon governmental institutions. Considers: "1. The governmental structure under which [the Nephite, Lamanite, and Jaredite] nations lived at different times in their history and the theoretical powers and duties of their officers. 2. The laws that were enacted and domestic policies that were pursued. 3. The rights enjoyed by the citizens. 4. The 'foreign policy' of these nations, where applicable, including military policy. 5. The teachings of Book of Mormon prophets and secular leaders of the various types of government . . . and the lessons which can be drawn from the political experiences of the Book of Mormon peoples." [A.T.]

C.063 Chadwick, Bruce A., and Thomas Garrow. "Native Americans." In *Encyclopedia of Mormonism*, edited by Daniel H. Ludlow, 3:981-85. 5 vols. New York: Macmillan, 1992. Presents an overview of the Book of Mormon story. Latter-day Saints believe that the Book of Mormon is a record of the ancestors of the native inhabitants of the Western Hemisphere. The message of the book is specifically for them. [J.W.M.]

C.064 Chadwick, Clinton. "Down the Dark Path: Sherem, Nehor, and Korihor as Archetypal Anti-heroes." *Insight* 8 (Fall 1992): 1-4. Looks at Book of Mormon anti-Christs within a model set up by Joseph Campbell showing some degree of reversal of the mythic hero type. They are depicted as counterfeits, and experience a tragic "ironic twist of the sacrificial archetype epitomized by Christ." [D.M.]

C.065 Chamberlain, Jonathan M. "I Have a Question: What is the meaning of Luke 16:18 and 3 Nephi 12:32?" *Ensign* 23 (January 1993): 59-60. A discussion about the permissibility of divorce on grounds other than adultery in the law of Moses as compared to the higher law Jesus offered. [S.H.]

C.066 Chandler, Rick D. "O Remember and Perish Not: A Scriptural Study of the Process of

Memory as a Vehicle to Exaltation." In *The Second Annual Church Educational System Religious Educators' Symposium: A Symposium on the Book of Mormon,* edited by The Church Educational System, 33-37. Salt Lake City, UT: Corporation of the President of the Church of Jesus Christ of Latter-day Saints, 1979. A treatment, in outline form, of the term "remember" in its various forms and its antonyms that occur in the Book of Mormon and the Doctrine and Covenants. The author lists dictionary definitions of remember, memory, and remembrance, lists citations from passages that are relevant to his study, and occasionally gives brief commentary to elicit the meaning of remembering or forgetting. [B.D.]

C.067 Charlesworth, James H. "Messianism in the Pseudepigrapha and the Book of Mormon." In *Reflections on Mormonism,* edited by Truman G. Madsen, 99-137. Salt Lake City: Bookcraft, 1978. Reviews five pseudepigrapha with Jewish origins and four pseudepigrapha with Christian origins that contain references to the Messiah, the anointed one, and the Christ. These references are then compared with the citations to the same titles in the Book of Mormon. [B.D.]

C.068 Chase, Daryl. *Sidney Rigdon—Early Mormon.* Ph.D. dissertation, University of Chicago, 1931. A historical examination of the life of Sidney Rigdon that discusses the theories concerning the origin of the Book of Mormon. Concludes that Sidney Rigdon had no contact with Joseph Smith nor the Spaulding Manuscript prior to 1830. [J.W.M.]

C.069 Chase, Lance D. "Spaulding Manuscript." In *Encyclopedia of Mormonism,* edited by Daniel H. Ludlow, 3:1402-3. 5 vols. New York: Macmillan, 1992. Also known as the *Manuscript Found.* The Spaulding manuscript was written by Solomon Spaulding, and consists of 175 handwritten pages. The work was first published in 1885. It is a fictional story about a group of Romans who were lost in a storm and settled in America about the fourth century A.D. Enemies of the LDS church claimed it was the basis for the Book of Mormon. This theory was propagated by Philastus Hurlbut and E. D. Howe in the early days of the Church when the manuscript was lost. The manuscript was found after forty-five years and that theory was proved invalid. [J.W.M.]

C.070 Chatburn, Mrs. T. W., and William Pooler. "Two Living Witnesses Who Saw David Whitmer." *The Iron Rod* 1 (May 1924): 19-20. Two individuals report that David Whitmer possessed a strong, personal testimony of the Book of Mormon gold plates. [J.W.M.]

C.071 Checketts, Darby, and Sharon Checketts. *Scripture Focus for Everyday Living.* Provo, UT: Cornerstone Pro-Dev Press, 1992. A scripture study program. Contains fifty-two post-on-the-wall scriptural thoughts (one for each week of the year) designed to inspire, teach, and motivate students of the Book of Mormon. [D.W.P]

C.072 Cheesman, Paul R. "Ancient Writing in the Americas." *BYU Studies* 13 (Autumn 1972): 80-90. Subsequent to Joseph Smith's statement that descendants of Hebrews in ancient America inscribed metal plates, many examples of ancient American writings on metal have been discovered. Examples include the Kinderhook plates, the Arizona tablets, the Metcalf stone, Newspaper Rock, a Peruvian gold plate, and a copper plate from Equador. [B.D.]

C.073 Cheesman, Paul R. "Ancient Writing on Metal Plates." *Ensign* 9 (October 1979): 42-47. A photographic essay of ancient writing on metal plates. The author notes that while many examples of ancient metal inscriptions exist in the Old World, examples of metal plates in the New World are just beginning to surface. This is in part due to the lack of archaeological study in the New World. [D.M.]

C.074 Cheesman, Paul R. *Ancient Writing on Metal Plates: Archaeological Findings Support Mormon Claims.* Bountiful, UT: Horizon, 1985. The Book of Mormon was translated from gold plates. Correspondingly, many examples of writings on metal plates and other pre-Columbian writings have been discovered since the time of Joseph Smith. Such items lend credence to the gold plates of the Book of Mormon. [B.D.]

C.075 Cheesman, Paul R. "Answers to Questions Regarding Archaeological Evidences of the Book of Mormon." *NE* 5 (March 1975): 49-50. Gives evidences of a high civilization in Meso and South America, including towers seen by Cortez, highways up to 9,000 miles in length that cross South America, and metallurgy including gold, silver, and copper all of which lend support to the Book of Mormon. [L.D.]

C.076 Cheesman, Paul R. "Archaeology and the Book of Mormon." *Instructor* 103 (November 1968): 428-32. The author reviews archaeological evidences of the Book of Mormon and other finds which clarify understanding of the Book of Mormon. The subjects reviewed include: ancestry of the American Indian, the calendar, iron, elephants, and horses. [B.D.]

C.077 Cheesman, Paul R. "Book of Helaman." In *Encyclopedia of Mormonism*, edited by Daniel H. Ludlow, 1:152-53. 5 vols. New York: Macmillan, 1992. The book of Helaman records the period preceding the birth of the Savior. It was written by Helaman and was abridged by Mormon who inserts his own commentary. The most prominent person in the book is $Nephi_2$. Also included are prophecies and teachings of Samuel the Lamanite and the rise of the Gadianton robbers. [J.W.M.]

C.078 Cheesman, Paul R. *Book of Mormon Lands: A Photographic Essay*. Salt Lake City: Blaine Hudson Printing, 1978. A photographic essay of Book of Mormon lands. "With a little effort the reader will become immersed in the beauty of the ancient citadels and landscapes and sense their relationship to the spirit of the scriptures [the Book of Mormon]." [B.D.]

C.079 Cheesman, Paul R. *The Book of Mormon: The Keystone Scripture*. Provo, UT: Brigham Young University Religious Studies Center, BYU, 1988. Collection of papers presented on the campus of Brigham Young University at the First Annual Book of Mormon Symposium. Individual selections appear in this bibliography under the names of the respective authors. [J.W.M.]

C.080 Cheesman, Paul R. "A Cultural Analysis of the Nephite-Lamanite-Mulekite Civilizations from the Book of Mormon." Project for Ph.D., Brigham Young University, 1967. "The purpose of this project is to analyze the cultural aspects of the ancient American people, part of whose history is presented in the text of the Book of Mormon. It is presented in such a manner that, hopefully, this analysis could serve as the basis of a reconstruction of the Book of Mormon civilizations which would be helpful in the production of motion pictures." [A.T.]

C.081 Cheesman, Paul R. "Cultural Parallels between the Old World and the New World." In *The Book of Mormon: The Keystone Scripture*, edited by Paul R. Cheesman, S. Kent Brown, and Charles D. Tate Jr., 206-17. Provo, UT: Brigham Young University Religious Studies Center, 1988. Argues for the theory of diffusion between the Old and the New World. Cites evidence of pre-Columbian transoceanic voyages, modern voyages by means of primitive craft, and cultural similarities. [B.D.]

C.082 Cheesman, Paul R. *Early America and the Book of Mormon: A Photographic Essay of Ancient America*. Salt Lake City: Deseret Book, 1972. A photographic essay of Mesoamerica and the narrow coastal region and highlands of the Middle Andes, which includes Peru, Ecuador, and Bolivia. [B.D.]

C.083 Cheesman, Paul R. "External Evidences of the Book of Mormon." In *By Study and Also by Faith,* edited by John M. Lundquist and Stephen D. Ricks, 2:73-90. Salt Lake City: Deseret Book and FARMS, 1990. Mentions practices, legends, ceremonies and beliefs of the Olmecs, Mayans, and Aztecs that support the stories contained in the Book of Mormon. Examples include Quetzalcoatl, the Bearded White God, the architecture of buildings, the existence of stone boxes and writings on metal, the religious beliefs of an afterlife and a heavenly kingdom, the evidences of Christian-like practices and rites, the legends of a dark and a light people, the existence of fortifications and weapons suggesting warfare, and the discovery of stelas and other carvings that make reference to the tree of life and other Book of Mormon themes. [A.A.]

C.084 Cheesman, Paul R. "Helaman$_2$." In *Encyclopedia of Mormonism*, edited by Daniel H. Ludlow, 2:584. 5 vols. New York: Macmillan, 1992. The second Helaman mentioned in the Book of Mormon was the eldest son of Alma the Younger. He became a High Priest, military commander, Nephite record keeper, and prophet. He is noted for preaching repentance. [J.W.M.]

C.085 Cheesman, Paul R. *The Keystone of Mormonism: Little Known Facts About the Book of Mormon*. Salt Lake City: Deseret Book, 1973. A review of the "primary and secondary accounts which pertain to the coming forth of the Book of Mormon." The author's goal is for readers to discover the divine literature of the Book of Mormon and to consider its historical and theological aspects. [R.M.]

C.086 Cheesman, Paul R. *The Keystone of Mormonism: Early Visions of the Prophet Joseph Smith*. Provo, UT: Eagle Systems International, 1988. Examines the details of the accounts of the early visions of Joseph Smith. Skeptics have a problem with the time that elapsed before the accounts were written. It is suggested that the sacred nature of the visions required a time of secrecy. Some of the accounts were written by intimate associates of the prophet who may have received details in the oral account given them that Joseph's own written account did not include, or these authors may have put in their own embellishments. There are some discrepancies, but the basic elements are consistent. Discusses the part played by the Urim and Thummin in the translation of the Book of Mormon. [J.W.M.]

C.087 Cheesman, Paul R. "Lehi's Journeys." In *The Book of Mormon: First Nephi, The Doctrinal Foundation*, edited by Monte S. Nyman and Charles D. Tate Jr., 241-50. Provo, UT: Brigham Young University Religious Studies Center, 1988. Examines the journey of the Lehite colony in the wilderness and attempts to determine the route taken and specific locations dealing with the journey. [A.T.]

C.088 Cheesman, Paul R. "Monuments of Vanished Peoples." *Ensign* 2 (September 1972): 43-45. A brief description of eight major Mesoamerican archaeological sites—Copan, Teotihuacan, Monte Alban, La Venta, Palenque, Tikal, Cuicuilco and Dzibilchaltun—is provided. [B.T.]

C.089 Cheesman, Paul R. "Origin of the American Indian and Why the Earth was Divided." In *A Symposium on the Book of Mormon*, 14-17. Salt Lake City: Church of Jesus Christ of Latter-day Saints, 1979. Writes concerning the origin of American Indians. Theorizes that the continents were divided because God desired a separated land for the proposed habitation by groups of righteous people. Such groups could leave their witness of Christ for subsequent generations. [N.K.Y.]

C.090 Cheesman, Paul R. "The Power to Repent." *Instructor* 104 (December 1969): 436-37. Writes concerning the doctrine of repentance. Helaman 13-15 (see especially Helaman 13:38) indicates that as individuals choose evil, their power to choose is taken away until destruction is made sure. As individuals choose righteousness, their power to choose increases. The concepts of freedom and free agency are directly related. [B.D.]

C.091 Cheesman, Paul R. "Q & A: Is there anything that has been found among the archaeological evidences that would sustain or support the Book of Mormon?" *NE* 5 (March 1975): 49-50. Proof of the Book of Mormon lies in the spiritual realm. However, there is evidence that supports it: architecture, cement, highways, weapons of war, metallurgy, medicine, and highly organized priesthood. There are many native legends that tell of a Christ-like god whose teachings resemble Christ's. [J.W.M.]

C.092 Cheesman, Paul R. "The Ruins of Monte Alban." *Instructor* 105 (July 1970): center insert. The ruins of Monte Alban ("sacred mountain") date back to 500 B.C. and a composite of peoples occupied it for two thousand years. Such peoples may be connected with those of the Book of Mormon. [J.W.M.]

C.093 Cheesman, Paul R. "The Stone Box." *IE* 69 (October 1966): 875-78, 900. Prior to Joseph

Smith's encounter with the stone box that contained the gold plates no record existed that described the stone boxes of antiquity. The author includes descriptions of various stone boxes that have subsequently been found in Central and South America. [J.W.M.]

C.094 Cheesman, Paul R. *These Early Americans: External Evidences of the Book of Mormon.* Salt Lake City: Deseret Book, 1974. Presents numerous archaeological, anthropological and ethnological data to support ideas found in the Book of Mormon. Discusses such topics as Quetzalcoatl, the wheel, stone boxes, language, and ancient writing. [B.D.]

C.095 Cheesman, Paul R. "Transatlantic Crossings: A New Look." *Ensign* 5 (January 1975): 50-51. A report of the findings of the 1973 Pre-Columbian Transatlantic Crossings Symposia held in Lumpkin, Georgia. Three important conclusions were drawn by the presenters: (1) Ancient Americans were literate and kept records. (2) Pre-Columbian Americans had the technology necessary for the production of iron. (3) Ancient Americans actually came from the Old World via the Atlantic as well as the Pacific. [D.H.M.]

C.096 Cheesman, Paul R. "The Wheel in Ancient America." *BYU Studies* 9 (Winter 1969): 185-97. Discusses ancient highways that have been uncovered, and the early uses of the wheel, wheeled toys, and other wheel-like objects found in Central America and Mexico. [L.D.]

C.097 Cheesman, Paul R. *The World of the Book of Mormon.* Salt Lake City: Deseret Book, 1978. Discusses many subjects concerning external evidences of the Book of Mormon, including the relevance of the bearded white God to Jesus Christ, geography of the Book of Mormon, ancient ruins from Central and South America, ancient writing, stone boxes, the wheel, horses, and medicine. [B.D.]

C.098 Cheesman, Paul R., and Barbara Hutchins. *Pathways to the Past: A Guide to the Ruins of Mesoamerica.* Bountiful, UT: Horizon, 1984. A tour guide intended for the novice LDS audience. Maps, photographs, and directions are provided. Also included are the author's interpretations of how certain Mesoamerican sites and ruins correspond to the Book of Mormon. [B.D.]

C.099 Cheesman, Paul R., and Millie F. Cheesman. *Ancient American Indians: Their Origins, Civilizations and Old World Connections.* Bountiful, UT: Horizon, 1991. The goals of the authors are to show "(1) the origins of the American Indians, (2) cultural parallels between the Old and the New World, and (3) temples, mounds, and ruins in prehistoric North America." Includes photographs and illustrations. [D.W.P.]

C.100 Cheesman, Paul R., and Millie Foster Cheesman. *Early America and the Polynesians.* Provo, UT: Promised Lands Publications, 1975. Through the employment of quotes from authorities of the Church, scientific data, and photographic presentations of Polynesia, the author discusses the possibilities that the Polynesians were descendants of Lehi. [B.D.]

C.101 Cheesman, Paul R., moderator, Noel B. Reynolds, John L. Sorenson, and Arthur Wallace. "External Evidences of Scripture: A Panel." In *Scriptures for the Modern World*, edited by Paul R. Cheesman and Wilfred C. Griggs, 121-35. Provo, UT: Brigham Young University Religious Studies Center, 1984. The panel fields several issues dealing with Book of Mormon external evidences, e.g., the persuasiveness of evidences to nonbelievers, the value of evidences to members with testimonies, the possibility that some alleged evidences are invalid, and whether or not non-Mormon scholars agree with Book of Mormon archaeology. [B.D.]

C.102 Cheesman, Paul R., S. Kent Brown, and Charles D. Tate Jr., eds. *The Book of Mormon: The Keystone Scripture.* Provo, UT: Brigham Young University Religious Studies Center, 1988. Contains fifteen papers from the First Annual Book of Mormon Symposium. Each of the articles are dealt with elsewhere in this bibliography. The volume deals with such Book of Mormon topics as Jesus Christ, fasting, faith, hope, charity, and Old and New World similarities. [B.D.]

C.103 Cheesman, Paul R., and Wilfred C. Griggs, eds. *Scriptures for the Modern World.* Provo, UT: Brigham Young University Religious Studies Center, 1984. Three Book of Mormon articles treated in this volume deal with Moroni, the allegory of the Olive Tree, and external evidences of scriptures. The three articles are dealt with elsewhere in this bibliography. [B.D.]

C.104 Cheney, Silas L., Roy A. Welker, J. Karl Wood. "A New Sacred Scripture Revealed." In *The Church: Its History and Mission*, edited by Cheney, Welker, and Wood, 83-147. Salt Lake City: LDS Department of Education, 1952. Details the coming forth of the Book of Mormon and provides many purposes for the book as identified by its prophets. [J.W.M.]

C.105 Cheville, Roy A. *Book of Mormon Speaks for Itself.* Independence, MO: Herald House, 1971. Explores twelve separate aspects of the Book of Mormon, investigating such topics as how "the book speaks of God in history, the book centers on the universal Christ, and the book predicts the ministry of the Holy Spirit." [L.D.]

C.106 Cheville, Roy A. *Meet Them in the Scriptures.* Independence, MO: Herald House, 1960. Examines the personalities of important persons in the scriptures, including characters of the Book of Mormon. [B.D.]

C.107 Cheville, Roy A. *Scriptures From Ancient America.* Independence, MO: Herald Publishing House, 1964. Establishes the criteria for religious writings that would be placed in a world Library of Sacred Writings—they must have a survival quality, an applicable conception of man, usability in ceremonies, devotions, and memorial occasions, quotability, elasticity and expandability (symbolic and figurative language), and a functional conception of Divinity. The Book of Mormon meets the criteria to belong in such a library. It is a Hebrew collection of scriptures that supplements and supports the Bible and contributes much to the modern world. The history and story of the Book of Mormon is included. [J.W.M.]

C.108 Chidester, C. Richard. "The Natural Man and Spiritual Rebirth." In *A Symposium on the Book of Mormon*, 12-17. Salt Lake City: Church of Jesus Christ of Latter-day Saints, Church Educational System, August 1986. Shows how a correct understanding of the doctrines of the fall, natural man, atonement, and spiritual rebirth can bring about a spiritual change that leads individuals to God. [A.T.]

C.109 Child, A. Lon. "Plates of the Book of Mormon." *Juvenile Instructor* 85 (August 1950): 256-57. Features a chart and explanation of the different sets of plates identified in the Book of Mormon, including the brass plates, the twenty-four gold plates, the small and large plates of Nephi, Mormon's abridgment of Nephi's large plates, and Moroni's abridgment of Jaredite record. [A.C.W.]

C.110 "Children's Section—Testimonies Regarding the Book of Mormon." *Juvenile Instructor* 52 (September 1917): 484-86. Students of Calvin S. Smith's theology class in the Latter-day Saints University bear testimony of the Book of Mormon. [J.W.M.]

C.111 Childs, Larry G. "Epanalepsis in the Book of Mormon." Provo, UT: FARMS, 1986. Also published in an abbreviated form in Childs, Larry G. "Epanalepsis in the Book of Mormon." In *Reexploring the Book of Mormon*, edited by John W. Welch, 165-66. Salt Lake City: Deseret Book and FARMS, 1992. Epanalepsis is a literary device utilized by at least fifteen Book of Mormon writers. Called "resumptive repetition," epanalepsis contains two identical or near identical phrases within a longer sentence. Between the two phrases is interjected a parenthetical expression that adds additional information to the principal statement being expressed. An example of epanalepsis is found in Alma 3:1. Narrative, rather than poetry, lends itself to this figure. An appendix containing a complete listing of references of epanalepsis in the Book of Mormon is appended to the article. [D.W.P.]

C.112 Choate, Jane McBride. "The Brother of Jared Saw the Finger of God." *Friend* 18 (November 1988): 48-49. The great faith of the brother of Jared permitted him to see the finger of God (Ether 1-6). [J.W.M.]

C.113 Choate, Jane McBride. "Teancum: Fighter for Freedom." *Friend* 18 (May 1988): 48-49. Teancum, Nephite military leader, fights and voluntarily gives his life for the liberty of his people. [J.W.M.]

C.114 Christensen, A. H. *Little Known Facts*, Volume 2. Denver, CO: n.p., 1955. Provides brief facts and statements regarding Book of Mormon geography. Deals with the location of the last battle, the location of the Hill Cumorah, the Nephite wilderness, and other geographical items. [D.W.P.]

C.115 Christensen, Ann Nicodemus. "Where Are the Prophets?" *Ensign* 19 (September 1989): 69. A conversion story of a young woman who studies the Book of Mormon and determines that there exist living prophets of God . [J.W.M.]

C.116 Christensen, Harold. "Speculations on Polynesian Origins." *IE* 38 (November 1935): 672-74, 711. Believes that the Polynesians are of the blood of Israel and that they journeyed from the American continent at the time Hagoth built his ships. [B.D.]

C.117 Christensen, James. "The Land of Promise" (photo essay). *NE* 5 (January 1975): 20-29. The aim of this photo essay is to help readers visualize Book of Mormon scenery. There are thirteen photographs with accompanying scriptures. The work is "not meant to suggest any real locations in the Book of Mormon." [A.T.]

C.118 Christensen, Joe J. "Everyman's Vital Questions." *Instructor* 103 (March 1968): 126-28. The Book of Mormon is "doctrinally relevant" in today's world as it provides answers to vital questions concerning Christ's divinity, mission, resurrection, the essential nature of baptism, the power of the Holy Ghost, God as a God of miracles, and the reality of a final day of judgment. [A.C.W.]

C.119 Christensen, Joe J. " 'In Conclusion.' " In *A Symposium on the Book of Mormon*, 111-12. Salt Lake City: Church of Jesus Christ of Latter-day Saints, 1979. Summarizes the proceedings of a Book of Mormon symposium. The purpose of the symposium was to stimulate scholarship, improve teaching, and provide fellowship among teachers. [N.K.Y.]

C.120 Christensen, Kevin. "The Big Picture." *Sunstone* 15 (April 1991): 3-4. Argues with John Kunich over the article "Multiply Exceedingly: Book of Mormon Population Sizes" (*Sunstone* 14 [June 1990]: 27-44). Suggests that Kunich fails to define the problem of population size, to control appropriately the statistics, and to understand Lamanite lifestyles. [J.W.M.]

C.121 Christensen, Kevin. " 'Nigh Unto Death': NDE Research and the Book of Mormon." *Journal of Book of Mormon Studies* 2 (Spring 1993): 1-20. "This article suggests that contemporary near-death research casts light on several episodes in the Book of Mormon." The conversions of Alma, Limhi, and Limhi's father all demonstrate elements of near death experiences. In addition, the dreams of Lehi and Nephi show elements of both ancient and modern "other world journey literature." Author concludes that "the Book of Mormon matches the revelatory literature of the great traditions." [A.T.]

C.122 Christensen, Leon N. *The Little Book: Why I Am a Mormon*. Boston: Branden Press, 1976. The Book of Mormon played a great role in the conversion of the great leaders in the early Church. Its philosophical content established a way of life for peaceful, God-fearing people. Its doctrines, including baptism, sacrament prayers, mode of conducting meetings, and the precise way of bestowing the Holy Ghost, restores correct truths that had been lost to the world. [J.W.M.]

C.123 Christensen, Robert J. "How the Book of Mormon Can Help Teachers Deal Kindly with Wayward students." In *The Sixth Annual Church Educational System Religious Educators' Symposium on the Book of Mormon*, 13-16. Salt Lake City: Church of Jesus Christ of Latter-day Saints, Church Educational System, 1982. Uses the lives of Laman, Lemuel, Alma the Younger, the four sons of Mosiah, and Alma as examples of how to deal with wayward students. [A.T.]

C.124 Christensen, Ross T. "Did Book of Mormon Peoples Reach Peru?" *UASN* 67 (7 July 1960): 1-7. Theorizes that the Central Andes of Peru may have been home to much of the Book of Mormon civilization. Also, the "narrow neck of land" may have been the Isthmus of Tehuantepec. Many "large-scale migrations" are recorded in the Book of Mormon. [J.W.M.]

C.125 Christensen, Ross T. "Geography in Book of Mormon Archaeology." *SEHA* 147 (December 1981): 1-4. The stricture of George Q. Cannon in 1890 against concern for Book of Mormon geography studies was appropriate because comparative secular knowledge was not then available. Now it is. If archaeology is to be considered at all in connection with the Book of Mormon then both geography and chronology of the scriptures must be specified then compared systematically with external information. Argues briefly that "the Tehuantepec correlation" of geography has come to be widely accepted among LDS students of the subject, as against "the Panama correlation." The SEHA should lead out in such geography study. [J.L.S.]

C.126 Christensen, Ross T. "Lehi's Landing Place." *UASN* 46 (17 December 1957): 4-5. No "official LDS view" of the place of Lehi's landing in ancient America exists. All views of Book of Mormon geography are personal, private interpretations, but the most popular contemporary view requires a landing for the Lehite company in Southern Central America. [J.W.M.]

C.127 Christensen, Ross T. "Mormon Archaeology." *New World Antiquity* 4 (July 1957): 105-6. Basic explanation of LDS beliefs and Book of Mormon migrations. Book of Mormon archaeologists need to correlate textual descriptions with New World archaeological sites and land configurations. [A.C.W.]

C.128 Christensen, Ross T. "On the Study of Archaeology by Latter-day Saints." *UASN* 64 (January 1960): 1-6. Latter-day Saints should be trained and active because we have "with archaeology and the Book of Mormon the one instance in the history of the world . . . in which it is possible to put a decisive scientific test to the key foundation stone of a major religious system." Archaeologists ought, moreover, to be interested in the Book of Mormon for what it potentially can tell them. [J.L.S.]

C.129 Christensen, Ross T. "The Place Called Nahom." *Ensign* 8 (August 1978): 73. A spot in Yemen on a 1763 map is called "Nehhm." It qualifies as the place "Nahom" mentioned by Nephi as Ishmael's burial place, alternative to the locus proposed by the Hiltons. Semiticists, and ultimately archaeologists, should examine this possibility carefully. [J.L.S.]

C.130 Christensen, Ross T. "Possible Routes Suggested for Mulek's Voyage." *Ensign* 3 (September 1973): 76-77. One route for Mulek's journey from Jerusalem to the New World may have been through the Mediterranean Sea and westward across the Atlantic Ocean. An alternative route may have been around Africa and the Cape of Good Hope, then northwest towards the Gulf of Mexico. The existence of strong ocean currents supports the plausibility of either of the two routes. [D.M.]

C.131 Christensen, Ross T. "Present Status of Book of Mormon Archaeology." *MS*, Part I, 114 (September 1952): 206-11, 218; Part II, 114 (October 1952): 234-37, 244; Part III, 114 (November 1952): 246-47, 263; Part IV, 114 (December 1952): 293-97, 304. Defines Book of Mormon archaeology as "that branch of general archaeology which studies the discoveries . . . [for] every fact which throws light upon the Book of Mormon." It can be expected both to elucidate the scripture and to confirm it. Using the study of the Bible through archaeology as a model, he lays out a logic and methods for doing so, notably by establishing "major" and "minor" correspondences. Major correspondences consist of geographical and chronological frameworks in the real (New) world that compare adequately with what the Book of Mormon says. Minor correspondences consider specific cultural elements such as the use of iron, the wheel, the horse, etc. Ultimately it should be possible to test "the historical claims" of the Book of Mormon by archaeology. The status thus far is reviewed and the interim conclusion is reached that "in large part the Book of Mormon is vindicated by archaeological science; but many points still remain . . . to challenge us." [J.L.S.]

C.132 Christensen, Ross T. *Progress in Archaeology (an Anthology)*. Provo, UT: Brigham Young University, 1963. Selections from 1951-1963 issues of the University Archaeology Society Newsletter that are scripture-related. Many deal with Book of Mormon subjects: transoceanic influences, Book of Mormon geography and chronology, the horse in ancient America, use of cement, Mayan writing. [A.C.W.]

C.133 Christensen, Ross T. "Renewed Latter-day Saint Interest in the Phoenicians." *IE* 73 (October 1970): 12-15. New evidence reveals Phoenician contact with the New World between 1000 to 500 B.C. Phoenician inscriptions record in remarkable detail the voyages of mariners, pinpointing both departure and arrival dates and places. Christensen hypothesizes that the guardian(s) of Mulek may have asked Phoenician friends to aid in their escape from the Babylonians. [J.W.M.]

C.134 Christensen, Ross T. "The River of Nephi: An Archaeological Commentary on an Old Diary Entry." *SEHA* 158 (December 1984): 1-8. An 1881 diary entry made by Charles Lowell Walker states that the Prophet Joseph Smith identified a key location to Book of Mormon geography. He spoke of a great temple that was located in Central America. The River Copan was anciently called the river of Nephi. A second account by Mosiah Lyman Hancock substantiates Walker's entry. Maps are included. [J.W.M.]

C.135 Christensen, Ross T. "The Seven Lineages of Lehi." *NE* 5 (May 1975): 40-41. Discusses the different "ites" of the Book of Mormon. The Nephites were divided into Nephites, Jacobites, Josephites, and Zoramites, and the Lamanites were divided into Lamanites, Lemuelites, and Ishmaelites. Defines several terms, including five different definitions of the term "Lamanite." [A.T.]

C.136 Christensen, Ross T. "A Tour and Brief Description of Some of the Ancient Ruined Cities of Central and Southern Mexico or 'Land Northward' of the Book of Mormon." *U.S.A.N.* 28 (10 August 1955): 3-5. Also in Christensen, Ross T. *Progress in Archaeology: An Anthology*, 149-152. Reports on a tour taken by several members of the BYU archaeological department. The archaeologists speculate on the possible connection between Book of Mormon cities and those visited, Teotihuac'an, Copilco, Cuicuilco, Cholula, Mitla, and Monte Alban. Many significant parallels were observed. [J.W.M.]

C.137 Christensen, Ross T. *The Tree of Life in Ancient America*. Provo, UT: Brigham Young University, 1968. Makes a comparison of the Stela 5, Izapa, stone with the tree of life described in the dream of Lehi. Provides a detailed description and analysis of Stela 5, Izapa, and concludes that the stone is a religious carving representing the events depicted in the Book of Mormon tree of life scene. Includes photographs of the stone. [J.W.M.]

C.138 Christensen, Ross T. "The Value and Development of Book-of-Mormon Archaeology as a Field of Study." *U.S.A.N.* 6.1 and 44.00 (27 September 1957): 1-2. Also in Christensen, Ross T. *Progress in Archaeology: An Anthology*, 144-147. Authentication and elucidation of the Book of Mormon is the purpose for Book of Mormon archaeology. It is as important as biblical archaeology or archaeology in the Aegean that sheds light on Homer's *Iliad* and *Odyssey* as important historical documents. [J.W.M.]

C.139 Christensen, Ross T., ed. *Papers of the Fifteenth Annual Symposium of the Archaeology of the Book of Mormon*. Salt Lake City: Church of Jesus Christ of Latter-day Saints, 1964. A collection of papers relating archaeology to the scriptures, many of which are relevant to Book of Mormon subjects: Joseph Smith's knowledge of archaeology, Mulek's migration, pyramid architecture, metals in the New World, etc. [A.C.W.]

C.140 Christensen, Ross T., ed. *Transoceanic Crossings to Ancient America*. Provo, UT: Brigham Young University Press, 1970. Contains selected articles from the *Newsletter and Proceedings of the Society for Early Historic Archaeology* (SEHA) that pertain to transoceanic crossings prior to Columbus. Determines that the ancient inhabitants of the New World consisted of multi-races. Sees a Phoenician influence in the Americas. Archaeologists have found artifacts of many cultures including those of Mediterranean descent who knew Christianity. [J.W.M.]

C.141 Christensen, Ross T., and Ruth R. Christensen. "Georgia Symposium Considers Transatlantic Contacts." *SEHA* 135 (August 1974): 1-9. Petroglyphs in Georgia, the Metcalf stone, the Bahaman ruins, coins from the Mediterranean scattered throughout the eastern U.S., the Batcreek stone, Roman artifacts in Arizona, and runes in Oklahoma all indicate the existence of pre-Colombian transoceanic contact between the Old and New World. [A.C.W.]

C.142 Christensen, Ross T., and Ruth R. Christensen. "Perspectives on the Route of Mulek's Colony." *SEHA* 131 (September 1972): 1-6. Proposes two possible routes for the transoceanic Mulekite journey: (1) The Mediterranean/North Atlantic route, or (2) the African/South Atlantic route. The first choice is seen as the more likely. [D.M.]

C.143 Christenson, Allen J. "Chiasmus in Mayan Texts." *Ensign* 18 (October 1988): 28-31. Christenson investigates the possibility of the use of chiasmus in Mayan writings. Of the thirty-seven Mayan documents examined, chiastic patterns are found in sixteen. [D.L.L.]

C.144 Christenson, Allen J. "Chiasmus in Mesoamerican Texts." In *Reexploring the Book of Mormon*, edited by John W. Welch, 233-35. Salt Lake City: Deseret Book and FARMS, 1992. Examines thirty-seven Mayan texts and discovers numerous simple and complex chiastic forms. [N.K.Y.]

C.145 Christenson, Allen J. "Maya Harvest Festivals and The Book of Mormon." In *Review of Books on the Book of Mormon*, edited by Daniel C. Peterson, 1-31. Provo, Utah: FARMS, 1991. Examines the harvest festival celebrated in Guatemala on November 11 that resembles Mayan traditions more than Christian ones. This is not only a harvest festival, but is also a New Year's celebration and a time of renewal of kingship. Many elements of the tradition parallel King Benjamin's address in the Book of Mormon. Discusses the tree of life motif and its association with the cross. [J.W.M.]

C.146 Christenson, Allen J. "Nephite Trade Networks and the Dangers of a Class Society." In *The Book of Mormon: Helaman through 3 Nephi 8, According to Thy Word*, edited by Monte S. Nyman and Charles D. Tate Jr., 223-40. Provo, UT: Brigham Young University Religious Studies Center, 1992. Proposes that one of the reasons for the deterioration of Nephite society described in Helaman and 3 Nephi 1-7 "was the establishment of elaborate trade networks with the express purpose of accumulating wealth and power. This in turn stimulated the rise of a class society and the desire among those of noble lineages to reinstitute kingship to control international trade." [D.M.]

C.147 Christenson, Allen J. "The Use of Chiasmus by the Ancient Quiché-Maya." Provo, UT: FARMS, 1989. Points out the use of chiasmus in several Quiché-Maya texts that were written in the Quiché-Mayan language using Latin letters. Also compares those texts that contain chiasms with those that do not. [B.D.]

C.148 Christianson, James R. "The Bering Strait and American Indian Origins." In *The Book of Mormon: The Keystone Scripture*, edited by Paul R. Cheesman, S. Kent Brown, and Charles D. Tate Jr., 218-36. Provo, UT: Brigham Young University Religious Studies Center, 1988. Examines the archaeological and ethnological evidence that supports the theory that the Americas were peopled via the Bering Strait. The author determines that the evidence that supports this theory is extremely lacking, and offers the Book of Mormon solution of transoceanic crossings of various peoples at differing times. [B.D.]

C.149 Christianson, James R. "Crawfish Tails, Possum, and Other Missionary Delights." *Ensign* 19 (April 1989): 48-51. Historic tidbits of Wilford Watts Jordan, who through prayer and reading the Book of Mormon received a testimony of it. [B.D.]

C.150 "Christopher Columbus." *Juvenile Instructor* 1 (15 April 1866): 29. Praises Christopher Columbus and shows how he fulfilled a prophecy by Nephi. [D.M.]

C.151 Church of Jesus Christ of Latter-day Saints. *Gold Plates Used Anciently*. Salt Lake City: Deseret News Press, 1963. A pamphlet describing a number of ancient metal plates containing writings on them. These findings support claims that the Book of Mormon was written on metal plates. [B.D.]

C.152 Church of Jesus Christ of Latter-day Saints. *History and Teachings of the Book of Mormon: Supplement for Religion 421 and 422*. Provo, UT: Brigham Young University, 1967-1968 [R]. This supplement is designed for university students of religion. It presents students with background information, doctrinal approaches, and bibliographical sources related to the Book of Mormon. [B.D.]

C.153 Church of Jesus Christ of Latter-day Saints. *A Sure Foundation: Answers to Difficult Gospel Questions*. Salt Lake City: Deseret Book, 1988. A selection of questions/answers dealing with Mormon belief. Representative Book of Mormon questions include: Why does the Book of Mormon use the terms "adieu," "Bible," and "baptize?" Why was Jesus was born at Jerusalem? Why have changes been made in editions of the Book of Mormon subsequent to the first edition? How is the Book of Mormon related to the writings of Spaulding and Ethan Smith? [B.D.]

C.154 Church of Jesus Christ of Latter-day Saints. *23 Questions Answered by the Book of Mormon*. Salt Lake City: Church of Jesus Christ of Latter-day Saints, 1977. A one page list of twenty-three questions concerning doctrine of the Church and God's dealings with humanity followed by references from the Book of Mormon that provide the answers. [J.W.M.]

C.155 Church of Jesus Christ of Latter-day Saints, Board of Education. *Selected References Concerning Lamanites from the Journal of Discourses and Extracts from the Comprehensive History of the Church*. Salt Lake City: Church of Jesus Christ of Latter-day Saints, 1960. A compilation of references dealing with the Lamanites taken from the *Journal of Discourses* and from the *Comprehensive History of the Church*. The references include prophecies about the Lamanites, a description of their Book of Mormon background, and the blessings that await them. [M.D.P.]

C.156 Church of Jesus Christ of Latter-day Saints, CES. *Book of Mormon Student Manual, Religion 121 & 122*. Salt Lake City: Church of Jesus Christ of Latter-day Saints, 1989. A manual for college students of the Book of Mormon, covering all chapters of the Book of Mormon. [B.D.]

C.157 Clark, David L. "Lehi and El Niño: A Method of Navigation." *BYU Studies* 30 (Summer 1990): 57-65. Also, Provo, UT: FARMS, 1991. Natural means might have been used to transport Lehi's group to the promised land. Under ordinary circumstances it would be difficult to traverse eastward from Indonesia to America as the ocean currents flow westerly. But a natural occurrence that happens every two to ten years changes the flow of currents to an easterly direction—it is called *El Niño*. Had Lehi traveled from the Arabian Peninsula in August at the height of the monsoonal cycle and reached the Pacific in time to catch the *El Niño* he would have landed on the west coast of Central America. [J.W.M.]

C.158 Clark, E. Douglas. *The Grand Design: America from Columbus to Zion*. Salt Lake City: Deseret Book, 1992. Asserts that history is often so obscure that God's help is needed to understand it. The Book of Mormon is the providential means to understand the history and future of America. It contains prophecies about Columbus, the discovery and establishment of America, and future events connected with America, including the establishment of Zion. [B.D.]

C.159 Clark, E. Douglas, and Robert S. Clark. *Fathers and Sons in the Book of Mormon*. Salt Lake City: Deseret Book, 1991. Describes the relationships between fathers and sons in the Book of Mormon. For instance, righteous fathers taught their sons and righteous sons followed the example of their fathers. The greatest father and son are represented to be God and Jesus Christ. The book reinforces and describes the most important role of a man—fatherhood. [B.D.]

C.160 Clark, George Edward. *Why I Believe: 54 Evidences of the Divine Mission of the Prophet Joseph Smith.* Salt Lake City: Bookcraft, 1952. The 54 evidences are divided into three sections: general evidences, doctrinal evidences, and Book of Mormon evidences. Book of Mormon evidences involve external evidence including the Savior in America, steel, horses and elephants, Hebrew language, literary style, and many others. [J.W.M.]

C.161 Clark, J. Reuben, Jr. " 'All Roads Lead to Rome.' " *IE* 63 (June 1960): 398-99. Discusses Lehi's vision, Christ's sermon at the temple to the Nephites, and emphasizes the correctness of the Book of Mormon translation. The Book of Mormon, when used in concert with the Bible, will guide individuals to the one and only road to heaven. [A.C.W.]

C.162 Clark, J. Reuben, Jr. "Eighth Period: The Benediction upon Our Lord's Ministry—His Visit to the Western Hemisphere." In Clark's *Our Lord of the Gospels,* 463-517. Salt Lake City: Deseret News Press, 1954. Uses scriptural references from 3 Nephi interspersed with commentary to tell about the Savior's visit to the American Continent. [J.W.M.]

C.163 Clark, J. Reuben Jr. "A Heavenly Being Brings Good Tidings." In Clark's *On the Way to Immortality and Eternal Life,* 127-35. Salt Lake City: Deseret Book, 1949. Describes the visit of angel Moroni to Joseph Smith and reception of the Book of Mormon. The best explanation of the Book of Mormon is the one delivered by Joseph Smith. The eleven witnesses have confirmed his testimony with their testimonies. [J.W.M.]

C.164 Clark, John E. "Book of Mormon Geography." In *Encyclopedia of Mormonism,* edited by Daniel H. Ludlow, 176-79. 5 vols. New York: Macmillan, 1992. Geographic features of the Book of Mormon, including the narrow neck of land, the east and the west seas, the hill Cumorah that figured in the final battles of two major civilizations, and the time of travel between areas by journeying groups and individuals permit some evaluation of Book of Mormon geography. Studies indicate the most dense population activity was west of the Yucatan Peninsula. No Church sanction has been given to any proposals regarding Book of Mormon geography. [N.K.Y.]

C.165 Clavey, Bruce W. "Biblical Messianism and the Book of Mormon." In *Restoration Studies III,* edited by Maurice L. Draper, 232-43. Independence, MO: Herald House, 1986. The Book of Mormon concept of kingship and messianism came from the world of the Bible, from which the Book of Mormon peoples originated. The early Book of Mormon prophets selected Old Testament passages to identify Jesus Christ as the Messiah who would suffer the atoning sacrifice for the sins of mankind. [J.W.M.]

C.166 Clawson, Rudger. Untitled talk. *CR* (April 1904): 42-45. A talk on prayer that emphasizes the fact that the coming forth of the Book of Mormon was greatly influenced by prayer. Doctrine and Covenants 10 clearly shows that the records of the Book of Mormon were preserved in answer to prayers offered by Nephite prophets up to 1400 years ago. [J.W.M.]

C.167 Clawson, Rudger. Untitled talk. *CR* (April 1929): 25-29. There are four scriptural works that stand as witnesses to the Gospel of Christ—the Bible, Book of Mormon, Doctrine and Covenants, and Pearl of Great Price. The Book of Mormon is a sacred history of the ancient inhabitants of America. The Three Witnesses, Eight Witnesses, and Joseph Smith all bear individual testimonies concerning the truth of the Book of Mormon. [J.W.M.]

C.168 Clayton, Corliss. "Mormon and the Book of Mormon." *Friend* 18 (October 1988): 48-49. A rebus (a story puzzle with pictures representing part of the words) of the story of Mormon. [J.W.M.]

C.169 Clement, Russell T. "Polynesian Origins: More Word on the Mormon Perspective." *Dialogue* 13 (Winter 1980): 88-98. Reviews the claims of the scientists and Mormon leaders regarding the origin of the Polynesians. The debate continues among scientists, some favoring American origins, while most tend to Asian origins. Mormon leaders have consistently held that the Polynesians came from the American continent. [B.D.]

C.170 Clemmer, Janice White. "A Testimony." In *Sidney B. Sperry Symposium: The Book of Mormon*, edited by A. Gary Anderson, 11-17. Provo, UT: Brigham Young University Religious Studies Center, 1981. A testimonial wherein the author states that knowledge of the Old and New Testaments prepared her for the Book of Mormon. The Book of Mormon explained her American Indian heritage and gave her dignity. [J.W.M.]

C.171 Clift, Frederic. "Book of Mormon Language: Hebrew and Egyptian." *IE* 8 (January 1905): 168-76. A stance defending the proposition that the Book of Mormon was written in Egyptian. Hints that neighboring alphabets, such as Hebrew, Arabic, Chaldean, and Assyriac are also found in the Book of Mormon. Charles Anthon's comments to Martin Harris regarding the Book of Mormon characters are also mentioned. [D.M.]

C.172 Cloward, Robert A. *The Joseph Smith Translation: The Restoration of Plain and Precious Things*, 163-200. Provo, UT: Brigham Young University Religious Studies Center, 1985. Also in "The Sermon on the Mount in the Joseph Smith Translation of the Bible and the Book of Mormon." Provo, UT: FARMS, 1985. Demonstrates how the Joseph Smith Translation of the Bible and the Book of Mormon enlarge one's understanding of the Sermon on the Mount. Examines such topics as: audience and setting, disciples and beatitudes, salt and light, and the old and the new law. The author highlights differences in the three versions and provides a short commentary. [A.T.]

C.173 Cloward, Robert A., and Kathleen P. Cloward. "Teaching the Divine Attribute of Mercy with the Book of Mormon." In *A Symposium on the Book of Mormon*, 18-23. Salt Lake City: Church of Jesus Christ of Latter-day Saints, CES, August 1986. Sets forth one approach that teachers of the Book of Mormon may utilize to teach mercy to their students. [A.T.]

C.174 Cluny, Russell F. "The Book of Mormon, The Testimony of the Witnesses." In Cluny's *Positive Evidence of the Restored Church*, 26-30. Salt Lake City, UT: Russell F. Cluny, 1953. Declares that both the Bible and the Book of Mormon are spiritual guides for the Church. The Book of Mormon is in harmony with the Bible and contains the everlasting gospel as preached to the Savior's "other sheep" in America. The Book of Mormon is an abridgment of several metal plates and the Three Witnesses testify of its truthfulness. [J.W.M.]

C.175 Cohen, Irving H. *The Jews in Relation to the Book of Mormon, Jews of Torah*. Scotia, NY: Cumorah, 1967. Shows how the Torah was revealed. Argues that the Bible is incomplete and that the Book of Mormon should be esteemed as highly as the Bible. Uses Ezekiel 37:16-17, 2 Nephi 29, and Moroni 10 in his discussion of the importance of the Book of Mormon. [B.D.]

C.176 Cole, Clarissa Katherine. "Promised Land, Concept of a." In *Encyclopedia of Mormonism*, edited by Daniel H. Ludlow, 3:1160. 5 vols. New York: Macmillan, 1992. The Book of Mormon gives special meaning to the land of promise. It is a land of inheritance belonging to the Lord, a place of freedom and refuge for those who serve the Savior. [J.W.M.]

C.177 Coleman, Clifford E. "The Book on My Closet Shelf." *Ensign* 19 (June 1989): 54-55. After searching for the answer to, "Which church is true?" the author remembered the book on the shelf. He found the answer to his question in the Book of Mormon and bears witness to its truthfulness. [J.W.M.]

C.178 Collier, Fred C. *The Nauvoo Doctrine in Light of Book of Mormon Prophecy*. Salt Lake City: Collier's Publishing, 1986. The Doctrine of Salvation (the Doctrine of Christ) and the Doctrine of Exaltation (the Nauvoo Doctrine or Doctrine of the Father), which deals with temple ordinances, are present in the Book of Mormon. The Book of Mormon does reveal and illuminate the "covenant which God the Father made to the Patriarchs Abraham, Isaac, and Jacob . . . the 'work of the Father' (1 Nephi 14:17)." [J.W.M.]

C.179 "The Coming Forth of the Book of Mormon." *Ensign* 13 (December 1983): 31-51. A pictorial collection of documents, artifacts, and old photographs related to the coming forth of the Book of Mormon, accompanied by written accounts of the circumstances surrounding this event. [S.P.S.]

C.180 "Coming Forth of the Book of Mormon." *Relief Society Magazine* 20 (January 1933): 52-53. Reviews the obtaining and the translation of the gold plates by Joseph Smith, the Anthon incident and the publication of the Book of Mormon. [J.W.M.]

C.181 Compier, Hendrik. "Inner Evidence." *Restoration Witness* 7 (May 1969): 4-5, 15. Author's testimony is not based on archaeology or history, but on the "plainness, honesty, simplicity, directness, boldness, and unapologizing approach" of the Book of Mormon. The Book of Mormon is a commentary on the Bible and clarifies its meaning. [J.W.M.]

C.182 *Compilation of the Book of Mormon.* Provo, UT: Department of Audio-Visual Communication BYU, n.d. Color diagram of the records that became the Book of Mormon, beginning with the brass plates to the finished product. [J.W.M.]

C.183 Compton, Todd M. "The Spirituality of the Outcast in the Book of Mormon." *Journal of Book of Mormon Studies* 2 (Spring 1993): 139-60. The outcast of the Book of Mormon—the Lamanite, the poor, or others—often lean toward becoming spiritual, while the rich classes sometimes become wicked. Author compares the "outcast" of the Book of Mormon to John Wesley and the beginnings of Methodism, the Dionysiac religion, the poor Christians of India, and other groups. [A.T.]

C.184 Condie, Spencer J. "A Mighty Change of Heart." *Ensign* 23 (November 1993): 15-17. Nephi, Mormon, King Benjamin, and others teach that the Holy Ghost actively participates in an individual's life by enticing, persuading, and influencing one to do good. We are admonished to cease contending with him because of pride and discouragement, which are strategies of Satan. Through the Spirit one may put the evils of pride and discouragement aside and experience the "mighty change of heart" (Mosiah 5:2) leading one toward perfection. [J.W.M.]

C.185 Condie, Spencer J. "Righteous Oaths, Reproofs, and Reconciliation (Alma 52-63)." In *Studies in Scripture: Alma 30 to Moroni*, edited by Kent P. Jackson, 8:80-91. Salt Lake City: Deseret Book, 1988. Discusses Captain Moroni, the Anti-Nephi-Lehies, the two thousand mothers and their stripling sons, Moroni's epistle to Pahoran, and Hagoth (Alma 52-63). Points out the importance of oaths, the proper exercise of authority, and how strength comes from unity. [J.W.M.]

C.186 Cong Ton Nu, Tuong-Vy. "Out of the Tiger's Den." *Ensign* 19 (June 1989): 44-47. The story and testimony of the courageous woman who translated the Book of Mormon into Vietnamese. [J.W.M.]

C.187 Conkling, Chris. "The Gentle Power of Jacob." *Ensign* 22 (February 1992): 7-10. Jacob's unique style as a poet-prophet demonstrates his "empathy for suffering" and "sensitivity to the challenges that women face." With sorrow and afflictions in his youth and his observance of sin in his own family, Jacob stresses the need for humility, denounces sin, and focuses on Israel's destiny. Jacob's writings show his "deep, personal witness of the suffering and sacrifice of the Savior" and of the atonement. [A.C.W.]

C.188 Connell, Maurice W. "The Prophet Said Silk." *IE* 65 (May 1962): 324-26, 338-40, 342, 344-45. The inclusion of the word "silk" in the Book of Mormon has been met with controversy. Evidence that there might have been silk production prior to the Spanish conquest is substantiated by excerpts from Thomas Gage's autobiography published in 1758. [J.W.M.]

C.189 "Conversions through the Book of Mormon." *IE* 63 (November 1960): 814-15, 836. The article reprints three earlier published recollections of the profound converting effects of the Book of Mormon in the lives of three prominent early LDS personalities—Wilford Woodruff, Willard Richards, and Parley P. Pratt. Wilford Woodruff received his testimony in a missionary meeting held in a village schoolhouse. Willard Richards was touched by the Lord after reading the entire Book of Mormon twice in just ten days. Parley Pratt read the Book of Mormon straight through, non-stop, day and night, and the Spirit of the Lord came upon him and he knew it was true. [R.C.D.]

C.190 Cook, Gene R. "Trust in the Lord." *Ensign* 16 (March 1986): 78-81. Challenges individuals to strive to reach their divine potential by trusting in Christ and following the Spirit's promptings. Provides an example of a young man who spoke regarding the controversial topic of the Book of Mormon for a school speech class and, trusting in the Lord, was able to bear testimony of the book and consequently touch lives. [J.W.M.]

C.191 Cook, Lyndon W., ed. *David Whitmer Interviews*. Orem, UT: Grandin Book, 1991. Presents a short biography and a collection of David Whitmer interviews and letters that date from March 1858 to January 1888. Many of the materials deal with his testimony of the truthfulness of the Book of Mormon. [J.W.M.]

C.192 Coons, Lela Bartlett. "Bright Scripture." *Ensign* 23 (February 1993): 54. A testimony of the warmth and bright feeling reading the Book of Mormon has given to the author since childhood. [S.H.]

C.193 "Corroborative Evidence." *MS* 62 (6 December 1900): 783-84. The historical and religious portions of the Book of Mormon cannot be separated. External evidence verifies the historical portions. *New York World* reports a mound where a tablet inscribed with the Ten Commandments, "sarcophagi," pottery and pictures that resemble that flood story, and characters resembling Egyptian and Assyrian writing were found. [J.W.M.]

C.194 Cottam, William. "I Have a Question: If both the Lamanites and the Nephites became wicked in the end, why was one group destroyed while the Lord allowed the other to remain?" *Ensign* 20 (June 1990): 15. The wickedness of the Nephites exceeded that of the Lamanites. The Nephites were cursed if they turned from the Lord. The Lamanites, wicked because of the traditions of their fathers, would be blessed with the gospel in the latter-days. [J.W.M.]

C.195 Cowan, Richard O. "American History Foreseen by Nephi." *Instructor* 101 (September 1966): 328-29. The remarkable vision of Nephi in 1 Nephi 13 speaks concerning the Savior's visit to America, Columbus' crossing the ocean, and the "plain and precious" truths of the gospel in the Book of Mormon that would come forth. [J.W.M.]

C.196 Cowan, Richard O. "Aztec History and the Book of Mormon." *Instructor* 102 (March 1967): 131-33. External evidences of the Book of Mormon provide an additional witness for the truth of the Book of Mormon. For instance, Aztec history has several parallels in the Book of Mormon. [B.W.J.]

C.197 Cowan, Richard O. "Historians of the Book of Mormon." *Instructor* 97 (December 1962): 444-45. A synopsis of the prominent record keepers of the Book of Mormon. A serviceable chart notes the authors, the time span they covered, and the amount of pages their writings occupy. [J.W.M.]

C.198 Cowan, Richard O. "In the Mouth of Two or Three Witnesses." *Instructor* 99 (August 1964): 328-29. The Book of Mormon is a witness of Christ. In accordance with the ancient biblical law of witnesses, the Book of Mormon complements the Old and New Testaments with its teachings and truths. [J.W.M.]

C.199 Cowan, Richard O. "The Lamanites—A More Accurate Image." In *The Book of Mormon: Helaman through 3 Nephi 8, According to Thy Word*, edited by Monte S. Nyman and Charles D. Tate Jr., 251-64. Provo, UT: Brigham Young University Religious Studies Center, 1992. Discusses Laman and Lemuel and the Lamanites of today. Points out that the Lamanites often superseded the Nephites in righteousness and that the Lamanites yet anticipate a glorious destiny. [D.M.]

C.200 Cowan, Richard O. "The Lehi Stone." *Instructor* 103 (March 1968): 132-33. A monument in Chiapas, Mexico (the Lehi Stone) has several correlations with the Book of Mormon tree of life pericope (1 Nephi 8, 11). Author provides a drawing and brief explanation of the monument. [B.W.J.]

C.201 Cowan, Richard O. "A New Meaning of 'Restoration': The Book of Mormon on Life after Death." In *The Book of Mormon: Alma, The Testimony of the Word*, edited by Monte S. Nyman and Charles D. Tate Jr., 195-210. Provo, UT: Brigham Young University Religious Studies Center, 1992. The Book of Mormon and modern prophets teach many things regarding life after death—there exists a probationary time after death before the resurrection; righteous spirits are separated from the wicked; the body will be restored to the spirit at the resurrection; physical defects present at death will eventually be removed. Further, at the day of judgment all will have a bright recollection of their earthly doings. [N.K.Y.]

C.202 Cowan, Richard O. "The Tame and Wild Olive Tree." *Instructor* 99 (October 1964): 415-16. The prophet Zenos outlined the history of Israel in the allegory of the olive tree in Jacob 5. Author includes a graph depicting the scattering and gathering of Israel. [J.W.M.]

C.203 Cowan, Richard O. " 'We Did Magnify Our Office unto the Lord.' " In *The Book of Mormon: Jacob through Words of Mormon, To Learn with Joy*, edited by Monte S. Nyman and Charles D. Tate Jr., 73-86. Provo, UT: Brigham Young University Religious Studies Center, 1990. The Doctrine and Covenants is not the only source of information on the Church's mission and organization. The Book of Mormon also contains valuable information on the organization of the Nephite church and it also "sets forth worthy examples we should follow in order to 'magnify our office unto the Lord' (Jacob 1:19)." [B.D.]

C.204 Cowan, Richard O. "When Jesus Visited Some 'Other Sheep.' " *Instructor* 96 (December 1961): 444-45. The "American Gospel" (3 Nephi), as recorded in the Book of Mormon, clarifies, and supports the teachings of the Bible and testifies of its authenticity. When Jesus Christ visited the American continent he blessed his people, organized his Church, and taught the gospel. [J.W.M.]

C.205 Cowan, Richard O. "Who Are the Lamanites?" *Instructor* 103 (May 1968): 211. The history of the term Lamanite is traced through the scriptures. "The 'Lamanite' nation, which was preserved, included descendants not only of Laman and Lemuel, but also of Nephi and his righteous brethren." A helpful chart shows the intermingling of family lines. [B.W.J.]

C.206 Cowdery, Oliver. "The Coming Forth of the Book of Mormon." In *Studies in Scripture: 1 Nephi to Alma 29*, edited by Kent P. Jackson, 7:10-16. Salt Lake: Deseret Book, 1987. A reprint of selected statements drawn from articles published in the *Messenger and Advocate* wherein Oliver Cowdery describes the events dealing with the coming forth of the Book of Mormon. [J.W.M.]

C.207 Cowdery, Oliver. "Delusion." *M&A* 1 (March 1835): 90-93. Title is taken from a pamphlet written by Alexander Campbell. Challenges Campbell's arguments and discusses the Aaronic versus the Nephite priesthood, the offering of sacrifice, a land of promise outside of Canaan, and the central role of the temple in Jerusalem. [D.M.]

C.208 Cowdery, Oliver. "Early Scenes and Incidents in the Church." *IE* 2 (July 1899): 652-58. Speaks of Joseph Smith's visions of Moroni, the last battles of the Jaredites, and of the Nephites on the hill Cumorah. [B.D.]

C.209 Cowdery, Oliver. "Letter." *M&A* 1 (October 1834): 13-16. Tells about meeting Joseph Smith for the first time and beginning his (Oliver Cowdery's) task as the scribe in the translation process of the Book of Mormon. Bears testimony to the genuine nature of the book. [D.M.]

C.210 Cowdery, Oliver. "Letter IV." *M&A* 1 (February 1835): 77-80. A recital of the events leading to the coming forth of the Book of Mormon, emphasizing Joseph Smith's encounter with the angel. [D.M.]

C.211 Cowdery, Oliver. "Letter VII." *M&A* 1 (July 1835): 155-59. Describes the Hill Cumorah, and identifies it with the final scenes of destruction for the Nephites and Jaredites. [D.M.]

C.212 Cowdery, Oliver. "Letter VIII." *M&A* 2 (October 1835): 195-202. Gives an account of when Joseph Smith Jr. went to find the plates in the Hill Cumorah. The box that contained the plates is described. [B.D.]

C.213 Cowdery, Oliver. *Letters of Oliver Cowdery to W. W. Phelps on the Origin of the Book of Mormon, and the Rise of the Church of Jesus Christ of Latter-day Saints.* Liverpool, England: n.p., 1844. Also in *Joseph Smith Jr.'s Rare Reprints, #23.* Independence, MO: n.p., 1990; and in *Letters of Oliver Cowdery: Showing the Rise and Progress of the LDS Church.* Lamoni, IA: RLDS Church, 189?. Seven letters (ca. 1839) containing testimony concerning Cowdery's scribal work for Joseph Smith during the translation of the Book of Mormon and other items of historical interest. Joseph's own narrative includes an account of the place and manner in which the records were deposited, the box that held the plates, his attempts to take the plates without authorization from the angel, and the angel's warning. [J.W.M.]

C.214 Cowdery, Oliver. "O. Cowdery's First Letter to W. W. Phelps." *MS* 3 (January 1843): 152-54. Letter also found in *M&A* 1 (October 1834): 13-16. A letter written to W. W. Phelps from Norton, Medina County, Ohio, Sabbath evening, September 7, 1834. Cowdery writes of his first meeting with the prophet and his immediate work began as scribe for Joseph Smith for the translation of the Book of Mormon. Then he writes of the manifestation of the angel to give the Aaronic Priesthood. [B.D.]

C.215 Cowdery, Oliver. "O. Cowdery's Letters to W. W. Phelps Letter #1." *The Gospel Reflector* 1 (15 March 1841): 137-40. Recalls his cherished relationship with the prophet Joseph Smith and tells of his gratitude to have been a part of the translation of the Book of Mormon. [J.W.M.]

C.216 Cowdery, Oliver. "Record of the Nephites; an Account of Joseph Smith's Receiving of the Gold Plates." *M&A* 2 (October 1835): 203-4. An account of the coming forth of the Book of Mormon and the receiving of the gold plates by Joseph Smith. [B.D.]

C.217 Cowdery, Oliver. "Rise of the Church: Letter VIII." *TS* 2 (May 1841): 391-97. Oliver Cowdery, in a letter to W. W. Phelps, describes how the plates were buried and how Joseph received them. [B.D.]

C.218 Cowdery, Oliver. "Trouble in the West." *M&A* 1 (April 1835): 104-7. Responds to attacks against the Book of Mormon dealing with the Spaulding manuscript, the birth of Jesus at Jerusalem, the ascription of Mary as the "mother of God," and the appearance of Jesus to the Lehites. [D.M.]

C.219 Cowley, Matthew. "Testimony through Reading the Book of Mormon." *Relief Society Magazine* 40 (January 1953): 6-12. Also published in *Matthew Cowley Speaks*, compiled and edited by Marba C. Josephson, 107-17. Salt Lake City: Deseret Book, 1954. A testimony of the Book of Mormon can be gained while reading the book. By reading the standard works, individuals can come to know God. [J.W.M.]

C.220 Cowley, M. F. "The Book of Mormon." In Cowley's *Talks on Doctrine*, 257-73. Chicago, IL: Northern States Mission, Church of Jesus Christ of Latter-day Saints, n.d. The Book of Mormon gives an account of God's dealings with many people. The prophecies of the book are being fulfilled such as no slavery or kings upon the land of America. Old theories that undermine the book's authenticity are exposed for the deceit that they contain, such as the Spaulding theory. Rejecting the book on its literary merits has no validity. [J.W.M]

C.221 Cowley, Matthias F. "The Book of Mormon." In *Cowley and Whitney on Doctrine,* compiled by Forace Green, 178-86. Salt Lake City: Bookcraft, 1963. Originally published as "Talks on Doctrine—the Book of Mormon." *MS* 100 (25 August 1938): 535. Tells of the origins of the Book of Mormon peoples. Discusses biblical passages that refer to the Book of Mormon (Matthew 13, Ezekiel 37, Isaiah 29 and Psalms 85). External evidences provide insight into the divinity of the book. The book's literary defects are explained. The divine nature of the Book of Mormon is affirmed by the witnesses. [J.W.M.]

C.222 Cowley, Matthias F. "Were All the Unsealed Records of the Book of Mormon Translated?" *IE* 5 (March 1902): 393-95. Gives a description of the gold plates, discusses the Urim and Thummim that were used by Joseph Smith to translate the Book of Mormon, and believes that the entire unsealed portion of the gold plates was translated. [L.D.]

C.223 Cracroft, R. Paul. "A Clear Poetic Voice." *Ensign* 14 (January 1984): 28-31. The author examines the traces of Hebrew literary forms found in the Book of Mormon—particularly the forms of parallelism and chiasmus. [S.P.S.]

C.224 Cracroft, Richard H. "The Gentle Blasphemer: Mark Twain, Holy Scripture, and the Book of Mormon." *BYU Studies* 11 (Winter 1971): 119-40. Examines Mark Twain's treatment of sacred writings and religious institutions in order to put into context his treatment of the Book of Mormon and Mormon practices. Twain is known for his exaggeration and misrepresentation of facts in order to give a humorous treatment of the subject. [B.D.]

C.225 Craig, Marshall R. "Father Lehi: Prophet and Patriarch." *Ensign* 6 (September 1976): 58-63. There are important teachings in the Book of Mormon regarding the role of Lehi as a prophet and a patriarch. He sees visions, cares for the welfare of his family, guides them physically and spiritually, and he blesses them. [B.D.]

C.226 Craig, Robert H. *The Book of Mormon at-a-Glance*. Sonora, CA: Yankee Hill Book, 1988. Gives a point-by-point precis of the Book of Mormon contents, from 1 Nephi to Moroni. [D.M.]

C.227 Craig, Robert H. *The Book of Revelation and the Vision of Nephi: (Compared Side-by-Side)*. Sonora, CA: Yankee Hill Book, 1988. Explains the relationship between Nephi's vision and the New Testament book of Revelation. Presents common themes by placing verses in parallel columns. [D.M.]

C.228 Cramer, Lew W. "Abinadi." In *Encyclopedia of Mormonism*, edited by Daniel H. Ludlow, 1:5-7. 5 vols. New York: Macmillan, 1992. Abinadi, the best-known martyr of the Book of Mormon, has his story recorded in the Book of Mosiah. He may have come from Zarahemla; he taught repentance to the royal court of King Limhi during his mock trials. His only recorded convert was Alma the Elder. His teachings, for which he was burned to death, included the Ten Commandments, interpretations of Isaiah, and prophecies of Christ. [J.W.M.]

C.229 Critchlow, William J., Jr. "Read the Book of Mormon." *IE* 68 (June 1965): 519-20. The Book of Mormon must be read slowly, personally, and purposefully. Reading the Book of Mormon will reveal the gospel of Jesus Christ. [J.W.M.]

C.230 Critchlow, William J., III. "Manuscript, Lost 116 Pages." In *Encyclopedia of Mormonism*, edited by Daniel H. Ludlow, 2:854-55. 5 vols. New York: Macmillan, 1992. The 116 pages of the original manuscript known as the "lost manuscript" were transcribed primarily by Martin Harris. They were translated by Joseph Smith from the record of Lehi abridged by Mormon. They were lost by Harris causing much grief for both translator and scribe. [J.W.M.]

C.231 "Crossing the Sea." *Friend* 19 (November 1989): 28-29. Cartoon depiction of Lehi's family crossing the sea designed for children. [J.W.M.]

C.232 Crowell, Angela. "Adieu: The Right Word After All." In *Recent Book of Mormon Developments: Articles from the Zarahemla Record*, 2:40. Independence, MO: Zarahemla Research Foundation, 1992. Explains that "adieu" in Jacob 5:48 (RLDS versification) is a proper translation of the Hebrew *barak*. "Adieu," according to the 1828 dictionary, is a common English loan word from French that means the same as the English *farewell*, or the Hebrew *barak*. [B.D.]

C.233 Crowell, Angela. A Comparative Study of Biblical Hebrew Sentence Structure in the Old Testament and in the Book of Mormon. M.A. thesis, Central Baptist Theological Seminary, August 1988. Describes some 50 forms of biblical Hebrew sentence structures, giving examples of its usage in the Bible and compares them to similar forms in the Book of Mormon (1908 RLDS edition). [B.D.]

C.234 Crowell, Angela. "Hebraisms in the Book of Mormon." In *Recent Book of Mormon Developments*, 55-62. Independence, MO: Zarahemla Research Foundation, 1982, pub.

1984. Also published in *ZR* 17 and 18 (Summer and Fall 1982), 1-7, 16. Introduces the reader to a broad coverage of Hebraisms in the Book of Mormon, such as numerals, the compound subject, compound prepositions, and the prophetic perfect. [D.W.P.]

C.235 Crowell, Angela. "Hebrew Poetry in the Book of Mormon: Part I and II." *ZR* 32-33 (1986): 2-9; 7-12. An introduction to Hebrew poetry in the Book of Mormon. The author introduces several poetic types, including synonymous, synthetic, staircase, alternate, chiastic, and antithetical parallelisms. Other poetic and literary patterns are also investigated. In most instances Crowell gives only one example of each poetic type from the Bible, followed by one from the Book of Mormon. [D.W.P.]

C.236 Crowell, Angela. "Lead Us Not into Temptation: A Hebrew Idiom." *ZR* 17 (Summer/Fall 1982): 13 Quotes several biblical scholars in support of Joseph Smith's translation of the Lord's prayer (3 Nephi 13:12), which differs slightly from Matthew's account (Matthew 6:14). [J.W.M.]

C.237 Crowell, Angela. "The Learning of the Jews." *ZR* 41 (February 1989): 2. Explains the use of *adieu* at the end of Jacob. Although a French word, its use is justified by its definition and as a fitting ending for the chiasmus in the last verse of Jacob. [A.T.]

C.238 Crowell, Angela. "The Learning of the Jews." *ZR* 47 (February 1990): 2. Examines the difference between the Joseph Smith Translation and the Book of Mormon version of the Lord's Prayer (3 Nephi 5:10-15). The author explains that Hebrew idiomatic usage resolves the differences. [A.T.]

C.239 Crowell, Angela. "Midrash: Ancient Jewish Interpretation and Commentary." In *Recent Book of Mormon Developments; Articles from the Zarahemla Record*, 2:27-30. Independence, MO: Zarahemla Research Foundation, 1992. Crowell identifies two forms of Midrash in the Book of Mormon that are common to the Bible. The two forms are Homiletic Midrash, including proem and yelammedenu homilies, and Narrative Midrash. [B.D.]

C.240 Crowley, Ariel L. "The Anthon Transcript." *IE* 45 (January-March 1942): 14-15, 58-60, 76-80, 124-125, 150-151, 182-183. Also in *A Book of Mormon Treasury*, 67-76. Salt Lake City: Bookcraft, 1959, 2nd printing 1976. Tells of Joseph Smith's desire to have someone examine characters copied from the gold plates. Reprints a portion of Joseph Smith's history dealing with the visit of Martin Harris to Charles Anthon. Also contains a letter sent to John A. Widtsoe by Frederick M. Smith of the Reorganized Church stating that the original copy of the Egyptian characters made by Joseph Smith is in the hands of the Reorganized Church. Tells of several different copies of the Egyptian characters in existence and gives examples of people verifying the genuineness of the characters as Egyptian. [A.T.].

C.241 Crowley, Ariel L. "The Anthon Transcript." *IE* 47 (September 1944): 542, 576-83. Presents a character-by-character analysis and interpretation of the Anthon transcript and concludes that a translation is still confronted with "formidable obstacles," but that it is clearly Egyptian and "most closely akin to demotic." [B.D.]

C.242 Crowley, Ariel L. "The Anthon Transcript and the Maya Glyphs." In *A Book of Mormon Treasury*, 77-80. Salt Lake City: Bookcraft, 1959, [R]1976. Also in *IE* 55 (September 1952): 644-45. A. Hiatt Verrill's work, *Old Civilizations of the New World*, reproduces an "inscription found at Sahhuayacu, Peru" that closely approximates "the script of the Anthon Transcript." Argues that the Mayan people did not progress from pictographs to a linear script, but possessed a linear, semicursive script from its early history. [A.T.]

C.243 Crowley, Ariel L. "The Escape of Mulek." *IE* 58 (May 1955): 324-26. An attempt to reconcile the biblical account of Zedekiah's capture and the implied extermination of all his male royal line, with the Book of Mormon account of an escape by one son, referred to as Mulek. Using logic the author makes a reconciliation between the two accounts. [R.C.D.]

C.244 Crowley, Ariel L. "Laman Found." *IE* 54 (February-March 1951): 80-82, 156-57, 205-6. Citing early Spanish writers and historians, the author demonstrates that the name "Laman" existed among the Indians at least as early as the time of Columbus' discovery of America. [R.C.D.]

C.245 Crowley, Ariel L. "Lehi's River Laman." *IE* 47 (January 1944): 14-15, 56-57, 59-61. Deals with Lehi's migration from Jerusalem and discusses the river Laman (1 Nephi 2:6). Quoting from the W. M. Flinders Petrie journal that recalls an expedition in Sinai, Crowley presents possible locations for the river Laman and the valley of Lemuel. A map of the region is included. [J.W.M.]

C.246 Crowley, Ariel L. "Metal Record Plates in Ancient Times." In Crowley's *Statement of Beliefs of the Church of Jesus Christ of Latter-day Saints*, 122-45. Idaho City, ID: Deseret News Press, 1961. Presents examples of written records on metal from the Romans, Greeks, Hittites, Egyptians, Babylonians, Chinese and Jews and demonstrates that the Jews were familiar with inscribing records on metal before the time of Moses. Such evidence of metal record plates suggests that the Book of Mormon may have been written on golden plates, according to the claim of Joseph Smith and others. [B.D.]

C.247 Crowley, Ariel L. *Metal Record Plates in Ancient Times*. N.p., 1947. Produces many evidences that ancient Israelites engraved their records upon metal plates. [B.D.]

C.248 Crowley, Elmer S. "An Angel from on High." *IE* 51 (September 1948): 556-57, 590. Discusses the life and mission of the angel Moroni, his visits with Joseph Smith, and his role in the translation of the Book of Mormon. [J.W.M.]

C.249 Crowther, Duane S. "Biblical Proof of the Book of Mormon." In Crowther's *Doctrinal Dimensions: New Perspectives on Gospel Principles*, 48-71. Bountiful, UT: Horizon Publishers, 1986. Talks on cassette tape (1980-1986). The Book of Mormon stands as a witness of Christ parallel with the Bible and is of equal significance. The Book of Mormon explains biblical references to "the other sheep," Jacob's prophecy in Genesis 49 of a "fruitful bough by a well," Ezekiel 37 concerning "the stick of Joseph," the psalmist's prophecy that "truth shall spring out of the earth," and Isaiah's prophecies of the Book of Mormon, i.e., the Anthon transcript, the destruction of the Nephite nation (Isaiah 29), and the great apostasy. [J.W.M.]

C.250 Crowther, Duane S. *Inspired Prophetic Warnings*. Bountiful, UT: Horizon, 1987. Prophetic warnings of the Book of Mormon directed to the inhabitants of the earth are discussed. The author enumerates the instruments of God's judgments and outlines the ways that individuals can prepare for survival. [J.W.M.]

C.251 Crowther, Duane S. *The Plan of Salvation and the Future in Prophecy*. Bountiful, Utah: Horizon Publishers, 1971. Combines Book of Mormon passages with others from the standard works of the Church to outline the plan of salvation. Many Book of Mormon passages foretell future conditions. [J.W.M.]

C.252 Crowther, Duane S. *The Prophecies of Joseph Smith*. Bountiful, UT: Horizon Publishers, 1983. An in-depth study of Joseph Smith's prophecies and their fulfillment, many of which apply to the Book of Mormon. Includes a history of Joseph Smith from Moroni's visit to the completion of the book's translation and publication. [J.W.M.]

C.253 Crowther, Duane S. *Prophetic Warnings to Modern America*. Bountiful, UT: Horizon, 1977. Refers to passages from the Book of Mormon that warn of perilous circumstances that will come to America, including the intrusion of secret combinations. [D.M.]

C.254 Crowther, Duane S. *Reading Guide to the Book of Mormon*. Bountiful, UT: Horizon, 1975. By dividing the reading of the Book of Mormon into twelve one-week periods, that book can be completely read in three months. Each major portion of the Book of Mormon is outlined, providing a preview for the reader. Also contains a doctrinal guide that references major doctrinal themes. [B.D.]

C.255 Crowther, Jean D. *Book of Mormon Puzzles and Pictures of Young Latter-day Saints*. Bountiful, UT: Horizon 1977. A book full of Book of Mormon games, puzzles and coloring pictures for children. [L.D.]

C.256 Cullimore, James A. "The Book of Mormon." *Ensign* 6 (May 1976): 84-86. The purpose of the Book of Mormon is outlined and those who take the book too lightly are condemned. Contains testimonies of the power of the book to change individual lives, nations, and the world. [J.W.M.]

C.257 Cummings, Horace H. "Eternal Evidences of the Book of Mormon." *Juvenile Instructor* 59 (September 1924): 466-67. External evidences of the Book of Mormon include the testimony of eleven witnesses, the fulfillment of many prophecies, and modern archaeological discoveries. The greatest evidence, however, comes from reading, praying, and pondering the message of the book. [J.W.M.]

C.258 Cummins, Lawrence. "Ammon the Valiant." *Friend* 15 (May 1985): 48-49. Deals with the story of Ammon, the son of Mosiah, who served King Lamoni, and the subsequent conversion of the king, his family, and the people (Alma 17-19). [J.W.M.]

C.259 Cummins, Lawrence. "Benjamin the Prophet King." *Friend* 18 (June 1988): 48-49. A narrative about King Benjamin and his address at the temple (Mosiah 1-6). [J.W.M.]

C.260 Cummins, Lawrence. "Nephi's Courage." *Friend* 16 (June 1986): 48-49. A narrative of Nephi's return with his brothers to obtain the brass plates from Laban (1 Nephi 2-4). [J.W.M.]

C.261 Curtis, Bardella Shipp. *Sacred Scriptures and Religious Philosophy: A Comparative Study*. Caldwell, ID: Caxton Printer, 1942. Explains sacred scripture found in various cultures with regard to the Book of Mormon. The Book of Mormon can be divided into four divisions: the plates of Nephi, Mormon, Ether, and the brass plates of Laban. Archaeological research supports the Book of Mormon. [J.W.M.]

C.262 Curtis, Delbert W. *Christ in North America*. Tigard, OR: Resource Communications, July 1993. Suggests that Book of Mormon lands are in the United States of America, particularly in the area of New York State. The narrow neck of land mentioned in the book lies between Lake Erie and Lake Ontario. The Spirit bears witness to the truthfulness of the Book of Mormon and a knowledge of the geography is not necessary. [J.W.M.]

C.263 Curtis, Lindsay R. *The Making of a Prophet*. Salt Lake City, UT: Deseret Book, 1967. An illustrated history of Joseph Smith for young readers. Presents a narrative of the coming forth of the Book of Mormon from the first visits of Moroni to the testimonies of the witnesses. [J.W.M.]

C.264 Cuthers, John. "The Book of Mormon Aspect of Preparedness." *IE* 19 (April 1916): 516-17. Quoting the book of Alma pericope regarding the refusal of the newly converted Anti-Nephi-Lehies to take up arms against their antagonists, the author pleads for peace during the World War. [D.M.]

C.265 Cutler, Ed. "Glad Tidings from Cumorah." In *The Restored Gospel and Applied Christianity: Student Essays in Honor of President David O. McKay, 1992*, 91-97. Provo, UT: Brigham Young University, Center of the Study of Christian Values in Literature and the Religious Studies Center, 1992. It is significant that the Restoration began in the spring, a period of rebirth. Moroni's message is a message of hope in Jesus Christ amid the despair of death (Moroni 10:27). The Book of Mormon is a call for all to come to Christ. [J.W.M.]

D.

D.001 Dahl, Larry E. "The Concept of Hell in the Book of Mormon." In *Doctrines of the Book of Mormon, 1991 Sperry Symposium*, edited by Bruce A. Van Orden and Brent L. Top, 42-56. Salt Lake City: Deseret Book, 1992. The concept of hell plays a prominent role in the Book of Mormon. The term "hell" is attested sixty-two times in the Book of Mormon. Addresses the following questions regarding hell: Is hell temporary or permanent? What does it mean to die in our sins? Can one repent in hell? Can one receive the gospel and improve his/her condition between death and the resurrection? [N.K.Y.]

D.002 Dahl, Larry E. "Faith, Hope, Charity." In *The Book of Mormon: The Keystone Scripture*, edited by Paul R. Cheesman, S. Kent Brown, and Charles D. Tate Jr., 137-50. Provo, UT: Brigham Young University Religious Studies Center, 1988. The Book of Mormon teaches that faith, hope, and charity are three distinct attitudes required for salvation and instructs individuals how to acquire these three attributes. [B.D.]

D.003 Dahl, Larry E. "The Plan of Redemption—Taught and Rejected." In *Studies in Scripture: 1 Nephi to Alma 29*, edited by Kent P. Jackson, 307-20. Salt Lake City: Deseret Book, 1987. The teachings of Alma and Amulek in Ammonihah are featured in Alma 9-16. Those who accepted the message of Alma and Amulek were cast out and their families burned. Repentance was the message rejected by those entrenched in priestcraft and false doctrine. Includes a list of questions that aid the reading of these chapters. [J.W.M.]

D.004 Daines, Robert H. "Cotton and the Book of Mormon." *IE* 65 (October 1962): 722-24, 751-53. Evidence indicates that cotton seeds from the Old World were transported across the ocean and interbred with wild cotton plants to produce a superior New World plant that was then cultivated. [B.D.]

D.005 Daines, Robert H. "The Globe-Trotting Sweet Potato." *Ensign* 5 (March 1975): 67. The South American sweet potato is cited as one possible proof "of the influence of Lehi's descendants on the Polynesian culture." Various theories are listed concerning how the potato arrived on the South Pacific Islands. [B.T.]

D.006 Darling, Joseph W. "The Book Will Prove Itself." *MS* 111 (September 1949): 282-83. Discusses attempts to discredit the Book of Mormon and Joseph Smith. Refers to Alexander Campbell, the Spaulding theory, and the Woodbridge Riley Theory. The best evidences of the divinity of the Book of Mormon are found within its own pages. [J.W.M.]

D.007 Darter, Francis M. *The Gathering of Israel: . . . From a Scriptural Standpoint*. Long Beach, CA: n.p., 1915. The Book of Mormon came by way of the Gentiles because of the destruction of the Nephites and rejection by the House of Israel. The book is to be used to gather Israel. [J.W.M.]

D.008 "David Whitmer and the Book of Mormon." *MS* 43 (December 1881): 785-89. An article reprinted from the *Chicago Times*, written after a reporter interviewed David Whitmer. David Whitmer confirms his testimony of the Book of Mormon and says that the Spaulding Theory is false. Sidney Rigdon did not know of the Book of Mormon until after it was published. Whitmer also showed the reporter the printer's manuscript of the Book of Mormon. [B.D.]

D.009 "David Whitmer's Last Hours and Testimony." *MS* 50 (27 February 1888): 139-40. Reprint of an article in the *Deseret News* that reprints portions from the Richmond *Democrat* of January 26. David Whitmer, the last of the Three Witnesses, told how he saw the plates and other objects. The article also reprints his last testimony of the Book of Mormon, recorded shortly before his death. [B.D.]

D.010 Davies, Legrande. "Isaiah: Texts in the Book of Mormon." In *Encyclopedia of Mormonism*, edited by Daniel H. Ludlow, 2:700-701. 5 vols. New York: Macmillan, 1992. Contains a chart listing Isaiah citations in the Book of Mormon and compares the Book of Mormon Isaiah to the Isaiah of the Masoretic Text, Septuagint, and Vulgate. The author argues that the Isaiah portions in the Book of Mormon show the error in the multiple authorship theories for the book of Isaiah. [A.T.]

D.011 Davis, Joseph H. "The Book of Mormon." *MS* 73 (21 December 1911): 804-6. Biblical prophets foretold the coming forth of the Book of Mormon. Includes a brief synopsis of the Book of Mormon story line. Mentions Martin Harris's visit to Professor Anthon. Joseph Smith had divine aid in translating. [A.C.W.]

D.012 Davis, Mark, and Brent Israelson. *International Relations and Treaties in the Book of Mormon*. Provo, UT: FARMS, 1982. A description of the civic and military characteristics of the Nephites and Lamanites. Shows ways in which political circumstances conform to observed customs in the Middle East. [D.M.]

D.013 Davis, Nora A. "Moroni the Faithful." *MS* 96 (7 June 1934): 358-59, 365. Gives biographical sketch of Moroni based on the account in the Book of Mormon. Praises his spirituality in time of turmoil and loneliness. Discusses his role in the restoration of the gospel. [A.C.W.]

D.014 Day, Afton J. "Then I Could Touch People's Hearts." *Ensign* 7 (September 1977): 72-73. As a tour guide at the Washington D.C. Temple, Linda Turman realized she needed to deepen her testimony of the Book of Mormon. She began reading and felt the Book of Mormon prophets teaching her. She was then able to bear testimony that touched the lives of others. [J.W.M.]

D.015 De Fuentes, Carmen Rodriguez. "A Lamp unto My Feet." *Ensign* 23 (October 1993): 68-69. The Book of Mormon assists individuals in every facet of life—when the teachings of the world contradict gospel teachings, in moments of discouragement, when faith needs strengthening, in marriage, and in times of fear and suffering. It is a good parental guide. [J.W.M.]

D.016 De Hoyos, Arturo. *The Old and the Modern Lamanite.* Provo, UT: Institute of the American Indian Services and Research, 1970. The term *Lamanite* applies to the native inhabitants (the Indians) of the American continent, the Eskimos, the Samoans of the Pacific Islanders, and other groups. [B.D.]

D.017 de Jagar, Jacob. Untitled talk. In *Official Report of the First Area General Conference for Germany, Austria, Holland, Italy, Switzerland, France, Belgium, and Spain*, August 1973, 102-5. Salt Lake City: Church of Jesus Christ of Latter-day Saints, 1973. Bears testimony of the truthfulness of the Book of Mormon and states that an angel taught and visited with Joseph Smith, and that the book that he brought forth contains the fullness of the gospel as it was taught to the inhabitants of ancient America. It is a missionary tool to convert both Jew and Gentile to Jesus' gospel. [J.W.M.]

D.018 Dee, Genet Bingham, ed. *A Voice from the Dust, A Sacred History of Ancient America.* Salt Lake City: Deseret News Press, 1939. A recreation of the entire text of the Book of Mormon. Contains commentary and pictures of sites in Mexico that may correspond with Book of Mormon lands. [L.D.]

D.019 Dellenbach, Robert K. "Hour of Conversion." *Ensign* 20 (November 1990): 23-24. A testimonial and exhortation in which the author relates his experience of finding out that the Book of Mormon contains the word of God. In order for an individual to receive a testimony of the Book of Mormon, he/she must have a desire, set forth good works, pray unto God, and trust in the Lord. [B.D.]

D.020 DeLong, Richard A. "Maya Glyphs May Identify Hill Cumorah." *The Witness* 67 (Winter 1989): 4-5, 14. The temple of inscriptions at Palenque in Mexico has a glyph that "can be interpreted as meaning Hill Ramah or Hill Cumorah." Delong believes that Cerro Rabon is a prime candidate for the Hill Cumorah in Mesoamerica. [B.D.]

D.021 DePillis, Mario S. "The Quest for Religious Authority and the Rise of Mormonism." *Dialogue* 1 (Spring 1966): 68-88. An attempt to understand how Mormonism's idea of "religious authority" appealed to early converts. Refers to the Book of Mormon to describe Mormonism's idea of religious authority. Discusses the role of the book in the formulation of Joseph Smith's philosophy and doctrine. [M.R.]

D.022 Derbidge, Gertrude. "The Women of the Book of Mormon." *Young Woman's Journal* 8 (November 1896): 80-82. Celebrates the noble women in the Book of Mormon, notably Sariah and the mothers of the stripling soldiers who fought under Helaman. [D.M.]

D.023 Despain, Goldie B. "The Tapestry of the Ages." *Instructor* 103 (November 1968): 458. Traces the succession of those who kept the records of the Book of Mormon until Moroni gave them to Joseph Smith. [B.D.]

D.024 "The Destruction of the Jaredites." *Friend* 20 (June 1990): 18-20. Children's illustrated story of Ether and the Jaredites. [M.R.]

D.025 Dibb, Dianne. "Ether Woke Us Up." *Ensign* 8 (July 1978): 58-59. Family readings of the Book of Mormon helped to arouse the children's interest in the book of Ether. After reading a chapter the family would draw the chapter's main idea on a large posterboard, an activity that served to help the children remember the important points of the book of Ether. [B.D.]

D.026 Dibble, Charles E. "Mexican and Mayan Codices." *IE* 43 (August 1940): 464-65, 504-6; "Ancient America in the Light of Recent Findings." *IE* 44 (January 1941): 1; "Some Facts Concerning Costa Rica and Its Inhabitants." *IE* 44 (February 1941): 68; "Metal Craft in Ancient America." *IE* 44 (April 1941): 218; "Compilation of the Indian Language of America." *IE* 44 (August 1941): 456; "Toltec Problems." *IE* 44 (September 1941): 538; "Chiapas Ruins." *IE* 44 (October 1941): 599; "The Olmec Influence in Ancient America." *IE* 45 (January 1942): 6; "Aztec Facts." *IE* 45 (February 1942): 69; "The Cuicuilco Excavation." *IE* 45 (March 1942): 135; "The Mayan Days . . . and Their Meaning." *IE* 45 (April 1942): 198; "Reconstructing Ruins." *IE* 45 (May 1942): 268; "Excavations in Mexico City." *IE* 45 (June 1942): 360; "Mexican Money-Axes." *IE* 45 (July 1942): 442; "Facts on Teotihuacan." *IE* 45 (August 1942): 483; "Priest's Dwellings in Teotihuacan." *IE* 45 (September 1942): 549, 593; "Copilco—Ancient Burying Ground." *IE* 45 (October 1942): 613; "Quetzalcoatl." *IE* 46 (January 1943): 6; "Aztec Recording—1518." *IE* 46 (February 1943): 71; "The Five Suns in Aztec Mythology." *IE* 46 (March 1943): 133; "La Venta Culture." *IE* 46 (April 1943): 197; "Pre-Colombian Irrigation." *IE* 46 (May 1943): 264; "Central American Migration Legend." *IE* 46 (June 1943): 330, 355; "The Arch and the Wheel in Ancient America." *IE* 46 (July 1943): 387; "Super Imposition in Central American Architecture." *IE* 46 (August 1943): 453; "Anthropological Conference." *IE* 46 (September 1943): 522; "Our Word Debt to the Aztecs." *IE* 46 (October 1943): 582; "Human Sacrifice Among the Indians." *IE* 46 (November 1943): 682; "The Religion of the Mayan Common Folk." *IE* 47 (July 1944): 391; "The Ten Commandments in Aztec." *IE* 49 (July 1946): 420; "Aztec Method of Recording History." *IE* 49 (October 1946): 613, 649. A series of brief comments in which the author presents archaeological findings, architectural notes, and myths and legends that deal indirectly with the Book of Mormon. Dibble discusses the wheel, ancient irrigation methods, metals, Mexican and Mayan codices, Quetzalcoatl, ancient buildings, and numerous other related items. [J.W.M.]

D.027 Dibble, Charles E. "Religious Beliefs of the Aztecs." *MS* 110 (October 1948): 296-97. The Aztecs of Mexico were religious fanatics who eventually were led to human sacrifice. The myths and legends of the Aztec people are perversions from the true gospel of Jesus Christ which was had in the first and second centuries A.D. [J.W.M.]

D.028 DiFrancesca, Vincenzo. "Burn the Book." *IE* 70 (May 1968): 4-7. Autobiographical sketch of DiFrancesca's life-long search for the Church after finding a damaged Book of Mormon in an ash barrel. [B.W.J.]

D.029 DiFrancesca, Vincenzo. "I Will Not Burn the Book!" *Ensign* 18 (January 1988): 18-21. An inspiring true story of a New York Italian Protestant minister in the early 1900s who finds a copy of the Book of Mormon that lacks the title page, and cannot be identified as the Book of Mormon. The minister gains a testimony of the Book of Mormon and spends the next twenty years looking for the Church "to which the book belonged." [D.L.L.]

D.030 Dixon, Riley Lake. *Just One Cumorah*. Salt Lake City: Bookcraft, 1958. Argues that the Hill Cumorah, where the Nephites and Lamanites fought their last battle, was the Hill Cumorah in New York state. The author also believes that the Nephites landed in Chile thirty degrees south latitude, according to a statement attributed to Joseph Smith. [B.D.]

D.031 "Do You Know?" *Friend* 18 (February 1988): 33. An activity for children concerning Lehi's son Nephi. [J.W.M.]

D.032 Dobson, J. Laverd, and J. D. Dobson. *Omni*. Salt Lake City: Dobson Family, 1980. An extensive discussion of the book of Omni. Examines the personalities, geography, and plates of Omni, and presents charts and illustrations. [D.M.]

D.033 Doddridge, David W. "Fertility, Right?" *Sunstone* 15 (October 1991): 9. Takes issue with John Kunich's theory that a 2 percent per year population growth in the Book of Mormon is "unheard of." According to newly issued population reports of May 1991, the Mideast is expanding at 2.8 percent, South Asia at 2.3 and Africa and 3 percent. It is possible that this type of population growth can occur. [J.W.M.]

D.034 "Domestic Life Among the Nephites." *Relief Society Magazine* 5 (February 1918): 107-11. Nephite women were descendants of Hebrew women, who had to adapt to a semi-tropical climate. The architecture of their homes was perhaps related to the Hebrew custom of hollow squares, flat roofs, and a courtyard in the center. While home life was simple and pleasant, the women were industrious. [J.W.M.]

D.035 Donaldson, Lee L. "Benjamin and Noah: The Principle of Dominion." In *The Book of Mormon: Mosiah, Salvation Only through Christ*, edited by Monte S. Nyman and Charles D. Tate Jr., 49-58. Provo, UT: Brigham Young University Religious Studies Center, 1991. The book of Mosiah offers a penetrating look at the differences between King Benjamin and King Noah, the former epitomizing righteousness and the latter wickedness. The two kings are contrasted in seven areas: their use of temples, conflicts with the Lamanites, plans for succession, sermons, physical labor and service, and their attitude toward scripture and the living prophet. [B.D.]

D.036 Doty, Donald B. "The Book of Mormon: 'The Most Correct Book.'" *Ensign* 18 (August 1988): 28-29. Rehearses two popular reasons why the Book of Mormon is called "the most correct book." Presents a list of doctrinal contributions of the Book of Mormon. [D.L.L.]

D.037 Dowding, Goff. "Word Portraits from Third Nephi." *IE* 51-52 (September-January 1948-49): 550, 614, 678, 782, 6. A series presenting narrative taken from 3 Nephi 1-28 with accompanying illustrations. Illustrations depict the events surrounding Christ's birth, death, and visit on the American continent. [B.D.]

D.038 Downs, Robert Bingham. "Joseph Smith's, 'The Book of Mormon.'" In *Books That Changed America*, 26-35. New York: Macmillan, 1970. Discusses twenty-five books that succeeded in shaping American thought. Chapter 4 is dedicated to the Book of Mormon. The author concludes that "the possession of their own scriptures . . . has proved to be the Mormons' greatest missionary tract, giving permanence and stability to their religion and providing them with a faith by which to live." [B.D.]

D.039 Doxey, Roy W. "I Have a Question: Some passages in the Book of Mormon seem to indicate that there is only one God and that he is a spirit only. How can we explain this?" *Ensign* 15 (August 1985): 11-13. Also in *A Sure Foundation: Answers to Difficult Gospel Questions*, 5-11. Salt Lake City: Deseret Book, 1988. Doxey explains, citing many scriptures, how the Book of Mormon "does indeed teach that God the Father, his Son Jesus Christ, and the Holy Ghost are three separate beings and that the Father and the Son are not personages of spirit." [B.D.]

D.040 Doxey, Roy W. "I Have a Question: What was the approximate weight of the gold plates from which the Book of Mormon was translated?" *Ensign* 16 (December 1986): 65. Also in *A Sure Foundation: Answers to Difficult Gospel Questions*, 50-52. Salt Lake City: Deseret Book, 1988. Citing Joseph Smith's own description of the physical appearance of the plates as well as several contemporary accounts of persons who were permitted to lift them, the author provides an approximate weight of the gold plates. [S.P.S.]

D.041 Doxey, Roy W. "Modern Fulfillment of a Book of Mormon Prophecy." *IE* 53 (November 1950): 879-80, 924. A prophecy made by Nephi (2 Nephi 30:3) states that many gentiles of the last days will believe the words of the Book of Mormon. The great numbers of persons who read and accept the Book of Mormon in this era demonstrate eloquent fulfillment of this prophecy. [R.C.D.]

D.042 Doxey, Roy W. "One of Joseph Smith's Contributions—Translation of the Book of Mormon." *Relief Society Magazine* 56 (November 1969): 857-62. The Book of Mormon is a witness to the Bible's truthfulness, proclaims the reality of Christ's resurrection, imparts and clarifies gospel truths, and is an instrument for salvation. Having faith in the Book of Mormon increases faith in Christ. [A.C.W.]

D.043 Doxey, Roy W. "Satan's Opposition to the Coming Forth of the Book of Mormon." *Relief Society Magazine* 44 (November 1957): 760-64. In opposition to the Lord's great work of saving the souls of mankind, Satan has sought to destroy the same. Joseph Smith was cautioned that temptations would arise concerning the gold plates. The loss of the manuscript was not a frustration to God's work, it was an important lesson. [J.W.M.]

D.044 Doxey, Roy W. "The Three Special Book of Mormon Witnesses." *Relief Society Magazine* 45 (January 1958): 49-55. The testimonies of the Three Witnesses were strengthened by their spiritual experiences with Joseph Smith and the Book of Mormon. Oliver Cowdery, Martin Harris, and David Whitmer never denied their testimonies. [J.W.M.]

D.045 Doxey, Roy W. Untitled talk. *CR* (October 1948): 104-6. The author tells the story of a man who visited his office who had served as an evangelist. He read the Book of Mormon, was touched by the spirit of God, and desired to obtain more copies to distribute. He felt greater faith could be had through the Book of Mormon than could be obtained through the Bible. [J.W.M.]

D.046 Draper, Melvin S. *Our Cousins the American Indian*. Santa Maria, CA: n.p., 1962. Draws upon cultural and anthropological relationships between ancient American peoples and the civilizations in the Book of Mormon. Discusses Ixtilixochitl, Quetzalcoatl, and the "Fair God" of Mesoamerica. [D.M.]

D.047 Draper, Richard D. "The Book of Mormon Teachings on the Gathering of Israel." In *A Symposium on the Book of Mormon*, 38-41. Salt Lake City: Church of Jesus Christ of Latter-day Saints, 1979. The Book of Mormon provides a host of materials regarding the gathering of Israel in the last days and God's promises to restore Israel to their ancient lands. [N.K.Y.]

D.048 Draper, Richard D. "The Mortal Ministry of the Savior Understood by the Book of Mormon Prophets." *Journal of Book of Mormon Studies* 2 (Spring 1993): 80-92. Examines Book of Mormon passages that concern Christ's mortal ministry, concluding that the revelations of Book of Mormon prophets contain the essential elements of Christ's ministry and character, providing the necessary information for Book of Mormon peoples to have faith in Christ. The paper focuses on Christ's uniqueness, "showing why he was neither human nor man, and the importance of His distinction from other mortals." [A.T.]

D.049 Driggs, Howard R. "Gospel Messages from the Book of Mormon." *Relief Society Magazine* 35 (September 1948): 640-47. Treasures of wisdom comparable to the biblical book of Proverbs may be found scattered throughout the Book of Mormon. The author presents many Book of Mormon examples of proverbial sayings. [J.W.M.]

D.050 Driggs, Jean R. *The Palestine of America*. Salt Lake City: n.p., 16 March 1928. Argues that the Book of Mormon lands were located in Honduras and Guatemala, extending "no further northward than southern parts of Mexico." Three maps are included. [B.D.]

D.051 Driggs, William King. *'The Liahona'; a Dramatic Cantata for Mixed Voices*. Los Angeles: The Liahona Choral Society, 1952. A cantata paraphrased from 1 and 2 Nephi. [B.D.]

D.052 Drummond, Peggy Ann. "One Good Conversion Deserves Another." *NE* 5 (March 1975): 43. A story of a girl who was converted by the Book of Mormon and she in turn helped convert ten other people. [M.D.P.]

D.053 Duckwitz, Norbert H. O. "Amulek." In *Encyclopedia of Mormonism*, edited by Daniel H. Ludlow, 1:38-39. 5 vols. New York: Macmillan, 1992. Amulek was a prominent and wealthy Nephite of the wicked city Ammonihah. Once rebellious toward God, he was called by an angel to assist Alma the Younger and became his missionary companion. His powerful and articulate testimony confounded lawyers and called many to repentance. [J.W.M.]

D.054 Duncan, Betty L. "The Invitation." *The Restoration Witness* 231 (March 1982): 6-10. Relates the events of her conversion through reading the Book of Mormon, and shares a personal experience and testimony regarding the coming of Christ to the Americas as recorded in 3 Nephi. [J.W.M.]

D.055 Dunford, C. Kent. "The Book of Mormon As a Record for the Future." In *A Symposium on the Book of Mormon*, 24-28. Salt Lake City: Church of Jesus Christ of Latter-day Saints, CES, August 1986. The Book of Mormon prophesies latter-day moral decay; it is a voice that warns against secret combinations and the denial of Christ; it solves religious confusion by supporting the Bible; it clarifies biblical doctrine and reveals plain and precious parts that have been taken out of the Bible; it is an additional witness of Jesus Christ. [B.D.]

D.056 Dunford, C. Kent. *A Testament for Our Times*. Salt Lake City: Bookcraft, 1993. The Book of Mormon was written for our day. The doctrines in the Book of Mormon are relevant to the twentieth century. It corrects a world in religious decline, gives counsel on war and politics, and guides against demonic influences, teaches of God and his dealings with the nations, clarifies the atonement, true conversion, the Christian way of life, the resurrection, judgment, and the afterlife. [B.D.]

D.057 Dunford, C. Kent, et. al. *Problems in Archaeology and Religion*. Provo, UT: LDS Institute, Brigham Young University, 1966. Poses many problems pertaining to scriptural archaeology and provides a number of tentative or positive solutions. [D.M.]

D.058 Dunn, Loren C. "Gaining a Testimony through the Book of Mormon." *CR* (October 1972): 95-97. Also found in *Ensign* 3 (January 1973): 84-85. Dunn presents two main points regarding a testimony of the Book of Mormon: (1) "The real strength of this Church is to be measured by the individual testimonies to be found in the total membership of the Church." (2) The Lord brought forth the Book of Mormon primarily to give individuals who study, ponder, and pray about it a testimony of its truthfulness. [R.C.D.]

D.059 Dunn, Loren C. "Read, Ponder, Pray." In *BYUSY* (7 March 1972). Provo, UT: BYU Press. The key to conversion and gaining a testimony of the mission and glory of Jesus Christ and the restoration of his gospel is found in the Book of Mormon. [J.W.M.]

D.060 Dunn, Loren C. "A Second Witness for Christ." *Ensign* 3 (July 1973): 44-46. Also found in *CR* (April 1973): 65-69. The Book of Mormon stands as a second witness of the nature, mission, and resurrection of Christ. [B.T.]

D.061 Dunn, Paul H. "Have Ye Inquired of the Lord?" In *BYUSY* (8 April 1969). Provo, UT: BYU Press. During a personal crisis of any kind individuals should remember the words of 1 Nephi 15:8, "Have ye inquired of the Lord?" Author cites several stories as examples. [R.J.L.]

D.062 Dunn, Paul H. *A Look at the Book of Mormon*. N.p.: n.p., 197?. Provides a series of tables and outlines identifying Book of Mormon time frames and events; includes Book of Mormon references to many archaeological and doctrinal passages. [D.M.]

D.063 Durham, A. Richards. "Antiquity, Scholarship, and the Prophet Joseph Smith." In *Papers of the Fifteenth Annual Symposium on the Archaeology of the Scriptures*, edited by Ross T. Christensen, 8-17. Provo, UT: Brigham Young University, 1964. When determining the competency of the prophet Joseph Smith, whether from a spiritual or a scholarly viewpoint, the same conclusion must be drawn: the Book of Mormon and the Book of Abraham are without question "genuine document[s] out of antiquity." [J.W.M.]

D.064 Durham, G. Homer. "The Christ of the Book of Mormon." In *Brigham Young University 1978 Devotional and Fireside Speeches*, 41-45. Provo, UT: Brigham Young University.

The Book of Mormon answers questions that plague humanity in the latter days. It provides key information concerning the divine role of Jesus Christ. [J.W.M.]

D.065 Durham, G. Homer. *Joseph Smith—Prophet-Statesman.* Salt Lake City: Bookcraft, 1944. The first section of this work focuses on "the political theory of the Book of Mormon." Several political aspects are treated, including the founding of the Nephite republic (Mosiah 29:10-29), the welfare of the state (Alma 4:11-12, 15-20), and the ideal Christian society (4 Nephi 1-3, 16-17). [R.J.L.]

D.066 Durham, Reed C. *A History of Joseph Smith's Revision of the Bible.* Ph.D. diss., Brigham Young University, 1965. Compares verses of the King James Version that are quoted in the Book of Mormon that are significantly different from the same verses in Joseph Smith's Revision of the Bible. The lack of harmony between the two works is "strong evidence that the revision was incomplete." [B.D.]

D.067 Durham, Reed C., Jr. *Some Recent Historical and Archaeological Evidences for the Book of Mormon.* R. C. Durham, 1980. An outline listing a number of Book of Mormon archaeological evidences, with an accompanying bibliography. Evidences include: Beit Lehi inscriptions, chiasmus, transoceanic influences, Mayan and Egyptian calendar parallels, Zuggurats, horses. [D.M.]

D.068 Durham, W. Cole, Jr. "Moroni." *Ensign* 8 (June 1978): 56-61. As a witness to the destruction of the entire Nephite civilization, Moroni's writings on the gold plates add special insights to today's society. [D.M.]

D.069 Dyer, Alvin R. "The Precepts of Men." *IE* 72 (June 1969): 39-42. Nephi once taught of the unfortunate condition of mankind when they cease to trust in God and to rely on "the precepts of men and denieth the power of God, and the gift of the Holy Ghost" (2 Nephi 28:26). One of the evil doctrines of our education system is sex education in our schools. The "new morality" fails to make the distinction between right and wrong. Personal agency is in jeopardy. [J.W.M.]

E.

E.001 E., A. "The Anthon Account." *MS* 113 (September 1951): 206-7, 224. Isaiah saw the great work of the Book of Mormon and prophesied concerning Martin Harris's visit with Professor Anthon (Isaiah 29:11-12). The article contains Martin Harris's account of this visit. Edward Stevenson wrote that Martin Harris saw his visit as a fulfillment to Isaiah's prophecy. Metallic sheets discovered in Iran buried in the palace of Darius verify the statements made by Joseph Smith and the Book of Mormon about metal records. [J.W.M.]

E.002 Eames, Rulon D. "Book of Mormon: First Book of Nephi." In *Encyclopedia of Mormonism*, edited by Daniel H. Ludlow, 1:144-45. 5 vols. New York: Macmillan, 1992. Summarizes the book of 1 Nephi and provides a map of the Arabian Peninsula that traces the possible route of Lehi. [A.T.]

E.003 Earl, Mary Hasler. "Bach, Beethoven, and the Book of Mormon." *NE* 13 (August 1983): 10-11. Offering a simple analogy to motivate individuals to read the Book of Mormon, the author compares piano practice to scripture study. "Just as I have to learn new piano techniques, I must review the Book of Mormon and learn eternal techniques." [R.J.L.]

E.004 Eastwood, Laura Teichert, and Robert O. Davis. *Rich in Story, Great in Faith: The Art of Minerva Kohlhepp Teichert.* Salt Lake City: Church of Jesus Christ of Latter-day Saints, 1988. A booklet containing a photographic essay on the life and paintings of Minerva Teichert. Created to accompany an exhibition at the Museum of Church History and Art, the work contains representations of several of Teichert's Book of Mormon paintings. [D.W.P.]

E.005 Edwards, Kay P. "The Kingdom of God and the Kingdoms of Men." In *Studies in Scripture: 1 Nephi to Alma 29*, edited by Kent P. Jackson, 7:270-82. Salt Lake City: Deseret Book, 1987. Examining Mosiah 25-29 provides insights into Alma's first address to the combined congregation of reunited Nephites and the people of Zarahemla. Alma taught the first principles and ordinances of the gospel and the process of spiritual rebirth. Discusses various forms of government, including government by the voice of the people and finds that government is important and is sanctioned by God, who does not necessarily endorse any particular system of government. [J.W.M.]

E.006 Edwards, Kay P. "What the Doctrine and Covenants Says about the Book of Mormon." *Ensign* 19 (January 1989): 34-37. In the Doctrine and Covenants the Lord testifies of the truthfulness of the Book of Mormon. The Doctrine and Covenants teaches that the Book of Mormon came forth under the direction of the Lord, that it should be studied by mankind, that woe will come to those who neglect it, that blessings of knowledge and eternal life are promised to those who receive it, that it will bring Lamanites and Jews to the Lord, and that it will bring to light the true points of Christ's doctrine. [A.A.]

E.007 Eggington, William. "Our Weakness in Writing": *Oral and Literate Culture in the Book of Mormon.* Provo, UT: FARMS, 1992. "Investigates aspects of the socio-cultural structure of the Nephite, Lamanite, and Mulekite people of the Book of Mormon from the point of view of those who study the nature of oral and literate societies." Lehi and his descendants functioned in an "Oral residual culture," a culture that writes to accomplish some very narrow functions, but acts, to a large extent, like an oral culture. "If we somehow can begin to understand the discourse and socio-cultural structures of the Book of Mormon authors, and the natures of their text production constraints and our text perception constraints, we may more clearly comprehend the text and its vital messages." [B.D.]

E.008 Eidmann, Karl. *Brief Studies of the Life and Times of Lehi.* St. Paul, MN: Liahona, 1947. A sketch of Lehi's life that draws heavily on Jewish sources and terminology. [D.M.]

E.009 "The Eight Witnesses" *Historical Record* 6 (1888): 195-219 Oliver Cowdery, David Whitmer, and Martin Harris desired the privilege and responsibility of being the Three Witnesses to the Book of Mormon. This article contains Joseph Smith's words concerning this event, the testimony of the Three Witnesses and a lengthy history of each. [J.W.M.]

E.010 Eldred, Phil. "Records Yet to Come Forth." *Witness* 79 (Winter 1992): 8-9. 14. Scriptural passages in the Book of Mormon refer to "other records" that have been lost or withheld that will be given at a later time. It is pointed out that the Book of Mormon must be received, embraced, and cherished before the promised records will be given. [J.W.M.]

E.011 Elledge, Helen. *Book of Mormon Stories for Children.* Independence, MO: Herald House, 1962. Simplified Book of Mormon stories are given for children, with illustrations. [B.D.]

E.012 Elliott, David C. "America: God's Promised Land for the Gathering and Redemption of Israel." *ZR* 29, 30, 31 (1985-86): 14-17, 22. Through Bible and Book of Mormon references, Elliott claims that "the history of America and the history of the Israelite peoples have been inseparably entwined together." Both the land of Israel and the land of America are lands of promise, both have a city called Jerusalem, and both are gathering places for the House of Israel. America will play a major role in the redemption of the world. [R.J.L.]

E.013 Elliott, Max B. "Hand in Hand: Indian Traditions and the Book of Mormon." *Instructor* 104 (January 1969): 30. LDS missionaries taught the Book of Mormon story to a Navajo spiritual leader and his family. The spiritual leader acknowledged that their story is true and already known in Navajo tradition. 3 Nephi 30:5-6 is applied to this event. [R.J.L.]

E.014 Ellis, Alvin R. *The Divinity of the Book of Mormon.* Grand Rapids: Evans, n.d. Lists many prophecies given in the Book of Mormon and gives historical and statistical facts to show how these prophecies have been realized. [B.D.]

E.015 Ellsworth, German E. Untitled talk. *CR* (April 1912): 89-93. Discusses the Apostasy, the Restoration, and the Book of Mormon. Though many reject its divinity, none have been able to disprove it. In the world there are many honest and good people who must be sought out and given the truths of the gospel. [J.W.M.]

E.016 Ellsworth, German E. Untitled talk. *CR* (April 1916): 79-83. Never has there been a book that has come forth with more evidences and testimonies of its truthfulness. Mentioned are the angel Moroni's visit, the testimony of the Three and Eight Witnesses, and the Book of Mormon prophets. [J.W.M.]

E.017 Ellsworth, Richard G. "Growing toward the Good." *NE* 16 (May 1986): 8-13. A testimonial by an individual in the navy who studied the Book of Mormon and felt a great spiritual power accompany the book. The promise in Moroni 10 had a long lasting effect upon him. [B.D.]

E.018 Enciso, N. Paul. "When a Lamanite Reads the Book of Mormon." In *The Sixth Annual Church Educational System Religious Educators' Symposium on the Book of Mormon*, 24-26. Salt Lake City: Church of Jesus Christ of Latter-day Saints, 1982. A testimonial by a Native American who gained a knowledge of the truthfulness of the Book of Mormon. Recalls statements by his grandparents concerning the migration of their ancestors to the American continents and the visit of the "Creator" to their ancestors. [A.T.]

E.019 England, Eugene. "Benjamin, the Great King." *Ensign* 6 (December 1976): 26-31. The life of King Benjamin is recounted. King Benjamin may be the greatest king who ever lived because he brought his people to both temporal and spiritual redemption. [B.D.]

E.020 England, Eugene. *Converted to Christ through the Book of Mormon*. Salt Lake City: Deseret Book, 1989. A compilation of various individuals' experiences with the Book of Mormon. The work is divided into three main sections: (1) the Book of Mormon family-to-family program in which families provide gift copies of the Book of Mormon to others; (2) stories of persons being converted to the Book of Mormon; and (3) reconversion stories of lifetime members of the Church. [B.D.]

E.021 England, Eugene. " 'Means Unto Repentance': Unique Book of Mormon Insights Into Christ's At-One-Ment." In *Rediscovering The Book of Mormon*, edited by John L. Sorenson and Melvin J. Thorne, 153-67. Salt Lake City: Deseret Book and FARMS, 1991. Explores the popular Christian theories about the atonement, the "satisfaction" and "moral influence" theories. Discusses the LDS view and finds that the fall of Adam was an essential part of the at-one-ment. The Book of Mormon makes this clear. [J.W.M.]

E.022 England, Eugene. "Moroni and His Captains: Men of Peace in a Time of War." *Ensign* 7 (September 1977): 29-36. While abridging ancient records, Mormon recorded many items dealing with wars in Alma 42-63. It was his desire to identify the righteous attributes of military captains Moroni, Helaman, Lehi, and Teancum. [B.D.]

E.023 England, Eugene. *The Quality of Mercy: Personal Essays on Mormon Experience*. Salt Lake City: Bookcraft, 1992. Several pages of this work are devoted to showing how the Book of Mormon teaches the principle of mercy in relationship to the atonement and the condition of the Lamanites. [D.M.]

E.024 England, Eugene. "A Second Witness for the Logos: The Book of Mormon and Contemporary Literary Criticism." In *By Study and Also by Faith*, edited by John M. Lundquist and Stephen D. Ricks, 2:91-125. Salt Lake City: Deseret Book and FARMS, 1990. Presents internal consistency of the Book of Mormon with respect to biblical patterns, metaphorical language, topological structures, Christ-centered content and eschatological meaning. These techniques, as used by the literary critics Frye and Girard on the Bible, show the presence and divinity of the Logos or redeeming Word of God in the Book of Mormon as well. Man's dark pilgrimage through life toward the ultimate tree of life, made possible by God's love and Christ's atonement, is considered in light of patterns in the Book of Mormon. Nephi's killing of Laban and God's use of violence is discussed. [A.A.]

E.025 England, Eugene. "Through the Arabian Desert to a Bountiful Land: Could Joseph Smith Have Known the Way?" In *Book of Mormon Authorship: New Light on Ancient Origins*, edited by Noel B. Reynolds, 143-56. Provo, UT: Brigham Young University Religious Studies Center, 1982. Compares the details of Lehi's journey across the Arabian desert to knowledge of the Arabian desert during Joseph Smith's time, showing that Joseph did not use worldly knowledge to translate the Book of Mormon. [B.D.]

E.026 England, Eugene. "Why Nephi Killed Laban: Reflections on the Truth of the Book of Mormon." *Dialogue* 22 (Fall 1989): 32-51. Violence and non-violence in the Book of Mormon is examined, including the killing of Laban (1 Nephi 4), the story of the Anti-Nephi-Lehies (Alma 24) and King Benjamin's address (Mosiah 4). [B.D.]

E.027 "Enos." *Friend* 11 (October 1981): 20-21. Cartoon pages for children telling the story of how Enos went into the wilderness to pray. [J.W.M.]

E.028 "Enos." *Friend* 20 (March 1990): 28-29. An illustrated story for children about Enos. [M.D.P.]

E.029 "Enos's Prayer." *Friend* 13 (July 1983): 48-49. A children's version of Enos and his prayer. [J.W.M.]

E.030 Ensign, Kathy. "One Thing I Remember from the Book of Mormon." *NE* 7 (May 1977): 41. A young woman was touched by Alma 34:28 as she read it to a group of deaf visitors to Temple Square who had requested that she read it. It speaks of those who turn away the needy and warns that their prayers are in vain. [M.D.P.]

E.031 Epperson, Steven. "Jewish Identity and Destiny in the Book of Mormon." In Epperson's *Mormons and Jews: Early Mormon Theologies of Israel*, 19-41. Salt Lake City: Signature, 1992. Joseph Smith's interest in the Jewish people was ever enduring and figured prominently in the Book of Mormon, which contains a worldview different than any other. The Book of Mormon holds future Israel and Judaism in high esteem as they preserve the biblical records, embrace the Messiah in the gathering to his place of refuge, reconcile to Christ and recognize his love and mercy. [J.W.M.]

E.032 Erickson, Einar C. "New Dates for the Reign of Zedekiah." In *Papers of the Fifteenth Annual Symposium on the Archaeology of the Scriptures*, edited by Ross T. Christensen, 39-46. Provo, UT: Brigham Young University, 1964. Nephi records that his family left Jerusalem during the first year of the reign of Zedekiah. The discovery of new archaeological evidence, the Babylonian Chronicle, makes possible the exact dating of Zedekiah's reign, the Babylonian conquest of Jerusalem, and therefore Lehi's and Mulek's migrations to America. [J.W.M.]

E.033 Ernst, Justus. "Translation Aids." In *Conference on the Language of the Mormons*, 95-138. Provo, UT: BYU Language Research Center, 8 April 1974. Provides aids for translators of the Book of Mormon, including a "scripture comparison list" that shows textual parallels to the Book of Mormon and the King James Version of the Bible and a "Book of Mormon translation guide" to give translators the best choices for Book of Mormon terminology. [B.D.]

E.034 Escobar, Victor. "A Book of Mormon Triptych Painting." M.F.A. thesis, Brigham Young University, 1969. Presents a triptych painting (a three-panel composition) depicting (1) Christ with the Nephites feeling his wounds; (2) Christ blessing Nephite children; (3) a harvest scene symbolizing that prosperity is the result of following Christ's teachings. [B.D.]

E.035 Essig, Fred, and Daniel Fuller. *Nephi's Slaying of Laban: A Legal Perspective*. Provo, UT: FARMS, 1982. A detailed examination of the legal ramifications of Nephi's execution of Laban. [D.M.]

E.036 Ettinger, Cecil. "A Testimony of the Book of Mormon." *Restoration Witness* 8 (April 1970): 6-7. Bears a testimony that is not based on archaeological evidences connected to the Book of Mormon, but on the contents of the book. [J.W.M.]

E.037 Etzenhouser, Rudolf. *The Book of Mormon and Its Translator*. Independence, MO: Ensign House, 1899. The Book of Mormon, like the Bible, is necessary for humanity. Joseph Smith translated the Book of Mormon from inscribed plates. Presents archaeological evidence of ancient cities, elephants, and horses. [B.D.]

E.038 Etzenhouser, Rudolf. *The Book Unsealed; An Exposition of Prophecy and American Antiquities.* Independence, MO: Ensign Print, 1892, [R]1895. Cites biblical prophecies and archaeological and other scientific studies to provide external evidence for many claims of the Book of Mormon concerning ancient American culture: evidence of highly civilized peoples, Hebrew customs, ancient writings, textiles, horses and elephants, metals, Egyptian influence, and the fulfillment of Psalms 85 and Isaiah 29. [B.D.]

E.039 Etzenhouser, Rudolf. *Engravings of Prehistoric Specimens from Michigan, U.S.A.* Detroit, Michigan: John Borman and Son, 1910. Contains depictions of stone, copper, and clay tablets, boxes and other objects upon which are found ancient engravings. [B.D.]

E.040 Etzenhouser, Rudolf. *From Palmyra, New York, 1830 to Independence, Missouri 1894.* Independence, MO: Ensign House, 1894. The book is divided into three parts, two of which contain a discussion of the Book of Mormon. Features a revised and enlarged edition of the author's *Book Unsealed* (1892) reviews eleven works written against Mormonism, and examines six United States school histories and four encyclopedias that deal with Mormonism. [B.D.]

E.041 Evans, John Frederick. *Remarkable Discoveries by Our Scientists of Book of Mormon Names on the Stone Ruins of Mexico, Central America and South America.* Salt Lake City: Vanity, 1940?. Relates names from New World inscriptions to names or titles in the Book of Mormon. Names of calendar months and other titles were associated with Book of Mormon words such as Laman, Mulek, Enos, Laban, Benjamin, Nephi, and so forth. [D.M.]

E.042 Evans, John Henry. "The Book of Mormon as a Motivating Force in 'Mormonism.'" *DN* (19 November 1932): 5, 7. Text of an address showing the power that the Book of Mormon exerts on human hearts. Gives conversion stories of early Church leaders, and relates the Book of Mormon teachings to the principles of personal knowledge, righteousness, and service that are the heart of the New Testament. [A.C.W.]

E.043 Evans, John Henry. "Book of Mormon Women and Their Work." *Relief Society Magazine* 15 (March 1928): 121-26. Women in the Book of Mormon were probably similar to women of all eras, the inspiration behind good men. Book of Mormon women that are referred to by name include Sariah, the wife of Lehi, and Abish, a Lamanite servant to King Lamoni. Women were held in high esteem, possessed great talents, and their work was important. [J.W.M.]

E.044 Evans, John Henry. "The Book with Golden Leaves," "Through Urim and Thummim," and "The Red Man's Bible." In Evans's *Our Church and People,* 67-86. Salt Lake City: Deseret Book, 1924. The author gives a very personal side of Joseph Smith's experience concerning the coming forth of the Book of Mormon. Observes that the translation of the Book of Mormon was a great period of training for the young prophet of God. There were two other purposes—to teach the gospel to the native inhabitants of America and to reinforce the teachings of the New Testament and make them easy to understand. [J.W.M.]

E.045 Evans, John Henry. "The Christ of the Book of Mormon." *Relief Society Magazine* 15 (April 1928): 179-90. The Book of Mormon presents a clearer understanding of Jesus Christ than does the Bible. It teaches regarding his pre-earth life, his Godhood, his godly attributes, and his appearance to the Nephites. [J.W.M.]

E.046 Evans, John Henry. "Conversions through the Book of Mormon" (Series). *Instructor* 78-79 (November 1943–December 1944): 565, 624, 25, 56, 120, 156, 211, 322, 374, 413, 469, 579. A series of accounts and stories of individuals who were converted through the Book of Mormon. Relates the stories of a hardened criminal, Thomas B. Marsh, George Ottinger, John Wells, Lester F. Bardin, Alvina Covert Turner, Robert Thomas Hill, Josephine and Otto Gaeth, A. William Lund, Heber J. Grant, and a Shoshone Indian, all of whom were converted by reading the Book of Mormon. [R.H.B.]

E.047 Evans, John Henry. "Form and Structure." *Relief Society Magazine* 19 (February 1932): 97–101. On the basis of its involved structure, the author argues that the Book of Mormon is a translation of an ancient document and not a modern composition. [S.H.]

E.048 Evans, John Henry. *Joseph Smith: An American Prophet.* Salt Lake City: Deseret Book, 1989. Chapter three deals specifically with the Book of Mormon, its coming forth and contents, and the positive effect it has had upon people. [J.W.M.]

E.049 Evans, John Henry. *Message and Characters of the Book of Mormon.* Salt Lake City: n.p., 1929. Written for young people. Details the historical background of the coming forth of the Book of Mormon, its translation, and then presents selected messages and characters from the Book of Mormon. [J.W.M.]

E.050 Evans, John Henry. "Nephite Philosophy of Life." *IE* 30 (September 1927): 955-59. Nephite leaders and teachers possessed a distinct philosophy regarding life. For instance, God demonstrates an impartiality towards the human race, the Holy Ghost is available to direct one's life, the principle of freedom is attached to obedience to divine law, an eternal view of things is advanced as opposed to the limited temporal view that mankind is prone to take. [D.M.]

E.051 Evans, John Henry. "Opening of the New Dispensation." In Evans's *One Hundred Years of Mormonism*, 1-120. Salt Lake City: n.p., 1905?. Recounts events taking place in America and Europe from 1815 to 1820, and sets forth the Smith family history relevant to the Prophet Joseph. The errors that had crept into the Bible and the arguments over doctrine are examined. Gives vivid accounts of the miracles surrounding the period of translation and provides many details concerning the coming forth of the Book of Mormon, the witnesses' testimonies, and accusations concerning the book's authenticity, contents, and the calling of Joseph Smith. [J.W.M.]

E.052 Evans, John Henry. "Side Lights on the Book of Mormon" (series). *Relief Society Magazine* 18 (October, November 1931; January, April, June 1932): 546-48, 606-10, 97-101, 218-22. June 1932 article is also in *MS* 94 (4 August 1932): 490-95. Between 1820 and 1830 Joseph Smith received a great spiritual education through contact with heavenly beings and learning of God's dealings with men in the Book of Mormon. The literary structure of the Book of Mormon is complex, filled exposition of doctrine and many details regarding people, events, and things. The Book of Mormon clears up many disputed doctrines of the Bible, such as baptism, the Godhood of Christ, pre-earth life, the nature of man, the purpose of life, and others. Hebrew culture, customs, ideas, and mode of thought is at the very root of the book. Early converts to the Church—Thomas Marsh, Parley P. Pratt, Willard Richards, and others—received their testimony from reading the Book of Mormon. [J.W.M.]

E.053 Evans, Richard L. "Communication." *IE* 66 (December 1963): 1074-76. The Book of Mormon is not a substitute but a supplement for the Bible, and a sacred record preserved by prophets of ancient America. [J.W.M.]

E.054 Evans, Richard P. "Another Evidence." *MS* 100 (27 October 1938): 674-75. Having spent most of his life in Shiprock, New Mexico, the author explains the history of the American Indian through his knowledge of the Book of Mormon. He cites a knowledge of the cross symbol among pre-Columbian Indians. [R.H.B.]

E.055 Evans, Richard P. "Mormonism for the Red Man." *MS* 99 (October 1937): 693-95, 700-701. Evans rejoices in the fact that missionaries are now being sent to preach to the Navaho Indians. The Navahos have many legends that are similar to biblical myths such as the flood, and Jonah in the great fish. Many have tried to determine the origin of the Native Americans. The Book of Mormon gives the answer that they descend from Lehi, a Jew from Jerusalem. [B.D.]

E.056 Evans, William. "The Origin of the American Indian." *MS* 100 (4 August 1938): 482-85. Studies the habits and customs of the Xlavajo Indians for forty years and concludes that the Book of Mormon represents the true explanation of their origin. [R.H.B.]

E.057 "An Excellent Book." *Deseret Weekly* 38 (19 January 1889): 112. Claims that archaeological evidences in the Americas substantiate the Book of Mormon. The book, *The American Indian*, by Elijah M. Haines, unwittingly supports the Book of Mormon. [D.M.]

E.058 "External Evidences of Scripture: A Panel... With Noel Reynolds, John L. Sorenson, Arthur Wallace, and Paul R. Cheesman, moderator." In *Scriptures For The Modern World*, edited by Paul R. Cheesman and C. Wilfred Griggs, 121-35. Provo, UT: Brigham Young University Religious Studies Center, 1984. Conversion depends upon the reception of the witness of the Holy Ghost, however, testimonies may be stimulated and strengthened by external evidence. Discusses the distinction between internal and external evidence of the Book of Mormon, who wrote the book, what is its purpose, what influence do external evidences have on nonbelievers, do external evidences prove anything about the existence of God, can Mormonism be proved experimentally, and many others. [J.W.M.]

E.059 "Extract." *TS* 3 (January 1842): 657-59. A proclamation to the inhabitants of America that Jesus Christ has appeared to the forefathers of the Indians, that God inspired Columbus to discover America, and that America became a free land "to prepare the way for the coming of the Book of Mormon." A warning for the same inhabitants to repent and believe in the words of Jesus Christ as presented in the Book of Mormon. [D.W.P.]

E.060 Eyre, Floyd G. "A Formula for Spiritual Knowledge." *MS* 98 (8 July 1937): 434-36, 444-45. Believes that the formula for understanding spiritual truth is found in Moroni 10:4-5, "by the power of the Holy Ghost ye may know the truth of all things." Some of the best tools to find spiritual truth are desire, sincerity, faith, pure living, and communication with God. [J.W.M.]

E.061 Eyring, Carl F. *The Book of Mormon Speaks: Service to Neighbor Is Service to God*. Salt Lake City: Church of Jesus Christ of Latter-day Saints, 1940. A transcript of the author's radio address on KSL Radio, May 5, 1940, wherein the author testifies that the Book of Mormon contains the word of God and is a true work, and recounts briefly how the book affected the lives of early Saints like Parley P. Pratt and Brigham Young. [B.D.]

E.062 Eyring, Henry B. "The Brother of Jared." *Ensign* 8 (July 1978): 62-65. Mahonri Moriancumer, or the brother of Jared (Ether 2), was humble, persistent, willing to work hard, and had great faith in the Lord. [B.D.]

F.

F.001 F., J. B. "American Antiquities." *Juvenile Instructor* 19 (15 July 1884, 1 August 1884, 15 August 1884): 222, 235, 250-51. Correct answers concerning the origins of past civilizations in the Americas were not found until the Book of Mormon was published. Discusses mounds in North and South America. Notes distinct historical periods in Mexico, Central America, and Peru. [D.M.]

F.002 FARMS Staff. *Book of Mormon Critical Text: A Tool for Scholarly Reference*, edited by Robert F. Smith. 3 vols. Provo, UT: FARMS, 1984-1987, Second ed. 1986-1987. Good for an overall view of the textual development of the Book of Mormon, but cannot be fully relied upon in specific instances. Its text is derived from a computerized 1830 edition, with changes based on visual examination of hard-to-read microfilms of the original and printer's manuscripts. The apparatus lists a good many textual variants (but not all), again based on a visual examination of most of the significant editions of the Book of Mormon. The apparatus also contains biblical and other ancient parallels and commentary. The appendices provide a number of valuable but preliminary lists of archaisms, names, textual errors, and page headings, as well as a manuscript register and a chronology. [R.S.]

F.003 FARMS Staff. "Martin Harris' Visit with Charles Anthon: Collected Documents on Short-Hand Egyptian." Provo, UT: FARMS, 1985. Using available historical information, this article serves to document the meeting between Harris and Anthon and to "illustrate the kind of information about Egyptian available to Anthon by 1828." Appendices contain reproductions of many relevant documents. [A.T.]

F.004 FARMS Staff. "Weights and Measures in the Time of Mosiah II." Provo, UT: FARMS, 1983. Examines the possible Akkadian and Sumerian origin of the terms *sheum* and *limnah* and uses the results of this study as one possible basis for deciphering weights and measurements in the Book of Mormon. [A.T.]

F.005 "Facts Are Stubborn Things." *TS* 3 (15 September 1842): 921-22. Comments on and quotes from Stephen's *Incidents of Travel in Central America*. It is claimed that the Toltecs were of the house of Israel, a concept that is seen as corroborating the existence of Nephites and Lamanites. [D.M.]

F.006 Fairchild, James Harris. "Manuscript of Solomon Spaulding and the Book of Mormon." *Magazine of Western History* 4 (1886): 30-39. A theory proposed by E. D. Howe (*Mormonism Unveiled*) purports that Sidney Rigdon stole Spaulding's manuscript and rewrote it for Joseph Smith to publish. It was research into the history of the manuscript that led to the conclusion that the Book of Mormon and Spaulding manuscript are not related. An excerpt from the manuscript is reprinted and Spaulding's religious beliefs are explored. Rigdon's denial is included. [J.W.M.]

F.007 Farley, J. Robert. *An Overview of the Book of Mormon*. Independence, MO: Zarahemla Research Foundation, 1980. A general overview of the main characters and events in the Book of Mormon, illustrated in color and probably intended for youth. [B.D.]

F.008 Farley, S. Brent. "The Appearance of Christ to the People of Nephi." In *Studies in Scripture: Alma 30 to Moroni*, edited by Kent P. Jackson, 8:149-60. Salt Lake City: Deseret Book, 1988. Christ's visit to the Nephites is "the apex of the Book of Mormon." Christ emphasized authority and ordinances, especially baptism, taught the people the Beatitudes and the Lord's Prayer, and showed them how to live the higher plane of the gospel. By building upon the rock of Christ, one can gain eternal rewards. [A.C.W.]

F.009 Farley, S. Brent. "Come Unto Christ (Moroni 9-10)." In *Studies in Scripture: Alma 30 to Moroni*, edited by Kent P. Jackson, 8:304-12. Salt Lake City: Deseret Book, 1988. Explains how a testimony may be gained from testing Moroni's promise (Moroni 10:3-5). Discusses the gifts given by the Spirit and the supreme challenge and goal offered by Moroni to "come unto Christ and be perfected in Him" (Moroni 10:32-33). [A.C.W.]

F.010 Farley, S. Brent. "Nephi, Isaiah, and the Latter-day Restoration." In *The Book of Mormon: Second Nephi, The Doctrinal Structure*, edited by Monte S. Nyman and Charles D. Tate Jr., 227-39. Provo, UT: Brigham Young University Religious Studies Center, 1989. Both Nephi and Isaiah prophesy of the restoration of the fullness of the gospel through the Book of Mormon, of the gold plates that will be delivered to Joseph Smith, of Charles Anthon, and of the Three and Eight Witnesses. [B.D.]

F.011 Farnsworth, Dewey, and Edith Wood. *The Americas Before Columbus*. El Paso, TX: Farnsworth Publishing, 1947. A presentation of photographs, notes, and comments dealing with ancient South and Central America. Discusses Hebrew and Egyptian parallels in the New World, four brothers as founders of the early South American culture, Christianity before Columbus, cement roads, and the use of metal. [B.D.]

F.012 Farnsworth, Dewey, and Edith Wood, comps. *Book of Mormon Evidences in Ancient America*. Salt Lake City: Deseret Book, 1953. Presents archaeological findings from ancient America that provide support for the Book of Mormon. [B.D.]

F.013 Farr, Beth Richards. *Jesus Christ Visits the Americas: A Book of Mormon Story for Children*. Salt Lake City: Little One's Books, 1977. Large drawings designed for children illustrate the text of 3 Nephi, wherein Jesus visited the Nephites and blessed the children. [B.D.]

F.014 Faulconer, James E. "The Olive Tree and the Work of God: Jacob 5 and Romans 11." In *The Allegory of the Olive Tree: The Olive, The Bible, and Jacob 5,* edited by Stephen D. Ricks and John W. Welch, 347-66. Salt Lake City:

Deseret Book and FARMS, 1994. Compares the use of olive symbolism in Romans 11 and Jacob 5. The focus in both is on grafting. There is a great deal of similarity, possibly indicating a common text underlying both Jacob 5 and Romans 11. These two passages are responses to different situations. Jacob 5 is a call to repentance, while Paul uses the occasion to warn the Gentiles not to think themselves superior to the Jews. [J.W.M.]

F.015 Faulring, Barbara, and Scott Faulring. "Revisions in the LDS Triple." *Seventh East Press* 2 (24 August 1982): B1-B8. Reviews the changes made in the 1981 edition of the triple combination. Book of Mormon changes are provided on pages B-1 and B-2. [B.D.]

F.016 Faunce, Edward. "Is the Book of Mormon Written in an Ancient Hebraic Poetic Style?" *ZR* 27-28 (1985): 1-4. Reproduces 1 Nephi 1:1, 1 Nephi 6:8-9; 2 Nephi 3:24-66 (RLDS versification) to demonstrate the elements of Hebrew poetry found in each passage. Briefly discusses poetic parallelism. [A.T.]

F.017 Faust, James E. "The Keystone of Our Religion." *Ensign* 13 (November 1983): 9-11. Also in *CR* (October 1983): 9-12. The Book of Mormon is the keystone of the Church of Jesus Christ of Latter-day Saints because it "establishes and ties together eternal precepts, rounding out the basic doctrines of salvation." Also claims that the book is not primarily a history, nor a geographical primer, but a confirming evidence of the life and work of Christ and the restoration of the gospel. The Book of Mormon brings individuals to Christ. [S.P.S.]

F.018 Featherstone, Vaughn J. "Moroni Example: Patriotism and Freedom in a Choice Land." *CR* (October 1975): 8-12. Speaking of America, Elder Featherstone encourages all citizens to greater loyalty to country and to stronger patriotism to the United States. If we all followed general Moroni's example (and his "title of liberty") we would all show by words and action how grateful we are for our freedom and our country here in this choice land. [R.C.D.]

F.019 Felt, Marie F. "A Chosen Servant: Mormon." *Instructor* 99 (April 1964): 149-51. For a juvenile audience, an account of Mormon's role in compiling the records of the Book of Mormon. [A.C.W.]

F.020 Felt, Marie F. "A Father's Love Rewarded." *Instructor* 96 (March 1961): 91-2. Children's flannel board story of Alma and the people he baptized at the waters of Mormon, and Alma the Younger's conversion. [A.C.W.]

F.021 Felt, Marie F. "How We Got the Book of Mormon." *Instructor* 103 (May 1968): 193-95, 197. Children's flannel board story concerning the coming forth of the Book of Mormon and its translation by Joseph Smith. [A.C.W.]

F.022 Felt, Marie F. "Our Heavenly Father Listens." *Instructor* 97 (June 1962): 199-200. Children's flannel board story about the Jaredites. [A.C.W.]

F.023 Felt, Paul E. *The Book of Mormon, the Lamanite, and His Prophetic Destiny*. Provo, UT: Brigham Young University Press, 1964. Contains four lectures given by the author at a Conference at BYU on the Indian program of the Church. Lecture one explains the curse on the Lamanites and explains how curses come through disobedience. Lecture two deals with the promised restoration of the Lamanites and their role in building the New Jerusalem. Lecture three discusses statements by Church Authorities on the Lamanite's role in the building of the New Jerusalem and missionary work among the Lamanites. Lecture four speaks concerning the era when the Lamanites will blossom as a rose (D&C 49:24). [B.D.]

F.024 Felt, Paul E. "Remnants of Israel Who? When Gathered? In *Sidney B. Sperry Symposium: The Book of Mormon*, edited by A. Gary Anderson, 83-95. Provo, UT: Brigham Young University Center, 24 January 1981. The Book of Mormon identifies the remnants of Israel and clarifies their destiny. [J.W.M.]

F.025 Ferguson, Larry S. "The Most Powerful Book." *Dialogue* 23 (Fall 1990): 9-10. A reaffirmation by Larry S. Ferguson on behalf of his father Thomas Stuart Ferguson that he (Thomas Stuart Ferguson) believed the Book of Mormon to be the word of God until the day that he died. [M.R.]

F.026 Ferguson, Thomas S. *Cumorah—Where?* Independence, MO: Zion's, 1947. Ferguson looks at the conflicting theories that the original Hill Cumorah was in New York or in Mesoamerica and concludes that it was in Mesoamerica. [B.D.]

F.027 Ferguson, Thomas S. "Gold Plates and the Book of Mormon." *IE* 65 (April 1962): 233-34, 270-71. Ferguson reports on the discovery of two Persian gold plates. One was engraved in the 4th century B.C. in the days of Darius II and the other dates to the 5th century B.C. [B.D.]

F.028 Ferguson, Thomas S. *Great Message of Peace and Happiness*. Orinda, CA: author, n.d. A book containing text and pictures that illustrate archaeological claims about the Book of Mormon. [D.M.]

F.029 Ferguson, Thomas S. "Joseph Smith and American Archaeology." *Bulletin of the UASN* 4 (March 1953): 19-25. Shows "striking agreements between the Book of Mormon history and the independent findings of modern archaeological-historical research." [D.M.]

F.030 Ferguson, Thomas S. *One Fold and One Shepherd*. San Francisco: Book of California, 1958. Comparisons are made between the stories and claims of the Book of Mormon and ancient American myths, legends, and archaeological finds. Includes a discussion of Quetzalcoatl. [G.A.]

F.031 Ferguson, Thomas S. "Some Important Book of Mormon Questions." *IE* 44 (September 1941): 528, 569-71. Advances several questions and answers about the Book of Mormon, including: Are all the Indians Lamanites? No. Did any white people survive the battle of Cumorah? Yes. Did the Book of Mormon people occupy the greater part of the western hemisphere? No. Is it true that the Nephites and Lamanites spent most of their time at warfare? No. Do archaeologists accept the Book of Mormon and use it as a guide in discovering ruined cities? No. [B.D.]

F.032 Ferguson, Thomas S. "The Wheel in Ancient America." *IE* 49 (December 1946): 785, 818-19. Argues against those that believe that the ancient Americans had no knowledge of the wheel by presenting five reproductions of wheeled toys and several scholarly views on the existence of such in Mesoamerica. [B.D.]

F.033 Ferguson, Thomas S. *The World's Strangest Book—The Book of Mormon*. n.p., 195?. A thirteen-page paper defending the Book of Mormon from an archaeological viewpoint. [D.M.]

F.034 Ferguson, Thomas S., and Milton R. Hunter. *Ancient America and the Book of Mormon*. Oakland, CA: Kolob, 1950. The Spanish conquest of Mexico resulted in the deliberate destruction of almost all written native records. Fortunately there were some who remembered the contents of the destroyed records. One of those was Ixtililxochitl who wrote as best he could a history of ancient America. This book uses parallel quotations from the *Works of Ixtililxochitl* and the Book of Mormon. Striking similarities confirm to a remarkable degree the story of the Book of Mormon. [R.H.B.]

F.035 "Fifty-two Quotes." *IE* 64 (January 1961): 28-30. A challenge to readers of the Book of Mormon to memorize scriptural quotes as they read the work. [J.W.M.]

F.036 Firmage, Edwin Brown. "Violence and the Gospel: The Teachings of the Old Testament, the New Testament, and the Book of Mormon." *BYU Studies* 25 (Winter 1985): 31-53. The use and misuse of war and bloodshed as seen from a study of the Bible and the Book of Mormon is treated. The study considers issues of force, war, repentance, the "Just War" theory, nonviolence, and pacifism. [D.L.L.]

F.037 First Presidency of the Church of Jesus Christ of Latter-day Saints. "Book of Mormon." In *Principles of the Gospel*, 92-115. Salt Lake City: Church of Jesus Christ of Latter-day Saints, 1943. Explains the content and history of the Book of Mormon, and provides evidences of the book's divine authenticity. The Bible does not conflict with the Book of Mormon's historical, prophetic, and doctrinal passages. [J.W.M.]

F.038 First Presidency of the Church of Jesus Christ of Latter-day Saints. "Modern Language Editions of the Book of Mormon Discouraged." *Ensign* 23 (April 1993): 74. An announcement of the number of copies sold in 1992 of the Book of Mormon followed by a discouragement of the publication of modern language editions of the Book of Mormon because they risk the introduction of doctrinal errors. [S.H.]

F.039 Fitzgerald, Heber Alvah. "Progressive Opinion of the Origin and Antiquity of the American Indian." M.A. thesis, Brigham Young University, 1930. Comprehensive study on the theories that have been held concerning the provenance of the American Indians from the time of Columbus to 1929. [D.M.]

F.040 Flake, Chad J., ed. *A Mormon Bibliography 1830—1930; Books, Pamphlets, Periodicals, and Broadsides Relating to the First Century of Mormonism.* Salt Lake City: University of Utah Press, 1978. An indexed bibliography of works dealing with the LDS Church. References concerning the Book of Mormon are included. [B.D.]

F.041 Flammer, Philip M. "A Land of Promise, Choice above All Other Lands." In *The Book of Mormon: First Nephi, The Doctrinal Foundation*, edited by Monte S. Nyman and Charles D. Tate Jr., 217-29. Provo, UT: Brigham Young University Religious Studies Center, 1988. Discusses the "promised land" covenant in the Book of Mormon and the divine intervention in the instances of Columbus, the Pilgrims, and the Revolutionary War. Concludes that the vision of the promised land must have been a sustaining force to Nephi and Lehi during their struggles in the wilderness. [A.T.]

F.042 Flanigan, J. H. *Mormonism Triumphant! Truth Vindicated, Lies Refuted, the Devil Mad, and Priestcraft in Danger!! Being a Reply to Palmer's Internal Evidences Against the Book of Mormon.* Liverpool: R. James, 1849. A systematic response to William Palmer's polemical tract. Contains documentary evidence from Sidney Rigdon that he had nothing to do with the Spaulding manuscript. Examines the language of the Book of Mormon, allegations of internal contradictions, and Book of Mormon inconsistencies with the Bible. [D.M.]

F.043 Fletcher, Lyle L. "Pronouns of address in the Book of Mormon." M.A. thesis, Brigham Young University, 1988. This thesis explores the second person pronominal usage of the English language in the Book of Mormon to discover the method of translation and the influence of God within the pages of the book. Fletcher finds "that the Book of Mormon is the word of God translated into the English of Joseph Smith" under the inspiration of God. [J.W.M.]

F.044 Fletcher, Rupert J. *The Way of Deliverance.* Independence, MO: Author, 1969. Writes concerning the coming forth of the Book of Mormon, the testimony of the Three and Eight Witnesses, the evils of the present world as presented in the scriptures, and the future establishment of the New Jerusalem. [D.W.P.]

F.045 Folsom, Marvin H., and Alan F. Keele. *Learn German through the Book of Mormon.* Provo, UT: Brigham Young University Press, 1978. Contains nine lessons for learning German using the German translation of the Book of Mormon as the text. Each lesson contains different rules of grammar plus exercises. [L.D.]

F.046 Foremaster, Philip. "Chastened, but Not Forgotten." *IE* 26 (September 1923): 995-97. The Mexican people are a chosen race of people. According to Isaiah 29:4 they have been brought down in the dust. However, they are descendants of Joseph, through Lehi (1 Nephi 5:14) and they will be redeemed (2 Nephi 30:5-6). [B.D.]

F.047 Fowler, Barbara. "Double Negatives in the Book of Mormon? Yes! Yes!" *ZR* 58 (December 1991): 2-4. Reprinted in *Recent Book of Mormon Developments; Articles From the Zarahemla Record*, 2:57-59. The restoration of the original text of the Book of Mormon has uncovered double negatives that offend the speaker of modern English. Previous to 1762, when Robert Lowth of Oxford created rules applying the mathematical rule of double negatives equaling a positive, double negatives were used in English. The double negatives in the original text are further evidence of Hebraisms in the Book of Mormon. Several examples are given. [J.W.M.]

F.048 Fowles, John L. "The Decline of the Nephites: Rejection of the Covenant and Word of God." In *The Book of Mormon: Helaman through 3 Nephi 8, According to Thy Word*, edited by Monte S. Nyman and Charles D. Tate Jr., 81-92. Provo, UT: Brigham Young University Religious Studies Center, 1992. Proposes that the downfall of the Nephites in the book of Helaman was caused by flouting their covenants. Emphasizes the debilitating nature of pride. Suggests some warnings appropriate to the latter days. [D.M.]

F.049 Fowles, John L. "Zenos' Prophetic Allegory of Israel." In *A Symposium on the Book of Mormon*, 29-36. Salt Lake City: Church of Jesus Christ of Latter-day Saints, CES, August 1986. Sets forth the reason individuals should study Jacob 5 and provides the keys to interpreting the allegory of the olive tree and a verse-by-verse commentary. [A.T.]

F.050 Frandsen, Russell M. "Antichrists." In *Encyclopedia of Mormonism*, edited by Daniel H. Ludlow, 1:44-45. 5 vols. New York: Macmillan, 1992. The title antichrist applies to those who deny essential parts of the gospel and the divinity of Jesus Christ. They actively oppose and/or seek to destroy the faith of the Savior's followers. The term is defined in the Book of Mormon and exemplified by Sherem, Nehor, and Korihor. [J.W.M.]

F.051 Frazier, Herb. "Helps in Teaching the Book of Mormon to Lamanites." In *A Symposium on the Book of Mormon*, 42-44. Salt Lake City: Church of Jesus Christ of Latter-day Saints, 1979. The promises of God to the Lamanites are great. The curse given to the Lamanites long ago has at times been lifted and will be removed as they become righteous. [N.K.Y.]

F.052 "From Lehi to Moroni." *Friend* 10 (February 1980): 20-21. An illustrated children's story of the Book of Mormon; includes one picture per book. [M.R.]

F.053 "From Stephens' *Incidents of Travel in Central America*." *TS* 3 (15 September 1842, 1 October 1842): 911-15, 927-28. Using extracts from the writings of Stephens, these articles suggest that the archaeological and historical observations of Stephens in Central America provide evidence that the Book of Mormon contains the truth. [J.W.M.]

F.054 Fronk, Camille. "Prophecy in the Book of Mormon." In *Encyclopedia of Mormonism*, edited by Daniel H. Ludlow, 3:1163-64. 5 vols. New York: Macmillan, 1992. Discusses various types of prophecy in the Book of Mormon including Messianic prophecy, prophecy of future Book of Mormon events, latter-day prophecy, and false prophecy. [A.T.]

F.055 Fronk, Camille. "Show Forth Good Examples in Me." In *Studies in Scripture: 1 Nephi to Alma 29*, edited by Kent P. Jackson, 7:321-34. Salt Lake City: Deseret Book, 1987. All things typify Christ—the ordinances, the law of Moses, the prophets, and all God's creations. Every creation of God assists in understanding the atonement and Christ's mission. This typology is replete in Alma 17-23. The sons of Mosiah exemplified Christ-like behavior following the mighty change of their hearts. Service, humility, unselfish sacrifice, and obedience were some of the Christ-like qualities Ammon typified. [J.W.M.]

F.056 Frost, S. E., Jr. *The Sacred Writings of the World's Great Religions*. New York: New York Home Library, 1943. One chapter of this work is dedicated to the sacred writings of Mormonism. Provides a brief history of the discovery and translation of the Book of Mormon, followed by a brief synopsis of each individual book. Reprints scriptural passages from the Book of Mormon. [B.D.]

F.057 Frye, Frank E. "The Principle of First Mention." In *Recent Book of Mormon Developments; Articles From the Zarahemla Record*, 2:201-203. Independence, MO: Zarahemla Research Foundation, 1992. The "principle of first mention" (Henry M. Morris, *Many Infallible Proofs*) is the idea that the first time an important word or concept is mentioned in the Bible provides the foundation for understanding its full development in later parts. Frye explains this principle and uses it to analyze the meaning of several Book of Mormon passages. [B.D.]

F.058 Frye, Frank Evan. "Who Are the Lamanites?" *The Witness* 79 (Winter 1992): 5-9, 14. Presents a concise summary of the origins and migrations of the three Book of Mormon peoples (Jaredites, Nephites, Mulekites). Describes the religious and political divisions of the Nephites that gave rise to the Lamanites. [R.H.B.]

F.059 Fuller, Barney R. *Stick of Joseph.* Pasadena, CA: Tri-Tech, 1969. Reviews Book of Mormon passages that deal with the earthly mission of Christ, his visit to the Americas, the restoration of the Church in this era, and the prophecies concerning the descendants of the Nephites and Lamanites in the last days. [A.T.]

F.060 Fyans, J. Thomas. "The Book of Mormon's Witness of Jesus Christ." *Ensign* 17 (May 1987): 28-29. Compares the body's need for oxygen to the soul's need for a sure knowledge of God and Jesus Christ. Author asserts that the best source for such knowledge is the Book of Mormon, and the witness of the book's truthfulness comes by the power of the Holy Ghost. [S.P.S.]

F.061 Fyans, J. Thomas. "The Lamanites Must Rise in Majesty and Power." *Ensign* 6 (May 1976): 12-13. Also in *CR* (April 1976): 16-18. The rapid growth of the Church in Mexico and Central America fulfills Book of Mormon prophecy. The Lamanites will again reach the spiritual heights their ancestors once attained. [B.D.]

F.062 Fyans, J. Thomas. "The Pattern." *NE* 18 (August 1988): 4-5. Mankind cannot follow what uninspired men teach because their perception of truth always changes, but the gospel truths, as outlined in the Book of Mormon, remain the same. [B.D.]

F.063 Fyans, J. Thomas. Untitled talk. In *Proceedings of the Stockholm Area Conference,* 36-40. Salt Lake City: Church of Jesus Christ of Latter-day Saints, 1974. The Book of Mormon is an important part of sharing the gospel and flooding the earth with the word of God. Its purpose is to bring all to Christ. The Lord told Joseph Smith that it would be as fruitless for man to try to stop the mighty Mississippi as to try to stop the heavens from pouring down knowledge. A great part of that knowledge comes through the Book of Mormon. [J.W.M.]

G.

G.001 G. "Old Bottles and Elephants." *Juvenile Instructor* 16 (1 April 1881): 82. Discusses earthenware manufacture in antiquity. Points out that some bottles and pottery vessels dug up on the American continent resemble elephants. Also mentions that the discovery of elephant bones in the United States tend to prove the truth of the Jaredite record. [A.C.W.]

G.002 Gabbott, Mabel Jones. "Abinadi." *Children's Friend* 61 (September 1962): 44-45. A children's story of Abinadi preaching to King Noah. [M.D.P.]

G.003 Gabbott, Mabel Jones. "Alma." *Children's Friend* 61 (October 1962): 12-13. A children's story of how Alma believed Abinadi and then organized the Church of Christ after preaching in secret to the people. [M.D.P.]

G.004 Gabbott, Mabel Jones. "Alma, the Younger." *Children's Friend* 61 (December 1962): 18-19. A children's story of the angel that appeared to Alma the Younger and the four sons of Mosiah and how they were converted by this experience. [M.D.P.]

G.005 Gabbott, Mabel Jones. "Ammon." *Children's Friend* 62 (February 1963): 18-19. A children's story of Ammon teaching among the Lamanites. [M.D.P.]

G.006 Gabbott, Mabel Jones. "Amulek." *Children's Friend* 62 (January 1963): 18-19. A children's story of Amulek. [M.D.P.]

G.007 Gabbott, Mabel Jones. "Circle of Fire." *Children's Friend* 62 (August 1963): 16-17. A children's story of Nephi and Lehi and the miracles that took place inside the Lamanite prison. [M.D.P.]

G.008 Gabbott, Mabel Jones. "Circle of Fire." *Friend* 7 (January 1977): 28-29. A children's story of Nephi and Lehi who were protected by a circle of fire in a Lamanite prison and converted all the Lamanites who were present. [M.D.P.]

G.009 Gabbott, Mabel Jones. "Famine in the Land." *Children's Friend* 62 (October 1963): 6-7. A children's story of how Nephi asked God to smite the earth with a famine instead of having the people destroyed by the sword so that the people might repent. [M.D.P.]

G.010 Gabbott, Mabel Jones. "Gideon." *Children's Friend* 61 (November 1962): 12-13. A story for children about Gideon who came up with a plan for King Limhi and his people to escape from the bondage of the Lamanites. [M.D.P.]

G.011 Gabbott, Mabel Jones. "Helaman and the Two Thousand." *Children's Friend* 62 (July 1963): 16-17. A children's story of Helaman and the two thousand stripling warriors. [M.D.P.]

G.012 Gabbott, Mabel Jones. *Heroes of the Book of Mormon*. Salt Lake City: Deseret Book, 1975. The author rewrites, on a child's level, topics such as Lehi's vision and journey into the wilderness, Nephi and the brass plates, Nephi building a ship, the faith of Jacob, Abinadi, Alma, Amulek, Ammon, the Anti-Nephi-Lehies, Helaman, Samuel the Lamanite, the brother of Jared, and Moroni hiding the brass plates. [B.D.]

G.013 Gabbott, Mabel Jones. "Jacob." *Children's Friend* 61 (August 1962): 34-35. A children's story of Jacob from the time he was born in the wilderness to his meeting with Sherem, the anti-Christ. [M.D.P.]

G.014 Gabbott, Mabel Jones. "Lehi." *Children's Friend* 61 (April 1962): 10-11. A story for children of Lehi leaving Jerusalem for the promised land. [M.D.P.]

G.015 Gabbott, Mabel Jones. "Mormon." *Children's Friend* 61 (January 1962): 32-34. A children's story of Mormon up to the time he received the plates. [M.D.P.]

G.016 Gabbott, Mabel Jones. "Moroni." *Children's Friend* 61 (February 1962): 16-17. A story for children about Moroni. [M.D.P.]

G.017 Gabbott, Mabel Jones. "The Murder of the Chief Judge." *Children's Friend* 62 (September 1963): 20-21. A children's story of Nephi prophesying of the murder of the chief judge. Many people thought Nephi was guilty, but Nephi shows that the chief judge's brother, Seantum, actually did it. [M.D.P.]

G.018 Gabbott, Mabel Jones. "Nephi and the Bow." *Children's Friend* 61 (June 1962): 14-16. A children's story of Nephi making a new bow to feed his family while they were in the wilderness. [M.D.P.]

G.019 Gabbott, Mabel Jones. "Nephi Builds a Ship." *Children's Friend* 61 (July 1962): 44-45. A children's story of Nephi building a ship to travel to the promised land. [M.D.P.]

G.020 Gabbott, Mabel Jones. "Nephi, Son of Nephi." *Children's Friend* 63 (December 1963): 22-23. A story for children. Nephi mourned for his people because of their wickedness and the Lord comforted him. Nephi saw the signs and wonders of Christ being born in Jerusalem. [M.D.P.]

G.021 Gabbott, Mabel Jones. "Nephi—The Plates of Brass." *Children's Friend* 61 (May 1962): 34-36. A children's story of Nephi getting the plates of brass from Laban. [M.D.P.]

G.022 Gabbott, Mabel Jones. "The Nephite Maiden." *Children's Friend* 62 (May 1963): 22-23. A children's story of a maid servant of Morianton who warned Moroni of Morianton's plans, which in turn allowed Moroni to stop the people of Morianton. [M.D.P.]

G.023 Gabbott, Mabel Jones. "One Thousand and Five." *Children's Friend* 62 (March 1963): 16-17. A story for children about the Anti-Nephi-Lehies and the 1005 that were killed by the Lamanites after they had taken an oath not to take up weapons against their brethren. [M.D.P.]

G.024 Gabbott, Mabel Jones. "Samuel, the Lamanite." *Children's Friend* 62 (November 1963): 10-11. A children's story of Samuel the Lamanite. [M.D.P.]

G.025 Gabbott, Mabel Jones. "The Three Generals." *Children's Friend* 62 (June 1963): 10-11. A story for children about three Nephite generals—Moroni, Teancum, and Lehi—during a war with the Lamanites. [M.D.P.]

G.026 Gabbott, Mabel Jones. "The Un-named Soldier." *Children's Friend* 62 (April 1963): 16-17. A story for children. One of Moroni's soldiers, during a war with the Lamanites, smote and raised Zerahemnah's scalp up with his sword, which led to a covenant of peace. [M.D.P.]

G.027 Gaer, Joseph. *The Legend of the Wandering Jew*. New York: Mentor, 1961. Chapter 12 discusses the tradition of "the wandering Jew among the Mormons," wherein the author cites examples of Mormons seeing one of the Three Nephites or the wandering Jew. [A.T.]

G.028 Gardner, Marvin K. "The Book Seemed to Cry Out to Her." *Ensign* 18 (December 1988): 20-21. The Book of Mormon was the motivating factor in the conversion of Marilu Ramirez to the LDS faith. She found and purchased it from a magazine rack when she was eight years old, believed it was true and later became a member of the Church. [B.D.]

G.029 Garmendia, Guillermo. Untitled talk. In *The Official Report of the First Mexico and Central America Area General Conference of the Church of Jesus Christ of Latter-day Saints*, August 1972, 38-41. Salt Lake City: Church of Jesus Christ of Latter-day Saints, 1972. Members of the Church with Lamanite heritage recall the origin and lineage of their progenitors. Inhabitants of the Huasteca area, which now constitutes the recently organized Tampico stake, were descendants of the Olmecas and the Maya-Quiches Indians. Great promises have been made to the Lamanite people (1 Nephi 2:18-20; Ether 1:38-43; Enos 1, 3-5, 15-18; 2 Nephi 1:6, 9, 10, 20). [J.W.M.]

G.030 Garner, Kent R. "Insights into the Old Testament from the Small Plates of Nephi." In *A Symposium on the Book of Mormon*, 37-46. Salt Lake City: Church of Jesus Christ of Latter-day Saints, CES, August 1986. The Book of Mormon "contributes considerably to [the] understanding of various things pertaining to the Old Testament," including the following areas—the book of Isaiah, Eden and the fall of Adam and Eve, prophecies of and references to Christ, the role of opposition and suffering, revelation and the ongoing process of scripture, and the scattering, gathering and apostasy of the house of Israel. [B.D.]

G.031 Garr, Arnold K. "Columbus: Fulfillment of Book of Mormon Prophecy." In Garr's *Christopher Columbus: A Latter-day Saint Perspective*, 1-5. Provo, UT: Brigham Young University Religious Studies Center, BYU, 1992. Columbus testified that he was guided to the New World by a divine hand. Orson Hyde testified that part of Moroni's ministry was to preside over the destiny of America and was with Columbus and protected his journey. Many Church authorities add their witness of the divine mission of Columbus and the Lord's intervention in his behalf. [J.W.M.]

G.032 Garrard, LaMar E. "Creation, Fall and Atonement." In *Studies in Scripture: 1 Nephi to Alma 29*, edited by Kent P. Jackson, 7:86-102. Salt Lake City: Deseret Book, 1987. A study of 2 Nephi 2, dealing with the concepts of creation, the fall, law and justice, and the atonement. [D.M.]

G.033 Garrard, LaMar E. "The Fall of Man." In *Principles of the Gospel in Practice, 1985 Sperry Symposium*, edited by Robert J. Matthews, 39-70. Salt Lake City: Randall, 1985. Discusses the manifold consequences of the fall, concluding that it was not a "negative or catastrophic event," but a necessary part of the Lord's program for mankind. Quotes liberally from the Book of Mormon. [D.M.]

G.034 Garrard, LaMar E. "Korihor the Anti-Christ." In *Studies in Scripture: Alma 30 to Moroni*, edited by Kent P. Jackson, 8:1-15. Salt Lake City: Deseret Book, 1988. Discusses different aspects of Korihor's philosophy using modern terms including: epistemology, the nature of the universe, and the nature of humanity. Refers to the viewpoint of Bertrand Russell. Finds absolute confidence in naturalism to be limited. [D.M.]

G.035 Garrett, H. Dean. "The Book of Mormon on War." In *A Symposium on the Book of Mormon*, 47-52. Salt Lake City: Church of Jesus Christ of Latter-day Saints, CES, August 1986. Author questions why so much of the Book of Mormon is dedicated to wars and warfare. The lessons to be learned from Book of Mormon warfare include: (1) It is important to always follow God's prophet; (2) God will reveal to the righteous when war is necessary; (3) An individual going to war for the correct reasons can live a righteous life. [A.T.]

G.036 Garrett, H. Dean. "Inspired By a Better Cause." In *Studies in Scripture: Alma 30 to Moroni*, edited by Kent P. Jackson, 8:69-79. Salt Lake City: Deseret Book, 1988. An essay justifying why so much space in the Book of

Mormon is devoted to war and warfare, and explaining when war is justified and when it is not. [D.M.]

G.037 Garrett, H. Dean. "Nephi's Farewell." In *The Book of Mormon: Second Nephi, The Doctrinal Structure*, edited by Monte S. Nyman and Charles D. Tate Jr., 377-90. Provo, UT: Brigham Young University Religious Studies Center, 1989. By reading Nephi's farewell address one can learn about his commitment to God, his love for his people, and his faith in the promises of God. [B.D.]

G.038 Garrett, H. Dean. "Peace Within." *Ensign* 18 (September 1988): 20-25. Many pages of Book of Mormon are devoted to warfare. Garrett discusses war in connection with the role of government, individual responsibility, and how war affects humanity today. [D.L.L.]

G.039 Garrett, H. Dean. "The Three Most Abominable Sins." In *The Book of Mormon: Alma, The Testimony of the Word*, edited by Monte S. Nyman and Charles D. Tate Jr., 157-72. Provo, UT: Brigham Young University Religious Studies Center, 1992. Discusses the three greatest sins against God as outlined by Alma. They are (1) the sin against the Holy Ghost, (2) the shedding of innocent blood, and (93) sexual sin. [N.K.Y.]

G.040 Garth, Norman V. "I Have a Question: What is the current status of research concerning the 'tree of life' carving from Chiapas, Mexico?" *Ensign* 15 (June 1985): 54-55. The Izapa Stela 5 seems to depict the tree of life discussed in 1 Nephi 8. A total of eighty-nine stone monuments similar to the Stela have been found. Theories as to their meaning include: there is an anthropomorphic god whose symbol is the sun, he is god of the tree of life, the tree relates to life after death, physical resurrection is implied, worship involves a divine atonement, and the spirit of a child originates in heaven. [J.W.M.]

G.041 Gates, Thomas J. "Succession of Book of Mormon Authors." *IE* 37 (March 1934): 162. Lists chronologically the succession of the authors of the Book of Mormon with dates. [L.D.]

G.042 Gaunt, LaRene. "The Book Changed My Life: Members Share Their Testimonies of the Book of Mormon." *Ensign* 12 (February 1991): 18-21. Members of the LDS church bear witness of the influence that the Book of Mormon had in their lives. It strengthened testimonies, brought personal witness of Christ, assisted in conversion, and helped to reactivate members. [J.W.M.]

G.043 Gaunt, LaRene. "Does the Book of Mormon count? For these families, the answer is an emphatic yes!" *Ensign* 21 (June 1991): 20-23. Church members share experiences they had following the council of President Benson to read the Book of Mormon with their families. Small children understood and loved the stories of the book, a husband was reactivated, etc. [J.W.M.]

G.044 Gaunt, LaRene. "Painting the Word." *Ensign* 22 (January 1992): 32-35. Depicts a selection of paintings and original artwork with Book of Mormon themes, the result of international art competition. [A.C.W.]

G.045 Gee, John. "Limhi in the Library." *Journal of Book of Mormon Studies* 1 (Fall 1992): 54-66. It was an ancient Near Eastern practice for kings to employ scribes to record all of their official statements, and it appears that all of the direct quotations of King Limhi were recorded by an official scribe. Limhi's quotations of documents precede the cited documents themselves and all quotations are from material chronologically preceding Limhi, and to which he could have had access. [R.H.B.]

G.046 Gee, John. "A Note on the Name 'Nephi.'" *Journal of Book of Mormon Studies* 1 (Fall 1992): 189-91. The name Nephi is a Syro-Palestinian Semitic form of an Egyptian man's name dating from the Late Period in Egypt. [R.H.B.]

G.047 Gee John, and Daniel C. Peterson. "Graft and Corruption: On Olives and Olive in the Pre-Modern Mediterranean." In *The Allegory of the Olive Tree: The Olive, The Bible and Jacob 5*, edited by Stephen D. Ricks and John W. Welch, 186-247. Salt Lake City: Deseret Book and FARMS, 1994. Philological evidence indicates that the olive originated in the area of Syro-Palestine. It was considered first among trees and its oil was an equivalent of money. The article explores methods of planting, grafting, pruning, digging, nourishing, dunging, and harvesting of the olive tree, and the pressing and storage of the oil, all in relation to Zenos's parable of Jacob 5. [J.W.M.]

G.048 "Genealogical Records Relationship." *IE* 23 (September 1920): 962-66. Book of Mormon accounts of Hagoth agree fully with Maori and Hawaiian traditions, legends, and genealogical records. [J.W.M]

G.049 Gentry, Leland H. "Early Reactions to the Book of Mormon." In *Mormon History Association 15th Annual Meeting.* Palmyra, N.Y.: n.p., May 1980. Explores events between September 22, 1827, and March 25, 1830, which shaped the course of Mormon history: the way the local populace responded to reports of the existence of the plates, the difficulties in obtaining a publisher, the fall of Martin Harris and the Whitmers, and the response of the media to the publication of the Book of Mormon. [J.W.M.]

G.050 Gentry, Leland H. "God Will Fulfill His Covenants with the House of Israel." In *The Book of Mormon: Second Nephi, The Doctrinal Structure*, edited by Monte S. Nyman and Charles D. Tate Jr., 159-76. Provo, UT: Brigham Young University Religious Studies Center, 1989. "One reason Latter-day Saints understand Isaiah better than other students is the excellent commentary provided by Nephite prophets." The Book of Mormon explains Isaiah's prophecies and shows how they will be fulfilled. [B.D.]

G.051 Gentry, Leland H. "Vengeance is Mine, Saith the Lord." In *A Symposium on the Book of Mormon,* 54-56. Salt Lake City: Church of Jesus Christ of Latter-day Saints, CES, August 1986. The Book of Mormon teaches members of the LDS Church how to deal with anti-Mormon works and workers. Members are to be humble, forgiving, and not to avenge their wrongs. [A.T.]

G.052 Gentry, Leland H. "Why So Much Isaiah in the Book of Mormon." In *A Symposium on the Book of Mormon*, 45-47. Salt Lake City: Church of Jesus Christ of Latter-day Saints, 1979. The Book of Mormon contains twenty-one chapters from the book of Isaiah. The prophet Isaiah had much to say about the history, scattering, and gathering of Israel. The Book of Mormon convinces the children of Israel that they are not forgotten and they will be gathered. [N.K.Y.]

G.053 Giacalone, Joseph. "Growing into the Church." *Ensign* 14 (June 1984): 64-65. A loving wife and children and other members of the Church brought this man closer to Church membership, but it was in discovering the beauty of the Book of Mormon that he gained his testimony. [J.W.M.]

G.054 Gibson, William. "Remarks on the Book of Mormon." *MS* 12 (15 July; 1 August; 1, 15 September; 1, 15 October 1850): 209-12, 225-28, 261-65, 283-86, 289-92, 313-15. Defends the Book of Mormon against current calumny. Cites reasons why God's communications are not limited to the Bible. Explains why the plates should not be available for inspection. Shows the harmony between the Book of Mormon and the Bible, using many prooftexts, including Zechariah 10:7-11, Hosea 11:9ff, and Isaiah 28. Discusses archaeological confirmations. [D.M.]

G.055 Gigena, Marcelo A. "My Surprising Senior Year." *NE* 22 (June 1992): 8-10. A conversion story of a young man who became interested in the Church through his friends' examples and received his testimony after reading the Book of Mormon. [M.D.P.]

G.056 Gilchrist, Donald B. "The Fullness of the Gospel As Found in the Book of Mormon and Other Written Sources." In *A Symposium on the Book of Mormon*, 48-54. Salt Lake City: Church of Jesus Christ of Latter-day Saints, 1979. The Book of Mormon contains the fullness of the gospel. The author discusses this idea and provides possible meanings. [N.K.Y.]

G.057 Gileadi, Avraham. *The Book of Isaiah: A New Translation with Interpretive Keys from the Book of Mormon.* Salt Lake City: Deseret Book, 1988. A poetic translation of Isaiah, utilizing four interpretive keys from Nephi and

Jesus. The keys are the "spirit of prophecy," or revelation by the Holy Ghost, the "letter of prophecy" or the "manner" of the Jews, searching Isaiah diligently, and seeing Isaiah's teachings as "types" within salvific history. [D.M.]

G.058 Gileadi, Avraham. "Isaiah—Key to the Book of Mormon." In *Rediscovering the Book of Mormon*, edited by John L. Sorenson and Melvin J. Thorne, 197-206. Salt Lake City: Deseret Book and FARMS, 1991. The Book of Mormon teaches four concepts that assist in understanding the Book of Isaiah: the spirit of prophecy, the manner of the Jews, search Isaiah's words, and types (events in the past that foreshadow events in Israel's future). A knowledge of Isaiah's influence in the Book of Mormon assists in its understanding as well. [J.W.M.]

G.059 Gileadi, Avraham. *The Last Days: Types and Shadows from the Bible and the Book of Mormon.* Salt Lake City: Deseret Book, 1991. Finds that Book of Mormon writers followed the manner of Jewish writers who built information into the structure of their writings, thus conveying messages through literary techniques. A prominent feature is the viewing of future events in the light of the past through typology. The "Great and Marvelous work of the Lord" is associated with the "Great and terrible day of the Lord" when two opposing forces meet in a "kind of showdown" as described in the Book of Mormon. Discusses the allegory of the olive tree in Jacob 5. The last days will be filled with more destruction than any other time in the history of the earth. To prepare for this time we keep God's commands and honor him. [J.W.M.]

G.060 Giles, John D. "Father Lehi's Children." *IE* 49 (September 1946): 556-59, 601-2. Describes President George Albert Smith's visit to Mexico city. Several prophecies concerning the Lamanites are quoted to show the importance of the Lamanites in the last days. [B.D.]

G.061 Gillum, Gary P. *Book of Mormon Books in Print, April 1984, with Published Book Reviews.* Provo, UT: FARMS, 1988. Lists two-and-a-half pages of citations of books on the Book of Mormon published before April 1984. Also includes reprints of published book reviews of many of the listed books. [B.D.]

G.062 Gillum, Gary P. "Book of Mormon Reviews through 1987." Provo, UT: FARMS, 1988. A collection of photocopies of book reviews from several sources such as *BYU Studies, U.A.S. Newsletter, Improvement Era, Dialogue,* and others.

G.063 Gillum, Gary P. *Hugh Nibley Quotes: Of the Book of Mormon.* Provo, UT: FARMS, 1982. A reprint of a number of quotes by Hugh Nibley on the Book of Mormon from Gillum's *Of All Things: A Nibley Quote Book.* Salt Lake City: Signature Books, 1981. [B.D.]

G.064 Gillum, Gary P. "Repentance Also Means Rethinking." In *By Study and Also by Faith,* edited by John M. Lundquist and Stephen D. Ricks, 2:406-37. Salt Lake City: Deseret Book and FARMS, 1990. Repentance involves a new way of thinking, a change of perspective to the way the Lord thinks. This change of perspective comes by way of the Holy Ghost, and with it comes a boost of self-confidence. The Book of Mormon emphasizes three concepts: all people must repent, there must be enough time for all to repent, and faith must be present. Repentance brings about a change of heart. [J.W.M.]

G.065 Gillum, Gary P. "Romans 11:17-24: A Bibliography of Commentaries." In *The Allegory of the Olive Tree: The Olive, The Bible, and Jacob 5,* edited by Stephen D. Ricks and John W. Welch, 367-72. Salt Lake City: Deseret Book and FARMS, 1994. An alphabetical list of biblical scholars and articles or books that have been written about the passage in Romans 11 that deals with the olive tree. [J.W.M.]

G.066 Gillum, Gary P. *Scripture Index to Hugh Nibley's Works: Book of Mormon: Preliminary Report.* Provo, UT: FARMS, 1984. Gives a list of Book of Mormon scriptures and their location as quoted and used in the writings of Hugh Nibley. [J.W.M.]

G.067 Goates, Claudia T. "Converted After Years of Membership." *Ensign* 7 (September 1977): 49-51. After reading Mosiah 3:19 in the Book of Mormon and attending the temple, the author's prayers were answered and she felt truly converted to the gospel. [B.D.]

G.068 Godfrey, Dale. "Can Forgiven Sins Be Returned?" *The Witness* 77 (Summer 1992): 11-12. Scriptural passages in the Book of Mormon, Bible, and Doctrine and Covenants suggest that forgiven sins may not always remain so. In order to bring safety to the soul one must forgive others and "endure to the end" (1 Nephi 7:69). [J.W.M.]

G.069 Godfrey, Kenneth W. "By the Gift and Power of God: The Remarkable Story of the Coming Forth of the Book of Mormon." In *A Symposium on the Book of Mormon*, 57-65. Salt Lake City: Church of Jesus Christ of Latter-day Saints, CES, August 1986. A history of the coming forth of the Book of Mormon beginning with Moroni's visit to Joseph Smith followed by four years of preparation, the acquisition of the gold plates, the divine protection of Joseph and the plates, the translation, and finally the publication of the Book of Mormon by E. B. Grandin. [B.D.]

G.070 Godfrey, Kenneth W. "A New Prophet and a New Scripture: The Coming Forth of the Book of Mormon." *Ensign* 18 (January 1988): 6-13. Retells the coming forth of the Book of Mormon from its inception (on September 21, 1823) to its first printing (advertised for sale on March 26, 1830). [D.L.L.]

G.071 Godfrey, Kenneth W. "Using the Book of Mormon to Better Prepare Missionaries." In *A Symposium on the Book of Mormon*, 55-57. Salt Lake City: Church of Jesus Christ of Latter-day Saints, 1979. The great missionary sections in the Book of Mormon detail how missionaries can be better prepared. Detailed study of the Book of Mormon and application to one's own condition can improve attitudes and knowledge and help make effective missionaries. [N.K.Y.]

G.072 Godfrey, Kenneth W. "The Zelph Story." *BYU Studies* 29 (Spring 1989): 31-56. This article presents all written accounts relating to the Zelph story. A detailed cross comparison of all features of the accounts are presented in tabular form. While Joseph Smith kept no record of the march of Zion's Camp, Willard Richards wrote an account in the first person, as though written by the prophet himself. Some facts are certain but "those who try to support a particular historical or geographical point of view about the Book of Mormon by citing the Zelph story are on inconclusive grounds." [R.H.B.] [B.D.]

G.073 Goff, Alan. "Boats, Beginnings, and Repetitions." *Journal of Book of Mormon Studies* 1 (Fall 1992): 67-84. Ancient writers relished repetition over originality. They cherished stories that were repeated in succeeding generations. The Bible is full of repeated or allusive stories, and the Book of Mormon often reinscribes this biblical emphasis on repetition. One such biblical reverberation in the Book of Mormon is Nephi's ocean voyage, which evokes biblical stories of origination: creation, deluge, and exodus. These three stories of beginnings are carefully alluded to in Nephi's own foundational story, exactly as would be expected in an ancient Hebraic text. [R.H.B.]

G.074 Goff, Alan. "Book of Mormon." In *Encyclopedia of Mormonism*, edited by Daniel H. Ludlow, 1:149-50. 5 vols. New York: Macmillan, 1992. This article is a overview of the Book of Mormon. The author identifies the theme of deliverance, the main groups that figure prominently in the text, and underlying textual sources. The book is divided into four sections: Benjamin's speech, Zeniff's record, Alma's record, and the annals of Mosiah. [A.T.]

G.075 Goff, Alan. "Book of Mosiah." In *Encyclopedia of Mormonism*, edited by Daniel H. Ludlow, 1:149. 5 vols. New York: Macmillan, 1992. The Book of Mosiah records events from 200 B.C. to 91 B.C. and is chronologically complex. It is filled with rich religious symbolism and significant political events. The text includes King Benjamin's address, the records of Zeniff, Alma the Elder, and Mosiah, and the first reference to the Jaredites. Its underlying theme emphasizes deliverance from physical and/or spiritual bondage. [J.W.M.]

G.076 Goff, Alan. "A Hermeneutic of Sacred Texts: Historicism, Revisionism, Positivism, and the Bible and Book of Mormon." M.A. thesis,

Brigham Young University, 1989. Biblical studies take two approaches—historical and literary. The latter focuses on the narrative. This study focuses on the narrative of the Book of Mormon, which is a collection of complex, interwoven texts, a canonical work and an ancient document. The author looks at the methods of those who want to see the Book of Mormon as a nineteenth-century document [J.W.M.]

G.077 Goff, Alan. "Mourning, Consolation, And Repentance At Nahom." In *Rediscovering The Book of Mormon*, edited by John L. Sorenson and Melvin J. Thorne, 92-99. Salt Lake City: Deseret Book and FARMS, 1991. The account of the death and burial of Ishmael contains suggestions of much deeper meaning than is apparent on the surface. The word *Nahom* carries the ideas of mourning, consolation, and repentance that link it with earlier biblical traditions. [J.W.M.]

G.078 Goff, Alan. "The Stealing of the Daughters of the Lamanites." In *Rediscovering The Book of Mormon*, edited by John L. Sorenson and Melvin J. Thorne, 67-74. Salt Lake City: Deseret Book and FARMS, 1991. Explores the connections between the Old World, Old Testament, and the Book of Mormon by means of the story found in Mosiah 20:1-5, the story of the wicked priests who kidnapped young Lamanite women for their wives. Finds a parallel in the book of Judges concerning the tribe of Benjamin. [J.W.M.]

G.079 Goff, Alan, and John W. Welch. "Nephi's Bows and Arrows." In *Reexploring the Book of Mormon*, edited by John W. Welch, 41-43. Salt Lake City: Deseret Book and FARMS, 1992. The bow is symbolic of political power. When Nephi fashioned a new one, his brothers accused him of having political ambition. [J.W.M.]

G.080 *Gold Plates Used Anciently.* Salt Lake City: Deseret News Press, 1963. Citing instances when gold plates were used anciently to record sacred and historical writings, this pamphlet includes photographs and lists findings of such plates. [J.W.M.]

G.081 Gonzales, Franklin S. "Teaching Helps and Insights for Alma 43-62." In *A Symposium on the Book of Mormon*, 58-60. Salt Lake City: Church of Jesus Christ of Latter-day Saints, 1979. Individuals can benefit from the Book of Mormon war chapters (Alma 43-62) by making an outline similar to the one Gonzales creates for the article. One can learn about heroes, results of internal dissension, the number killed in battle, the value of liberty, how drinking wine lost wars, religion and revelation helpful while going to war, and other topics of interest. [N.K.Y.]

G.082 Goodson, J. "Letter." *M&A* 3 (October 1836): 397-99. Answers objections to the Book of Mormon concerning writing styles, quotations from the Bible contained in the Book of Mormon, non-Egyptian words such as "Jesus" and "Christ," Ezra's overlooking of Lehi's writings, and Jesus not acknowledging the fulfillment of Lehi's prophecies in his own life. [D.M.]

G.083 Gordon, Cyrus H. "A Hebrew Inscription Authenticated." In *By Study and Also by Faith: Essays in Honor of Hugh Nibley*, edited by John M. Lundquist and Stephen D. Ricks, 1:67-80. 2 vols. Salt Lake City: Deseret Book and FARMS, 1990. Discusses the pre-Columbian Old World contacts with the New World. Finds that the Bat Creek Inscription is early Hebrew dating back to before 686 B.C. Cites evidence of transatlantic ocean crossing by Phoenicians and others. Notes that seafaring peoples have had great skill in the ancient world. [J.W.M.]

G.084 Gordon, Cyrus H. "Pre-Columbian Discoveries Link Old and New Worlds." *Ensign* 1 (October 1971): 56-63. Adaptation of *SEHA* 125 (July 1971): 1-10. The greatest growth of civilization in the New World after its discovery took place in Central America because the New World civilization there is an extension of the civilization of the Near East. Religiously and linguistically the two civilizations are closely connected. An examination of Genesis 10 discloses world-wide settlement. Ancient historians as well as archaeological evidences bear record of transoceanic crossings. [J.W.M.]

G.085 Gordon, Steven H., and Thomas H. Patterson. *Study Maps of the Book of Mormon.* Provo, UT: FARMS, 1985. A collection of maps of proposed Book of Mormon geographical sites in Mesoamerica and archaeological sites in relation to contemporary locations. [J.W.M.]

G.086 Gorton, H. Clay. "If There Be Faults." *Latter-day Digest* 2 (March 1993): 30-38. Moroni's concern over scriptural faults or errors was due to the fact that the Book of Mormon plates were written in reformed Egyptian rather than modified Hebrew. Mistakes in the Book of Mormon were corrected using the corrective form of the appositive *or* followed by the corrective phrase. This appears 69 times in the Book of Mormon but only once in the Doctrine and Covenants and only once in the Bible. [J.W.M.]

G.087 Graham, Pat. "Follow Righteous Leaders." *Friend* 18 (July 1988): 36-37. Children's story of Captain Moroni and Amalickiah, based on Alma 46. [A.C.W.]

G.088 Graham, Pat. "Fun With Favorites." *Friend* 18 (October 1988): 46-47. Children's game based upon the Book of Mormon Liahona. [A.C.W.]

G.089 Graham, Pat. "Helaman and the Two Thousand Young Men of Faith." *Friend* 16 (May 1986): 37. A brief summary for children of the story of Helaman and the two thousand stripling warriors. [M.D.P.]

G.090 Graham, Pat. "Search the Scriptures." *Friend* 18 (March 1988): 42-43. Children's activity to enhance knowledge of Book of Mormon by arranging the books in the correct order. [A.C.W.]

G.091 Graham, Pat, and Elise Niven Black. "Study the Book of Mormon." *Friend* 18 (September 1988): 40-41. Children's pictures of noted Book of Mormon figures that may be cut out and placed in chronological order. [A.C.W.]

G.092 Graham, Pat, and Laurie K. Hutchinson. "Hold to the Rod." *Friend* 18 (June 1988): 24-25. Children's game based on Lehi's vision (1 Nephi 8). [A.C.W.]

G.093 Grant, Carter E. "An Angel Visited This Home." *IE* 66 (March 1963): 168-72, 190-91. A photographic essay regarding the Joseph Smith Jr. home, where the angel Moroni visited. Includes details of activities outside the home as well as a discussion of the translation of the gold plates. [B.W.J.]

G.094 Grant, Carter E. *The Kingdom of God Restored.* Salt Lake City: Deseret Book, 1955. Presents a history of the events that led to the coming forth of the Book of Mormon using Joseph Smith's own words and historical accounts of Oliver Cowdery, Lucy Mack Smith, and others. There are facts about the Hill Cumorah and the monument placed there in honor of Moroni, and the translation of the Book of Mormon. [J.W.M.]

G.095 Grant, Heber J. "Nephi: Exemplar of Faith." *Liahona* 14 (15 August 1916): 112. Nephi's life and character was a guiding star in Grant's personal life. Nephi's example demonstrates the Lord's power and his fulfillment of promises. [A.C.W.]

G.096 Grant, Heber J. "The Treaty of Peace—Restoration of the Gospel." *IE* 23 (December 1919): 107-24. Relates Joseph Smith's vision of the angel Moroni, his revelation of where the golden plates were hidden and Joseph's yearly visits to the Hill Cumorah for instruction. [B.D.]

G.097 Grant, Heber J. Untitled talk. *CR* (April 1924): 152-60. Grant's recent reading of the Book of Mormon as an adult had a great impact upon his understanding of the Savior and his divine mission, and has increased his testimony of the book. He expressed gratitude for his boyhood readings and his assurance of its truthfulness. Nephi's obedience to the Lord, his confidence in the Lord, and his uncomplaining nature has been an example to Brother Grant. [J.W.M.]

G.098 Grant, Heber J. Untitled talk. *CR* (April 1929): 128-31. A testimony of the Book of Mormon. In a court of law the testimony of the Three Witnesses and the Eight Witnesses would make the case. A man ridiculed the Book of Mormon because it says the ancients used cement and the voice of the Lord could be heard over the whole land. Archaeologists have dug up cement that the ancients used and if the radio can carry man's voice over the whole land, surely the Lord could do it. [B.D.]

G.099 Grant, Heber J. Untitled talk. *CR* (October 1935): 2-12. As a youth, Heber J. Grant was ridiculed by a man for his belief in the Book of Mormon because the Book of Mormon said that there was cement in ancient Mexico and that the Lord's voice was heard throughout the land. Grant proclaimed his faith in the divinity of the book and said that time would prove its validity. Cement has now been found in Mexico, and through radio and telephones voices have been heard throughout the land. [B.D.]

G.100 Grant, Heber J. Untitled talk. *CR* (October 1937): 97-99. External evidences are being uncovered more and more each year to confirm the divinity of the Book of Mormon. Grant states that this book is the greatest preacher of the gospel of Jesus Christ that exists and that it brings an everlasting testimony that remains beyond the grave. [J.W.M.]

G.101 Grant, Heber J., and Melvin J. Ballard. "The Mission of the Book of Mormon." *IE* 37 (March 1934): 160-61. Includes testimonies of Melvin J. Ballard and Heber J. Grant and features photographs of the building in which the Book of Mormon was published, the first edition of the book, the home of Isaac Hale where the translation began, and the Hill Cumorah where the plates were deposited. [J.W.M.]

G.102 "The Greatest of All American Books." *Relief Society Magazine* 14 (September 1927): 437. This article claims that the Book of Mormon is the most important of all American books. [J.W.M.]

G.103 Green, Dee F. "Ancient Trans-Pacific Migration." *UASN* 70 (25 November 1960): 1-6. Also in Christensen, Ross T. *Progress in Archaeology: An Anthology,* 71-80. Recent finds have renewed consideration of the possibility of transoceanic crossings and Old World influence in the New World in pre-Columbian times. A new theory is emerging that looks at three possibilities: the influence of the Old World via the Bering Strait, independent origins, and transoceanic crossings. [J.W.M.]

G.104 Green, Dee F. "Book of Mormon Archaeology: The Myths and the Alternatives." *Dialogue* 4 (Summer 1969): 71-80. Explores archaeological trends in Book of Mormon research and finds that past efforts have been naive and have often caused more harm than good. Sets forth a number of myths related to archaeology that need to be dispelled. Holds that the Book of Mormon cannot be proven through scientific means. [J.W.M.]

G.105 Green, Dee F. "Mormonism and Anthropology." *Instructor* 96 (September 1961): 298-99. Discusses the intent of archaeology, anthropology, and biology in providing evidences to the truthfulness of the Book of Mormon. [L.D.]

G.106 Green, Lynn M. "Political and Economic Practices of the Nephites and Lamanites." In *A Symposium on the Book of Mormon,* 61-63. Salt Lake City: Church of Jesus Christ of Latter-day Saints, 1979. Reviews the types of government of both the Jaredites and Nephites, the manner in which anarchy destroyed the Nephite government just before Christ came, and the final annihilation of both civilizations. Also views the united order of the Nephites. [N.K.Y.]

G.107 Green, Lynn M. "Seership in the Book of Mormon." In *The Sixth Annual Church Educational System Religious Educators' Symposium on the Book of Mormon,* 30-32. Salt Lake City: Church of Jesus Christ of Latter-day Saints, 1982. The responsibilities and powers of a seer include calling people to repentance, possessing revelatory powers and the power to translate, preparing a "righteous people to enter into the rest of the Lord," establishing the Church of Christ, and recording the history of people for future generations. [A.T.]

G.108 Greene, John T. "Evidences of the Divinity of the Book of Mormon." *MS* 73 (9-16 February 1911): 85-87, 100-103. The coming forth of the Book of Mormon fulfills a prophecy made by David that the truth would spring forth from the earth. It is the record of the "other sheep" spoken of by the Savior. The book fulfills other scriptural prophecies in Ezekiel, Genesis, and Isaiah. There are eleven witnesses as well as

Joseph Smith and thousands of others bear testimony of its truthfulness. [J.W.M.]

G.109 Greenhalgh, Joseph H. "Book of Mormon Recorders." *DN Church Section* (2 March 1940): 1, 4. Contains details about the 25 writers of the Book of Mormon, including who they were, where and when they lived, what they wrote, and their relationship to each other. Includes photographs of the first edition of the Book of Mormon and an artist's conception of Nephi obtaining the plates from Zoram. [J.W.M.]

G.110 Grey Owl and Little Pigeon. *Cry of the Ancients*. Independence, MO: Herald House, 1974. In this collection of articles Grey Owl, an Indian, tells that he holds sacred the message of hope given in the Book of Mormon to his people. It is their history, it may be read as you would read the wampum or listen to the traditions. [J.W.M.]

G.111 Grey, Robert Avery Jr. "The Daring Book Report." *NE* 19 (September 1989): 12-14. A teenager in Germany discusses the Book of Mormon in his high school class with positive results. [D.M.]

G.112 Griffin, Edith. "The Two Books." *MS* 77 (March 4, 1915): 134-35. Two books of scripture used by members of the Church are the Bible and the Book of Mormon. Both present God's dealings with the human family and both testify of Jesus Christ. [D.W.P.]

G.113 Griffith, Michael T. *The Book of Mormon as Ancient History: A Response to the Tanners, Larry Jonas, and Other Critics*. United States: Vanity, 1981. LDS scholars respond to a number of objections to the Book of Mormon, i.e., Jesus was born "at Jerusalem," Book of Mormon parallels with the work entitled *View of the Hebrews*, the alleged Shakespearean quotation in the Book of Mormon, and the allegation that there are no external evidences in favor of the Book of Mormon. Also compares the Itzas and the Nephites. [D.M.]

G.114 Griffith, Michael T. "The Lehi Tree of Life Story in the Book of Mormon Still Supported by Izapa Stela 5." *SEHA* 151 (December 1982): 1-13. A detailed defense of Wells Jakeman's interpretation of the Stela 5 carving as it relates to Lehi's vision of the tree of life. [D.M.]

G.115 Griggs, C. Wilfred. "The Book of Mormon as an Ancient Book: Gold Plates and the Tree of Life from the Ancient Mediterranean." *BYU Studies* 22 (Summer 1982): 259-78. Also in *Book of Mormon Authorship: New Light on Ancient Origins*, edited by Noel B. Reynolds, 75-102. Provo, UT: Brigham Young University Religious Studies Center, 1982. Challenges the theories of the so-called "environmentalists" who declare that the Book of Mormon was a product of Joseph Smith's nineteenth-century environment. The Book of Mormon cannot accurately be compared to contemporary writings or incidents for it is an ancient text. "The challenge of the Book of Mormon lies elsewhere. It claims to be an ancient book, and it must be examined and criticized in terms of this claim." If the book is indeed an ancient book with Near Eastern origins, it will contain an adequate portrayal of Near Eastern society, law, religion, literary forms, and so on. In light of this Griggs speaks of gold plates and the tree of life. [D.W.P.]

G.116 Griggs, C. Wilfred. "The Tree of Life in Ancient Cultures." *Ensign* 18 (June 1988): 26-31. The tree of life as a religious symbol is found in all ancient Near Eastern societies. Its symbols and religious significance are explained in many of the ancient religious writings of Mesopotamia, Egypt, Greece, and in the writings of the early Christian Fathers. Further, ancient texts and writings from Central America contain pictorial depictions or expositions concerning the tree of life. However, references found in the Bible and the Book of Mormon represent the truest and purest explanations of the sacred tree, with the most complete commentary being found in the Book of Mormon. Griggs's goal of demonstrating that the Book of Mormon tree of life is an ancient work by comparing its symbols with other religious writings of the period is achieved. [D.W.P.]

G.117 Groberg, John H. "The Beauty and Importance of the Sacrament." *Ensign* 19 (May 1989): 38-40; Also in *CR* (1-2 April 1989): 49-52. We can come near to the Lord through the sacrament. 3 Nephi 18 warns against partaking of the emblems unworthily. The Spirit instructs individuals as to their worthiness. [J.W.M.]

G.118 "A Group of Six Prophecies." *Young Woman's Journal* 32 (February 1921): 101-13. Discusses prophecies found in the Book of Mormon including: the Lamanites would be a scourge to the Nephites; the Lamanites would not be utterly destroyed; there would be an apostasy from the truth; the Jaredites would be destroyed; readers of the Book of Mormon will receive a testimony of its truthfulness if they follow the proper steps. The Book of Mormon was preserved for the benefit of those of the latter days. [D.M.]

G.119 Grover, Roscoe A. "Moroni Lives Again." *IE* 38 (September 1935): 542-45. Provides "an account of the dedication of the Angel Moroni Monument at Hill Cumorah, near Palmyra, New York," and discusses the significance of this dedication to the Church. [L.D.]

G.120 "Guide to Applying Book of Mormon Scriptures in Your Life." *NE* 23 (January 1993): 34. A list of scriptures organized by topic to help in applying the Book of Mormon to everyday life. [S.H.]

G.121 Gunn, Stanley R. *Oliver Cowdery, Second Elder and Scribe.* Salt Lake City: Bookcraft, 1962. Provides "an unbiased history of the life and times of Oliver Cowdery." Chapter 3 discusses Cowdery as a scribe during the translation of the Book of Mormon and chapter 5 relates his experience of viewing the gold plates. [A.T.]

G.122 Gunnell, Wayne C. "Martin Harris—Witness and Benefactor to the Book of Mormon." M.A thesis, Brigham Young University, 1955. A biographical treatise on the life of Martin Harris that discusses his personal involvement in the coming forth of the Book of Mormon. [J.T.]

H.

H.001 Haag, Eldon C. "By the Gift and Power of God." *Instructor* 105 (March 1970): 82-83. The Lord did not need an educated man to translate the Nephite records, but one like Joseph Smith who would capture the spirit and message of the original document through divine aid. [A.C.W.]

H.002 Hadley, Thomas M. "A Thousand Copies of the Book." *Ensign* 19 (September 1989): 68-69. Converted through reading the Book of Mormon, Mr. Morgensen of Denmark purchased one thousand copies of the Book of Mormon to share with others, even before he received his baptism. [J.W.M.]

H.003 Haight, David B. "Joseph Smith the Prophet." *Ensign* 9 (November 1979): 22-24. The Prophet Joseph Smith was divinely commissioned to restore the Lord's Church after a profound apostasy left mankind in darkness. He worked to bring forth the Book of Mormon in order to dispel the darkness. [J.W.M.]

H.004 Haight, David B. "Remembering the Savior's Atonement." *Ensign* 18 (April 1988): 6-13. From the Book of Mormon and the New Testament significant truths are learned about the sacrament and the atonement of Jesus—Jesus gave himself for the sins of the world and the sacrament was given to remind individuals of that atonement. [J.W.M.]

H.005 Hainsworth, Jerome Child. "The Book of Mormon as an Instrument in Teaching the Historicity of Old Testament Events and Characters." M.R.E. thesis, Brigham Young University, 1964. Analysis of Book of Mormon passages dealing with Old Testament characters and events is made to establish the historical validity of the Bible. Several historical characters and events are mentioned, such as Adam, Eve, Moses, and the parting of the Red Sea. [J.T.]

H.006 Hale, Lynette Burke. "Real Testimony." *Friend* 23 (August 1993): 43-45. A story for children about gaining a real testimony of the Book of Mormon by reading it. [S.H.]

H.007 Hales, Robert E., and Sandra L. Hales. *A Standard unto My People: How to Hiss Forth with the Book of Mormon.* 2 vols. Orange, CA: Seven Up Publishing, 1990-91. A guide for parents on how to teach their children about the doctrinal concepts in the Book of Mormon. Book of Mormon concepts are supported with scriptural references from the standard works of the LDS Church. [J.W.M.]

H.008 Hall, Glade A. "The Book of Mormon As a Second Witness for What Jesus Christ Taught in the New Testament." In *A Symposium on the Book of Mormon*, 66-71. Salt Lake City: Church of Jesus Christ of Latter-day Saints, CES, August 1986. In an era that lacks faith in the divinity of Christ, the witness of the Book of Mormon is especially needed. The Book of Mormon confirms the teachings of the New Testament and sheds additional light on the first principles of the gospel and the nature of Christ. [A.L. & P.H.]

H.009 Hall, John Franklin. "The Olive in Greco-Roman Religion." In *The Allegory of the Olive Tree: The Olive, The Bible, and Jacob 5*, edited by Stephen D. Ricks and John W. Welch, 248-61. Salt Lake City: Deseret Book and FARMS, 1994. Explores the use of the olive and olive oil in Greek and Roman religions in comparison with Eastern religions. Athena was first considered as the rocky mound of the Acropolis and later as the olive tree upon the mound. In time the olive was considered only as a tree sacred to her and her gift to the Athenians. [J.W.M.]

H.010 Halverson, Sandy. *Book of Mormon Activity Book.* Bountiful, UT: Horizon, 1982. Book of Mormon oriented exercises designed for children. Includes mazes, scrambled words, and fill in the blanks. [D.M.]

H.011 Ham, Wayne. "A Textual Comparison of the Isaiah Passages in the Book of Mormon with the Same Passages in the St. Mark's Isaiah Scroll of the Dead Sea Community." M.A. thesis, Brigham Young University, 1961. A textual comparison between the Isaiah texts in the Dead Sea Scrolls and the Book of Mormon. [M.R.]

H.012 Hamblin, William J. "Armor in the Book of Mormon." In *Warfare in the Book of Mormon*, edited by Stephen D. Ricks and William J. Hamblin, 400-425. Salt Lake City: Deseret Book and FARMS, 1990. Discussed the history of body armor and its usage in the Book of Mormon. Mesoamerican documents confirm that such armor existed in antiquity and Book of Mormon descriptions are technically correct. [N.K.Y.]

H.013 Hamblin, William J. "Basic Methodological Problems with the Anti-Mormon Approach to the Geography and Archaeology of the Book of Mormon." *Journal of Book of Mormon Studies* 2 (Spring 1993): 161-200. Analyzes issues of the difficulties of reconstructing ancient geographies, problems with the discontinuity of Mesoamerican toponyms, the historical development of the idea of a limited geography model, and difficulties of textual and artifactual interpretation when trying to relate the Book of Mormon to archaeological remains. [A.T.]

H.014 Hamblin, William J. "Book of Mormon, History of Warfare In." In *Encyclopedia of Mormonism*, edited by Daniel H. Ludlow, 1:162-66. 5 vols. New York: Macmillan, 1992. Sacral warfare was extensive among the Nephites who frequently consulted prophets before going into war. At least eighty-five armed conflicts are mentioned in the Book of Mormon. No animals are mentioned in connection with Nephite warfare. The major compiler of the Book of Mormon was a general and included warfare in the record to show how it changed societies and fulfilled prophecies and how important it was to have faith in God in order to win. [N.K.Y.]

H.015 Hamblin, William J. "The Bow and Arrow in the Book of Mormon." In *Warfare in the Book of Mormon*, edited by Stephen D. Ricks and William J. Hamblin, 365-99. Salt Lake City: Deseret Book and FARMS, 1990. Provides a history of the development and use of the bow and arrow in the Book of Mormon. The weapon is depicted in ancient Assyrian documents, and the atlatls, much used in Mesoamerica, is another form of the bow and arrow. Hamblin also provides reasons why Nephi needed a new arrow for his wood bow. [N.K.Y.]

H.016 Hamblin, William J. "Directions in Hebrew, Egyptian, and Nephite Language." In *Reexploring the Book of Mormon*, edited by John W. Welch, 183-86. Salt Lake City: Deseret Book and FARMS, 1992. Cardinal directions were not expressed by ancient Egyptian and Israelite peoples as they are today. The

Israelite and Egyptian directional systems differed and it is not clear which system was used by the Nephites since they were familiar with both. Hence caution is needed when one makes directional assumptions. [N.K.Y.]

H.017 Hamblin, William J. "The Importance of Warfare in Book of Mormon Studies." In *Warfare in the Book of Mormon*, edited by Stephen D. Ricks and William J. Hamblin, 481-500. Salt Lake City: Deseret Book and FARMS, 1990. Looks at Book of Mormon warfare and such topics as the influence of ecology; military technology; the social and economic foundations of ancient warfare; military operations; the political, cultural, and legal norms of warfare; the influence of religion; and Book of Mormon parallels to ancient warfare patterns. [N.K.Y.]

H.018 Hamblin, William J. "Warfare in the Book of Mormon." In *Rediscovering the Book of Mormon*, edited by John L. Sorenson and Melvin J. Thorne, 241-48. Salt Lake City: Deseret Book and FARMS, 1991. The features of warfare in Joseph Smith's day differed from ancient warfare due to the development of gunpowder. Book of Mormon warfare resembles that of the ancient Near East and Mesoamerica. [J.W.M.]

H.019 Hamblin, William J., and A. Brent Merrill. "Notes on the Cimeter (Scimitar) in the Book of Mormon." In *Warfare in the Book of Mormon*, edited by Stephen D. Ricks and William J. Hamblin, 360-64. Salt Lake City: Deseret Book and FARMS, 1990. Cimeters described in the Book of Mormon could have been similar to those depicted in Mayan pictures with flint blades. They may also have reference to the jaguar claws mounted on a club thought to be used in ceremonies. [N.K.Y.]

H.020 Hamblin, William J., and A. Brent Merrill. "Swords in the Book of Mormon." In *Warfare in the Book of Mormon*, edited by Stephen D. Ricks and William J. Hamblin, 329-51. Salt Lake City: Deseret Book and FARMS, 1990. Examines swords in the Book of Mormon and reviews ancient Near East pictures and descriptions of swords. Jaredite references to swords and the making of copies of Laban's sword by Nephi add to our knowledge of Book of Mormon swords. [N.K.Y.]

H.021 Hammond, Fletcher B. *Geography of the Book of Mormon*. Salt Lake City: Utah Printing Company, 1959, [R]1964. Presents information to support the idea that the Book of Mormon lands are located in Central America or Mexico. Suggests that a Hill Cumorah was located both in Palmyra New York and in Central America. A number of maps and diagrams are presented. [L.D.]

H.022 Hamson, Robert L. *The Signature of God: A Positive Identification of Christ and His Prophets by Computer Wordprints*. Solana Beach, CA: Sandpiper Press, 1982. Computer analysis of the personal words of Jesus Christ as found in the New Testament and in the revelations of Joseph Smith shows them to be similar, suggesting that Jesus Christ is the author of both of the works mentioned. Hamson also points out that the wordstyles of Christ are different than the writings of Matthew, Mark, Luke, John, and Joseph Smith (who have their own unique writing styles), allowing a positive identification of authorship in a given text. The Book of Mormon is examined and the results showed multiple authorship and that the Book of Mormon wordprints were nowhere near that of Joseph Smith or his contemporaries. [J.T.]

H.023 Hand, Wayland Debs. "The Three Nephites in Popular Tradition." *Southern Folklore Quarterly* 2 (September 1938): 123-29. Recounts legendary stories concerning the three Book of Mormon Nephite apostles who were given power over death until the return of Jesus Christ in the last days. [J.T.]

H.024 Hanks, Marion D. "Alone in the Moonlight." *IE* 64 (April 1961): 238-39, 262. Experiencing soul satisfying circumstances is better when one is not alone. Sharing such experiences with loved ones increases the satisfaction, as is exemplified in the Book of Mormon. Examples of such phenomena include Lehi, who tastes of the fruit of the tree of life and desires to share; Enos, who prays for his brethren; and the sons of Mosiah and Alma, who shared their experiences as missionaries following their conversion. [J.W.M.]

H.025 Hanks, Marion D. "Fathers to Teach Sons." *CR* (October 1975): 35-38. The Book of Mormon teaches that fathers have the sacred responsibility to teach their children. For instance, Alma taught, counseled, reprimanded, and bore testimony to his sons. [R.C.D.]

H.026 Hanks, Marion D. "Hard to Be Understood." *IE* 64 (August 1961): 586-87. The only way to clearly understand the great teachings and doctrines of the Book of Mormon is through the Holy Spirit. Science, study, and pure human intellectual pursuits, without God's spirit, will not adequately relay the full message of the Book of Mormon. [R.C.D.]

H.027 Hanks, Marion D. "'I, Johnny, Parent-to-be.'" *IE* 64 (February 1961): 97, 113. Although being born of "goodly parents" (1 Nephi 1:1) is an ideal situation, not all children have this opportunity and privilege. However, everyone may become "goodly parents" to their own children in ways that the Book of Mormon teaches. [J.W.M.]

H.028 Hanks, Marion D. "Lessons for Living." *IE* 64 (January 1961): 26-27. There are many rewarding approaches to the Book of Mormon. One can approach the Book of Mormon historically, through the external evidence, through its marvelous theological teachings, and through its application to life. [J.W.M.]

H.029 Hanks, Marion D. "Mormon, Compiler of the Book of Mormon, Author, Soldier, Man of God." *IE* 71 (April 1968): 13-14. A biographical sketch of Mormon, who served as prophet, editor, soldier, and author. [B.W.J.]

H.030 Hanks, Marion D. "Steps to Learning." In *BYUSY* (4 May 1960). Provo, UT: BYU Press. Quoting an Episcopalian prayer book, the author gives "five steps to wisdom"—read, hear, mark, learn, and digest. Application of the five steps should be made to the Book of Mormon, so that one's love of the book will grow. [J.W.M.]

H.031 Hanks, Marion D. "Travels between Nephi and Zarahemla." *Instructor* 102 (September 1967): 372-73, 376. In this response to the criticism that Joseph Smith authored the Book of Mormon, Hanks claims that the Book is so intricate, with numerous migrations, expeditions, flashbacks, interpolations, and other plot complexities, that it would have been amazing for an untutored boy to have written it. He includes a chart of travels between Zarahemla and the land of Nephi. [C.C.]

H.032 Hanks, Marion D. "Why Are They Not Chosen?" *IE* 65 (April 1962): 260-61. Alma 31:16-18 contains the prayer offered by the apostate Zoramites. They declare themselves the chosen and elect of God. 1 Nephi 1:20 tells us that the chosen are such because of their faith. Alma adds repentance and good works to faith (Alma 13:1, 3-4, 10). "The Lord chooses those who in faith choose him!" [J.W.M.]

H.033 Hanks, Marion D., and Elaine Cannon. "Era of Youth." *IE* 68 (November 1965): 1041-52. This article tells youth that they can find answers in the scriptures and uses stories and quotes from the Book of Mormon and the Bible to show this. [M.D.P.]

H.034 Hansen, Eric. "I Asked, He Answered." *NE* 22 (September 1992): 23. A story of a young man who took Moroni's challenge (Moroni 10:3-5). After he prayed, the Spirit manifested the truth of the Book of Mormon to him. [M.D.P.]

H.035 Hansen, Gerald, Jr. "The Book of Alma as a Prototype for Teaching the Word of God." In *The Book of Mormon: Alma, The Testimony of the Word*, edited by Monte S. Nyman and Charles D. Tate Jr., 263-80. Provo, UT: Brigham Young University Religious Studies Center, 1992. The Book of Alma emphasizes the power of preaching the word of God to accomplish much good. In Alma, the word of God is used for church reformation, conversion of people by missionary work, dealing with anti-Christs, teaching members of Alma's family, and bringing peace to a war-torn nation. [N.K.Y.]

H.036 Hansen, Gerald, Jr. "The Terrifying Book of Helaman." In *The Book of Mormon: Helaman through 3 Nephi 8, According to Thy Word*, edited by Monte S. Nyman and Charles D. Tate Jr., 163-76. Provo, UT: Brigham Young University Religious Studies Center, 1992. An exposition on the grim message in the Book of Helaman, wherein the prophets warn against the sins of pride, aspirations for riches, crime, pseudopatrotism, and injustice. [D.M.]

H.037 Hansen, L. Taylor. *He Walked the Americas*. Amherst: Amherst Press, 1963. This is a collection of more than fifty Indian legends concerning the Healer, the Mighty, and the Prophet. The sequence of these legends, particularly vivid among the wild tribes, form a curious pattern matching the stories told in the Book of Mormon. They tell of a saintly white teacher who performed miracles of healing. His symbols are woven into blankets, carved on canyon walls, and burned in pottery. [R.H.B.]

H.038 Hanson, Paul M. "Book of Mormon Geography." In *Recent Book of Mormon Developments*, 77-80. Independence, MO: Zarahemla Research Foundation, 1984. Also in *ZR* 10 (Fall 1980): 4-8. Reports a shift in RLDS Church attitudes toward Book of Mormon geography, comparing an 1894 map to a 1980 map of proposed Book of Mormon lands. Argues for the Isthmus of Tehuantepec as the "narrow neck" of land. Also addresses Book of Mormon population shifts and believes that that placing Book of Mormon events in Central America makes things too crowded. [A.T.]

H.039 Hanson, Paul M. *In the Land of the Feathered Serpent*. Independence, MO: Herald House, 1949. Argues that Quetzalcoatl, a major deity of pre-Columbian Mexico and Central America, may have been Christ. Presents a pictorial tour of archaeological sites—including the Toltec ruins at Tlaxcala, the ruins at Mitla, and the Temple of Quetzalcoatl at Tula, in which this deity, also known as the Feathered Serpent, is represented. [C.C.]

H.040 Hanson, Paul M. *Jesus Christ among the Ancient Americans*. Independence, MO: Herald House, 1945, [R]1947 & 1959. Submits archaeological, anthropological, and historical evidence to validate the Book of Mormon. Topics include Israelite origin of Native Americans, native American myths, Quetzalcoatl—the tall white god who may have been Jesus Christ—and linguistic similarities between Hebrew words and words from Mayan, Incan, and Mexican languages. [C.C.]

H.041 Hanson, R.A. "The Rod of Iron." *MS* 77 (8 April 1915): 223-24. Recalls Lehi's dream of the rod of iron that leads to the tree of life. Likens those who occupied the great and spacious building and mocked those who partook of the tree of life to people of the present age who scoff at the existence of the Book of Mormon. [D.W.P.]

H.042 Harder, Erika. "An Answer Like a Splash of Fire." *Ensign* 13 (December 1983): 22-23. The author's conversion to the restored gospel through the Book of Mormon is told. Recounts specifically how she wanted to receive a sign but learned through a passage in Alma 32 regarding the importance of faith. [S.P.S.]

H.043 Harding, Robert George. *The Gadianton Robbers*. Salt Lake City: Promised Land Publications, 1969. Traces the rise and growth of organized crime in Nephite-Lamanite culture. The author discusses how, through conspiracy and murder, the Gadianton Robbers gained seats in the government and became the ruling force. Claims they originated with Cain. Shows how the Jaredites, 2300 B.C.–A.D. 200, were destroyed by a similar group. Draws parallels with present-day society and warns that history repeats itself and that liberty requires vigilance. [C.C.]

H.044 Hardy, Bud G. "A Study to Identify and Isolate the Principles and Lessons of the Book of Mormon Record as Inserted by the Writers and Abridgers." M.A. thesis, Brigham Young University, 1975. Maintains that the Book of Mormon contains key phrases, like "it came to pass" and "thus we see," that point out the messages of the various Book of Mormon authors and abridgers. These phrases can be historical in nature, explaining events, or polemic, explaining teachings, or they can be direct statements to the reader. The author includes tables and summaries that list the phrases. [C.C.]

H.045 Hardy, Grant. "Columbus: By Faith or Reason." In *Reexploring the Book of Mormon*, edited by John W. Welch, 32-36. Salt Lake City: Deseret Book and FARMS, 1992. Recent research has overturned the idea that Columbus was led by science, reason, restlessness, and conquest to discover America. Columbus was "deeply influenced by prophecy and revelation." The Book of Mormon's claim that Columbus was inspired by the Spirit of God was in opposition to the intellectual trend of 1830. Columbus wrote, but never completed, a book that set forth his views of himself as a "fulfiller of biblical prophecies" recorded in Isaiah. [J.W.M]

H.046 Hardy, Grant. "Gold Plates." In *Encyclopedia of Mormonism*, edited by Daniel H. Ludlow, 2:555. 5 vols. New York: Macmillan, 1992. Presents a description of the gold plates on which the Book of Mormon was written. It includes an estimate of the size of the plates. [A.T.]

H.047 Hardy, Grant. "Mormon's Agenda." In *Reexploring the Book of Mormon*, edited by John W. Welch, 245-47. Salt Lake City: Deseret Book and FARMS, 1992. As an editor of the Book of Mormon, Mormon devoted much of the record to warfare and to the spiritual interpretation of political events. His work shows an effort to draw uplifting lessons from mean and ugly events. His effort at simplification of complex events is remarkable where sizable groups of people are involved. [N.K.Y.]

H.048 Hardy, Grant R. "Mormon As Editor." In *Rediscovering The Book of Mormon*, edited by John L. Sorenson and Melvin J. Thorne, 15-28 Salt Lake City: Deseret Book and FARMS, 1991. Compares editing that was done by Mormon in the Book of Mormon with that done by biblical editors. Tries to determine Mormon's biases and purposes as he made selections from massive amounts of material. Mormon makes spiritual meanings out of historical events by the use of flashbacks, simplification, narrative, deletions, and commentary to make his messages clear. [J.W.M.]

H.049 Hardy, Grant R., and Robert E. Parsons. "Book of Mormon Plates and Records." In *Encyclopedia of Mormonism*, edited by Daniel H. Ludlow, 1:195-201. 5 vols. New York: Macmillan, 1992. The complicated history of the Book of Mormon is taken from many records: the twenty-four Jaredite plates, Nephi's small and large plates, and the brass plates of Laban. A description of the contents of each is given. Quotations from the brass plates are almost the same as quotes from biblical records but have significant textual differences and mention many prophets not found in the Bible. [N.K.Y.]

H.050 Hardy, Rufus K. Untitled talk. *CR* (9 April 1939): 131-32. A testimony that fifteen hundred years ago the Book of Mormon was penned by the hand of a prophet and contains the words of the Lord and Savior Jesus Christ. Joseph Smith translated it correctly, according to the will of God. Quoting Moroni's discourse on faith, hope, and charity, the author calls to the meek and lowly in heart to read the Book of Mormon. [J.W.M.]

H.051 Harper, Bruce T. "The Church Publishes a New Triple Combination." *Ensign* 11 (October 1981): 8-19. An announcement and discussion concerning the publication of the new Triple Combination (Book of Mormon, Doctrine and Covenants, and Pearl of Great Price) in 1981. Various new features in the Triple Combination are designed to assist the student in understanding the scriptures. [D.M.]

H.052 Harris, Franklin S. "Agricultural Conditions in Book of Mormon Times." *IE* 17 (December 1913): 97-100. Book of Mormon references and archaeological evidences (i.e. complex irrigation systems and terraces) from early agricultural sites demonstrate advanced knowledge and practice in tilling the land among the Nephite peoples. [D.M.]

H.053 Harris, Franklin S. "Ancient Records on Metal Plates." In *13th Annual Symposium on Archaeology of the Scriptures*, edited by Dee F. Green, 41-51. Provo, UT: Brigham Young University, Department of Extention Publications, 1962. Joseph Smith described the metal plates from which came the Book of Mormon as having the appearance of gold. The use of metals appeared early in world history. A recent excavation at a cemetery in Ur (approx. 2500 B.C. or earlier) uncovered sheets made of gold that could be bent and folded like paper. Similar finds are also reported in various parts of the world, including ancient America, where metallurgy was highly sophisticated. [J.W.M.]

H.054 Harris, Franklin S. "Biological Conditions in Book of Mormon Lands." *IE* 13 (March 1910): 385-90. Harris claims that the references in the Book of Mormon, with regard to both the Jaredite and Lehite peoples, concerning the use of timber and cement are corroborated by studies published in a bulletin from the U.S.D.A. Similar claims are made of the fauna and flora in America. [D.M.]

H.055 Harris, Franklin S. "More Book of Mormon Evidence." *Young Woman's Journal* 36 (January 1925): 16-17. The inhabitants of ancient America had Christian traditions in pre-Columbian times and their ancestors crossed the Pacific Ocean in boats, landing somewhere on the coast of present day Mexico. [J.W.M.]

H.056 Harris, Franklin S. "They Collected Legends." *Ensign* 7 (February 1977): 80-82. Legends and stories were gathered by early Spanish settlers several centuries ago, many of which correspond to Book of Mormon history. [D.M.]

H.057 Harris, Franklin S., Jr. *The Book of Mormon Messages and Evidences.* Salt Lake City: Deseret News Press, 1953, [R]1961. An argument for the authenticity of the Book of Mormon. The author asserts that the biblical passages of the Book of Mormon represent a translation of an ancient text and that the language of the Book of Mormon indicates multiple authorship. Also discusses discoveries of metal records, the origin of the Native Americans and Christ's visit to America. [C.C.]

H.058 Harris, Franklin S., Jr. "Confirmatory Evidences of 'Mormonism': Baptism Early in America." *MS* 96 (4 January 1934): 9-11. Catholic missionaries who arrived in America found the natives practicing baptism and were horrified. Some cultures sprinkled while others immersed the infant, but always it was meant to lead the individual toward a better life and salvation in the kingdom of God. These practices are explain by the Book of Mormon text that informs the reader that baptism was introduced early in America's history. [J.W. M.]

H.059 Harris, Fanklin S., Jr. "Confirmatory Evidences of 'Mormonism': The Book of Mormon." *MS* 96 (8 February 1934): 91-93. Joseph Smith described the gold plates as having "the appearance of gold." The word "appearance" is significant as plates of pure gold would have been in danger of easy destruction. Most likely it was a gold and copper alloy. The Book of Mormon could have been written in Hebrew on just 21 pages or plates; in Phoenician characters about 45 plates would have been necessary, even taking into account the loss of the 116 pages. [J.W.M.]

H.060 Harris, Franklin S., Jr. "Confirmatory Evidences of 'Mormonism': The Calendar in America." *MS* 96 (11 January 1934): 25-27. The calendar developed by the Maya Indians began somewhere between 613 and 580 B.C., though it dates back to 3373 B.C., and was arranged by the deity Quetzalcoatl. The Book of Mormon people reckoned their time from the Savior's birth. The date when Mayan history began and the correlation with the sign of the birth of deity are evidence of the authenticity of the Book of Mormon. [J.W.M.]

H.061 Harris, Franklin S., Jr. "Confirmatory Evidences of 'Mormonism': Eastern Culture in America." *MS* 95 (7 December 1933): 793-95. Growing amount of evidence shows that Columbus was late in his discovery of America. Ancient manuscripts indicate that the first inhabitants of America came from the East and that they had elephants as reported in the *Sheffield Weekly Telegraph,* November 4. [J.W.M.]

H.062 Harris, Franklin S., Jr. "Confirmatory Evidences of 'Mormonism': Traditions of the Virgin Birth in America." *MS* 95 (December 1933): 826-27. Lord Kingbrough (1830–1848), H. H. Bancroft, D. G. Brinton, Torquemanda, and Angus W. McKay found traditions of the virgin birth in the traditions of Mexico, the Otomies, and Navajo Indians.

Other ancient peoples such as the Aztecs and the Indians of Paraguay believed in the virgin birth of their gods. This same belief was taught to ancient Americans in the Book of Mormon. [J.W.M.]

H.063 Harris, Franklin S., Jr. "Confirmatory Evidences of 'Mormonism': Transliteration—Hebrew in 'Reformed Egyptian.'" *MS* 96 (8 March 1934): 154-56. Harris cites many examples of one language being written with another alphabet—transliteration. This he does to support the claim of the Book of Mormon that Hebrew was written with Reformed Egyptian characters (Mormon 9:32-33; 1 Nephi 1:2). Mentions the discovery by Sir Flinders Petrie of some writings in the Peninsula of Sinai that were in the Hebrew language but written "in Egyptian hieratic characters somewhat changed." [B.D.]

H.064 Harris, Franklin S., Jr. "Confirmatory Evidences of 'Mormonism': Writing on Metal Plates in the Old World." *MS* 96 (25 January 1934): 57-59. The Book of Mormon records that Lehi's colony took brass plates upon which were recorded the record of the Jews and the genealogy of their forefathers. The British Museum has metal plates that are engraved with records of several different cultures. [J.W.M.]

H.065 Harris, Franklin S., Jr. "Confirmatory Evidences of 'Mormonism': Writing on Metal Plates in the New World." *MS* 96 (1 February 1934): 74-76. Metal plates prepared by the ancients have been found in several locations in America. There are many historical accounts of metal plates that no longer exist as they were melted down to be used in other ways. Melvin J. Ballard describes plates seen in a museum in Lima, Peru, that were gold sheets, the size of the Book of Mormon plates (*DN* April 30, 1932). [J.W.M.]

H.066 Harris, Franklin S., Jr. "Confirmatory Evidences of 'Mormonism': The Urim and Thummim." *MS* 96 (1 March 1934): 134-35, 139-41. Harris cites evidence that many ancient American cultures used "seer stones" and breastplates that suggest a corrupt form of the Urim and Thummim used with the breastplate. He shows how many Indians from North America to Peru in South America used clear stones or crystals for divination. [B.D.]

H.067 Harris, Franklin S., Jr. "Others Left Records on Metal Plates, Too." *Instructor* 92 (October 1957): 318-21. Book of Mormon peoples kept records on metal plates. Early critics claimed that this was impossible since ancient metallurgy was not sufficiently advanced, but many other metal records have been discovered since the days of Joseph Smith. Includes a table of plates found and a map of sites. [C.C.]

H.068 Harris, James R. "The 'I Am' Passages in the Gospels and in 3 Nephi." In *The New Testament and the Latter-day Saints, Sperry Symposium, 1987*, edited by H. Dean Garrett, et. al., 89-114. Salt Lake City: Randall, 1987. Lists passages in the Four Gospels and in 3 Nephi where Jesus uses the expression "I am." Such pronouncements of self-identification underscore Jesus' divinity, in contrast to the views of Nicodemus and his modern counterparts, who see Jesus only as a great man. [D.M.]

H.069 Harris, James R. *Patterns of Conversion in the Book of Mormon*. Provo, UT: Brigham Young University, 1968. Conversion is the key to salvation. Conversion can be gained, in part, by reading the Book of Mormon and reliving its many conversion experiences. Harris identifies six patterns in these conversion experiences and suggests ways to implement them in daily life. Includes a chart of typical conversion events and a graph of steps in sanctification. [C.C.]

H.070 Harris, James R. *Southwestern American Indian Rock Art and the Book of Mormon*. Orem, UT: Harris House, 1991. Links inscriptions on rocks in the American Southwest with Book of Mormon themes. [D.M.]

H.071 Harris, Martin. "The Testimony of Martin Harris." *MS* (1 January 1877): 4-5. Two letters of Martin Harris written to a Mr. Emerson, with an editorial introduction. Harris testifies that an angel showed him the plates containing the Book of Mormon and that the translation copied from them was approved by Professor Anthon. Harris states that Joseph Smith could not have translated the plates by himself. He denies that he preached against the Book of Mormon in England. [C.C.]

H.072 Harris, Russell C. "A Converter of Souls." *Instructor* 97 (July 1962): 232-33. On many occasions the Book of Mormon has converted practicing Christians to the LDS faith. Moroni's promise (Moroni 10:3-5) applies to all. [A.C.W.]

H.073 Harrison, Elias L.T. "The 'Spaulding Story' Refuted from Itself." *MS* 19 (24 January 1857): 49-56. Harrison argues that it is impossible that the Book of Mormon be even remotely related to the *Manuscript Found* by Solomon Spaulding. The *Manuscript Found* is a fictitious account of the lost ten tribes and the Book of Mormon is an account of one family of the tribe of Joseph. [B.D.]

H.074 Harrison, Grant Von. *The Conversion Power of the Book of Mormon.* Orem, UT: Accor, 1988. A handbook for missionary-minded people who want to use the Book of Mormon as a tool of conversion. [D.M.]

H.075 Harrison, Grant Von. *Converting with the Book of Mormon: A Guide for Missionaries.* Woods Cross, UT: Publishers Book Sales, 1981. A twenty-one page booklet designed to assist the missionary in becoming skilled in "using the Book of Mormon in every aspect of his proselytizing activities." Missionaries are told of the importance of reading the Book of Mormon with investigators and committing investigators to read the Book of Mormon. [A.T.]

H.076 Hart, Charles H. "Joseph the Prophet." *IE* 23 (April 1920): 491-95. It is more difficult to think Joseph Smith could invent the Book of Mormon, given his youth, limited experience, and opportunities, than to believe he was inspired. Joseph would have needed extensive research to have learned, for example, that Native Americans used stone boxes for the burial of valuables, a fact virtually unknown in his day. Not until 1906 were such boxes discovered in the areas of Toronto, Tennessee, Illinois, and New Mexico. [C.C.]

H.077 Hart, Charles H. "Steadfast Testimony of the Three Witnesses." *MS* 89 (1 September 1927): 545-51. Refutes the claim made in the 1911 edition of the *Catholic Encyclopedia* that the Three Witnesses denied their testimonies of the Book of Mormon plates. As evidence, he cites an 1883 interview of David Whitmer, the dying declaration of Martin Harris, and an affidavit testifying that, in a Michigan murder trial, Oliver Cowdery defended the Book of Mormon. [C.C.]

H.078 Hart, Charles H. Untitled talk. *CR* (April 1907): 96-99. As a guide in the Kirtland temple, Martin Harris bore his testimony of the Book of Mormon. He proclaimed that he had seen the plates, handled them with his hands, seen the angel, and heard his voice. He bore this same testimony at the time of his death. [J.W.M.]

H.079 Hart, Charles H. Untitled talk. *CR* (April 1923): 150-52. The author calls for a reliance on the Book of Mormon and points out its value in understanding the "Hebrew scriptures" (the Bible). [J.W.M.]

H.080 Hart, Charles H. Untitled talk. *CR* (April 1924): 53-57. Two great sources of testimony are "the divine witness" and "human witnesses." The divine witness is the Holy Ghost. The Lord called human witnesses to the Book of Mormon—the Three Witnesses, Joseph Smith, and others. [J.W.M.]

H.081 Hart, Charles H. Untitled talk. *CR* (April 1928): 100-1. The Book of Mormon, which came from the Hill Cumorah, supports the doctrine of life after death especially as it tells of the visit of Christ to the American Continent. [J.W.M.]

H.082 Hartley, William G. "Close Friends as Witnesses: Joseph Smith and the Joseph Knight Families." In *Joseph Smith: The Prophet, the Man*, edited by Susan Easton Black and Charles D. Tate Jr., 271-83. Provo, UT: Brigham Young University Religious Studies Center, 1993. Though the family of Joseph Knight Sr. were never allowed to view the gold plates, they were of great assistance in bringing forth the Book of Mormon. Father Knight gave Joseph provisions to help until the translation was complete and donated paper needed for the translation. It was Father Knight's wagon that was used to retrieve the plates on September 23, 1827. Brother Knight observed that Joseph's excitement over the Urim and Thummim seemed to supersede his excitement over the plates. [J.W.M.]

H.083 Hartley, William G. "Every Member Was a Missionary." *Ensign* 8 (September 1978): 21-24. Early members of the Church were armed with strong testimonies, biblical understanding, firsthand relationships with Joseph Smith, and copies of the Book of Mormon. Before publication of the book, informal missionary work began using hand-copied teachings from the manuscript. Many were converted by its words. [J.W.M.]

H.084 Hartman, Adrienne. "Nephi's Ship." *Friend* 7 (September 1977): 23. A story for children about Nephi building a ship to cross the seas to the promised land. Illustrations included. [M.D.P.]

H.085 Hartshorn, Chris B. *Commentary on the Book of Mormon*. Independence, MO: Herald House, 1966. A verse-by-verse doctrinal commentary on the Book of Mormon. The commentator's sources include histories, archaeological findings, personal religious beliefs, and other sources. [J.T.]

H.086 Hauck, F. Richard. *Deciphering the Geography of the Book of Mormon*. Salt Lake City: Deseret Book, 1988. A geographical and historical approach to the Book of Mormon that attempts to "document the settlement and route networks of the Book of Mormon." The author "examines the interaction and relationships between settlements, transportation routes, and cultural technology and environment for any given people, time, and place" and then creates "an actual, physical correlation of the places in the Book of Mormon. . . . The model fit into the portion of Ancient America that is known as southern Mesoamerica comprising portions of the modern nations of Mexico, Belize, and Guatemala." Presents numerous maps and charts. [A.T.]

H.087 Hauck, Forrest R., ed. *Papers of the Fourteenth Annual Symposium on the Archaeology of the Scriptures*. Provo, UT: Department of Extension Publications, Brigham Young University, 1963. Transcriptions of papers presented at a symposium April 13, 1963. Book of Mormon topics include Egyptian and Mayan calendars, geography, the tree of life symbols, and the Anthon transcript. [J.W.M.]

H.088 Hawes, Allison M. "Performing the Book of Mormon." *Ensign* 23 (September 1993): 78-79. A description of the success of "Stories from the Book of Mormon" as a missionary tool. [S.H.]

H.089 Hawkes, John D. *Book of Mormon Digest and 1700 Questions with Answers*. Salt Lake City: Hawkes, 1968. A new revised edition of the author's *Book of Mormon Digest and 1600 Study Questions with Answers*. An abridgment of the Book of Mormon for quick reading and reference. Reviews the story regarding the coming forth of the Book of Mormon, presents study questions with answers, explanations of Isaiah, and a system for memorizing. [J.T.]

H.090 Hawkes, John D. *Story-Talks for Primary*. Salt Lake City: Hawkes Publishing, 1985. A collection of forty-seven illustrated Book of Mormon stories for Primary children. [R.H.B.]

H.091 Hawkins, Lisa Bolin, and Gordon Thomasson. *I Only Am Escaped Alone to Tell Thee: Survivor Witnesses in the Book of Mormon*. Provo, UT: FARMS, 1984. Compares survivor witnesses in the Book of Mormon with other survivor witnesses that are described in Des Pres, "Survivors and the Will to Bear Witness." *Social Research* 40 (1973): 668-69. [B.D.]

H.092 Haworth, Walter J. *The Book of Mormon on Trial*. Wallsend, Australia: Hutton, 1900. An apologetic work that answers numerous charges against the Book of Mormon. He reviews Emma Smith's testimony that while translating the Book of Mormon, Joseph Smith "had neither manuscript nor book to read from." An attempted refutation of Bay's work, *Doctrines and Dogmas of Mormonism*. [M.R.]

H.093 Hayes, John. "The Spaulding Manuscript and the Book of Mormon." *MS* 50 (27 August 1888): 548-50. Hayes compares the contents of the Spaulding manuscript with the Book of Mormon. The Spaulding manuscript is a story of a Roman named Fabius who was blown off course traveling from Britain to America in the 4th century A.D. Hayes writes that nothing is similar in the Book of Mormon to what is contained in the Spaulding Manuscript. [B.D.]

H.094 Heady, Gordon. "Time and the Calendar in the Book of Mormon." *Witness* 71-72 (Winter, Spring 1990): 9–10, 10-14. Investigates textual clues to determine what type of calendrical system was used by the Nephites and the Jaredites and when these systems commenced and fell into disuse. [A.C.W.]

H.095 Heater, Dennis. "More 'No Erasers' in the Book of Mormon." *ZR* 39-40 (1988): 9-13. Examines Book of Mormon passages wherein the original author or editor added additional words for clarification. Since the custodians of the gold plates did not possess erasers, they used terms or phrases such as "or," "rather," and "or in other words" when adding clarifying remarks to the text. Includes a list of all the verses where this is noted. [A.T.]

H.096 Heater, Shirley R. "The 1830 Edition's History and Manuscript Comparison." In *Recent Book of Mormon Developments; Articles from the Zarahemla Record*, 2:89-98. Independence, MO: Zarahemla Research Foundation, 1992. A comparison of the 1830 edition with the Printer's Manuscript and the Original Manuscript showing editorial changes and variants. Heater explains the history of the 1830 edition up to the donation of the original "form proofs" by the Wilford Wood family to the LDS Church in 1991. [B.D.]

H.097 Heater, Shirley R. "The 1837 Edition Introduced Significant Editorial Changes." In *Recent Book of Mormon Developments; Articles from the Zarahemla Record*, 2:99-105. Independence, MO: Zarahemla Research Foundation, 1992. An analysis of the significant editorial changes introduced in the 1837 edition of the Book of Mormon. Heater explains the history of the publication of the 1837 edition then describes several changes that were introduced. The different changes include "Englishized" grammar, modernization of archaic words and word changes, omissions, and additions. [B.D.]

H.098 Heater, Shirley R. "Beyond the Stone Anchor Mystery." *ZR* 24-26 (Spring, Summer, Fall, 1984): 18-20. A follow-up to "Chinese Stone Anchors in the New World" (*ZR* 15 [Winter 1981-1982]: 1-3) by the same author. Writes concerning the origin of stone anchors discovered off the coast of California. Discusses the implications that this discovery has on the Book of Mormon. [J.T.]

H.099 Heater, Shirley R. "Chiasmus Brings New Understanding of Geography." *ZR* 46 (December 1989): 3. Examines the chiastic structure of Alma 13:68-14:1 (RLDS versification) to better understand the geographical information contained in the passage. [A.T.]

H.100 Heater, Shirley R. *The Chinese Jaredite Connection*. Independence, MO: Foundation for Research on Ancient America, 1984. A pamphlet that points out that pre-Christian Chinese ships recall the form of the Jaredite barges. Also, the recent "discovery of ancient stone anchors from Asia on the shores of the New World" suggests an early contact that may point to Jaredite migration. [D.W.P.]

H.101 Heater, Shirley R. "Chinese Stone Anchors in the New World." *ZR* 15 (Winter 1981-82): 1-3. A report and discussion of ancient stone anchors (approx. 2000-3000 years old) discovered off the California coastline and their possible connection to China. Argues for a Jaredite cultural influence in China and pre-Columbian oceanic crossings. [J.T.]

H.102 Heater, Shirley R. "An Experiment with Desire." In *Recent Book of Mormon Developments; Articles from the Zarahemla Record*, 2:166-67. Independence, MO: Zarahemla Research Foundation, 1992. The author describes how she applied the words of Alma 16 (Alma 32 in LDS versification) to her life and the new spiritual heights she reached. [B.D.]

H.103 Heater, Shirley R. "Gold Plates, Foolscap, and Printer's Ink." *ZR* 35-38 (1987): 3-15. Contains a history and description of the original and printer's manuscripts of the Book of Mormon. The author uses photographs to show the differences between the two manuscripts, including changes, omissions, and punctuation additions. Also presents a "study of five editions of the Book of Mormon—the 1830, 1837 and 1840 edition and the 1874 and 1908 editions, which were published during the reorganization period." Includes a number of charts and tables. [A.T.]

H.104 Heater, Shirley R. "Hebrew Poetry Brings a New Understanding of Joy." *ZR* 34 (1986): 14-15. Poetic analysis of Alma's words in the Book of Mormon provides insight into the meaning of word "joy." [J.T.]

H.105 Heater, Shirley R. "History of the Manuscripts of the Book of Mormon." In *Recent Book of Mormon Developments; Articles from the Zarahemla Record*, 2:66-79. Independence, MO: Zarahemla Research Foundation, 1992. A detailed history of the original manuscript and the printer's manuscript. Sets forth many of their differences. [B.D.]

H.106 Heater, Shirley R. "Lehi's Blessing to His Son Joseph." *ZR* 44 (August 1989): 2-3, 7. Lehi's blessing of Joseph in 2 Nephi follows a chiastic structure that emphasizes the importance of coming to a knowledge of the covenants of the fathers. [A.T.]

H.107 Heater, Shirley R. "Manuscripts and Editions." *ZR* 48 (April 1990): 2-3. Details of the history of Book of Mormon manuscripts and RLDS editions are summarized in a chart. Concludes with the suggestion that a corrected text is needed. [A.C.W.]

H.108 Heater, Shirley R. "Moroni's Title Page." *ZR* 43 (June 1989): 3-4. Moroni wrote the title page of the Book of Mormon. The poetic structure of the title page emphasizes that its purpose is for the Lamanites, Jews, and Gentiles to "know the covenants of the Lord." [A.T.]

H.109 Heater, Shirley R. "The Power of the Word." *ZR* 62 (July/August 1992): 1, 4. Notes that the phrase "state of awful woundedness" (1 Nephi 13:32) in the original and printer's manuscripts was replaced in the 1837 edition of the Book of Mormon with the phrase "state of awful blindness." Then Heater references Alma 32 and writes concerning the power of the word. [D.M.]

H.110 Heater, Shirley R. "A Preview of Textual Corrections in the New Corrected Edition of the Book of Mormon: Variances Between the Printer's Manuscript and the 1830 Edition." *ZR* 51-52 (December, October 1990): 2-4, 2-4. Results of the author's textual comparison research detailing differences between the printer's manuscript and the 1830 edition of the Book of Mormon. [A.C.W.]

H.111 Heater, Shirley R. "Report on Book of Mormon Research." *ZR* 27-28 (Winter-Spring 1985): 5-7, 16. A detailed summary of John L. Sorenson's two-part article "Digging into the Book of Mormon," *Ensign* (September 1984): 26-37 and (October 1984): 12-23. Studies in the areas of geography, archaeology, war, demographics, metallurgy, and writing are discussed. [J.T.]

H.112 Heater, Shirley R. "Rio Azul: Archaeological Research Sheds Light on Book of Mormon Subject." *ZR* 32-33 (1986): 10-13. Discusses excavations at Rio Azul (Mayan city, 250 B.C.–A.D. 400 to 500) and possible Book of Mormon connections. Five archaeological firsts are also reported in detail: (1) locking lid jars, (2) directional hieroglyphs, (3) the hieroglyph of the verb "bury," (4) ancient Maya fabric "1000 years older than any . . . previously found," and (5) carving on the jaw of a wild pig. [J.T.]

H.113 Heater, Shirley R. "Variances between the Original and Printer's Manuscripts." In *Recent Book of Mormon Developments; Articles from the Zarahemla Record*, 2:80-88. Independence, MO: Zarahemla Research Foundation, 1992. Briefly summarizes variants between the original manuscript and the printer's manuscript of the Book of Mormon. Two tables show words on the original manuscript that were omitted from the printer's manuscript and words copied incorrectly on the printer's manuscript. [B.D.]

H.114 Heater, Shirley R., and Mary Lee Treat. "A Literal Manuscript Version of the Book of Mormon." In *Recent Book of Mormon Developments; Articles From the Zarahemla Record*, 2:65. Independence, MO: Zarahemla Research Foundation, 1992. An update of the Zarahemla Research Foundation's work on producing a text of the Book of Mormon that is "restored to read as the manuscripts read" and that is organized in "poetry-like style." [B.D.]

H.115 Hedengren, Paul. "Nephite Coins." In Hedengren, *In Defense of Faith: Assessing*

Arguments against Latter-day Saint Belief, 109-30. Provo, UT: Bradford & Wilson, 1985. An apologetic work dealing with common criticisms of Mormon beliefs. Pages 109-30, for instance, discuss the problem of Nephite weights and measures. [M.R.]

H.116 Heidenreich, John F. "It Taught Me the Bible." *Ensign* 6 (September 1976): 22-23. After reading the Book of Mormon five times in seven months in a comparative study with the Bible, this divinity student of another faith found the Book of Mormon to be a great help in understanding the Bible. The divinity of Jesus Christ became more apparent through the Spirit of the Lord, which permeates the book. [J.W.M.]

H.117 Heinerman, Jacob. *Stories of Conversion through the Reading of the Book of Mormon.* Manti, UT: Mountain Valley, 1974. A collection of journal extracts and writings that report the influence of the Book of Mormon in the lives of various individuals in the nineteenth and twentieth centuries and their conversion to the LDS faith. Includes the conversion stories of Brigham Young and Parley P. Pratt. [J.T.]

H.118 "Helaman and the Two Thousand Young Men of Faith." *Friend* 16 (May 1986): 37. Retelling of the stripling warrior story for children, with pictures and brief commentary. [A.C.W.]

H.119 Hemingway, Donald W. *Christianity in America before Columbus?* Salt Lake City: Hawkes, 1988. Treats the symbols, practices, and beliefs of ancient America that appear to be related to Christianity that were prevalent before Columbus discovered America. Includes the cross; the use of keys, stones, and mountains in their temples; baptism; sacrament; fasting; prayer; life after death; the creation; the flood; the tower of Babel; the ten lost tribes; and many others. [J.W.M.]

H.120 Hemingway, Donald W. *An Introduction to Mormon: A Native American Prophet.* Salt Lake City: Publishers Press, 1978. A biographical treatise on the prophet Mormon (b. approx. 311 A.D.). Includes details surrounding his compilation of the gold plates from which the Book of Mormon was translated, his personal teachings and sermons, and other historical events surrounding his life. [J.T.]

H.121 Hepworth, Joseph Thomas. "Watermelons, Alma 32, and the Experimental Method." *BYU Studies* 23 (Fall 1983): 497-511. Likening the planting of watermelon seeds in his garden to Alma's analogy of planting a seed of the word of God in one's heart (Alma 32), the author finds that some spiritual seeds fail to grow while others are successful. The procedures for experimentation are contained within the scriptures and the results can be replicated. [J.W.M.]

H.122 Hess, Wilford M. "Botanical Comparisons in the Allegory of the Olive Tree." In *The Book of Mormon: Jacob through Words of Mormon, To Learn with Joy,* edited by Monte S. Nyman and Charles D. Tate Jr., 87-102. Provo, UT: Brigham Young University Religious Studies Center, 1990. Provides a detailed examination of Zenos's allegory of the olive tree in light of present-day knowledge of horticulture and determines that from the standpoint of science the allegory is accurate. Also presents an interpretation of the allegory in relation to the house of Israel. [D.M.]

H.123 Hess, Wilford M., Daniel J. Fairbanks, John W. Welch, and Jonathan K. Driggs. "Botanical Aspects of Olive Culture Relevant to Jacob 5." In *The Allegory of the Olive Tree: The Olive, The Bible, and Jacob 5,* edited by Stephen D. Ricks and John W. Welch, 484-562. Salt Lake City, Deseret Book and FARMS, 1994. Examines olive culture in agricultural Palestine and the rest of the Near East, analyzing the botanical and horticultural aspects that are inherent in Jacob 5. Includes domestication, planting, seasonal attributes, flowering, grafting, root systems, and pruning procedures. The ancients had an excellent knowledge of olive culture and the Book of Mormon closely follows those patterns. [J.W.M.]

H.124 Hickman, Josiah E. *Romance of the Book of Mormon.* Salt Lake City: Deseret Book, 1937. An anthropological/archaeological approach to the Book of Mormon with emphasis on cultural parallels between Book of Mormon people and American Indians. Hebrew origins of early American aborigines and possible evidence of Christ's visit to the Americas are also discussed. [J.T.]

H.125 Higginson, Mollie. "How We Obtained the Book of Mormon." *MS* 78 (6 July 1916): 417-22. A six-page synopsis of the Book of Mormon. Encourages researchers of the origin of the American Indians to read the Book of Mormon and end their research there. Through prayer all can know the truth of the Book of Mormon. [B.D.]

H.126 Hight, Dan. "Gustav and the Golden Plates." *The Witness* 77 (Summer 1992): 14. Gustav Koehn seriously questioned the Book of Mormon. He had a dream in which an angel showed him the plates of gold, leafed through them, and declared the book to be true. He was baptized into the RLDS Church and continued to testify of the Book of Mormon. [J.W.M.]

H.127 "The Hill Cumorah and Ancient Records." In *Stories from Mormon History*, edited by Alma P. Burton and Clea M. Burton, 87-116. Salt Lake City: Deseret Book, 1960. An anthology of texts concerning the Hill Cumorah, the gold plates, the stone box, Urim and Thummim, and other ancient records. These accounts are recorded by early leaders of the Church, such as Brigham Young, Heber C. Kimball, Oliver Cowdery, Orson Pratt, George Q. Cannon, Lucy Mack Smith, Martin Harris, and Edward Stevenson. [J.W.M.]

H.128 Hill, Donna. "Part Two: New York." In Hill's *Joseph Smith: The First Mormon*, 41-125. Garden City, NY: Doubleday, 1977. Provides an historical account of the coming forth of the Book of Mormon. Shortly after his marriage he received the plates and translation began, first with Emma as scribe then Martin Harris, Oliver Cowdery, and others. It seemed at first the book would be poorly received, but that proved untrue and the Church was established. [J.W.M.]

H.129 Hill, George W. "Message from an Indian Prophet." *Juvenile Instructor* 14 (15 April 1879): 91-92. Report of a prophecy concerning the coming of Johnston's army and of U.S. soldiers in Utah Territory, delivered by a messenger considered to be one of the Three Nephites. [D.M.]

H.130 Hill, Keith K. "Sorrow and Joy: What We Can Learn from Lehi." *Ensign* 18 (January 1988): 30-33. The problems of adversity in the lives of active believing Church members are recounted. Compares the problems of parenthood in today's world to Lehi's experience in the wilderness. [D.L.L.]

H.131 Hill, Theresa Snow. *Stories from the Book of Mormon*. Salt Lake City: Deseret Book, 1948. Presents the Book of Mormon in a narrative style, written primarily for juvenile audiences. [J.T.]

H.132 Hillam, Ray C. "The Gadianton Robbers and Protracted War." *BYU Studies* 15 (Winter 1975): 215-24. A history of the formation, leaders, and depredations of the Gadianton robbers. Discusses the relevancy to modern rebellions, assassinations, and insurgencies. [R.H.B.]

H.133 Hillam, Ray C. "Secret Combinations." In *Encyclopedia of Mormonism*, edited by Daniel H. Ludlow, 3:1290-91. 5 vols. New York: Macmillan, 1992. Describes the basic elements of a secret combination, and how they were manifest in the Bible, the Book of Mormon, and in the contemporary world. [A.T.]

H.134 Hills, Louis Edward. *Geography of Mexico and Central America from 2234 B.C. to 421 A.D.* Independence, MO: n.p., 1917. A booklet attempting to identify the geography named in the Book of Mormon with sites in Mexico and Central America. Places the Hill Cumorah in Mexico. Refers to Indian legends and Quetzalcoatl. Several maps are included. [D.M.]

H.135 Hills, Louis Edward. *Historical Data from Ancient Records and Ruins of Mexico and Central America*. Independence, MO: n.p., 1919. Quotes many sources, including the Quiche legends and the Popol Vuh, demonstrating anthropological and archaeological connections and correspondences with the Book of Mormon. [D.M.]

H.136 Hills, Louis Edward. *New Light on American Archaeology*. Independence, MO: Lambert

Moon, 1924. Discusses the origin of the early inhabitants of America, Jaredite movements, the Mulekite migration, archaeological evidences that support the Book of Mormon, Jesus Christ among the ancient Americas, stories of Quetzalcoatl, and possible Book of Mormon lands and sites. [D.W.P.]

H.137 Hills, Louis Edward. *A Short Work on the Popol Vuh and the Traditional History of the Ancient Americans by Ixt-xochitl.* Independence, MO: n.p., 1918. Describes the contents of the Popol Vuh and relates the four mythological founders of Mesoamerica to the four sons of Lehi. Draws on several anthropologists and archaeologists for various proposed evidences of the Book of Mormon. [D.M.]

H.138 Hilton, Hope A., and Lynn M. "The Lihyanites." *Sunstone* 9 (January-February 1984): 4-8. Discusses Lehi's eight year journey in Saudi Arabia and the possibility that he preached to and converted a group of people who later named themselves the "Lihyanites." [D.L.L.]

H.139 Hilton, John L. "On Verifying Wordprint Studies: Book of Mormon Authorship." *BYU Studies* 30 (Summer 1990): 89-108. Based on research conducted in Berkeley, California, by scholars who were attempting to authenticate the validity of wordprinting, this paper explores their conclusions. The results of Book of Mormon wordprints demonstrates that it is "statistically indefensible to propose Joseph Smith or Oliver Cowdery or Solomon Spaulding as the author of the . . . Book of Mormon." "The Book of Mormon measures multiauthored, with authorship consistent to its own internal claims." [A.T.]

H.140 Hilton, John L. "Wordprints and the Book of Mormon." In *Reexploring the Book of Mormon*, edited by John W. Welch, 221-26. Salt Lake City: Deseret Book and FARMS, 1992. Longer version available as "Some Book of Mormon 'Wordprint' Measurements using 'Wraparound' Block Counting." Provo, UT: FARMS, 1988. Wordprint studies confirm the Book of Mormon claim of multiauthorship. Usage of the terms "and," "the," "of," and "that" statistically confirm writing styles in 325 test runs of known authors. Texts by individual authors are significantly different from others. Joseph Smith, Oliver Cowdery, Solomon Spaulding, and others have no wordprints in common with the writings of the Book of Mormon. [N.K.Y.]

H.141 Hilton, John L., and Janet F. Hilton. "A Correlation of the Sidon River and the Lands of Manti and Zarahemla with the Southern End of the Rio Grijalva (San Miguel)." *Journal of Book of Mormon Studies* 1 (Fall 1992): 142-62. The authors construct a detailed geographical model of the Nephite homeland areas of Manti, Zarahemla, and the river Sidon using the Book of Mormon text of around 80 B.C. They nominate the southern end of the Grijalva river basin, located across the southern part of the Mexico-Guatemala border, as a possible candidate for the ancient Nephite homeland because it corresponds to the text's topography from the most general to the most detailed parts of the description. [R.H.B.]

H.142 Hilton, John L., and Ken Jenkins. "All Book of Mormon References by Author and Literary Form." Provo, UT: FARMS, 1983. A preliminary study that details the five primary literary forms found in the Book of Mormon: chapter headings, didactic sermons, first and third persons narratives, and dialogues. The study lists, for each of the five literary forms, the scriptural book, chapter, verse, author, literary form, and the number of words found therein. No mention is made of poetic forms found in the Book of Mormon text. [D.W.P.]

H.143 Hilton, Lynn M., and Hope A. "In Search of Lehi's Trail." *Ensign* 6 (September-October 1976): 32-54, 34-63. Attempts to identify specific sites and routes followed by Lehi's party as they traveled from Jerusalem to the coast of the Indian Ocean of the Arabian Peninsula. They believe that modern Salalah, Oman, is the Book of Mormon Bountiful. [D.M.]

H.144 Hilton, Lynn M., and Hope A. *In Search of Lehi's Trail.* Salt Lake City: Deseret Book, 1976. An endeavor to discover Lehi's trail in the Middle East. The authors attempt to identify such places as the Frankincense Trail, Lehi's route from Jerusalem, the Valley of

Lemuel, the place of the broken bow, and the land Bountiful. [L.D.]

H.145 Hilton, Matthew. *Preliminary Summary of Nephite Armed Conflict in the Book of Mormon.* Provo, UT: FARMS, 1987. Outlines a "rough summary of the basic information about Nephite wars and warfare in the Book of Mormon." Includes scriptural quotations that touch upon the subject of war and gives the corresponding date. [B.D.]

H.146 Hilton, Matthew, and Neil J. Flinders. "The Impact of Shifting Cultural Assumptions on the Military Policies Directing Armed Conflict Reported in the Book of Alma." In *Warfare in the Book of Mormon*, edited by Stephen D. Ricks and William J. Hamblin, 237-65. Salt Lake City: Deseret Book and FARMS, 1990. Family conflicts and conflicting ideological issues evolve into war. Accepting the theistic principles taught by the Nephites or accepting agnostic principles espoused by followers of Nehor led to repeated conflicts. We should be aware of this conflict potential in our day. [N.K.Y.]

H.147 Hinckley, Gordon B. "An Angel from on High, the Long, Long Silence Broke." *Ensign* 9 (November 1979): 7-8. Summarizes the conversion of Parley Pratt by reading the Book of Mormon. The Book of Mormon is the scripture of the New World, as the Bible is of the Old. No other book so clearly illustrates that righteous nations prosper and that disregard for God's word leads to impotence and death. [R.H.B.]

H.148 Hinckley, Gordon B. "As One Who Loves the Prophet." In *Joseph Smith: The Prophet, the Man*, edited by Susan Easton Black and Charles D. Tate Jr. Provo, UT: Brigham Young University Religious Studies Center, 1993. Author expresses gratitude for the Prophet Joseph Smith who was instrumental in bringing forth the Book of Mormon. Mentions that the Bible was recently rated the most influential book in America, and the Book of Mormon was rated eighth most influential. The author states his belief that the Book of Mormon will be rated number two in time. [J.W.M.]

H.149 Hinckley, Gordon B. "Book of Mormon Message and Challenge." *CR* (October 1979): 8-11. The coming forth of the Book of Mormon was remarkable and miraculous; one of its major teachings is that it predicts tragic consequences to all societies who become wicked. The book stands (with the Bible) as a witness of the mission and atonement of Jesus Christ. [R.C.D.]

H.150 Hinckley, Gordon B. "The Cornerstones of Our Faith." *Ensign* 14 (November 1984): 50-53. Also in *CR* (October 1984): 65-70. The cornerstones of the Church are: (1) Jesus Christ (the chief cornerstone), (2) the vision of the Father and the Son to the Prophet Joseph Smith, (3) the Book of Mormon, and (4) the Priesthood. Each cornerstone relates to the others and all are "tied to the chief cornerstone, Jesus Christ." [S.P.S.]

H.151 Hinckley, Gordon B. "Metal Plates in the British Museum." *IE* 39 (March 1936): 154. Research has shown that the Egyptians, Hebrews, and Greeks used tablets of metal to record important documents. The Inca-ruled natives of Peru and the Aztecs of Mexico engraved records on metal sheets. Engraved records are also found among relics of North American Indians. The British Museum possesses a set of twenty-five silver plates containing Buddha's first sermon and a gold tablet containing the dedication of the temple to Osiris by Ptolemy Eureregetes, 242-222 B.C. [R.H.B.]

H.152 Hinckley, Gordon B. "Mormon Should Mean 'More Good.'" *Ensign* 20 (November 1990): 51-54. The name *Mormon* is an honorable name, borne by one who was a great prophet on the American continent. Joseph Smith said that the name meant "more good" (*TJS*, pp. 299-300). The book that Mormon prepared bears his name—the Book of Mormon. It has touched the lives of thousands for good, for it witnesses of the Savior and Redeemer of the world, Jesus Christ. [J.W.M.]

H.153 Hinckley, Gordon B. "My Testimony." *Ensign* 23 (November 1993): 51-53. Reiterates testimony that Joseph Smith is a prophet, that he conversed with God the Father and Jesus

Christ, his Son, and that the Book of Mormon was written by ancient prophets and not by a young farm boy from New York. The complex and harmonious nature of the Book of Mormon does not resemble the Spaulding manuscript or the *View of the Hebrews* from which opponents of the Church say it is taken. [J.W.M.]

H.154 Hinckley, Gordon B. "The Power of the Book of Mormon." *Ensign* 18 (June 1988): 2-6. The conversion of Parley P. Pratt and others to the restored gospel through the Book of Mormon is recited. The article also discusses the role of the Book of Mormon as a witness to the Bible. [D.L.L.]

H.155 Hinckley, Gordon B. "Praise to the Man." *Ensign* 13 (August 1983): 2-6. Briefly recounts the legacy of the Prophet Joseph Smith and the early Church. Confirms that the Book of Mormon stands as a witness to the divinity of the Prophet's mission and that it should be read with earnest inquiry. Reminds readers that the book has outlasted its critics for over 150 years. [S.P.S.]

H.156 Hinckley, Gordon B. "Praise to the Man." In *Brigham Young University 1979 Devotional and Fireside Speeches,* 202-7. Provo, UT: BYU Press. In dealing with the critics of Joseph Smith, three questions must be asked: What do you do with the Book of Mormon? How do you explain Joseph Smith's power to influence strong men to follow him, even to death? How do you rationalize the fulfillment of his prophecies? The author answers these questions. [J.W.M.]

H.157 Hinckley, Gordon B. "The Stick of Joseph." *IE* 62 (December 1959): 958-60. The Book of Mormon converts people to the gospel of Jesus Christ and since its first printing a number of great individuals have been converted by its message. Once the Book of Mormon is accepted as true, other truths become evident. These are that God lives, the Church is true, Joseph was a prophet, and the Bible contains the word of God. [J.W.M.]

H.158 Hinckley, Gordon B. *Truth Restored.* Salt Lake City: LDS Church and Deseret Book, 1979. A history of the LDS Church that includes the story of the coming forth of the Book of Mormon. Photographs of historical events and places are included. [J.W.M.]

H.159 Hinckley, Gordon B. "A Unique and Wonderful University." In *Brigham Young University 1988 Devotional and Fireside Speeches,* edited by Karen Seely, 47-52. Provo, UT: BYU Press. Members of the Church have the responsibility to take the message of the Book of Mormon to a spiritually troubled world. Presents a testimony of a young missionary who found a copy of the Book of Mormon and was converted. The author makes a plea for those belonging to Brigham Young University to "learn to love the Book of Mormon and to love to learn from it." [J.W.M.]

H.160 Hinckley, Helen (Jones). *Columbus: Explorer for Christ.* Independence, MO: Herald House, 1977. A short biography on Christopher Columbus in light of the prophecy written about him by Nephi. [D.M.]

H.161 Hinton, Gary D. "This I Believe." *IE* 68 (August 1965): 714-15. A young man gave a Book of Mormon to his history teacher and told him that the American Indians were descendants of the people in the Book of Mormon. [M.D.P.]

H.162 "Historians of the Nephites." *Contributor* 1 (March 1880): 137-38. Also *MS* 82 (24 June 1920): 405-7. A listing and analysis of the historians in the Book of Mormon and where they stood relative to Nephite history. [D.M.]

H.163 *History of America B.C. 2200-420 A.D. Book of Mormon: An authentic account of the origin of the American Indian. Translated from the original by Joseph Smith, Jr."* Independence, MO: Missions of the Church of Jesus Christ of Latter-day Saints, 1912? Presents a brief overview of the Book of Mormon story and declares that it is in complete harmony with all other known truths including religious, historical, or scientific. Writes concerning charity, service, baptism, and other topics. [J.W.M.]

H.164 Hlavaty, Lauri. "The Religion of Moses and the Book of Mormon." In *The Book of Mormon: Jacob through Words of Mormon, To Learn with Joy,* edited by Monte S. Nyman and Charles D. Tate, 103-24. Provo, UT: Brigham Young University Religious Studies Center,

1990. Discusses Book of Mormon instruction on the religion of Moses and its emphasis on the Savior and his atonement. The insights in the Book of Mormon are crucial to understanding the religion Moses taught. Nephi taught that all things typify Jesus Christ. The purpose of the law of Moses was to bring the children of Israel to Christ. [J.W.M.]

H.165 Hobby, June M. "Jaredite-Nephite Armor and Weaponry: Reflections upon the Work of Christopher Reinhold." *Zarahemla Quarterly* 2/3 (1988): 30-31. The Zapotec Indians are identified as the Western Jaredites and the Maya, the Eastern Jaredites. Artifacts have been found that depict men wearing helmets. [J.W.M]

H.166 Hobby, Michael M. "The Mulekite Connection." *Zarahemla Quarterly* 2/1 (1988): 34-46. There was a four-century cohabitation of Mulekite and Jaredite societies before the latter was destroyed. This geographical study concludes that the Mulekites landed north of the narrow neck of land, encountered the Jaredites later and adopted their religion and culture, but fled when the final battle began and established the city where the Nephites found them. [J.W.M.]

H.167 Hobby, Michael M., and Troy J. Smith. "The Narrow Necks of Panama." *Zarahemla Quarterly* 2/3 (1988): 4-21. Hydrogeologist and geoarchaeologist Michael Hobby and geoarchaeologist Troy Smith recount experiences as they investigate the Panama region for possible evidence for the narrowest point in pre-Columbian times. This report includes maps and photographs. [J.W.M]

H.168 Hogan, Mervin B. *Freemasonry and the Book of Mormon.* Salt Lake City: Research Lodge of Utah F. and A.M., 1976. Explains the Book of Mormon from several angles. Quotes liberally from Robert B. Downs who wrote *Books That Changed America.* Downs says: "Throughout the history of Mormonism, the Church's most powerful and effective weapon has been the Book of Mormon.... The possession of their own scriptures . . . has proved to be the Mormons' greatest missionary tract." Hogan presents an outline summary of the narrative of the Book of Mormon and a summary of its theological teachings, and he concludes by discussing the importance of being creative in interpreting symbolism in ancient scripture. [B.D.] [D.M.]

H.169 Holbrook, Brett L. "The Sword of Laban as a Symbol of Divine Authority and Kingship." *Journal of Book of Mormon Studies* 2 (Spring 1993): 39-72. This article explains the importance of the sword of Laban in the Book of Mormon and the restoration. The sword is a "symbol of divine authority and kingship." The sword of Laban was used by rulers in the Book of Mormon and for Joseph Smith was a "witness of his authority and of the divine sanction for his work." [A.T.]

H.170 Holdaway, Annie W. "Redemption of the Lamanites." *IE* 27 (March 1924): 418-23. A brief article explaining some of the persecutions as well as progress that the Indians have experienced. When Melvin J. Ballard visited Ft. Peck and Blackfoot reservations the Indians knew him and were waiting for the "Book" because they had seen him in dreams. Ballard, Holdaway writes, believed the Three Nephites had labored among those Indians for years. [B.D.]

H.171 Holland, Jeffrey R. "Alma, Son of Alma." *Ensign* 7 (March 1977): 79-84. Similar to the New Testament Paul, Alma, the son of Alma, was converted from an opponent of Christ to a disciple of Christ. Much of the Book of Mormon is devoted to his life story, which includes messages of the anguish of a parent over a wayward child, the reality of repentance and its accompanying suffering, and the power of Christ. [R.H.B.]

H.172 Holland, Jeffrey R. "An Analysis of Selected Changes in Major Editions of the Book of Mormon: 1830-1920." M.A. thesis, Brigham Young University, 1966. Compares the changes of a number of LDS editions of the Book of Mormon, including the first three editions (1830, 1837, and 1840) published under the direction of Joseph Smith, the third British edition (1852) edited by Franklin D. Richards, Orson Pratt's 1879 revision that introduced a new chapter and verse system, and James E.

Talmage's 1920 version. The author displays 156 textual differences between these editions. Only a sampling of differences is provided with no intent to be systematic or complete. [R.S.]

H.173 Holland, Jeffrey R. "Conclusions and Charge." In *The Book of Mormon: First Nephi, the Doctrinal Structure*, edited by Monte S. Nyman and Charles D. Tate Jr., 315-23. Provo, UT: Brigham Young University Religious Studies Center, 1988. Mentions the loss of the 116 pages as a vehicle for bringing about 1 Nephi. Draws doctrinal conclusions from the first twenty verses of the Book of Mormon, and charges believers to cling to the rod of iron. [A.T.]

H.174 Holland, Jeffrey R. "Daddy, Donna, and Nephi." *Ensign* 6 (September 1976): 7-11. The Book of Mormon needs to be read with a questioning mind and each verse needs to be examined critically for its meaning. Every chapter is charged with meaning, often with many meanings. From the first, the book forces the serious reader to recognize divine direction from God. [R.H.B.]

H.175 Holland, Jeffrey R. "I Have a Question: 'How can I explain Nephi's killing Laban to my non-member friends? Some really reject it as scriptural.'" *Ensign* 6 (September 1976): 83-84. These seven things help us understand: Nephi gives a detailed account so he would not be misunderstood; he had no desire to take Laban's life; Old Testament prophets were likewise commanded; Laban was guilty of atrocities toward Nephi's family; modern revelation condones taking the life of a wicked man; Nephi was commanded by the Lawgiver; obedience was the focal point of the story. [J.W.M.]

H.176 Holland, Jeffrey R. "Mormon: The Man and the Book." *Ensign* 8 (March-April 1978): 15-18, 57-59. Mormon, the prophet/historian, was uniquely qualified for the task of editing the gold plates. Under the direction of the Spirit, Mormon carefully included only those items that would be of the greatest value to our generation in his abridgment of the Nephite records. [D.M.]

H.177 Holmes, Reed M. "Christ and Our Day." In Holmes's *Seek This Christ, 1954*, 29-44. Independence, MO: Herald Publishing House, 1954. Jesus is the Christ, the Son of God. He can be traced through the testimony of the Book of Mormon. The Book of Mormon is not a substitute for the Bible but is a supplement to it. This chapter investigates the passages of the Book of Mormon that relate to the Savior's ministry. [J.W.M.]

H.178 Holmes, Reed M. *The Social and Moral Message of the Book of Mormon*. Gospel Quarterly Series, #3. Independence, MO: Herald House, 1951. When nations or individuals are peaceful, the indication is that they have a committed, loving relationship with Deity. The opposite is also true. Evidence of this is abundant in the Book of Mormon. [J.W.M.]

H.179 Holmes, Samuel L. "The Christ Story in the Book of Mormon." *MS* 101 (5 October 1939): 630-31, 638-39. The Nephite people knew of Christ, his birth, mission, and death. When Mexico was conquered in 1520, Cortez found a fallen Christian Church, but the descendants of Lehi had not entirely forgotten their great white god and his wondrous miracles and teachings, which had become the worship of Quetzalcoatl. Thinking he had returned, the people welcomed the Spaniards. [J.W.M.]

H.180 Homer, William H., Jr. "The Passing of Martin Harris." *IE* 29 (March 1926): 468-72. Martin Harris, one of the Three Witnesses to the Book of Mormon, was persuaded to move from Kirtland, Ohio, to Utah in 1870. A prominent part of the article is devoted to Harris's tenacious adherence to his testimony of the Book of Mormon. [D.M.]

H.181 Homer, William H., Jr. "Publish It Upon the Mountains." *IE* 58 (March-May 1955): 144-45, 310-11, 344. Reviews Martin Harris's role in bringing forth the Book of Mormon, and discusses Harris's testimony of the Book of Mormon. [R.C.D.]

H.182 Hopfenbeck, G. Martin. "The Book of Mormon Manuscripts." *MS* 85 (27 December 1923): 820-23. The history of Book of Mormon manuscripts is set forth. Includes mention of various scribes, the loss of 116 manuscript pages, publication of the Book of Mormon, and nineteen manuscript pages found in the Nauvoo House cornerstone. [A. C.]

H.183 Hopkin, Fred W. "Conversion in Honduras." *Friend* 18 (October 1988): 32-33. A picture story illustrating the conversion of a Central American girl through the Book of Mormon. [D.M.]

H.184 Hopkins, N. Gaylon. "The Condescension of the Father and the Son." In *Sidney B. Sperry Symposium: The Book of Mormon*, edited by A. Gary Anderson, 48-59. Provo, UT: Brigham Young University Religious Studies Center, 1981. The Book of Mormon reveals the paternity of Jesus Christ, his divinity as Creator, and his condescension, or his subjection into the hands of mortal men. The book also reveals the temptations that the Savior had to endure. [J.W.M.]

H.185 Hoppe, Edward W. "What We Learned from Our Book of Mormon Project." *Ensign* 3 (March 1973): 47. Report of successes and failures in a Brigham Young University project to send copies of the Book of Mormon to foreign missions. [A.C.W.]

H.186 "The Horse in Ancient America." *MS* 90 (26 April 1928): 268-69. Through historical, scientific, and scholarly evidence, this article shows that there were indeed horses in ancient America, well before Spaniards. Nephi stated in the Book of Mormon that horses were found upon their arrival in the promised land. [M.D.P.]

H.187 Horton, George A., Jr. "Book of Mormon—Transmission from Translator to Printed Text." In *The Book of Mormon: The Keystone Scripture*, edited by Paul R. Cheesman, S. Kent Brown, and Charles D. Tate Jr., 237-55. Provo, UT: Brigham Young University Religious Studies Center, 1988. Reviews the history of the English text of the Book of Mormon by discussing textual changes made or authorized by Joseph Smith and transmissional problems such as orthography, haplography, dittography, homoeoteleuton, and homoeoarchton. Concludes that "the basic meaning of the text has not been changed [and] the changes and corrections are not only correct but appropriate." [B.D.]

H.188 Horton, George A., Jr. "Understanding the Textual Changes in the Book of Mormon." *Ensign* 13 (December 1983): 24-28. Gives a history of the many textual changes made in various editions of the Book of Mormon (spelling, grammatical, punctuation, and clarification). Discusses the circumstances that made the changes necessary and how these changes should be viewed in light of Joseph Smith's statement that the Book of Mormon is the most correct book. [S.P.S.]

H.189 Hoskisson, Paul Y. "The Allegory of the Olive Tree in Jacob." In *The Allegory Of The Olive Tree: The Olive, The Bible, and Jacob 5*, edited by Stephen D. Ricks and John W. Welch, 70-104. Slat Lake City: Deseret Book and FARMS, 1994. Examines four aspects of the allegory of the olive tree: what are the symbols, why Jacob used the allegory in his writings, what historical events does it allude to, and what does it say to latter-day people? Concludes that the allegory refers to actual events in the history of the house of Israel. The message of the allegory is that Father in Heaven is a caring God. Jacob included this allegory to show that reconciliation with God comes through Jesus Christ. [J.W.M.]

H.190 Hoskisson, Paul Y. "The Ancient Near Eastern Background of the Language of the Book of Mormon." In *The Sixth Annual Church Educational System Religious Educators' Symposium on the Book of Mormon*, 40-42. Salt Lake City: Church of Jesus Christ of Latter-day Saints, 1982. Finds "indications of an ancient Near Eastern influence on the received text of the Book of Mormon [in the form of] lexemes, style, and onomastics." 1 Nephi 2:9 is an example of a lexeme. Lehi's statement that the river "emptied into the fountain of the Red Sea" does not make sense until one realizes that the "ancients of the Near East saw the oceans and subterranean waters to be the source of rivers and steams." [A.T.]

H.191 Hoskisson, Paul Y. "Book of Mormon Names." In *Encyclopedia of Mormonism*, edited by Daniel H. Ludlow, 1:186-87. 5 vols. New

York: Macmillan, 1992. "The Book of Mormon contains 337 proper names and 21 gentilics (or analogous forms) based on proper names." Of the 337 proper names, "188 are unique to the Book of Mormon." Some semantic names have translated meanings that would be more meaningful if linguistic origins were available. [N.K.Y.]

H.192 Hoskisson, Paul Y. "Explicating the Mystery of the Rejected Foundation Stone: The Allegory of the Olive Tree." *BYU Studies* 30 (Summer 1990): 77-87. Relates the allegory of the olive tree (Jacob 5) to biblical eras and dispensations and demonstrates that "many of the historical metaphors" can represent actual time periods in the history of the house of Israel. However, there is a far greater purpose for the allegory than to assign time frames to its sequence of events. The deeper meaning is that it is possible for the Jewish people to build upon the foundation stone of Christ after having once rejected him. [J.W.M.]

H.193 Hoskisson, Paul Y. "An Introduction to the Relevance of and a Methodology for a Study of the Proper Names of the Book of Mormon." In *By Study and Also by Faith,* edited by John M. Lundquist and Stephen D. Ricks, 2:126-35. Salt Lake City: Deseret and FARMS, 1990. This well-footnoted article discusses the significance of proper names in the Book of Mormon and presents a methodology for the study of such names. Proper names can convey meaning, lead to the identity of the language of origin, preserve sounds of a mother tongue, give clues to the nature of peoples or events of the past, and help to identify times at which writings took place. Example etymologies of a few names are suggested and a caution raised regarding multiple languages of origin, commingling of languages, unknown languages of origin, Jaredite names, and multiple spellings of names in early Book of Mormon manuscripts. [A.A.]

H.194 Hoskisson, Paul Y. "Scimitars, Cimeters! We Have Scimitars! Do We Need Another Cimeter?" In *Warfare in the Book of Mormon,* edited by Stephen D. Ricks and William J. Hamblin, 352-59. Salt Lake City: Deseret and FARMS, 1990. The term "cimeter" (now spelled scimitar) is mentioned eleven times in the Book of Mormon. The Book of Mormon cimeter is discussed and compared with those used in Near Eastern areas, and its usage and description is not improper. [N.K.Y.]

H.195 Hoskisson, Paul Y. "Textual Evidences for the Book of Mormon." In *The Book of Mormon: First Nephi, the Doctrinal Foundation*, edited by Monte S. Nyman and Charles D. Tate Jr., 283-95. Provo, UT: Brigham Young University Religious Studies Center, 1988. Uses textual material from the Book of Mormon to demonstrate its ancient Near Eastern background and style. Compares Book of Mormon phrases to Ugaritic, Akkadian, and Hebrew texts, and notes that this was information not available to Joseph Smith. [A.T.]

H.196 Hoskisson, Paul Y. "Urim and Thummim." In *Encyclopedia of Mormonism*, edited by Daniel H. Ludlow, 4:1499-1500. 5 vols. New York: Macmillan, 1992. Lists different prophets that have been in possession of the Urim and Thummim, Joseph Smith's description of them, the meaning of the words *Urim and Thummim,* and future uses of the Urim and Thummim. [A.T.]

H.197 "How Are the American Indians Related to the Jews?" *IE* 23 (March 1920): 453-55. Discusses the idea that the American Indians are descendants of Lehi, Ishmael, and Mulek, the former two being of the house of Joseph and the latter, the house of Judah. [J.W.M.]

H.198 "How the Book of Mormon Was Translated: How God Uses Human Agencies to Give His Word to Mankind." *MS* 68 (March 1906): 205-6. The authors know of no record from the prophet himself on exactly how he translated the Book of Mormon. They suggest that Joseph Smith's mind was quickened by the Urim and Thummim and that after getting the idea of the message, he wrote it in his own words. Thus the grammatical errors are his own. [B.D.]

H.199 "How We Got the Book of Mormon." *Friend* 10 (April 1980): 30-32. An illustrated children's story of Joseph Smith receiving the golden plates. [M.R.]

H.200 Howard, F. Burton. "Come Back to the Lord." *Ensign* 16 (November 1986): 76-78. Also in *CR* (4-5 October 1986): 97-100. Stresses the importance of repentance. Mentions the stories of Alma the Younger and Aminidab, showing how they repented and returned to the Lord. [A.C.W.]

H.201 Howard, Richard P. *Restoration Scriptures: A Study of Their Textual Development*. Independence, MO: Herald House, 1969. Discusses the development of the Book of Mormon, the "Inspired Version" of the Bible, and the Doctrine & Covenants. With regard to the Book of Mormon, the author attempts to "establish the relationship between the two (original) manuscripts produced prior to publication in 1830," to "demonstrate the continuing concern of Joseph Smith, Jr. for the refinement of the Book of Mormon text," and to discuss the textual developments of various editions of the Book of Mormon. Includes in parallel columns portions of Book of Mormon texts from different editions to show changes. [A.C.W.]

H.202 Howells, Rulon S. "The Book of Mormon Story." In Howells's *The Mormon Story: A Pictoral Account of Mormonism*, 17-25. Salt Lake City: Bookcraft, 1957. Tells Joseph Smith's story using his own words, with pictures, maps, and photographs to emphasize the historical account of the coming forth of the Book of Mormon. [J.W.M.]

H.203 Howells, Rulon S. *Compilation of the Book of Mormon*. Salt Lake City, UT: Bookcraft, 1961. A large fold-out chart depicting the way in which the Book of Mormon was compiled and abridged. Includes a facsimile of the characters on the plates, the translation of the records, and an account of the method of translation. [J.W.M.]

H.204 Howells, Rulon S. *The Way to Happiness*. Salt Lake City: Bookcraft, 1967. This full-color illustrated booklet begins with the organization of the primitive church by Christ, and moves through the Apostasy to the Restoration of the Latter-day Church. It presents the Joseph Smith story in Smith's own words. Includes doctrines taught in the Book of Mormon on baptism, divine authority, the sacrament, and temple marriage. [J.W.M.]

H.205 Howells, Rulon S. *Where the Book of Mormon Story Took Place*. Salt Lake City, UT: Bookcraft, 1961. A fold-out map of the Americas marked with Book of Mormon story events and dates showing the location where Book of Mormon peoples landed in South and Central America. To be used as a teaching aid. [J.W.M.]

H.206 Hubble, M. J. "Interview with David Whitmer." *BYU Studies* 14 (Summer 1947): 483-86. Transcript and copy of a hand-written document, reporting information David Whitmer gave regarding the translation of the Book of Mormon. [D.M.]

H.207 Huber, Jay H. "Lehi's 600 Year Prophecy and the Birth of Christ." Provo, UT: FARMS, 1982. Using historical data to date the time that Lehi left Jerusalem and the time of Christ's birth and death, the author concludes that the Nephites used a 360-day year and Christ was born on or near 11 April, 4 B.C., or September/October of 5 B.C. "The 360-day hypothesis agrees with all historical data dealing with Zedekiah and Herod, is consistent with the Book of Mormon account, and allows us a plausible explanation for the heavenly signs inferred from the Nephite account." [A.T.]

H.208 Hunter, Howard W. "The Book of Mormon Testifies of Christ." *CR* (April 1983): 17-20. The greatest message of all is the gospel—the good news, which is Jesus Christ. It is the message of the Bible. It is also the message of the Book of Mormon. The Book of Mormon is a second witness for Christ. Reading it "will have a profound effect on your life." [R.C.D.]

H.209 Hunter, Howard W. "Evidences of the Resurrection." *Ensign* 13 (May 1983): 15-16. The Book of Mormon is the record of Christ's "other sheep" (John 10:14-16). It provides evidence of the resurrected Lord through its record of Christ's appearance in America following his crucifixion and resurrection. It is a confirming and harmonious testimony of the biblical record. [J.W.M.]

H.210 Hunter, Howard W. " 'No Less Serviceable.' " *Ensign* (April 1992): 64-67. Helaman and his brethren are "no less serviceable unto the people" (Alma 48:19) than Moroni (Alma 48:17). Elder Hunter talks about other scriptural individuals that did not hold the limelight of attention. These include: Sam, Ishmael, Ishmael's daughters, Mother Sariah, Abish, Mosiah, Limhi, Amulek, Pahoran, and Shiblon. [A.T.]

H.211 Hunter, Milton R. "Archaeology and the Book of Mormon." In *Book of Mormon Talks by General Authorities*, 32-45. Provo, UT: FARMS, 1990. Also published in *BYUSY* (19 July 1966). Provo, UT: BYU Press. This is an address given at BYU, July 19, 1966. The author gives archaeological evidences supporting the Book of Mormon. Discusses ancient civilizations, gold and silver, clothing and jewelry, stela 5 (Izapa, Mexico), which depicts Lehi's dream, and the story of the White God visiting America. [B.D.]

H.212 Hunter, Milton R. *Archaeology and the Book of Mormon.* Salt Lake City: Deseret Book, 1956. Printed as a series in *IE* 58-59 (April-October 1955, January-May 1956): 229, 280, 282, 316-19, 338, 340-43, 496-98, 520-23, 561, 576, 578, 580, 582-86, 638-39, 654, 656, 658, 724-40, 26-27, 42, 44-47, 82-84, 98, 100, 102, 168-70, 172-74, 176, 178-79, 239-41, 282, 324-26, 328, 330, 332, 334. A comprehensive compilation of archaeological artifacts in Mesoamerica that relate to Book of Mormon places and peoples. Copiously illustrated with photographs of buildings, pottery, statues, and carvings. Includes evidences of Christ's appearance to the Americas. Reviews ancient Mayan writings, including Title of the Lords of Totonicapan, the Popol Vuh, the annals of the Cakehiquels, and the words of Ixtlilxochitl. Discusses white and dark people in ancient America. [R.H.B.]

H.213 Hunter, Milton R. "Book of Mormon Evidences." *IE* 57 (December 1954): 912-14, 916, 918. Vast amounts of marvelous evidences for the Book of Mormon have accumulated. Archaeological evidences include the many discoveries in the Americas—La Venta, Izapa stone, Quetzalcoatl, bearded-men statues, Egyptian type burials, arts, metals, and textiles. The writings of sixteenth-century Indian historians, such as the *Totonicapan, Popol Vuh, Annals of the Cakchiquels,* and the *Works of Ixtlilxochitl,* and the writings of the sixteenth-century Catholic priests Bernardino de Sahagun, Bishop Bartholome de Las Casas, Diego de Landa, and Juan de Torquemad present correlations and correspondences to the Book of Mormon. [R.C.D.]

H.214 Hunter, Milton R. "Book of Mormon Evidences." In *BYUSY* (21 January 1958). Provo, UT: BYU Press. The Book of Mormon is unique, for it is the only book written completely in accordance to divine command. No other book was written by a succession of prophets. It was written for a divine purpose, preserved by a Divine Being, and stands the test of time. No other book has had more testators. Archaeology bears witness of its truthfulness. [J.W.M.]

H.215 Hunter, Milton R. *Christ in Ancient America.* Salt Lake City: Deseret Book, 1959. Chapters deal with Quetzalcoatl—the white bearded God—Christ the good shepherd, Teotihuacán, and the plumed serpent. These topics are carefully related to Jesus' visit to the ancient Americas. Copiously illustrated. [R.H.B.]

H.216 Hunter, Milton R. "Gospel Dispensations in Ancient America." In *The Gospel through the Ages*, 82-89. Salt Lake City: Stevens and Wallis, 1945. There are two gospel dispensations identified in the Book of Mormon—the Jaredite and the Nephite. The Nephites lived the law of Moses in concert with the gospel of Christ under the direction of both the Aaronic and Melchizedek Priesthoods for 600 years before Christ's visit. [J.W.M.]

H.217 Hunter, Milton R. "A Great and Marvelous Work." *IE* 72 (June 1969): 87-88. The Book of Mormon is unique because Jesus Christ initiated and supervised its production. It was written under divine guidance by prophets specifically for the last days. The gold plates were in the custody of an angel. The translation was conducted by an unlearned man and completed in approximately sixty days. The Lord proclaimed its divinity and truthfulness. [J.W.M.]

H.218 Hunter, Milton R. *Great Civilizations and the Book of Mormon.* Salt Lake City: Bookcraft, 1970. Deals with the Olmec civilization, Indian culture, the Maya civilization, Tikal, Copan, Uxmal, Kabah, Chichen Itza, Teotihuacan, and the origin of American Indians. [R.H.B.]

H.219 Hunter, Milton R. "The Greatest Event in Ancient America." *IE* 64 (June 1961): 408-9. Various Indian traditions and practices suggest that Jesus Christ visited the American continent, as the Book of Mormon indicates. Author points out archaeological and historical similarities between Jesus and Itzamna, the god of the Mayas, and Quetzalcoatl, the "Fair God" of ancient America. [J.W.M.]

H.220 Hunter, Milton R. "Indian Traditions of the Book of Mormon." *IE* 58 (June 1955): 430-32. Compares oral traditions of Indian tribes that correspond to Book of Mormon stories. Two ancient Mayan writings, the *Works of Ixtlilxochitl* and the *Popol Vuh,* possess remarkable parallels with the Book of Mormon. [R.C.D.]

H.221 Hunter, Milton R. "Marriage Customs of the Quiché Maya." *IE* 59 (June 1956): 413-15. A careful study of the religious beliefs and practices of the Quiché Maya indicate that their roots may be found in the Book of Mormon narrative. Discusses marriage customs of the Quiché Maya. [J.W.M.]

H.222 Hunter, Milton R. "A Marvelous Work and a Wonder." *IE* 61 (December 1953): 930-33. The Book of Mormon fulfills prophecies of Isaiah. The phrase "marvelous work and a wonder" (used by both Isaiah and Nephi) has a three-fold meaning: the true gospel of Jesus Christ would be restored, the covenants the Lord made with the children of Israel would be fulfilled, and the records of the ancient American people would be given to all of the world. [J.W.M.]

H.223 Hunter, Milton R. "The Modern Scriptures—Our Greatest Aids." *IE* 58 (December 1955): 940-41. Joseph Smith's contributions to the scriptural canon include the Book of Mormon and the Doctrine and Covenants. Both are added witnesses of Jesus Christ and clarify the teachings and doctrines of Jesus Christ, including the conditions for eternal life or exaltation. [R.H.B.]

H.224 Hunter, Milton R. "Prophecies and Blessings to the Lamanites." *IE* 62 (December 1959): 928-31. God is beginning to fulfill his promises as recorded in the Book of Mormon that the gospel will be opened unto the Lamanites. [R.C.D.]

H.225 Hunter, Milton R. Untitled talk. *CR* (October 1958): 26-30. A testimony that the Book of Mormon fulfills prophecy found in both Isaiah 29 and 1 Nephi 13. In reference to Isaiah 2:3, Hunter writes that the word of the Lord came from Jerusalem in the Holy Bible and the law came from Zion in the Book of Mormon, the Doctrine and Covenants, and the Pearl of Great Price. [B.D.]

H.226 Hunter, Milton R. Untitled talk. *CR* (April 1969): 82-84. A testimony of the Book of Mormon. In D&C 17:6 the Lord himself testified of the Book of Mormon. In D&C 17:1 the Lord granted that Oliver Cowdery, David Whitmer, and Martin Harris would be the chosen Three Witnesses of the gold plates. Only through the Holy Ghost can anyone receive a testimony of the truth (1 Corinthians 2, Moroni 10:2-5). [B.D.]

H.227 Hunter, Milton R. "Witnesses to the Book of Mormon." *IE* 73 (June 1970): 100-101. Also found in *CR* (April 1970): 136-38. Histories produced by American Indians during the colonial period of America contain accounts similar to those in the Book of Mormon. The Works of Ixtlilxochitl appears to be a Lamanite history. Four other books that correspond with the Book of Mormon are *The Annals of the Cakchiquels, Title of the Lords of Totonicapan,* the *Popul Vuh,* and *Anales do los Xahil.* [B.D.]

H.228 Hunter, Milton R., and Thomas Stuart Ferguson. *Ancient America and the Book of Mormon.* Oakland, CA: Kolob Book, 1950. A comparison between the Book of Mormon and Spanish, Mexican, and Guatemalan sources, such as *Works of Ixtlilxochitl, Popul Vuh,* and *Totonicapan.* Joseph Smith translated the Book of Mormon independently, with no help from historical sources, as most lay unpublished in archives or had not reached the United States. [J.W.M.]

H.229 Hurd, Jerrie W. *Our Sisters in the Latter-Day Scriptures.* Salt Lake City: Deseret Book, 1987. Though few women are named in the Book of Mormon, they have had great power and influence. Specifically named are Sariah and Abish; many other women—sisters, mothers, queens—are unnamed. [J.W.M.]

H.230 Hutchins, Barbara, and Paul R. Cheesman. *Pathways to the Past.* Bountiful: Horizon, 1984. A travel guidebook to Middle America that links several Book of Mormon sites with present day locations. [C.C.]

H.231 Huttinger, Beverly. "Asking in Faith." *Ensign* 17 (December 1987): 34-35. An account of an individual who gained a testimony of the Book of Mormon and converted to the LDS faith. [A.C.W.]

H.232 Hyde, W. A. "The Spirit and Influence of the Book of Mormon." *IE* 30 (September 1927): 988-92. The Book of Mormon is full of the Spirit of Truth. This Spirit carries the book's message to the hearts of its readers. [D.M.]

H.233 Hyland, Richard. "The Gospel in the South Seas." *MS* 99 (25 November 1937): 758-59, 766. Believes that the Hawaiians, Samoans, Maoris, and other south sea peoples originated on the American Continent. The three native foods of Polynesia—the coconut, sweet potato, and taro root—are of American origin. The genealogical name lines of such widely separated peoples as New Zealand Maoris and Hawaiians unite 65 generations back to Hema who led a migration to New Zealand. Prior to Hema, the names in both Hawaiian and Maori legends are similar. [R.H.B.]

I.

I.001 "I Have a Question: Questions Relating to the Book of Mormon." Provo, UT: FARMS, 1991. A collection of questions and answers that relate to the Book of Mormon reprinted from issues of the *Ensign* 1985-91. Subjects include the tree of life, the Godhead, the "fulness of the gospel," eternal hell, and Hebraisms. [J.W.M.]

I.002 Iba, Stephen K. "Elements of Effective Teaching: King Benjamin's Address." In *The Sixth Annual Church Educational System Religious Educators' Symposium on the Book of Mormon,* 43-44. Salt Lake City: Church of Jesus Christ of Latter-day Saints, 1982. Examines chapters of King Benjamin's speech for "elements of effective teaching." The elements include preparation, setting, use of rapport and examples, analogies, personal experiences, testimony, and challenges. [A.T.]

I.003 "Illustrated Stories of the Scriptures and Church History" (Series). *Friend* 14-21 (1984-1991). The editions that pertain to the Book of Mormon are: 1984, Vol. 14: January, June, August. 1989, Vol. 19: May, June, July, August, September, October, November. 1990, Vol. 20: January, February, March, April, May, June, August, October. 1991, Vol. 21: January, March, May, July, September, November. This series includes full-page, full-color cartoon stories from the scriptures and Church history for children. [J.W.M.]

I.004 *The Indian Bible. Book No. 1: The Book of Nephi.* Alexandria, VA: American Indian Restoration Enterprises, 1962. A typewritten paraphrase of 1 and 2 Nephi geared especially for the American Indian. Divided into 300 verses. Emphasizes Indians as the audience to whom the messages are addressed. Refers to God and Christ as "the Great Spirit." [D.M.]

I.005 *Introduction to the First Book of Nephi.* Independence, MO: Zarahemla Research Foundation, 1986. Gives a brief overview of the setting and author of 1 Nephi up to the period of Lehi's examination of the plates of brass. Includes notes and comments on the first several verses of 1 Nephi, including a discussion of Hebrew terms. [D.M.]

I.006 "An Invitation." *IE* 26 (August 1923): 951. An invitation to read the Book of Mormon. Presents an overview of the coming forth of and contents of the Book of Mormon. [L.D.]

I.007 Ireland, H. "The Book of Mormon." *MS* 74 (11 July 1912): 440-42. A testimony of the Book of Mormon. The Book of Mormon is not superior or inferior to the Bible—it contains the will of the same God. Many truths lost from the Bible are restored in the Book of Mormon. Through prayer a sincere person can know if it is true. [B.D.]

I.008 Ireland, H. "Good Roads in Book of Mormon Times." *Liahona* 24 (7 September 1926): 132-33. Draws a parallel between archaeological finds and 3 Nephi. Evidence indicates that the Mayan civilization flourished near the beginning of the Christian era. For instance, Mayan road building rivaled that of Rome in the same period. This period coincides with 3 Nephi 6:8, A. D. 29-30, which describes the advanced state of civilization and large scale road building. [C.C.]

I.009 "Iron Sword from the Time of Jeremiah Discovered near Jericho." *Ensign* 17 (June 1987): 57. Reports an archaeological find of an iron (or primitive steel) sword, perhaps dating to the time of King Josiah. Demonstrates that such workmanship as the sword of Laban existed at the time. [D.M.]

I.010 Iverson, Heber C. "The Three Witnesses." *MS* 97 (June 1935): 386-87, 394-96. Includes a reprint of the testimony of the Three Witnesses from the Book of Mormon, a report of Oliver Cowdery's testimony given at the conference at Council Bluffs, his testimony at the time of his death in David Whitmer's home, David Whitmer's rebuttal to John Murphy, William Harrison Homer's interview with Martin Harris, and Harris's testimony given in Salt Lake City and in Clarkston, Utah, just prior to his death. [J.W.M.]

I.011 Ivins, Anthony W. "Are the Jaredites an Extinct People?" *IE* 6 (November 1902): 43-44. Argument for Book of Mormon authenticity. The Mayan and Egyptian hieratic alphabets are similar. The Chiapas claim descent from the "Lord of the Hollow Wood" who was at the tower of Babel. Jared was at the tower and crossed the ocean in "hollow wood" that was tight like a dish. [C.C.]

I.012 Ivins, Anthony W. "The Book of Mormon." *Relief Society Magazine* 14 (August 1927): 384-88. Retells the story of the angel Moroni showing the gold plates to Joseph Smith. The recent discovery of gold plates and steel represent external evidences of the truthfulness of the book. [J.W.M.]

I.013 Ivins, Anthony W. "The Book of Mormon Bears Witness of Christ." *MS* 89 (29 September, 6 October 1927): 609-14, 625-31. Church members are exhorted to live righteously and to know doctrine and Church history well enough to defend their faith. Testifies that the Redeemer appeared on this continent. [B.D.][C.C.]

I.014 Ivins, Anthony W. "The Book of Mormon Divine." *MS* 91 (30 May 1929): 337-43, 345-47. Addresses criticisms of the Book of Mormon, especially by John Fisk, who wrote that the Book of Mormon in "blissful ignorance, introduces oxen and sheep, as well as the knowledge of smelting iron, into pre-Columbian America." Ivins quotes A. Hyatt Verril who found "a steel or hardened iron implement" on the Isthmus of Panama, cites evidence of oxen and horses discovered in the asphalt pits of Los Angeles, and gives evidence of the use of pearls and the use of engraven metal plates not only by ancient Americans but by many peoples throughout the world. [B.D.]

I.015 Ivins, Anthony W. "Cumorah: A Mute Witness of Epochal Events." *MS* 90 (May 1928): 289-95. In connection with the 1928 Church acquisition of the Hill Cumorah, Ivins speaks concerning the records that make up the Book of Mormon, including the brass plates, consisting of the Pentateuch, Isaiah, and Jeremiah; the large and small plates of Nephi; and the twenty-four gold plates of the Jaredites. [C.C.]

I.016 Ivins, Anthony W. "The Hill Cumorah." *IE* 31 (June 1928): 675-811. A report reviewing historical events dealing with the Hill Cumorah. The author recounts the history of the Nephite plates from the time Nephi began inscribing on them to when Ammaron turned them over to Mormon, followed by Moroni's acquisition of the plates and their placement in Hill Cumorah. Reference is also made to the sealed plates yet to be translated. [D.M.]

I.017 Ivins, Anthony W. "Multiplicity of Evidences Prove Divine Authenticity of the Book of Mormon." *Liahona* 14 (October 1916): 241-47. Response to criticism that Joseph Smith fabricated the Book of Mormon from his own milieu. It is unlikely that Joseph Smith could have realized the following points: the American Indians possess a number of legends that suggest an Israelite origin, including stories regarding the creation of the earth, the temptation of the first man and woman by a serpent, and Cain and Abel. Cement, mentioned in the Book of Mormon (Helaman 3:7, 9), was the primary building material of an ancient community that existed 40 miles north of present day Mexico City. [C.C.]

I.018 Ivins, Anthony W. *The Relationship of "Mormonism" and Freemasonry.* Salt Lake City: Deseret News, 1934. The LDS Church is founded upon the principles of the Book of Mormon. The Book of Mormon is not a "Golden Bible" nor does it take the place of the Bible. It is not associated with secret societies, but condemns the same. [J.W.M.]

I.019 Ivins, Anthony W. Untitled talk. *CR* (April 1909): 57-62. A refutation of an attack on Mormonism and a testimony that the Book of Mormon is true. Hubert Howe Bancroft saw a tablet of stone with the ten commandments inscribed on it in Hebrew, which was found in a mound in Ohio. The pyramids of ancient America resemble the pyramids of the Egyptians and the Maya language resembles the Egyptian language according to professor Leplongeon. [B.D.]

I.020 Ivins, Anthony W. Untitled talk. *CR* (October 1920): 46-53. Teaches concerning the doctrine of mercy, repentance, and forgiveness, using Corianton, the son of Alma, as an example. [D.W.P.]

I.021 Ivins, Anthony W. Untitled talk. *CR* (April 1921): 18-21. Announces changes to the 1921 edition of the Book of Mormon. It has double columns, which reduced the size by one hundred pages, brief synopses of the books' contents, a list of the names and order of the books, revised footnotes, a pronouncing vocabulary, and an improved index. [J.W.M.]

I.022 Ivins, Anthony W. Untitled talk. *CR* (October 1923): 139-47. Refutes the charge of Mormon critics that Mormons do not teach Christ. Cites the title page and several passages of the Book of Mormon to indicate that the basic purpose of the book is to stand with the Bible as a second witness of Jesus Christ. [R.C.D.]

I.023 Ivins, Anthony W. Untitled talk. *CR* (April 1929): 8-16. Defends the Book of Mormon by answering major objections raised by critics. Cautiously he presents evidences of precolumbian usage of steel, domesticated animals (sheep, ox, horse), beautiful pearls, goldsmithing, and writings on plates of gold (with metal rings). Book of Mormon geography is also considered. [R.C.D.]

I.024 Ivins, Antoine R. "The Gospel and the Lamanites." *Relief Society Magazine* 25 (July 1938): 433-35. The Church has long been interested in the American Indians because they are descendants of Book of Mormon people. [K.M.]

I.025 Ivins, Antoine R. "The Lamanites." *Relief Society Magazine* 37 (August 1950): 507-14. The Book of Mormon devotes a major part of its account to discussing the Lamanite nation. It is a mistaken idea that all the indigenous groups of people who were found in America following the landing of Christopher Columbus were Lamanites. A testimony is not based on the external but internal evidences of the Book of Mormon. [J.W.M.]

I.026 Ivins, Antoine, R. Untitled talk. *CR* (9 April 1939): 128-31. The greatest knowledge one receives concerning Christ comes from the New Testament and the Book of Mormon, which is "a new witness for God." The sure way to know of the Book of Mormon's veracity is through Moroni's promise. [J.W.M.]

J.

J.001 J., W. "Stray Thoughts." *Juvenile Instructor* 18 (15 June 1883): 182-83. Notes the ill treatment and antagonistic attitude of the white people toward the Indians. According to the

Book of Mormon the Indians have a glorious destiny and the Latter-day Saints are urged to treat them with consideration. [D.M.]

J.002 Jackson, Kent P. "The Beginnings of Christianity in the Book of Mormon." In *The Book of Mormon: The Keystone Scripture*, edited by Paul R. Cheesman, S. Kent Brown, and Charles D. Tate Jr., 91-99. Provo, UT: Brigham Young University Religious Studies Center, 1988. Gives scriptural reasons why the Book of Mormon prophets who lived before Jesus' birth possessed and taught Christian teachings. Christological understanding was new to Lehi and Nephi and their knowledge unfolded at intervals. The sermons and reflections about Christ by Lehi, Nephi, and Jacob influenced subsequent Lehite prophets. [D.M.]

J.003 Jackson, Kent P. "Christ and the Jaredites." In *Studies in Scripture: Alma 30 to Moroni*, edited by Kent P. Jackson, 245-58. Salt Lake City: Deseret Book, 1988. Comments on how the Nephites and Mulekites became aware of the Jaredites. Focuses on Ether 1-4 and the supreme role played by the brother of Jared (Mahonri Moriancumer). Discusses Ether 3:15, the appearance of Jesus to the brother of Jared. [D.M.]

J.004 Jackson, Kent P. "The Lamanite Converts Firm in the Faith of Christ." In *Studies in Scripture Vol. 7: 1 Nephi to Alma 29*, edited by Kent P. Jackson, 335-45. Salt Lake City: Deseret Book, 1987. A chronicle of events found in Alma 24-29, which contrasts the behavior of the Amalekites and Amulonites with the converted Lamanites. Many spiritual lessons are to be learned in these chapters. [D.M.]

J.005 Jackson, Kent P. "Latter-day Saints: A Dynamic Scriptural Process." In *The Holy Book in Comparative Perspective*, edited by F. Denny and R. Taylor, 63-83. Columbia, SC: University of South Carolina Press, 1985. An essay dealing with the Latter-day Saint concept of scripture. Contains a section on the Book of Mormon, describing its origin, contents, and intention. Emphasizes its truthfulness and equality with the Bible in the LDS canon. [D.M.]

J.006 Jackson, Kent P. "Nephi and Isaiah." In *Studies in Scripture: 1 Nephi to Alma 29*, edited by Kent P. Jackson, 131-45. Salt Lake City: Deseret Book, 1987. Discusses the idea of likening scripture to one's own situation. Lists Isaiah's three major themes and explains why modern people have difficulty understanding the prophet. Outlines the Isaiah passages quoted in the Book of Mormon by topic. [D.M.]

J.007 Jackson, Kent P. "Neum." In *Encyclopedia of Mormonism*, edited by Daniel H. Ludlow, 3:1006. 5 vols. New York: Macmillan, 1992. Neum, mentioned once in the Book of Mormon, was an Israelite prophet that prophesied of different aspects of Christ's mortal mission. [A.T.]

J.008 Jackson, Kent P. " 'Never Have I Shown Myself unto Man.' A Suggestion for Understanding Ether 3:15a." *BYU Studies* 30 (Summer 1990): 71-76. A presentation of several interpretations of Ether 3:15, which discusses the appearance of Jesus to the brother of Jared. Jackson holds that while Christ had previously appeared to several pre-Jaredite prophets as Jehovah, the Father, he appeared for the first time in his role as Jesus Christ, the Son, and this was because of the exceeding faith of the brother of Jared. [J.W.M.]

J.009 Jackson, Kent P. "Nourished by the Good Word of God." In *Studies in Scripture: 1 Nephi to Alma 29*, edited by Kent P. Jackson, 185-95. Salt Lake City: Deseret Book, 1987. Refers to the prophet Zenos and discusses the importance of the scattering and gathering of Israel in salvation history, and then gives a brief step by step interpretation of the allegory of the olive tree in Jacob 5. [D.M.]

J.010 Jackson, Kent P. "Teaching from the Words of the Prophets." In *Studies in Scripture: Alma 30 to Moroni*, edited by Kent P. Jackson, 196-207. Salt Lake City: Deseret Book, 1988. Deals with Jesus' quotations of Malachi in 3 Nephi 24-25. Several themes are emphasized, including the purification of the sons of Levi, and the significance of the sealing keys restored by Elijah. [D.M.]

J.011 Jackson, Kent P. "The Tree of Life and the Ministry of Christ." In *Studies in Scripture: 1 Nephi to Alma 29*, edited by Kent P. Jackson, 34-43. Salt Lake City: Deseret Book, 1987. Features an overview of the images in Lehi's vision of the tree of life and presents specific concepts about Jesus and his mission in the same vision. Discusses the condescension of both the Father and the Son. [D.M.]

J.012 Jackson, Kent P. "Zenock." In *Encyclopedia of Mormonism*, edited by Daniel H. Ludlow, 4:1623. 5 vols. New York: Macmillan, 1992. Nephi, when teaching his family from the words of previous Israelite prophets, mentions Zenock as prophesying about the earthly mission of Jesus Christ. [A.T.]

J.013 Jackson, Kent P., ed. *Studies in Scripture Vol. 7: 1 Nephi to Alma 29*. Salt Lake City: Deseret Book, 1987. An collection of essays on themes from the first half of the Book of Mormon. [D.M.]

J.014 Jackson, Kent P., ed. *Studies in Scripture Vol. 8: Alma 30 to Moroni*. Salt Lake City: Deseret Book, 1988. A collection of essays on themes found in the second half of the Book of Mormon. [D.M.]

J.015 Jackson, Kent P., and Darrell L. Matthews. "Built upon Christ's Gospel." In *Studies in Scripture: Alma 30 to Moroni*, edited by Kent P. Jackson, 208-17. Salt Lake City: Deseret Book, 1988. Deals with the final four chapters of 3 Nephi, specifically analyzing the name of the Church, a definition of the gospel, the translated Three Nephites, and Mormon's counsel to modern readers not to reject revelation and miracles. [D.M.]

J.016 Jackson, Kent P., and Darrell L. Matthews. "The Lamanite Converts Firm in the Faith of Christ." In *Studies in Scripture: 1 Nephi to Alma 29*, edited by Kent P. Jackson, 335-45. Salt Lake City: Deseret Book, 1988. A chronicle of events found in Alma 24-29, which includes the contrasting behavior of the Amalekites and Amulonites with the converted Lamanites. Many lessons can be learned from these chapters by the modern-day reader. [D.M.]

J.017 Jackson, Kent P., and Morgan W. Tanner. "Zeniff and Noah." In *Studies in Scripture: 1 Nephi to Alma 29*, edited by Kent P. Jackson, 230-39. Salt Lake City: Deseret Book, 1987. Contrasts the righteous ways of Zeniff with the evil doings of King Noah, and then discusses the consequences of righteousness and evil. Provides comments on the character and message of Abinadi. [D.M.]

J.018 "Jacob and Sherem." *Friend* 20 (February 1990): 8-10. An illustrated story for children about Jacob and Sherem. [M.D.P.]

J.019 Jacobs, L. R. *Mormon Non-English Scriptures, Hymnals and Periodicals 1830-1986: A Descriptive Bibliography*. Salt Lake City: n.p., 1991. An alphabetical listing of translations of the Book of Mormon, including editions from both the LDS and RLDS Churches. Also includes an example of the script of the language and photocopies of the cover and/or title page. [J.W.M.]

J.020 Jacobs, Leone O., and Edith S. Elliot. "Visiting Teaching Messages: Book of Mormon Gems of Truth." *Relief Society Magazine* 38-44 (July 1951–February 1957). Monthly Book of Mormon lessons for adult women (Relief Society). Each month a verse of Book of Mormon scripture is presented with accompanying quotes from General Authorities and writers of the Church. [J.W.M.]

J.021 Jakeman, M. Wells. "Ancient American Religious Art." *UASN* 4 (20 January 1952): 9. Ancient art objects in the Americas correspond to Book of Mormon symbols, i.e., the brazen serpent and the tree of life. [D.M.]

J.022 Jakeman, M. Wells. "Ancient Maya Hieroglyphic Writings and Their Decipherment and Study." *UASN* 44 (27 September 1957): 2-4. Also in Christensen, Ross T. *Progress In Archaeology: An Anthology*, 128-30. The Book of Mormon records that there are records "of every kind" written (Helaman 3:15). Ancient Maya hieroglyphs are found on stelae, codices, vases, and on walls and steps of temples. The Mayan calendar found to be more accurate than its European counterpart dates to pre-Book of Mormon times. It is difficult to correlate it with the European calendar. [J.W.M.]

J.023 Jakeman, M. Wells. "The Ancient Middle-American Calendar System: Its Origin and Development." *UASN* 31 (9 December 1955): 1-2. Evidence shows that in middle America the calendar was first developed in the Lehite-Mulekite period. Calendars duplicate the ancient Israelite system. There is evidence of a final migration from Central America into Mexico that corresponds with the final migration of the Nephites in A.D. 327. The birth of the Christ-like god took place on April 6, A.D. 2, in correspondence with Joseph Smith's revelation (D&C 20:1). [J.W.M.]

J.024 Jakeman, M. Wells. "The Book of Mormon Civilizations in Space and Time." *UASN* 22 (August 1954): 1-5. An abstract of lectures given June 21-24. Before applying the "comparative archaeological test to the Book of Mormon," one must first be sure to deal with the correct area and period. The Tehuantepec area in Mesoamerica is by far the likely area. A sketch of the history of Mesoamerican archaeology establishes that only in recent years has material of the correct (Pre-Classic) era been available for analysis. Definite correspondences (not detailed) with the Book of Mormon account are evident. [J.L.S.]

J.025 Jakeman, M. Wells. "The City Bountiful Found?" *UASN* 22 (23 August 1954): 4-6. Defends the thesis that Bountiful was located in the "northernmost part of Central America, including the Isthmus of Tehuantepec." [D.M.]

J.026 Jakeman, M. Wells. *The Complex "Tree of Life" Carving on Izapa Stela 5.* Provo, UT: n.p., 1958. A booklet containing an analysis of the tree of life and other figures and depictions on Izapa Stela 5. Illustrations are provided. [D.M.]

J.027 Jakeman, M. Wells. *Discovering the Past: Introductory Readings and Visual Studies in Archaeology.* Provo, UT: University Archaeological Society, 1954. Guide for the beginning archaeology student. The Book of Mormon stands in conflict with popular explanations of the origins of the American people. Archaeology has confirmed the value of Homer's writings as well as the Bible. It has similar value for the Book of Mormon. Cultures found by archaeologists seem to fit Nephite cultures. [J.W.M.]

J.028 Jakeman, M. Wells. "Is Book of Mormon Archeology Valid? An Exchange of Letters." *UASN* 34-35 (30 April 1956; 8 June 1956): 4-6, 1-4. An anonymous Los Angeles physician inquires as to the historicity of the Book of Mormon. Jakeman replies that archaeological evidences of Mexico and Central America do not "disprove the Book of Mormon history" but appear "to establish it, to a high degree of probability." Jakeman admits that his findings are preliminary. [D.W.P.]

J.029 Jakeman, M. Wells. "Izapa Stela 5 and the Book of Mormon." In *Book of Mormon Institute*, edited by Dee F. Green, 47-53. Provo, UT: Extension Publications, 5 December 1959. See also *Instructor* 96 (December 1961): 410-11, 429. Three useful areas of correspondence between the Book of Mormon and modern science are geography, chronology, and similarities in culture traits. The Stela 5 depiction of the tree of life presents an arbitrary correspondence to the images in 1 Nephi 8. [D.M.]

J.030 Jakeman, M. Wells. "The Main Challenge of the Book of Mormon to Archaeology; and a Summary of Archaeological Research to Date Giving a Preliminary Test of Book of Mormon Claims." *UASN* 22.01 (23 August 1954): 2-4. Finding vast numbers of remains of both cultural and skeletal materials at archaeological sites is the main challenge to Book of Mormon archaeology. Further, these materials must match with Book of Mormon accounts in dating period, geographical area, and description. Excavations in Mexico and Central America have been made since 1830 that actually date according to the Book of Mormon period. [J.W.M.]

J.031 Jakeman, M. Wells. "Non-Mormon Archaeologists and the Book of Mormon, a Further Reply." *UASN* 57 (25 March 1959): 4-5. Non-Mormon archaeologists do not use the Book of Mormon as an archaeological guide, as some well-meaning Mormons have claimed. The Book of Mormon does not claim that all Indians are Lamanites. [D.M.]

J.032 Jakeman, M. Wells. "A Possible Remnant of the Nephites in Ancient Yucatan." In *Papers of the Fifteenth Annual Symposium on the Archaeology of the Scriptures*, edited by Ross T. Christensen, 110-19. Provo, UT: Brigham Young University, 1964. Evidences from archaeology and early historical sources are provided that show that the "Itzas," an ethnic group in prehispanic Yucatan, show at least nineteen similarities to the Nephites of the Book of Mormon. "We are justified in concluding that there is much more than a possibility that the Itzas were a remnant of the Nephites . . . who had migrated to Yucatan in the third century A.D., thereby escaping" the destruction of their fellows. [J.L.S.]

J.033 Jakeman, M. Wells. "Progress of 1961 Excavations at Aguacatal." *13th Annual Symposium on Archaeology of the Scriptures* (1 April 1961): 60-68. There are many possible sites for the Book of Mormon city Bountiful and its temple. One possible site is Aguacatal, which in many respects is similar to the descriptions of Bountiful in the Book of Mormon. [J.W.M.]

J.034 Jakeman, M. Wells. "Progress of Archaeology in Book of Mormon Lands." *UASN* 22 (23 August 1954): 2-4. Archaeological information about Book of Mormon lands has come to light largely since 1830. Since 1910 excavations have revealed the existence of two pre-classic periods in Mexico and Central America: "Early pre-classic" or "lower archaic" and "late pre-classic" or "upper archaic." Correspondences in these sites have been found in the Book of Mormon in areas, time or period, number and order, and characteristics. [D.M.]

J.035 Jakeman, M. Wells. "Stela 5, Izapa, as 'The Lehi Tree of Life Stone'; A Reply to Recent Attacks." *SEHA* 104 (29 November 1967): 2-11. Response to a critic who attempts to discredit Jakeman's study proposing that the Stela 5 is a depiction of Lehi's vision of the tree of life. Points out that the critic is unaware of the technical intricacies of Mesoamerican archaeology. [D.M.]

J.036 Jakeman, M. Wells. *Stela 5, Izapa, Chiapas, Mexico.* Provo, UT: UASN, 1958. A detailed commentary on Stela 5, beginning with some comparisons of Near Eastern depictions of the tree of life and continuing with a long section identifying points of contact with the tree of life parable in 1 Nephi. Some illustrations are included. [D.M.]

J.037 Jakeman, M. Wells. "Volcanoes in the Book of Mormon." *UASN* 8 (25 November 1952). Theorizes that the cataclysm in 3 Nephi resulted from a volcano (or several volcanoes) that are located near the central part of the narrow neck of land. [D.M.]

J.038 Jakeman, M. Wells. "Which Is the Way? A Reply to Dee F. Green's *Book of Mormon Archaeology: The Myths and the Alternatives*." *SEHA* 117 (December 1969): 1-6. A response to Green's 1969 attack (in *Dialogue*) on the "geographical-historical" approach to the Book of Mormon, which he attributed to Jakeman. Jakeman defends the logic and accomplishments of his approach (that he prefers to call "historic-archaeological"), taking umbrage at Green's implications of intellectual dishonesty in his labor. Ends by emphasizing his aim "for a conclusive determination of the authenticity of the Book of Mormon," which can only be done his way. [J.L.S.]

J.039 Jakeman, M. Wells. "Who Were The Mayas?" *IE* 43 (February 1940): 78-79, 119-20. Also in *A Book of Mormon Treasury*, 157-66. Salt Lake City: Bookcraft, 1959, 2nd printing 1976. Recounts some of the archaeological discoveries found in Central and South American sites that date before the advent of the Aztecs and the Mayas. Archaeological exploration and the Book of Mormon provide clues as to the origin of the Maya people. [A.T.]

J.040 Jakeman, M. Wells, and Bernhart Johnson. "Israelite-Phoenician Commercial Relations and the Voyage of Mulek to the New World." *SEHA* 140 (March 1977): 1-9. During the Solomonic period and after, Israel enjoyed international trade alliances with the Phoenicians. The Phoenician influence is found in the architecture of Israel as well as religious symbols. The authors conclude that Mulek, the son of King Zedekiah, fled Israel with

Phoenicians to the New World. There are several artifacts in the New World of Phoenician origin. [W.D.M.]

J.041 James, Rhett Stephens. "Harris, Martin." In *Encyclopedia of Mormonism*, edited by Daniel H. Ludlow, 2:574-76. 5 vols. New York: Macmillan, 1992. Contains a brief summary of Martin Harris's life. It includes details concerning his involvement with the Book of Mormon: assistance with the translation, taking a transcription to Charles Anthon, work as scribe, his 1829 prophecy that the Book of Mormon would be preached in England, and his experiences in becoming a witness to the Book of Mormon. [A.T.]

J.042 James, Uncle. "God's Great Men: Nephi." *MS* 50 (27 February 1888): 132-34. Nephi was young, probably under twenty years old, when he became a "pioneer and leader of the family." He was obedient, he was courageous in confronting Laban, and he never questioned or complained. [J.W.M.]

J.043 "The Jaredites Leave Babel." *Friend* 20 (April 1990): 20-21. An illustrated story for children about the Jaredites leaving Babel and preparing to cross the sea. [M.D.P.]

J.044 Jennings, Lillie, et. al. *Stories from the Book of Mormon*. Independence, MO: Herald House, 1956. Book of Mormon stories, geared to small children, are written by several authors. [D.M.]

J.045 Jensen, De Lamar. "The Popol Vuh and the Book of Mormon." *UASN* 16 (1 December 1953): 1-2. A discussion of the sacred *Popul Vuh,* or "book of the People," written in Maya-Quiché by a learned Quiché in the 16th century. The Popul Vuh deals with the history of the world and of the Quiché people. It has etiologic similarities with the Book of Mormon and points of contact with the Bible and the Pearl of Great Price. By way of example, the Quiché people trace their ethnic beginnings to four wandering brothers who were joined with two other families. [D.M.]

J.046 Jensen, Elwin W. *Captain Cook as the Fair God Lono*. Bountiful, UT: author, 1974. At the time that Captain Cook landed in Hawaii the local people assumed that he was the god Lono. On other occasions and with different characters similar scenes occurred in Mexico and Peru. Such occurrences recall the story that Jesus would someday return to the peoples of the Americas. [D.M.]

J.047 Jensen, Jay E. "Why We Ask People to Read the Book of Mormon." *Ensign* 14 (August 1984): 18-20. Claims that the doctrines of the gospel are taught more clearly in the Book of Mormon than anywhere else. The Book of Mormon has the ability to bring people closer to God and to convince them of the divinity of Jesus Christ and his mission. [S.P.S.]

J.048 Jensen, Joan Tondro. "Records of the Ancient People of the American Continents." In *A Symposium on the Book of Mormon*, 72-75. Salt Lake City: Church of Jesus Christ of Latter-day Saints, CES, August 1986. The Nephite leaders and prophets accumulated a large treasury of records and plates, and the Book of Mormon in its present form represents only a fraction of the corpus. [D.M.]

J.049 Jensen, Margie Calhoun, comp. *Stories of Insight and Inspiration*. Salt Lake City, UT: Bookcraft, 1976. A compilation of testimonies by numerous authors indexed according to gospel topics. Those under the heading of "Book of Mormon" were written by Gregory G. Vernon, Barbara Gail Mikeska, Rex D. Pinegar, an unnamed author, and Gregg Weaver. [J.W.M.]

J.050 Jensen, Nephi. "First Nephi and Archaeology." *IE* 22 (August 1919): 855-58. Specific archaeological findings and a number of legends that deal with the book of 1 Nephi are discussed. Neither Solomon Spaulding nor Joseph Smith could have known about the archaeological findings nor the legends. [D.M.]

J.051 Jensen, Nephi. "Isaiah 29." *IE* 13 (April 1910): 512-15. Jenson testifies that the Book of Mormon fulfills the prophecy in Isaiah 29. It is a record of a fallen nation, it was a marvelous work and a wonder that the boy Joseph Smith translated the book, and it has caused the meek to increase their joy in the Lord. [B.D.]

J.052 Jensen, Nephi. "Ten Outstanding Proofs of the Divinity of the Book of Mormon." *Liahona*

21 (8 April 1924): 399-400. Lists several proofs of the divinity of the Book of Mormon. For instance, the book contains historical information not known in 1830, it gives a substantial account of Jesus' ministry among his "other sheep," prophecies in the book have been fulfilled, and twelve witnesses saw the gold plates. [D.M.]

J.053 Jensen, Therald N. "Fragments of Social and Ethical Teachings of the Book of Mormon." *Week-day Religious Educator* 1 (March 1937): 3-5. Although the Book of Mormon does not contain definitive statements regarding ethical and social precepts, it does contain useful teachings regarding ethics, including statements on joy, the criteria and sanction of the good, freedom of the will, and guidelines for social problems. [D.M.]

J.054 Jenson, Andrew. "The Career of the Book of Mormon." *IE* 26 (September 1923): 963-68. A rehearsal of primary events connected with the Book of Mormon, including Joseph Smith's work with the gold plates, the conversion of several individuals (including Thomas B. Marsh, Willard Richards, Parley P. Pratt, and Sidney Rigdon) through the power of the book, and a discussion of the various translations of the Book of Mormon into foreign languages. [D.M.]

J.055 Jenson, Andrew. "David Whitmer." *The Historical Record* 7 (October 1888): 622-24. An obituary of David Whitmer that emphasizes his recollections of the emergence of the Book of Mormon. [D.M.]

J.056 Jenson, Andrew. "The Eight Witnesses." *The Historical Record* 7 (October 1888): 609-22. A biographical sketch of each of the Eight Witnesses of the Book of Mormon (with the exception of Hyrum Smith, and Joseph Smith Sr.). Underscores the fact that the witnesses never denied their experience of handling the plates. Mary Musselman Whitmer, the mother of the five Whitmer sons who were witnesses, is also identified. [D.M.]

J.057 Jenson, Andrew. "History and Genealogy." In *Collected Discourses Delivered by President Wilford Woodruff, His Two Counselors, The Twelve Apostles, and Others (1896-1898)*, edited by Brian H. Stuy, 5:36-46. Woodland Hills, UT: B. H. S. Publishing, 1992. The Book of Mormon records the importance of keeping records—Nephi returned for the brass plates to preserve the language and the law, men will be judged out of the records. [J.W.M.]

J.058 Jenson, Andrew. "Nephi—An Impressive Lesson." *IE* 30 (October 1927): 1093. Many examples from the life of Nephi impress the author to follow the example of Nephi. [J.W.M.]

J.059 Jenson, Andrew. "The Three Witnesses." *The Historical Record* 6 (May 1887): 195-219. A documentary recounting the lives of the Three Witnesses of the Book of Mormon. Attention is given to the Church careers of the men, with special emphasis on their experiences and testimonies relative to the Book of Mormon. [D.M.]

J.060 Jenson, Janet. "Variations Between Copies of the First Edition of the Book of Mormon." *BYU Studies* 13 (Winter 1973): 214-22. Not only are there differences between the several editions of the Book of Mormon, but there exist variations between copies of the first edition itself. The author compares seventy copies of the first edition and finds a number of variations (as illustrated in three tables), which include misspelled words or differences in capital and lower case words. [D.M.]

J.061 Jesclard, Paul Richard. "A Comparison of the Nephite Monetary System with the Egyptian System of Measure." *SEHA* 134 (October 1973): 1-5. Argues that there is "a connection between the Nephite monetary system, as detailed in the Book of Mormon (Alma 11:3-19), and the Egyptian *wedjat*-eye system of measuring grain." The Nephites altered a pattern of measuring money from the Near East. [D.M.]

J.062 Jessee, Dean C. "Joseph Smith Jr. in His Own Words, Part 1." *Ensign* 14 (December 1984): 22-31. Reprints 6 letters and refers to twenty-nine letters or documents and parts of two diaries that were written in the prophet Joseph Smith's own handwriting. Tells about the publication of the Book of Mormon. [J.W.M.]

J.063 Jessee, Dean C. "New Documents and Mormon Beginnings." *BYU Studies* 24 (Fall 1984): 397-428. Contains an evaluation of letters purportedly written by Joseph Smith to Josiah Stowell (June 18, 1825) and by Martin Harris to William W. Phelps (October 23, 1830). The first letter offers advice on trying to find a mine and the other deals with Book of Mormon origins. [D.M.]

J.064 Jessee, Dean C. "The Original Book of Mormon Manuscript." *BYU Studies* 10 (Spring 1970): 259-78. Discusses the preservation and handwriting of the original Book of Mormon manuscript. Contains pictures of sections of the original manuscript and a list of the original Book of Mormon holdings in the Church Historian's office. [L.D.]

J.065 Jessee, Dean C. "Solomon Spaulding and the Book of Mormon." In *The First Annual CES Religious Symposium: LDS Church History.* 57-68. Provo, UT: Brigham Young University, 1977. Reviews how Doctor Philastus Hurlbut suggested the connection between the Spaulding manuscript and the Book of Mormon. Offers reasons why the Spaulding explanation is untenable, even though it is constantly cited as the actual origin of the Book of Mormon. [D.M.]

J.066 Jessee, Dean C., comp. *The Personal Writings of Joseph Smith.* Salt Lake City: Deseret Book, 1984. Contains primary source material from Joseph Smith's writings and includes references to the coming forth of the Book of Mormon, as indicated in the index. Spelling in the original documents is retained. [D.M.]

J.067 "Jesus Lives and Loves Us All." *Friend* 7 (April 1977): 40-41. A story for children about Christ's ministry to the Nephites after his resurrection. [M.D.P.]

J.068 John, David. "Prophecies of the Coming Forth of the Book of Mormon and Their Fulfillment." *Young Woman's Journal* 2 (April 1891): 310-13. Quotes Isaiah 29 and prophecies within the Book of Mormon concerning its eventual appearance in the latter days. Recounts events surrounding its preparation for publication, with emphasis on the experiences of the Three Witnesses. [D.M.]

J.069 Johnson, Bernhart, and M. Wells Jakeman. "Israelite-Phoenician Commercial Relations and the Voyage of Mulek to the New World." *SEHA* 140 (March 1977): 1-9. Summarizes "extensive evidence, both literary and archaeological, of long and close . . . relations between ancient Israel and Phoenicia," resulting in a "partial 'Phoenicianization' " of the Israelites. Thus Book of Mormon Israelites in the New World must have had many Phoenician traits in their culture. Moreover it is likely that a Phoenician ship carried Mulek and his group to America. [J.L.S.]

J.070 Johnson, Clark V. "Alma's Counsel to His Sons." In *Studies in Scripture: Alma 30 to Moroni,* edited by Kent P. Jackson, 41-47. Salt Lake City: Deseret Book, 1988. Brief comments regarding the advice given by Alma the Younger to his first two sons, Helaman and Shiblon (Alma 36-38). Items taught by Alma include prosperity, the liahona, and Alma's own conversion story. [D.M.]

J.071 Johnson, Clark V. "The Beatitudes: Eight Qualities That Savor the Eternal Guest." In *The New Testament and the Latter-day Saints, Sperry Symposium, 1987,* edited by H. Dean Garrett, et. al., 115-28. Salt Lake City: Randall, 1987. An analysis and comparison of the beatitudes found in Matthew and 3 Nephi. [D.M.]

J.072 Johnson, Clark V. "From Small Means the Lord Brings about Great Things." In *The Book of Mormon: First Nephi, The Doctrinal Foundation,* edited by Monte S. Nyman and Charles D. Tate Jr., 231-39. Provo, UT: Brigham Young University Religious Studies Center, 1988. Demonstrates how the colony of Lehi was taught obedience to parents and to the Lord and the importance of the scriptures. The trials faced by the Lehites in the wilderness helped them to grow stronger physically and spiritually. [A.T.]

J.073 Johnson, Clark V. "Jacob: In Harmony with God." In *Studies in Scripture: 1 Nephi to Alma 29,* edited by Kent P. Jackson, 175-84. Salt Lake City: Deseret Book, 1987. A retelling of the incidents and comments in Jacob 1-3, 7. The Lord commissioned Jacob with the unenviable task of reproving the Nephites for unrighteous attitudes toward wealth, the sin of pride, and the practice of unchastity. The anti-Christ Sherem challenged Jacob regarding Christ's mission and thus met an ignominious end. [D.M.]

J.074 Johnson, Clark V. "Prophetic Decree and Ancient Histories Tell the Story of America." In *The Book of Mormon: Jacob through Words of Mormon, To Learn with Joy*, edited by Monte S. Nyman and Charles D. Tate Jr., 125-39. Provo, UT: Brigham Young University Religious Studies Center, 1990. Compares features of cosmology and salvation history (including the existence of a righteous and an evil power figure) in the Book of Mormon with the *Popol Vuh* (a sacred history of the Quiche Indians that was codified by an unknown writer to preserve generations of oral tradition shortly after the Spanish conquest of Guatemala in 1524). [D.M.]

J.075 Johnson, Marion Ashby. "Minverva Teichert: Scriptorian and Artist." *BYU Studies* 30 (Summer 1990): 66-71. Features fifty-four Book of Mormon paintings by Minverva Teichert and gives insights concerning the paintings. Also presents background information into Teichert's life. [J.W.M.]

J.076 Johnson, Marjorie G. *Book of Mormon Stories for Little Children*. Bountiful: Horizon, 1976. Selected stories from the Book of Mormon for young children, with illustrations. [D.M.]

J.077 Johnson, Orville S. "Irrefutable Evidence." *Relief Society Magazine* 19 (October 1932): 577-80. A story about Oliver Cowdery, who never denied his testimony of the Book of Mormon. [J.W.M.]

J.078 Johnson, R. Val. "Sage's Song." *Ensign* 19 (August 1989): 30-35. Tells the story of the badly burned Sage Volkman and her struggle for life. Sage tells of her visit with Christ while comatose. She bears testimony of the Book of Mormon. [J.W.M.]

J.079 Johnson, Roy. "Oaths in the Old Testament and Book of Mormon." Provo, UT: FARMS, 1982. The oath in ancient Israel and other ancient civilizations was important in political, religious, social, and legal life. It included two parts—a covenant and a curse—and was a binding force, irrevocable, and needed no social or civil enforcement, for God would mete out punishment on the false swearer. [J.W.M.]

J.080 Johnson, Sherrie. "Abish, Lamanite Woman of God." *Friend* 18 (February 1988): 48-49. A story for children depicting Ammon teaching the gospel to King Lamoni and recounting the testimony of Abish (Alma 19). [J.W.M.]

J.081 Johnson, Sherrie. "A Change of Heart." *Friend* 16 (January, February 1986): 48-49, 48. A story for children telling of the conversion of Alma the Younger and the sons of Mosiah (Mosiah 27, 29 and Alma 2-8) and relating the ministry of Alma the Younger in Ammonihah (Alma 13-15). [J.W.M.]

J.082 Johnson, Sherrie. "Convert to the Truth." *Friend* 16 (August 1986): 48-49. A children's story of Alma, Amulek, and Zeezrom (Alma 11-15, 31). [J.W.M.]

J.083 Johnson, Sherrie. "Courage to Believe." *Friend* 15 (October 1985): 48-49. The conversion of Alma, priest of Noah and his ministry at the waters of Mormon (Mosiah 18:23-25) is the topic of this children's story. [J.W.M.]

J.084 Johnson, Sherrie. "Cumorah Treasure." *Friend* 23 (February 1993): 48, ibc. A summary for children of the history of the Book of Mormon from the first vision to translation and publication. Illustrated. [S.H.]

J.085 Johnson, Sherrie. "Enos Prays." *Friend* 18 (January 1988): 48-49. A story for children that recounts Enos's experiences as he went into the forest and prayed (Jacob 7:27; Enos). [J.W.M.]

J.086 Johnson, Sherrie. "Gideon." *Friend* 18 (July, August 1988): 48-49, 48-49. A children's story recalling the experiences of Gideon (Mosiah 19-22; Alma 1; 2:20; 6:7). [J.W.M.]

J.087 Johnson, Sherrie. "Gidgiddoni: Prophet and Commander." *Friend* 18 (March 1988): 48-49. A story for children describing Gidgiddoni, the Nephite military leader (3 Nephi 3-4). [J.W.M.]

J.088 Johnson, Sherrie. "Lehi: Man of Vision." *Friend* 17 (October, November 1987): 48-49, 48-49. A child's story describing the prophet Lehi and his visions. [J.W.M.]

J.089 Johnson, Sherrie. "Martyr for Truth." *Friend* 15 (July 1985): 48-49. For children, the courageous story of Abinadi as he bears witness before King Noah (Mosiah 11-17). [J.W.M.]

J.090 Johnson, Sherrie. "Nephi, Man of Faith." *Friend* 18 (September 1988): 48-49. A story for children recalling when Nephi's brothers bound him, the power of the Lord loosened the cords, and Nephi forgave his brothers (1 Nephi 7). [J.W.M.]

J.091 Jolley, Katy. "A Calming Answer." *NE* 23 (April 1993): 49. Though her parents are divorcing, author finds peace and calm in reading the Book of Mormon. [S.H.]

J.092 Jones, Carl Hugh. "The 'Anthon Transcript' and Two Mesoamerican Cylinder Seals." *SEHA* 122 (September 1970): 1-8. A comparison of the "characters" from the Anthon transcript with two Mesoamerican scripts. The author concludes that the characters are similar. [D.M.]

J.093 Jones, Carl Hugh. "The Archaeological Paintings of George M. Ottinger." *14th Annual Symposium on Archaeology of the Scriptures* (13 April 1963): 5-11. Paintings and illustrations that include Lehi preaching in Jerusalem, the destruction of Zarahemla, Nephi's vision, building the temple at Nephi, offering sacrifice as a token of gratitude, and others. [J.W.M.]

J.094 Jones, Carl Hugh. "An LDS View of the Apparent Jomon-Valdivia Contact." *SEHA* 115 (8 September 1969): 4-6. Discusses possible travel routes of the Book of Mormon peoples. Points out that other groups may well have landed in the Americas. [D.M.]

J.095 Jones, Helen Hinckley. "A Writer Looks at the Book of Mormon." *IE* 63 (November 1960): 798-801, 834-35. A testimony of the Book of Mormon from the point of view of a successful and professional writer, Helen Hinckley Jones. In order to write an excellent book, it takes tremendous research, painstaking effort to build distinct characters, a complex form, a unique style of writing, and an appropriate theme, followed by laborious retracing, redoing, and revising. Joseph Smith had neither the talent nor the time to author the Book of Mormon. Jones concludes that Joseph Smith "was reading the Book of Mormon, not writing it." [R.C.D.]

J.096 Jones, Irene. *Know Your Scriptures: A Reading Program.* Independence: Herald Publishing House, 1966. Provides an outline for reading Book of Mormon passages as they refer specifically to the Old and New Testaments, then continues with a chapter-by-chapter content outline, a narrative outline, and a check-up quiz. [J.W.M.]

J.097 Jones, Miles L. Untitled talk. *CR* (April 1930): 123-25. When asked what publication we have that is the most reliable, or rather that gives us the most reliable information regarding the origin of the American Indian, a radio announcer replied that the Book of Mormon was. Jones gives a brief history of the Book of Mormon and its final publication. [B.D.]

J.098 Jones, Milton Jenkins. *Book of Mormon Chart Book.* Salt Lake City: Visual Arts Press, 1961. Four different charts show the Book of Mormon timeline, the historical setting of the books of the Book of Mormon, the angel Moroni's visits, and the translation of the book. [J.W.M.]

J.099 Jones, S. S. "Our Indian Brother." *MS* 35 (13 May 1873): 296-97. The author compares the rights given to the Negro with the rights given to the Native American Indian. The Negro is now made equal with his former master and has all rights of citizenship while the Indian is still pursued and persecuted by the U.S. Government. The Lamanite "is yet to go through 'to tear in pieces and none shall deliver' and yet to 'become a light and delightsome people.'" [B.D.]

J.100 Jorgensen, Bruce W. "The Dark Way to the Tree: Typological Unity in the Book of Mormon." In *Literature of Belief: Sacred Scripture and Religious Experience*, edited by Neal E. Lambert, 217-31. Provo, UT: Brigham Young University Religious Studies Center,

1981. A partial thematic interpretation of the Book of Mormon. The author seeks to uncover the book's "typological or figural unity" and finds this in the dream of the tree of life in 1 Nephi. Many themes emerge from the images in this dream. The themes show up in Jacob's allegory of the olive tree and in various conversion narratives. The dream symbolizes the process of moving through the wilderness and of reaching fulfillment. [D.M.]

J.101 "Journey to the Tower." *NE* 12 (November 1982): 46-47. Reader is asked to match a scriptural reference in Mosiah with nine different hypothetical situations. An activity for youth. [A.T.]

J.102 Judd, Ella Mae. *Sunday Afternoon Workbook for Study of the Book of Mormon.* 3 vols. Phoenix: n.p., 1978. A Book of Mormon workbook designed for children 9-16 years of age. Contains questions, fill in the blanks, and charts. [D.M.]

K.

K.001 Kapp, Ardeth G. "Captains of Ten." *NE* 13 (November 1983): 48-50. A youth oriented challenge to read the Book of Mormon. Youth relate testimonial experiences they had while reading the Book of Mormon. [A.T.]

K.002 Kee-Pi-Po-Kayo (One Hundred Bears) (J. J. Galbreath). "The Book of Mormon." *IE* 37 (March 1934): 139. A brief testimony of the truthfulness and value of the Book of Mormon, written by a man who is part Scottish and part Blackfoot Indian. [D.M.]

K.003 Keim, Laurence H. "My Odyssey Of Faith." *Ensign* 21 (April 1991): 28-30. A few months after baptism this author was given "anti-Mormon material." It was then that with earnest prayer, he turned to the Book of Mormon. He was called to serve as a mission trainer in Ecuador where he gained a testimony of the antiquity of the Book of Mormon. [J.W.M.]

K.004 Keller, Roger R. "Mormon and Moroni as Authors." In *Reexploring the Book of Mormon*, edited by John W. Welch, 269-71. Salt Lake City: Deseret Book and FARMS, 1992. Mormon and Moroni served as authors, compilers, and editors of the Book of Mormon. Wordprint studies and textual analyses demonstrate a distinction between their writings. For example, Mormon used an editorial expression "and thus we see" on twenty occasions, but Moroni utilized the expression once only. [N.K.Y.]

K.005 Kelley, E. L. *Antiquarian Evidences Concerning the Book of Mormon.* Independence, MO: Ensign, 1896. Speaks about the validity of the Bible and argues that God has spoken to the ancient western world as well as set forth in the Book of Mormon. Adduces archaeological evidence and arguments of reason to defend the Book of Mormon. [D.M.]

K.006 Kelley, William H. "Modern Scientific Disclosures Corroborate the Statement of Joseph Smith, Jr." In *Presidency And Priesthood: The Apostasy, Reformation, And Restoration,* 252-93. Lamoni, IA: Herald Publishing House, 1895. All of the Mediterranean languages had their birth in Mesopotamia and were transmitted by the descendants of Noah. Many archaeological finds substantiate that many languages derived form one common source. The Book of Mormon peoples had a very advanced civilization and show signs of borrowing from that common source. [J.W.M.]

K.007 Kelson, John H. "Wars of the Nephites and Lamanites." *Deseret Weekly* 43 (17, 24, 31 October 1891; 14 November 1891): 521-22, 561-62, 593-94, 657-58. Gives ethnic descriptions of Book of Mormon peoples and discusses them as inventors, explorers, and warriors. Cites archaeological findings that relate to the Book of Mormon. [D.M.]

K.008 Kerr, Todd R. "Ancient Aspects of Nephite Kingship in the Book of Mormon." *Journal of Book of Mormon Studies* 1 (Fall 1992): 85-118. Nephite kings were expected to fulfill the same roles that kings played in other ancient civilizations—commander of the military forces, chief judicial official, and leader of the national religion. A king's success depended not only on the extent to which he performed each role, but also on the motives behind his service. Some Nephite kings ruled selflessly (like Benjamin) and commanded the respect and praise of the people, while others (like Noah) sought for wealth and fame and roused Old World disdain. [R.H.B.]

K.009 Kienke, Asa Solomon. *Fourteen Objectives for the Reading and Study of the Book of Mormon.* N.p., 1920. Lists fourteen objectives with scriptural references for reading the Book of Mormon. Objective examples include: records and plates, prophecy yet to be fulfilled, and Christ's ministry among the Nephites. [D.M.]

K.010 Kimball, Spencer W. "Book of Mormon Message to the Lamanite." *CR* (October 1959): 57-62. Reviews the history of Israel and the Book of Mormon from the perspective of the Lamanite people. Describes the prophetic destiny of the Lamanites as a chosen people. [R.C.D.]

K.011 Kimball, Spencer W. "A Book of Vital Message." In *Faith Precedes the Miracle*, 329-37. Salt Lake City: Deseret Book, 1972. Also published in *IE* 66 (June 1963): 490-95. The contents of the Book of Mormon are multi-faceted. It contains elements pertaining to drama, archaeology, exploration, travel, anthropology, astronomy, geology, psychology, political science, scientists, military strategy, and many other subjects. The major value of the book is its religious influence upon individuals. [D.M.]

K.012 Kimball, Spencer W. "Conference Report, October 1977." In *Book of Mormon Talks by General Authorities*, 84-85. Provo, UT: FARMS, 1987. The liahona (1 Nephi 16) directed Lehi's family according to their faith. Every individual may have that kind of faith. [B.D.]

K.013 Kimball, Spencer W. "The Lamanite." In *BYUSY* (15 April 1953). Provo, UT: BYU Press. Quoting the Book of Mormon, the author points out the destiny of the Lamanite people and suggests that it is the responsibility of members of the Church to assist in the great work of recovering the Lamanites. Recounts the maltreatment of the Cherokee Nation and other Indian nations. [J.W.M.]

K.014 Kimball, Spencer W. "The Lamanite." *IE* 58 (April 1955): 226-28, 246, 250-58. An impassioned retelling of the horrible maltreatment by the white man of the Lamanites (more especially of the Cherokee, Sioux, Navajo, and Apache Indian Nations). This maltreatment was prophesied in the scriptures. President Kimball extends a poignant plea for Church members to possess an active concern for the Lamanites by giving them opportunity, understanding, and warm fellowship. [R.C.D.]

K.015 Kimball, Spencer W. "The Lamanite and the Gospel." In *Faith Precedes the Miracle*, 339-49. Salt Lake City: Deseret Book, 1972. The white man has exploited the American Indians and owes a debt to them. Prophecies regarding the Lamanites are recited. The condition of the Indian is improving, their numbers are improving and their standard of living is improving. [D.M.]

K.016 Kimball, Spencer W. "Lamanite Prophecies Fulfilled." Provo, UT: Brigham Young University Press, 13 April 1965. In a devotional address the speaker shares personal memories of his official ecclesiastical involvement with the American Indian. He reviews the progress they have made, both in joining the Church and in attaining a relatively high standard of living. President Kimball cites a number of scriptures and statements of Church leaders that deal with the future of the Lamanites. [D.M.]

K.017 Kimball, Spencer W. "The Lamanites: 'And They Shall Be Restored.' " *IE* 50 (November 1949): 717, 762-65. The Book of Mormon prophesies much concerning the Lamanites. It is the responsibility of the Church to help them to fulfill their great destiny. Many are receiving the gospel and are bearing fervent testimonies and living the gospel. A letter from a father to his son counsels the son to look for the "Mormons," who have the record of his people. The son then writes of his search for this book that would teach him the true gospel, which he found in the Book of Mormon. [J.W.M.]

K.018 Kimball, Spencer W. "The Lamanites Are Progressing." *IE* 56 (June 1953): 432-35. A testimony of the redemption of the Lamanites. Kimball gives examples of certain Lamanites who are progressing in the Church. [B.D.]

K.019 Kimball, Spencer W. "A Personal Liahona." *CR* (October 1976): 114-17. Speaking about the Book of Mormon Liahona, President Kimball describes how Lehi and Nephi "worked it" according to their "faith and diligence." The Liahona dictated to the Nephite group the direction of travel and the manner in which to act. President Kimball likens the Liahona to one's conscience, teaching that when an individual heeds the conscience, it will guide that person to righteousness. [R.C.D.]

K.020 Kimball, Spencer W. "Redemption of the Lamanites." In *The Teachings of Spencer W. Kimball*, edited by Edward L. Kimball, 594-620. Salt Lake City: Bookcraft, 1982. The term "Lamanite" "includes all Indians and Indian mixtures." The Lamanites have been greatly persecuted, especially in America. It is the Church's responsibility to help them. [B.D.]

K.021 Kimball, Spencer W. Untitled talk. *CR* (6 April 1960): 62-68. The Book of Mormon was Spencer Kimball's traveling companion and it thrilled him with its stories. Men of many professions would find the excitement of a life's work in this book, but its greatest power is to transform the lives of individuals and to bridge eternity. [J.W.M.]

K.022 Kimball, Spencer W. Untitled talk. *CR* (April 1963): 62-68. Many people may have interest in the Book of Mormon: gentiles, Jews, archaeologists, navigators, students and teachers, astronomers and geologists, politicians, and military men. It is most of all a sacred book, with the record of Christ's appearance in America. It is a second witness for Christ. [J.W.M.]

K.023 Kimball, Spencer W. Untitled talk. In *Proceedings of the LaPaz, Bolivia Area Conference*, 4-5, 14-15. Liverpool, England: Church of Jesus Christ of Latter-day Saints, March 1977. "Jesus did come and for some days he explained to the Lamanites and the Nephites, who are the parents of the Indians, the same doctrines that he had given the people in Jerusalem." [J.W.M.]

K.024 Kimball, Spencer W. Untitled talk. In *Proceedings of the New Zealand Area Conference*, 2-6. Salt Lake City: Church of Jesus Christ of Latter-day Saints, February 1976. In recent history, the Maoris came from Hawaii. Before that, however, they originated from the Book of Mormon seafarer called Hagoth (Alma 63). [D.M.]

K.025 Kimball, Spencer W. Untitled talk. In *Proceedings of the Tonga Area Conference*, 2-4. Salt Lake City: Church of Jesus Christ of Latter-day Saints, February 1976. A brief history of the scattering and gathering of God's people is given. A dispersion with relevancy to the Book of Mormon is detailed in Alma 63, where Hagoth the seafarer led a group of people from the American continent. Groups eventually settled in Hawaii, Tonga, and other islands of the South Pacific. [D.M.]

K.026 Kimball, Spencer W. "The Work among the Lamanites Must Not Be Postponed, If We Desire to Retain the Approval of God." *IE* 53 (December 1950): 980-82. An exhortation to work more towards redeeming the Lamanites. Kimball encourages the saints to remember them in their prayers and do their utmost to preach to them. He includes a prophecy of Joseph Smith that the saints will go to the Rocky Mountains and there open the door for establishing the gospel among the Lamanites. Wilford Woodruff designated the Zuni, Laguna and Isletas Indians of Southwest New Mexico as Nephite people. [B.D.]

K.027 Kimball, Stanley H. B. "The Anthon Transcript: People, Primary Sources, and Problems." *BYU Studies* 10 (Spring 1970): 323-52. Addresses a number of questions incidental to the Harris-Anthon episode, such as who encouraged Harris to consult Anthon (as well as Mitchell), what were the qualifications of the learned men, what was the value of their observations, how reliable was Harris's report, when was the transcript made, and when did the incident become public and become a missionary tool? [D.M.]

K.028 Kimball, Stanley H. B. "Charles Anthon and the Egyptian Language." *IE* 63 (October 1960): 708-10, 765. Knowledge concerning the Egyptian language was underdeveloped in the 1820s when Martin Harris presented the Book of Mormon characters and translation to

Dr. Charles Anthon. While Anthon was a known Egyptian scholar of the period, he nonetheless lacked sufficient knowledge to vouch for the accurate translation of the characters. [R.C.D.]

K.029 Kimball, Stanley H. B. "I Cannot Read a Sealed Book." *IE* 60 (1957): 80. Also in *A Book of Mormon Treasury*, 19-29. Salt Lake City: Bookcraft, 1959, 2nd edition 1976. Tells of Martin Harris's visit with Charles Anthon and Dr. Mitchell in New York City in February 1828. Presents a historical profile on Anthon and Mitchell. Answers why Martin Harris went to these men instead of any others and how valid their testimony was respecting the characters shown to them. [R.C.D.]

K.030 Kimball, William Clayton. "Partaking of the Fruit." *Ensign* 10 (July 1980): 16-19. A discussion concerning Alma's sermon (Alma 32) to the Zoramites about the seed of faith. A greater understanding of this pericope can be gained through an examination of the context, structure, and substance of the sermon. [D.M.]

K.031 "King Benjamin." *Friend* 12 (January 1982): 28-29. King Benjamin's address is recalled in cartoon form for children. [A.T.]

K.032 "King Benjamin." *Friend* 20 (August 1990): 18-21. Children's illustrated story of King Benjamin's tower. [M.R.]

K.033 "King Limhi and His People Escape." *Friend* 12 (May 1982): 30-31. Eleven cartoon drawings for children depicting the escape of Limhi's people. [A.T.]

K.034 King, Arthur Henry. "Language Themes in Jacob 5: 'The Vineyard of the Lord of Hosts Is the House of Israel' (Isaiah 5:7)." In *The Allegory of the Olive Tree: The Olive, the Bible, and Jacob 5*, edited by Stephen D. Ricks and John W. Welch, 140-73. Salt Lake City: Deseret Book and FARMS, 1994. An analysis of the rhetorical language of Jacob 5. The scriptures are to be read aloud to gain their full benefits. Jacob 5 is best understood when read in paragraphs as found in the 1830 edition. There are twenty-one paragraphs, each of which is introduced by ritualistic wording and shows a passage of time. [J.W.M.]

K.035 King, David S. "'Proving' the Book of Mormon: Archaeology Vs. Faith." *Dialogue* 24 (Spring 1991): 143-46. Reflects on the methodology and goals of Thomas Stuart Ferguson in his aspiration to discover the archaeological proofs of the Book of Mormon. Suggests that there are already accumulated numerous evidences of the Book of Mormon and that others will surface within science's "own inflexible timetable." While external evidences may be fascinating and illuminating, "our principle effort should be not so much to seek knowledge about the Book of Mormon as to seek knowledge of the Book of Mormon." [D.M.]

K.036 Kirkham, Francis W. "Attempts to Prove the Book of Mormon Man-made." *IE* 54 (October 1951): 726-28. Since the Book of Mormon was first published it "has withstood a century of attempts to prove it man-made." Gives examples of different attempts and shows how each has failed. [M.D.P.]

K.037 Kirkham, Francis W. "Attempts to Prove the Book of Mormon Man-Made." In *BYUSY* (23 February 1954). Provo, UT: BYU Press. Reviews published reports dating between the years 1829-1951 that attempt to prove that the Book of Mormon was a fraudulent work, and then points out the varied reasons people have for claiming the book to be man-made. [J.W.M.]

K.038 Kirkham, Francis W. "The Book of Mormon, Evidence that Jesus Is the Christ." *Instructor* 98 (February 1963): 70-71. Examines the title page of the Book of Mormon in view of other Hebrew writings. Discusses what the Book of Mormon tells of Christ. [L.D.]

K.039 Kirkham, Francis W. "Early Knowledge of America's Strangest Book." *IE* 47 (September 1944): 552. Discusses the publication and printing process of the Book of Mormon, the present location of the original manuscript of the book, and the statement of the Three Witnesses regarding the authenticity of the Book of Mormon. [L.D.]

K.040 Kirkham, Francis W. "The Manner of Translating the Book of Mormon." *IE* 42 (October 1939): 596-97, 630-32. Quotes Joseph Smith,

Oliver Cowdery, and other contemporary accounts to show how and where Joseph obtained the plates. Also quotes Emma Smith and the Three Witnesses to explain that the Book of Mormon was translated with divine aid and with the use of the Urim and Thummim. [A.C.W.]

K.041 Kirkham, Francis W. *A New Witness for Christ in America.* 2 vols. Independence, MO: Zion's, 1951, 2nd ed, Salt Lake City: Utah Printing, 1960. Volume 1 consists of a collection of primary documents from individuals, both sympathetic and antagonistic toward the Book of Mormon who were involved in the coming forth of the book. The documents deal with the circumstances in which Joseph Smith obtained the plates and the process of translation and printing the work. Volume 2 continues the compiler's selection of primary documents relative to varied opinions about the coming forth of the Book of Mormon. Most of the views set forth assume that the Book of Mormon came about in ways other than the process claimed by Joseph Smith. Included are early newspaper notices by Obadiah Dogberry and Alexander Campbell's resentful evaluation. [D.M.]

K.042 Kirkham, Francis W. *Suggestions for the Reading, Study, and Prayerful Consideration of the Book of Mormon.* Salt Lake City: Vanity, 1965. Three-page essay that encourages readers of the Book of Mormon to study the volume in such a way that they will receive a testimony. [D.M.]

K.043 Kirkham, Francis W. "Why the Book of Mormon?" *Instructor* 99 (December 1964): 472-73. Discusses the purpose and coming forth of the Book of Mormon, presents personal testimony regarding the truthfulness of the book, and speaks about how it helps humanity in their "search for happiness." [L.D.]

K.044 Kirkham, Francis W. "Why the Book of Mormon? Revealed Reasons for the Coming Forth of the Book of Mormon." *MS* 111 (June 1949); 168-69, 188-89. The Book of Mormon came forth in the midst of an unbelieving world that by faith and diligent study, mankind could come to know Jesus Christ by revelation. If the book had been a fraud, mistakes would have occurred on every page because of the complexity of the book. [J.W.M.]

K.045 Kirkham, Francis W. "The World's New Scripture." *MS* 98 (28 October 1937): 690-92. When the Book of Mormon was published, a local newspaper called it "The greatest piece of superstition that has come to our attention." Orson Pratt observed that the book was either true or "one of the most cunning, wicked, bold, deep-laid impositions ever palmed off upon the world." By 1937, the book was translated into sixteen languages and selling 50,000 copies a year. This should be adequate evidence of the divine nature of the book. [J.W.M.]

K.046 Kirkham, Francis W. "The Writing of the Book of Mormon." *IE* 44 (June 1941): 341-43, 370-75. An examination of the people and dates involved in translating the Book of Mormon. Very little of the translation occurred between the time Martin Harris lost the 116 pages of the Book of Lehi and Oliver Cowdery began serving as scribe on April 7, 1829. Information is provided regarding the hand-written manuscripts of the Book of Mormon. [D.M.]

K.047 Kirkham, James M. Untitled talk. *CR* (April 1936): 89-91. The author bears testimony of the divine nature of the Book of Mormon and that it comes from God, and he exhorts members to read and teach the Book of Mormon more. [J.W.M.]

K.048 Kirkland, Harriet Rosser. "A Book Different from Any Other." *Ensign* 16 (July 1986): 38-39. The personal conversion story and testimonial of a Jewish girl from New Jersey who converted to Mormonism through reading the Book of Mormon. [L.D.]

K.049 Knowlton, Clark S. "Problems in Book of Mormon Archaeology." *13th Annual Symposium on Archaeology of the Scriptures* (1 April 1961): 52-54. Book of Mormon archaeology presents many problems: the location of Book of Mormon lands is unknown; many researchers are not qualified and have made serious mistakes; some use writings that support LDS theology and ignore unsupportive writings. There is a need to test theories carefully and slowly create a basis of tested and proven evidence to support the Book of Mormon. [J.W.M.]

K.050 Kocherhans, Arthur J. *Lehi's Isle of Promise.* Fullerton, CA: Et Cetera, Et Cetera Graphics, 1989. A word study and commentary on the Book of Mormon, with maps and pictures. Defines words such as *knowledge, prophecy,* and *understanding* according to their 1828 meanings. The Nephites fulfilled the promises of God to Abraham, Isaac, Jacob, and Joseph who was sold into Egypt. [D.M.]

K.051 Kocherhans, Gib. "The Need for a Book of Mormon History." In *The Second Annual Church Educational System Religious Educators' Symposium: A Symposium on the Book of Mormon,* 71-73. Salt Lake City: Church of Jesus Christ of Latter-day Saints, 1979. Proposes that the Book of Mormon is an artistic work, compared to a symphony. Suggests outlining the book to make it more meaningful—gives examples of outlines for 1 and 2 Nephi. For example, an outline of 2 Nephi would highlight the patriarchal blessings, the doctrines of the fall and the atonement, the testimonies of Christ, and the coming forth of the Book of Mormon. [D.M.]

K.052 "Korean Book of Mormon." *IE* 70 (June 1967): 15. Discusses the translation of the Book of Mormon into Korean, published in Seoul, Korea. [L.D.]

K.053 "Korihor." *Friend* 23 (July 1993): 20-22. An illustrated story for children of Korihor (Alma 30). There is a caption under each picture summarizing the related scriptures. [S.H.]

K.054 Kotchongva, Dan. "Where Is the White Brother of the Hopi Indian?" *IE* 39 (February 1936): 82-84, 116, 118-19. Discusses the Hopi Indians and their connection with the Book of Mormon. An interpreted version of the Hopi Indian story as told by their chief in Salt Lake City. [L.D.]

K.055 Kraut, Ogden. *The Three Nephites.* Salt Lake City: Kraut, 1988. A collection of stories and testimonials from individuals who have claimed to have experienced encounters with the Three Nephites. [M.R.]

K.056 Kruckenberg, Janet. "Rummage-Sale Book of Mormon." *Ensign* 20 (February 1990): 69. A conversion story of a man and his family who were baptized after a Book of Mormon was discovered at a rummage sale. [L.D.]

K.057 Krueger, John R. *An Analysis of the Names of Mormonism.* Bloomington: Selbstverlag Press, 1979. A study of the proper names extant in the Book of Mormon. Author notes that over 140 biblical names occur in the Book of Mormon, while over 188 Book of Mormon names are nonbiblical. After a technical analysis the writer suggests that efforts "should be directed towards linking up the non-biblical names with names found in post-biblical literature, Talmudic materials, other Semitic languages; and particularly, in materials about South American and North American proto-languages." [M.R.]

L.

L.001 Lamb, David. "Behold, He Is the Word of Truth." *ZR* 50 (August 1990): 2. Shows the correlation between the Book of Mormon identification of Christ as the "Word of Truth" (Alma 18:12, RLDS versification) and the Hebrew term for truth (*'emeth*). [A.T.]

L.002 Lamb, David. "The Four-Part Pattern in Prophecies." *ZR* 44 (August 1989): 1, 8. In the Old Testament there is a four-part pattern used by prophets in prophesying: "(1) identification of sin, (2) need for repentance, (3) judgment of God (if people do not repent), and (4) future in Christ." The article shows how Samuel the Lamanite, Alma$_2$, Lehi, and Abinadi followed this pattern. [A.T.]

L.003 Lamb, David. "Friend: A Covenant Term." *ZR* 49 (June 1990): 1, 3-4. Also in *Recent Book of Mormon Developments; Articles From the Zarahemla Record,* 2:50-51. Independence, MO: Zarahemla Research Foundation, 1992. The term friend is often used to express a covenantal agreement between two individuals. Such was the case between Zoram and Nephi (2 Nephi 1:55, RLDS versification). Other examples include Isaiah 41:8, 2 Chronicles 20:7, and Zechariah 13:6. [A.T.]

L.004 Lamb, David. "The Meaning Behind Moroni's Title of Liberty." *ZR* 45 (November 1989): 1-2. Moroni and the Title of Liberty feature a "step-by-step procedure on preparation for spiritual warfare through the upholding of Jesus Christ." These steps are: despise evil, humble ourselves, put on the armor of God, seek God's instruction through prayer, work to save the nation, and look to the Lord. [A.T.]

L.005 Lamb, David. "The Meaning of the Name 'Mormon.'" *ZR* 43 (June 1989): 1-2. Suggests that the Book of Mormon was not named after a man, but after a place called Mormon where the Nephites once covenanted to observe the laws of God. This important place was very suitable as a name for a book of scripture. [A.T.]

L.006 Lamb, David. "Priests and Teachers." *ZR* 59 (January/February 1992): 1, 4. Points out several doublets in the Bible and Book of Mormon: parents and teachers, priest and scribe (teacher), Lord and master (teacher), ruler and teacher, and teacher and king. It is characteristically Hebraic to think of a vocation or calling in connection with being a teacher; thus the emphasis on teacher is an evidence for the authenticity of the Book of Mormon. [D.M.]

L.007 Lamb, David. "The Righteous Branch." *ZR* 48 (April 1990): 64. Both Lehi and Jeremiah denominate Joseph of Egypt (2 Nephi 3) as the "righteous branch," an expression that generally refers to Christ. This fact suggests that Lehi possessed or had access to a copy of Jeremiah's writings or that Nephi and Jeremiah were acquaintances. [A.T.]

L.008 Lamb, David. "Search the Words of Isaiah." *ZR* 60 (March/April 1992): 1, 4. Suggests following the directive of Jesus to take the writings of Isaiah seriously. To accomplish this assignment one must learn the manner of the Jews. [D.M.]

L.009 Lamb, David. "A Turnabout in the Meaning of Repentance." In *Recent Book of Mormon Developments; Articles From the Zarahemla Record*, 2:224-25. Independence, MO: Zarahemla Research Foundation, 1992. Lamb explains the Hebrew meaning of the verb "to repent" (*shub*) and shows that the Book of Mormon treatment of repentance is in accordance with the Hebrew. For example, 3 Nephi 8:65 (RLDS versification) says "return and repent." *Shub* means to turn around or return. [B.D.]

L.010 Lamb, David. "What's in a Number?" In *Recent Book of Mormon Developments; Articles From the Zarahemla Record*, 2:41. Independence, MO: Zarahemla Research Foundation, 1992. Examines Mosiah 11 (RLDS versification) in light of the symbolism of numbers. Alma's people first traveled eight days (Mosiah 11:1-4). Eight symbolizes new beginnings. In Mosiah 11:72 Alma's people travel one day. One symbolizes unity. They arrived in Zarahemla 12 days later (Mosiah 11:75-76). Twelve symbolizes perfection of government. Finally their total journey of 21 days symbolizes divine completion. [B.D.]

L.011 Lambert, James R. *Objections to the Book of Mormon and the Book of Doctrine and Covenants Answered and Refuted.* Lamoni, IA: Herald Publishing House, 1894. [R] 1898. Responds to critics of the Book of Mormon. Writes concerning metal plates, manner of translation, poor grammar, rapid population growth, dark color of Lamanites, modern words used in the translation, polygamy, place of Christ's nativity, Holy Spirit given before Christ came in the flesh, the charge of plagiarism, and the Spaulding theory. [B.D.]

L.012 Lambert, L. Gary. "Allegory of Zenos." In *Encyclopedia of Mormonism*, edited by Daniel H. Ludlow, 1:31-32. New York, NY: Macmillan Publishing Company, 1992. A brief description of the allegory of Zenos from Jacob 5. The allegory reinforces Jacob's teachings about Jesus Christ and the house of Israel's anticipated unresponsiveness toward the coming Redeemer, and instructs the people about the promised future gathering of Israel. [B.D.]

L.013 Lambert, L. Gary. "Alma$_1$." In *Encyclopedia of Mormonism*, edited by Daniel H. Ludlow, 1:32-33. New York, NY: Macmillan Publishing Company, 1992. A brief description of Alma the Elder's life and ministry including his genealogy, occupation, how he was converted to God through Abinadi, his leadership, and the influence he and his descendants had on the Church. [B.D.]

L.014 Lambert, R. G. "Hawaiian Mythology." *Juvenile Instructor* 11 (15 October 1876): 235. Sees some elements of Hawaiian myth as correlative to the Book of Mormon. Sites some particulars of Captain Cook. [D.M.]

L.015 Lambert, Roy. *The Weight of an Angel*. Salt Lake City: Bookcraft, 1961. A biography of Moroni, based on the Book of Mormon and comments from LDS authorities. [D.M.]

L.016 Lambert, William O. G. "The Earth's Interior." *Our Desert Home* 2 (June-July 1883): 126-29, 152-53. Argues that the scriptures, including the Book of Mormon, refer to places inside the earth. Makes reference to the parable of the olive tree and to the habitation of the lost tribes of Israel. [D.M.]

L.017 Lamoreaux, Adam. "Book of Mormon Bibliography." In *Review of Books on the Book of Mormon* 2 (1990): 267-73. Provides a bibliography of books and articles that have been written about the Book of Mormon between the years 1984 and 1989. Listed by author. [J.W.M]

L.018 Lancaster, James E. "The Method of Translation of the Book of Mormon." In *Restoration Studies III*, edited by Maurice L. Draper, 220-31. Independence, MO: Herald House, 1986. Reprint from the *John Whitmer Historical Association Journal* 3 (1983): 51-61. Analyzes the method of translation by Joseph Smith of the Book of Mormon. Joseph Smith gave no specific details about the translation process, but simply stated that the book was translated by the "gift and power of God." Witnesses relate that there were two translational aids, first the Urim and Thummim and later the "seer stone." [J.W.M.]

L.019 "A Land of Promise." *Relief Society Magazine* 5 (April 1918): 233-36. The Book of Mormon taught that America is a land of promise and the hope of the world. All other lands stretch out their hands for the material, political, and spiritual wealth that America offers. [J.W.M.]

L.020 Landon, Donald D. *The Book of Mormon is Christian*. Independence, MO: Herald House, 1962. A tract designed to persuade the reader that Christology in the Book of Mormon qualifies the book to be Christian scripture, consistent with the Bible. [D.M.]

L.021 Landon, Donald D. *How the Book of Mormon Confirms the Message of Christ*. Independence, MO: Herald House, 196?. A tract published by the Reorganized Church designed to introduce interested readers to the Book of Mormon. Teachings from the Book of Mormon are consistent with and in agreement with biblical doctrines. [D.M.]

L.022 Lane, Keith H. "Symbolic Action and Persuasion in the Book of Mormon." M.A. thesis, Brigham Young University, 1990. Takes the methodology of Kenneth Burke to plead that Mormons read some passages of the Book of Mormon as rhetorical devices and accept Christ and live by his code. The rhetoric is couched within "scenes" from the Book of Mormon. [D.M.]

L.023 "Languages of the Book of Mormon." *Ensign* 22 (August 1992): 80. By the end of 1991 the Book of Mormon had been translated into ninety languages. [A.C.W.]

L.024 Largey, Dennis L. "The Book of Mormon, an Interpretive Guide to the New Testament." In *The New Testament and the Latter-day Saints, Sperry Symposium, 1987*, edited by H. Dean Garrett, et. al., 129-47. Salt Lake City: Randall, 1987. Demonstrates through several examples how the Book of Mormon clarifies doctrines only tacitly dealt with in the New Testament. Comments on President Benson's statements that the Book of Mormon confounds false doctrine and that members of the Church should know it better than any other text. [D.M.]

L.025 Largey, Dennis L. "Built Upon the Rock." *Ensign* 22 (January 1992): 47-51. Study of the Book of Mormon makes a difference in testimony, gospel knowledge, and lays a firm foundation for faith in Christ. The Book of Mormon contains the "words of life" and is a "voice of warning," supports and enhances biblical teachings and was vital to the Restoration. [A.C.W.]

L.026 Largey, Dennis L. "Enduring to the End." In *Doctrines of the Book of Mormon, 1991 Sperry Symposium*, edited by Bruce A. Van Orden and Brent L. Top, 57-69. Salt Lake City: Deseret Book, 1992. The principle of enduring to the end is specifically taught 22 times throughout the Book of Mormon. Endurance might be considered the fifth of the first principles and ordinances. God's children are to endure afflictions and temptations, to continue in the faith, and are entitled to divine help. Enemies of endurance include Satan's inspiration, murmuring, hardness of heart, immorality, apostasy, and priestcraft. [N.K.Y.]

L.027 Largey, Dennis L. "The Enemies of Christ: 2 Nephi 28." In *The Book of Mormon: Second Nephi, The Doctrinal Structure*, edited by Monte S. Nyman and Charles D. Tate Jr., 287-305. Provo, UT: Brigham Young University Religious Studies Center, 1989. Discusses how 2 Nephi 28 exemplifies President Benson's proposition that the Book of Mormon reveals Christ's enemies. The following forms of enemies are treated: (1) the precepts of men or false doctrines, (2) spurious teachers, (3) pride, and (4) Satan. [D.M.]

L.028 Largey, Dennis L. " 'Enemies of Righteousness': The Book of Mormon Identifies Latter-day Forces That Oppose the Lord." *Ensign* 19 (December 1989): 6-11. Shows how 2 Nephi 28 exposes the enemies of Christ. They are identified as false doctrines, false teachers, priestcrafts, pride, apathy, and Satan. [D.M.]

L.029 Largey, Dennis L. "Enos: His Mission and His Message." In *The Book of Mormon: Jacob through Words of Mormon, To Learn with Joy*, edited by Monte S. Nyman and Charles D. Tate Jr., 141-56. Provo, UT: Brigham Young University Religious Studies Center, 1990. Enlarges on several themes in Enos including forgiveness as a consequence of a "wrestle before God," concern for other people, revelation, confidence that the Lord honors his covenants with his disciples, and the importance of parents teaching their children. [D.M.]

L.030 Largey, Dennis L. "Lessons from the Zarahemla Churches." In *The Book of Mormon: Mosiah, Salvation Only through Christ*, edited by Monte S. Nyman and Charles D. Tate Jr., 59-71. Provo, UT: Brigham Young University Religious Studies Center, 1991. The materials in Mosiah 25-27 were selected for the benefit of members of the Church: the standard of truth is set forth for a darkened world; the Nephites dealt with flattery, teaching the rising generation, persecution, transgression in the Church; and the conversion of Alma the Younger and the Sons of Mosiah is a model for hope. [D.M.]

L.031 Larsen, Dean L. "Likening the Scriptures unto Us." In *The Book of Mormon: Alma, The Testimony of the Word*, edited by Monte S. Nyman and Charles D. Tate Jr., 1-13. Provo, UT: Brigham Young University Religious Studies Center, 1992. The Book of Mormon bears a primary role in standing as a second witness of Jesus' divinity. It also holds a great value by virtue of what we can learn from the experiences of the people in the record by finding vivid parallels for our own day. For instance, the people of the Book of Mormon sometimes dwindled in unbelief and apostasy, often followed periods of righteousness and prosperity. [N.K.Y.]

L.032 Larsen, Dean L. "Looking Beyond the Mark." *Ensign* 17 (November 1987): 11-12. Makes an analogy between the shot put of an athlete and the scripture that states that "blindness came by looking beyond the mark" (Jacob 4:14). The mark needs to be faith in Jesus Christ. Replacing faith in the Savior with other goals, including pursuing the mysteries, pride, and reading scriptural commentaries only is the downfall of mankind. [J.W.M.]

L.033 Larsen, Dean L. *You and the Destiny of the Indian*. Salt Lake City: Bookcraft, 1966. Largely concerned with the identity of the American Indians, their noble heritage, and their role in the events of the latter days. Several Book of Mormon passages dealing with the Lamanites are reviewed and listed. [D.M.]

L.034 Larsen, Wayne A., and Alvin C. Rencher. "Response to Book of Mormon 'Wordprints' Reexamined" *Sunstone* 6 (March-April 1981): 22-26. A reaction to an article by D. James Croft (*Sunstone*, March-April 1981) who challenges the methodology of an earlier article by Larsen and Rencher (*BYU Studies*, Spring 1980). Larsen and Rencher claim that different word styles of each Book of Mormon author can be reasonably maintained, though they recognize that their studies have limitations. [D.M.]

L.035 Larsen, Wayne A., Alvin C. Rencher, and Tim Layton. "Multiple Authorship of the Book of Mormon." *NE* 9 (November 1979): 10-13. Results of the author's use of statistical analysis to determine how many individuals authored the Book of Mormon. Results: "The odds against these books being the work of one author exceeded 100 billion to one!" Also compares Book of Mormon authors with Joseph Smith's contemporaries, specifically men suggested as having been authors of the Book of Mormon. Result: "None of the wordprints of the modern authors resembled the Book of Mormon wordprints at all." Also did cluster analysis, discriminant analysis, and classification analysis. A brief description is given of each with the results. [A.T.]

L.036 Larsen, Wayne A., Alvin C. Rencher, and Tim Layton. "Who Wrote the Book of Mormon? An Analysis of Wordprints." *BYU Studies* 20 (Spring 1980): 225-51. Also in *Book of Mormon Authorship: New Light on Ancient Origins*, edited by Noel B. Reynolds, 157-88. Provo, UT: Brigham Young University Religious Studies Center, 1982. Tests the claim that the Book of Mormon was written by a number of ancient authors using an analysis called "wordprint" or the science of stylometry. Discusses potential non-Book of Mormon authors, Manova, cluster analysis, and classification analysis. [L.D.]

L.037 Larson, Anthony E. *Parallel Histories: The Nephites and the Americans.* Orem, UT: Zedek Books, 1989. Suggests ways in which incidents and historical situations in the Book of Mormon are similar to those of the present era. Twelve parallels may be drawn between the Book of Mormon society and modern American society that may predict future events in America. Both nations had similar origins and crossed the ocean as a result of difference of religion and philosophy. Both degenerated in morality. [J.W.M.] [D.M.]

L.038 Larson, Clinton F., Stuart Heimdal, and Paul R. Cheesman. *Illustrated Stories from the Book of Mormon.* Provo, UT: Promised Land Publications, 1967. This is a sixteen-volume work for young readers. Major events are narrated and illustrated. [B.D.]

L.039 Larson, Stanley R. "Changes in Early Texts of the Book of Mormon." *Ensign* 6 (September 1976): 77-82. Makes comparisons between the original hand-written printer's manuscript and subsequent editions of the Book of Mormon, pointing out changes in the Book of Mormon texts. Author examines the changes made and comes to the conclusion that these corrections, when properly reviewed, become a testimony for the truthfulness of the book rather than witnessing against it. Photographs of the original manuscripts are included. [J.W.M.]

L.040 Larson, Stanley R. "Conjectural Emendation and the Text of the Book of Mormon." *BYU Studies* 18 (Summer 1978): 563-69. Proposes a number of plausible conjectural emendations for the text of the Book of Mormon, namely: "sun of righteousness" rather than "son of righteousness," rights for rites, raiment rather than remnant in 2 Nephi 24:19, travail versus travel, Shiblom versus Shiblon, year instead of yea (in several cases), desert versus dissent, and possible examples of accidental word loss. [R.S.]

L.041 Larson, Stanley R. "Early Book of Mormon Texts: Textual Changes to the Book of Mormon in 1837 and 1840." *Sunstone* 1 (Fall 1976): 44-55. Classifies and discusses the main types of textual changes in the 2nd (1837, Kirtland) and 3rd (1840, Nauvoo) editions of the Book of Mormon, including corrections of typos from the 1st (1830, Palmyra) edition, revisions by Joseph Smith for the 2nd edition, corrections in the 3rd edition by reference to the original manuscript, and accidental errors in both editions. [R.S.]

L.042 Larson, Stanley R. "I Have a Question: Chronological dates are recorded at the bottom of the pages in the Book of Mormon. How reliable are these dates? Are there any that need to be corrected?" *Ensign* 7 (September 1977): 38-39. The Book of Mormon gives a fairly accurate chronological dating system. The notes are provided to assist the reader in converting that system into the dating system used in the present era. [J.W.M.]

L.043 Larson, Stanley R. "A Most Sacred Possession: The Original Manuscript of the Book of Mormon." *Ensign* 7 (September 1977): 89-91. Provides a brief historical outline of the original manuscript, during and after the translation, a detailed description of the appearance of the manuscript, and a synopsis of its value. He points out four examples of corrections that have been made. Church historian Leonard Arrington believes that this document is the most sacred possession of the Church. [J.W.M.]

L.044 Larson, Stanley R. "A Study of Some Textual Variations in the Book of Mormon Comparing the Original and the Printer's Manuscripts and the 1830, the 1837, and the 1840 Editions." M.A. thesis, Brigham Young University, 1974. A horizontal columnar comparison of the original manuscript, the printer's manuscript, corrections in the printer's manuscript for the 1830, 1837, and 1840 editions. Also presents a review of the bringing forth of the Book of Mormon, and six appendices. [D.M.]

L.045 Larson, Stanley R. "Textual Variants in the Book of Mormon Manuscripts." *Dialogue* 10 (Autumn 1977): 8-30. Examines fifty textual changes found in the currently published Book of Mormon in contrast with the original hand-copied printer's manuscript. There are three categories of variations: (1) corrections within the manuscripts themselves, (2) transcription errors, and (3) differences between the manuscript version and the printed copy. [J.W.M.]

L.046 Lassetter, Courtney, J. "Lehi's Dream and Nephi's Vision: A Look at Structure and Theme in the Book of Mormon." *Perspective: A Journal of Critical Inquiry* (Winter 1976): 50-54. A challenge to the idea that the Book of Mormon is composed of discreet, unrelated episodes, but rather it is literarily unified. The vision of the tree of life, for example, unfolds themes that appear throughout the book. The symbolism of the tree of life as the love of God as manifested in Christ is seen dramatically through a chronological view of Jesus' role on earth—from his condescension, to the crucifixion, to his personal visit to the Lehites. [D.M.]

L.047 Laub, Normand D. "He Knew David Whitmer." *Ensign* 11 (September 1981): 63. While laboring as a missionary in Jackson County, Missouri, this author met a man who as a child had known David Whitmer and was present when Whitmer bore witness of the Book of Mormon prior to his death. [J.W.M.]

L.048 Layton, Lynn C. "An 'Ideal' Book of Mormon Geography." *IE* 41 (July 1938): 394-95, 439. Contains a map of the proposed geography of the Book of Mormon but does not super-impose this geography over a present-day map. The author makes an analysis of the geographical descriptions in the Book of Mormon text. [J.W.M.]

L.049 Layton, Lynn C., and H. J. Layton. *Book of Mormon Lands*. n.p., 194?. Speculates on Book of Mormon geography. Defends the view that Moroni hid the plates in upstate New York. [D.M.]

L.050 Lea, Leonard J. *Compendium of the Scriptures: Including Texts of the Standard Books of the Church*. Independence, MO: Herald Publishing House, 1951. Compendium of scriptural references from the Book of Mormon and other standard works of the RLDS church appear under subject headings to assist greater understanding of doctrinal topics. Topics include the divine nature of God, the Book of Mormon, divine revelation, authority and priesthood. [J.W.M.]

L.051 "The Learning of the Peoples of the Book of Mormon." *The Relief Society Magazine* 5 (September 1918): 534. The Book of Mormon peoples had access to the early teachings of the Bible. They had great opportunities of learning and built complex and important civilizations. The tedious task of record keeping on plates of metal seriously hampered their ability to pass on their learning. [J.W.M.]

L.052 Leavitt, Janit Perry. "Prized Possession." *Friend* 23 (June 1993): 15-17. A story for children teaching that the Book of Mormon is a "prized possession" that should be shared with friends. [S.H.]

L.053 LeBaron, E. Dale. "The Book of Mormon: Pattern in Preparing a People to Meet the Saviour." In *Doctrines of the Book of Mormon, 1991 Sperry Symposium*, edited by Bruce A. Van Orden and Brent L. Top, 70-79. Salt Lake City: Deseret Book, 1992. One of the purposes of the Book of Mormon is to provide guidance in preparing individuals and groups for the Second Coming of Jesus. The editors (Nephi, Mormon, Moroni) saw our day and selected materials that are germane to this era. The signs of the coming are becoming so common that we scarcely recognize them. [D.M.]

L.054 LeBaron, E. Dale. "The Role of the Book of Mormon in Preparing a Generation to meet the Savior." In *The Sixth Annual Church Educational System Religious Educators' Symposium on the Book of Mormon*, 48-51. Salt Lake City: Church of Jesus Christ of Latter-day Saints, 1982. Discusses the great experiences of Nephi, Mormon, and Moroni that qualified them to write and abridge the Book of Mormon. All three were personally visited by Jesus Christ and received a clear vision of the latter days. Therefore, their input to the Book of Mormon is geared specifically for the latter days and preparing individuals for the Second Coming. The article includes two charts illustrating Book of Mormon references regarding latter-day challenges and "Mormon's Abridging Methods—Ratio of Pages to Years." [A.T.]

L.055 Lee, Harold B. "Communion with Deity." *IE* 69 (December 1966): 1142-44. Aaron chided Ammon for boasting, but Ammon reminded his brother that he did not boast in his own strength, but in the strength of God. Spiritual strength is needed to serve in our earthly missions thus we must be attuned to God through repentance, faith, good works, and continual prayer. [J.W.M.]

L.056 Lee, Harold B. "The Iron Rod." *Ensign* 1 (June 1971): 5-10. See also *CR* 141 (April 1971): 89-94. Lehi's vision of the tree of life provides the best antidote for the modern malady known as aimlessness. The rod of iron or the word of God gives direction to those who are seeking. Liberals both in the Church and out are like those who scoffed in the vision. Hold fast to the iron rod and continue to learn the truths of the Savior to remain steadfast. [J.W.M.]

L.057 Lee, Hector. *The Three Nephites: The Substance and Significance of the Legend in Folklore*. Albuquerque, NM: University of New Mexico Press, 1949. A scholarly analysis of the legend of the Three Nephites among Latter-day Saints in Utah. Lee explains the history of the Three Nephites and shows the chronological frequency and distribution of the legends. Lee analyzes the dominant motifs of the legends and discusses their historical, sociological, and psychological impact. More than thirty legends of the Three Nephites are included in the appendix. [B.D.]

L.058 Lee, Rex E. "The Book of Mormon: Another Testament of Jesus Christ," in Lee's, *What Do the Mormons Believe?* 11-18. Salt Lake City: Deseret Book, 1992. Gives an overview of Book of Mormon contents in one chapter. Notes that external evidences of the Book of Mormon are interesting but not critical, for they are as yet tentative. Emphasizes the spiritual power generated in the book. [D.M.]

L.059 "Lehi Leaves Jerusalem." *Friend* 19 (June 1989): 40-41. For children, contains illustrative cartoon panels narrating Lehi and his family fleeing Jerusalem. [D.M.]

L.060 "Lehi Warns the People." *Friend* 19 (May 1989): 15. For children, cartoon illustrations and written narrative explains Lehi's dealings with the people of Jerusalem. [D.M.]

L.061 "Lehi's Dream." *Friend* 19 (September 1989): 20-22. For children, depicts cartoon drawings of Lehi's vision of the tree of life. [D.M.]

L.062 "Lehi's Warning." *Friend* 11 (January 1981): 20-21. Story of Lehi designed for children in cartoon form. [J.W.M.]

L.063 Leigh, Samuel F. *Testimony of the Three Witnesses*. Samuel F. Leigh, 191?. A brief tract recounting the testimony of the Three Witnesses to the Book of Mormon and their

L.064 LePoidevin, Cecil George. *Zion, Land of Promise: An Atlas Study of Book of Mormon Geography.* N.p.: n.p., 1977. An atlas containing numerous drawings of maps in which various geographical locations in the Book of Mormon are identified. Migration patterns, battle sites, missionary routes, and the paths of explorations are mapped. Relevant Book of Mormon verses are offered with some commentary. [D.M.]

L.065 Lesh, Ralph F. *Ancient Mesoamerica: A Preliminary Study of Book of Mormon Geography.* Independence, MO: Zarahemla Research Foundation, 1980. Large map of Central America showing the migration routes of the Book of Mormon peoples. Uses double arrows to indicate a northward direction as well as a true north to accommodate directions used in the Book of Mormon. Identifies the "Narrow Neck" with the Isthmus of Tehuantepec. [J.W.M.]

L.066 Lesh, Ralph F. "Is North, North?" In *Recent Book of Mormon Developments*, 86-89. Independence, MO: Zarahemla Research Foundation, 1984. Also published in *ZR* 19/20/21 (Winter/Spring/Summer 1983): 21-24. The author published *Ancient Mesoamerica* in 1980 in which he used a double north arrow—one labeled "northward" and the other "true north" to show that they may not have meant the same thing for the Nephites. After the publication of this book, authors challenged his theory. After a review of the other theories, the author continues to support his theory that the north of the Nephites was true north. [A.T.]

L.067 "Lesser Lights of the Book of Mormon." *Contributor* 1 (April 1880): 149-51. Focuses on the book of Enos, first describing the contrasting lifestyles of the Nephites and Lamanites of his day, then retelling the events Enos recorded about his life. [D.M.]

L.068 Lesueur, James W. *Indian Legends.* Independence, MO: Zion, 1928. The legends of Indians who dwelt in North, Central, or South America are compiled. The legends concern the Indians' origin, migrations, wars, cosmogonic stories, recitals of a universal flood, the building of a great tower, and visitations of a god and white prophets. Religious beliefs of the Indians are listed. One section juxtaposes selected passages in the Book of Mormon with analogous Indian legends. [D.M.]

L.069 Lesueur, James W. Untitled talk. *CR* (7 April 1918): 118-20. Proposes external evidences of the Book of Mormon by claiming that in the Salt River Valley, Arizona, there exist ruins of a great Nephite city, fifteen miles wide and thirty or forty miles long and a Nephite irrigation canal that is still used. [B.D.]

L.070 "Letters from the West." *TS* 2 (15 February 1841): 322-24. Reprint of an article from the *Upper Mississippian* that relates some aspects concerning the Book of Mormon. Says that Joseph Smith found brass plates and was instructed by the Lord to employ people to translate them. The translation contained a prophecy about the condition of the Latter-day Saints, including their persecutions in Missouri. The *Times and Seasons* editor notes that some of the views about the Book of Mormon in the article are off quite "widely from the mark." [D.M.]

L.071 Lewis, Ben E. "The Most Correct Book." In *BYUSY* (18 January 1972). Provo, UT: Brigham Young University, 1971. An admonitional speech encouraging individuals to regard the Book of Mormon with resolution. The stories relating Alma's encounter with Korihor and Alma's parting words to his three sons are recalled. The Book of Mormon is vital to our spiritual condition. [D.M.]

L.072 "The Liahona." *Friend* 13 (November 1983): 48-49. For children. Describes the account of the liahona. [A.T.]

L.073 Lindgren, A. Bruce. "Sin and Redemption in the Book of Mormon." In *Restoration Studies*, edited by Maurice L. Draper and A. Bruce Lindgren, 201-6. Independence, MO: RLDS Temple School, 1983. The Book of Mormon portrays humanity as being sinful and depraved. Far from depicting an optimistic view that man is capable of progressing in righteousness to great heights, the Book of Mormon outlines the cyclical model of people ultimately succumbing to pride and sin after a period of righteousness and resultant prosperity. Enduring to the end is required but difficult. The predicament graphically presented in the Book of Mormon is answered in the redemption motif of Romans 8. [D.M.]

L.074 Little, James A. "The Book of Mormon as History." *Juvenile Instructor* 13 (15 July 1878): 158-59. Briefly discusses the Book of Mormon as inspired history. [D.M.]

L.075 Little, James A. "Book of Mormon Sketches" (Series). *Juvenile Instructor* 14-15 (1, 15 January, 15 September 1879–15 December 1880): 8-9, 14-15, 209, 218-19, 232, 249, 256-57, 266-67, 284-85, 10-11, 20-21, 35, 39-40, 57-58, 62-63, 75-76, 86-87, 98-99, 116-17, 124-25, 134-35, 152-53, 164-65, 178, 189, 201-2, 212-13, 221, 237-38, 244-45, 262-63, 266-67, 281. Retells Book of Mormon stories: priests of Noah, Mosiah and Alma's ministries, Amlici's civil war, Alma and Amulek's mission, Ammon's mission, Korihor and the Zoramites, Zarahemnah's battle with Moroni, war with Amalickiah, Moroni's warfare tactics, Pahoran and the king-men, Teancum's exploits, Hagoth's expedition, Gadianton and Kishkumen, Nephi and Cezoram, Samuel the Lamanite's prophecies, signs of Christ's birth, war between Giddianhi and Gidgiddoni, destruction at the time of Christ's crucifixion, Christ's ministry among the Nephites, subsequent righteousness, ensuing wickedness, Mormon and Moroni's abridgments, and the Nephite destruction. [A.C.W.]

L.076 Little, James A. "A Family Dialogue." *Juvenile Instructor* 17 (15 May 1882): 155. Discusses fulfillment of prophecy given in 1 Nephi 13:14. Columbus and Indian oppression was foretold centuries ago, and prophecies yet remain to be fulfilled in the future. [A.C.W.]

L.077 Little, James A. "The Jaredite Colony to America." *Juvenile Instructor* 13 (15 September 1878): 208-9. Retelling of the story of the voyage of the Jaredites to America. [D.M.]

L.078 Little, James A. "Reflections on Reading the Book of Mormon." *MS* 39 (30 July 1877): 501-3. A testimony of the Book of Mormon. The Book of Mormon exposes false doctrine and guides men in the proper course of their lives. Consistent with God's divine justice and mercy, God had guided his peoples on both the eastern and western continents. The Book of Mormon is not a history of a people, for that would not have changed human affairs, but it is a book of doctrine. [B.D.]

L.079 Lloyd, D. Clyde. *Is That in the Book of Mormon?* Salt Lake City: Deseret Book, 1962. A book containing trivia questions about the Book of Mormon. [D.M.]

L.080 Lloyd, T. E. *Carroll-Lloyd Expose: Elder T. E. Lloyd Replies to Rev. Carroll, Defending the Book of Mormon and Prophetic Mission of Joseph Smith.* N.p., 1895. The Bible does not indicate a cessation of revelation, and was not intended to be the last and only rule of faith and practice. Joseph Smith received revelation that the Book of Mormon was a divine document. Hurlbut originated the Spaulding theory. Professor Anthon's statement is examined. Discusses the witnesses to the Book of Mormon and finds their testimonies valid. [J.W.M.]

L.081 Logan, Cordell Eckre. "A Voice From the Ground." In Logan's *Spiritual Matter*, 55-64. U.S.A.: n.p., 1980. The story of the Book of Mormon begins with those who came out from Babylon in the days of the Tower of Babel and then completes the story with Lehi's and Ishmael's families who were Joseph's seed who left Jerusalem. [J.W.M.]

L.082 Longden, John. "A Marvelous Work." *IE* 63 (June 1960): 436-37. Faithful men and women all over the world bear witness of the authenticity of the Book of Mormon. The message can be spread throughout the world through Church members. Two stories, one of a Methodist minister and another of a young Baptist, reveal the value of this concept. [J.W.M.]

L.083 "The Lord Leads the Jaredites to a Promised Land." *Friend* 20 (May 1990): 19-22. An illustrated story for children. The brother of Jared saw the Lord and the Jaredites were led across the sea to the promised land. [M.D.P.]

L.084 Lovalvo, V. James. *It Is Written: Truth Shall Spring Out of the Earth.* Fresno, CA: Mid-Cal Publishers, 1980. Both the Apostasy and the Restoration are prophesied of in the Book of Mormon. The book is an important part of the Restoration. This work discusses Old World apostasy, then retells the history of the coming forth of the book, its story, the testimony of the witnesses, and a brief analysis of its teachings. [J.W.M.]

L.085 Loveland, Jerry K. "Hagoth and the Polynesian Tradition." *BYU Studies* 17 (Autumn 1976): 59-73. Accepts the common LDS belief that the Polynesians are descended from expeditions spearheaded by Hagoth, although there is not irrefutable evidence in Polynesian lore that links them with Hagoth. The traditions voiced by current Polynesians are not totally reliable due to changes that could enter into the legends, but there are some possible parallels arising out of Polynesian legends. [D.M.]

L.086 "A Lover of Truth." *Evening and Morning Star* 3 (September 1842): 86-88. The author tells of series of lectures that he attended delivered by G. J. Adams in which he testified and gave evidence of the truthfulness of the Book of Mormon. [M.D.P.]

L.087 Loving, Albert L. *From the Tower of Babel to the Hill Ramah Cumorah in Mexico.* Independence, MO: Author, 1976. Speaks concerning the Jaredites and the Lehites, with emphasis on the Tower of Babel and the dispersion. Claims that the Hill Cumorah is located in the state of Morelos in Mexico. [D.M.]

L.088 Lowe, Gareth W. "The Book of Mormon and Early Southwest Cultures" *UASN* 19 (12 April 1954): 1-3. Believing that Book of Mormon events took place in Mesoamerica, the author speculates that peoples of the southwest section of the United States had connections and correspondences with their Mesoamerican neighbors. Other Asiatic peoples also likely played a part in the development of North American Indian culture. [D.M.]

L.089 Lowe, Gareth W. "The Book of Mormon and the Late Southwest Archaeology." *University Archaeological Newsletter* 18 (25 February 1954):1-2. Discourages students of the Book of Mormon from associating all archaeological remains in the Americas with the Book of Mormon, since many of them differ in time and space. [D.M.]

L.090 Ludlow, Daniel H. "The Book of Mormon was Written for Our Day." *Instructor* 101 (July 1966): 265-66. Lists Book of Mormon passages that demonstrate that the book was written for our day. Also lists twelve Book of Mormon subjects that are particularly relevant for the people of the latter days. [D.M.]

L.091 Ludlow, Daniel H. "The Challenge of the Book of Mormon." In *The Book of Mormon: The Keystone Scripture*, edited by Paul R. Cheesman, S. Kent Brown, and Charles D. Tate Jr., 1-20. Provo, UT: Brigham Young University Religious Studies Center, 1988. Challenges both the believer and non-believer to take the Book of Mormon seriously, receive a testimony, and live in harmony with its teachings. [D.M.]

L.092 Ludlow, Daniel H. *A Companion to Your Study of the Book of Mormon.* Salt Lake City: Deseret Book, 1976. A Book of Mormon study guide that includes a verse-by-verse commentary, five appendices, a number of charts and maps, and several expositions discussing the history behind the Book of Mormon, the purposes of the Book of Mormon, the major plates, a historical overview of biblical history preceding the Book of Mormon period, and a secular history of the peoples in the Book of Mormon. [D.M.]

L.093 Ludlow, Daniel H. *A Guide to the Reading of the Book of Mormon.* Provo, UT: Brigham Young University, 1964. A study guide of thirty-five sections on the Book of Mormon. Each section contains objectives, a prospectus for the assigned reading material, and study questions. Four appendices conclude the work. [D.M.]

L.094 Ludlow, Daniel H. "I Have a Question: Shouldn't Moroni's promise in the Book of Mormon (Moroni 10:4) always work?" *Ensign* 16 (March 1986): 50-51. Also in *A Sure Foundation: Answers to Difficult Gospel Questions* 18-21. Salt Lake City, UT: Deseret Book, 1988. Ludlow analyzes Moroni's promise in Moroni 10 and includes verses 1-5, which seem to indicate that it is necessary to study more than just the Book of Mormon. Biblical study is required, then ponder and pray with sincerity and faith, which makes one capable of recognizing the truths and promptings as the Holy Ghost manifests them. [J.W.M.]

L.095 Ludlow, Daniel H. "I Have a Question: Why do we say that the Book of Mormon contains the fulness of the gospel (D&C 20:9) when it doesn't contain some of the basic teachings of the Church? Why doesn't it include such doctrines as the three degrees of glory, marriage for eternity, premortal existence of spirits, and baptism for the dead?" *Ensign* 15 (September 1985): 17-19. Also in *A Sure Foundation: Answers to Difficult Gospel Questions*, 11-15. Salt Lake City, UT: Deseret Book, 1988. The Book of Mormon definition of the gospel of Christ is revealed in 3 Nephi 27:13-22: the atonement, faith in Jesus Christ, repentance, baptism, and the gift of the Holy Ghost. None of the four compilers intended to include all of the teachings and ordinances of Christ. Important doctrines are restored when the church membership is ready to accept them. [J.W.M.]

L.096 Ludlow, Daniel H. "The Message to the Jews with Special Emphasis on 2 Nephi 25." In *The Book of Mormon: Second Nephi, The Doctrinal Structure*, edited by Monte S. Nyman and Charles D. Tate Jr., 241-57. Provo, UT: Brigham Young University Religious Studies Center, 1989. Defines various meanings of "Jew." Notes that 2 Nephi 25 is a synthesis of materials Nephi had learned from the plates of brass, personal revelation, instructions from Lehi and Jacob, and his own experience. [D.M.]

L.097 Ludlow, Daniel H. "A Priceless Possession: How to Gain a Testimony of the Book of Mormon." *NE* 16 (October 1986): 46-50. Pointing out that "signs follow them that believe," Ludlow distinguishes some of the signs that do follow believers and shows that the Lord is not adverse to signs. Signs follow faith. An outlined method of study is given. Knowing the book is true is different than being able to live by its precepts. [J.W.M.]

L.098 Ludlow, Daniel H. *A Series of Discussions on the Book of Mormon*. Provo, UT: Brigham Young University Extension Publications, 1964. An outline organized into three discussions: "The Book of Mormon as a Part of God's System of Witnesses," "The Teachings in the Book of Mormon of the Resurrected Jesus Christ," and "Modern Messages of the Book of Mormon." [D.M.]

L.099 Ludlow, Daniel H. "The Title Page." In *The Book of Mormon: First Nephi, The Doctrinal Structure*, edited by Monte S. Nyman and Charles D. Tate Jr., 19-33. Provo, UT: Brigham Young University Religious Studies Center, 1988. Reviews statements by Joseph Smith that the title page of the Book of Mormon was translated from the last leaf of the gold plates. Notes changes in the title page between various editions of the Book of Mormon and proposes that one portion of the title page was written by Mormon and another by Moroni. [A.T.]

L.100 Ludlow, Daniel H. "Zenos." In *Encyclopedia of Mormonism*, edited by Daniel H. Ludlow, 4:1623-24. 5 vols. New York: Macmillan, 1992. "Zenos is one of four Israelite prophets of Old Testament times cited in the Book of Mormon whose writings appeared on the plates of brass but who are not mentioned in the Old Testament." [A.T.]

L.101 Ludlow, Daniel H., comp. "The Holy Scriptures." In *Latter-day Prophets Speak: Selections from the Sermons and Writings of the Presidents of the Church of Jesus Christ of Latter-day Saints*, 343-56. Salt Lake City: Bookcraft, 1948. Quotes Latter-day prophets Brigham Young, George Albert Smith, Wilford Woodruff, Joseph Smith, Heber J. Grant, and John Taylor on a variety of topics concerning the scriptures. These include "The scriptures are the word of God," "Read the Scriptures," "The Book of Mormon . . . the American Scripture," "We Believe the Book of Mormon to Be The Word of God," "The Bible and The Book of Mormon Agree," and many others. [J.W.M.]

L.102 Ludlow, Douglas Kent. "Liahona." In *Encyclopedia of Mormonism*, edited by Daniel H. Ludlow, 2:829-30. 5 vols. New York:

Macmillan, 1992. A brief description of the Liahona, also referred to as the ball, compass, or director that was shown to Joseph Smith and the Three Witnesses along with the Book of Mormon plates. [B.D.]

L.103 Ludlow, Victor L. *Isaiah: Prophet, Seer and Poet*. Salt Lake City: Deseret Book, 1982. Author analyzes the book of Isaiah "in terms of historical context, literary style, scriptural context, and doctrinal application." Emphasis is placed upon Isaiah's cultural and historical surroundings and his use of parallelism. LDS perspectives are employed where possible (e.g., wide use of the Book of Mormon Isaiah passages is made), yet passages are interpreted in an open-ended fashion, with the assumption that Isaiah's pronouncements may typically refer to more than one event. Isaiah is affirmed as the sole author of the text. [A.L. & P.H.]

L.104 Ludlow, Victor L. *Jesus' "Covenant People Discourse" in 3 Nephi: With Old Testament Background and Modern Application*. Provo, UT: Brigham Young University Religious Studies Center, 1988. The first purpose of the Book of Mormon as stated on the title page is to demonstrate to the remnant of the House of Israel the great things the Lord has done for their fathers, and to show that because of past covenants latter-day generations are not excluded from divine interest. [D.M.]

L.105 Ludlow, Victor L. "Jesus' Covenant Teachings in Third Nephi." In *Rediscovering the Book of Mormon*, edited by John L. Sorenson and Melvin J. Thorne, 177-85. Salt Lake City: Deseret Book and FARMS, 1991. At least 113 passages in the Book of Mormon contain important information about the Lord's covenants with his people. Most of these are concentrated in 3 Nephi. The Lord gives key signs and events that demonstrate that his covenants are being fulfilled in the Book of Mormon. [J.W.M.]

L.106 Ludlow, Victor L. "Scribes and Scriptures." In *Studies in Scripture: 1 Nephi to Alma 29*, edited by Kent P. Jackson, 196-204. Salt Lake City: Deseret Book, 1987. Addresses Enos, Jarom, Omni, and the Words of Mormon. Themes considered are prayer, the importance of records, and the procedures followed by Nephi and Mormon that later compensated for the loss of the 116 pages from the Book of Lehi. [D.M.]

L.107 Ludlow, Victor L. "Secret Covenant Teachings of Men and the Devil in Helaman through 3 Nephi 8." In *The Book of Mormon: Helaman through 3 Nephi 8, According to Thy Word*, edited by Monte S. Nyman and Charles D. Tate Jr., 265-82. Provo, UT: Brigham Young University Religious Studies Center, 1992. Shows the counterfeit covenants members of secret combinations entered into with Lucifer, as recorded in Helaman and 3 Nephi. Includes several tables. [D.M.]

L.108 Lund, Anthon, H. "Discourse by Elder Anthon H. Lund." *MS* 62 (25 January 1900): 49-53. A testimony that a prophet of God guides the Church. Similar to the dream of Lehi, mists of darkness surround individuals today. The rod of iron, relied on in faith, leads to the tree of life. Lund explains that he reveres the Bible, but he also believes the Book of Mormon. [B.D.]

L.109 Lund, Anthon H. Untitled talk. *CR* (April 1902): 87-89. The Book of Mormon has been translated into Tahitian, Samoan, Maori, Hawaiian, and Turkish. There are many external and internal evidences of its authenticity and the Holy Ghost will tell individuals that it is true. The discovery of the Spaulding manuscript destroys the Spaulding theory, though some wrongly say there was another manuscript. Sidney Rigdon did not know about the Book of Mormon until after it was published. The writing style of the Book of Mormon differs from Sidney Rigdon's. [B.D.]

L.110 Lund, Anthon H. Untitled talk. *CR* (April 1908): 115-20. The Lord told the Prophet Joseph Smith he was to perform a marvelous work. The publication of the Book of Mormon took moral courage. It proved to be a good missionary tool and many received a testimony of the truths it contained. Brigham Young, Joseph Young, Phineas Young, Lorenzo Young, and John Young are among the first converts because of the convincing power of the book. [J.W.M.]

L.111 Lund, Anthon H. Untitled talk. *CR* (October 1912): 11-15. Bearing testimony that Latter-day Saints esteem the Bible as the word of God as highly as any people on earth, this author calls attention to some discrepancies in the various translations to show the possibility of errors in the text and offers the Book of Mormon as an answer to know how correctly the Bible has been preserved. The Latter-day scriptures are as important as are the ancient ones that they support and sustain. [J.W.M.]

L.112 Lund, Gerald N. "An Anti-Christ in the Book of Mormon—the Face May Be Strange, but the Voice Is Familiar." In *The Book of Mormon: Alma, The Testimony of the Word*, edited by Monte S. Nyman and Charles D. Tate Jr., 107-28. Provo, UT: Brigham Young University Religious Studies Center, 1992. An entire chapter of the Book of Mormon is dedicated to Korihor, an example of an anti-Christ. Korihor acts as a negative example of the "power of the word" in contrast to the positive side, which is illustrated and discussed in the chapters before and after Alma 30. Points out that Korihor's views in three branches of philosophy—metaphysics, axiology, and epistemology—are still taught today. [D.M.] [N.K.Y.]

L.113 Lund, Gerald N. "Countering Korihor's Philosophy." *Ensign* 22 (July 1992): 16-21. Relates Korihor's philosophical foundations and rationalizations to current beliefs and arguments used against the gospel. Alma's answer used revelation and true doctrine, not academic debate, and exposed Korihor's lies. [A.C.W.]

L.114 Lund, Gerald N. "Divine Indebtedness and the Atonement." In *The Book of Mormon: Mosiah, Salvation Only through Christ*, edited by Monte S. Nyman and Charles D. Tate Jr., 73-89. Provo, UT: Brigham Young University Religious Studies Center, 1991. Mosiah taught that as a result of our nothingness and of constant blessings, especially that of the atonement, we are indebted to our "heavenly King," for which we should be profoundly grateful. [D.M.]

L.115 Lund, Gerald N. "An Exploration of the Process of Faith As Taught in the Book of Mormon." In *The Second Annual Church Educational System Religious Educators' Symposium: A Symposium on the Book of Mormon*, 74-80. Salt Lake City: Church of Jesus Christ of Latter-day Saints, 1979. An essay on the dynamic relationship of faith with hope, knowledge, power, and perfection. Exposition is based on Alma 32, Ether 12, Moroni 7, and the *Lectures on Faith*. [D.M.]

L.116 Lund, Gerald N. "The Fall of Man and His Redemption." In *The Book of Mormon: Second Nephi, The Doctrinal Structure*, edited by Monte S. Nyman and Charles D. Tate Jr., 83-106. Provo, UT: Brigham Young University Religious Studies Center, 1989. Focus is on 2 Nephi 2. Outlines aspects that deal with the fall and the redemption. Illustrates with charts the role of the Messiah, the place of grace and works, and the difference between one who has a broken heart and a contrite spirit and one who does not. Discusses the importance of opposition. [D.M.]

L.117 Lund, Gerald N. " 'Knowest Thou the Condescension of God?' " In *Doctrines of the Book of Mormon, 1991 Sperry Symposium*, edited by Bruce A. Van Orden and Brent L. Top, 80-92. Salt Lake City: Deseret Book, 1992. Notes that the word "condescension" relative to God's relationship to the world is used three times by Nephi, twice in his dream of the tree of life, and once in his psalm (2 Nephi 4:26). Proposes that there are three applications to this word in those passages: (1) the birth of Christ, (2) his mortal ministry, and (3) his mercies. Discusses the significance of the christological hymn in Philippians 2:5-8. [D.M.] [N.K.Y.]

L.118 Lund, Gerald N. "The Mysteries of God Revealed by the Power of the Holy Ghost." In *The Book of Mormon: First Nephi, The Doctrinal Foundation*, edited by Monte S. Nyman and Charles D. Tate Jr., 151-59. Provo, UT: Brigham Young University Religious Studies Center, 1988. Examines 1 Nephi 9:6, 1 Nephi 10:17, and 1 Nephi 10:18-21, as prelude to Nephi's vision. The vision of Nephi is used as a basis for discussing the question, "When Nephi says the Lord knows all things, does that truly imply that he has all knowledge in the

Universe?" The author then describes the vastness of the universe and discusses time and relativity in relation to Nephi's vision. [A.T.]

L.119 Lund, Gerald N. "Sanctification and Justification Are Just and True." In *Sidney B. Sperry Symposium: The Book of Mormon*, edited by A. Gary Anderson, 28-38. Provo, UT: BYU Religious Instruction, 24 January 1981. A vigorous doctrinal discussion on sanctification and justification, clarifying the terms by examining their Semitic and Greek roots. Explains practical application, arguing that the terms are not abstruse but easily understandable. [D.M.]

L.120 Lund, Herbert Z. "Joseph Smith and the Book of Mormon." *MS* 95 (26 October 1933): 689-95. Argues against statements that Joseph Smith produced the Book of Mormon by way of "visionary seizures." The testimony of the Three Witnesses is reprinted, as is a description of David Whitmer's testimony before he died. [A.T.]

L.121 Lundgren, Alice. " 'In the Learning of the Jews': A Testimony." *ZR* 27-28 (1985): 14-15. Refers to mourning rituals enacted by Jews upon the death of a loved one and demonstrates how the rituals apply directly to the pattern given in Alma 30:2, where fasting, mourning, and prayer are mentioned. [D. M.]

L.122 Lundquist, John M., and John W. Welch. "Ammon and Cutting Off the Arms of Enemies." In *Reexploring the Book of Mormon*, 180–81. Salt Lake City: Deseret Book and FARMS, 1992. Compares similar practices in the Near East to Ammon's cutting off the arms of enemies in Alma 17:39, explaining possible reasons for this prevalent phenomena in the ancient world. [A.C.W.]

L.123 Lundquist, John M., and John W. Welch. "Kingship and Temple in 2 Nephi 5-10." In *Reexploring the Book of Mormon*, edited by John W. Welch, 66-68. Salt Lake City: Deseret Book and FARMS, 1992. In antiquity kings and temples were closely related. Nephi's intent to build a temple paved the way toward his kingship. It was necessary for covenant ceremonies at the temple to establish a legitimate state. [J.W.M.]

L.124 Lundquist, John M., and Stephen D. Ricks, eds. *By Study and Also by Faith*. 2 vols. Salt Lake City: Deseret Book and FARMS, 1990. These two volumes contain essays written by various authors in honor of Hugh W. Nibley. Many of the articles are related to Book of Mormon topics, such as the sacramental covenants, the Lamanite view, external evidences of the Book of Mormon, Lehi's family and others. [J.W.M.]

L.125 Lundstrom, Harold. "Original Words of the Book of Mormon." *IE* 51 (February 1948): 84-86, 116. During the period of 1820-1830 coining words was less common than at any subsequent time in America. The fact that the Book of Mormon contains so many unfamiliar words is a testimony of its divinity. B. H. Roberts studied the names in the Book of Mormon and found that Jaredite names end with consonants and Nephite names in vowels. One hundred eighty-one new words came forth out of seventy-five working days of translation. [J.W.M.]

L.126 Lundstrom, Joseph. *Book of Mormon Personalities*. Salt Lake City: Deseret Book, 1969. A collection of more than fifty profiles of Book of Mormon personalities. Each sketch originally appeared in the *CN* as a series. [D.M.]

L.127 Lyman, Albert R. *A Voice Calling*. Salt Lake City: Deseret News Press, 196?. A pamphlet directed to the American Indians as a missionary message. Summarizes the contents of the Book of Mormon and invites the Indians to investigate the book. [D.M.]

L.128 Lyman, Melvin A. *Out of Obscurity into Light*. Salt Lake City: Albany Books, 1985. Using President Kimball's definition of Lamanite, this book focuses upon the native American inhabitants as descendants of Lehi and Ishmael. The author tells of the evil treatment that these children of Lehi have received in North and Latin America. Archaeological, historical, and traditional evidence reinforce the Book of Mormon. The Book of Mormon records the Lord's promises to the Lamanites and those who are under obligation to aid in the fulfillment of these blessings. [J.W.M.]

L.129 Lynn, Ervin. "The Book That Would Not Burn." *Ensign* 16 (October 1986): 61-62. A Book of Mormon had been delivered to a home in New Mexico by two missionaries. Some time later the home burned and among the ashes was found the "untouched Book of Mormon." This miracle converted and strengthened many. [J.W.M.]

L.130 Lynn, Wayne B. *The Book of Mormon Our Unpaid Debt*. Salt Lake City: Church of Jesus Christ of Latter-day Saints, Church Schools, Dept. of Seminaries and Institutes of Religion, 198?. Noting that the Book of Mormon came from the ancestors of the Lamanites, the author admonishes Church members to take more seriously the mandate to inform the Lamanites of their book and their great role in the latter days. [D.M.]

L.131 Lyon, Warren H. "Book of Mormon Studies." *MS* 66 (3 March 1904): 140-41. The Book of Mormon explains the concept of Godhead, and treats "vital questions of theology . . . with startling clearness," explaining the Bible and correcting false traditions. [A.C.W.]

M.

M.001 M., M. R. "Sacred Stones in the Vicinity of Near, Licking County, Ohio." *MS* 28 (1, 8 December 1866): 753-59, 769-74. "The Two Bibles" refers to the discovery of "sacred stones of Ohio," upon which were inscribed Hebrew phrases (*MS* 28/41: 641-43). This article analyzes the inscriptions further, showing that the decalogue was poorly written. It suggests the tribes of Dan, Reuben, Zebulun, or Joseph could have wandered to America and deposited the stones in Ohio. [B.D.]

M.002 M., W. A. "The Book of Mormon in Prophecy." *MS* 69 (16 May 1907): 305-11. Old Testament prophecies of Christ are conclusive proofs of his divinity; therefore, biblical prophecies of Book of Mormon are conclusive proofs of its divinity as well. [A.C.W.]

M.003 M., W. A. "Lessons from the Life of Nephi." *MS* 70 (November 1908): 705-8. The account of Nephi's conduct and Laman and Lemuel's treatment of him while crossing the ocean teaches important principles of the gospel. A righteous person will prosper and the unrighteous will not. We bind ourselves by cords that hinder us by evil speaking, neglect of prayer, disobedience, and failure to pay tithing. [B.D.]

M.004 Mabey, Charles R. "Let Its Words Be Judged." *MS* 64 (October 1902): 641-47. Though external evidence validates the Book of Mormon, it is the internal evidence that reveals its divinity. Like the Bible, the Book of Mormon rebukes sin, explains the existence of mankind, is filled with the "pure spirit of inspiration," explains the law of opposition, and discusses the philosophy that brings one to believe in God. [J.W.M.]

M.005 Mabey, John Hicksen. "The Book of Mormon as an Instrument in Teaching the Concept of Prayer." M.A. thesis, Brigham Young University, 1963. A comprehensive report on the teachings of prayer in the Book of Mormon. A primary interest of the author is to provide teachers in the Church with a source for teaching prayer. [D.M.]

M.006 Macgregor, Maggie. "The Restoration Accomplished." In Macgregor's *Light At Evening Time: The Gospel Restored*, 183-254. Independence, MO: Board of Publication of The Church of Christ, 1942?. Provides Joseph Smith's own testimony of the coming forth of the Book of Mormon. The Book of Mormon is the sign of the Restoration, and fulfills all the criteria of the biblical prophecies concerning the sign. Presents the witnesses' testimonies, archaeological evidences, internal evidences, literary and moral features of the book. [J.W.M.]

M.007 Mackay, Thomas W. "Mormon and the Destruction of Nephite Civilization." In *Studies in Scripture: Alma 30 to Moroni*, edited by Kent P. Jackson, 231-44. Salt Lake City: Deseret Book, 1988. Begins by reflecting on Mormon's feelings concerning Nephite heroes and scoundrels. Describes the degeneration and social disintegration of the Nephite society as witnessed by Mormon. Comments on Mormon's message to the present world. Concludes by discussing Moroni's role in winding up his father's record. [D.M.]

M.008 Mackay, Thomas W. "Mormon's Philosophy of History: Helaman 12 in the Perspective of Mormon's Editing Procedure." In *The Book of Mormon: Helaman through 3 Nephi 8, According to Thy Word*, edited by Monte S. Nyman and Charles D. Tate Jr., 129-46. Provo, UT: Brigham Young University Religious Studies Center, 1992. The concerns and cosmology of Mormon as a historian and editor coalesce in Helaman 12. History is explained providentially rather than mechanistically or apart from God's intervention as a reaction to human behavior. [D.M.]

M.009 Mackenna, Irma de. "The Book of Mormon Taught Me to Read." *Ensign* 5 (February 1975): 40-41. An elderly lady in Chile learned to read from the Book of Mormon through the help of the Lord. She prayed for help, and had her daughter read a few lines, which she then memorized and then began to study line by line to learn to read. [J.W.M.]

M.010 Maddox, Julie Adams. "Lehi's Vision of the Tree of Life: An Anagogic Interpretation." M.A. thesis, Brigham Young University, 1986. A look at Lehi's vision from a literary-critical point of view. Emphasis is placed on symbolic aspects of the tree of life, especially as it relates to death and renewal of life. [D.M.]

M.011 Madsen, Ann N., and Susan Easton Black. "Joseph and Joseph: 'He Shall Be Like unto Me' (2 Nephi 3:15)." In *The Old Testament and the Latter-day Saints; Sperry Symposium, 1986*, 125-40. U.S.A.: Randall, 1986. The Book of Mormon contains information about ancient Joseph that is found in no other place. There are many similarities between Joseph Smith and the ancient prophet Joseph. Each traveled with their families, experienced time in prison, each had a divine calling, and had dreams in their youth. [J.W.M.]

M.012 Madsen, John M. "Jesus Christ, the Son of the Living God." *Ensign* 23 (May 1993): 26-27. The Book of Mormon is the "instrument" with which to "flood the earth" with a knowledge of the divine mission of Jesus Christ so that the inhabitants may "be of good cheer." [S.H.]

M.013 Madsen, Truman G. "B. H. Roberts after Fifty Years: Still Witnessing for the Book of Mormon." *Ensign* 13 (December 1983): 10-19. A brief history of the life of B. H. Roberts and his work as a defender of the Book of Mormon. Argues that Roberts never lost his testimony of the Book of Mormon as some critics have claimed. Roberts's goal was to prepare future defenders of the book by showing where critics could attack it. [S.P.S.]

M.014 Madsen, Truman G. "B. H. Roberts and the Book of Mormon." *BYU Studies* 19 (Summer 1979): 427-45. Also in *Book of Mormon Authorship: New Light on Ancient Origins*, edited by Noel B. Reynolds, 7-32. Provo, UT: Brigham Young University Religious Studies Center, 1982. Discusses B. H. Roberts's dedication in analyzing the Book of Mormon throughout his life. Discusses Roberts as a historian, analyst of translation, defender, teacher, and writer. [L.D.]

M.015 Madsen, Truman G. "B. H. Roberts: The Book of Mormon and the Atonement." In *The Book of Mormon: First Nephi, The Doctrinal Structure*, edited by Monte S. Nyman and Charles D. Tate Jr., 297-314. Provo, Utah: Brigham Young University Religious Studies Center, 1988. Gives a brief description of the preparation of *The Truth, the Way, the Life*, a six-volume work by B. H. Roberts, then examines this work in relation to the Book of Mormon. The specific topics covered are: "The Presuppositions of the Atonement," "Four Kinds of Suffering," and "The Law of Opposites." [A.T.]

M.016 Madsen, Truman G. "Facets of Prayer." *IE* 69 (February 1966): 157-59. An essay for youth about prayer, using Enos as the model. [D.M.]

M.017 Madsen, Truman G. "Ye Are My Witnesses." In *Christ and the Inner Life*, 43-54. Salt Lake City: Bookcraft, 1978. A short story based on events surrounding the appearance of Christ in 3 Nephi. [D.M.]

M.018 Madsen, Truman G., and John W. Welch. "Did B. H. Roberts Lose Faith in the Book of Mormon?" Provo, UT: FARMS, 1985. Although Roberts was aware of some potential objections to the Book of Mormon, and was not always prepared to answer them, his conviction regarding its truthfulness never wavered. His views were recorded in several journals of people he interacted with, especially his missionaries in the eastern states. [D.M.]

M.019 Maeser, Karl G. "Sketches from the Book of Mormon: Abinadi." *MS* 30 (January 1868): 6-8. A brief description of the mission of Abinadi. He was the Stephen of that dispensation, sent by God in response to the wickedness of King Noah. [B.D.]

M.020 Maeser, Karl G. "Sketches from the Book of Mormon: Alma the Great." *MS* 30 (February 1868): 69-71. A brief description of the life and mission of Alma: He was of pure blood of Nephi and became one of the greatest prophets and leaders of the Nephites. [B.D.]

M.021 Maeser, Karl G. "Sketches from the Book of Mormon: The Expedition of Ammon." *MS* 29 (December 1867): 818-20. A brief summary of the events recorded in the Book of Mosiah. Maeser mentions King Mosiah$_2$, Abinadi, Limhi, Gideon, and King Noah, and the expedition of Ammon. [B.D.]

M.022 Maeser, Karl G. "Sketches from the Book of Mormon: Jacob, the Brother of Nephi." *MS* 29 (November 1867): 695-96. Just as Moses had appointed Joshua as the secular leader and Aaron as the spiritual leader of the people, so too had Nephi anointed a king as the secular leader and Jacob the spiritual leader. Jacob provides valuable lessons on polygamy and the outcome of the anti-Christ such as Sherem. [B.D.]

M.023 Maeser, Karl G. "Sketches from the Book of Mormon: Nephi." *MS* 29 (October 1867): 673-74. A short description of Nephi's character. Maeser writes that Nephi had a strong character and was an excellent servant of God because of his temperance caused by his submission to the will of God and the promptings of the Holy Spirit. [B.D.]

M.024 Maeser, Karl G. "Sketches from the Book of Mormon: The Seven Prophets of the House of Jacob." *MS* 29 (November 1867): 759-60. A brief discussion of the seven prophets after Jacob and before King Benjamin. Maeser also summarizes the events that these prophets recorded. [B.D.]

M.025 Maestas, John R., and Jeff Simons. *The Lamanite*. Provo, UT: Brigham Young University, n.d. This work contains statements by prophets from Joseph Smith to Spencer W. Kimball concerning the Lamanites. Topics treated include: "Nephites Found in New Mexico," "Lamanites a shield to us," "Blessings Promised to Lamanites," and "Zelph–White Lamanite." [J.W.M.]

M.026 Maestas, John R., and Jeff Simons. *The Lamanites—In the Words of the Prophets*. Utah: n.p., 1980. Discusses the origin and history of the American Indians (Lamanites), mistreatment of Indians, God's directing hand in their affairs, and the latter-day responsibility of the Church to take the gospel to them. [L.D.]

M.027 Magleby, Kirk A. "And the Waters Prevailed: Some Andean Indian Versions of the Flood." *NE* 13 (January-February 1983): 9-12. North, Central, and South American Indians all "preserved the story of the flood." Their deluge accounts share with the Bible three main themes: "(1) mankind becomes wicked and offends the Gods, (2) a worldwide flood destroys sinners and purifies the earth, and (3) one righteous family or group is spared to begin a new, improved human race." Samples of the writings of early American explorers relating to Indian traditions about the flood are given. [A.T.]

M.028 Magleby, Kirk A. "Four Peruvian Versions of the White God Legend." *NE* 8 (December 1978): 14-17. Chronicles recorded shortly after the Spaniards reached South America describe Peruvian legends of a great white god. Author parallels four prominent versions of the white god legend with the account of Christ's visit to the Nephites shortly after his resurrection. [D.M.]

M.029 Magleby, Kirk A. "A Survey of Mesoamerican Bearded Figures." Provo, UT: FARMS, 1983. A detailed study of bearded men as found in artifacts and historical accounts of Mexico and Central America. Relates findings to the Book of Mormon, concluding that the groups mentioned in that book resided in Mesoamerica. [D.M.]

M.030 Mahoney, W. LeRoy. "A Comparison of the Egyptian and Mayan Calendars." In *14th Symposium on Archaeology of the Scriptures*, edited by Forrest R. Hauck, 87-94. Provo, UT: Brigham Young University, 1963. Lehi's measurement of time was influenced by the Egyptian calendric system, a system that was ultimately handed down to the Mayans. Several points of similarity between the Egyptian and Mayan calendars are noted, such as a luni-solar year consisting of twelve months of thirty days. [D.M.]

M.031 Maley, Thomas S. *Why I Believe in the Book of Mormon*. Minneapolis, MN: n.p., 197?. A brief statement on how the Book of Mormon answers vital questions. [D.M.]

M.032 Mangelson, David R. "The Book of Mormon as an Instrument in Teaching the Historicity of the New Testament of Events of Christ's Life." M.A. thesis, Brigham Young University, 1968. The Book of Mormon is a corroborating witness with the New Testament concerning the events of the pre-mortal and historical Jesus. Thematically similar passages from the New Testament and Book of Mormon are juxtaposed in parallel columns, an exercise that allows readers to view the manner in which the Book of Mormon stands as another witness of Jesus Christ. [D.M.]

M.033 Mangelson, David R. "The Book of Mormon As Another Witness of Jesus Christ." In *A Symposium on the Book of Mormon*, 76-80. Salt Lake City: Church of Jesus Christ of Latter-day Saints, CES, August 1986. Certain Christian groups exist who do not believe in the divinity of Jesus. The Book of Mormon, with the Bible, stands as a witness that Jesus is the Christ. The Book of Mormon testifies of Jesus Christ with regard to his pre-mortal existence, divine birth, ministry, trials, suffering, death, and resurrection. [D.M.]

M.034 Mansfield, M. W. "Jacob's Isle." *IE* 7 (January 1904): 264-67. Discusses the writings in the Bible and Book of Mormon that use the term "isles" and discusses what land is referred to by the prophets. [L.D.]

M.035 "Manuscript of Solomon Spalding" *Journal of History* 17 (April 1924): 169-82. An RLDS publication, containing primary documents relative to the Spaulding manuscript, including letters from L. L. Rice and a lecture by James H. Fairchild of Oberlin College. Concludes that it is unlikely that Spaulding had anything to do with the Book of Mormon. [D.M.]

M.036 Maples, Evelyn. *The Brass Plates Adventure*. Independence, MO: Herald House, 1972. Short, illustrated storybook for children about the acquisition of the plates of brass. [D.M.]

M.037 Maples, Evelyn. *Lehi, Man of God*. Independence, MO: Herald House, 1972. Illustrated children's storybook about Lehi. [D.M.]

M.038 Markham, Julie Cannon. "Chapter-a-Week Home Evening." *Ensign* 20 (February 1990): 72. Describes several successes in reading a chapter of the Book of Mormon at each family home evening. Gives specific examples. [D.M.]

M.039 Marler, Ezra L. "The Book of Mormon: The Bible. Is It Enough? A New Volume of Scripture." In Marler's *High Way Helps: Lights along Lifes Great Highway*, 152-59. Independence, MO: Zion's Printing, 1945. Quoting 2 Nephi 28:29–29:10, the author calls attention to what would be lacking if the Bible were our only religious literature: the nature of God, the meaning and plan of life, origin and destiny of man, the mode of baptism, the destiny of righteous dead. The Book of Mormon does not detract from or contradict the Bible, it adds clarity to the Bible. [J.W.M]

M.040 Marler, Ezra L. *Christ in the Book of Mormon*. Salt Lake City: Deseret Book, 1956. An anthology of scriptural quotations from the Book of Mormon. The brief work is divided into two main sections—the predictions of Christ's birth in the holy land and his visit to the Americas. No commentary is supplied by the compiler. [D.M.]

M.041 Marler, Ezra L. *Gospel Teachings in the Book of Mormon.* Salt Lake City: Deseret Book, 1956. A topically arranged ready reference on gospel subjects taken from the Book of Mormon. The compiler offers no commentary. [D.M.]

M.042 Marler, Ezra L. *History and Stories in the Book of Mormon.* Salt Lake City: Deseret Book, 1956. Historical narratives are extracted from the Book of Mormon and quoted verbatim to create a Book of Mormon history. The selections are arranged in historical order from 1 Nephi to Mormon, with the exception of the book of Ether, which is placed last. [D.M.]

M.043 Marquardt, H. Michael. *Book of Mormon Cross Reference.* Bountiful, UT: Restoration Research, 1983. This pamphlet cross references the LDS 1981 edition with the RLDS 1908 and 1966 editions of the Book of Mormon. [J.W.M.]

M.044 Marriott, Dean L. "I Have a Question: Is the book of Revelation the remainder of the vision Nephi recorded in 1 Nephi?" *Ensign* 17 (June 1987): 25–26. Both Nephi and John beheld similar visions but each wrote only a portion of what he saw. It is not entirely clear if the book of Revelation is that portion of Nephi's vision that the apostle John was commanded to write. Differences and similarities between the two records are examined. [S.P.S.]

M.045 Marsh, Herbert J. *Book of Mormon Reference.* Houston, TX: Texas Mission, 10 April 1943. A small handbook of references for missionaries. The scriptural references are placed according to topic: "Where does faith come from?" "Is sincerity of belief enough?" "Who should be baptized?" and "Are revelations continuous?" [J.W.M.]

M.046 Marshall, Craig G. "Father Lehi." *Ensign* 6 (September 1976): 58-63. An overview of the life and personality of Lehi. Lehi was an exceptional prophet, a visionary character who prophetically foresaw events concerning his family down through the ages. [B.T.]

M.047 Martineau, Theodore. "Voices from the Dust." *IE* 36 (January 1933): 146-47. Chihuahua, Mexico was once inhabited by a brilliant civilization. A visit to the ruins shows remarkable skills in masonry, textiles, and pottery, as well as a preoccupation with warfare and ingenious designs for protection. The inhabitants of this civilization may have been the Gadianton robbers. [D.M.]

M.048 Martinez, Arturo R. Untitled talk. In *The Official Report of the First Mexico and Central American Area General Conference of the Church of Latter-day Saints*, August 1972, 140-42. Salt Lake City: Church of Jesus Christ of Latter-day Saints, 1972. Expresses gratitude for ancestors who received the testimony of the truthfulness of the Book of Mormon. They followed the council of Moroni to pray to God in the name of Christ and after much study received a manifestation of the truth through the Holy Ghost. A great and mighty people lived at one time in Guatemala. The Book of Mormon unfolds their history. They were they of whom the Savior testified were his "other sheep." [J.W.M.]

M.049 Masters, George F. "3 Nephi 12:1-12: The Savior's Emphasis on the Weightier Matters." In *A Symposium on the Book of Mormon*, 81-85. Salt Lake City: Church of Jesus Christ of Latter-day Saints, CES, August 1986. The beatitudes of the sermon at Bountiful may signify the weightier matters neglected by the Pharisees (Matthew 23:23). Each succeeding beatitude represents a step toward perfection. [D.M.]

M.050 Matheny, Ray T. "An Analysis of the Padilla Gold Plates." *BYU Studies* 19 (Fall 1978): 21-40. Discusses the circumstances of the discovery of the Padilla gold plates, their physical description, means of production, and the content of the engravings on them. The article attempts to determine the plates' historical value. "If authentic [the Padilla gold plates] represent the most significant archaeological evidence of the Book of Mormon yet to appear." Author concludes that the plates are not authentic. [L.D.]

M.051 Matthews, Robert J. "Abinadi: Prophet and Martyr." *Ensign* 22 (April 1992): 25-31. Abinadi's forceful ministry "influenced the entire second half of the Nephites' history." Discusses the man and the prophet Abinadi, his trial and conviction, his death and his doctrinal teachings about the law of Moses, the atonement, and the resurrection. [A.C.W.]

M.052 Matthews, Robert J. "Abinadi: The Prophet and Martyr." In *The Book of Mormon: Mosiah, Salvation Only through Christ*, edited by Monte S. Nyman and Charles D. Tate Jr., 91-111. Provo, UT: Brigham Young University Religious Studies Center, 1991. Article is divided into two parts: (1) a historical sketch of Abinadi, including the circumstances he faced before King Noah's court; (2) A consideration of Abinadi's doctrinal teachings, with emphasis on the *raison d'etre* of the law of Moses and clarifications on the atonement and resurrection. [D.M.]

M.053 Matthews, Robert J. "An Appreciation for the Book of Mormon." In *Sidney B. Sperry Symposium: The Book of Mormon*, edited by A. Gary Anderson, 18-27. Provo, UT: BYU Religious Instruction, 24 January 1981. Speaks about themes covered in the Book of Mormon: the mission of Christ, the fall and the atonement, salvation only through Christ, the nature of God, the devil, spiritual gifts, the ministry of angels, and the philosophies of men. Includes a table listing the names of Christ in the Book of Mormon. [D.M.]

M.054 Matthews, Robert J. "The Atonement of Jesus Christ: 2 Nephi 9." In *The Book of Mormon: Second Nephi, The Doctrinal Structure,* edited by Monte S. Nyman and Charles D. Tate Jr., 177-99. Provo, UT: Brigham Young University Religious Studies Center, 1989. Rehearses information about the Book of Mormon prophet Jacob, but expends most of the essay on the atonement, using 2 Nephi 9 as well as other scriptures. The atonement paid for the original sin, and is "infinite." [D.M.]

M.055 Matthews, Robert J. *A Bible! A Bible!* Salt Lake City: Bookcraft, 1990. Joseph Smith taught that the Book of Mormon is a witness for the Bible. It testifies of Jesus Christ and His divinity, teaches a wide range of secular and religious topics, and identifies the enemies of Christ. The Book of Mormon is the most correct of any book on earth, the keystone of the LDS religion, and individuals will "get nearer to God by abiding by its precepts than by any other book." [J.W.M.]

M.056 Matthews, Robert J. "The Bible and Its Role in the Restoration." *Ensign* 9 (July 1979): 40-45. The Bible played a vital role in the Restoration of the gospel. The angel Moroni used biblical verses to instruct Joseph Smith. Many basic doctrines of the Church, including the age of accountability, three degrees of glory, and celestial marriage, were developed as a result of Joseph's efforts to translate the Bible. The literary style of the Book of Mormon was adopted from the Bible. [D.M.]

M.057 Matthews, Robert J. "The Book of Mormon a Witness for the Bible." *Instructor* 101 (April, May 1966): 160, 205. Compilation of quotes from scripture and Church leaders that demonstrate how the Book of Mormon is a witness for the Bible. Charts of scriptures comparing Old Testament, New Testament, and Book of Mormon show unity of doctrine. [A.C.W.]

M.058 Matthews, Robert J. "The Book of Mormon as a Co-Witness with the Bible and as a Guide to Biblical Criticism." In *The Sixth Annual CES Religious Educators' Symposium on the Book of Mormon*, 55-58. Salt Lake City: Church of Jesus Christ of Latter-day Saints, 1982. Explains what the eighth article of faith means with regard to the Bible. The paper describes variations in biblical texts and the ways in which those variations came about. The Book of Mormon clarifies and restores the text of the Bible. [A.T.]

M.059 Matthews, Robert J. "Christ's Authority, His Other Sheep, and the Redemption of Israel." In *Studies in Scripture: Alma 30 to Moroni*, edited by Kent P. Jackson, 161-71. Salt Lake City: Deseret Book, 1988. A discussion of 3 Nephi 15-16, with elaboration of the biblical Sermon on the Mount, dealing with the question of Christ's authority, the "other sheep" referred to in John 10:16, and the meaning of "gentile." [D.M.]

M.060 Matthews, Robert J. "The Doctrine of the Resurrection as Taught in the Book of Mormon." *BYU Studies* 30 (Summer 1991): 41-56. Discusses aspects of the resurrection as taught by each prophet in the Book of Mormon, while noting that every writer on the subject emphasized peculiar features. There is no one place in the Book of Mormon where the complete teachings on the resurrection are brought together. The author lists 23 separate components of resurrection scattered throughout the Book of Mormon. [D.M.]

M.061 Matthews, Robert J. "Establishing the Truth of the Bible." In *The Book of Mormon: First Nephi, The Doctrinal Foundation*, edited by Monte S. Nyman, and Charles D. Tate Jr., 193-215. Provo, UT: Brigham Young University Religious Studies Center, 1988. References Book of Mormon statements to Old and New Testament events to show how the Book of Mormon supports Biblical events and historical figures such as the creation, Noah, Babel, and Abraham. The Book of Mormon tells the history of the Bible. [A.T.]

M.062 Matthews, Robert J. "I Have a Question: Why do the Book of Mormon selections from Isaiah parallel the King James Version and not the older—and presumably more accurate—Dead Sea Scrolls text?" *Ensign* 10 (March 1980): 40. For two reasons the Isaiah passages in the Book of Mormon parallel the King James Version rather than the Dead Sea Scrolls. First, the Dead Sea Scrolls have been found to differ considerably from texts of the same vintage. Second, the translation in the Book of Mormon may not reflect the "minute and highly detailed analysis of every word on the gold plates." [J.W.M.]

M.063 Matthews, Robert J. "I Have a Question: Why have changes been made in the printed editions of the Book of Mormon?" *Ensign* 17 (March 1987): 47-49. The changes and corrections made in various editions of the Book of Mormon were necessary to correct "typographical errors, misspellings, misplaced or dropped words, and ambiguities." These original textual errors arose from non-standardized spelling in the 1800s, errors made by various scribes, editors and typesetters, and from the difficulty of communicating the things of God in the language of man. [S.P.S.]

M.064 Matthews, Robert J. "Jacob: Prophet, Theologian, Historian." In *The Book of Mormon: Jacob through Words of Mormon, To Learn with Joy*, edited by Monte S. Nyman and Charles D. Tate Jr., 33-53. Provo, UT: Brigham Young University Religious Studies Center, 1990. Compiles the historical information available on Jacob, discusses his and his brother Joseph's calling as priest and a teacher, and summarizes his style of speaking and the content of his message. [D.M.]

M.065 Matthews, Robert J. "Joseph Smith—Translator." In *Joseph Smith: The Prophet, the Man*, edited by Susan Easton Black and Charles D. Tate Jr., 77-87. Provo, UT: Brigham Young University Religious Studies Center, 1993. A prophet is an instrument of God to bring forth scripture. The Prophet Joseph Smith brought forth many scriptures, many through the gift of translation: the Book of Mormon, the Doctrine and Covenants, the Joseph Smith Translation of the Bible, the Book of Abraham translated from papyri, and the scroll of Joseph of Egypt part of which was also translated from papyri. [J.W.M.]

M.066 Matthews Robert J. "Modern Revelation: Window to the Old Testament." *Ensign* 3 (October 1973): 20-23. Latter-day revelation is the key to understanding the Old Testament. The Book of Mormon, Doctrine and Covenants, and the Pearl of Great Price give an expanded view of certain writings of Old Testament prophets and supplement the doctrine. [J.W.M.]

M.067 Matthews, Robert J. "The New Publications of the Standard Works—1979, 1981." *BYU Studies* 22 (Fall 1982): 387-424. Discusses the changes in format of the Book of Mormon, Doctrine and Covenants, Pearl of Great Price, and the Bible in their new editions. There was a need for publication of an LDS edition of the Bible and that led to an update of the other standard works of the Church. Contains photographs of the printer's copy of the Book of Mormon, the original Book of Mormon manuscript, the "Kirtland Revelation Book," and Joseph Smith translations. [L.D.]

M.068 Matthews, Robert J. "Notes on Lehi's Travels." *BYU Studies* 12 (Spring 1972): 312-14. Sets forth the sources that declare that the course of Lehi ended up in "South America, in Chile, thirty degrees south latitude." [L.D.]

M.069 Matthews, Robert J. "Patterns of Apostasy in the Book of Helaman." In *The Book of Mormon: Helaman through 3 Nephi 8, According to Thy Word*, edited by Monte S. Nyman and Charles D. Tate Jr., 65-80. Provo, UT: Brigham Young University Religious Studies Center, 1992. A discussion of identifiable characteristics that led to a spiritual degeneration of large groups as recorded in the book of Helaman. Notes the uncompromising righteousness of Helaman, brothers Nephi and Lehi, and Samuel the Lamanite, and the unrighteousness of Kishkumen, Gadianton, and the Gadianton robbers. [D.M.]

M.070 Matthews, Robert J. "The Probationary Nature of Mortality." In *The Book of Mormon: Alma, The Testimony of the Word*, edited by Monte S. Nyman and Charles D. Tate Jr., 47-60. Provo, UT: Brigham Young University Religious Studies Center, 1992. A commentary on Alma 12. Expounds on the idea that greater truth is given to those who are prepared, the lesser truth to those who are not. Elaborates on the "chains of hell," the second death, the probationary period, and the "rest of the Lord." [D.M.]

M.071 Matthews, Robert J. "Resurrection." *Ensign* 21 (April 1991): 6-11. Examines the doctrine of the resurrection in the Old and New Testaments. The teachings in the Book of Mormon clarify why the death and resurrection of Jesus Christ are vital. Explores the teachings of Lehi, Jacob, Benjamin, Abinadi, Amulek, Alma, and those given at the temple when Christ appeared. Jesus atoned for man's sins and the resurrection was an important part of the plan. [J.W.M.]

M.072 Matthews, Robert J. "The Savior's Sermon to the Nephites Compared with the Sermon on the Mount." In *The Sixth Annual Church Educational System Religious Educators' Symposium on the Book of Mormon*, 52-54. Salt Lake City: Church of Jesus Christ of Latter-day Saints, 1982. The two sermons are compared and contrasted using the KJV, JST, and Book of Mormon. The elements examined include: the Beatitudes, the Lord's prayer, the law of Moses, and Scribes and Pharisees. The author concludes that the Nephite sermon is "fresh and independent, totally adapted to the particular situation of the Nephite people to whom it was given." [AT.]

M.073 Matthews, Robert J. "Some Comparisons of the Book of Mormon with the Old and New Testaments." In *A Symposium on the Book of Mormon*, 18-23. Salt Lake City: Church of Jesus Christ of Latter-day Saints, 1979. Cites the promise of 3 Nephi that the records of Judah and those of the Nephites would be combined. Compares Matthew 5 with 3 Nephi 12; Matthew 6 with 3 Nephi 13 and JST Matthew 6; JST Matthew 7 with Matthew 7. [N.K.Y.]

M.074 Matthews, Robert J. "Some Thoughts on the Atonement." Provo, UT: FARMS, 1989. Uses the greater knowledge presented in the Book of Mormon to clarify Jesus' "points of doctrine" concerning his atonement. The dimensions of the atonement include elements of love, service, legality, and debt payment. A divine redeemer of mortal and immortal parentage was needed to offer the holy sacrifice. [J.W.M.]

M.075 Matthews, Robert J. "Two Ways in the World: The Warfare between God and Satan." In *Studies in Scripture: 1 Nephi to Alma 29*, edited by Kent P. Jackson, 146-61. Salt Lake City: Deseret Book, 1987. 2 Nephi 26-30 contrasts the ways of God and Satan. Shows the *modus operandi* of the two and refers to prophecies about how they would be (and are being) expressed in the latter days. [D.M.]

M.076 Matthews, Robert J. "What the Book of Mormon Tells Us about Jesus Christ." In *The Book of Mormon: The Keystone Scripture*, edited by Paul R. Cheesman, S. Kent Brown, and Charles D. Tate Jr., 21-43. Provo, UT: Brigham Young University Religious Studies Center, 1988. A variety of Christological roles of Jesus found in the Book of Mormon are discussed, including Jesus Christ as the universal Savior, the resurrected Lord, and as the figure who wrought the atonement. [D.M.]

M.077 Matthews, Robert J. "What the Book of Mormon Tells Us about the Bible." In *Doctrines of the Book of Mormon, 1991 Sperry Symposium*, edited by Bruce A. Van Orden and Brent L. Top, 93-113. Salt Lake City: Deseret Book, 1992. The Book of Mormon declares the Bible to be a sacred and true record, but it sustained serious losses in its early stages, which has caused considerable stumbling. Many biblical scholars today reject the authenticity of many of the teachings of Jesus. The Book of Mormon confirms the truthfulness of the Bible. [D.M.]

M.078 Matthews, Robert J. *Who's Who in the Book of Mormon?* Salt Lake City: Deseret Book, 1964, [R]1976. A *Who's Who* of Book of Mormon personalities. Part 1 presents a listing of each person named; part 2 contains a listing of all people not specifically named. Appendix 1 provides a description of the Book of Mormon plates; appendix 2 presents random facts about the Book of Mormon; appendix 3 names the categories of people in the Book of Mormon. [D.M.]

M.079 Matthews, Robert J. "Why Have Changes Been Made in the Printed Editions of the Book of Mormon?" In *A Sure Foundation: Answers to Difficult Gospel Questions*. 33-39, Salt Lake City: Deseret Book, 1988. Translating from one language to another is difficult at best; spelling errors and dropped or misplaced words are common. The process is complex and with each edition small mistakes are corrected. Spelling had not been standardized at Joseph Smith's time. The same kind of process took place with the Bible. [J.W.M.]

M.080 Matthews, Robert J. "Why the Book of Mormon Is the Keystone of Our Religion." In *A Symposium on the Book of Mormon*, 86-90. Salt Lake City: Church of Jesus Christ of Latter-day Saints, CES, August 1986. While not depreciating the Bible, the author sees the Book of Mormon as being a more correct work, since its language was not at the mercy of so many generations of translations with their inevitable errors. The Book of Mormon testifies profoundly about Christ and his atonement, and other crucial aspects of life that weigh heavily on mankind. [D.M.]

M.081 Mattson, Vernon W., Jr. *The Dead Sea Scrolls and Other Important Discoveries*. Brandon, FL: Buried Records, 1978. A compilation of quotations by different people on the Dead Sea Scrolls and other ancient records. The author ties the archaeological discoveries in both hemispheres to the Book of Mormon and retells the story of the gold plates from Joseph Smith's point of view. [D.M.]

M.082 Maxfield, M. Richard. "The Book of Mormon and the Conversion Process to the Church of Jesus Christ of Latter-day Saints: A Study of Recent Converts." Ph.D. diss., Brigham Young University, 1977. Examines the conversion stories of a number of LDS converts and attempts to determine the precise role of the Book of Mormon in the conversion process. Determines that personal prayer, the witness of the Spirit, and the spirit of the missionaries tended to be more formidable determinants in the conversion process than did the influence of the Book of Mormon. [D.M.]

M.083 Maxwell, Neal A. "An Ancient Record—with Relevancy." *Instructor* 105 (July 1970): 240-41. Discusses the Book of Mormon as an ancient record that was predestined to come forth in this day and is a work relevant to our day. [L.D.]

M.084 Maxwell, Neal A. "The Book of Mormon: A Great Answer to 'The Great Question.'" In *The Book of Mormon: First Nephi, The Doctrinal Structure*, edited by Monte S. Nyman and Charles D. Tate Jr., 1-17. Provo, Utah: Brigham Young University Religious Studies Center, 1988. The Book of Mormon answers the great question, "Is there really a redeeming Christ?" The Book of Mormon restores truth lost from the Bible, is important for our time, and provides and defines a plan and purpose for our existence. Reviews Moroni's promise, the way Book of Mormon peoples observed the law of Moses and the importance of searching the scriptures. [A.T.]

M.085 Maxwell, Neal A. "The Book of Mormon is Relevant Today." *Instructor* 105 (July, August,

September, October, November 1970): 240-41, 306-7, 316-17, 370-71, 404-5. Five-part series showing how the Book of Mormon is relevant today: all generations need to learn from the past for it teaches of the sorrowing of the damned and the danger of unchastity. Author details some of the "magnificent miscellany" contained in the Book of Mormon, such as the erosion of spiritual experience, reason vs. inspiration, and the importance of two-way communication; shows how the Book of Mormon is congruent with the Bible; details some milestones for modern Christians found in the Book of Mormon in the areas of charity, prayer, and testimony. [A.C.W.]

M.086 Maxwell, Neal A. "The Children of Christ." In *The Book of Mormon: Mosiah, Salvation Only through Christ*, edited by Monte S. Nyman and Charles D. Tate Jr., 1-22. Provo, UT: Brigham Young University Religious Studies Center, 1991. Explores the divine declaration of Jesus Christ as found in the book of Mosiah in the Book of Mormon and the manner in which mortals may become children of Christ. The author explains the value of exploring all of the rooms and corridors of the Book of Mormon, which he likens to a vast mansion. The Restoration has produced a great feast of gospel messages. [J.W.M.]

M.087 Maxwell, Neal A. "The Children of Christ." *BYUSY* (4 February 1990):79-91. Focuses on Christology in the Book of Mosiah, using the teachings of King Benjamin, Mosiah, Abinadi, and Alma the Younger. There are significant insights into Christ's role and ministry and the process by which mortals may become his children and receive eternal life. The atonement is relevant because it opens the way to reconciliation with Father. Book of Mormon prophets exemplify the way. [J.W.M.]

M.088 Maxwell, Neal A. "A Choice Seer." *Ensign* 16 (August 1986): 6-15. Also in *Brigham Young University 1985-1986 Devotional and Fireside Speeches*, 113-21. Provo, UT: Brigham Young University Press, 1985. An essay about the Prophet Joseph Smith as a seer. Referring to the translation of the Book of Mormon, the author writes that, "since Joseph, who knew the 'particulars' [of the translating process], chose not to describe them in detail, we cannot presently be definitive about methodology." [D.M.]

M.089 Maxwell, Neal A. "Endure It Well." *Ensign* 20 (May 1990): 33-35. Also in *CR* (March/April 1990): 42-46. Commentary on 2 Nephi 31:15 wherein it is written that "he that endureth to the end, the same shall be saved." Testing is an integral part of life; endurance is more than merely putting up with a problem. It is learning from what we experience, loving and proceeding in spite of fatigue. It enlarges the mind and the heart. [J.W.M.]

M.090 Maxwell, Neal A. "King Benjamin's Manual of Discipleship." *Ensign* 22 (January 1992): 8-13. In Mosiah 2-5, King Benjamin describes how to be a true disciple of Christ. The process begins with casting away the tendencies of the natural man and intently striving to become a follower of Christ through obtaining godly characteristics, giving service to fellowmen, and rendering all that we have to God. "The qualities of a disciple haven't changed since King Benjamin spoke centuries ago." [B.D.]

M.091 Maxwell, Neal A. *Looking Beyond the Mark*. Salt Lake City: University of Utah Institute of Religion, 1976. A devotional address concentrating on Jacob's observation of people who "miss the point" or "look beyond the mark." [D.M.]

M.092 Maxwell, Neal A. *Plain and Precious Things*. Salt Lake City: Deseret Book, 1983. The purpose of the Book of Mormon is to support the Bible in bearing witness of Christ. Though it is a highly complex instructional book in its plot, structure, and symbolism, its greatest value lies in its spiritual message. The purpose of scriptures is to remove stumbling blocks, to elevate our minds, hearts, and standards, and to deepen our trust by revealing the purposes of God. [J.W.M.]

M.093 Maxwell, Neal A. "The Reality of the Living Scriptures." In Maxwell's *Things As They Really Are*, 83-109. Salt Lake City, UT: Deseret

Book, 1978. Attempting to encourage greater scripture study, the author testifies that the Book of Mormon is the "most correct book," a second witness for Christ, and that there is "a seamless structure of truths" in the scriptures. The scriptures define reality in very profound ways. The Book of Mormon passages sustain and clarify many biblical teachings. [J.W.M.]

M.094 Maxwell, Neal A. *That Ye May Believe.* Salt Lake City: Bookcraft, 1992. A collection of letters written to the author's grandchildren with Book of Mormon scriptures interspersed throughout. Early members of the Church had received a firm testimony in spite of limited amounts of leisure time to study its contents. The author bears his own witness of the timeliness in which the Book of Mormon came forth. [J.W.M.]

M.095 Maxwell, Neal A. "Three Jaredites." *Ensign* 8 (August 1978): 6-11. A didactic essay, demonstrating positive and negative qualities of Ether, Shiz, and Coriantumr. Traits to be emulated and avoided are indicated. [D.M.]

M.096 McAllister, Jack. "The Unlikely Daniel Webster Jones: First Spanish Translations from the Book of Mormon." *Ensign* 11 (August 1981): 50-52. Daniel Webster Jones went with a company of men from Missouri to fight in the war with Mexico. He was taken to Provo to recuperate from a gun accident and was introduced to the Book of Mormon. He was the first to translate portions of the book into Spanish with Mileton G. Trejo. [J.W.M.]

M.097 McBride, W. C. "The Cliff Dwellers and The Mormon Theory." *Pacific Monthly* (June 1907): 697-713. Written by a non-Mormon, the bulk of the article describes the terrain of the American Southwest. Last few pages deal with Book of Mormon origins. The author associates the migration of the Jaredites with a statement by Josephus, and he speculates on where the Book of Mormon peoples landed and settled. [D.M.]

M.098 McConkie, Bruce R. "Article 8: We believe the Bible to be the word of God as far as it is translated correctly; we also believe the Book of Mormon to be the word of God." In McConkie's *A New Witness for the Articles of Faith*, 389-471. Salt Lake City: Deseret Book, 1985. The Bible contains the fulness of the gospel, however, it has been perverted. Those who believe the Bible believe the Book of Mormon. The Book of Mormon is the record of Joseph, and it comes to us as a voice from the dust. The sealed portion of the Book of Mormon will be opened during the millennium. The restoration of the gospel will be effected as a result of the Book of Mormon. Moroni 10:3-5 teaches how to know the Book of Mormon is true, which knowledge is necessary because the Book of Mormon is the keystone of the Church of Jesus Christ of Latter-day Saints. [B.D.]

M.099 McConkie, Bruce R. "The Book of Mormon." *IE* 64 (June 1961): 402-5. The best possible missionary tool is the Book of Mormon combined with the power of the Holy Ghost. Joseph Smith said the Book of Mormon is the "most correct of any book on earth" and it is "the keystone of our religion." Author explains how anyone can find out for himself if the Book of Mormon is true. [M.D.P.]

M.100 McConkie, Bruce R. "The Book of Mormon: A Missionary Tool." *CR* (April 1961): 38-40. The Book of Mormon is the "most effective, compelling, and persuasive missionary tool ever given to any people in any age." It is the keystone of the LDS religion. With a testimony of it, the verity of the three greatest truths of the entire Restoration—Jesus Christ is the Son of God, Joseph Smith was a true prophet, and that the Church is true—will also be confirmed. [R.C.D.]

M.101 McConkie, Bruce R. " 'Book of Mormon' and Others." In McConkie's *Mormon Doctrine*, 92-94. Salt Lake City, UT: Bookcraft, 1958. Discusses the purposes of the Book of Mormon and presents a number of encyclopedic entries on Book of Mormon topics, including the brass plates, gold plates, Jaredites, Lamanite curse, Moroni, Mulekites, Nephites and Lamanites, Stick of Ephraim, Three Nephites, and the witnesses of the Book of Mormon. [D.W.P.]

M.102 McConkie, Bruce R. "The Book of Mormon and the Second Coming." In McConkie's *The Millennial Messiah*, 146-58. Salt Lake City: Deseret Book, 1982. The Book of Mormon was brought forth to prepare all of God's children for the Second Coming of Jesus Christ. The Book of Mormon, along with the Bible testifies to all that Jesus is the Christ. The sealed portion of the Book of Mormon will not be revealed until after the restoration of all things. [G.A.]

M.103 McConkie, Bruce R. *The Book of Mormon— Its Eternal Destiny*. N.p., n.d. Excerpts from an address on 18 August 1978 at BYU, and an October 1983 General Conference address. The 8th Article of Faith verifies LDS value of the Bible. Book of Mormon passages concerning the Jesus Christ's doctrine surpass their counterparts in the Bible. The Book of Mormon's destiny is to be a witness of Christ, to bring men to Christ, to aid in the gathering of Israel, and to offer salvation to people. [J.W.M.]

M.104 McConkie, Bruce R. "The Book That Prepares the Way." In McConkie's *The Millennial Messiah*, 169-181. Salt Lake City: Deseret Book, 1981. The Book of Mormon prepares humanity for the Second Coming of Jesus Christ. The Bible and the Book of Mormon work together in gathering the children of Israel, in both a spiritual and a temporal manner. [G.A.]

M.105 McConkie, Bruce R. "The Book That Welcomes the Second Coming." In McConkie's *The Millennial Messiah*, 159-68. Salt Lake City: Deseret Book, 1982. The Book of Mormon bears witness of Jesus Christ, sustains the teachings of the Bible, gathers scattered Israel into the true fold, and prepares humanity for the Second Coming of the Lord. Further, the Book of Mormon is a threat to Satan and will diminish his power. Therefore, Satan tries to convince individuals that revelation has ceased, and that the Book of Mormon is not necessary. [G.A.]

M.106 McConkie, Bruce R. "Come: Hear the Voice of the Lord." *Ensign* 15 (December 1985): 54. Tells about some of the features of the 1979 edition of the Book of Mormon, including some of the changes. [D.M.]

M.107 McConkie, Bruce R. "The Keystone of Our Religion." *IE* 68 (June 1965): 500-1. Those who seek truth may find it in the same way Joseph Smith did. The way has been prepared through the Book of Mormon, it is the witness of the divinity of the work of Jesus Christ and his Church. [J.W.M.]

M.108 McConkie, Bruce R. "The Keystone of Our Religion." *IE* 71 (June 1968): 46-48. Delineates the role of the Book of Mormon as the keystone of the LDS religion. [B.W.J.]

M.109 McConkie, Bruce R. "Scattering and Gathering of Israel." In *Proceedings of the Mexico and Central America Area Conference, August 1972*. Salt Lake City: Church of Jesus Christ of Latter-day Saints, 1973. The Book of Mormon contains a number of teachings regarding the scattering and gathering of Israel. [G.A.]

M.110 McConkie, Bruce R. "This Generation Shall Have My Word through You." *Ensign* 10 (June 1980): 54-59. Joseph Smith had the responsibility of giving the Lord's word to the world. That word is found in the scriptures, the chief of which is the Book of Mormon, another witness of Christ comparable to the Bible. [J.W.M.]

M.111 McConkie, Bruce R. Untitled talk. *CR* (October 1949): 75-80. The Book of Mormon is a tool for carrying the message of salvation to the world in this generation through Joseph Smith. The Book of Mormon is a witness that Joseph Smith is a prophet of God. The LDS message centers on three truths: Jesus is the divine Christ, his messages have been restored through Joseph Smith, and the LDS Church is the kingdom of God on earth. The Book of Mormon is the living witness to these truths. Those who read the Book of Mormon will "grow in faith and in righteousness until they become the sons of God, heirs to his eternal kingdom." [B.D.]

M.112 McConkie, Bruce R. Untitled talk. *CR* (April 1965): 27-29. Every person may receive answers in the same way Joseph Smith did. God is no respecter of persons, he answers prayers.

The way to receive the answer is through personal faith, prayer, and reading the Book of Mormon. This message was delivered by a holy angel and contains the record of a fallen people and the fullness of the gospel of Jesus Christ. It is the keystone of the LDS religion. [J.W.M.]

M.113 McConkie, Bruce R. Untitled talk. *CR* (April 1968): 19-21. The Book of Mormon contains the voice, mind, and will of God concerning his dealings with a people who possessed the fullness of the gospel of Jesus Christ. Its teachings conform with those of the Bible. Salvation is not found in a book, it is only found in Christ through his atoning sacrifice—it comes by the grace of God. Many prophets assisted in bringing forth the Book of Mormon. All may verify its truthfulness by following Moroni's counsel. [J.W.M.]

M.114 McConkie, Bruce R. Untitled talk. In *Proceedings of the Santiago, Chile Area Conference*. Salt Lake City: Church of Jesus Christ of Latter-day Saints, March 1977. Since all must hear the gospel, the Lord makes available his greatest missionary tool, the Book of Mormon. The message of the Church centers on three truths—Jesus is the divine Christ, his messages have been restored through Joseph Smith, and the LDS Church is the kingdom of God on earth. The Book of Mormon is the living witness to these truths. [J.W.M.]

M.115 McConkie, Bruce R. "What Think Ye of the Book of Mormon?" *Ensign* 13 (November 1983): 72-74. In order for an individual to know for certain whether or not the Book of Mormon is true, that individual must read the book, then ponder and pray about it. Individuals should not rely solely upon the testimony of others, but receive one's own testimony regarding the Book of Mormon. Outlines two tests that the reader can apply while reading the book to know if it is true. [S.P.S.]

M.116 McConkie, Bruce R. "What Think Ye of the Book of Mormon." In *Doctrines of The Restoration: Sermons and Writings of Bruce R. McConkie*, edited by Mark L. McConkie, 257-75. Salt Lake City, UT: Bookcraft, 1989. Relating an experience with ministers of other faiths, the author points out the problems and importance of presenting the Book of Mormon to the world. The Book of Mormon is an essential part of the restitution of all things, and coupled with the Bible comprises that portion of the Gospel that people are willing to receive. Neither is the complete record of God. The Book of Mormon is a correction text and proves the truthfulness of the Bible. [J.W.M.]

M.117 McConkie, Joseph Fielding. "The Book of Mormon and the Doctrinal Restoration." In *A Symposium on the Book of Mormon*, 91-96. Salt Lake City: Church of Jesus Christ of Latter-day Saints, CES, August 1986. The Book of Mormon contains the fullness of the gospel. It teaches the plan of salvation and the necessity of gospel ordinances. One mission of the Book of Mormon was to bring about the doctrinal restoration, thus ending the apostasy. [G.A.]

M.118 McConkie, Joseph Fielding. "A Comparison of Book of Mormon and Bible Teachings on the Doctrines of Salvation." In *The Book of Mormon: The Keystone Scripture*, edited by Paul R. Cheesman, Kent S. Brown, and Charles D. Tate Jr., 73-90. Provo, UT: Brigham Young University Religious Studies Center, 1988. The Bible delivers a detailed account of events, but does not provide reasons why the events occurred. The Book of Mormon provides detailed reasons why events occurred and explains doctrines with completeness and clarity. [G.A.]

M.119 McConkie, Joseph Fielding. "The Final Gathering to Christ." In *Studies in Scripture: Alma 30 to Moroni*, edited by Kent P. Jackson, 184-95. Salt Lake City: Deseret Book, 1988. A commentary on the theme of gathering as taught in 3 Nephi 20-22. Defines "gentiles," and points out their role in the last days; shows how the gathering is connected with the Abrahamic covenant; discusses the New Jerusalem and the role the Jews will have in the gathering. [D.M.]

M.120 McConkie, Joseph Fielding. "The Gathering of Israel and the Return of Christ." In *The Sixth*

Annual Religious Educator's Symposium on the Book of Mormon, 59-62. Salt Lake City: Church of Jesus Christ of Latter-day Saints, 1982. Uses the Book of Mormon as a guide for understanding the scattering and gathering of Israel. Discusses why the scattering took place, when the gathering will occur, when the old and new Jerusalems will be built/rebuilt, the role of Christ, and other related items. [A.T.]

M.121 McConkie, Joseph Fielding. *His Name Shall Be Joseph: Ancient Prophecies of the Latter-day Seer*. Salt Lake City: Hawkes, 1980. An elaboration of the prophecy of Lehi in 2 Nephi 3, which is similar to the prophecy in JST Genesis 50. A useful study on prophetic anticipations of Joseph Smith. [D.M.]

M.122 McConkie, Joseph Fielding. "The Promise of Eternal Life." In *Studies in Scripture: 1 Nephi to Alma 29*, edited by Kent P. Jackson, 162-74. Salt Lake City: Deseret Book, 1987. Reflections on 2 Nephi 31-33. Discusses the first principles and ordinances of the gospel and how Christ set the perfect example by being baptized. Treats the blessings derived from the Holy Ghost and the importance of prayer. Nephi's testimony is solemn and binding. [D.M.]

M.123 McConkie, Joseph Fielding. "The Testimony of Christ Through the Ages." In *The Book of Mormon: Jacob through Words of Mormon, To Learn with Joy*, edited by Monte S. Nyman and Charles D. Tate Jr., 157-73. Provo, UT: Brigham Young University Religious Studies Center, 1990. Jacob 4 teaches that all prophets testified of Christ; all prophets worshipped the father in the name of Christ; Abraham's offering of Isaac was a representation of Christ (as was the law of Moses); we should not look beyond the mark; and someday the Jews will recognize the Christ known to their fathers. [D.M.]

M.124 McConkie, Joseph Fielding, and Donald W. Parry. *A Guide to Scriptural Symbols*. Salt Lake City: Bookcraft, 1990. Discusses seven principal figures of speech that assist in understanding scriptural symbols: metaphors, similes, implication, symbols revealed in plain language, metonymy, synecdoche, and parallelism. Examples of these principles are found in the Book of Mormon as well as the other books of the standard works. [J.W.M.]

M.125 McConkie, Joseph Fielding, and Robert L. Millet. *Doctrinal Commentary on the Book of Mormon: Volume 1—First and Second Nephi*. Salt Lake City: Bookcraft, 1987. Verse-by-verse doctrinal comments on 1 and 2 Nephi. Introductory essays include "Why the Book of Mormon," "Doctrinal Contributions of the Book of Mormon," and "Testimony of the Book of Mormon." [D.M.]

M.126 McConkie, Joseph Fielding, and Robert L. Millet. *Doctrinal Commentary on the Book of Mormon: Volume 2—Jacob through Mosiah*. Salt Lake City: Bookcraft, 1988. Consideration of doctrines taught in the books of Jacob to Mosiah, discussed verse-by-verse or in clusters of verses. Each section includes a heading, one or more verses quoted from the Book of Mormon, and then a commentary by the authors. [D.M.]

M.127 McConkie, Joseph Fielding, and Robert L. Millet. *Doctrinal Commentary on the Book of Mormon: Volume 3—Alma through Helaman*. Salt Lake City: Bookcraft, 1991. Authors make topical comments on each verse (or cluster of verses) of Alma and Helaman. Alma 43-62, dealing with war, do not contain a detailed discussion of verses, but a six-page exposition on various subthemes. The work is doctrinally oriented. [D.M.]

M.128 McConkie, Joseph Fielding, Robert L Millet, and Brent L. Top. *Doctrinal Commentary on the Book of Mormon: Volume 4—3 Nephi through Moroni*. Salt Lake City: Bookcraft, 1992. The final volume of the series, consisting of commentary on verses from 3 Nephi through Moroni. A reflective essay culminates the work. [D.M.]

M.129 McConkie, Kathleen. "Defending Against Evil." *Ensign* 22 (January 1992): 19-21. Explains why Mormon used valuable space on the plates to record military intrigue and battle strategy. Satan's war "against truth and righteousness" occurring today requires divine guidance as found in the Book of Mormon, "the Lord's combat manual for the latter days." By using warfare chapters as a " 'type and shadow' of the eternal war between good and evil," individuals can prevail against Satan's forces. [A.C.W.]

M.130 McConkie, Oscar W. "Book of Mormon." In McConkie's *The Kingdom of God,* 285-92. Salt Lake City: Church of Jesus Christ of Latter-day Saints, 1962. A priesthood manual for priests. Recounts the events and facts surrounding angel Moroni's visit in September 1823, gives a short synopsis of the Book of Mormon and of references from the Old and New Testaments that refer to the Book of Mormon: Ezekiel 37, Isaiah, and Revelation 14. The testimony of the witnesses reinforce Moroni's challenge to read the book and ask concerning the truth. [J.W.M.]

M.131 McConkie, Oscar W. "The Witnesses to the Book of Mormon." *MS* 96 (15 February 1934): 97-103. The legal status of the testimony of the witnesses to the Book of Mormon is important. "Their witness stands unimpeached before the world." Despite apostasy, none ever denied his testimony; all were honorable, upstanding men. [A.C.W.]

M.132 McCormick, Marjorie A. "You Bring Them and I'll Read Them." *Ensign* 7 (September 1977): 75-76. A friend at work gave some LDS tracts to this author's husband. The couple purchased and read the Book of Mormon, and the Holy Ghost testified of its truthfulness in a miraculous way. [J.W.M.]

M.133 McDonald, A. Melvin. *The Day of Defense.* Denton, TX: Alpha, 1974. Places the Book of Mormon in a hypothetical trial situation with a judge (Jewish rabbi), prosecutors (members of religious denominations), and defendants (LDS missionaries). The verdict is that the Book of Mormon was truly revealed of God. [J.W.M.]

M.134 McDonald, Angus. *Prophetic Numbers: Or the Rise, Progress, and Future Destiny of the Mormons by a Free Thinking Optical Professor, Who Will Deliver Lectures on the Subject, Illustrated by Stereopticon Dissolving Views, and Zodiacal Map.* Salt Lake City: W. M. Egan, 1885. Shows how using the prophetic numbers may prove that the establishment of the LDS church and the coming forth of the Book of Mormon fits the prophetic timetable found in the scriptures such as those in Daniel and the book of Revelation. Advocates that the Book of Mormon substantiates plural marriage. [J.W.M.]

M.135 McDonald, Carolyn. "The Textbook Was a Revelation." *Ensign* 19 (March 1989): 10-11. A personal story of conversion to the Book of Mormon and the Church through attendance at religion class. [D.M.]

M.136 McDonnell, John. "Lehi's Vision and the Parable of the Sower." In *Recent Book of Mormon Developments*, 145-47. Independence, MO: Zarahemla Research Foundation, 1984. Also published in *ZR* 11 (Winter 1981): 3, 6, 8. Divides the parable of the sower and Lehi's vision into four responses: the first is unbelief, represented by Laman and Lemuel and the seeds that fell by the wayside; second is "partial belief; no effort"; the third is "more belief; some effort"; and the fourth is "belief leads to faith with assurance." [A.T.]

M.137 McGavin, E. Cecil. *An Apology for the Book of Mormon.* Salt Lake City: Deseret News Press, 1930. The relationship of the Book of Mormon to the Bible from the standpoint of literary accuracy is discussed. The author justifies the textual changes in the Book of Mormon by rehearsing a historical trail of changes made in the English Bible. [D.M.]

M.138 McGavin, E. Cecil "Book of Mormon and Peace." *MS* 104 (19 November 1942): 738-39, 749. From the Nephites we learn the importance of self-defense to protect one's homeland, freedom, and religion, but also the necessity of finding lasting peace. Contrasts two individuals—Moroni and Zerahemnah. [A.C.W.]

M.139 McGavin, E. Cecil. *How We Got the Book of Mormon.* Salt Lake City: Deseret Book, 1960. Details the coming forth of the Book of Mormon by naming its authors and their records, the transferal of the gold plates from generation to generation, the nature of metal records, and Joseph Smith's role in the process. [D.M.]

M.140 McGavin, E. Cecil. "Indian Traditions of the Book of Mormon." *Instructor* 66 (August 1931): 449-52. Traditions of the Indians tell of "a book" that their forefathers once possessed. It was taken from them, buried, and promised that it would come forth at a later time. Accounts from letters and journals of early missionaries of the Church as well as scholars of ancient Indians tell of these traditions. [J.W.M.]

M.141 McGavin, E. Cecil. "The Lord's Promise to the Lamanites." *IE* 30 (October 1927): 1095-97. Contrasts the benighted condition of the Indians when the European colonists arrived in America with the glorious promises that are yet to come as prophesied in the Book of Mormon. [D.M.]

M.142 McGavin, E. Cecil. "A Man of Destiny." *IE* 42 (October 1939): 600, 628. The voyage of Christopher Columbus was foreseen by the Book of Mormon prophets. The spirit of the Lord "wrought upon the man." Columbus wrote to King Ferdinand of his desire to spread the word of God as foretold by the prophet Isaiah in chapters 24 and 64. His journal excerpts show his loyalty to God and his own knowledge of his divine appointment. He recorded that an angel appeared to him and gave him keys to "bind the oceans" and to link the continents. [J.W.M.]

M.143 McGavin, E. Cecil. "Martin Harris and the Lost Manuscript." In McGavin's *The Historical Background of the Doctrine and Covenants*, 23-39. Salt Lake City: Paragon, 1949. Martin Harris was changeable and fickle, while his wife was strong willed and aggressive. She was convinced that the new religious movement started by Joseph Smith was fraudulent. No one knows the real story of how the Book of Mormon manuscript pages were lost. The small plates of Nephi filled the gap made by the loss. So strong was the impression of this lesson on Joseph Smith's mind that from that time forward copies were made of all written material. [J.W.M.]

M.144 McGavin, E. Cecil. *A Marvelous Work and a Wonder*. Salt Lake City: KSL radio, 1941. A series of radio addresses on the Book of Mormon discussing metal plates, the Spaulding manuscript, Hebrew traits and Bible quotations within it, the antiquity of the book, its current relevance, the Book of Mormon as a witness of the Bible, and the witnesses. [D.M.]

M.145 McGavin, E. Cecil. "Moroni Looks Down upon a World at War." *IE* 47 (January 1944): 6, 37. Moroni experienced two aspects of war—he rallied his soldiers in defense of their liberties and later witnessed the destruction of his people. Moroni later wrote concerning the destruction of his people. [D.M.]

M.146 McGavin, E. Cecil. "Whitmer Hospitality." In McGavin's *The Historical Background of the Doctrine and Covenants,* 55-60. Salt Lake City: Paragon, 1949. The final work of translation of the Book of Mormon took place in the home of Oliver Cowdery's good friends, the Peter Whitmers. The final task of translation was done in relative silence and great care was taken so as to create no contention in the home or the neighborhood. The Whitmer sons were given a special witness of the divinity of the work and later as a reward their mother was favored to see the plates at the hands of Moroni. [J.W.M.]

M.147 McGavin, E. Cecil, and A. S. Reynolds. "The Coming Forth of the Book of Mormon." *MS* 101 (17 August 1939): 517-18, 523. Because of fear, the people of Palmyra tried to prevent publication of the Book of Mormon. For this reason two copies of the translation were made and only portions went to the publisher at a time. A covenant was made among people in the community that not a single copy would be bought. Despite this difficult beginning, the Book of Mormon has become the second best seller in the nation, published also in Braille. [J.W.M.]

M.148 McGavin, E. Cecil, and A. S. Reynolds. "The Consistency of the Book of Mormon." *MS* 101 (21 September 1939): 602-3, 606. It would have been impossible for an uneducated farm boy to have written the text of the Book of Mormon without provincialism upon every page. Anachronisms and other errors are not part of it. Much information that has recently been uncovered by archaeologists support the book. Though Shakespeare was an accomplished writer his works contain modernized character's attire. [J.W.M.]

M.149 McGavin, E. Cecil, and A. S. Reynolds. "Literary Aspects of the Book of Mormon." *MS* 101 (19 October 1939): 667-68. A literary study of the Bible assists in understanding its origin, purpose, and interpretation; the same is true of the Book of Mormon. Religious truths are conveyed in a distinctive way. The Book of Mormon is mainly narration of a pedantic style with a universal appeal. It was far more important to both recorder and translator that the book be understood than to be a literary masterpiece. [J.W.M.]

M.150 McGavin, E. Cecil, and Willard W. Bean. "Cumorah-Land, An Ancient Battlefield." *IE* 44 (September 1941): 526, 571-72. Discusses the authors' point of view concerning the identity of the Hill Cumorah as an ancient battlefield. Authors conclude that the scholars "need not search for (Cumorah) in Mexico or Yucatan." [L.D.]

M.151 McGavin, E. Cecil, and Willard W. Bean. *The Geography of the Book of Mormon*. Salt Lake City: Bookcraft, 1948. Argues that the Hill Cumorah and Hill Ramah as geographical locations in the Book of Mormon were located in upstate New York. It therefore challenges the theory that the Hill Cumorah was located somewhere in Latin America. At least some Book of Mormon history took place in southeast Canada and the northeast United States. [D.M.]

M.152 McKay, David O. "Three Witnesses of the Book of Mormon." *IE* 63 (November 1960): 790-91, 855. A review of the lives of Oliver Cowdery, David Whitmer, and Martin Harris, the Three Witnesses of the Book of Mormon. Although the Three Witnesses later left the Church, none of them ever denied their testimony of the Book of Mormon. [R.C.D.]

M.153 McKay, David O. "Witnesses to the Truth." *IE* 54 (July 1951): 493-94, 542. There are many witnesses to the truth. The Three Witnesses saw the plates and bore witness of the validity of the Book of Mormon. The Holy Spirit also is a witness to the truth. [J.W.M.]

M.154 McKean, Jerry. " 'Just Cut My Hair and Don't Preach!' " *Ensign* 20 (April 1990): 63-65. A touching and humorous conversion story, in which the Book of Mormon was the converting agent. [D.M.]

M.155 McKiernan, F. Mark. "Advent of Mormonism into the Western Reserve." In McKiernan's *The Voice of One Crying in the Wilderness, 1971*, 25-42. Lawrence, KS: Coronado Press, 1971. Gives an historical account of the life of Sidney Rigdon, his conversion through the Book of Mormon to the LDS church, and refutes the theory that Sidney Rigdon had any connection with the Spaulding manuscript or authorship of the Book of Mormon. Family members offer proof that Matilda Davidson and Ellen E. Dickinson had reported falsely about Rigdon's involvement. [J.W.M.]

M.156 McNeely, Brent E. "The Book of Mormon and the Heavenly Book Motif." In *Reexploring the Book of Mormon*, edited by John W. Welch, 26-28. Salt Lake City: Deseret Book and FARMS, 1992. Joseph Smith's reception of the gold plates from the angel Moroni fits a common pattern of the ancient Near East. Many writings, both biblical (i.e., Exodus 31:18, Ezekiel 2:9-10, Revelation 10:8), and non-biblical (i.e., the Vision of Hermas) were delivered to individuals from a heavenly being. [N.K.Y.]

M.157 Meek, Shirleen. "Inosi's Golden Book." *Ensign* 21 (August 1991): 64-66. After almost two years of excuses and avoiding the missionaries and their "golden book," the loss of a newborn son made Inosi think about religion and God. Soon he accepted the challenge of baptism. [J.W.M.]

M.158 Mehew, Randall K. *Historical Outline of the Book of Mormon*. Orem, UT: Millennial Press, 1983. Contains a thumbnail sketch of several important personalities in the Book of Mormon. Provides Book of Mormon maps, tables, and materials dealing with chronology. [D.M.]

M.159 Mehew, Randall K. *A Most Convincing Witness: Reasons Why the Book of Mormon Is the*

True Word of God. Orem, UT: Keepsake Paperbacks, 1990. Presents arguments dealing with the authenticity of the Book of Mormon, including discussions about Jesus, the Shepherd, the witnesses, revelation from God, the translation of the work, ancient discoveries, and testimonials. [R.H.B.]

M.160 "Melchizedek Priesthood: Book of Mormon Is Special Witness." *IE* 68 (July 1965): 634. Members should "bear their witness of the truth of the restoration of the gospel" and of the Book of Mormon. [M.D.P.]

M.161 Melonakos, Christine. *Turn Your Little Ones into Book of Mormon Whiz Kids.* Bountiful, UT: Horizon, 1990. Activities for young children designed to increase their fine and gross motor skills while teaching them about the Book of Mormon. [D.W.P.]

M.162 Melville, Alton C. "Quetzalcoatl." *IE* 32 (December 1928): 122-26. Provides several legends and descriptions of the "feathered serpent" god called Quetzalcoatl and links Jesus Christ and his visit to the Americas (3 Nephi) with him. Quetzalcoatl was known as a light complexioned wise benefactor. After having spent some time with the ancestors of the Aztecs, he promised to return to them. [D.M.]

M.163 Melville, Alton C. "Recent Scientific Investigations: They Substantiate the Book of Mormon." *IE* 30 (February 1927): 311-14. A study of archaeological remains in Panama lead one archaeologist from New York to call it "the Pompeii of ancient America." Melville believes Panama finds corroboration with the Book of Mormon in such issues as location and size, commerce, industries, cloth, tools, and elephants. [D.M.]

M.164 Melville, Alton C. "The Reign of the Judges: An Outline of Nephite Government." *IE* 31 (January 1928): 240-41. Discusses King Mosiah's political discourse in which he introduces a democratic government and does away with the autocratic government system of kings. Democratic laws that were implemented into the Nephite judicial system at this time include the right to appeal, capital punishment, cross examination, and religious freedom. [L.D.]

M.165 Menzies, James S., Merle P. Guthrie, and Richard M. Reid. *Christ in America.* Independence, MO: Herald House, 1965. A tract that briefly recites the account of Jesus' ministry to the Lehites. Offers archaeological and other evidences to substantiate the event. [D.M.]

M.166 Menzies, James S., Merle P. Guthrie, and Richard M. Reid. *Evidences of the Book of Mormon.* Independence, MO: Herald House, 1966. Authors make reference to secular evidences related to the Book of Mormon that are offered by non-LDS scholars in such matters as medicine and astronomy. They also relate the Book of Mormon to passages in Ezekiel 37, Jeremiah 49, Genesis 49, and Isaiah 29. [D.M.]

M.167 Merrill, A. Brent. "Nephite Captains and Armies." In *Warfare in the Book of Mormon*, edited by Stephen D. Ricks and William J. Hamblin, 266-95. Salt Lake City: Deseret Book and FARMS, 1990. Compares the organization of armies of the Book of Mormon to those of the ancient Near East. Discusses the Nephite captains and chief captains. Fifties, hundreds, thousands, and ten thousands were the usual army units. The Book of Mormon depicts war as being sordid, tedious, destructive, exhausting, and boring. It depicts great military leaders who deplored war and may help us see the futility of it in our day. [N.K.Y.]

M.168 Merrill, Amos N., and Alton D. Merrill. "Changing Thought on the Book of Mormon." *IE* 45 (September 1942): 568. A published summary of Merrill's thesis, written in 1940 (see above), wherein the author examined publications dealing with the Book of Mormon and noted the themes emphasized during the periods 1830-1855 and 1915-1940. [L.D.]

M.169 Merrill, Byron R. "Government by the Voice of the People: A Witness and a Warning." In *The Book of Mormon: Mosiah, Salvation Only through Christ*, edited by Monte S. Nyman and Charles D. Tate Jr., 113-37. Provo, UT: Brigham Young University Religious Studies Center, 1991. Provides a history and definition of the Nephite system of government and shows parallels and differences with the American political system. The warnings outlined in Mosiah 29 are relevant to the present condition in America. [D.M.]

M.170 Merrill, Byron R. "Joseph Smith and the Lamanites." In *Joseph Smith: The Prophet, the Man*, edited by Susan Easton Black and Charles D. Tate Jr., 187-202. Provo, UT: Brigham Young University Religious Studies Center, 1993. Joseph taught that the aboriginal inhabitants of North America were literal descendants of Abraham, people of the covenant. Following the first interview with Moroni, Joseph related to his family detailed descriptions of their mode of dress, travel, animals, cities, buildings, warfare and religious worship. He left them a great legacy in the form of the translation of the record of their ancestry, which has done more for the Lamanite than any other effort made in their behalf. [J.W.M.]

M.171 Merrill, Byron R. "To Become as a Little Child: The Quest for Humility." In *Doctrines of the Book of Mormon, 1991 Sperry Symposium*, edited by Bruce A. Van Orden and Brent L. Top, 114-26. Salt Lake City: Deseret Book, 1992. To be humble in the scriptural sense does not mean to be obsequious but to obey God cheerfully in all things, to possess the traits of a child, i.e., submissiveness, meekness, patience, being filled with love, and to discard the negative trappings of adulthood. Pride is the opposite of humility, as exemplified by the Rameumptom. Other examples, positive and negative, are given. [D.M.]

M.172 Merrill, Hyde M. "Christopher Columbus and the Book of Mormon." *IE* 69 (February 1966): 96-98, 135-36. Discusses Lehi's prophecy regarding "a man among the Gentiles" (Columbus) who would be "wrought upon" by the Holy Ghost and travel "forth upon many waters" (1 Nephi 13:12). Presents evidence from Columbus's journals and letters that support the claim that he was an inspired man who accomplished "a thing more divine than human to have found that way never before known to go to the east where the spices grow" (Sebastian Cabot). [B.W.J.]

M.173 Merrill, Joseph F. *The Truth Seeker and Mormonism*. Independence, MO: Zions, 1946. Transcripts of radio messages, two of which relate to the Book of Mormon. Speaks concerning the truthfulness of the Book of Mormon; contains the testimony of the Eight Witnesses, the final statements of the Three Witnesses, and explores the possibility of collusion. [J.W.M.]

M.174 Merrill, Joseph F. Untitled talk. *CR* (April 1930): 147-48. The Book of Mormon is physical evidence of the divinity of the Church of Jesus Christ of Latter-day Saints. If the Book of Mormon is true then God is a personal being and has visited the earth. If the Book of Mormon is false, then Mormonism is a fraud. [B.D.]

M.175 Merrill, Joseph F. Untitled talk. *CR* (April 1937): 37-42. Discusses Joseph Smith's first vision, the appearance of the angel Moroni, the restoration of the Priesthood, and the Book of Mormon as the best evidence of Joseph Smith's prophetic call. The book came forth by the power of God and cannot be refuted. [J.W.M.]

M.176 Meservy, Keith H. "The Book of Mormon, Biblical Prophecies about." In *Encyclopedia of Mormonism*, edited by Daniel H. Ludlow, 1:159-60. New York: Macmillan, 1992. The Book of Mormon fulfills many Bible prophecies: Joseph, who was sold into Egypt, later prophesied about his numerous descendants; Jesus referred to other sheep of his fold; Isaiah predicted cities like Ariel (Jerusalem) would be destroyed but her speech would whisper as a voice out of the ground; Ezekiel prophesied about two records, one of Ephraim and another of Judah. [N.K.Y.]

M.177 Meservy, Keith H. "Discoveries at Nimrud and the 'Sticks' of Ezekiel." *SEHA Newsletter* 142 (November 1978): 1-10. The word for "stick" in Ezekiel 37 (Hebrew *etz*) is normally translated "wood." The word corresponds to the Babylonian *is le'u*, referring to a writing tablet. Etymologically and culturally, it is likely that Ezekiel wrote about joining the tablets of Judah and Joseph to form what would eventually be called the Bible and the Book of Mormon. [D.M.]

M.178 Meservy, Keith H. "Ezekiel's Sticks." *Ensign* 7 (September 1977): 22-27. Discusses how Ezekiel knew that Joseph's stick (the Book of Mormon) would be joined to Judah's stick (the

Bible) from Ezekiel 37:16-17. Provides scriptural and archaeological notes. [L.D.]

M.179 Meservy, Keith H. "Ezekiel's Sticks and the Gathering of Israel." *Ensign* 17 (February 1987): 4-13. Links a 1948 discovery—that ancient scribes kept records on wax-covered, wooden writing boards—to the sticks of Joseph and Judah spoken of in Ezekiel 37. The coming together of these two records mark the beginning of the physical gathering of Israel (gathering to lands and countries) and the spiritual gathering of Israel (return to God). [S.P.S.]

M.180 Meservy, Keith H. "Jerusalem at the Time of Lehi and Jeremiah." *Ensign* 18 (January 1988): 22-25. Quotes from the Old Testament book of Jeremiah and the Book of Mormon in order to summarize the history of Jerusalem during the time of Nebuchadnezzar's rule. [D.L.L.]

M.181 Meservy, Keith H. "The 'Writing Boards' of Ezekiel and What They Mean." In *A Symposium on the Book of Mormon*, 81-92. Salt Lake City: Church of Jesus Christ of Latter-day Saints, 1979. An exposition of Ezekiel 37. In order to bring about the Lord's program of restoration it was necessary to remedy five problem areas: (1) the scattering of Israel, Judah included; (2) Judah's nonacceptance of the Messiah; (3) the floundering of Joseph's descendants resulting from a loss of identity; (4) the need to call Israel back to the Lord; and (5) replacement of false doctrine with true doctrine. The two sticks of Joseph and Judah may be seen as writing tablets or boards. [D.M.]

M.182 Mesle, Carl. "The Fifth and Sixth Gospels." *Restoration Witness* 7 (April 1969): 4-5. The Book of Mormon is an account of God's dealings with his people in America and is a second witness for Christ. 3 Nephi may be considered the "Fifth Gospel" and the Doctrine and Covenants represents the "Sixth Gospel" of Christ. Together these works set forth the correct way of life. [J.W.M.]

M.183 Michelsen, Rasmus. "Paleontology and the Book of Mormon." *IE* 36 (January 1933): 150-52. Provides information regarding a number of recent paleontological discoveries that shed light on Book of Mormon statements regarding oxen, sheep and other animals, and the smelting of iron. [D.M.]

M.184 Mickelson, Lynn A. "What Is Truth?" *Ensign* 20 (November 1990): 27-29. Anti-Mormon literature destroyed the faith of one individual but strengthened a second individual. When dealing with religious literature, the right questions need to be asked, hearts must be prepared, truth must be sought with the aid of the spirit. [J.W.M.]

M.185 Midgley, Louis C. "The Challenge of Historical Consciousness: Mormon History and the Encounter with Secular Modernity." In *By Study and Also by Faith,* edited by John M. Lundquist and Stephen D. Ricks, 2:502-51. Salt Lake City: Deseret Book and FARMS, 1990. Relates the tensions that have arisen between two types of Mormon historians: those who see history naturalistically and those who perceive a divine dimension. The Book of Mormon is explained on either basis, and the implications of one's approach yields significant implications. [D.M.]

M.186 Midgley, Louis C. " 'O Man Remember, and Perish Not' Mosiah 4:30." In *Reexploring the Book of Mormon,* edited by John W. Welch, 127-29. Salt Lake City: Deseret Book and FARMS, 1992. Elements of the phrase "remember" is repeated some 200 times in the Book of Mormon and emphasized on its title page and in the sacramental prayers. To remember one's covenants is an essential gospel principle that is taught both in the Book of Mormon and in the Old Testament. [N.K.Y.]

M.187 Midgley, Louis C. "Ways of Remembrance." In *Rediscovering The Book of Mormon,* edited by John L. Sorenson and Melvin J. Thorne, 168-76. Salt Lake City: Deseret Book and FARMS, 1991. Over two hundred times the Book of Mormon uses terms related to "remembering" and "forgetting." The word remembrance seems to carry the connotations of not only recalling past information but also involves an active participation linked with covenant keeping. [J.W.M.]

M.188 Mikeska, Barbara Gail. "The Morning After." In *Stories of Insight and Inspiration,* edited by Margie Calhoun Jensen, 34-37. Salt Lake City: Bookcraft, 1976. A conversion story of a woman raised in a Catholic home who, during a time of great despair, sought the Lord in prayer and was introduced to the Book of Mormon by a friend. [J.W.M.]

M.189 Miller, Anita. "If You're Having Trouble Getting Started." *Ensign* 2 (December 1972): 71. A story of conversion through the Book of Mormon. A teacher advised that if anyone had trouble getting started reading the Book of Mormon that they should begin with 3 Nephi. Mrs. Miller did and gave the book to her husband to do the same. Within six months he had completed the entire book and was baptized. [J.W.M.]

M.190 Miller, Helen M. "Now I Wake Early." *Ensign* 6 (September 1976): 21-22. Two young men with a Book of Mormon answered a desire of the author to know the origin of the ancient inhabitants of America. As a hungry person feasting, the author feasts upon the words of Christ in the Book of Mormon each morning. [J.W.M.]

M.191 Miller, Jeanette W. "The Tree of Life, A Personification of Christ." *Journal of Book of Mormon Studies* 2 (Spring 1993): 93-106. The author proposes "that the tree of life is a personification of Jesus Christ." Compares some of the basic elements of Lehi's dream and its subsequent interpretation with other passages of scripture and with symbolism of the tree of life in other cultures, and writes concerning the tree of life in connection with the temple and temple typology. [A.T.]

M.192 Miller, Ken. "The Book of Mormon." In Miller's *Mormonism: A Happy Way to Live!* 97-109. Bountiful, UT: Horizon, 1977. Also published as "The Book of Mormon." In Miller's *What the Mormons Believe: An Introduction to the Teachings of the LDS Church*, 97-109. Bountiful, UT: Horizon Publishers, 1981. "The purpose of the Book of Mormon is to help us come to know and live the plan of our Heavenly Father, to believe in Jesus Christ, and to learn and practice his teachings." This chapter includes a synopsis of the coming forth of the Book of Mormon, declares the Book of Mormon to be a second witness for Christ, discusses the appearance of Jesus in the Americas, and exhorts the readers to study, pray about, and learn of the truthfulness of the Book of Mormon for themselves. [J.W.M.]

M.193 Miller, M. Lee. "Priesthood Principles and Church Organization in the Book of Mormon." In *The Sixth Annual CES Religious Educator's Symposium on the Book of Mormon*, 63-65. Salt Lake City: Church of Jesus Christ of Latter-day Saints, 1982. The Church was organized and functioned with common priesthood principles in Book of Mormon times similar to the way in which the LDS church is now organized. Author provides evidence of organizational principles, priesthood functions and priesthood keys, apostolic power, and similar items. [A.T.]

M.194 Millet, Robert L. "Abinadi's Messianic Sermon (Mosiah 12-16)." In *A Symposium on the Book of Mormon*, 97-103. Salt Lake City: Church of Jesus Christ of Latter-day Saints, CES, August 1986. Covers several points in Mosiah 12-16: the relationship between the law of Moses and the atonement; Abinadi's exposition on Isaiah's suffering servant (Isaiah 53); the ways in which Christ embodies the roles of Father and Son; and teachings on the resurrection. [D.M.]

M.195 Millett, Robert L. "Alma$_2$." In *Encyclopedia of Mormonism*, edited by Daniel H. Ludlow, 1:33-35. 5 vols. New York: Macmillan, 1992. A description of Alma, the son of Alma, and his activities for and against the Church. [B.D.]

M.196 Millet, Robert L. "Another Testament of Jesus Christ." In *The Book of Mormon: First Nephi, the Doctrinal Foundation*, edited by Monte S. Nyman and Charles D. Tate Jr., 161-75. Provo, Utah: Brigham Young University Religious Studies Center, 1988. Addresses the need for the Book of Mormon as an additional testament to the Bible and as another witness of Christ, the identity of the guide in the vision of Nephi, the condescension of God (1 Nephi 11:13-16), and the importance of the tree of life in the visions of Nephi and Lehi. [A.T.]

M.197 Millet, Robert L. "The Brass Plates: An Inspired and Expanded Version of the Old Testament." In *The Old Testament and the Latter-day Saints*, 415-43. Provo, UT: Randall, 1986. Discusses the influence of the brass plates in the Book of Mormon, their nature and origin, and information from the plates that is not contained in the Bible. This new information strongly resembles "in subject and specific language" the Joseph Smith Translation of the Bible. [A. L. & P. H.]

M.198 Millet, Robert L. *By Grace Are We Saved.* Salt Lake City: Bookcraft, 1989. Elaborates on the Book of Mormon theme of grace as it applies to salvation. Relates it to justification, sanctification, perfection, and acknowledging God's hand in all things. [D.M.]

M.199 Millet, Robert L. "The Gathering of Israel in the Book of Mormon: A Consistent Pattern." In *Rediscovering the Book of Mormon*, edited by John L. Sorenson and Melvin J. Thorne, 186-96. Salt Lake City: Deseret Book and FARMS, 1991. The Book of Mormon passages concerning the gathering of Israel paint a picture consistent with biblical ones. Joseph Smith and the Book of Mormon and those who possess it play a key role in the gathering. [J.W.M.]

M.200 Millet, Robert L. "The Holy Order of God." In *The Book of Mormon: Alma, The Testimony of the Word*, edited by Monte S. Nyman and Charles D. Tate Jr., 61-88. Provo, UT: Brigham Young University Religious Studies Center, 1992. A study on the priesthood as found in Alma 13. The priesthood of the Nephites was patriarchal, and many leaders were foreordained. The priesthood is "from eternity to all eternity." Explains the concept of "entering into the rest of God." Defines various properties of the priesthood and then describes Melchizedek as a prototype. [D.M. & N.K.Y.]

M.201 Millet, Robert L. "The Influence of the Brass Plates on the Teachings of Nephi." In *The Book of Mormon: Second Nephi, The Doctrinal Structure*, edited by Monte S. Nyman and Charles D. Tate Jr., 207-25. Provo, UT: Brigham Young University Religious Studies Center, 1989. The Nephites learned a great deal from the brass plates and incorporated teachings from them in their scriptures. [D.M.]

M.202 Millet, Robert L. "Joseph Smith among the Prophets." In *Joseph Smith: The Prophet, the Man,* edited by Susan Easton Black and Charles D. Tate Jr., 15-31. Provo, UT: Brigham Young University Religious Studies Center, 1993. Joseph Smith as the head of the final dispensation is a revealer of Christ. Gives evidence that Joseph Smith was ordained of God to bring forth the Book of Mormon. Joseph Smith was not just given the scriptures but was taught and tutored by the authors themselves. [J.W.M.]

M.203 Millet, Robert L. "Joseph Smith and Modern Mormonism: Orthodoxy, Neoorthodoxy, Tension, and Tradition." *BYU Studies* 29 (Summer 1989): 49-68. Challenges the assertion by Mormon revisionist historians related to "Mormon neoorthodoxy" that Joseph Smith taught a trinitarian concept in the Book of Mormon, but became progressively more liberal after 1835, when he evolved a view of Godhead describing three distinct beings. Disputes the "neoorthodoxy" thesis regarding the view of the fall, nature of man, and pathways to redemption. [D.M.]

M.204 Millet, Robert L. "Joseph Smith, the Book of Mormon, and the Nature of God." In *To Be Learned Is Good If. . .,* edited by Robert L. Millet, 59-76. Salt Lake City: Bookcraft, 1987. Argues that the Book of Mormon is valuable in illuminating the Bible. Seeming New Testament doctrinal anachronisms in the Book of Mormon are brought about by the loss of "plain and precious truths" from the original Bible. Defends the Book of Mormon as an inspired record, not as an aspect of Joseph Smith's evolving theology. Discusses the doctrine of the Father and the Son in the Book of Mormon. [D.M.]

M.205 Millet, Robert L. "Justice, Mercy, and the Life Beyond." In *Studies in Scripture: Alma 30 to Moroni*, edited by Kent P. Jackson, 56-68. Salt Lake City: Deseret Book, 1988. Treats the subjects dealt with when Alma was instructing Corianton (Alma 40-42): restoration, resurrection, justice, and mercy. Points out that what for Paul in Galatians is the law of the harvest for is restoration Alma. If justice were destroyed, God would cease to be God. [D.M.]

M.206 Millet, Robert L. *Lifting the Condemnation: The Sanctifying Power of the Book of Mormon.* Provo, UT: BYU Continuing Education, 1990.

A seminar presentation. The Latter-day Saints are under condemnation for not paying sufficient attention to the Book of Mormon. The Book of Mormon was written for our day and shows the manner in which individuals can sanctify their souls and draw closer to God. [D.W.P.]

M.207 Millet, Robert L. "The Love of God and of All Men: the Doctrine of Charity in the Book of Mormon." In *Doctrines of the Book of Mormon, 1991 Sperry Symposium*, edited by Bruce A. Van Orden and Brent L. Top, 127-44. Salt Lake City: Deseret Book, 1992. Considers various strands of charity or love. God loves us and we are to love one another. Comments on ingredients of charity mentioned in Moroni 7 and 1 Corinthians 13. Notes that there are obstacles to charity, such as immorality and crudeness. Charity is a fruit of the spirit and a key to enduring to the end. [D.M.]

M.208 Millet, Robert L. "The Ministry of the Father and the Son." In *The Book of Mormon: The Keystone Scripture*, edited by Paul R. Cheesman, S. Kent Brown, and Charles D. Tate Jr., 44-72. Provo, UT: Brigham Young University Religious Studies Center, 1988. Expounds on the differences between the Father and the Son, but also emphasizes that they are united. Shows the ways in which Jesus is the Eternal God, and the various ways in which he takes on the role of Father. [D.M.]

M.209 Millet, Robert L. "The Natural Man: An Enemy to God." In *The Book of Mormon: Mosiah, Salvation Only through Christ*, edited by Monte S. Nyman and Charles D. Tate Jr., 139-59. Provo, UT: Brigham Young University Religious Studies Center, 1991. Bases his exposition on King Benjamin's discourse, "the natural man is an enemy to God." Provides an in-depth discussion of the fall: its definition, its characteristics, and several misconceptions concerning it. Mankind is fallen and lost without the Redeemer and his atonement. [D.M.]

M.210 Millet, Robert L. "Nephi on the Destiny of Israel." In *Studies in Scripture: 1 Nephi to Alma 29*, edited by Kent P. Jackson, 73-85. Salt Lake City: Deseret Book, 1987. A study of 1 Nephi 19-22. States some possible theories of the origin of Laban's plates of brass and then discusses Nephi's teachings of the future of Israel as outlined by Zenos and Isaiah. [D.M.]

M.211 Millet, Robert L. "The Only Sure Foundation: Building on the Rock of our Redeemer." In *The Book of Mormon: Helaman through 3 Nephi 8, According to Thy Word*, edited by Monte S. Nyman and Charles D. Tate Jr., 15-37. Provo, UT: Brigham Young University Religious Studies Center, 1992. Discusses the doctrines taught by Helaman to his sons Nephi and Lehi in Helaman 5. Comments on the significance of deliverance from sin. Expounds on the role of the Father in the process of redemption, and of the stability of recognizing Jesus as our rock. [D.M.]

M.212 Millet, Robert L. "The Path of Repentance." In *Studies in Scripture: Alma 30 to Moroni*, edited by Kent P. Jackson, 48-55. Salt Lake City: Deseret Book, 1988. A discussion of Corianton's sin and Alma's response to it in Alma 39. Of the three most grievous sins, only the first two are not covered by the atonement. For all others repentance is possible. [D.M.]

M.213 Millet, Robert L. "The Plates of Brass: A Witness of Christ." *Ensign* 18 (January 1988): 26-29. Prophetic records, such as the brass plates, are important for the preservation of God's people. This article discusses the possible origins and the contents of the plates of brass. Gospel teachings of Israelite prophets not mentioned in the Bible (Zenos, Zenock, Neum, and Ezias), who were descendants of Joseph, show that the witness of Christ in the brass plates is more explicit than in our Old Testament. The Joseph Smith Translation of the Bible may, in fact, "contain some of the information found on the plates of brass." [A.A.]

M.214 Millett, Robert L. "Redemption through the Holy Messiah." In *Studies in Scripture: 1 Nephi to Alma 29*, edited by Kent P. Jackson, 115-30. Salt Lake City: Deseret Book, 1987. A consideration of 2 Nephi 6-10. The doctrine of the redemption of the dead in Israel was understood earlier than current scholars are willing to allow. The atonement is infinite in three ways: (1) it circumvents death, (2) it extends to all of Christ's creations, (3) it was performed by an infinite being. All will be judged, but Jesus suffered to enable us to choose life. Jacob taught how to take advantage of the atonement. [D.M.]

M.215 Millet, Robert L. "Sherem the Anti-Christ." In *The Book of Mormon: Jacob through Words of Mormon, To Learn with Joy*, edited by Monte S. Nyman and Charles D. Tate Jr., 175-91. Provo, UT: Brigham Young University Religious Studies Center, 1990. Identifies characteristics of the anti-Christ as exhibited through Sherem: (1) denies the need for a Christ figure, (2) uses flattery, (3) accuses brethren of false teachings, (4) has a naturalistic frame of reference, (5) distorts scripture, and (6) seeks after signs. Shows how Jacob prevailed over Sherem, illustrating the tragic end of sign-seekers. The downfall of Sherem provides a warning for today. [D.M.]

M.216 Millet, Robert L. " 'So Glorious a Record.' " *Ensign* 22 (December 1992): 7-11. Emphasizes that the Book of Mormon was written and has relevance for our day. MIllet pleads for the members of the Church not take it lightly. [D.M.]

M.217 Millet, Robert L., and Joseph Fielding McConkie. *Our Destiny: The Call and Election of the House of Israel*. Salt Lake City: Bookcraft, 1993. Traces the call and election of the house of Israel from its pre-mortal existence through its temporal history until and including the era of the millennium. Explores doctrines related to the house of Israel, including the scattering, gathering, blessings as a covenant people, concepts concerning the ten tribes, the lands of promise, the role of the priesthood, and the role of Jesus Christ. The authors demonstrate the Book of Mormon's clarity, import, and message regarding the house of Israel. [D.W.P.]

M.218 Mills, John M. *Pronouncing Vocabulary*. Salt Lake City: Deseret Sunday School Union, 1920. Pamphlet containing pronouncing guide for Book of Mormon names, designed to be taped into the back of the 1920 edition of the scriptures. [J.W.M.]

M.219 "Mohawk Singer and the Book of Mormon." *MS* 98 (20 August 1936): 535. A famous Mohawk singer, Os-ke-non-ton, was told the story of the Book of Mormon and his ancestors and said, "Of the many anthropological explanations of the origin of the American Indian the Mormon one impresses me as the briefest and most feasible." [M.D.P.]

M.220 Monch, Elder L. F. "The Book of Mormon, and the End of the World." *MS* 48 (29 March, 5, 12, 19, 26 April, 3 May 1886): 193-96, 209-13, 235-40, 243-47, 267-71, 283-88. Six-part series discussing how Mormonism fulfills biblical prophecy concerning the last days: the coming of Elijah, restoration of the gospel and correct ordinances such as baptism by immersion and the sacrament, Church organization, and continuing revelation. [A.C.W.]

M.221 Monson, Leland H. *Ancient America Speaks*. Salt Lake City: Deseret Book, 1958. This book wishes to motivate members of the Church to read the Book of Mormon with greater benefit. The Book of Mormon is directed to the Lamanites, Jews, and Gentiles; the author provides biographical sketches of prominent figures, expounds on character traits, and treats selected doctrinal themes. [D.M.]

M.222 Monson, Leland H. "An Appreciation of the Book of Mormon." *Relief Society Magazine* 39 (June 1952): 364-66. A lessening of belief in "the divine Christ" began in the seventeenth century. By Joseph Smith's day "higher criticism" of the Bible, like a snake coiled, was squeezing the life blood out of Christianity. The Book of Mormon came forth to reaffirm the divinity of Christ. In 1946, the New York Times Book Review listed the Book of Mormon thirty-eighth on the list of books that have most influenced America. [J.W.M.]

M.223 Monson, Leland H. "Long Road of Corianton." *Instructor* 94 (June 1959): 178-79. Discusses Corianton's trip to Antionum to teach the gospel of Jesus Christ to the Zoramites. [L.D.]

M.224 Monson, Leland H. "Mormon." *IE* 48 (September, October 1945): 512, 550-51, 576, 612-13. Also in *Instructor* 98 (October 1963): 344-45. Writes concerning the conditions of the people and era when Mormon grew up and the manner in which Mormon's family influenced him for good. Discusses Ammaron's influence on Mormon, and Mormon as a record keeper, teacher, and warrior. [L.D.]

M.225 Monson, Leland H. "Moroni Addresses the Future." *IE* 49 (March 1946): 149, 181-82. Discusses Moroni's abridgment of the gold plates, his wanderings, his address concerning the future, the war at Cumorah, and how to gain a testimony of the Book of Mormon (Moroni 10:4). [L.D.]

M.226 Monson, Leland H. "Moroni Spoke Also to Us." *Instructor* 103 (June 1968): 216-17. Discusses Moroni's closing words in the Book of Mormon (Moroni 10:1, 10:24). Discusses the admonitions and promises he left for those who read the Book of Mormon. [L.D.]

M.227 Monson, Leland H. "The Nephite Pattern of Personality." *Instructor* 97 (November 1962): 363, 365. Analyzes the physical being, the intellectual being, and the emotional being in relation to the Nephites in the Book of Mormon. Several Book of Mormon scriptures describe the character of the people, including Alma 7:10-11, 4 Nephi 1:3, and 4 Nephi 1:15. [L.D.]

M.228 Monson, Leland H. "The Structure of the Book of Mormon." *IE* 49 (July 1946): 436-37, 474-75. Discusses the plates of Mormon, source material, and the use made of the plates. Explains the general structure of the Book of Mormon and how to identify different writers in the Book of Mormon. [L.D.]

M.229 Monson, Thomas S. "You Make A Difference." *Ensign* 18 (May 1988): 41-43. Also *CR* (April 1988): 49-53. Follow the prophets and study the Book of Mormon. Sins are like barnacles that fasten themselves to the hull of a ship, weighing it down, slowing its progress, and decreasing its efficiency. Repentance will rid us of these. [J.W.M.]

M.230 Moody, William A. "Origin of the Samoans." *MS* 59 (September 1879): 587-88. Argues that the Samoans originate from American shores, namely from Hagoth (Alma 63:5-8). [B.D.]

M.231 Moore, C. E. "Anachronisms and the Book of Mormon." *IE* 52 (October 1949): 644, 659-60. This article argues that there is a marked absence of anachronisms in the Book of Mormon. One method of detecting a fraudulent historical document is to examine it for anachronisms. It is almost impossible to keep such errors from slipping into documents when one is producing the document in a time period other than that about which it is being written. [J.W.M]

M.232 Moore, June A. "Tests of the Truth of the Book of Mormon." *MS* 91 (8 August 1929): 507-9. The four fundamental tests that may be used to determine the truthfulness of the Book of Mormon are science, history, doctrine, and prophecy. Moore gives an example of each of these four tests. [R.H.B.]

M.233 Moore, Sidney. *Stories from the Book of Mormon*. Independence, MO: Herald House, 1956. A collection of 20 Book of Mormon stories for children, illustrated by Sidney Moore and written by different authors. This work contains such stories as "The Alter of Stones," "The Rod of Iron," "The Strange Ball," and "Gideon's Plan." [J.W.M]

M.234 "More Than One Way to Study the Book of Mormon." *Ensign* 21 (Feb. 1991): 21. Gives suggestions on methods of studying the Book of Mormon: write down important principles, listen to the Spirit and gain strength from the messages hidden between the lines, and pray over passages not understood. [J.W.M.]

M.235 Morgan, John. "The Book Of Mormon." In *Opinions of the Leading Statesmen of the United States on the Edmunds Law and Refutation of the Spaulding Story Tract #3, 1884?*, 20-23. Salt Lake City: Juvenile Instructor Office, 1884?. Refutes the Spaulding theory by providing a reprint of James H. Fairchild's letter admonishing that the theory be repealed. Believes that the Spaulding manuscript shows no similarity to the Book of Mormon. [J.W.M.]

M.236 "Mormon and the 'Small Plates' of Nephi." *Instructor* 75 (August 1940): 344. Gives an explanation of the lost 116 pages and how the small plates of Nephi were substituted for these lost pages that had been translated from the large plates of Nephi. [J.W.M.]

M.237 "The 'Mormon Bible.'" *MS* 40 (4 February 1878): 68-70. Reprint from the *Deseret News*. An article written in the *Post and Tribune* contains much false information about the Book of Mormon, including that the witnesses had denied their testimonies and the book was written by Spaulding. The Book of Mormon corroborates and supports the Bible, but does not replace it. [J.W.M.]

M.238 "Mormon Relics." *Weekly Inter Ocean* (26 October 1886): 9. Article about David Whitmer's memories of his early role in the coming forth of the Book of Mormon. Also discusses the original Book of Mormon manuscript. [D.M.]

M.239 "Mormonism: Authentic Account of the Origin of this Sect from one of the Patriarchs." *Harper's Weekly* (11 June 1881): none given. Reprint from *Kansas City Journal* (5 June 1881): none given. Gives the testimony of David Whitmer, the manner of translation, and an account of the loss of the 116 pages of Book of Mormon manuscript—the Book of Lehi. Also an account of the events surrounding the Three Witnesses seeing the plates, as well as the eight who saw them later. [J.W.M]

M.240 "Moroni Raises the Title of Liberty." *Friend* 12 (July 1982): 48. The story of Captain Moroni is retold for children. [A.T.]

M.241 Morris, George Q. *What Is the Book of Mormon?* Salt Lake City: Church of Jesus Christ of Latter-day Saints, 1940. A KSL radio presentation presenting an overview of the contents of the Book of Mormon. [D.W.P.]

M.242 Morris, Nephi Lowell. "Book of Mormon Prophecy I & II." In Morris's *Prophecies of Joseph Smith and Their Fulfillment*, 217-58. Salt Lake City, UT: Deseret Book, 1926. Discusses America's role as a choice and promised land and how latter-day events have confirmed Book of Mormon prophecies: God fights for America, he will fortify it, it will be free from bondage, and there will be no kings upon it. [A.C.W.]

M.243 Morris, Nephi Lowell. *Prophecies of Joseph Smith and Their Fulfillment*. Salt Lake City: Deseret Book, 1920. The Book of Mormon is a volume of prophecy and also a fulfillment of other prophecies. Morris cites many passages that prophesy of the greatness of America and the liberty to be enjoyed on the American continent. These passages have been fulfilled particularly noting the Monroe Doctrine and the ill success of Emperor Maximilian over Mexico and Dom Pedro of Brazil. [B.D.]

M.244 Morris, Nephi Lowell. "What Prophecy Asserts, History Affirms." *IE* 4 (October 1901): 895-900. The Monroe Doctrine states that the United States government will overthrow any type of monarchy set up on the western continent. This corresponds with the Book of Mormon in 2 Nephi 10:11-14 where it says that no king will be set upon the American continent. The south side of the pyramid of Zochicako tells of a destruction in the land, which Morris relates to the destruction before Christ appeared on the American continent (3 Nephi 8-9). [B.D.]

M.245 Morrise, Mark J. "Simile Curses in the Ancient Near East, Old Testament, and Book of Mormon." *Journal of Book of Mormon Studies* 2 (Spring 1993): 124-38. Also published as "Simile Curses in the Ancient Near East, Old Testament and Book of Mormon." Provo, UT: FARMS, 1981. Simile curses, a combination of the literary feature called "simile" and an oath of malediction, are common elements in ancient Near Eastern texts, including the Old Testament and Book of Mormon. Simile curses occur most often in three contexts—treaties, religious covenants, and prophecies. A Book of Mormon example of a simile curses is found in Alma 44:1-4 where the simile "even as this scalp has fallen to the earth" is followed by the curse, "so shall ye fall to the earth." A ritualistic act or visual action often accompanies the curse, such as rending garments, felling a tree, or breaking a weapon, making the symbolism of the curse more effective. The attestation of simile curses in the Book of Mormon may suggest a historical connection between the new world scripture and the ancient records of the old world. [D.W.P.]

M.246 Morrow, Cherry L. "My Nonmember Missionary." *Ensign* 19 (July 1989): 53-54. Personal conversion story based upon the Book of Mormon. The author was given a Book of Mormon by a nonmember friend. After reading and praying about the contents of the book Morrow became a member of the Church of Jesus Christ of Latter-day Saints. [A.C.W.]

M.247 Mortimer, Wm. James. "The Coming Forth of the LDS Editions of Scripture." *Ensign* 13 (August 1983): 35-41. An account of the work that led to the publication of the LDS edition of the King James Version of the Bible, and new editions of the Book of Mormon, the Doctrine and Covenants, and the Pearl of Great Price. [S.P.S.]

M.248 Morton, William A. "The Bible and the Book of Mormon." *MS* 83 (July 1921): 468-71. Includes a very lengthy quote of the book, *God's Message to the Human Soul*, by John Watson. The Bible's main theme is the fellowship of man with God. The same can be said of the Book of Mormon. To show this the author quotes 1 Nephi 6:4-6 and Moroni 10:30-32. [B.D.]

M.249 Morton, William A. "The Book of Mormon in Prophecy." *MS* 69 (16 May 1907): 305-11. The author's purpose is to "prove, from the holy scriptures, the divine authenticity of the Book of Mormon." The Book of Mormon peoples are a fulfillment of the prophecies in Deuteronomy 28:63-64, and Genesis 49:22, 26; Christ's visit to America is a fulfillment of John 10:16; and the coming forth of the Book of Mormon a fulfillment of Isaiah 29:4-6; 45:8, Psalm 85:11, Ezekiel 37:16-19, Isaiah 29:11-12, and Revelation 14:6, 7. [A.T.]

M.250 Morton, William A. *Book of Mormon Ready References*. Salt Lake City: Geo. Q. Cannon & Sons, 1898. [R]1914. A collection of passages from the Book of Mormon that deal with subjects incidental to the restored gospel, such as the atonement and the gathering of Israel. Includes "traditions and discoveries confirming the Book of Mormon." [D.M.]

M.251 Morton, William A. "Concerning the Testimony of the Three Witnesses." *MS* 84 (7 September 1922): 570-71. The author responds to an article that claimed that the Three Witnesses "afterwards renounced Mormonism and said that their testimony was false." The Witnesses never denied their testimony of the Book of Mormon. [M.D.P.]

M.252 Morton, William A. "A Little More Evidence." *MS* 70 (13 August 1908): 513-17. Those who refuse to believe the Book of Mormon because Joseph Smith did not show the plates to more witnesses are not much different than the Jews who would not believe the resurrection because Jesus did not show himself to them. Believing the Solomon Spaulding theory is foolish. The true story about Martin Harris's visit to Professor Anthon is explained. [J.W.M.]

M.253 Morton, William A. *Mother Stories from the Book of Mormon*. Salt Lake City: W. A. Morton, 1911. Twenty stories from the Book of Mormon designed for children. [D.M.]

M.254 Morton, William A. "Objections to the Book of Mormon Answered." *MS* 83 (13 October 1921): 641-45. Morton responds to three objections to the Book of Mormon. Mr. Rought Brooks of the *Burnley News* maintains that the Book of Mormon is weakened because Joseph Smith used a "peek-stone" to search for money, and the Book of Mormon mentions the use of "precious steel," domesticated horses, cows and oxen, and the compass. Morton counters that the Chinese used magnetic directors in 2634 B.C., ancient iron remains have been dug up in the New World, as have remains of horses. Buffaloes are domesticated cows and oxen gone wild. [B.D.]

M.255 Morton, William A. "Why I Believe The Book of Mormon To Be The Word Of God." *MS* 83 (8 September 1921): 561-66. A testimony of the Book of Mormon. The Spaulding theory is absurd. Spaulding was a Presbyterian minister who would never preach against infant baptism as is preached in Moroni 8:90-21. Joseph Smith translated the Book of Mormon by the aid of God. There are many prophecies relating to the Book of Mormon in the Bible:

Genesis 49:22-26, Isaiah 29:4, 11-14, Psalms 85:11, Ezekiel 37:15-20, John 10:14-16, and Revelations 14:6-7. [B.D.]

M.256 Morton, William A. *Why I Believe the Book of Mormon to Be the Word of God.* Salt Lake City: Church of Jesus Christ of Latter-day Saints, 1918. [R]1925, 1949, 1957. Also "Why I Believe the Book of Mormon to Be the Word of God." In *Handbook of the Restoration*, 392-411. Independence, MO: Zions, 1944. A testimonial of the truthfulness of the Book of Mormon. Discusses the origin of the Book of Mormon and uses the Bible to prove the Book of Mormon to be of God. The Bible prophesies of the Book of Mormon, and the Lord gave eleven witnesses to verify its authenticity. The Book of Mormon assists in the solving of theological problems. [L.D.]

M.257 Morton, William A. "Why the Plates of the Book of Mormon Were Not Shown to the World." *Young Woman's Journal* 24 (October 1913): 613-15. The gold plates were not/are not available for inspection because acceptance of the Book of Mormon is a matter of faith. Those predisposed to disbelieve the Book of Mormon would not be converted to the Gospel even if they saw the plates. [D.M.]

M.258 Moss, James R. "Six Nephite Judges—a Study in Integrity." *Ensign* 7 (September 1977): 61-65. Evaluates and praises the integrity of several Nephite judges. Brings out four principles that they observed: (1) law, not personality, authority or force, governs society; (2) law was to be determined by the voice of the people; (3) prophets as God's agents communicate proper principles of law; (4) laws were established through a spiritual foundation. [D.M.]

M.259 Moyle, Henry D. "He Saw the Golden Plates." *Instructor* 95 (July 1960): 226-27, 229. An account of an interview between David Whitmer and the author's father, James H. Moyle, in which Whitmer reaffirmed the validity of the plates and the angel who showed them to him. [B.D.]

M.260 Moyle, Henry D. "To the End He Held that He Saw the Golden Plates." *Instructor* 95 (July 1960): 226-27, 229. Contains a reproduction of the testimony of the Three Witnesses. David Whitmer, after being excommunicated from the Church, still testifies of the truthfulness and divinity of the Book of Mormon. [L.D.]

M.261 Moyle, James H. Untitled talk. *CR* (April 1929): 18-22. Moyle writes of archaeological evidence of the Book of Mormon. Doctor Spinden of the Peabody Museum of Boston proclaimed that the excellence of cloth manufacture in ancient Peru was not equaled by any other nation of that time. The Book of Mormon explains clearly the high culture to which the ancient Americans attained. [B.D.]

M.262 Moyle, James H. Untitled talk. *CR* (April 1930): 118-23. When returning home from the University of Michigan in 1885 Moyle spoke with David Whitmer. Whitmer affirmed his testimony of the Book of Mormon. [B.D.]

M.263 Mulholland, David H. *A Reading Guide to the Book of Mormon.* Salt Lake City: Deseret Book, 1989. A reading guide and study aid that asks questions of the Book of Mormon chapter by chapter. Answers are given in the back. [D.M.]

M.264 Mulliner, H. L. "Internal Evidences of the Truth of the Book of Mormon." *IE* 9 (October 1906): 913-23. Provides several examples to show that the Book of Mormon taught against many of the popularly held views and practices of Joseph Smith's day. He, therefore, was not an impostor who desired to have his views accepted and approved. [D.M.]

N.

N.001 N., W. N. "'Then Shall They Rejoice.'" *MS* 91 (31 January 1929): 72-73. Describes episodes in which modern-day Lamanites of Mexican descent rejoiced upon receiving the Book of Mormon. [R.H.B.]

N.002 Nackos, Louis J. "Judah in the Days of Jeremiah and Lehi." In *Papers of the Fifteenth Annual Symposium on the Archaeology of the Scriptures*, edited by Ross T. Christensen, 30-37. Provo, UT: Brigham Young University, 1964. Explores the events that led up to the destruction of Jerusalem and the reign of

Zedekiah who was king when Lehi left Jerusalem. Lehi was one of the prophets that the Lord sent to call the people to repentance. Accounts found by archaeologists suggest that the Israelites were confident that no harm would come to them in spite of the prophets' warnings. [J.W.M.]

N.003 Neeley, Dela Petersen. *Child's Story of the Book of Mormon*. 4 vols. Salt Lake City: Deseret News Press, 1949-53. Published by Deseret Book in 1987. A presentation of the Book of Mormon to young children. The stories of the Book of Mormon are dramatized and told in a simple language. [L.D.]

N.004 Negaard, Sadi. *Heroes for God*. 4 parts. Independence, MO: Herald House, 1961. Parts 2-3 feature Book of Mormon stories for youth, with illustrations. [D.M.]

N.005 Nelson, Fred W., Jr. "The Colossal Stone Heads of the Southern Gulf Coast Region of Mexico." *SEHA* 103 (12 August 1967): 2-8. Analyzes the features of several stone heads discovered in Veracruz and speculates that they might belong to the Jaredite culture. A map, table, and pictures are supplied. [D.M.]

N.006 Nelson, Nels Lars. "The Dictionary of Slander." *Mormon Point-of-View* 1 (1 January 1904, 1 April 1904): 73-100, 157-96. Catalogs several charges against the Mormons including the Spaulding connection to the Book of Mormon. Shows in detail how this explanation is untenable. Discusses Book of Mormon witnesses. [D.M.]

N.007 Nelson, Nels Lars. "The Harris-Anthon Episode." *Mormon Point-of-View* 1 (1 July 1904): 282-92. Weighs the probabilities of the viewpoints of Martin Harris and Charles Anthon with regard to their interview concerning the Book of Mormon characters. [D.M.]

N.008 Nelson, Nels Lars. "Human Side of the Book of Mormon." *Mormon Point-of-View* 1 (1 April 1904): 105-56. Treats the possibility of errors existing in the Book of Mormon. Points out that revelation coming through human media is bound to be imperfect, by the very nature of human weakness. Shows areas where mistakes might have been made by Mormon the compiler, and Joseph Smith the translator. Discusses anachronisms and affinities with the Bible in phraseology. Considers Joseph Smith's method of translating. Concludes that the Book of Mormon is a divine record. [D.M.]

N.009 Nelson, Reed. "That Book is True!" *Ensign* 13 (December 1983): 23. A story of divine coincidences in which a young man was exposed to the Book of Mormon and became a convert to the Church. [S.P.S.]

N.010 Nelson, Russell M. "Jesus Christ—Our Master and More." In *The Book of Mormon: Helaman through 3 Nephi 8, According to Thy Word*, edited by Monte S. Nyman and Charles D. Tate Jr., 1-14. Provo, UT: Brigham Young University Religious Studies Center, 1992. Comments on several Christological titles in the Book of Mormon and other scriptures. Jesus Christ is the creator and Jehovah of the Old Testament. He is the advocate with the Father, the Son of God. He is the promised Immanuel, the Anointed One, Savior and Redeemer. He is both judge and exemplar. He is the Millennial Messiah. [J.W.M.] [D.M.]

N.011 Nelson, Russell M. "Thanks for the Covenant." In *Brigham Young University 1988-89 Devotional and Fireside Speeches*, 53-61. Provo, UT: Brigham Young University Publications, 1989. A discussion of the Abrahamic covenant. Points out that the patriarch Joseph received the birthright in Israel and that the land allotted to him was not Canaan but the Americas. "America was to serve as the repository of sacred records written on metallic plates. It one day was to become the location for the restoration of the gospel. It was to host headquarters of the Lord's restored Church." [D.M.]

N.012 Nelson, Russell M. "A Treasured Testament." *Ensign* 23 (July 1993): 61–65. Declares the translation of the Book of Mormon by Joseph Smith a "marvelous miracle." The many different forms of Hebraisms in the book attest to its Semitic origins. The book stands as another testament of Christ. [S.H.]

N.013 Nelson, Ted, Glen Scott, Lyle Smith, Brenda Trimble, and Linda Trimble. "Archaeology

Alert." *The Witness* 67 (Winter 1989): 15. Points out two different findings in Mexico that show how archaeology converges with the Book of Mormon. The two excavations uncovered a Maya Codex in a city close to San Salvador and a lost fort found in Guatemala. [L.D.]

N.014 Nelson, Ted, Glen Scott, Lyle Smith, Brenda Trimble, and Linda Trimble. "La Mojarra: A Voice from the Dust." *The Witness* 64 (February 1989): 4-6. A large engraved stone with hieroglyphics and a picture of a fully clothed man was discovered in the Acula River, southeast of Veracruz, Mexico in 1986. Many scholars believe the hieroglyphics represent an earlier version of the Maya language, probably Olmec. [L.D.]

N.015 "Nephi and the Exodus." *Ensign* 17 (April 1987): 64-65. Asserts that "one of the most important of all Hebrew motifs, the exodus cycle, is woven throughout 1 Nephi." "The exodus cycle is a pattern of enslavement and divine rescue used often in the Bible and other Jewish writings." Because Nephi was raised a Jew and knew Hebrew literary styles, he used this literary method in writing his own record. [S.P.S.]

N.016 "Nephites." In *Encyclopedia of Mormonism,* edited by Daniel H. Ludlow, 3:1006. 5 vols. New York: Macmillan, 1992. A brief description of the term "Nephite" in the Book of Mormon. A Nephite is distinguished by his belief in the gospel of Jesus Christ. [B.D.]

N.017 Neser, Arlin P. "A Witness From the Holy Ghost." *Ensign* 14 (July 1984): 22-25. Explains how an investigator in Yugoslavia knew by looking at a German Book of Mormon, especially the pictures, and by praying that it was true, even though she was not able to read it. [D.M.]

N.018 "New and Interesting Discovery in South America." *TS* 5 (1 December 1844): 733-34. Reports the discovery of "extraordinary ruins" by Judge Neito in Peru. The proportions were immense with the remains of ancient dead within. It "must be the greatest building in the world in point of size." The workmanship is exquisite. This is archaeological evidence that the Book of Mormon is true. [J.W.M.]

N.019 "New Developments in Book of Mormon Research." *Ensign* 18 (February 1988): 12-17. A compilation of research reports on the Book of Mormon discussing such topics as Jesus Christ, law, biblical and Near Eastern studies, archaeology, anthropology, language, and literature. [L.D.]

N.020 "New Home in the Promised Land." *Friend* 11 (July 1981): 21-22. For children, cartoon story of the animosity that Laman and Lemuel felt toward Nephi, and Nephi's need to leave and find a new home after Lehi's death. Depicts the way the records were kept by Lehi, Nephi, Jacob, and Enos. [J.W.M.]

N.021 "A New Home in the Promised Land." *Friend* 20 (January 1990): 20-21. An illustrated story for children about the Nephites and Lamanites after they arrived at the promised land. [M.D.P.]

N.022 "New Issue of the Book of Mormon." *IE* 24 (February 1921): 352-54. Official announcement of the LDS Church First Presidency (Heber J. Grant, Anthon H. Lund, and Charles W. Penrose) reporting a new printing of the Book of Mormon. The issue features new typesetting, larger printed type, two columns of text per page, chapter headings, and an updated footnotes and index. [A.C.W.]

N.023 "New Light on the Shining Stones of the Jaredites." Provo, UT: FARMS, 1992. Research by Sandia National Laboratories produced radioluminescent light sources. These may provide light without electrical power supplies for as long as 20 years. Such technology shows a possible answer as to how the Lord touched Jared's 16 stones in response to his faith. [J.W.M.]

N.024 "The New Scripture." *Relief Society Magazine* 15 (January, February 1928): 46-48, 104-6. Three lesson outlines for Relief Society that focus on the prophecies concerning the Book of Mormon, its guardian messenger and his mission, the Urim and Thummim, and the method of translation. [J.W.M.]

N.025 Newberry, S. "Ancient American Civilizations." *Deseret Weekly* 44 (4 June 1892): 771-72. Refers to an article in the June, 1892 issue of *Popular Science Monthly* by S. Newberry, whose description of ancient civilizations of

Latin America harmonize with information in the Book of Mormon. [D.M.]

N.026 Newell, Linda King, and Valeen Tippetts Avery. "Emma and Joseph 1825-1827, The 'Elect Lady' 1827-1830." In Newell's and Avery's *Mormon Enigma: Emma Hale Smith, Prophet's Wife, "Elect Lady," Polygamy's Foe*, 15-30. Garden City, NY: Doubleday, 1984. Describes the family backgrounds of Joseph Smith and Emma Hale, and the relationship between the families. There is a detailed narration of the coming forth, translation, and publication of the Book of Mormon. [J.W.M.]

N.027 Nibley, Hugh W. *An Approach to the Book of Mormon*. Salt Lake City: Council of the Twelve Apostles of the Church of Jesus Christ of Latter-day Saints, 1957. 2nd ed. Salt Lake City: Deseret Book, 1964. 3rd ed. vol. 6 of *CWHN*, edited by John W. Welch. Salt Lake City: Deseret Book and FARMS, 1988. This book was originally published as the lesson manual for the Melchizedek Priesthood quorums of the Church of Jesus Christ of Latter-day Saints. Compares the Book of Mormon to the world of Lehi's day, Lehi's training and profession, travel, relations with Egypt, politics in Jerusalem and with Laban, sects living in the wilderness, the Dead Sea scrolls, the apocrypha, ancient warfare, the ideologies of intellectuals and the wicked, and the sobering message of the Book of Mormon regarding the downfall of civilizations. [J.W.W.]

N.028 Nibley, Hugh W. "Archaeology and Our Religion." *Seventh East Press* (18 January 1982): 4-7. Methodological musings on the inadequacies and interpretive pitfalls of archaeology against a setting of the general debate between science and religion. [J.W.W.]

N.029 Nibley, Hugh W. "The Atonement of Jesus Christ." *Ensign* 20 (July-October 1990): 18-23, 30-34, 22-26, 26-31. A four-part series that emphasizes that the Book of Mormon teaches the correct principles of the atonement. The power of resurrection is provided only by the Savior. Only the Book of Mormon teaches the fulness of the truth of the atonement, why life is as it is, and how one may approach God to be at one with him. Since all fall short, the blood sacrifice of the Savior was the indispensable step. Atonement is both individual and collective and so God's people must be "of one heart and one mind." "The Atonement is one of the grand constants in nature." [J.W.M.]

N.030 Nibley, Hugh W. "Bird Island." *Dialogue* 10 (Autumn 1977): 120-23. Satirical lecture on some of the excesses and weaknesses of archaeology and theories of Book of Mormon geography. [J.W.W.]

N.031 Nibley, Hugh W. "The Book of Mormon and the Ruins: The Main Issues." Provo, UT: FARMS, 1980. Lecture notes regarding Mesoamerican ruins, pre-Columbian, American races, Cumorah, and the disappearance of ancient cultures. [J.W.W.]

N.032 Nibley, Hugh W. "Book of Mormon as a Mirror of the East." *IE* 51 (April 1948): 204-6, 249-51. Reprinted, without illustrations, in *IE* 73 (November 1970): 115-20, 122-25. Revised version appears in *Lehi in the Desert* (1952). Book of Mormon proper names are related to Egyptian etymologies. [J.W.W.]

N.033 Nibley, Hugh W. "The Book of Mormon as a Witness." In Nibley's *The World and the Prophets*. 189-96. Salt Lake City: Deseret Book, 1954. Radio talk on the Book of Mormon as a witness of continuing revelation and God's dealings with mankind. [J.W.W.]

N.034 Nibley, Hugh W. "The Book of Mormon: Forty Years After." A talk given at the Sunstone 1988 Book of Mormon Lecture Series, May 10, 1988. Reprinted in *CWHN* 8:533-69. Even after forty years of research, new insights are still to be found in the Book of Mormon. Examples come from the episode at the waters of Sebus, wordprinting, Enos and the princes of India, Isabel as a Phoenician name, the Zoramites as dissenters, and clear statements about God and man, riches, economics, and repentance. [J.W.W.]

N.035 Nibley, Hugh W. "Book of Mormon Near Eastern Background." In *Encyclopedia of Mormonism*, edited by Daniel H. Ludlow, 1:187-90. 5 vols. New York: Macmillan, 1992. The main Book of Mormon groups migrated at different times from the Near East and Asia to the Americas. External and circumstantial evidence exists to confirm such ties. Narratives discovered closely parallel recently discovered manuscripts, describe desert travel, customs, and terrain characteristics, duplicate intricate ancient coronation ceremonies, sustain the Near Eastern custom of writing on gold plates for special documents, and other unusual features. [N.K.Y.]

N.036 Nibley, Hugh W. "The Book of Mormon: True or False?" *MS* 124 (November 1962): 274-77. Reprinted in *CWHN* 8:219-42. Argues that if Joseph Smith was not telling the truth when he provided the world with the Book of Mormon, then he recklessly exposed his forgery and fraud to public discovery. The Book of Mormon is authentic history, not a forgery, and not a product of the tendencies of Joseph Smith's day. [J.W.W.]

N.037 Nibley, Hugh W. "The Boy, Nephi, in Jerusalem." *Instructor* 96 (March 1961): 84-85. Reprinted in *CWHN* 8:207-11. Historical fiction about the possible thoughts on a day in the life of the twelve-year-old Nephi in Jerusalem. [J.W.W.]

N.038 Nibley, Hugh W. "Censoring the Joseph Smith Story." Provo, UT: FARMS, 1961. Reprinted in *CWHN* 11:55-101. Explains how Joseph Smith's critics in the 1840s and also Fawn Brodie rewrote Joseph's story to suit their perceptions of the Book of Mormon and the First Vision. [J.W.W.]

N.039 Nibley, Hugh W. "Christ Among the Ruins." *Ensign* 13 (July 1983): 14, 16-19. Compare *CWHN* 8:407-34. Subtitled, "A comparison of the Old World early Christian 'forty-day ministry' story with the New World 3 Nephi accounts." Compares Jesus' post-resurrection words to his disciples in Galilee with accounts in the Book of Mormon. [J.W.W.]

N.040 Nibley, Hugh W. "Christ Among the Ruins." In *Book of Mormon Authorship*, edited by Noel B. Reynolds, 121-41. Provo, UT: Brigham Young University Religious Studies Center, 1982. Compares Jesus' words in 3 Nephi with Jesus' post-resurrection words to his disciples in Galilee as reported in several apocryphal sources. [J.W.W.]

N.041 Nibley, Hugh W. "Churches in the Wilderness." In *Nibley on the Timely and Timeless*, edited by Truman D. Madsen. Provo, UT: Brigham Young University Religious Studies Center, 1978. Reprinted in *CWHN* 8:289-327. Compares passages in the Enoch Scroll and the Manual of Discipline from Qumran with the Book of Moses and the Book of Mormon regarding the establishment of churches of anticipation, worship, baptism, and hymns. [J.W.W.].

N.042 Nibley, Hugh W. "Columbus and Revelation." *Instructor* 88 (October 1953): 319-20. Reprinted in *CWHN* 8:49-53. Relevant to 1 Nephi 13:11-12, this brief article gives historical evidence showing that Columbus was moved upon by the Holy Ghost. [J.W.W.]

N.043 Nibley, Hugh W. "The Comparative Method." *IE* 62 (October-November 1959): 744-47, 759, 848, 854, 856. Reprinted in *CWHN* 8:193-206. Rejects the idea that the Book of Mormon copies Ethan Smith's *View of the Hebrews*. [J.W.W.]

N.044 Nibley, Hugh W. "Dark Days in Jerusalem: The Lachish Letters and the Book of Mormon." In *Book of Mormon Authorship*, edited by Noel B. Reynolds, 103-20. Provo, UT: Brigham Young University Religious Studies Center, 1982. Makes a comparison between the Lachish Letters, discovered in 1935 and translated by Harry Torczyner, and the narrative found in 1 Nephi 1. Finds many parallels: the same time and place framework, similar classes of society confronted with same difficult circumstances, similar writing techniques, and other items. [J.W.M.]

N.045 Nibley, Hugh W. "Dear Friend of the Book of Mormon." Provo, UT: FARMS, 1983. An open letter praising the formation of the Foundation for Ancient Research and Mormon Studies as an important work, providing an opportunity for serious study of the Book of Mormon. [J.W.W.]

N.046 Nibley, Hugh W. "Freemen and Kingmen in the Book of Mormon," in *CWHN* 8:328-79. Captain Moroni was a man of peace. Analyzes war, government, management, the political tactics and strategies of Amalickiah, and the constant struggle between those who follow the ways of righteousness and those who promote wicked political agendas. Includes notes about similar political problems in ancient Mesoamerican societies. [J.W.W.]

N.047 Nibley, Hugh W. "The Grab Bag." *IE* 61 (July 1959): 530-33, 446-48. Reprinted in *CWHN* 8:170-81. Shows that Book of Mormon critics have made an art of explaining a very large and complex text by focusing only on a very small part of it. [J.W.W.].

N.048 Nibley, Hugh W. "Howlers in the Book of Mormon." *MS* 125 (February 1963): 28-34. Reprinted in *CWHN* 8:243-58. Lists over twenty Book of Mormon points that may have seemed ridiculous in 1830 but that "appear very different" in light of modern scholarship, including transoceanic voyaging, gold plates, steel, elephants, coins, names, literary and ritual patterns, execution, modes of prophecy and revelation. [J.W.W.]

N.049 Nibley, Hugh W. "Just Another Book." *IE* 62 (May-July 1959): 345-47, 388-91, 412-13, 501-3, 530-31, 565. Reprinted in *CWHN* 8:148-69. Shows ways in which the Book of Mormon was out-of-sorts with the nineteenth century and thus not just another book of that time. [J.W.W.]

N.050 Nibley, Hugh W. "Kangaroo Court." *IE* 62 (March-April 1959): 145-48, 184-87, 224-26, 300-301. Reprinted in *CWHN* 8:127-47. A witty exposé of anti-Mormon methods of Book of Mormon criticism. [J.W.W.].

N.051 Nibley, Hugh W. "The Lachish Letters: Documents from Lehi's Day." *Ensign* 10 (December 1981): 48-54. Reprinted in *CWHN* 8:380-406. Suggests connections between the Lachish letters written at the time Jerusalem was destroyed by the Babylonians and events associated with Lehi's departure. Includes political pressures on prophets, types of proper names, and a possible identification of Mulek. [J.W.W.]

N.052 Nibley, Hugh W. "Last Call: An Apocalyptic Warning from the Book of Mormon." *Sunstone* 12 (January 1988): 14-25. Reprinted in *CWHN* 8:498-532. The Book of Mormon's message of Christ specifically is to "show" and "convince" by a bulwark of historical evidence through which the doctrine must be considered. The ascension motif—righteous man rising above the wicked world by supplicating God—is repeated over and over. It is symbolic and warns mankind to spiritually break away from his real enemy, himself, in the world of sin. [J.W.M.]

N.053 Nibley, Hugh W. "Lehi in the Desert." *IE* 53 (January-October 1950): 14-16, 66-72, 102-4, 155-59, 200-2, 222, 225-26, 229-30, 276-77, 486-87, 516-19, 566-67, 587-88, 640-42, 670, 706-8, 744, 804-6, 824, 826, 828, 830. Reprinted, without illustrations, as the first half of *Lehi in the Desert and the World of the Jaredites*. Salt Lake City: Bookcraft, 1952. Reprinted, with illustrations, in *CWHN* 5:1-149. A classic reflection on Lehi's world in Arabia: poetry, tree of life, family affairs, politics, imagery, travel, tents, and foods. One of the first attempts to test the Book of Mormon against known geographical and cultural details in the regions where Lehi probably traveled in the Old World. [J.W.W.]

N.054 Nibley, Hugh W. "The Lesson of the Sixth Century B.C." Provo, UT: FARMS, 1956. Lehi, Solon, Thales, Buddha, Confucius, Lao Tze, Zarathustra, and Pythagoras are discussed as contemporaries living in an important and booming "axial" era, the seminal 6th century B.C. [J.W.W.]

N.055 Nibley, Hugh W. "The Liahona's Cousins." *IE* 64 (February 1961): 87-89, 104-6, 108-11. Reprinted in *CWHN* 7:251-63. Analysis of the Liahona, especially in light of Arabic divination arrows. Proposes an etymology for this name. [J.W.W.].

N.056 Nibley, Hugh W. "Literary Style Used in the Book of Mormon Insured Accurate Translation." *DN Church Section* (29 July 1961): 10, 15. Reprinted in *CWHN* 8:212-18. Discusses why the Book of Mormon uses King James English to communicate effectively with Joseph Smith's audience. [J.W.W.].

N.057 Nibley, Hugh W. "Mixed Voices: A Study in Book of Mormon Criticism." *IE* 62 (March-November 1959): 145-48, 184-87, 224-26, 300-1, 345-47, 388-91, 412-13, 501-3, 530-33, 546-48, 565, 590-92, 610, 612, 614-15, 744-

47, 759, 848, 854, 856. Reprinted in *CWHN* 8:127-206. A series about the Book of Mormon and its nineteenth-century American critics. David Marks, who heard the story of the book from the Whitmer family, dismissed it as deception that he could not support by purchasing the book. Alexander Campbell, Origen Bacheler, E. D. Hose, and Professor Rafinesque joined him. The critics could not believe in angelic visits, visions, and further revelation from God. They criticized the grammar and content, rebuked the translator as a fraud, a liar, and a money-digging, peep-stone looking cheat. One critic relied upon the words of another without checking to see if there was any truth. [J.W.W.]

N.058 Nibley, Hugh W. "The Mormon View of the Book of Mormon." *Concilium Int'l Revue of Theology* 10 (December 1967): 82-83. Also in *Concilium: Theology in the Age of Renewal* 30 (1968): 170-73, and in other foreign-language editions of this Catholic journal in French, 151-53; Portuguese, 144-47; German, 855-56. Reprinted as "The Book of Mormon: A Minimal Statement," in *Nibley on the Timely and the Timeless,* 149-53. Provo, UT: Brigham Young University Religious Studies Center, 1978. Reprinted in *CWHN* 8:259-64. A summary statement of the content and purpose of the Book of Mormon prepared for *Concilium,* a journal devoted to an examination of the Christian scriptures. Explains it as an ancient record, a companion to the Bible with revealed Christianity before Christ and 40-day literature from the appearance of Christ among the Nephites. [J.W.W.]

N.059 Nibley, Hugh W. "New Approaches to the Book of Mormon Study." *IE* 56, 57 (November 1953-July 1954): 830-31, 859-62, 919, 1003, 30-32, 41, 88-89, 125-26, 148-50, 170, 232-33, 246, 248-50, 252, 308-9, 326, 330, 389, 447-48, 450-51, 506-7, 521. Reprinted in *CWHN* 8:54-126. Vividly displays internal and external evidences to test whether the Book of Mormon is or is not a forgery, using the standard scholarly criteria for detecting forged writings. Very insightful comments on methodology for studying the Book of Mormon, evaluating evidence, using newly discovered documents, metal plates, literary criticism, poetry, lower criticism, and history. Also comments on animals, weights and measures, and the use of the Bible in the Book of Mormon. [J.W.W.]

N.060 Nibley, Hugh. "Of The Book of Mormon." In *Of All Things!: Classic Quotations from Hugh Nibley,* edited by Gary P. Gillum, 125-59. Salt Lake City: Deseret Book and FARMS, 1993. Using quotes from various sources, the editor brings to the reader a greater understanding of Nibley's perception of the Book of Mormon. The quotes range from humorously witty to serious appraisals of the great value of the book. Nibley's testimony of the Book of Mormon is clearly put: "It is carefully organized, specific, sober, factual, and perfectly consistent." [J.W.M.]

N.061 Nibley, Hugh W. "Old World Ritual in the New World." In Nibley's *An Approach to the Book of Mormon,* 243-56. Salt Lake City: Deseret Book, 1957. Compares King Benjamin's speech with the ancient Year Rite festivals. [J.W.W.].

N.062 Nibley, Hugh W. "Paul and Moroni." Letter to *Christianity Today* 5 (22 May 1961): 727. A response to a letter by C. Sumter Logan of the Trinity Presbyterian Church in Ogden, Utah, that had appeared in *Christianity Today* 5 (27 March 1961): 551. Comments on Moroni 7 and Paul's praise of charity in 1 Corinthians 13. [J.W.W.]

N.063 Nibley, Hugh W. "The Prophetic Book of Mormon." *Seventh East Press* 1 (27 March 1982): 6-8, 16-17. Reprinted in *CWHN* 8:435-69. This 1981 lecture relates present-day political circumstances to the "polarizing" that caused the collapse of the Nephites and that has been a major cause in the sudden and complete downfall of many civilizations. [J.W.W.]

N.064 Nibley, Hugh W. *The Prophetic Book of Mormon.* Vol. 8 of *CWHN,* edited by John W. Welch. Salt Lake City: Deseret and FARMS, 1989. Explores the many ways in which the Book of Mormon is a true, prophetic, historical, and apocalyptic book. [J.W.W.]

N.065 Nibley, Hugh W. "Rediscovery of the Apocrypha." Provo, UT: FARMS, 1965. Transcript of a talk about patterns of prophecy and early Israelite traditions about the plan of salvation found in newly discovered apocryphal writings and in the Book of Mormon. [J.W.W.]

N.066 Nibley, Hugh W. "Rediscovery of the Apocrypha and the Book of Mormon." In *Temple and Cosmos*, edited by Don E. Norton, 212-63. Salt Lake City: Deseret Book, 1992. Nibley describes images that are important in the Apocrypha and the Book of Mormon. The imagery discussed is as follows: desert imagery, the plan, heavenly treasures, apocalyptic imagery, the right and left hand of God, the white garment, the strait way, the filthy and pure waters, looking beyond the mark, flight into the wilderness, the tree of life, Zenos/Zenez, Olive culture, Redeemer of Israel, likening the scriptures, ritual war, and kings and covenants. [B.D.]

N.067 Nibley, Hugh W. "Review essay of *Bar-Kochba: The Rediscovery of the Legendary Hero of the Second Jewish Revolt against Rome,* by Yigael Yadin." *BYU Studies* 14 (Autumn 1973): 115-26. Reprinted in *CWHN* 8:274-88. Points out that Yadin's discoveries seem to show, among other things, that the presumably feminine name Alma was also used by Jews as a masculine name, just as it was in the Book of Mormon. Draws a number of parallels between the Bar Kochba artifacts and the Lehi colony. Compares materials in the Book of Mormon about Lehi, Captain Moroni, and the name Alma with Palestinian warfare and practices from the first century A.D. [J.W.W.]

N.068 Nibley, Hugh W. "Scriptural Perspectives on How to Survive the Calamities of the Last Days." *BYU Studies* 25 (Winter 1985): 7-27. Reprinted in *CWHN* 8:470-97. Repentance, humility, and righteousness, not weapons, are essential for surviving the last days. The Nephite response to war and to challengers is analyzed. Good guys and bad guys are identified by individual religious virtues. [J.W.W.]

N.069 Nibley, Hugh W. *Since Cumorah.* Vol. 7 of *CWHN*, edited by John W. Welch. Salt Lake City: FARMS and Deseret Book, 1967, [R]1988. Examines the Book of Mormon in light of the discoveries at Qumran, Nag Hammadi, and throughout the ancient world, challenging many traditional scholarly assumptions and opening avenues of inquiry regarding the Book of Mormon and its present-day implications. [J.W.W.]

N.070 Nibley, Hugh W. "Since Cumorah: New Voices from the Dust." *IE* 67, 68, 69 (October 1964-December 1966): 816-21, 844-47, 924-28, 974-75, 977,78, 980-83, 1032, 35, 1126-28, 34-37, 60-64, 100-103, 146-47, 210-13, 227, 228, 230-32, 234, 308-11, 326, 328-32, 406-7, 444, 482-83, 574-76, 616-17, 916-17, 974-77, 1013, 1040, 1090-91, 1165-68, 32-34, 44-46, 118-22, 196-97, 334-36, 419-20, 422, 424, 582-83, 636-38, 710-12, 794-95, 799-800, 802, 804-5, 884-85, 974-75, 1028-31, 1084-85, 1162-65. Reprinted as *CWHN* 7. The changing attitudes of biblical scholars toward basic questions about scripture allow room for claims made by the Book of Mormon. Discusses external evidences, the primitive church, Lehi, Zenos, the olive tree, and the Dead Sea Scrolls. [J.W.W.]

N.071 Nibley, Hugh W. "The Stick of Judah and the Stick of Joseph." *IE* 56 (January-May 1983): 16-17, 38-41, 90-91, 123-27, 150-52, 191-95, 250, 267, 331-32, 334, 336, 338, 341, 343, 345. Reprinted in *CWHN* 8:1-48. Writing on tally sticks is related to Ezekiel 37 and the meaning of the prophecy that two sticks shall become one. Extensive commentary on the traditional interpretations given to Ezekiel 37. [J.W.W.]

N.072 Nibley, Hugh W. "A Strange Order of Battle." In Nibley's *An Approach to the Book of Mormon,* 169-80. Salt Lake City: Deseret Book, 1957. Reprinted as a FARMS paper, 1964. Compares Captain Moroni's military practices, title of liberty, and oath, with descriptions from the Near East. [J.W.W.].

N.073 Nibley, Hugh W. "Strange Ships and Shining Stones." In *A Book of Mormon Treasury: Selections from the Papers of the Improvement Era,* 133-51. Salt Lake City: Bookcraft, 1959. Included in Nibley's *An Approach to the Book of Mormon,* 2nd ed. Compares the ships of the Jaredites with boats from Mesopotamia and the Gilgamesh Epic, and the sixteen stones of the brother of Jared with shining stones reported in the pseudepigrapha, Jerusalem Talmud, and by Greek historians. [J.W.W.]

N.074 Nibley, Hugh W. "Strange Ships and Shining Stones (A Not So Fantastic Story)." *IE* 59 (July-September 1956): 509-11, 415, 516, 566-67, 602, 630-32, 672-75. Revised as a chapter in *An Approach to the Book of Mormon*, 340-58, 2nd ed., 1964. Demonstrates some striking similarities between the Jaredite account of their barges with sixteen light-giving stones and old legends about Noah's ark and epic literature from Babylonia. [J.W.W.].

N.075 Nibley, Hugh W. *Teachings of the Book of Mormon: Semester 1-4*. Provo, UT: FARMS, 1989-1990. Tanscripts of lectures by Hugh Nibley presented to an Honors Book of Mormon class at Brigham Young University during the years 1989-1990. Semester 1 covers 1 Nephi–Mosiah 5; semester 2 covers Mosiah 6–Alma 41; semester 3 covers Alma 45–3 Nephi 20; semester 4 covers the rest of the book. Contains historical, biblical, and traditional insights from ancient times that assist in understanding events and doctrine within the Book of Mormon. [B.D.]

N.076 Nibley, Hugh W. "There Were Jaredites." *IE* 59-60 (July 1956–February 1957): 509-11, 514, 516, 566-67, 602, 630-32, 672-75, 710-12, 745-53, 818-19, 857-58, 906-7, 26-27, 41, 94-95, 122-24. Reprinted in *CWHN* 5:283-454. This wide-ranging series discusses the "epic milieu" of the second millennium B.C. and places the Jaredites in their historical context alongside the Babylonians, Egyptians, early Greeks and others. Makes a comparison between the Book of Ether and ancient writings of Babylon, Egypt, Sumer, and others. The description of the Jaredite boats seem to resemble the boat of Ut-Napitshtim who was the Sumerian counter-part of Noah. Old Jewish and even older Indian sources record the use of shining stones that protect the owner beneath the water. These have been traced back to Babylonian tales of the deluge. Since the Jaredite record reports that their boats were patterned after Noah's ark, ancient myths that surely have their foundation in real events help to provide greater understanding of the book of Ether. The book of Ether meets all the criteria of epic traditions of heroic societies. The remains of heroic societies are difficult to identify. [J.W.W.]

N.077 Nibley, Hugh W. *Tinkling Cymbals and Sounding Brass: The Art of Telling Tales about Joseph Smith and Brigham Young*. Vol. 11 of *CWHN*, edited by David J. Whittaker. Salt Lake City: Deseret Book and FARMS, 1992. A collection of answers to the works of Mormon critics Fawn Brodie, J. B. Turner, John C. Bennett, Henry Caswell, Pomeroy Tucker, and many others, pointing out their inconsistencies, and unconfirmed and distorted historical claims. Their attacks are confirmed by unreliable witnesses. Joseph Smith's opponents often played by no rules of fairness and often changed the rules as they argued. [J.W.M.]

N.078 Nibley, Hugh W. "Two Shots in the Dark: i. Dark Days in Jerusalem; ii. Christ among the Ruins." In *Book of Mormon Authorship: New Light on Ancient Origins*, edited by Noel B. Reynolds, 103-42. Provo, UT: Brigham Young University Religious Studies Center, 1982. Reprinted in *CWHN* 8:380-434. Presents information about the names used and the political and the social conditions of Lehi's Jerusalem based on contemporaneous messages written on pottery found at Lachish. [J.W.W.]

N.079 Nibley, Hugh W. "Warfare and the Book of Mormon." In *Warfare in the Book of Mormon*, edited by Stephen D. Ricks and William J. Hamblin, 127-45. Salt Lake City: Deseret and FARMS, 1990. Compares the descriptions of warfare in the Book of Mormon with the writings and axioms of Karl von Clausewitz's military treatise, *Vom Kriege*, that served the military as a bible for 150 years and was published in 1833. Descriptions of Book of Mormon warfare match von Clausewitz's principles very well. Again the internal evidence of the Book of Mormon establishes its accuracy in describing technical subjects unknown to Joseph Smith. [N.K.Y.]

N.080 Nibley, Hugh W. "What Frontier, What Camp Meeting?" *IE* 62 (August 1959): 590-92, 610, 612, 614-15. Reprinted in *CWHN* 8:182-92. Responds to the assertion that the Book of Mormon is a product of the religious and political milieu of the American frontier. [J.W.W.]

N.081 Nibley, Hugh W. "The World of the Jaredites." *IE* 54, 55 (September 1951–July 1955): 628-30, 673-75, 704-6, 752-55, 786-87, 833-35, 862-63, 946-47, 22-24, 92-94, 98, 100, 102, 104-5, 162-65, 167-68, 236-38, 258, 260-65, 316-18, 340-342, 344, 346, 398-99, 462-64, 510, 550. Reprinted as the second half of *Lehi in the Desert and the World of the Jaredites*. Salt Lake City: Bookcraft, 1952. Reprinted in *CWHN* 5:151-282. A detailed reconstruction of the epic milieu and ancient historical setting in the third millennium B.C. in Mesopotamia and Asia relative to details about the Jaredites: their ships, shining stones, government, wars, society, and worldview. [J.W.W.]

N.082 Nibley, Preston. "The Book of Mormon Manuscripts." In *BYUSY* (9 April 1957). Provo, UT: BYU Press. Explores the character of Joseph Smith and the conditions of poverty under which he translated of the Book of Mormon. Gives excerpts of journals written by those who knew Joseph at the time of translation to show the great humility, prayer, and determination of the Prophet. A lengthy discussion on the fate of the original manuscripts is given. [J.W.M.]

N.083 Nibley, Preston. "The Three Witnesses of the Book of Mormon." *Relief Society Magazine* 31 (August 1944): 431-34. A historical account of the vision the Three Witnesses received on the Peter Whitmer farm during the latter part of June 1829. Includes the testimonies of Oliver Cowdery, David Whitmer, and Martin Harris. [J.W.M.]

N.084 Nibley, Preston. *The Witnesses of the Book of Mormon*. Salt Lake City: Stevens and Wallis, 1946. 2nd and 3rd eds. Salt Lake City: Deseret Book, 1953, 1968. Features verses in the Doctrine and Covenants and Book of Mormon pertaining to the witnesses of the Book of Mormon. Discusses statements by the Prophet Joseph Smith and others concerning the witnesses of the Book of Mormon. Gives brief histories of the Three Witnesses and the Eight Witnesses. [L.D.]

N.085 Nichols, Robert E. "Beowulf and Nephi: A Literary View of the Book of Mormon." *Dialogue* 4 (Autumn 1969): 40-47. The life and character of Beowulf, the great hero of the epic age, parallels that of Nephi. Both were mighty in their deeds, both enjoyed great powers of strength and endurance, and both possessed various "manly skills." The Book of Mormon is "a work laden with promise for the literary analyst." More than a century has elapsed since the Book of Mormon has come forth and "literary scholarship" has all but ignored the literary aspects of this sacred text. [D.W.P.]

N.086 Nicholson, John. "Discourse on the Book of Mormon." *JD* 22:17-27. Discusses the remarkable nature of the Book of Mormon. Refers to prophecies in the book, especially those relative to the conversion of the Latter-day Lamanites, and the menace of secret combinations. Notes that "in the early rise of this Church the Lord manifested his displeasure with the Saints because they did not pay sufficient attention to the revelations contained in the Book of Mormon." [D.M.]

N.087 Nicholson, John. "The Lamanites." *Juvenile Instructor* 9 (21 November 1874; 5, 19 December 1874): 274-75, 280-81, 291-92, 303. Discusses the prophecy that the Lamanites will become a "white and delightsome people," and conjectures that the Three Nephites are ministering to them. [D.M.]

N.088 Nicholson, John. "The Lamanites." *MS* 37 (16, 23 February; 2, 9 March 1875): 97-99, 113-14, 131-32, 150-51. Nicholson tells of two instances in which, in his opinion, the Three Nephites appeared to Indian chiefs. Indian Chief Torbuka was visited by three men who mysteriously disappeared after giving their messages. He then arranged to have members of his tribe baptized. An Indian leader of the Uintah Reservation relates that while in Washington to speak with government officials he was visited by a personage on three different evenings who told him to trust the Mormons and told him about the Book of Mormon. [B.D.]

N.089 Nicholson, John. *The Latter-day Prophet.* Liverpool: William Budge, 1880. Writes concerning the need for a true prophet. The Book of Mormon was given by the power of God to clarify misunderstood passages in the Bible. Isaiah foretold of Martin Harris's visit to Professor Anthon. The Book of Mormon is the story of the ancient American inhabitants, whose descendants are receiving the truth in vast numbers. [J.W.M.]

N.090 Nicholson, John. "The Modern Prophet." In *Joseph Smith: Was He a Prophet of God? An Investigation and Testimony*, edited by J. M. Sjodahl. Salt Lake City: Deseret Book, 1891. Discusses why prophets are needed, the organization of the Church, evidences that the Book of Mormon is authentic, and modern day prophecy and the fulfillment of that prophecy. [L.D.]

N.091 Nicholson, John. *The Modern Prophet.* Salt Lake City: Deseret News Co., 189?. A work about Joseph Smith that devotes considerable space to the Book of Mormon. Tells about Joseph Smith's encounter with Moroni and the translation of the plates. Quotes separate testimonies of the Three Witnesses. Discusses the important role of the American Indians. [D.M.]

N.092 Nicholson, John. "Thoughts on the Indian Question." *MS* 53 (2 March 1891): 138-42. A reprint of an article from the *Young Woman's Journal.* Writes concerning the Indians, their lands, and Book of Mormon prophecies. [B.D.]

N.093 Nielsen, C. M. "Oliver Cowdery for the Defense." *IE* 46 (August 1943): 464, 504. Excerpted from the *Deseret News,* February 21, 1910. Recital of Oliver Cowdery's testimony of the Book of Mormon before a court in Michigan. [D.M.]

N.094 Nielsen, F. Kent. *Book of Mormon Teachings.* Provo, UT: Brigham Young University, 1960. A series of four lectures. Makes connections and correspondences between the land of promise and God, Zion, gentiles, and descendants of Joseph. Also points out differences between the LDS view of the Second Coming and those of the world in general. [D.M.]

N.095 Nielson, Harold K. *Mapping the Action Found in the Book of Mormon.* Orem, UT: Cedar Fort, 1987. Contains synopses of each chapter in the Book of Mormon, 32 hypothetical maps to illustrate where events took place, and listings of geographical references. [D.M.]

N.096 Ninnis, Ernest W. *The Marred Servant of the Book of Mormon.* Melbourne: n.p., n.d. A tract attempting to prove the truthfulness of the Book of Mormon through a discussion of the marred servant (Isaiah 52:13-15). [D.W.P.]

N.097 Nordgren, Weston N. "Taught by Their Mothers." *MS* 91 (9 May 1929): 297-98. Compares modern-day missionaries to the stripling warriors of Helaman. [R.H.B.]

N.098 Nordgren, Weston N. " 'Then Shall They Rejoice.' " *MS* 91 (31 January 1929): 72-73. Speaks of the prophecy in the Book of Mormon that the Lamanites, or the American Indians, shall rejoice of the Book of Mormon and its message. Gives several examples of American Indians that have read the Book of Mormon and were baptized because of their faith in its truthfulness. [M.D.P.]

N.099 Norman, V. Garth. "I Have a Question: What is the current status of research concerning the 'Tree of Life' carving from Chiapas, Mexico?" *Ensign* 15 (June 1985): 54-55. The author is cautious and tentative, but believes that the "stela 5 may prove to be the first deciphered artifact from the Nephite civilization." [D.M.]

N.100 Norman, V. Garth. "San Lorenzo as the Jaredite City of Lib." *SEHA Newsletter* 153 (June 1983): 1-9. Agrees with archaeologist Michael D. Coe that there are no direct archaeological evidences of the Book of Mormon. Proposes that the Olmec civilization corresponds to the Jaredite nation and that the present San Lorenzo is located at the site of the Jaredite city Lib. [D.M.]

N.101 Norman, V. Garth. "The Tree of Life Symbol in Ancient Israel." In *Papers of the Fourteenth Annual Symposium on the Archaeology of the*

Scriptures, edited by Forrest R. Hauck, 37-51. Provo, UT: BYU Dept. of Extension, 1963. Compares various symbols of the tree of life found throughout the world to the Israelite representation of the tree of life. Briefly offers some insight into Lehi's dream. [B.D.]

N.102 Norton, Walter A. "Comparative Images: Mormonism and Contemporary Religions as Seen by Village Newspapermen in Western New York and Northeastern Ohio, 1820-1833." Ph.D dissertation, Brigham Young University, 1991. Includes quotations and references from early newspapers referring to Joseph Smith and the Book of Mormon in the formative stages in Church history. [D.M.]

N.103 Novak, Gary F. "Naturalistic Assumptions and the Book of Mormon." *BYU Studies* 30 (Summer 1990): 23-40. This well-documented and didactic essay examines selected assumptions and consequences of naturalistically written history. "Naturalistic" explanations of the Book of Mormon are those that offer an "environmental" (instead of a theological) answer to its coming forth. Focuses on the writings of Dale Morgan and Fawn M. Brodie while also discussing the New Mormon History and one of its historians, Marvin S. Hill. [D.L.L.]

N.104 Numano, Jiro. "The Japanese Translation of the Book of Mormon: A Study in the Theory and Practice of Translation." M. A. thesis, Brigham Young University, 1976. Discusses theory of translation and applies it to the Book of Mormon. Argues that the Japanese translation of the book, although it is claimed to be colloquial, is too literal and hard to read. Considers the translation not sufficiently aware of Hebrew idioms or of the Jewish and Egyptian cultures from which the Book of Mormon originated. [D.M.]

N.105 Nyman, Monte S. "Abinadi's Commentary on Isaiah." In *The Book of Mormon: Mosiah, Salvation Only through Christ*, edited by Monte S. Nyman and Charles D. Tate Jr., 161-86. Provo, UT: Brigham Young University Religious Studies Center, 1991. An exegetical exercise, discussing Abinadi's prophetic message to King Noah's court, in relation to Isaiah 52:7-10 and 53. Themes include Christology and beautiful feet that bring good tidings. Tables and appendices are included. [D.M.]

N.106 Nyman, Monte S. "Appendix C. Isaiah in the Book of Mormon." In Nyman's *Great Are the Words of Isaiah*, 283-87. Salt Lake City: Bookcraft, 1980. Nineteen of the sixty-six chapters of the text of Isaiah from the King James Version of the Bible are quoted in their entirety in the Book of Mormon, two others lack two verses, others are partially quoted. A list of references compares the Book of Mormon passages with their counterparts in Isaiah. [J.W.M.]

N.107 Nyman, Monte S. "Bondage and Deliverance." In *Studies in Scripture: 1 Nephi to Alma 29*, edited by Kent P. Jackson, 260-69. Salt Lake City: Deseret Book, 1987. Retells the story of how Zeniff's colony of Nephites fell into bondage under the Lamanites at the end of King Noah's reign. Recalls the spiritual circumstances under which they were delivered. [D.M.]

N.108 Nyman, Monte S. "The Book of Mormon: A Blessing or a Curse?" In *To the Glory of God*, edited by Truman G. Madsen and Charles D. Tate Jr., 219-30. Salt Lake City: Deseret Book, 1972. Discusses the three phases of judgment that will come to all that possess the Book of Mormon. They are: the gathering of the "seed of Ephraim"; a "cleansing of the Lord's people"; and the judgments of God upon the nations that rejected the Book of Mormon. The Book of Mormon will be either a blessing or a curse depending on how individuals have received it. [A.T.]

N.109 Nyman, Monte S. "The Book of Mormon, Why?" *IE* 65 (July 1962): 530-31, 538-39. Relates the important role of the Book of Mormon as a witness not only for Christ but also for the Bible. The Book of Mormon's value in helping to understand the book of Isaiah is unlimited. [J.W.M.]

N.110 Nyman, Monte S. "By the Book of Mormon We Know." In *Doctrines of the Book of Mormon, 1991 Sperry Symposium*, edited by Bruce A. Van Orden and Brent L. Top, 145-57. Salt

Lake City: Deseret Book, 1992. Comments on the twenty doctrines enumerated in Doctrine and Covenants 20:17-36, and shows that the Book of Mormon enlightens every one. Examples include: existence of God, the commandment to love God, the creation of male and female in God's image, the fall and the atonement; the crucifixion, death, and resurrection, justification and grace, and the gift of the Holy Ghost. [D.M.]

N.111 Nyman, Monte S. "Come to Understanding and Learn Doctrine." In *The Book of Mormon: Second Nephi, The Doctrinal Structure*, edited by Monte S. Nyman and Charles D. Tate Jr., 19-31. Provo, UT: Brigham Young University Religious Studies Center, 1989. 2 Nephi is one of the most doctrinal books of the Book of Mormon. Author gives a chapter-by-chapter overview of doctrines contained in 2 Nephi. [D.M.]

N.112 Nyman, Monte S. "Confirmed to Others by the Ministering of Angels." In *A Symposium on the Book of Mormon*, 104-8. Salt Lake City: Church of Jesus Christ of Latter-day Saints, CES, August 1986. Presents a discussion about angels. Presents definitions and shows the role of angels in the coming forth of the Book of Mormon and the restoration of the gospel. [D.M.]

N.113 Nyman, Monte S. *An Ensign to All People: The Sacred Message and Mission of the Book of Mormon*. Salt Lake City: Deseret Book, 1987. Illuminates certain features of the Book of Mormon to encourage the reading of the book. The Book of Mormon is intended to be an ensign to the nations, Joseph Smith was the "choice seer" designated to bring it forth. Comments on how the Book of Mormon relates to the remnant of Ephraim, the gentiles, the Lamanites, the Jews, and the lost tribes. Includes a study of the allegory of the olive tree, and the building of two Zions, one in New Jerusalem, one in Jerusalem. [L.D. & D.M.]

N.114 Nyman, Monte S. "Hope, Faith, and Charity." In *Studies in Scripture: Alma 30 to Moroni*, edited by Kent P. Jackson, 293-303. Salt Lake City: Deseret Book, 1988. A meditation on Moroni 7, a sermon by Mormon, which deals with the Christian traits faith, hope and charity. Includes a section on the spiritual status of little children. [D.M.]

N.115 Nyman, Monte S. "I Have a Question: Why is the Book of Mormon the 'most correct book,' and how does it contain the fulness of the gospel?" *Ensign* 6 (September 1976): 87. The Book of Mormon is the "most correct book." This is not to be understood as "perfect." The words "correct" and "perfect" are not necessarily synonymous. The book is correct in far greater ways than in grammar, spelling, punctuation, and so on. It speaks of restored doctrines of the gospel, faith, repentance, the atonement, baptism, and the Holy Ghost. These are the saving principles and ordinances that bring one back into the presence of the Father. [J.W.M.]

N.116 Nyman, Monte S. "I Have a Question: Why were the Book of Mormon gold plates not placed in a museum so that people might know Joseph Smith had them?" *Ensign* 16 (December 1986): 64-65. Also in "Why Weren't the Gold Plates Placed in a Museum?" In *A Sure Foundation: Answers to Difficult Gospel Questions*, 52-54. Salt Lake City: Deseret Book, 1988. Asserts that the golden plates were never made available for public view for two reasons: (1) the Lord did not want the plates—with their impressive monetary value—to be used for personal or commercial gain, and (2) to test the faith of those who receive the record. [S.P.S.]

N.117 Nyman, Monte S. "Lehi and Nephi: Faith Unto Salvation." In *The Book of Mormon: First Nephi, The Doctrinal Structure*, edited by Monte S. Nyman and Charles D. Tate Jr., 67-77. Provo, Utah: Brigham Young University Religious Studies Center, 1988. Refers to the "Lectures on Faith" by Joseph Smith. Briefly discusses the three principles of faith and how Nephi and Lehi exemplified these attributes. The three principles are "faith as a principle of action, faith as a principle of power, and faith unto life and salvation." [A.T.]

N.118 Nyman, Monte S. "The Most Correct Book." *Ensign* 14 (June 1984): 20-23. As Joseph Smith stated that the Book of Mormon was the "most correct book," any errors in it are due mostly to the inadequacies of present languages. As the keystone of the LDS religion the book is important in uniting the Church, thus preventing a splintering like that of early Christianity. The Book of Mormon teaches the doctrines that will draw men and women to God. [S.P.S.]

N.119 Nyman, Monte S. *The Most Correct Book: Why the Book of Mormon is the Keystone Scripture.* Salt Lake City: Bookcraft, 1991. A three-pronged discussion of Joseph Smith's statement that the Book of Mormon (1) is the most correct book, (2) is the keystone of the LDS religion, and (3) enables a person to get close to God by abiding by its precepts. Subthemes deal with the translation of the book, a warning to the inhabitants of the promised land, how the book contains a fulness of the Gospel, how the book is scripture, what it has to say about the ministering of angels, how the book testifies of the Bible, and how the world is to be judged by the book. [D.M.]

N.120 Nyman, Monte S. "The Necessity of the Book of Mormon in Teaching the New Testament." In *The Eleventh Annual Sidney B. Sperry Symposium: The New Testament,* 73-83. Provo, UT: Church Educational System, 1983. Various aspects of the New Testament, such as the authenticity of certain books, the integrity of the Sermon on the Mount, and the reality of miracles are confirmed in the Book of Mormon, in spite of skepticism on the part of modern biblical criticism. [D.M.]

N.121 Nyman, Monte S. "Priesthood Versus Priestcraft among the Nephites." In *The Sixth Annual Religious Educator's Symposium on the Book of Mormon,* 66-69. Salt Lake City: Church of Jesus Christ of Latter-day Saints, 1982. Author demonstrates that Lehi held the Melchizedek priesthood. Uses the Book of Mormon to demonstrate some of the duties of an individual that holds the Melchizedek priesthood. Then the author defines priestcraft, and describes how it is different from anti-Christ. He outlines the stories of men who used priestcraft in the Book of Mormon such as Nehor and Amlici. [A.T.]

N.122 Nyman, Monte S. "The Restoration of Plain and Precious Parts: The Book of Helaman." In *The Book of Mormon: Helaman through 3 Nephi 8, According to Thy Word,* edited by Monte S. Nyman and Charles D. Tate Jr., 147-61. Provo, UT: Brigham Young University Religious Studies Center, 1992. Lists four areas in which the book of Helaman restores lost parts of the Bible or verifies what was not lost: (1) personages and incidents, (2) prophets, (3) prophecies and (4) New Testament precepts traced to the Old Testament. [D.M.]

N.123 Nyman, Monte S. "The Same God Yesterday, Today, and Forever." In *Sidney B. Sperry Symposium: The Book of Mormon,* edited by A. Gary Anderson, 117-26, Provo, UT: BYU Religious Instruction, 1981. Shows how God is the same yesterday, today, and forever through his personal appearances, the manner of his manifestations, and the fact that he is no respecter of persons. [D.M.]

N.124 Nyman, Monte S. "Source Book of Suggestions for Teaching the Book of Mormon." D.Ed. thesis, Brigham Young University, 1965. Consists of teaching suggestions for Book of Mormon classes, along with teacher responses to questionnaires. Also contains an elaborate teaching guide with statements of purpose, outlines, and questions. Includes handouts for students. [D.M.]

N.125 Nyman, Monte S. "The State of the Soul between Death and the Resurrection." In *The Book of Mormon: Alma, The Testimony of the Word,* edited by Monte S. Nyman and Charles D. Tate Jr., 173-94. Provo, UT: Brigham Young University Religious Studies Center, 1992. Expounds on Alma's instruction to Corianton (Alma 40:6-7, 11-14) regarding the spirit world. Sets forth where and what it is, writes concerning the wicked and righteous spirits who dwell there, and teaches concerning the work of salvation there. [D.M. & N.K.Y.]

N.126 Nyman, Monte S. "To Learn with Joy: Sacred Preaching, Great Revelation, Prophesying." In *The Book of Mormon: Jacob through Words of Mormon, To Learn with Joy,* edited by Monte S. Nyman and Charles D. Tate Jr., 193-208. Provo, UT: Brigham Young University Religious Studies Center, 1990. Shows how the writings of Jacob through the Words of Mormon on the small plates of Nephi followed the admonition and example set by Nephi—to devote the greater space to sacred things, and but little to historical events. [D.M.]

N.127 Nyman, Monte S. *Two Sticks One in Thine Hand.* Salt Lake City: Gen-Dex Press, 1973. "This treatise is an attempt to show how utterly false are the suppositions that the Church has its own Bible or that the Church fails to accept the Christian world's Bible. It will further endeavor to show that the Church not only accepts the Bible but is much concerned that modern Christianity maintains its faith in this sacred volume of scripture." Author uses the Book of Mormon as a basis for examining Old Testament authorship, Bible history, text, and interpretation. [A.T.]

N.128 Nyman, Monte S. "Two Sticks: One in Thine Hand." In *The Third Annual Church Educational System Religious Educators' Symposium: A Symposium on the Old Testament*, 243-51. Salt Lake City: Church of Jesus Christ of Latter-day Saints, 1979. Argues that the Book of Mormon corrects the false views about the Bible held by Bible critics. The Book of Mormon verifies the historicity and authorships of the Bible. [D.M.]

N.129 Nyman, Monte S. "Why Study Isaiah." In *The Second Annual Church Educational System Religious Educators' Symposium: A Symposium on the Book of Mormon*, 93-97. Salt Lake City: Church of Jesus Christ of Latter-day Saints, 1979. Rather than being discouraged by Isaiah, Latter-day Saints should take great interest in the prophet, because the Book of Mormon expressly commands its study. Isaiah testified of the Messiah and foresaw the future of Israel. The Book of Mormon joins the New Testament and Doctrine and Covenants in helping individuals to understand Isaiah. [D.M.]

N.130 Nyman, Monte S., and Charles D. Tate Jr. "Proving the Holy Scriptures Are True." In *"To Be Learned Is Good If . . .,"* edited by Robert L. Millet, 77-114. Salt Lake City: Bookcraft, 1987. Shows how the Book of Mormon, Doctrine and Covenants, Pearl of Great Price, and Joseph Smith Translation clarify the contents of the Bible. Includes an extensive table. [D.M.]

N.131 Nyman, Monte S., and Charles D. Tate Jr., eds. *The Book of Mormon: Alma, The Testimony of the Word: Papers from the Sixth Annual Book of Mormon Symposium, 1991.* Provo, Utah: Brigham Young University Religious Studies Center, 1992. Presenters included Dean L. Larsen, Rex C. Reeve Jr., Robert J. Matthews, Robert L. Millet, and others. The topics include the "New Meaning of 'Restoration,'" anti-Christs, faith and freedom, and others, all based on the book of Alma. [J.W.M.]

N.132 Nyman, Monte S., and Charles D. Tate Jr., eds. *The Book of Mormon: First Nephi, the Doctrinal Foundation.* Provo, UT: Brigham Young University Religious Studies Center, 1988. A collection of lectures delivered at a Brigham Young University-sponsored symposium. Subjects include Jesus in the Book of Mormon, Christianity in the Book of Mormon, fasting, love, Columbus, Old World contacts, and more. Talks are listed under the names of the respective authors in this bibliography. [D.M.]

N.133 Nyman, Monte S., and Charles D. Tate Jr., eds. *The Book of Mormon: Helaman through 3 Nephi 8, According To Thy Word: Papers from the Seventh Annual Book of Mormon Symposium, 1992.* Provo, Utah: Brigham Young University Religious Studies Center, 1992. Presenters included Russell M. Nelson, Robert Millet, Robert J. Matthews, Thomas W. Mackay, Monte S. Nyman, and others. The topics include sanctification, secret covenant teachings of men, the dangers of a class society, and many others found in the books of Helaman and 3 Nephi. [J.W.M.]

N.134 Nyman, Monte S., and Charles D. Tate Jr., eds. *The Book of Mormon: Jacob through Words of Mormon, To Learn with Joy.* Provo, UT: Brigham Young University Religious Studies Center, 1990. A compilation of addresses delivered at a Book of Mormon Symposium at Brigham Young University. Subjects include Jacob, the allegory of the Olive Tree, the religion of Moses, Enos, Sherem, the small plates, and more. Individual talks are listed in this bibliography under the names of the contributors. [D.M.]

N.135 Nyman, Monte S., and Charles D. Tate Jr., eds. *The Book of Mormon: Mosiah, Salvation Only through Christ.* Provo, UT: Brigham Young University Religious Studies Center, 1991. A group of speeches given at an annual Book of Mormon symposium at Brigham Young University. Subjects include King Benjamin, Noah, the atonement, government, the natural man, Abinadi, priesthood, church discipline in Mosiah, and more. Titles of talks are listed in this bibliography under the names of the contributors. [D.M.]

N.136 Nyman, Monte S., and Charles D. Tate Jr., eds. *The Book of Mormon: Second Nephi, The Doctrinal Structure.* Provo, UT: Brigham Young University Religious Studies Center, 1989. Compilation of Book of Mormon symposium addresses delivered at Brigham Young University. Subjects include free agency, the promised land, the fall of man, the Lamanite mark, God's covenants with the house of Israel, the atonement, the brass plates, the law of witnesses, and more. Specific titles are listed in this bibliography under the name of each contributor. [D.M.]

N.137 Nyman, Monte S., and Charles D. Tate Jr., eds. *The Book of Mormon: 3 Nephi 9-30, This Is My Gospel: Papers from the Eighth Annual Book of Mormon Symposium, 1993.* Provo, UT: Brigham Young University Religious Studies Center, 1993. Presenters at this symposium included Robert L. Millet, Robert J. Matthews, Monte S. Nyman, S. Kent Brown, Joseph Fielding McConkie, and numerous others. The subjects covered include prayer, the doctrine of translation, the gathering at the temple, service, and more. Papers are based on the book of 3 Nephi and Christ's visit to America. Specific titles are listed in this bibliography under the name of each contributor. [J.W.M.]

N.138 Nyman, Monte S., and Lisa B. Hawkins. "Book of Mormon Overview." In *Encyclopedia of Mormonism*, edited by Daniel H. Ludlow, 1:139-43. 5 vols. New York: Macmillan, 1992. Joseph Smith was quoted as saying the Book of Mormon was the most correct of any book on earth and that a person would get nearer to God by abiding by its precepts than by any other book. It confirms and supplements the Bible and stands as another testament of Jesus Christ. It deals primarily with the history of the Nephites and Lamanites from 600 B.C. to 400 A.D., the Jaredites from the tower of Babel until about 300 B.C., and the people of Mulek beginning at 300 B.C. and later merging with the Nephite history. [N.K.Y.]

O.

O.001 O., G. M. "Old America: Jared." *MS* 37 (March 1875): 197-99, 212-13, 231. Gives a brief synopsis of Jaredite history including their sailing to the American continent from the Tower of Babel. Also cites many ancient American flood myths that relate to the biblical story of the flood at the time of Noah. [B.D.]

O.002 Oaks, Dallin H. "The Desires of Our Hearts." In *Brigham Young University 1985–86 Devotional and Fireside Speeches of the Year,* edited by Karen Seely, 27-31. Provo, UT: Brigham Young University, 1986. Also in *Ensign* 16 (June 1986): 64-67. Desires are the foundation of all actions, and thus righteous desires must be cultivated. Quotes Mormon's teachings in Moroni 7 and King Benjamin's sermon to illustrate that hearts must be right with God. [E.G.]

O.003 Oaks, Dallin H. "Free Agency and Freedom." In *The Book of Mormon: Second Nephi, The Doctrinal Structure*, edited by Monte S. Nyman and Charles D. Tate Jr., 1-17. Provo, UT: Brigham Young University Religious Studies Center, 1989. Distinguishes two terms: free agency is "an exercise of the will, the power to choose." Freedom is the ability and "privilege to carry out our choices." Shows both the doctrine and application of these two principles. [D.M.]

O.004 Oaks, Dallin H. "The Historicity of the Book of Mormon." Provo, UT: FARMS, 1993.

Questions concerning the historicity of the Book of Mormon should be resolved with scholarship, faith, and revelation. All issues of content, vocabulary, revelation, and archaeology must be examined. [E.G.]

O.005 Oaks, Dallin H. "The Light and Life of the World." *Ensign* 17 (November 1987): 63-65. Also in *CR* (October 1987): 75-79. Emphasizes that Jesus Christ is the Light and Life of the world, that the Church of Jesus Christ of Latter-day Saints teaches love of Christ, and that the Book of Mormon bears witness of him. [L.D.]

O.006 Oaks, Dallin H. "What Think Ye of Christ?" *Ensign* 18 (November 1988): 65-68. Members of the Church must turn to the Book of Mormon to protect themselves from many of the heresies that exist about Christ. Many individuals challenge the divinity of Christ and declare that man must save himself. The Book of Mormon presents the complete doctrine of the atonement, Christ's divinity, and the fullness of the gospel he taught. Christ is the only way to salvation and life. [J.W.M.]

O.007 Oaks, Stella Harris. *Martin Harris—The Third Witness*. Provo, UT: Brigham Young University, August 1974. Relates Harris's connection with the coming forth of the Book of Mormon and his unfaltering testimony regarding seeing the gold plates and the angel. [D.W.P.]

O.008 "An Objection to the Book of Mormon Answered." *MS* 58 (27 August 1896): 557-58. Cites archaeological evidence that iron was used by ancient American inhabitants, supporting the claim made by the Book of Mormon concerning steel and iron. [A. C.]

O.009 O'Brien, T. C. "Book of Mormon." In *Encyclopedic Dictionary of Religion*, edited by Paul Kevin Meagher, et. al., 1:498. Washington, DC: Corpus, 1976. An encyclopedic entry that provides a brief description of the origin and contents of the Book of Mormon. [D.W.P.]

O.010 "Of Good Report." *Ensign* 23 (June 1993): 79-80. A report of the benefits of Book of Mormon "marathons" where participants read the entire book in one sitting. [S.H.]

O.011 Ogden, D. Kelly. "Answering the Lord's Call." In *Studies in Scripture: 1 Nephi to Alma 29*, edited by Kent P. Jackson, 17-33. Salt Lake City: Deseret Book, 1987. Reviews the historical background of Lehi's family and their exodus from Israel. Many new insights may be gained by studying Israel's history in conjunction with 1 Nephi 1-7. Lehi's family must have been inspired as they compared their experiences to Moses and the exodus that he led from Egypt. [J.W.M.]

O.012 Ogden, D. Kelly. " 'As Plain as Word Can Be.' " In *Doctrines of the Book of Mormon, 1991 Sperry Symposium*, edited by Bruce A. Van Orden and Brent L. Top, 158-65. Salt Lake City: Deseret Book, 1992. Points out that Book of Mormon prophets made rich use of figurative language, but inasmuch as they delighted in plainness, they often explained the meaning of the figurative language that they used. Examples include the chains of hell, lake of fire and brimstone, seed (in Alma 32), and kingdom of the devil. [D.M.]

O.013 Ogden, D. Kelly. "Why Does the Book of Mormon Say that Jesus Would Be Born in Jerusalem?" In *A Sure Foundation: Answers to Difficult Gospel Questions*, 3-5. Salt Lake City: Deseret Book, 1988. Deals with Alma 7:10 that states that Jesus would be born at Jerusalem. Explains that Alma wrote that Jesus would be born at Jerusalem (i.e., the land of Jerusalem) and not in Jerusalem (i.e., the city of Jerusalem). [J.W.M.]

O.014 Olsen, Steven L. "Cosmic Urban Symbolism in the Book of Mormon." *BYU Studies* 23 (Winter 1983): 79-92. Cosmic urban symbolism is one way that complex societies dramatize their belief that the perceived order of territorial environment, in its "natural" and built-up features, reveals the structure of a sacred universe. The society personifies this belief by building reduced embodiments of the cosmos usually in the form of a capital city or a ceremonial center. In this article, the author first describes and defines cosmic urban symbolism as found in ancient civilizations, and then writes concerning the concepts of centripetality, cardinality, and inductance as found in the text of the Book of Mormon. [D.L.L.]

O.015 Olsen, Steven L. "Patterns of Prayer: Humility or Pride." *Ensign* 22 (August 1992): 8-11. Mormon's abridgment of the records of the Zoramite mission teach a powerful lesson on prayer. The contrast between the proud Zoramite prayers on the Rameumptum and Alma's humble supplication shows what true worship should be like. [A.C.W.]

O.016 Olson, Earl E. "Book of Mormon." In *The Encyclopedia Americana*, edited by Mark Cummings, 4:246. 30 vols. Danbury, CT: Grolier, 1993. Sets forth the origin and contents of the Book of Mormon in a brief, encyclopedic manner. [D.W.P.]

O.017 Olson, Eric C. "The 'Perfect Pattern': The Book of Mormon as a Model for the Writing of Sacred History." *BYU Studies* 31 (Spring 1991): 7-18. Takes issue with Robert Millet's proposition that Mormon historians should take the Book of Mormon as the "perfect pattern" for writing history in the sense of recognizing God's hand, while not dwelling on mortal weaknesses. The small plates are not history (Millet had cited Nephi and Jacob as model historians), and much of the large plates is instruction. The Book of Mormon should serve as a historical guide only to a limited degree. [D.M.]

O.018 Olson, Ernest. *The Story of the Book of Mormon*. Orem, UT: Mil-Bur, 1967. A coloring book depicting Book of Mormon life. Includes pages illustrating the role of Joseph Smith in the coming forth of the Book of Mormon. [D.M.]

O.019 Oman, Richard G. "Lehi's Vision of the Tree of Life: A Cross-Cultural Perspective in Contemporary Latter-day Saint Art." *BYU Studies* 32 (Fall 1992): 5-34. Examines eight artists' representations of Lehi's vision of the tree of life and "shows how the differences in the artists cultural background actually enlarge our understanding of this ancient vision. In addition, an analysis of eight of these pieces can provide some insights into the current state of Latter-day Saint art." [B.D.]

O.020 " 'On the Morrow Come I Into the World'—The Book of Mormon Christmas Story." *Ensign* 16 (December 1986): 44-45. Discusses the account of Jesus' birth in the Book of Mormon and the events that occurred during that time in the American continent. Quotes extensively Helaman 12, 13, and 14 and 3 Nephi 1. [L.D.]

O.021 Ord, Gayle Gable. "The Book of Mormon Goes to Press." *Ensign* 2 (December 1972): 66-70. A detailed and technical account of the printing of the Book of Mormon, including a description of the physical process used by the printers, Egbert Grandin of the *Wayne Sentinel*, and John H. Gilbert, the compositor. [B.T.]

O.022 *Origin of the Book of Mormon*. Plano, IL: RLDS Church, 1876?. Argues that the Book of Mormon was not part of the Spaulding Manuscript. The fact that there were Three Witnesses to the gold plates presents an argument against the Spaulding theory for the origin of the Book of Mormon. [D.W.P.]

O.023 "The Original Manuscript." *Contributor* 8 (October 1887): 441, 474. A reproduction, explanation, and description of a page of the original Book of Mormon manuscript. [A.T.]

O.024 "Original Manuscript of the Book of Mormon." *IE* 3 (March 1900): 389-90. Gives an account about the possibility that David Whitmer or the Whitmer family possessed the original manuscripts of the Book of Mormon. [L.D.]

O.025 Orion. *Book of Mormon Talks*. Lamoni, IA: Board of Publication of the Reorganized Church of Jesus Christ of Latter Day Saints, 1912. This book, for older children, is in the form of a dialogue between a father and his three children. The children ask questions about the Book of Mormon and the father answers. Some topics discussed are: where did the Book of Mormon come from, who were the peoples in it, what does it say about them, what does the Bible say about the Book of Mormon, what prophecies does the Book of Mormon contain, and which prophecies have been fulfilled? [B.D.]

O.026 Orme, Gilbert Charles. *L.D.S. Scriptures*. Salt Lake City: Bookcraft, 1974. Teaching aid. Compilation of 1900 scriptural passages organized alphabetically under 300 subject headings. [J.W.M.]

O.027 Osmond, Waldo L. "The Three Witnesses." *MS* 89 (12 May 1927): 298-300. The Three Witnesses fulfilled the function of bearing living testimonies of the truthfulness of the Book of Mormon. They became witnesses when they received a heavenly manifestation in June 1829. [D.W.P.]

O.028 Ostler, Blake T. "The Covenant Tradition in the Book of Mormon." In *Rediscovering the Book of Mormon*, edited by John L. Sorenson and Melvin J. Thorne, 230-40. Salt Lake City: Deseret Book and FARMS, 1991. Discusses the two covenant renewal festivals of the Book of Mormon—King Benjamin's address and the account of King Limhi—and finds that the ancient origins of the Book of Mormon are revealed in the similarity of the traditions of Israel and the Book of Mormon records. [J.W.M.]

O.029 Ostler, Blake T. "The Development of the Mormon Concept of Grace." *Dialogue* 24 (Spring 1991): 57-84. An in-depth examination of grace, comparing the Book of Mormon concept with that of Augustine and the major instigators of the Reformation. The doctrines related to grace were largely carried through into the Nauvoo period. [D.M.]

O.030 Ostler, Blake T. "The Throne-Theophany and Prophetic Commission in 1 Nephi: A Form-Critical Analysis." *BYU Studies* 26 (Fall 1986): 67-95. Compares the throne theophany of Lehi in 1 Nephi 1 with similar visions in the Old Testament pseudepigrapha. Concludes that the Book of Mormon account more closely corresponds to ancient sources than to nineteenth-century religious experiences whose reports would have been available to Joseph Smith. Contains three appendices. [D.M.]

O.031 Otten, Leaun G., and E. A. McKenna. *Selected Statements from General Authorities Concerning Book of Mormon Passages*. 3 vols. Provo, UT: BYU Press, 1971. A collection of statements made by General Authorities of the Church of Jesus Christ of Latter-day Saints concerning Book of Mormon passages. Volume one begins with statements by Church leaders concerning 1 Nephi to Words of Mormon; volume two contains statements dealing with Mosiah and Alma; volume three with the books Helaman to Moroni. [J.W.M.]

O.032 Ottinger, G. M. "Old America." *Juvenile Instructor* 10-11 (9, 23 January, 6, 20 February, 6, 20 March, 3, 17 April, 1, 15, 29 May, 12, 26 June, 10, 24 July, 7, 21 August, 4, 18 September, 2, 16, 30 October, 13, 27 November, 11, 25 December 1875, 1, 15 January, 1, 15 February, 1, 15 March, 1, 15 April, 1, 15 May, 1, 15 June 1876): 3-4, 14-15, 32-33, 40-41, 52-53, 63-64, 80-81, 87-88, 98-99, 110-111, 131-132, 142-43, 155-56, 167-78, 178-89, 182-83, 194-95, 206-7, 220-21, 230-31, 244-45, 254-55, 266-67, 287-88, 290-91, 302-3, 8-9, 15, 27-28, 41-41, 51-52, 63-64, 74-75, 87-88, 98-99, 111-12, 128-29, 134-35. Series of articles dealing with archaeological, anthropological, geographical, societal, religious, and historical aspects of ancient America and their connections to the Book of Mormon, which is the key to understanding "old American" studies. [A.C.W.]

O.033 Ottinger, G. M. "Votan, the Culture-Hero of the Mayas." *Juvenile Instructor* 14 (1 March 1879): 57-58. Points out "remarkable" similarities between the Book of Mormon and the *Popol Vuh*, relating it to the Nephites, Mulekites, Jaredites, and various geographical locations from Book of Mormon. Compares the river Sid to the Rio Usumasint and Zarahemla to the ruins of Palenque. [A.C.W.]

O.034 *Outline Illustrating the Historical Evolution of the Book of Mormon*. N.p.: n.p., 1939. An illustrated outline of Book of Mormon history beginning with the exodus of the Jaredite people to Joseph Smith's visit from angel Moroni and the publication of the book. Gives a summary of the "Manuscript Found" by Solomon Spaulding and a reprint of the letter of President Fairchild of Oberlin College saying that the Spaulding manuscript bears no resemblance to the Book of Mormon. [J.W.M.]

P.

P.001 P. "The Indians." *MA* 2 (January 1836): 245-48. Relates the Book of Mormon to American Indians and the gathering of Israel. [A.C.W.]

P.002 P. "Untitled." *TS* 3 (1 September 1842): 906-8. A transcription of part of a conversation between a clergyman and a "saint" discussing the Book of Mormon as a revelation, why the gold plates are not on display, and the propriety of angelic visitations in this enlightened age. [D.M.]

P.003 Pack, Frederick J. "A New Scripture." *MS* 98 (9 July 1936): 434-36. Gives logical evidences that support the Book of Mormon, including the short amount of time it took Joseph Smith to translate the Book of Mormon, the Three Witnesses testified of it's truth to their dying day, archaeological discoveries, and more. [M.D.P.]

P.004 Pack, Frederick J. "Revelation Ante-Dating Scientific Discovery—An Instance." *IE* 10 (February, June 1907): 241-47; 595-97. Investigates geological evidence that horses were present on the American Continent during the Book of Mormon period. [J.W.M.]

P.005 Pack, Frederick J. "Route Traveled by Lehi and His Company." *Instructor* 73 (April 1938): 160. All American editions of the Book of Mormon after 1882 contain a notation, written possibly by Frederick G. Williams, that identifies the location of the landing place of Lehi's company. It is not properly verified as to authenticity and should be avoided. [J.W.M.]

P.006 Pack, Frederick J. "The Spalding Argument." *IE* 16 (February 1913): 333-41. Answers F. S. Spalding's allegations that the Book of Mormon is not true and Spalding's claims that the Book of Abraham was falsely translated and therefore both documents are fraudulent. [J.W.M.]

P.007 Pack, Frederick J. "Time Involved in Translating the Book of Mormon." *Instructor* 70 (February 1935): 49. That the bulk of the translation was done from 7 April 1829 to June 1829 is evidence that the Book of Mormon was of divine origin. The book agrees in doctrine with the Bible and with archaeological facts that were virtually unknown in backwoods New York in 1830. [J.W.M.]

P.008 Pack, Frederick J. "Valid Testimony of the Three Witnesses." *MS* 90 (6 December 1928): 769-75. Discusses the men who are the Three Witnesses to the Book of Mormon, their continued testimony after leaving the Church, and the reconversion of Oliver Cowdery and Martin Harris. [L.D.]

P.009 Pack, Melvin Deloy. "Possible Lexical Hebraisms in the Book of Mormon: the Words of Mormon to Moroni." M.A. thesis, Brigham Young University, 1967. Gives many examples of idioms used in the Book of Mormon that translate naturally back into Hebrew. Covers Words of Mormon through Moroni, continuing a similar study by E. Craig Bramwell. Includes a table of Book of Mormon verses that contain wording similar to biblical passages. [D.M.]

P.010 Packard, Dennis J. "The Beginning of Wisdom." *BYU Studies* 24 (Winter 1984): 53-60. One helpful method of studying the Book of Mormon is to read the scriptures aloud. The scriptures are meant to be heard like great music. [J.W.M.]

P.011 Packer, Boyd K. "Atonement, Agency, Accountability." *Ensign* 18 (May 1988): 69-72. Also in *CR* (2-3 April 1988): 80-84. The Book of Mormon clarifies the New Testament in regards to the atonement, agency, the accountability of mankind, and repentance. [J.W.M.]

P.012 Packer, Boyd K. "The Book of Mormon." In Packer's, *Let Not Your Heart Be Troubled*, 268-85. Salt Lake City: Bookcraft, 1991. Jesus Christ is the central message of the Book of Mormon. Gives suggestions of items to tell investigators when giving them a Book of Mormon. [D.M.]

P.013 Packer, Boyd K. "Book of Mormon Military Service and War." *CR* (April 1968): 33-36. Those who go to war should keep the commandments and not become "conscientious objectors." The Book of Mormon justifies war when defending lives, country, and religion. Being prepared for war is not warmongery. [R.C.D.]

P.014 Packer, Boyd K. "Book of Mormon Origin: Scriptures a Blessing." *CR* (April 1974): 135-39. Reaffirms the divine origin of the Book of Mormon and the reality of continuing revelation. Defends textual corrections and sets forth a formula for ascertaining truth of the Book of Mormon, that of spiritual inquiry coupled with a lifetime of sincerity and humility. [E.G.]

P.015 Packer, Boyd K. " 'The Law and the Light.' " In *The Book of Mormon: Jacob through Words of Mormon, To Learn with Joy*, edited by Monte S. Nyman and Charles D. Tate Jr., 1-27. Provo, UT: Brigham Young University Religious Studies Center, 1990. Man is unique in the animal kingdom (3 Nephi 15:9). Opposes organic evolution as the explanation for the origin of mankind. Points out intellectual and moral implications of accepting evolution. Admonishes that there are to be "no manner of -ites" (4 Nephi 1:15), but instead seekers after truth, looking to Christ as "the law and the light" (3 Nephi 15:9). [D.M.]

P.016 Packer, Boyd K. "The Library of the Lord." *Ensign* 20 (May 1990): 36-38. Reports on scriptural innovations: new editions of the standard works published in the early 1980s, increased numbers of translations, LDSView computer software, and the correlation of Church curriculum to the scriptures. Affirms the Book of Mormon's importance in testifying of Christ and validating the Old and New Testaments. [E.G.]

P.017 Packer, Boyd K. "Publication of LDS Edition of the Scriptures." *CR* (October 1982): 73-77. With the publication of the new LDS edition of the scriptures, the complete fulfillment of Ezekiel's prophecy of two sticks (records) has come to pass. The Book of Mormon will now have the title, "Another Testament of Jesus Christ," so the two sticks are now one. [R.C.D.]

P.018 Packer, Boyd K. "Scriptures." *Ensign* 12 (November 1982): 51-53. Also in *CR* (October 1982): 73-77. Ezekiel 37 tells of the sticks of Judah and Joseph that will become one in the hands of the user. This prophecy began to come true when the Book of Mormon was published. Gives the historical setting of the printing of the book and the progressive steps toward the new edition of the scriptures. This massive undertaking draws the Bible and the Book of Mormon into one. [J.W.M.]

P.019 Packer, Boyd K. "The Things of My Soul." *Ensign* 16 (May 1986): 59-61. Also in *CR* (5-6 April 1986): 73-78. Gives an introduction to the Book of Mormon for those who have never read it. The book is not fictional, biographical, or historical, nor is it merely a novel. It has profound value as a book and possesses a sacred message and a promise. [J.W.M.]

P.020 Packer, James S. "John Lloyd Stephens and the Mayas." *Ensign* 2 (September 1972): 50-53. John Lloyd Stephens's discoveries of 1839 are a physical witness to the Book of Mormon. In Honduras he discovered magnificent structures that dispelled the belief that native Americans were mere savages. [J.W.M.]

P.021 Page, John E. *The Spaulding Story Concerning the Origin of the Book of Mormon, Duly Examined, and Exposed to the Righteous Contempt of a Candid Public*. Pittsburgh: Author and Church of Jesus Christ of Latter-day Saints, 1843. Argues against the idea that Sidney Rigdon borrowed the Spaulding manuscript, altered the manuscript to fit his purposes, and used Joseph Smith to publish it as the Book of Mormon. [J.W.M.]

P.022 Palmer, David A. "Cumorah." In *Encyclopedia of Mormonism*, edited by Daniel H. Ludlow, 1:346-47. 5 vols. New York: Macmillan, 1992. Cumorah in the Book of Mormon is the hill upon which the Nephites and Lamanites fought their last battle and also where the Jaredites were destroyed. Many ancient records were deposited in it that will someday be revealed. Moroni buried the Book of Mormon plates in an unspecified site. No specific site is identified as the Book of Mormon Hill Cumorah. [B.D.]

P.023 Palmer, David A. "Has the City of Nephi Been Found?" *ZR* 22-23 (1984): 6-7, 15-16. Asserts that Kaminaljuyu, ancient ruins located within the present city of Guatemala, is the city of Nephi. Archaeologists and scholars have found evidence "that meets all the criteria with respect to geography and topography which the Book of Mormon gives for the city of Nephi." [D.S.T.]

P.024 Palmer, David A. *In Search of Cumorah: New Evidences for the Book of Mormon from Ancient Mexico.* Bountiful, UT: Horizon Publishers, 1981. Presents evidence regarding various geographical and archaeological aspects of the Book of Mormon. Points out similarities between the culture and history of the Jaredites, Mulekites, Nephites, and the Mesoamericans. Believes that Cerro Vigia was Mormon's Hill Cumorah. [C. W.]

P.025 Palmer, David A. "A Survey of Pre-1830 Historical Sources Relating to the Book of Mormon." *BYU Studies* 17 (Autumn 1976): 101-7. Discusses historical and religious internal reconstructions of Book of Mormon geography in Mexico and Guatemala. Discusses what authentic information on pre-400 A.D. Mesoamerican history was available in western New York in 1829. [L.D.]

P.026 Palmer, David A. "Warfare and the Development of Nephite Culture in America." Provo, UT: FARMS, 1985. The three causes of warfare are economic, political, and religious. Book of Mormon accounts of warfare seem to parallel the analysis of archaeologists concerning warfare in Mesoamerica. [J.W.M.]

P.027 Palmer, David A. "The World and Times of the Jaredites." In *A Symposium on the Book of Mormon*, 98. Salt Lake City: Church of Jesus Christ of Latter-day Saints, 1979. Uses parallel columns to compare archaeological finds and descriptions from the Book of Ether on construction of cities, the development of cities in the narrow neck of land, mining, metal work, and civil war. [N.K.Y.]

P.028 Palmer, Spencer J., and William L. Knecht "View of the Hebrews: Substitute for Inspiration?" *BYU Studies* 5 (Winter 1964): 105-13. Fawn Brodie claimed that when Joseph Smith's literary creativity dissipated in 2 Nephi he simply borrowed Isaiah passages referred to in Ethan Smith's *View of the Hebrews*. Using statistical methods, these authors challenge Brodie's opinion and find that the correlation between the Book of Mormon and *View of the Hebrews* is insignificant. [D.M.]

P.029 Palmer, William Rees. *Two Pahute Indian Legends: "Why the Grand Canyon Was Made" and "The Three Days of Darkness," External Evidences of the Book of Mormon Examined.* London: Bristol, 1849. The Indian legend "Why the Grand Canyon Was Made" tells of the great shaking and trembling of the earth that came after many generations and created the Grand Canyon. The account sounds very much like 3 Nephi 10:9-10. "The Three Days of Darkness" tells that at the time of the death of Shinob, younger God of the Pahute Indians, they could not light a fire. Later Shinob came back to life. This legend sounds like the account in the Book of Mormon in 3 Nephi 8:17-23. [J.W.M.]

P.030 Parker, Aubrey J. "B: The Bible and the Book of Mormon." In Parker's *ABC of Mormonism*. N.p.: by the author, 1953, 17-28. The Book of Mormon is a "history of the aborigines of the Americas." It contains the fullness of the gospel and supports and corrects the errors in the Bible. [J.W.M.]

P.031 Parker, Jimmy B. "A Record of Our Kingdoms." *Ensign* 6 (August 1976): 22-25. 1 Nephi 9:2-3 provides a good pattern for keeping records. One's own personal record of spiritual experiences may be likened to the small plates of Nephi. [J.W.M.]

P.032 Parkin, Max H. "Untitled Talk on Church History and the Book of Mormon." *Mormon History Association Newsletter* 45 (November 1980): 2-4. A brief analysis of several clues that have been used to argue possible dates that Joseph Smith received D&C 10, which scripture deals with "instructions to replace the 116 pages of the manuscript lost by Martin Harris in 1828 with another record, which God has prepared in antiquity for that purpose." [D.S.T.]

P.033 Parkinson, David. "A Study to Compare a Programmed Approach to Reading the Book of Mormon with the Traditional Reading Method." M.A. thesis, Brigham Young University, 1969. A work involving the comparison of "a programmed approach to reading the Book of Mormon with the traditional reading method based upon student ability to relate Book of Mormon persons with Book of Mormon events." Summary of findings, conclusions, and recommendations of the study are included. [D.S.T.]

P.034 Parkinson, David P. "Engraving the Image of God upon Our Countenances." In *The Sixth Annual CES Religious Educators Symposium on the Book of Mormon.* 70-72. Salt Lake City: Church of Jesus Christ of Latter-day Saints, 1982. A commentary on Alma 5, especially Alma 5:19 ("the image of God engraven upon their countenances"), is studied to determine its meaning. [A.T.]

P.035 Parrish, Alan K. "Laman." In *Encyclopedia of Mormonism,* edited by Daniel H. Ludlow, 2:801-2. 5 vols. New York: Macmillan, 1992. Identifies Laman and describes what became of his descendants including the "noteworthy future for them in the latter days." [B.D.]

P.036 Parrish, Alan K. "Lehi and the Covenant of the Promised Land: A Modern Appraisal." In *The Book of Mormon: Second Nephi, The Doctrinal Structure*, edited by Monte S. Nyman and Charles D. Tate Jr., 39-59. Provo, UT: Brigham Young University Religious Studies Center, 1989. Details the covenant between Lehi and the Lord concerning the promised land and indicates the high expectations for those who now live in the land of liberty. Relates rise and fall of Book of Mormon civilizations as a warning to latter-day American society. Concludes that Americans value freedom but need increased spiritual commitment to fulfill covenantal obligations. [E.G.]

P.037 Parrish, Alan K. "Stela 5, Izapa: A Layman's Consideration of the Tree of Life Stone." In *The Book of Mormon: First Nephi, the Doctrinal Foundation*, edited by Monte S. Nyman and Charles D. Tate Jr., 125-50. Provo, UT: Brigham Young University Religious Studies Center, 1988. Gives background information on the Stela 5, Izapa, the tree of life stone. Summarizes the works of V. Garth Norman, M. Wells Jakeman, and others and concludes that Stela 5, Itzapa, seems to coincide with the Book of Mormon both in dating and location. LDS Church members should expect to see Book of Mormon themes in ancient American art, especially the tree of life motif because of its message, origin, and importance to Lehi and Nephi. [A.T.]

P.038 Parrish, Mary Pratt. *The Book of Mormon Story.* Salt Lake City: Deseret Book, 1965. A factual, adult storybook version of the Book of Mormon. It is written in the same style of language that is found in the Book of Mormon so the reader will become accustomed to its "lofty expressions and peculiar phraseology" and be able to more fully understand and enjoy the original version. [C.W.B.]

P.039 Parry, Donald W. "Antithetical Parallelism in the Book of Mormon." In *Reexploring the Book of Mormon*, edited by John W. Welch, 167-69. Salt Lake City: Deseret Book and FARMS, 1992. The writer of Proverbs 13:9 uses contrasting elements to emphasize an idea. The same technique is found in Alma 5:40, 9:28, and 36:21 and other Book of Mormon scriptures. Such antithetical parallelisms invoke the readers' involvement and teach them about opposite ideas in the Book of Mormon. [N.K.Y.]

P.040 Parry, Donald W. *The Book of Mormon Text Reformatted according to Parallelistic Patterns.* Provo, UT: FARMS, 1992. The entire text of the Book of Mormon formatted into (1) historical narrative and (2) parallelistic forms (consisting of a number of parallel and repetitious types). The narrative portions are formatted into regular blocked style. The introduction includes explanations of the forms of poetic parallelisms found in scripture. [B.D.]

P.041 Parry, Donald W. "Climactic Forms in the Book of Mormon." In *Reexploring the Book of Mormon*, edited by John W. Welch, 290-92. Salt Lake City: Deseret Book and FARMS, 1992. Climactic composition occurs when successive clauses, sentences, or a same word or words form the end of a text and begin another. Examples are found in Joel 1:3-4 and in

Moroni 8:25-26. There are a score of other passages using this form in the Book of Mormon. Joseph Smith can be commended in his translation work for leaving the passages structurally intact. [N.K.Y.]

P.042 Parry, Donald W. "Hebrew Literary Patterns in the Book of Mormon." *Ensign* 19 (October 1989): 58-61. Surveys, defines, and gives specific examples of scriptural poetic forms found in the Book of Mormon, including synonymous, synthetic, antithetical, contrasting, alternate, numeric, climactic, and repeating parallelisms. These poetic literary patterns identify important passages, add emphasis to messages, define and enlarge upon main points, make certain information more memorable, and structure the text so that important material can be more easily understood and remembered. Beyond the examples given in the text, a list of several Book of Mormon scriptural references are given to illustrate the extensive use of these forms by the prophets, witnessing the divinity of the Book of Mormon. [A.A.]

P.043 Parry, Donald W. "I Have A Question: Why is the phrase 'and it came to pass' so prevalent in the Book of Mormon?" *Ensign* 22 (December 1992): 29. The Hebrew word *wayehi* is translated as "and it came to pass" numerous times in the King James Version of the Old Testament, but occurs even more frequently in the Hebrew Bible, since the King James Version translators also used alternate translations of the term. Its frequent repetition in various passages of the Book of Mormon is "further evidence [of] ties to the Hebrew language" that Joseph Smith would have been unaware of. [A.C.W.]

P.044 Parry, Donald W. "Parallelisms according to Classification." Provo, UT: FARMS, 1988. Book of Mormon scriptures are categorized according to their parallelistic structures. The categories of classification include simple alternate, anaphora, anabasis, antithetical as well as many others. These are examples of Hebrew poetry found in the Book of Mormon. [J.W.M.]

P.045 Parry, Donald W. "Parallelisms Listed in Textual Sequence." Provo, UT: FARMS, 1988. Hebrew poetic forms found in the Book of Mormon are listed in chronological order and noted according to type of poetic structure. [J.W.M.]

P.046 Parry, Donald W. "Poetic Parallelisms in the Book of Mormon." Provo, UT: FARMS, 1988. Parallelism is often used in Hebrew poetry. There are many examples in the Bible and the Book of Mormon: synonymous, identical words or phrases, antonyms, complementaries, different inflections of the same root, gradations, and superordinates. Examples of these structures are provided. [J.W.M.]

P.047 Parry, Donald W. "Symbolic Action as Prophetic Curse." In *Reexploring the Book of Mormon*, edited by John W. Welch, 206-8. Salt Lake City: Deseret Book and FARMS, 1992. Isaiah and Ezekiel and other prophets of the Old Testament used symbolic actions to represent prophetic curses in the Old Testament. Similar symbolic actions are found in the Book of Mormon, including Moroni's rending of his garment, and the hanging of Zarahemnah on a tree. [N.K.Y.]

P.048 Parry, Donald W. "Teaching in Black and White: Antithetic Parallel Structure in the Book of Alma, Its Form and Function." In *The Book of Mormon: Alma, The Testimony of the Word*, edited by Monte S. Nyman and Charles D. Tate Jr., 281-90. Provo, UT: Brigham Young University Religious Studies Center, 1992. Book of Mormon prophets teach in black and white and never leave gray areas, a result of the objective of teaching in plainness set forth by Nephi. The technique of antithetical parallelism is an excellent way to make things black or white. It is characterized by an opposition of thoughts, or an antithesis between two or more contiguous lines. It is used in the Bible, by Alma, and other prophets of the Book of Mormon. [N.K.Y.]

P.049 Parry, Donald W. " 'Thus Saith the Lord': Prophetic Language in Samuel's Speech." *Journal of Book of Mormon Studies* 1 (Fall 1992): 181-83. Six prophetic speech forms present in Samuel's speech—the messenger formula, the proclamation formula, the oath formula, the woe oracle, the announcement formula, and the revelation formula—are indicative of prophetic authority and prerogative. These speech forms and others dealing with the commission and divine workings of a prophet are also present in other sections of the Book of Mormon and Bible. [N.K.Y.]

P.050 Parry, E. F. "The Book of Mormon." In *Scrapbook of Mormon Literature*, edited by Ben E. Rich, 2:260-90. Chicago: Etten, 1917. Evidence of the authenticity of the Book of Mormon includes testimonials from Joseph Smith and the Eleven Witnesses, archaeological discoveries (coins, ancient cities), historical consistency with regard to the Bible, similarities between the Indian and Book of Mormon cultures, and others. [C.W.B.]

P.051 Parry, E. F. "The Book of Mormon Corroborated." *MS* 58 (December 1896): 836-38. Quotes William Niven's description of ancient ruins at Yerba Buena in the state of Guerrero, Mexico. Niven theorizes that the city was destroyed by being suddenly submerged in water and later coming up again. Parry quotes 3 Nephi 8:5-17, which describes the violent destruction in the Nephite and Lamanite land. The Book of Mormon is supported by Niven's theory. [B.D.]

P.052 Parry, E. F. *A Prophet of Latter Days: His Divine Mission Vindicated*. Liverpool: Millennial Star Office, 1897?. Joseph Smith was a true prophet, and the Book of Mormon is one of the fruits of his labors—all of which testify of his inspiration. Many external evidences are cited to demonstrate the authenticity of the Book of Mormon, including newly discovered evidence of ancient cities, and the fact that many Mesoamerican scholars support the idea that the ancient Mesoamericans' culture reflected Near Eastern relations. [B.D.]

P.053 Parry, E. F. "The Urim and Thummim." *MS* 59 (August 1897): 540-41. Parry argues that Joseph Smith's description of the Urim and Thummim coincide with the Bible's description. Since this and other statements of Joseph Smith coincide with the Bible, Joseph Smith was divinely inspired. [B.D.]

P.054 Parson, Michael K. "Sherem and Korihor: Sign Seekers Then and Now." In *The Sixth Annual CES Religious Educator's Symposium on the Book of Mormon*, 73-75. Salt Lake City: The Church of Jesus Christ of Latter-day Saints, 1982. Explains that signs are gifts from God and when Satan inspires individuals, such as Sherem and Korihor, to seek for signs it is a perversion of God's gift. Examines the relationship between sign seeking and faith and sign seeking and adultery. [A.T.]

P.055 Parson, Michael K. "Why Are These Things Not Recorded in Your Journal?" *Ensign* 19 (October 1989): 20-21. The Savior's admonition to include the writings of Samuel in the sacred records of the Nephites verifies President Kimball's plea to "write it down." [J.W.M.]

P.056 Parsons, Alonzo H. *Parson's Text Book*. Lamoni, IA: Herald Publishing House, 1902. Herald Heritage, [R]1971. As evidence that the Book of Mormon is a true document, the author quotes early works on the antiquities of America and gives Book of Mormon references that compare with the findings of early American explorers. [J.W.M.]

P.057 Parsons, Robert E. "Becoming Perfect in Christ." In *Sidney B. Sperry Symposium: The Book of Mormon*, edited by A. Gary Anderson, 39-47. Provo, UT: BYU Religious Instruction, 24 January 1981. Treats the subject of perfection from several angles, the role of grace, and how individuals can become perfect in Jesus Christ. [D.M.]

P.058 Parsons, Robert E. "The Game's in the Name." *Ensign* 2 (December 1972): 74-78. Riddles about Book of Mormon people to be played to assist in remembering the important characters of the book. [J.W.M.]

P.059 Parsons, Robert E. "The Great and Abominable Church." In *Studies in Scripture: 1 Nephi to Alma 29*, edited by Kent P. Jackson, 44-59. Salt Lake City: Deseret Book, 1987. There is a tremendous contrast between the church of Christ and Satan's kingdom. The Gentiles who crossed the sea to discover America were inspired of God. Anyone trying to identify the great and abominable church find that it cannot be identified with a specific church. [J.W.M.]

P.060 Parsons, Robert E. "Hagoth and the Polynesians." In *The Book of Mormon: Alma, The Testimony of the Word*, edited by Monte S. Nyman and Charles D. Tate Jr., 249-62. Provo, UT: Brigham Young University Religious Studies Center, 1992. In 55 B.C., Hagoth built a large ship, launched it into the West Sea, and sailed north with many families (Alma 63:4-9). Theories suggest that they were lost at sea or they sailed to Japan or Hawaii. It is possible that the Hawaiians or Polynesians are descended from Hagoth and his followers. [N.K.Y.]

P.061 Parsons, Robert E. "The Practices of the Church." In *Studies in Scripture: Alma 30 to Moroni*, edited by Kent P. Jackson, 282-92. Salt Lake City: Deseret Book, 1988. The practices of the church found in Moroni 1-6 are common to Latter-day Saints. The procedures Joseph Smith taught concerning priesthood ordinations, authority, and sacred ordinances essential for the salvation of mankind were uncommon in his day. Moroni also taught important principles like faith, proper attitude, nourishing new members, and how to conduct meetings. [J.W.M.]

P.062 Parsons, Robert E. "The Prophecies of the Prophets." In *The Book of Mormon: First Nephi, The Doctrinal Foundation*, edited by Monte S. Nyman and Charles D. Tate Jr., 271-81. Provo, UT: Brigham Young University Religious Studies Center, 1988. Reviews the prophecies of Zenos, Zenock, and Nehum as found in the Book of Mormon. Also questions why Nephi quoted Isaiah 48-49 in 1 Nephi 20-21 and provides assistance in understanding these two chapters. [A.T.]

P.063 Partridge, E. D. "A Book of Mormon Sent on a Mission." *IE* 23 (February 1920): 373. Prompted by an article written by Mrs. Minnie Moore Wilson entitled, "Indians who Avoid Civilization to Save Their Souls," donations were taken from class members and a Book of Mormon was sent to Mrs. Wilson. [J.W.M.]

P.064 Partridge, Edward. "Letter." *MA* 1 (January 1835): 56-61. Bears testimony that the Book of Mormon proclaims the same gospel the apostles taught. [D.M.]

P.065 Patch, Robert C. "The Fifth Gospel." *Instructor* 103 (April 1968): 171-73. Shows more than 25 agreements between 3 Nephi and the Gospels of the New Testament. Gives reasons that 3 Nephi should be referred to as the "fifth gospel." [L.D.]

P.066 Patch, Robert G. "I Have a Question: Does the 'Pronouncing Vocabulary' in the Book of Mormon represent the way the Nephites and Lamanites actually pronounced their names?" *Ensign* 10 (February 1980): 68. It is thought that Joseph Smith knew the proper way to pronounce Book of Mormon names, but never recorded it. A committee suggested rules of pronunciation in 1903, and John M. Mills created a guide using those rules in 1910. [J.W.M.]

P.067 Paul, Charles Randall. "Third Nephi." In *Encyclopedia of Mormonism*, edited by Daniel H. Ludlow, 1:153-55. 5 vols. New York: Macmillan, 1992. A synopsis of the book of 3 Nephi in the Book of Mormon. This book is the climax in Nephite history. It focuses on three advents of Jesus: his birth, his resurrection and appearance to the Nephites, and his Second Coming. [B.D.]

P.068 Paul, George F. "The Mystery of the Pacific." *IE* 36 (January 1933): 148-49. A chatty travelogue of visitors to Easter Island. The underlying question is whether or not certain aspects of the island reflect cultural characteristics of the Nephite voyagers during the time of Hagoth. [D.M.]

P.069 Paul, James P. "The Ancient Mounds of Ohio." *Young Woman's Journal* 29 (March 1918): 133-36. Considers that the mounds in Ohio had their origins with Book of Mormon peoples. [D.M.]

P.070 "A Peaceful Heart." *Friend* 4 (September 1974): 7. A children's story of the translation of the Book of Mormon. [M.D.P.]

P.071 Peak, W. E. *Concordance and Reference Guide to the Book of Mormon*. Lamoni, IA: n.p., 1890?. Small booklet that lists and indexes topics, names, and places according to page numbers from an RLDS edition of the Book of Mormon. [J.W.M.]

P.072 Pearce, Virginia. "Alma and Amulek Teach the Zoramites to Pray." *Friend* 22 (February

1992): 12-13. Alma and Amulek preached to the Zoramites and taught them how to pray. Stresses the importance of prayer and gives the basic steps of how to offer a prayer. [M.D.P]

P.073 Pearce, Virginia. "I Feel Reverent When I Read the Scriptures." *Friend* 22 (April 1992): 12-13. A story of a boy who enjoyed reading the Book of Mormon with his family and how it made him a better person. [M.D.P.]

P.074 Pearce, Virginia. "Nephi Builds a Ship." *Friend* 22 (March 1992): 44-45. A children's story of how Nephi built a ship because he was commanded to by the Lord. It is important to obey the commandments. [M.D.P.]

P.075 Pearson, Cyril Drew. "Columbus: 'The Spirit Wrought upon the Man.' " *IE* 52 (October 1949): 640-42, 672, 674. Presents the events and inspirations of Christopher Columbus's life. From his birth Columbus certainly felt the call of the Lord and God's protective hand over all things. Surely it was Columbus whom Nephi foretold would cross the waters. [J.W.M.]

P.076 Pearson, Glen L. "The Book of Mormon as a Witness of the Old Testament." *Ensign* 16 (June 1986): 14-18. As the world devalues the Bible more and more, the Book of Mormon becomes an even more valuable witness of the truthfulness of the Bible. Doctrines found in the Book of Mormon clarify and substantiate the Bible—the divinity of Christ, the purpose of the law of Moses, and the true authorship of the books of Moses (the Pentateuch) and Isaiah. [J.W.M.]

P.077 Pearson, Glen L. *The Book of Mormon in Its Own Defense*. Provo, UT: BYU Extension Division, 1954. A series of five lectures. Topics include: why we should have new revelation in addition to the Bible; mission of Jesus Christ clarified; the gathering of the house of Israel must be accomplished; one who reads the Book of Mormon must read it faithfully and know if it is true or false; the book of Mosiah is important in explaining the doctrine of the final judgment. [B.D.]

P.078 Pearson, Glen L. *The Book of Mormon, Keystone to Conversion*. Salt Lake City: Bookcraft, 1963. An instructional aid for the missionary offering the "single answer" system of response in confronting objections from both Christians and non-Christians. Using this system, the missionary is to show that all objections are in fact objections to revelation. In this manner the Book of Mormon is set forth as a true revelation from God that may result in conversion. [C.W.B.]

P.079 Pearson, Glen L. *Significance of the Book of Mormon*. Provo, UT: Brigham Young University, 1953. A series of lectures covering the following topics: "Book of Mormon Chronology," "The Mosiah Dynasty," "Abinadi," "Great Missionaries," and "Book of Mormon Theology." [D.M.]

P.080 Pearson, Glen L., and Reid E. Bankhead. *Building Faith with the Book of Mormon*. Salt Lake City: Bookcraft, 1986. Enlarged and revised edition of authors' *Teaching with the Book of Mormon*. "Our main purpose in writing this book is to help the reader to begin to fill up his 'bag' with treasures of knowledge out of the Book of Mormon that he can bring out whenever he is called upon to teach or preach." The book is divided into sections based upon such topics as faith, repentance, and baptism. [A.T.]

P.081 Pearson, Glen L., and Reid E. Bankhead. *A Doctrinal Approach to the Book of Mormon*. Salt Lake City: Bookcraft, 1962. A new method of studying the Book of Mormon is proposed in finding some of the more important passages of the Book of Mormon and starting a structured cross-reference system. In the book, a series of doctrinal topics are addressed by brief explanations, thought provoking questions, cross references and incorporating this doctrine into their marking system. Their goal is to help the user to be more fluent with the scriptures. [C. W.]

P.082 Pearson, Glen L., and Reid E. Bankhead. *Teaching with the Book of Mormon*. Salt Lake City: Bookcraft, 1976. A revised edition of *A Doctrinal Approach to the Book of Mormon*, containing the authors' Book of Mormon study system. [C. W.]

P.083 Pearson, Glen L., and Reid E. Bankhead. *The Word and the Witness: The Unique Mission of the Book of Mormon.* Salt Lake City: Bookcraft, 1970. An instructional aid that provides effective missionary techniques and gives directions on how to approach different types of people and controversial issues. It also provides a series of hypothetical door approaches that result in the contact reading the Book of Mormon with the missionary. [C.W.B.]

P.084 Penrose, Charles W. "Book of Mormon Teachings on Resurrection." *JD* 21:220-32. Compares passages from the Book of Mormon, Doctrine and Covenants, and Bible concerning the resurrection. The Church believes in the literal resurrection of the body as opposed to many other religions that reason it away by using philosophy. [J.W.M.]

P.085 Penrose, Charles W. "The Coming Forth of the Book of Mormon." *IE* 26 (September 1923): 953-57. Moroni's visits to Joseph Smith in September 1823 stand second only in importance to the First Vision. It is significant that Moroni's visitations preceded the restoration of the priesthood and the organization of the Church. [D.M.]

P.086 Penrose, Charles W. "The Dead Spaulding Story Buried Out of Sight." *MS* 47 (20 April 1885): 248-50. James H. Fairchild of the Oberlin College library recovered the *Manuscript Found* written by Solomon Spaulding. Fairchild claims that after comparing the Book of Mormon and Spaulding's manuscript the theory that the two are related "will probably have to be relinquished." [B.D.]

P.087 Penrose, Charles W. "The Edict of a Century." *IE* 23 (April 1920): 484-87. Contains an account of the first vision received by Joseph Smith and the importance of other visions leading up to the publication of the Book of Mormon and the organization of the Church of Jesus Christ of Latter-day Saints. [L.D.]

P.088 Penrose, Charles W. "The Egyptian Hieroglyphs in Yucatan." *MS* 72 (2 June 1910): 344-46. It is most remarkable that "modern scientists" could overlook the Book of Mormon while so much of their research in the Americas and Egypt adds evidences to the divinity of the work. The *London Magazine* reports that there is a connection between the hieroglyphs of the Mayas and those of the Egyptians. Could these hieroglyphs have originated with Adam and Eve, or was it Lehi's company who brought them? [J.W.M.]

P.089 Penrose, Charles W. "An Old Slander Revived and Refuted." *MS* 70 (4 June 1908): 360-64. Sidney Rigdon did not work for publisher Patterson who had the Spaulding manuscript nor did he know Joseph Smith until after the Book of Mormon was published. The manuscript has no significant similarities to the Book of Mormon. The testimonies of the Three Witnesses cannot be refuted as they were reaffirmed in the last years of the witnesses' lives. These final testimonies appear in this article. [J.W.M.]

P.090 Penrose, Charles W. "There are Only Two Churches." *MS* 70 (November 1908): 744-46. Commenting on 1 Nephi 13-14, Penrose identifies the great and abominable church as "all the institutions among mankind in all ages that are led into error . . . and which lead mankind away from the true God and the true faith." [B.D.]

P.091 Penrose, Charles W. "Truth Out of the Earth." *MS* 100 (13 January 1938): 26-28. See also "Rays of Living Light: The Book of Mormon." In *Handbook of the Restoration*, 146-51. Independence, MO: Zion's Printing and Publishing, 1944. A testimony of the Book of Mormon. Truth has sprung out of the earth as Psalms 85:11 prophecies. The lost sheep of the house of Israel (Matthew 25:24) are the Nephites and Lamanites or the "voice out of the dust" (Isaiah 29:4-19). Professor Anthon fulfilled Isaiah 29:11 by saying he could not read a sealed book. The Book of Mormon is the stick of Joseph spoken of in Ezekiel 37:15-22. [B.D.]

P.092 "The People of Ammon." *Friend* 23 (May 1993): 89. A series of pictures for children illustrating the repentance of the people of Ammon. [S.H.]

P.093 Perkins, Keith W. "Francis W. Kirkham: A 'New Witness' for the Book of Mormon." *Ensign* 14 (July 1984): 52-57. Tells the story of Francis W. Kirkham and his work as a defender of the Book of Mormon. Recounts

Kirkham's examination of "five explanations for the origin of the Book of Mormon, showing the strengths and weaknesses of each." [S.P.S.]

P.094 Perkins, Keith W. "I Have A Question: Some historical records indicate that Mary Musselman Whitmer was privileged to see the gold plates, in addition to Joseph Smith and the 3 and 8 Witnesses. Do we know of any other persons who may have seen or handled the plates?" *Ensign* 22 (July 1992): 53-5. In addition to the Three and Eight Witnesses of the Book of Mormon, Lucy Harris and Emma Smith also viewed the gold plates. [A.C.W.]

P.095 Perkins, Keith W. "Thou Art Still Chosen." *Ensign* 23 (January 1993): 14-19. Uses Joseph Smith's loss of the 116 pages of the Book of Mormon and his repentance process to teach repentance. [S.H.]

P.096 Perkins, Keith W. "True to the Book of Mormon: The Whitmers." *Ensign* 19 (February 1989): 34-41. Examines the lives, roles, contributions, testimonies, and apostasy of the five sons of Peter Whitmer, Sr.—David, Christian, Jacob, Peter Jr., and John—all of whom were special witnesses of the Book of Mormon plates. For a time, they were all very instrumental in building, defending and leading the Church. Despite their eventual estrangement from the Church, they all remained true to their testimonies regarding seeing and hefting the Book of Mormon plates and proclaiming the truthfulness of the Book of Mormon. [A.A.]

P.097 Perkins, Keith W. "Whitmer, David." In *Encyclopedia of Mormonism*, edited by Daniel H. Ludlow, 4:1564-66. 5 vols. New York: Macmillan, 1992. A short biography of David Whitmer, one of the Three Witnesses to the Book of Mormon. [B.D.]

P.098 Perrie, C. Johann. *What Every Christian Should Know About—The Restoration of Christ's True Gospel.* Provo, UT: Author, 1990. Complete apostasy in the early Church created the need for a restoration. The events that led to the Restoration were orchestrated by the Lord. Joseph Smith's own words tell of his calling to translate and publish the Book of Mormon. Books that have been written to discredit Joseph Smith and the Book of Mormon are listed by title and author. The Book of Mormon and modern revelation identify false teachings concerning revelation, the Godhead, the eternal nature of man, priesthood authority, original sin, infant baptism, authority, mode of baptism, paid clergy, eternal marriage, heaven and hell, and Church politics. [J.W.M.]

P.099 Perry, David E. "Mormon—A Man for Our Time." In *A Symposium on the Book of Mormon*, 99-101. Salt Lake City: Church of Jesus Christ of Latter-day Saints, 1979. Presents an outline about the prophet Mormon, his ministries, his military efforts, and his role as editor/writer. Perry also cites eleven major purposes of the Book of Mormon. [N.K.Y.]

P.100 Perry, David E. "The Relevance and Effectiveness of Four Book of Mormon Prophets and Their Teachings." Ph.D. diss., Brigham Young University, 1974. Analyzes the prophets Lehi, Nephi, Alma, and Mormon to discover the effect that they and their teachings had upon certain peoples. Considers whether the personality of each Book of Mormon prophet caused him to be significantly qualified and effective in coping with the problems he faced, and whether the teachings of each Book of Mormon prophet were directly relevant to his problems, assisting him to be effective in fulfilling his assignments. [A.T.]

P.101 Perry, L. Tom. "Becoming Self-Reliant." *Ensign* 21 (November 1991): 64-66. Nephi was resourceful when he inquired of the Lord where to find ore to make the tools instead of asking where the tools were. The Lord "expects His children to be self-reliant to the degree they can be." [J.W.M.]

P.102 Perry, L. Tom. "The Book of Mormon, Another Testament of Jesus Christ." Salt Lake City: University of Utah Institute of Religion, 1990. Speaks of the Book of Mormon as the instrument of missionary work. Compares its translation with that of the King James Bible. Discusses its purpose, promise, and philosophy. Retells and personalizes the story of Nephi. [D.M.]

P.103 Perry, L. Tom. "Book of Mormon Messages of Decision Making." *CR* (October 1979): 48-52. Individuals all must learn to make the correct decisions in order to have a happy, fulfilled life. Follow the example of Nephi who chose to follow the Lord and his father Lehi. [R.C.D.]

P.104 Perry, L. Tom. "Example of Alma the Younger." *CR* (April 1979): 15-18. Alma the Younger lived by his own law and was in the depths of hell. Upon his conversion (meaning that he now obeyed a higher law) his joy was unfathomable. [R.C.D.]

P.105 Perry, L. Tom. "I Will Go and Do the Things Which the Lord Hath Commanded." *Ensign* 4 (January 1974): 51-53. Lehi and his family were commanded of the Lord to return to Jerusalem for the brass plates. This difficult task was assigned to Lehi's sons. Nephi recognized it to be the inspiration of the Lord and willingly obeyed. Nephi was a lamplighter—because of his faith he brought light to an entire nation. [J.W.M.]

P.106 Perry, L. Tom. "Proclaim My Gospel from Land to Land." *Ensign* 19 (May 1989): 13-14. *CR* (1-2 April 1989): 15-17. Discusses bringing the Book of Mormon to all mankind. The Book of Mormon is a second witness to Jesus Christ. [L.D.]

P.107 Perry, L. Tom. Untitled talk. In *Proceedings of the Colombia Area Conference.* Salt Lake City: Church of Jesus Christ of Latter-day Saints, March 1977. Nephi considered the request to return to obtain the brass plates as an assignment from the Lord. Laman and Lemuel felt it to be a burdensome task. Lehi's family saw the immense value of the scriptures. The same is true today. We must teach the scriptures to our families. [J.W.M.]

P.108 Petersen, Emma Marr. *Book of Mormon Stories for Young Latter-day Saints.* Salt Lake City: Bookcraft, 1951. Contains brief stories designed for children, with illustrations. [D.M.]

P.109 Petersen, Emma Marr. *The Story of Our Church for Young Latter-day Saints.* Salt Lake City: Bookcraft, 1952. Retells stories for children. Book of Mormon topics include the Three Witnesses, the restoration of the Priesthood, the scribal work of Oliver Cowdery, Moroni's visits to Joseph Smith, Martin Harris's loss of the 116 pages of the Book of Mormon manuscript, and Joseph Smith's reception and translation of the gold plates and its publication. [J.W.M.]

P.110 Petersen, Mark E. *Alma and Abinadi.* Salt Lake City: Deseret Book, 1983. Contains narration and commentary on Book of Mormon passages about Alma and Abinadi. Chapters include: "Abinadi the Martyr," "Alma's Ministry," "Alma the Younger," "Amlici's Rebellion," and "The Zoramite Apostasy." [A.T.]

P.111 Petersen, Mark E. "America Testifies of Christ." *IE* 70 (June 1967): 98-101. For the general reader, testimonies of Christopher Columbus, George Washington, Abraham Lincoln, and ancient traditions from Alaska to Chile regarding the Great White God are discussed. Limited references. [B.W.J.]

P.112 Petersen, Mark E. "Ancient Records and the Book of Mormon." *IE* 60 (June 1957): 431-32. A testimony of the Book of Mormon comes by the Spirit (Moroni 10:4) and not from scientific research, nor from argument. And yet modern findings are vindications or supports to one's testimony. Such evidences are cement buildings, gold plates with ancient inscriptions, and stone boxes as depositories of metal records. [R.C.D.]

P.113 Petersen, Mark E. "Angels, Plates, Boxes and Joseph Smith." *CR* (October 1983): 40-44. See also *Ensign* 13 (November 1983): 29-31, and *Book of Mormon Talks by General Authorities,* (Provo, UT: FARMS, n.d.), 149-51. Moroni visited Joseph Smith on September 21, 1923, and commenced the restoration of the gospel. From this restoration came many things that shocked the world: the visitation of angels, revelation, modern day prophets, and records kept on gold plates and buried in stone boxes. The author lists examples of metal plates and stone boxes as containers for them that have been found. [B.D.]

P.114 Petersen, Mark E. *Book of Mormon Addresses.* Provo, UT: FARMS, 1986?. Reprints of several addresses: "The Great Prologue," *BYU*

Speeches of the Year, September 24, 1974, and conference addresses given 6 April 1968, 4 October 1970, 1 October 1977, 2 April 1978, 1 October 1978, 1 October 1983. Individual annotations are found in this bibliography. [J.W.M.]

P.115 Petersen, Mark E. "The Book of Mormon Converts." In Petersen's *Why the Religious Life*, 176-78. Salt Lake City: Deseret Book, 1966. The Book of Mormon is the most effective tool in missionary work; thousands have born witness to this fact. It is God's greatest witness to the truth and everyone needs this witness. Those who earnestly and prayerfully read its message will know of its truthfulness. [J.W.M.]

P.116 Petersen, Mark E. "Book of Mormon: Origin and Background." *CR* (October 1977): 15-18. Joseph Smith, the Book of Mormon, and the restoration of the gospel were all envisioned and spoken of by the prophet Isaiah. Joseph Smith was the unlearned man; the Book of Mormon is the familiar spirit out of the dust; the great and marvelous work is the restoration spoken of by Isaiah. [R.C.D.]

P.117 Petersen, Mark E. *Christ in America*. Salt Lake City: Church of Jesus Christ of Latter-day Saints, 1983. Writes of archaeological and historical evidence of "the Great White God" of ancient America. The coming of a tall, blue-eyed, bearded man from heaven was documented in several different groups of Indians and Polynesians. Petersen proposes that this great white god was Jesus. This can be documented in the Book of Mormon. [C.W.B.]

P.118 Petersen, Mark E. "Evidence of Things Not Seen." *Ensign* 8 (May 1978): 61-63. Also in *CR* (April 1978): 94-98. The Bible was never considered to be all of the word of God—the Book of Mormon is necessary. The Book of Mormon and modern-day prophets add new and valuable scripture that is designed to protect the Church from false teachings. The Book of Mormon is "tangible evidence of both the seen and the unseen," and the only plausible explanation for its origin is that Moroni delivered the plates to Joseph Smith. [A.C.W.] [J.W.M.]

P.119 Petersen, Mark E. "Gold from Ancient America." In Petersen's *Why the Religious Life*. 73-75. Salt Lake City: 1966. The use of metal plates to record sacred and governmental writings is not unique to the Book of Mormon peoples. Archaeologists have found plates made of a variety of metals including silver and gold in various locations around the world. [J.W.M.]

P.120 Petersen, Mark E. "The Great Prologue." In *Brigham Young University 1974 Devotional and Fireside Speeches,* 459-72. Provo, UT: Brigham Young University, 1975. Explains the restoration of the gospel and the events that led up to it. The Book of Mormon played a prominent role in the restoration. [B.D.]

P.121 Petersen, Mark E. "The Great White God Was a Reality." *IE* 72 (September 1969): 6-9. A discussion of the Great White God of ancient America—he was known by various names, provided teachings that contained elements similar to Christian religion, and may have been Jesus Christ who visited the Nephites of Bountiful. [J.W.M.]

P.122 Petersen, Mark E. "It Was a Miracle!" *Ensign* 7 (November 1977): 11-13. Author bears testimony concerning the prophetic office of Joseph Smith and the divine translation of the Book of Mormon and discusses the usage of metal plates and stone boxes in ancient civilizations. [J.W.M.]

P.123 Petersen, Mark E. *The Jaredites*. Salt Lake City: Deseret Book, 1984. Explains the story of the Jaredites; includes biblical references and charts listing the Jaredite kings. [C.W.B.]

P.124 Petersen, Mark E. "The Last Words of Moroni." *Ensign* 8 (November 1978): 57-59. Retells the story of the destruction of the Nephites, which came about to fulfill the prophecy that those who live on the American continent "must obey God or be swept off." Author also tells of the wickedness that Moroni saw in the present era and concludes by saying that humanity should read the Book of Mormon and obey its counsels. [M.D.P.]

P.125 Petersen, Mark E. "More Gold Plates Found." In Petersen's, *Why The Religious Life*. 147-51. Salt Lake City: Deseret Book, 1966. Archaeologists working in an Etruscan site found inscribed sheets of gold that contained tributes to a pagan goddess. The plates date to the 6th century B.C., an era that parallels Lehi's departure from Jerusalem. Modern allegations that ancient records were not kept on metal plates are no longer valid. [J.W.M.]

P.126 Petersen, Mark E. "Mormon and the Book of Mormon." *Friend* 14 (May 1984): 34-35. A story for children that deals with Mormon, abridger of the Nephite records. [J.W.M.]

P.127 Petersen, Mark E. "Moroni's Warning to America." *CR* (October 1978): 85-88. Also in *Book of Mormon Talks by General Authorities*, 147-48. Provo, UT: FARMS, 1990. The last words of Moroni are important for those living in America. Both Mormon and Moroni indicate that Americans must abandon pride, money, substance, and fine apparel (Mormon 8:35-36) in order to not be swept off the land as the ancient Nephites were. [B.D.]

P.128 Petersen, Mark E. "New Evidence for the Book of Mormon." *IE* 63 (June 1962): 456-59. Cites the studies of numerous scientists and anthropologists (especially Thor Hyerdahl) that seem to confirm the general LDS belief that Polynesians migrated from the Americas. [R.C.D.]

P.129 Petersen, Mark E. "Origin and Plight of Indians." *CR* (October 1970): 138-42. Also in *Book of Mormon Talks by General Authorities*, 140-42. Provo, UT: FARMS, 1990. All the peoples of the Americas shared a common belief in the visitation of a white God who taught them and ministered to them. The names differed—Quetzalcoatl, Votan, Gucumatz, Verachoeha, Sume, Kon-tiki, Kukulcan—but he was the same God, Jesus Christ, whose appearance is recorded in the Book of Mormon. [R.C.D.]

P.130 Petersen, Mark E. "Our Divine Destiny." In *BYUSY* (20 February 1968). Provo, UT: BYU Press. The promise given in 1 Nephi serves as a reminder of the importance of preserving America and its great destiny. An emphasis is placed on the inspiration of God in this great work and the need for his continued aid in these troubled times. [J.W.M.]

P.131 Petersen, Mark E. *Polynesians Came from America!* Salt Lake City: Deseret Book, 1962. The great faith of the Polynesian people indicates that they are of the blood of Israel. Evidence that they are descendants of Lehi lies in the structure of their temples, baptismal fonts, stone roadways, and the plant life with origins in North America. The first white men in these islands were greeted with great reverence because of the traditions of the people concerning their white god whose teachings resembled those of Jesus Christ. [J.W.M.]

P.132 Petersen, Mark E. *Sons of Mosiah*. Salt Lake City: Deseret Book, 1984. Discusses the missionary activities of the sons of Mosiah in twenty chapters. [R.H.B.]

P.133 Petersen, Mark E. "Their Greatest Tragedy." *IE* 68 (December 1965): 1128-30. The greatest tragedy that happened to the Jews was the rejection of their King, Jesus Christ. The people of the modern world may reject his Second Coming. Signs described in the Book of Mormon show that the Second Coming will not be unexpected. [M.D.P.]

P.134 Petersen, Mark E. *Those Gold Plates!* Salt Lake City: Bookcraft, 1979. Addresses the issue of the authenticity of the gold plates delivered to Joseph Smith. Author gives many examples of inscribed plates, and a list of 62 such findings. He also presents the testimonies of the Three and Eight Witnesses and their contemporaries. [C.W.B.]

P.135 Petersen, Mark E. "Three New Volumes of Scriptures Revealed." *IE* 67 (December 1964): 1093-95. Three new volumes of sacred literature, the Book of Mormon, the Doctrine and Covenants, and Pearl of Great Price sustain the Bible and add their own witness that divine guidance from God continues. [J.W.M.]

P.136 Petersen, Mark E. Untitled talk. In *Book of Mormon Talks by General Authorities*, 138-39. Provo, UT: FARMS, 1990. The United States of America is headed for ruin unless its citizens turn to God. Alma 61:13 and Ether 2:12 indicate that if Americans will turn to God they will receive again God-given freedom in America. [B.D.]

P.137 Petersen, Mark E. Untitled. In *Children of Promise: The Lamanites: Yesterday and Today*. Salt Lake City: Bookcraft, 1981. The Book of Mormon opens the doors for Lamanites who have been long oppressed. Though unjustly treated, scattered, and persecuted, they now have begun to fulfill their great destiny. Nephi prophesied that the mixture of his seed would be preserved and a remnant would receive the gospel. The Book of Mormon is a great instrument in gathering these children of Lehi to Jesus Christ. [J.W.M.]

P.138 Petersen, Mark E. Untitled talk. *CR* (April 1962): 111-15. The great faith of the Polynesian people is evidence that they are people of the blood of Israel and relatives of the American Indians. They are heirs to the promises made in the Book of Mormon. [J.W.M.]

P.139 Petersen, Mark E. Untitled talk. *CR* (April 1967): 111-14. Writes concerning Jesus Christ, Columbus, George Washington, native American traditions and legends that testify of the "Great White God," the Book of Mormon, and Joseph Smith who translated it. The Book of 3 Nephi records Christ's appearance in America. [J.W.M.]

P.140 Petersen, Mark E. "Who Was the Great White God?" *IE* 73 (December 1970): 117-20. Discusses various native traditions of the Western Hemisphere and Pacific region that refer to a "Great White God." Several sources are cited and their common points are discussed and compared to 3 Nephi 11. Jesus Christ was the Great White God referred to in all instances. [B.W.J.]

P.141 Petersen, Roger K. "Joseph Smith: Prophet-Poet." In *The Eighth Annual Sidney B. Sperry Symposium*, 265-79. Provo, UT: Religious Instruction, 26 January 1980. A literary analysis of selected writings of Joseph Smith, using the archetypal theories of Northrop Frye. A number of Book of Mormon passages are examined. [D.M.]

P.142 Petersen, Roger K. "Joseph Smith Prophet-Poet: A Literary Analysis of Writings Commonly Associated with His Name." Ph.D. diss., Brigham Young University, 1981. Shows how Joseph Smith used numerous literary patterns that are well known today but were not in his lifetime, and how this literary output reveals genius. Discusses archetypal patterns found in the Book of Mormon. [D.M.]

P.143 Peterson, Bruce Eldon. "Evaluation of the Use of Selected Book of Mormon Filmstrips in Improving the Learning of the Book of Mormon History." M.A. thesis, Brigham Young University, 1966. Evaluates the use of Book of Mormon filmstrips in youth classrooms to determine their pedagogical effectiveness. [D.M.]

P.144 Peterson, Clark A. *Using the Book of Mormon to Combat Falsehoods in Organic Evolution*. San Jose, CA: Clark A. Peterson, 1992. Cites Book of Mormon, scientific, and other sources to argue against the theories dealing with organic evolution. Believes that the Book of Mormon is opposed to organic evolution. [D.M.]

P.145 Peterson, Daniel C. "Authority in the Book of Mosiah." Provo, UT: FARMS, 1991. Priests in the Book of Mormon were consecrated, anointed, and commissioned to teach the law of Moses, the early Nephite king being the High Priest, political, and religious leader. Alma the Elder established a limited separation of church and state, where priesthood functions were severed from the political structure, and the Spirit of God, not human authority, made legitimate calls to the priesthood. [J.W.M.]

P.146 Peterson, Daniel C. "Book of Mormon Economy and Technology." In *Encyclopedia of Mormonism*, edited by Daniel H. Ludlow, 1:172-75. 5 vols. New York: Macmillan, 1992. The economics of Book of Mormon peoples were relatively simple. Dry measures and metal-weight units were used in a simple, efficient binary system. Trade is mentioned at times but was limited by wars. Agriculture involved livestock, horticulture, and sown crops. Horses and chariots are mentioned as are highways, cloth, silk, fine-twined linen, and steel weaponry. [N.K.Y.]

P.147 Peterson, Daniel C. "The Gadianton Robbers as Guerrilla Warriors." In *Warfare in the Book of Mormon*, edited by Stephen D. Ricks and William J. Hamblin, 146-73. Salt Lake City: Deseret and FARMS, 1990. Argues that the warlike behavior of the Gadianton robbers is plausible and believable. Shows chilling resemblances between their tactics of guerrilla warfare and those used by Mao Tsetung, Vo Nguyen Giap, and Ernesto "Che" Guevara. Compares secret combinations with the Masons. [D.M.]

P.148 Peterson, Daniel C. "Notes on 'Gadianton Masonry.'" In *Warfare in the Book of Mormon*, edited by Stephen D. Ricks and William J. Hamblin, 174-224. Salt Lake City: Deseret and FARMS, 1990. Cites authors who assert that the secret society of Gadiantons was based on the 1820 controversy about the Freemasons being a secret society and claim this is where Joseph Smith's Book of Mormon ideas came from. The Masonic controversy may have been published in Palmyra, but it has not been proved that Joseph Smith even knew of it. Book of Mormon critics have grasped another feeble straw to explain how Joseph Smith wrote the Book of Mormon. [N.K.Y.]

P.149 Peterson, Daniel C. "Priesthood in Mosiah." In *The Book of Mormon: Mosiah, Salvation Only through Christ*, edited by Monte S. Nyman and Charles D. Tate Jr., 187-210. Provo, UT: Brigham Young University Religious Studies Center, 1991. Detailed treatment of priesthood offices, functions, and prerogatives, as carried out by Zeniff, Noah (in a negative sense), and both $Alma_1$ and $Alma_2$. [D.M.]

P.150 Peterson, Daniel C. "'Secret Combinations' Revisited." *Journal of Book of Mormon Studies* 1 (Fall 1992): 184-88. Addresses the argument that the Gadianton robbers were merely nineteenth-century Freemasons, transparently disguised by the term "secret combinations." In 1828 Andrew Jackson used the term "secret combinations" in a vitriolic response to allegations made by Henry Clay. Jackson was a prominent Mason and would not have used the term in this fashion had it been known to refer uniquely to Freemasonry. [R.H.B.]

P.151 Peterson, Daniel C. "Text and Context." In Peterson's *Review of Books on the Book of Mormon*, 6:524-62. Provo, UT: FARMS, 1994. Examines the historical context out of which the book *New Approaches to the Book of Mormon*, edited by Brent Lee Metcalfe, developed. The authors of the book question the traditional view of the Book of Mormon held by the LDS church; their logic is tainted by prejudices and unclear motives and is based upon information that is questionable and built upon a naturalistic, irreligious world view. [J.W.M.]

P.152 Peterson, Daniel C. "Their Own Worst Enemies." In *Studies in Scripture: Alma 30 to Moroni*, edited by Kent P. Jackson, 92-106. Salt Lake City: Deseret Book, 1988. The narrative in Helaman 1-6 is the best example of how Mormon the editor worked. As Mormon abridged, he was surrounded by centuries of records and under the inspiration of the Lord chose what was important. He taught that his people were ripening for destruction and pointed out the causes and the efforts to stop it through preserving the appropriate records. [J.W.M.]

P.153 Peterson, Daniel C., ed. *Review of Books on the Book of Mormon*. Vol. 1. Provo, UT: FARMS, 1989. Contains reviews by various reviewers of books published on the Book of Mormon. Every type of book dealing with the Book of Mormon is reviewed including the following approaches—polemic, devotional, apologetic, evangelical, historical, and theological. Includes an introductory essay by the editor, and a bibliography of works written on the Book of Mormon. [D.M.]

P.154 Peterson, Donald H. "Great Ministers of the Book of Mormon." *Restoration Witness* 8 (April 1970): 10-14. Many Book of Mormon prophets delivered a sacred message to God's people, including Lehi, Nephi, King Benjamin, Alma, and Moroni. When Christ visited the Nephites, he revealed his own message and that of his Father. [J.W.M.]

P.155 Peterson, H. Donl. "Answer to Question Regarding Use of 'Lord' in Book of Mormon." *Ensign* 8 (October 1978): 16-17. Deals with the question of how to distinguish between the name/titles *Father* and *Son* and the word *Lord* in the Book of Mormon. Notes that sometimes the distinction is blurred, especially when the Son speaks on behalf of the Father in the first person. Discusses the different roles of both members of the Godhead. [D.M.]

P.156 Peterson, H. Donl. "Book of Mormon Commentaries." In *Encyclopedia of Mormonism*, edited by Daniel H. Ludlow, 1:171-72. 5 vols. New York: Macmillan, 1992. George Reynolds, Janne M. Sjodahl, and B. H. Roberts have produced Book of Mormon commentaries. Hugh Nibley, and Sidney B. Sperry have contributed many scholarly books on the subject. [N.K.Y.]

P.157 Peterson, H. Donl. "Church Discipline in the Book of Mosiah." In *The Book of Mormon: Mosiah, Salvation Only through Christ*, edited by Monte S. Nyman and Charles D. Tate Jr., 211-26. Provo, UT: Brigham Young University Religious Studies Center, 1991. Takes Mosiah 26 as the model and basis for Church discipline in its various facets, and points out that the steps described there are followed today in the LDS Church. Uses quotations from scripture and General Authorities to support his argument. [D.M.]

P.158 Peterson, H. Donl. "Father Lehi." In *The Book of Mormon: First Nephi, The Doctrinal Foundation*, edited by Monte S. Nyman and Charles D. Tate Jr., 55-66. Provo, UT: Brigham Young University Religious Studies Center, 1988. Discusses the importance of Lehi as a man, prophet, record keeper, man of faith, "father of nations," seer, and explorer. Honors Lehi as a leader, man of great courage, and exemplary patriarch. [A.T.]

P.159 Peterson, H. Donl. "I Have a Question: What is the meaning of the Book of Mormon passages on eternal hell for the wicked?" *Ensign* 16 (April 1986): 36-38. Also in *A Sure Foundation: Answers to Difficult Gospel Questions*, 45-50. Salt Lake City: Deseret Book, 1988. Points out that there are two hells identified in the Book of Mormon writings: one is the intermediate existence between death and the resurrection and the other is the never-ending state of the wicked. [D.M.]

P.160 Peterson, H. Donl. "The Law of Justice and the Law of Mercy." In *The Book of Mormon: Alma, The Testimony of the Word*, edited by Monte S. Nyman and Charles D. Tate Jr., 211-22. Provo, UT: Brigham Young University Religious Studies Center, 1992. Alma's instructions to his wayward son contain teachings on the fall of Adam and Eve, the atonement of Christ, and the justice and mercy of God. Justice, Alma teaches, exercises all of its demands and mercy claimeth all which is her own. God cannot bless one over another by allowing individuals to sin and not be required to fully repent. Alma summarizes his teachings on mercy and justice in Alma 42. [N.K.Y.]

P.161 Peterson, H. Donl. "Moroni$_2$." In *Encyclopedia of Mormonism*, edited by Daniel H. Ludlow, 2:956-57. 5 vols. New York: Macmillan, 1992. A short description of Moroni, his role in preserving and revealing the Book of Mormon, and his depiction as an angel blowing a trumpet. [A.T.]

P.162 Peterson, H. Donl. *Moroni: Ancient Prophet, Modern Messenger*. Bountiful: Horizon Publishers, 1983. Uses Moroni's example to teach "(1) the resurrection is a reality, (2) the state of a celestial being is truly glorious, (3) there is opportunity for continued service in the kingdom of God beyond the veil, (4) the knowledge and intelligence one attains in mortality does rise with that person in the resurrection, and (5) this dispensation has great destiny to fulfill." [A.T.]

P.163 Peterson, H. Donl. "Moroni and the Restoration: A Closer Look." In *Scriptures for the Modern World*, edited by Paul R. Cheesman and C. Wilfred Griggs, 13. Provo, UT: Brigham Young University Religious Studies Center, 1984. The author outlines the character, calling, and message of Moroni and his role in training Joseph Smith for to his prophetic calling. [B.D.]

P.164 Peterson, H. Donl. "Moroni: Joseph Smith's Tutor." *Ensign* 22 (January 1992): 22-29. Describes Moroni's visits to Joseph Smith; discusses the finding of the plates at Cumorah, the lost manuscript, and the Three and Eight

Witnesses. Moroni provided Joseph Smith with heavenly instruction and taught him line upon line on how to perform his prophetic tasks. [A.C.W.]

P.165 Peterson, H. Donl. "The Nephites and the Law of Moses." In *Sidney B. Sperry Symposium*, 103-16. Provo, UT: Brigham Young University, 24 January 1981. Discusses the law of Moses and the Aaronic and Melchizedek Preisthoods using both biblical and Book of Mormon references, and explains the fulfillment of the law of Moses through the crucifixion of Christ and his visit to the Nephites. [C.W.B.]

P.166 Peterson, H. Donl. "We Had a Hope of His Glory." *Instructor* 104 (August 1969): 300-301. The ancient Israelites, the Jaredites, and the Nephites all knew of Christ and benefited from following his gospel. Jesus is the Savior of all mankind and hope and happiness come through living his teachings. [L.M.]

P.167 Peterson, J. W. "The Urim and Thummim." *Rod of Iron* 1 (February 1924): 6-7. Reports a conversation he had with William B. Smith, brother of Joseph Smith, relative to the Urim and Thummim, the breastplate, and the "two rims of a bow." Gives a fairly detailed statement about the instruments. [D.M.] 16

P.168 Peterson, Janet. "Clay's Present for Jesus." *Ensign* 20 (March 1990): 62-63. Clay, a young man with Down's syndrome, was taught to read to his mother. In less than one year, Clay read the entire Book of Mormon from cover to cover. Clay stands as an example of the manner in which all individuals can read the book. [J.W.M.]

P.169 Pew, W. Ralph. "For the Sake of Retaining a Remission of Your Sins." In *The Book of Mormon: Mosiah, Salvation Only through Christ*, edited by Monte S. Nyman and Charles D. Tate Jr., 227-45. Provo, UT: Brigham Young University Religious Studies Center, 1991. An exposition on the sermon by King Benjamin. Avers that Benjamin's audience already understood the principles of faith and repentance and had been baptized. Author focuses on retaining forgiveness of sins after the initial forgiveness at baptism and in feeding the hungry and clothing the naked. [D.M.]

P.170 Pew, W. Ralph. " 'Yield Your Heart to God'—the Process of Sanctification." In *The Book of Mormon: Helaman through 3 Nephi 8, According to Thy Word*, edited by Monte S. Nyman and Charles D. Tate Jr., 207-22. Provo, UT: Brigham Young University Religious Studies Center, 1992. An essay on the doctrine of sanctification. Includes comments on the Holy Ghost as a sanctifier and a discussion of the significance of grace. [D.M.]

P.171 Phelps, William W. "The Book of Mormon." *The Evening and the Morning Star* 1 (January 1833): 57-59. An evangelical article testifying about the Book of Mormon, using such prooftexts as Psalm 85, Ezekiel 37, and John 10:16. Points out the textual purity of the book as opposed to the Bible and emphasizes the book as a new covenant to Israel. [D.M.]

P.172 Phelps, William W. "Discovery of Ancient Ruins in Central America." *The Evening and the Morning Star* 1 (February 1833): 71-72. Refers to ruins in Central America, extending more than twenty miles, that is seen as evidence for the Book of Mormon. [D.M.]

P.173 Phelps, William W. "The Indians." *The Evening and the Morning Star* 1 (December 1832): 54. The American Indians are portrayed as remnants of Joseph. Quotations about them from the Book of Mormon are supplied. [D.M.]

P.174 Phelps, William W. "The Jews." *The Evening and the Morning Star* 1 (December 1832): 51-53. Addresses the prospect of the return of the Jews to Jerusalem to rebuild the holy city. Light is thrown on the subject by quoting passages from the Book of Mormon. [D.M.]

P.175 Phelps, William W. "Letter No. 10 to Oliver Cowdery Concerning the Book of Mormon with Comment." *M&A* 1 (September 1835): 177-79. An appreciation and defense of the Book of Mormon by an early Church member who sees the Book of Mormon as "the foundation, or starting point of the Church of Christ." [D.M.]

P.176 Phelps, William W. "Letter No. 11 to Oliver Cowdery Concerning the American Indians." *M&A* 2 (October 1835): 193-95. Exults over the spiritual promises for the American Indians and contrasts their glorious destiny with the downfall of the Nephites at the time of Mormon. Refers to Zenos's allegory of the olive tree in Jacob 5. [D.M.]

P.177 Phelps, William W. "Letter No. 12 to Oliver Cowdery Concerning Early Aspects about the Book of Mormon." *M&A* 2 (November 1835): 221-23. Speaks of the Hill Cumorah, "which must become as famous among the latter-day saints, as Sinai was among the former day saints." Refers to criticisms of the Book of Mormon. [D.M.]

P.178 Phelps, William W. "The Resurrection of the Just." *The Evening and the Morning Star* 1 (December 1832): 49-51. Discusses the principle of resurrection as taught in the Bible and the Book of Mormon, a substantial part coming from Alma's instruction to Corianton. [D.M.]

P.179 Phelps, William W. "The Ten Tribes." *The Evening and the Morning Star* 1 (October 1833): 33-34. Discussion of the place of the ten tribes in salvific history, drawing on Jesus' allusion to "other sheep" in 3 Nephi and Jacob's allegory of the olive tree. [D.M.]

P.180 Phelps, William W. "The Tribe of Joseph." *The Evening and the Morning Star* 1 (November 1832): 41-43. An examination of the role of the tribe of Joseph in the latter days, quoting passages from 2 Nephi 3. Discusses the Book of Mormon relative to the stick of Joseph. [D.M.]

P.181 Phillips, G. F. "Skepticism and the Book of Mormon." *MS* 52 (10 February 1890): 104-5. Cites as evidence of the Book of Mormon a story by Montessini who visited America in the fifteenth century and discovered some Indians who "pronounced the words of Deuteronomy: *Schemah Israel Adonai Elohenu Adoni Ehad* (Hear O Israel, the Lord our God is one Lord)." Furthermore, he cites "Basnage's *Histoire des Jeufs* written in 1694," where Basnage writes that "Tis sufficiently certain that a vessel driven thither [Americas] by a tempest landed some Jews." [B.D.]

P.182 Phillips, R. Douglas. "Why Is So Much of the Book of Mormon Given Over to Military Accounts?" *Ensign* 8 (January 1978): 17-18. Also in *Warfare in the Book of Mormon*, edited by Stephen D. Ricks and William J. Hamblin, 25-28. Salt Lake City: Deseret and FARMS, 1990. Book of Mormon wars fulfill Lehi's prophecies about the terms and conditions for people to remain in the promised land. [D.M.]

P.183 Pierce, Florence. *The Golden Plates*. Salt Lake City: by the author, 1946. A detailed examination of the Book of Mormon plates, their contents and the story behind them. [D.M.]

P.184 Pierce, Florence. *Gospel Messages*. Salt Lake City: by the author, 1951. Thorough listing of scriptural quotations addressing many themes from the standard works, including Lehi's dreams, the coming forth of the Book of Mormon, King Benjamin's speech, and Christ's ministry in America. [D.M.]

P.185 Pierce, Florence. *Story of the Book of Mormon*. Salt Lake City: Deseret News Press, 1947. Pierce tells chronologically the story of the Book of Mormon with added explanations and correlating archaeological evidence of the events that occurred. Photographs are included from various sites and findings in Mexico that correspond to Book of Mormon history. [C.W.B.]

P.186 Pierce, Norman C. *Another Cumorah, Another Joseph*. N.p., 1954. A geographical and archaeological look at events found in the Book of Mormon. Author argues for the existence of two Cumorahs, one in Palmyra, New York, and the other in Central America. Suggests that the existing oceanic currents aided the Nephites and Jaredites in their destinations from the Old to the New World. Sees a connection between the mound builders of the Mississippi and Ohio Valleys and the mass migration of Hagoth and the other boats to the land northward. [C.W.B.]

P.187 Pierce, Norman C. "The Legend of Quetzalcoatl." *IE* 36 (December 1933): 858-59. A comparison of Quetzalcoatl, the Book

P.188 Pierce, Norman C. "The Legend of Quetzalcoatl." *MS* 96 (4 January 1934): 7, 11-13. Legends of Quetzalcoatl bear great resemblance to the account of Christ's ministry to the Nephites. [A.C.W.]

P.189 Pinegar, Ed J. *You, Your Family, and the Scriptures.* Salt Lake City: Deseret Book, 1975. Suggested program for studying the scriptures that provides a list of scriptural passages for studying with a specific subject in mind. Subjects include prayer, fasting, the value of the Book of Mormon, searching the scriptures, and keeping records and journals. [J.W.M.]

P.190 Pinegar, Rex D. "Voices from the Book of Mormon." In *Stories of Insight and Inspiration*, edited by Margie Calhoun Jensen, 38. Salt Lake City, UT: Bookcraft, 1976. A story of conversion of a young husband. Reading the Book of Mormon assisted him in his search for truth. [J.W.M.]

P.191 *Plain Fact for Students of the Book of Mormon with a Map of the Promised Land.* Salt Lake City: N.p., 1886. Five page booklet attempts to depict the exact geographical location of Book of Mormon lands and cities. Emphasis is placed on "Bountiful and four-sea regions." [D.W.P.]

P.192 "Plates, Metal." In *Encyclopedia of Mormonism*, edited by Daniel H. Ludlow, 3:1091. 5 vols. New York: Macmillan, 1992. The Book of Mormon was translated from a record kept on plates of metal. Other records were also kept on metal plates. [J.W.M.]

P.193 Pledger, Arthur G. "The W and I (Book of Mormon Names)." *Ensign* 6 (September 1976): 24-25. It is significant that the letter *w* is omitted in the 200 names introduced in the Book of Mormon, reflecting the Hebrew background of the text. The same is true of biblical names. [J.W.M.]

P.194 Poelman, Ronald E. "Companions from the Scriptures." In *BYU 1979 Devotional and Fireside Speeches of the Year,* 135-42. Provo, UT: BYU Press, 1980. Study of the scriptures is easier when one feels companionship with the people in them. Discusses the lives of Joseph of Egypt, Nephi, Paul, Moroni, and other scriptural figures. One develops a personal relationship with Jesus Christ through diligent study of the scriptures. [L.M.]

P.195 "Policies and Announcements." *Ensign* 16 (July 1986): 79. A letter from the First Presidency of the Church encouraging prospective missionaries to read the entire Book of Mormon. [L.D.]

P.196 "Policies and Announcements: Book of Mormon Placements." *Ensign* 15 (November 1985): 109. Directs members to do all they can to distribute copies of the Book of Mormon among non-members by directly giving them as gifts, through the family-to-family program, or offering them in public places. [J.W.M.]

P.197 Poll, Richard. "Liahona and Iron Rod Revisited." *Dialogue* 16 (Summer 1983): 69-78. Discusses Lehi's dream from the Book of Mormon, and reviews symbols and types of Liahonas and iron rods in Mormonism. [L.D.]

P.198 Pollard, Glen O. "The Book of Lehi." *Ensign* 7 (December 1977): 62. The book of Lehi was the source of the 116 pages of the gold plates that were translated by Joseph Smith and subsequently lost by Martin Harris. [D.H.M.]

P.199 Pope, John Keith. *Launching the Lehi.* San Francisco: Academy Phototype Service, 1955. Pope foretells an expedition that will sail on a raft without food or water from Saudi Arabia to Guatemala, manned by a crew of five or six persons. The purpose of the trip is to show that a voyage such as the one that brought Lehi and his family to America is possible. [L.M.]

P.200 Porter, L. Aldin. "Follow the Brethren." *Ensign* 17 (November 1987): 73-74. Also in *CR* (October 1987): 49-52. Issues a call to follow the brethren and to develop greater love for the prophets by reading the scriptures, especially the Book of Mormon. [J.W.M.]

P.201 Porter, Larry C. "The Book of Mormon: Historical Setting for Its Translation and Publication." In *Joseph Smith: The Prophet, the Man*, edited by Susan Easton Black and Charles D. Tate Jr., 49-64. Provo, UT: Brigham Young University Religious Studies Center, 1993. A detailed discussion of the translation and publication of the Book of Mormon. The bulk of the work of translation was completed in a relatively short time. The process of finding a printer was difficult. Some pages of the Book of Mormon were used by missionaries prior to the book's publication. A pact was made by "Christians" in the neighborhood that none would purchase the book. Nonetheless, the 5,000 copies of the Book of Mormon were used as great missionary tools. [J.W.M.]

P.202 Porter, Larry C. "The Church in New York and Pennsylvania, 1816–1831." In *The Restoration Movement: Essays in Mormon History,"* edited by F. Mark McKierman, 27-61. Independence, MO: Herald House, 1979. Explores the historical background of the coming forth of the Book of Mormon with excerpts from personal journals of Joseph Smith and many who knew him. Covers the early years of the prophet, the First Vision, the religious climate of Vermont and New York, Moroni's visit, Joseph's "money digging activites," and acquisition, translation, and publication of the golden plates. [J.W.M.]

P.203 Porter, Larry C. "The Colesville Branch and the Coming Forth of the Book of Mormon." *BYU Studies* 10 (Spring 1970): 365-85. Also published in *A New Light Breaks Forth: Essays in Mormon History*, edited by Lyndon W. Cook and Donald Q. Cannon, 75-96. Salt Lake City: Hawkes, 1980. The employment of Joseph Smith in the Colesville area of New York state brought him into contact with very important individuals of Church history. Josiah Stowell and Joseph Knight Jr. purposely planned to be at the Smith home when Joseph brought the plates home. There were many others who were equally important including Orson Pratt and Newell Knight as well as those who became the most prominent persecutors of the Church. [J.W.M.]

P.204 Porter, Larry C. " 'The Field is White Already to Harvest': Earliest Missionary Labors and the Book of Mormon." In *The Prophet Joseph: Essays on the Life and Mission of Joseph Smith*, edited by Larry C. Porter and Susan Easton Black, 73-89. Salt Lake City: Deseret Book, 1988. Details how the contents of the Book of Mormon were used in proselytizing prior to its publication in March 1830. [D.M.]

P.205 Porter, Larry C. "From a Book Coming Forth." *Ensign* 18 (July 1988): 42-46. Surveys letters, journals and other early Church historical writings concerning the missionary use of Book of Mormon passages from the beginning of its translation until its publication and the organization of the Church. By April, 1830, early members of the Church were instructed from and proselytized with passages from the Book of Mormon. Elements of this missionary work included written letters from Joseph Smith and Oliver Cowdery, angelic visitations and testimonies, handwritten excerpts from the translation, manuscripts and proof sheets from the printing, and finally the first edition of the Book of Mormon. [A.A.]

P.206 Porter, Larry C. "I Have A Question: Some scholars have implied that the Book of Mormon and LDS theology are products of Joseph Smith's environment. To what extent did Joseph Smith's environment influence the theological developments of the Church?" *Ensign* 22 (June 1992): 27-29. Rejects the so-called environment theory for the origin of the Book of Mormon. Discredits Indian, philosophical, historical, and literary influences (such as the Spaulding manuscript) upon the Book of Mormon. Contemporary religious thought appears to have been influential because the Book of Mormon answers and clarifies fundamental theological issues, but the only true source of influence upon the Book of Mormon was that of the Holy Ghost. [A.C.W.]

P.207 Porter, Larry C. "Palmyra/Manchester, New York." In *Encyclopedia of Mormonism,* edited by Daniel H. Ludlow, 3:1058. 5 vols. New York: Macmillan, 1992. An explanation of the importance of the Palmyra/Manchester area to LDS history. The first vision took place near there, the angel Moroni appeared there, the Hill Cumorah is only three miles southeast, and the Book of Mormon was printed there in Egbert B. Grandin's bookstore. [B.D.]

P.208 Porter, Larry C. "William E. McLellan's Testimony of the Book of Mormon." *BYU Studies* 10 (Summer 1970): 485-87. Contains a letter written by William E. McLellan in response to an inquiry made by James T. Cobb. Though McLellan had become a severe critic of the Church his testimony of the purity of the Book of Mormon and its divine origin remained in tact. [J.W.M.]

P.209 "Possible Routes Suggested for Mulek's Voyage." *Ensign* 3 (September 1973): 76-77. Discusses two possible routes of the voyage of the Mulekites to the "promised land" and sets forth reasons why they think the Mulekites took one of these routes. [M.D.P.]

P.210 Poulsen, George W., Jr. *Generations of the Nephites and Lamanites.* Salt Lake City: n.p., 1962. A pedigree chart of the Book of Mormon families of Lehi, Ishmael, and Mulek that provides brief information with scriptural references about Book of Mormon characters and the time and location where each resided. [J.W.M.]

P.211 "The Power of a Prophet." *Friend* 12 (October 1982): 48-49. Tells the story of Nephi$_3$ (prophet during the time of Christ). For children. [A.T.]

P.212 Pratt, David Leon. *The Prehistoric Hebrews of New England.* Salem, MA: Praetorian Press, 1985. Unorthodox presentation of the Book of Mormon text (1 Nephi–Jarom) as a history of the Hebrews. Says nothing about Joseph Smith or the origin of the Book of Mormon. Places the ancient Nephites in the present day New England area of the United States. Numerous footnotes provide commentary. [D.W.P.]

P.213 Pratt, Helaman. "Indian Customs and Traditions." *Juvenile Instructor* 15 (15 February 1880): 47. Writes about encounters with Indians in the Southwest and Mexico. The author was told that the Apaches would possess the land again, as the Book of Mormon describes. A tradition among the Pueblos listed three great events: the white race would conquer the Indians (fulfilled by Cortez), the Indians would rise up and regain their independence, and another group of white people would come with truth. [D.M.]

P.214 Pratt, John P. "Book of Mormon Chronology." In *Encyclopedia of Mormonism*, edited by Daniel H. Ludlow, 1:169-71. 5 vols. New York: Macmillan, 1992. Nephite history had three time references—time since they left Jerusalem, time from the commencement of the reign of the judges, and time from the birth of Christ. A table compares events in the three time references. [N.K.Y.]

P.215 Pratt, Noel B. *Prophecies of the American Indians.* Independence, MO: Zion, 1966. A booklet comprising 1 Nephi of the Book of Mormon, with several headings. [D.W.P.]

P.216 Pratt, Orson. "Accounts of Book of Mormon History: Records." *JD* 16:47-59. Discusses the meeting of Adam with his posterity in the valley of Adam-Ondi-Ahman, the location of the valley, the covenant with Enoch, records of God's dealings with men since creation, methods of preserving ancient records, Christ among the Nephites, and the fulfillment of prophecy in the fullness of times. [L.D.]

P.217 Pratt, Orson. "America, A Choice Land: Its Aborigines." *JD* 12: 338-46. Discusses America as a choice and promised land and the early inhabitants of America (aborigines) or Indians who are known to members of the Church as the Nephites, Lamanites, and the Jaredites of the Book of Mormon. [L.D.]

P.218 Pratt, Orson. "The Ancient Prophecies Fulfilled." *JD* 2: 284-98. Discusses the ancient prophecies in relation to the present generation, including prophecies about the coming forth of the Book of Mormon. [L.D.]

P.219 Pratt, Orson. "Background and Role of Book of Mormon." *JD* 21:128-36. Discusses the Book of Mormon and the "destiny of the kingdom of God and the Saints," the spreading of the Book of Mormon to the whole world, and presents the Book of Mormon as a divine revelation of God. [L.D.]

P.220 Pratt, Orson. "Bible Prophecy Fulfilled by Book of Mormon." *JD* 19:165-78. Joel's prophecy that young men will see visions and old men will dream dreams will be fulfilled only in the latter days when all men and women will be revelators. The translation of the Book of Mormon is the stick of Joseph coming forth to strengthen the Bible, the stick of Judah. [J.W.M.]

P.221 Pratt, Orson. "The Book of Mormon an Authentic Record." *JD* 21:168-78. Also in *Masterful Discourses and Writings of Orson Pratt*, compiled by N. B. Lundwall, 394-410. Salt Lake City, UT: Lundwall, n.d. A summary of how the Book of Mormon came into Joseph Smith's hands. Pratt bears his testimony to the truthfulness of the Book of Mormon. The Three Witnesses beheld the golden plates and will condemn the world through their words. [A.L.]

P.222 Pratt, Orson. "Book of Mormon and Redemption of Zion." *JD* 17:289-306. Recounts many of the trials through which the Saints passed and teaches that blessings follow the trials. The redemption of Zion is one of the anticipated blessings. When the Savior spoke of his "other sheep" he spoke of the American Indian. The Saints fulfilled prophecy when they moved to the Rocky Mountains at which time the work among the other sheep commenced. [J.W.M.]

P.223 Pratt, Orson. "Book of Mormon and the Restoration." *JD* 14:289-99. Reports on evidences of the Book of Mormon. Mentions the works of Stevens and Catherwood on ruins of ancient cities, a mound located in Licking County in which a stone tablet was found that had a representation of Moses and the ten commandments written in ancient Hebrew. [B.D.]

P.224 Pratt, Orson. "The Book of Mormon: Autograph Letter of Orson Pratt." *DN* 32 (28 November 1883): 707. Letter written by Orson Pratt May 2, 1876, bearing testimony to a friendly inquirer of the gospel. Advises the correspondent that he can know that the Book of Mormon is true. [D.M.]

P.225 Pratt, Orson. "Book of Mormon. Evidences of Its Divine Authenticity." In *A Compendium of The Doctrines of the Gospel*, edited by Franklin D. Richards and James A. Little, 95-101. Salt Lake City: Deseret News, 1882. The Book of Mormon fulfills Enoch's prophecy that "truth would come forth from the earth and would sweep it as a flood." Old Testament scriptures bear witness of the authenticity of the Book of Mormon as do archaeological evidences. There is an agreement between biblical and Book of Mormon doctrines. [J.W.M.]

P.226 Pratt, Orson. "Divine Authenticity of the Book of Mormon." *JD* 18:155-68. Gives evidences concerning the divinity of the Book of Mormon. Pratt covers such topics as the history of Joseph Smith's acquisition of the plates, the use of the Urim and Thummim to translate, Charles Anthon's statement concerning the characters, the witnesses who were shown the plates by the angel and a brief lifetime history showing that they never denied their testimony, the Eight Witnesses, and Isaiah's and Ezekiel's prophecies concerning the Book of Mormon. [B.D.]

P.227 Pratt, Orson. "Divinity of the Book of Mormon." *MS* 28 (16 June 1866): 369-71. Also in *Masterful Discourses and Writings of Orson Pratt*, compiled by N. B. Lundwall, 387-90. Salt Lake City, UT: Lundwall, n.d. The gospel writers of the New Testament fix the time of day of the Savior's crucifixion at noon and at three o'clock he was removed from the cross. The Book of Mormon records that the sign was given in the morning. The time difference is not contradictory, rather it offers proof that the Book of Mormon was not written by Joseph Smith, who could not have put such detail into the record. Three o'clock in the afternoon in Jerusalem would have been seven-thirty in the morning in America at one hundred twelve degrees west of Jerusalem. [J.W.M.]

P.228 Pratt, Orson. Editorial. *MS* 19 (September 1857): 600-605. A report on a visit to the Isle of Man where Pratt and others gave lectures on the divine authenticity of the Book of Mormon. They quoted from Isaiah 29 and explained how these verses apply to the Book of Mormon. [B.D.]

P.229 Pratt, Orson. "Evidences of Bible and Book of Mormon." *JD* 7:22-38. Author makes a scholarly comparison between the evidences supporting the Bible and the Book of Mormon. Evidences supporting the Book of Mormon include the twelve witnesses and doctrine in the Book of Mormon that is consistent with biblical doctrine. [B.D.]

P.230 Pratt, Orson. "Evidences Relating to the Divine Authority of the Bible and the Book of Mormon Compared." *JD* 16: 209-20. The people of this world will be judged according to the doctrines in both the Bible and the Book of Mormon. The testimonies of the Three Witnesses, manifestations of the Holy Ghost, and fulfilled prophecies testify of the truth of the Book of Mormon, whereas the Bible lacks similar evidences due to mistranslations. [A.L.]

P.231 Pratt, Orson. "The Gospel Restored from Heaven." *JD* 17:264-77. Discusses the truthfulness of the Book of Mormon and compares the evidences of Book of Mormon witnesses, etc., to those of the Bible. They are both true with or without man's acceptance. [A.L.]

P.232 Pratt, Orson. "The Hill Cumorah." *MS* 28 (July 1866): 417-19. Also in *Masterful Discourses and Writings of Orson Pratt*, compiled by N. B. Lundwall, 390-94. Salt Lake City, UT: Lundwall, n.d. A few notes on the Hill Cumorah. It was the site of the final battles of both Nephite and Jaredite nations, and contains a repository of plates and records. [B.D.]

P.233 Pratt, Orson. *An Interesting Account of Several Remarkable Visions, and of the Late Discovery of Ancient American Records*. New York: J. W. Harrison, 1841. Also published as *Interesting Account of Several Remarkable Visions and of the Late Discovery Of Ancient American Records*. Edinburgh: Ballyntyne and Hughes, 1840. Discusses the history of the American continent from the time of the tower of Babel to the present (1840). Also deals with the rise of the Church of Jesus Christ of Latter-day Saints and the coming forth of the Book of Mormon. [L.D.]

P.234 Pratt, Orson. "Joseph Smith: Coming Forth of Book of Mormon." *JD* 15:178-91. A brief synopsis of how Joseph Smith obtained the plates of gold. The stick of Joseph and the stick of Ephraim come together in the fullness of times of the gentiles for the purpose of gathering the tribes of Israel. [A.L.]

P.235 Pratt, Orson. "Joseph's Blessing: The American Indian." *JD* 14:7-12. Identifies the Book of Mormon as "an account of the first settlement of this country by these inhabitants [the native Indians], showing that they are not the ten tribes, but they are the descendants of one tribe, and they came into this country about 600 years before Christ." Included is a geographical history of the peoples of the Book of Mormon, following their movements from South America, through Central America, to North America wherein the Nephites were destroyed being "gathered together south of the great lakes in the country which we term New York." [B.D.]

P.236 Pratt, Orson. "King Limhi's Enquiry, Etc., Delivered on December 9, 1877." *JD* 19:204-19. Ammon's response to Limhi taught that the gift of seership is a high gift from God. By the use of the Urim and Thummim prophets translated and received revelation. The revelation the brother of Jared received cannot be revealed to mankind because of their lack of faith. The sealed portion of the Book of Mormon contains the full account of the instructions given to the brother of Jared. [J.W.M.]

P.237 Pratt, Orson. "The Knowledge of God Shall Cover the Earth As the Waters Cover the Deep." In *Masterful Discourses and Writings of Orson Pratt*, compiled by N. B. Lundwall, 410-24b. Salt Lake City, UT: Lundwall, n.d. All things from past dispensations are to be revealed so that truth and the knowledge of God shall flood the earth in this dispensation of the fullness of times. Many great prophets kept records. The records that Lehi's family brought with them contain a greater account than does the Bible. Jesus also taught many things when he visited in America that have not been revealed. All these records combined with those of the Eastern continents will be revealed in due time, and the heavens and the earth will reveal their knowledge of God. [J.W.M.]

P.238 Pratt, Orson. "The Latter-day Kingdom of God." *JD* 13:126-35. Explains what the Book of Mormon is and offers some evidences, including the timing of Jesus' crucifixion. Notes that Book of Mormon peoples had access to the scriptures, both those from the plates of brass and contemporary preachings, due to the copying of many scribes and the spreading of the manuscripts. [D.M.]

P.239 Pratt, Orson. "A Marvelous Work, etc." *JD* 19: 350-57. Many prophets through the ages have conversed with God. It is absurd to believe the heavens are closed to revelation. The Lord did not allow the Book of Mormon to be published until he had established the testimony of several witnesses who have never denied their testimonies. After publication of the book thousands of others testify by the Spirit of the book's truthfulness. [J.W.M.]

P.240 Pratt, Orson. *Masterful Discourses and Writings of Orson Pratt*, edited by N. B. Lundwall. Salt Lake City: Bookcraft, 1962. Contains many of the important works of Orson Pratt. Subjects include elephants of the Jaredite nation, darkness upon the American continent following the crucifixion, the Hill Cumorah, the Book of Mormon is consistent with the Bible, the witnesses to the Book of Mormon, and the Jaredite origins and records. [J.W.M.]

P.241 Pratt, Orson. "The Mastodon of the Book of Ether." *MS* 28 (8 December 1866): 776-77. Omer, a descendant of Jared, departed the Jaredite lands to a place by the seashore. His community's domesticated animals consisted of elephants and other unidentified animals that had perished by the time the Nephites arrived. Pratt muses about the disappearance of these animals and the remnants of curious animals found in New York. [J.W.M.]

P.242 Pratt, Orson. "More Evidence to Establish the Divine Authenticity of the Book of Mormon." *MS* 10 (15 November 1848): 341-43. Publishes an article entitled "Discoveries in America" from the *Edinburgh Evening Courant* 16 October 1848. Considers the discovery of Egyptian hieroglyphics in Central America and of Egyptian-style mummies in Mexico as external evidences of the Book of Mormon. [D.M.]

P.243 Pratt, Orson. "Nephite America—The Day of God's Power." *JD* 14:332-35. Contains a narrative of the Book of Mormon and descriptions of geographical locations that the author identifies as those where the events occurred. [J.W.M.]

P.244 Pratt, Orson. "Preparations for the Second Advent." *The Seer* 2 (August 1854): 305-20. In 1827 an angel of the Lord appeared in fulfillment of the revelations provided in Daniel and Revelation. The Book of Mormon contains the fullness of Christ's gospel, and the kingdom that was established upon the principles taught in the Book of Mormon has begun to roll forth from the tops of the mountains to establish the Lord's Zion. It is through this book that the guests are being called to the Lord's marriage feast. [J.W.M.]

P.245 Pratt, Orson. "Questions and Answers on Doctrine." *The Seer* 2 (February 1854): 212-15. Answers questions concerning the Book of Mormon. The Book of Mormon agrees with the Bible because they are both of divine origin and God does not disagree with himself. The Bible has been robbed of plain and simple truths. All are required to repent and accept the message of the Book of Mormon. [J.W.M.]

P.246 Pratt, Orson. "Reply to a Pamphlet, Printed in Glasgow, Entitled 'Remarks on Mormonism.'" *MS* 11 (15 March, 1 April, 1 May 1849): 85-88, 100-5, 129-33. Response to a polemical pamphlet against several aspects of Mormonism. Defends Joseph Smith's use of the Urim and Thummim, discusses the meaning of "other sheep" and "fold," and of the Book of Mormon as a covenant. [D.M.]

P.247 Pratt, Orson. "Sacred Metalic [sic] Plates." *MS* 28 (1, 8 December 1866): 761-64, 777-81. Refers to the discovery of "sacred stones" upon which are inscribed Hebrew characters, one of which reads "may the Lord have mercy upon me a Nephite." Scholars wonder where these people who spoke Hebrew came from, and the Book of Mormon provides the answers. The Nephites landed in Chile near the city of Valparaiso. Later Hagoth and others sailed to North America (Alma 63:4-12 and Helaman 3:3-16). The Nephites knew Hebrew and Egyptian and wrote in reformed Egyptian. [B.D.]

P.248 Pratt, Orson. "Sacred Stones in the Vicinity of Newark, Licking County, Ohio." *MS* 28 (December 1866): 753-59, 769-74. Features a quotation from the *Occident*, a contemporary American paper. In it the findings of four stones are described that contain what the non-Mormon author claims are unmistakably Hebrew inscriptions. One reads, "King of the Earth, Law of the Lord, the Word of the Lord, and the Holy of Holies," and the other contains the ten commandments. [K.M.]

P.249 Pratt, Orson. "Stick of Joseph, Etc., Delivered on January 25, 1874." *JD* 16:339-53. The prophecy of the two sticks in the book of Ezekiel refers to the Book of Mormon and the Bible. [J.W.M.]

P.250 Pratt, Orson. "True Christmas and New Year." *JD* 15:253. A reflection on the true meaning of Christmas and how the Book of Mormon shows the signs of the birth and crucifixion of Jesus Christ. [A.L.]

P.251 Pratt, Orson. "The Two Bibles." *MS* 28 (13 October 1866): 641-43. The two Bibles of the world are the Eastern Bible (Holy Bible) and the Western Bible (Book of Mormon). The Western Bible is the most correct book, but the Eastern Bible has been worked on by uninspired men and contains many errors. The discovery of stones inscribed with Hebrew found in ancient mounds in Ohio indicate that the ancient Indians of America had an alphabet and a written language. [B.D.]

P.252 Pratt, Orson. Untitled talk. *JD* 19 (October 1867): 311-21. Uses Book of Mormon references to discuss the nature of God. The brother of Jared saw Jesus Christ before his coming and thus learned that the God of the Old Testament was in the form of a man. Jacob teaches that Christ's atonement frees everyone from temporal and spiritual bondage, and Nephi teaches that through Adam's fall all mankind are fallen. [B.D.]

P.253 Pratt, Orson. Untitled talk. *JD* 19 (October 1877): 111-19. The Lord instructed the Nephite twelve disciples to "be even as I am." Pratt discusses his assignment to go to England and print the Book of Mormon and the Doctrine and Covenants in a phonetic shorthand method known as Pitman's phonotype system. [B.D.]

P.254 Pratt, Orson. "Was Joseph Smith Sent of God?" *MS* 10 (15 August; 1, 15 September; 1 October 1848): 247-51, 257-60, 273-78, 289-93. Pratt states that the Book of Mormon was revealed through Joseph Smith, that it contains the everlasting gospel and the writings of the tribe of Joseph. Explains Ezekiel 37:18-21 and Isaiah 29. Book of Mormon explains that America is the land of promise of Joseph. Thousands and tens of thousands of witnesses have accepted the Book of Mormon and witness concerning its truthfulness. [D.W.P.]

P.255 Pratt, Orson. "Yucatan." *MS* 10 (15 November 1848): 346-48. Takes issue with a statement from the *New York Sun* that "Yucatan is the grave of a great nation that has mysteriously passed away and left behind no history." Pratt claims that the Jaredites and descendants of Lehi inhabited that area and left their history in the Book of Mormon. Identifies the region of the Yucatan as the land of Desolation. Rejects the Spaulding theory. [D.M.]

P.256 Pratt, Parley P. "An Address By a Minister of the Church of Jesus Christ of L.D.S., To the People of England." In *Pre-Assassination Writings of Parley P. Pratt*, edited by Jerry Burnett and Charles Pope, 1-4. Salt Lake City: Mormon Heritage, 1976. Following a discourse on the basic beliefs and doctrines of the LDS Church, the author declares the Book of Mormon to be a true book. The Book of Mormon contains the same doctrines and principles that were revealed to the Jews and corroborates and sustains them. [J.W.M.]

P.257 Pratt, Parley P. "Address to the Red Man and Ancient Records of the Western Hemisphere." In *Pre-Assassination Writings of Parley P. Pratt*, edited by Jerry Burnett and Charles Pope, 8-15. Salt Lake City: Mormon Heritage, 1976. Calls pagans, Jews, and all people to repent, call on the name of the Lord, and read the Book of Mormon. He tells "the Red Men of America" that they are of the house of Israel, and from the tribe of Joseph as is recorded in the Book of Mormon. [J.W.M.]

P.258 Pratt, Parley P. "The Bible and the Book of Mormon Contrasted." *The Prophet* 1 (12 April 1845): 2-3. The Book of Mormon is superior to the Bible since the Book of Mormon is more simple and definite in its prophecies and doctrines. Nevertheless the Bible should be used as a companion record to the Book of Mormon despite its flaws and loss of plain truths. [A.C.W.]

P.259 Pratt, Parley P. "The Book of Mormon." *IE* 30 (August 1927): 938. Excerpt from *JD* 3:179, 308. Pratt rejoices in the Book of Mormon and says that if the world accepted its gospel all evil would cease. [A.C.W.]

P.260 Pratt, Parley P. "Book of Mormon." *MS* 1 (February 1841): 263-64. Announces the printing of a European edition of the Book of Mormon, a book that is worth more than "the gold and silver of Europe." [D.M.]

P.261 Pratt, Parley P. "The Book of Mormon—Origin of the American Indians, etc." In *A Voice of Warning and Instruction to All People or, An Introduction to the Faith and Doctrine of the Church of Jesus Christ of LDS*, 81-117. 9th edition. Salt Lake City: Deseret News Steam Printing, 1874. The Book of Mormon is the most misinterpreted and least understood book that has ever been published. The author presents a brief overview of the Book of Mormon and quotes Orson Pratt concerning its coming forth, a description of the stone box that contained the gold plates, the angel's declaration of their spiritual value and his admonition to use them properly. [J.W.M.]

P.262 Pratt, Parley P. "A Dialogue Between Tradition, Reason, and Scriptus." In *Pre-Assassination Writings of Parley P. Pratt,* edited by Jerry Burnett and Charles Pope, 11-16. Salt Lake City: Mormon Heritage, 1976. A play in which the characters Mr. Tradition, Mr. Reason, and Mr. Scriptus discuss the need for further revelation. Mr. Reason is willing to look for further evidence from all of the scriptures, including the Book of Mormon, but Mr. Tradition says that the "canon of scripture is full." Mr. Scriptus compares evidences of the New Testament and the Book of Mormon. [J.W.M.]

P.263 Pratt, Parley P. "Discovery of an Ancient Record in America." *MS* 1 (June 1840): 30-37. Tells how the Book of Mormon was made known to Joseph Smith. Contains passages from Jesus' ministry in 3 Nephi. [D.M.]

P.264 Pratt, Parley P. "Editorial Remarks." *MS* 3 (July 1842): 44-47. Various verses from Isaiah 29 are applied to the Book of Mormon. Refers to the work as a "record of the house of Joseph." [D.M.]

P.265 Pratt, Parley P. "Interesting Discoveries." *MS* 1 (August 1840): 101-3. Two articles on archaeological discoveries from *Athenaeum* and the *Manchester Guardian*. Asks if it is any more astonishing that plates hidden by Moroni should be preserved than that relics in America and England should survive to be discovered centuries after they were used. [D.M.]

P.266 Pratt, Parley P. *Key to the Science of Theology*. Salt Lake City: Deseret Book, 1973. The western hemisphere rose, progressed, declined, and fell as is recorded by the Book of Mormon. In the latter days Joseph Smith restored the keys to the science of theology through the Book of Mormon and divine revelation. [J.W.M.]

P.267 Pratt, Parley P. "A Letter to the Queen of England (Queen Victoria)." *TS* 3 (15 November 1841): 593-96. See also *IE* 4 (October 1901): 883-94, and in *Pre-Assassination Writings of Parley P. Pratt*, edited by Jerry Burnett and Charles Pope, 7-14. Salt Lake City: Mormon Heritage, 1976. A missionary proclamation including an account of the origin of the Book of Mormon and its purpose. Quotes from 1 Nephi, concerning the "great and abominable Church." [D.M.]

P.268 Pratt, Parley P. "Mormonism Unveiled!" In *Pre-Assassination Writings of Parley P. Pratt*, edited by Jerry Burnett and Charles Pope, 1-49. Salt Lake City: Mormon Heritage, 1976. Pratt compares the miracles recorded in the Bible and those of the Book of Mormon. When John gave the warning to not add to the book, he was not referring to the New Testament, but only to his book, the Revelation of John. That same warning is found in Deuteronomy. [J.W.M.]

P.269 Pratt, Parley P. "The Mormonites." *TS* 1 (January 1840): 45-46. A response to an article by Matilda Davidson. The LDS scripture is not called the "Mormon Bible" (as if to replace the well-known Bible), it is called the "Book of Mormon." The Book of Mormon corroborates the Bible. Pratt refutes Sidney Rigdon's connection with the Spaulding manuscript. [D.M.]

P.270 Pratt, Parley P. "Opposition to the Book of Mormon." *MS* 1 (November 1840): 185-87. Answers J. Curran's poorly reasoned objections to the Book of Mormon, published in the *Manx Journal,* that the New Testament forbids adding to the word of the Lord. [D.M.]

P.271 Pratt, Parley P. *Plain Facts, Showing the Falsehood and Folly of the Rev. C. S. Bush (A Church Minister of the Parish of Peover): Being a Reply to His Tract against the Latter-Day Saints.* Manchester: W. R. Thomas, 1840. Also published as "Plain Facts, Showing the Falsehood and Folly of the Reverend C. S. Bush." In *Pre-Assassination Writings of Parley P. Pratt,* edited by Jerry Burnett and Charles Pope, 1-16. Salt Lake City: Mormon Heritage, 1976. Rebuttal to Rev. Bush's publication "Plain Facts, Showing the Falsehood and Folly of The Mormonites or Latter-day Saints." Pratt confirms the Church's belief in the Bible as the word of God, but stresses that God is a God of continuous revelation. He denies that Emma Smith had signed a document stating that the Book of Mormon was false. The doctrines in the Book of Mormon are pure and holy. Whatever the medium upon which the scriptures are written or by what man of God they are recorded, their principles are the same. [J.W.M.]

P.272 Pratt, Parley P. "Present Condition and Prospects of the American Indians, Lamanites." *MS* 2 (July 1841): 40-42. The Book of Mormon prophesies that the Lamanites will be no longer persecuted but nourished by the gentiles beginning in 1830 when the Book of Mormon was published. In fulfillment of that, the United States government has apportioned an area of gathering for all the Indians; the tribes were paid money and given provisions at the expense of the United States. [B.D.]

P.273 Pratt, Parley P. "Proclamation! To the People of the Coasts and Islands of the Pacific (Ocean), of Every Nation, Kindred, and Tongue." *MS* 14 (18 September 1852, 25 September 1852): 465-70, 481-85. An apostolic manifesto enunciating basic principles of the Restoration. Addresses the "red man" identifying the Book of Mormon as a record of their people. Admonishes them to respond to the gospel and promises that they will thereby feel joy. Refers to the Book of Mormon as "that book of books, that Ensign to the nations." [D.M.]

P.274 Pratt, Parley P. *Proclamation!: To the People of the Coasts and Islands of the Pacific; of Every Nation, Kindred and Tongue.* Sydney, Australia: C. W. Wandell, 1851. See also *MS* 14 (18 September 1852, 25 September 1852): 465-70, 481-85. Treats the Book of Mormon as an essential element in the new dispensation of the gospel. Notifies the "red man" that the Book of Mormon is a record of their ancestors. [D.M.]

P.275 Pratt, Parley P. "Reminiscences and Testimony of Parley P. Pratt." *JD* 5:193-201. A testimony of the Church, Book of Mormon, and of Joseph Smith as a true prophet of God. [A.L.]

P.276 Pratt, Parley P. "A Reply to Mr. Thomas Taylor's 'Complete Failure' etc., and Mr. Richard Livesey's 'Mormonism Exposed.'" In *Pre-Assassination Writings of Parley P. Pratt,* edited by Jerry Burnett and Charles Pope, 1-12. Salt Lake City: Mormon Heritage, 1976. The reply to Mr. Taylor does not pertain to the Book of Mormon, however the response to Mr. Livesey is an attempt to disprove allegations that the Book of Mormon shows no "evidence of prophecy, of miracles, of purity of doctrine." [J.W.M.]

P.277 Pratt, Parley P. "Reply to the Anthenaeum: Being An Exposition of the Ignorance and Folly of Men Who Oppose the Truth." *MS* 2 (May 1841): 1-5. Response to an article in the *Edinburgh Intelligencer* (7 April 1841), which accused the Book of Mormon of being "a pretended revelation." Pratt calls the Book of Mormon "a marvelous work and a wonder." Defends against the accusation that the Book of Mormon is a forgery of Spaulding's manuscript. [J.W.M.]

P.278 Pratt, Parley P. "Ruins in Central America." *MS* 2 (March 1842): 161-65. A book review of Stephen's *Incidents of Travel,* which includes comments concerning archaeology and the Book of Mormon. [D.M.]

P.279 Pratt, Parley P. *A Voice of Warning*. Salt Lake City: Deseret News Press, 1874. Discusses fulfillment of prophecy and the Restoration, outlines the Book of Mormon's contents and the historical circumstances of Joseph Smith's translation. The Book of Mormon describes the origin of the American Indians. [E.G.]

P.280 Pratt, Parley P. "Wholesale Conversion of Methodists to Infidelity." *MS* 2 (December 1841): 114-15. Replies to several objections to the Book of Mormon listed by a minister, including that God commanded Nephi to kill Laban, that 3,000 Lamanites were killed in a battle and only seventy Nephites, that in John 17:4 Jesus says he had finished all that he was sent to do but the Book of Mormon attributed to him further duties. Pratt chides the minister for rejecting the Bible while trying to discredit the Book of Mormon. [D.M.]

P.281 Pratt, Rey L. "Book of Mormon Prophecies and the Mexican Situation." *Young Woman's Journal* 25 (September 1914): 529-40. Shows how the history of Mexico, beginning with the slaughters of Cortez, demonstrates the fulfillment of Book of Mormon prophecy that the Lamanites would "be scattered and smitten." [D.M.]

P.282 Pratt, Rey L. "Gospel Tidings For the Southland." *MS* 88 (15 April 1926): 225-30. Pratt, who has been called to conduct missionary work in "the southland," quotes 2 Nephi 1:1-11, 1 Nephi 13, 2 Nephi 30, and 3 Nephi 21 that speak of the fall, final gathering, and redemption of the Lamanites. [B.D.]

P.283 Pratt, Rey L. "The Gospel to the Lamanites." *IE* 16 (March, April, May, June, August 1913): 497-503, 577-85, 686-90, 796-801, 1021-25. Traces the origin, Book of Mormon prophecies regarding, subsequent conditions of, and ultimate destiny of the Lamanites. [D.M.]

P.284 Pratt, Rey L. Untitled talk. *CR* (October 1924): 142-45. Rejoices that the Lamanites are being brought the gospel, and says that people in Mexico and Central and South America are of the house of Israel. Those seeking to disprove the historical truth of the Book of Mormon will be unable to do so. Future archaeological excavations will strengthen its stance. [E.G.]

P.285 Pratt, Rey L. Untitled talk. *CR* (October 1925): 169-74. The Book of Mormon records that the Lamanites will be severely persecuted but not utterly overcome, the gentiles will bring the gospel to the Lamanites, and the time will arrive when the Lamanites will be redeemed. [B.D.]

P.286 Pratt, Rey L. Untitled talk. *CR* (April 1929): 70-76. Pratt speaks in conference about external evidences of the Book of Mormon. The ruins he has seen in his travels in South and Central America testify of great civilizations as described in the Book of Mormon. Many of the natives have legends that are similar to Christian myths. [B.D.]

P.287 Pratt, Rey L. Untitled talk. *CR* (October 1929): 18-22. A testimony of the Book of Mormon; Moroni 10:25 shows the way to find the truth of the Book of Mormon. [B.D.]

P.288 Pratt, Rey L., and Junius Romney. *The Book of Mormon—A Divine Record Prepared by Rey L. Pratt and Junius Romney*. N.p.: n.p., n.d. Many external evidences of the truthfulness of the Book of Mormon are presented—the horse, cement, paved streets, pyramids. The pamphlet seems to accompany a slide presentation presented by Rey L. Pratt. There are 47 items of archaeological evidence described. [J.W.M.]

P.289 Preece, Derek. " 'What If This Is Really True?' " *Ensign* 20 (September 1990): 20-21. A conversion story of a young man who received a testimony of the Book of Mormon while preparing stories to present as a home teacher. [J.W.M.]

P.290 "Presentation of the Book of Mormon to Rulers of the World." *IE* 43 (July 1940): 391. A list of kings, presidents, and statesmen of the world to whom a Book of Mormon has been presented, with the date and name of the presenter. [J.W.M.]

P.291 "President Benson Counsels New Mission Presidents in Annual Seminar." *Ensign* 16 (September 1986): 76. President Benson advises mission presidents to use the Book of Mormon as a part of their own personal study, preaching, and missionary work. [L.D.]

P.292 "Presiding Bishopric's Page: Young Men Can See Further." *IE* 64 (October 1961): 758-59,

767. The Book of Mormon is an instrument more valuable than binoculars—it will give a clear view of the pitfalls and traps of the enemy and prepare Aaronic priesthood boys for missionary service. The life of Nephi is an excellent example of a young man of faith with clear and righteous vision. [J.W.M]

P.293 Presler, Vi. "Humility, A Gem with Many Facets." *ZR* 29-31 (Summer, Fall 1985, Winter 1986): 6-10, 22. The author narrates 1 Nephi 1-10, pointing out the instances where pride or humility played an important part in the narrative. [A.T.]

P.294 Prestwich, Larry Berg. "A Visual Interpretation of Events and Personalities from the Book of Mormon." M.A. thesis, Brigham Young University, 1966. This thesis consists of drawings illustrating men and events in the Book of Mormon, with an attempt to capture emotional and spiritual expressions. Illustrations include Nephi, Enos, Omni, Mormon and Moroni. The author/artist explains in detail the techniques he used in the drawings. [D.M.]

P.295 Price, Rex Thomas Jr. "The Mormon Missionary of the Nineteenth Century." Ph.D. diss., University of Wisconsin, 1991. Tracks Mormon missionaries from 1830 to 1900, observing the place of the Book of Mormon in early LDS thought. The book shaped much of the ideological backdrop for the Church. Author explores the missionary call, finances, housing, and other items. [J.W.M]

P.296 Priddis, Venice. *The Book and the Map: New Insights into Book of Mormon Geography.* Salt Lake City: Bookcraft, 1975. A geographical investigation of Book of Mormon lands. Author believes that the Book of Mormon civilization inhabited western South America spanning the countries of Columbia, Equador, Peru, and Chile. Thirty-three maps and several illustrations are included. [C.W.B.]

P.297 Priest, Josiah. "American Antiquities." *MS* 7 (1 March 1846): 67-71. Large pyramids and mounds discovered in the eastern United States are described. Several references are cited confirming the use of metal in antiquity. Quotes Book of Mormon descriptions of Moroni's fortifications to show how recent discoveries support the Book of Mormon. [B.D.]

P.298 Priest, Josiah, and Thomas Ward. "American Antiquities." *MS* 9 (1 March 1846): 67-71. Tells of ancient American Indian ruins that show remnants of several large cities. This, as well as other American antiquities, helps support the Book of Mormon. Joseph Smith did not get his idea "to write" the Book of Mormon from this evidence because it did not come out until after the Book of Mormon was published. [M.D.P.]

P.299 Pritchett, Bruce. "Lehi's Theology of the Fall in Its Preexilic/Exilic Context." Provo, UT: FARMS, 1989. Explores preexilic and exilic literature that discuss the fall of Adam to determine how Lehi received his theology on the subject of the fall—was it solely from the brass plates or did he receive personal revelation to direct him? Concludes that the theology explained by Lehi was the same as that of the preexilic and exilic texts, and it offers the best explanation recorded. [J.W.M.]

P.300 Proctor, Paul Dean. "American Book of Mormon Map." N.p., 1988. A color-coded, detailed map suggesting locations of cities, lands, and places recorded in the Book of Mormon text. [J.W.M.]

P.301 "Prophecy and History." *IE* 28 (January–April 1925): 249-51, 362-63, 479-80, 582-83. A study guide. Several lessons address the Book of Mormon and prophecy. Deals with the Book of Mormon as fulfillment of ancient prophecy, prophecies in the Book of Mormon that have been fulfilled, are now being fulfilled, and others that have not yet been fulfilled. Also looks at prophecies dealing with the American Indian, the United States, and the Latter-day Saints. [L.D.]

P.302 "Prophecy and the Book of Mormon." *Relief Society Magazine* 5 (March 1918): 166-69. The prophetic teachings in 2 Nephi offer great hope and comfort as America is threatened by the crisis of World War I. Other prophecies in the Book of Mormon add to the testimony that Joseph Smith is a prophet of God. [J.W.M.]

P.303 "A Prophecy Come True." *Friend* 9 (December 1979): 39. A children's story: the prophecy of Samuel the Lamanite came true, for during the night it was like day and the people knew that Christ was born. [M.R.]

P.304 "Prophets of God Bear Testimonies of the Sacred Record." *IE* 63 (November 1960): 794-95. The testimonies of the Book of Mormon borne by the Presidents of the Church—from the Prophet Joseph Smith through President David O. McKay—are recited. [R.C.D.]

P.305 Pugh, Kaye Lynne. "Things They're Saying." *NE* 1 (May 1971): 37. A future missionary decided the best way to learn German was to read the Book of Mormon in German. This experience helped strengthen his testimony of the book. [M.D.P.]

P.306 Putnam, Reed H. "Were the Golden Plates Made of Tumbaga?" *IE* 69 (September 1966): 788-89, 828-31. Also in *Papers of the Fifteenth Annual Symposium of the Archaeology of the Scriptures*, edited by Ross T. Christensen, 101-9. Provo, UT: Extension Publications, Division of Continuing Education, BYU, 1964. Considers the physical properties of the golden plates of Nephi, the engraving of metal plates, and the stone box that stored the plates. Suggests that the plates may have been made of tumbaga, an alloy of gold and copper. [B.W.J.]

Q.

Q.001 "Questions and Answers." *Juvenile Instructor* 10 (9 January–11 December 1875): 5, 23, 34, 46, 58, 70, 82, 99, 106, 116, 130, 137, 154, 166, 190, 214, 227, 239, 250, 262, 275, 286, 293. Series that discusses the "Reign of the Judges." Based strictly on text, deals with details such as names, dates, and specific events. [A.C.W.]

Q.002 "Questions from the Field." *MS* 91 (11 April 1929): 237-38. Answers objections to the use of the word *steel* in the Book of Mormon. [R.H.B.]

Q.003 "Questions from the Field." *MS* 91 (25 April 1929): 271. Answers the question "Did Jesus appear to the people on the American continent before or after his ascension?" 3 Nephi 11:12 and 10:18 indicate he appeared after his final ascension in Palestine. [R.H.B.]

Q.004 Quinn, D. Michael. "The First Months of Mormonism: A Contemporary View by Diedrich Willers." *New York History* 54 (July 1973): 317-33. A response to an attack on the Church by Willers, a minister of the German Reformed Church. This article contains important insights into the role of the Urim and Thummim in the translation of the Book of Mormon. Ten locations are cited as places for translation besides the Whitmer home. [J.W.M.]

Q.005 Quinn, D. Michael. "The Mormon Church and the Spanish-American War: An End to Selective Pacifism." *Dialogue* 17 (Winter 1984): 11-30. The Book of Mormon's declarations concerning war dispense with the concepts of the war-like Jehovah of the Old Testament as well as the pacifistic Christ of the New Testament. Early Latter-day Saints were ambivalent with respect to war until they were leaving the United States and the Mexican War developed. Although peaceful solutions were always sought, there was no opposition to the defense of liberty. A strong military stance was maintained in Utah for the sole purpose of defense. [J.W.M.]

R.

R.001 R. "The Interpretation of Scripture." *MS* 49 (31 January 1887): 72-75. Peter teaches that prophecy is not to be interpreted privately. In spite of this counsel many have done so causing discord and contention. The Book of Mormon says that many of the plain and precious truths have been taken out of the Bible. A comparison of scriptures will provide an accurate understanding of difficult passages. [J.W.M.]

R.002 R. "Lesser Lights of the Book of Mormon." *Contributor* 1 (May–September 1880): 177-79, 206-9, 230-33, 243-45, 269-71. A series that tells the stories of some of the lesser-known figures in the Book of Mormon: Jacob a Nephite apostate, Jarom, Zoram, Muloki, Samuel the Lamanite, Antipas, and Teancum. [A.T.]

R.003 R., C. E. "Visit to an Ancient Indian Village." *Juvenile Instructor* 14 (15 November 1879): 257. Report of an inspection of an archaeological site in Arizona, which may corroborate the Book of Mormon. [D.M.]

R.004 Rabe, Julie T. "I Will Read the Book of Mormon." *Friend* 18 (January 1988): 28. A poster for children with a reading schedule for the Book of Mormon. [M.D.P.]

R.005 Raeithel, Gert. "Nephiten and Lamaniten: Mormonen and Indianerals Vettern und Nachbarn." *Merkur* 38 (April 1984): 316-22. Explanation of LDS beliefs concerning Indian descent from the house of Israel as set forth in the Book of Mormon. Connects those beliefs to LDS missionary work with the Indians, the Word of Wisdom, polygamy, racial discrimination, and work with Indian reservations in Canada. [A.C.W.]

R.006 Raish, Martin. "All That Glitters: Uncovering Fool's Gold in Book of Mormon Archaeology." *Sunstone* 6 (January 1981): 10-15. Poor LDS scholarship has damaged Book of Mormon credibility. Raish points out several types of errors: reliance on archaeologists to lend credibility, faulty footnotes, the use of pictures not related to scriptures with which they are associated, and publishing unauthenticated artifacts that sometimes turn out to be fraudulent. [J.W.M.]

R.007 Raish, Martin. "Tree of Life." In *Encyclopedia of Mormonism*, edited by Daniel H. Ludlow, 4:1486-88. 5 vols. New York: Macmillan, 1992. Describes how the tree of life is portrayed in the Book of Mormon, both in Lehi's vision (1 Nephi 8) and in Alma's allegory (Alma 32). Two mesoamerican representations of the tree of life are described: Stela 5 Izapa, Mexico, and the sarcophagus cover of King Pacal in the Mayan Temple of Inscriptions, Palenque. [B.D.]

R.008 Ralston, Russell. "Challenged to Examine." *Restoration Witness* 164 (August 1976): 7. An attempt to prove the Book of Mormon through external evidence led to a study of the book, which opened the author's mind to concepts that had previously been blind spots: the peace of God, prayer, and man's relationship with God. [J.W.M.]

R.009 Rannie, Edward. "Is the Book of Mormon a Help to Solve Present-day Problems?" *The Rod of Iron* 1 (July/August/September 1924): 27. The Book of Mormon offers the solution to every great problem the world ever encountered with such clarity and simplicity that even children can understand the messages. [J.W.M.]

R.010 Rasmussen, Della Mae, and B. Keith Christensen, illustrator. *The Illustrated Story of President Joseph Smith*. Provo, UT: Eagle Systems, 1982. Gives an historical account of the coming forth of the Book of Mormon with color illustrations for children. [J.W.M.]

R.011 Rasmussen, Ellis T. "I Have a Question: What are the best evidences to support the authenticity of the Book of Mormon?" *Ensign* 17 (January 1987): 53-55. Also in *A Sure Foundation: Answers to Difficult Gospel Questions*. Salt Lake City: Deseret Book, 1988, 27-33. Three evidences for the Book of Mormon are available—external, internal, and spiritual. Offers "seven key concepts" for identifying various internal evidences that "carry within them a spirit of authenticity." [D.L.L.]

R.012 Rasmussen, Ellis T. "Sidney B. Sperry: Student of the Book of Mormon." *Ensign* 16 (July 1986): 24-27. This synopsis of Brother Sperry's life explains that he was the first Latter-day Saint to earn his doctorate in biblical languages. His life's work was the defense of the Book of Mormon. [J.W.M.]

R.013 Rasmussen, James L. "Blood Vengeance in the Old Testament and Book of Mormon." Provo, UT: FARMS, 198?. A study on capital punishment in the Old Testament and Book of Mormon. Concludes that "the concept of blood guilt is pervasive in each of the scriptures studied. Innocent blood shed cries from the ground for vengeance that will be taken ultimately by God if not by execution of the murderer." [D.M.]

R.014 "Read Book of Mormon in One Day." *IE* 31 (April 1928): 528. Clyde B. Crandall had several reasons for trying to read the Book of Mormon in one day: to understand the story in sequence, to prove that reading the Book of Mormon is not a tedious task, and to meet the challenge and accomplish it. [J.W.M.]

R.015 Read, Lenet H. "A Book about God's Love." *Ensign* 18 (January 1988): 40-44. Shows how the development, history, structure, and teachings of the Book of Mormon manifest the pure love of God. God's everlasting love is evident in the vision of Nephi, in the birth, ministry, and sacrifice of Jesus Christ (Christ's atonement), in the redemptive experiences of Alma the younger, in the peaceful society following Christ's personal visit to the Nephites, and in the final teachings of Mormon and his son Moroni. [A.A.]

R.016 Read, Lenet H. "I Have a Question: Can you give me some keys to help me understand the parable of the tame and wild olive tree that Jacob tells?" *Ensign* 7 (April 1977): 30-32. The parable of the olive tree in Jacob 5 is best understood by reading 1 Nephi 15:7-20. Jacob explains the motives and emotions of the Lord and presents a clear historical and prophetic view of God's dealings with the house of Israel. [J.W.M.]

R.017 Read, Lenet H. "King Lamoni." *Ensign* 7 (August 1977): 60-63. This examination of King Lamoni's character presents new insights into the story of Ammon and Lamoni's conversion. [J.W.M.]

R.018 "Read the Book of Mormon." *Friend* 18 (January 1988): 1. A collection of testimonies by prophets of God (from Moroni to Ezra Taft Benson) for children concerning the value of reading the Book of Mormon. [J.W.M.]

R.019 *Read the Book of Mormon: It Can Change Your Life*. Salt Lake City: Church of Jesus Christ of Latter-day Saints, 1975. A tract encouraging people to study the Book of Mormon. Gives a brief overview of the book's contents and supplies direct quotations on several different themes. [D.M.]

R.020 *A Reader's Guide to the Book of Mormon*. Provo, UT: BYU, 1967. A booklet that presents a book-by-book summary of the contents of the Book of Mormon from 1 Nephi–Moroni. Suggests that young people may be wise to devote their attention to the lives of Book of Mormon prophets and leave the words of Isaiah until they have more background to aid their understanding. [D.W.P.]

R.021 Reay, Don. "The Book of Mormon." In Reay's *The Gospel of Jesus Christ According to My Understanding*, 62-69. New York: Exposition Press, 1969. Gives a brief account of the story of the Book of Mormon and states that the Book of Mormon is the "Stick of Joseph" referred to in Ezekiel 37. [J.W.M.]

R.022 "Recent Studies on the Book of Mormon." *Ensign* 19 (June, July 1989): 50-53, 62-65. Short quotes from scholars. Various topics include metal alloys in the Book of Mormon, principles found in both the Book of Mormon and the Bible, synagogues in the Book of Mormon, Mulek, Jewish festivals, King Benjamin's address, and many others. [J.W.M.]

R.023 Rector, Hartman, Jr. "The Gospel." *Ensign* 15 (November 1985): 74-76. Also in *CR* (October 1985): 95-98. The gospel of Christ (3 Nephi 27) centers upon Jesus Christ, his willingness to pay the price for all of the sins of humanity, to be lifted upon the cross giving his life for mankind, and to draw all men to him through repentance, baptism, and gift of the Holy Ghost. [J.W.M.]

R.024 Rector, Hartman, Jr. "Overcoming the Natural Man." *CR* (6 April 1970): 139-41. King Benjamin's teachings about the natural man are illuminated by Ether 12:27, which informs the reader that the Lord gives weaknesses to individuals to teach humility. The responsibility each bears is to become teachable, then the Lord gives assistance to overcome the sins that result from the weakness. [J.W.M.]

R.025 Reed, William C. "A Model for Parenting from the Book of Mormon." In *The Sixth Annual CES Religious Educators Symposium on the Book of Mormon*, 55-58. Salt Lake City: Church of Jesus Christ of Latter-day Saints, 1982. Elements of the stories of Lehi, Benjamin, Alma, and the two thousand Ammonite soldiers are used to illustrate actions and characteristics of model parents. [A.T.]

R.026 Rees, Robert A. "Ammon." *Ensign* 7 (June 1977): 72-77. Repentance is the theme of the story of Ammon. He shows a mighty change as he was transformed from a rebellious prince into a heroic missionary. [J.W.M]

R.027 Rees, Robert A. "Melville's Alma and the Book of Mormon." *Emerson Society Quarterly* 2/43 (1966): 41-46. A comparison of the character of Alma in Melville's *Mardi* and the two Almas in the Book of Mormon. [D.M.]

R.028 Rees, Robert A. Review of the Book of Mormon Collection in the William Andrews Clark Library. *Dialogue* 4 (Spring 1969): 119-20. Reviews the collection of sixty-two separate editions of the Book of Mormon purchased from Charles N. Kessler and placed in the William Andrews Clark Library in Los Angeles. [J.W.M.]

R.029 Reeve, Rex C., Jr. "Book of Mormon." In *Encyclopedia of Mormonism*, edited by Daniel H. Ludlow, 1:156. 5 vols. New York: Macmillan, 1992. Gives a synopsis of the book of Mormon, written by the prophet Mormon, who describes the fall of the Nephites and includes his final plea to future generations. [B.D.]

R.030 Reeve, Rex C., Jr. "The Book of Mormon Plates." In *The Book of Mormon: Second Nephi, the Doctrinal Structure*, edited by Monte S. Nyman and Charles D. Tate Jr., 99-111. Salt Lake City: Bookcraft, 1988. The gold plates Joseph Smith received from Moroni consisted of Mormon's abridgment of the large plates of Nephi, an unabridged set of the small plates of Nephi, an abridgment of the Jaredite record made by Moroni, and a sealed portion that remained untranslated. This article contains commentary on the contents of these plates as well as the brass plates, also identified in the Book of Mormon. [J.W.M.]

R.031 Reeve, Rex C., Jr. "Brother of Jared." In *Encyclopedia of Mormonism*, edited by Daniel H. Ludlow, 1:235-36. 5 vols. New York: Macmillan, 1992. A description of the brother of Jared, Mahonri Moriancumer, who led the Jaredite people by revelation under his brother, Jared. [B.D.]

R.032 Reeve, Rex C., Jr. "Dealing With Opposition to the Church." In *The Book of Mormon: Alma, The Testimony of the Word*, edited by Monte S. Nyman and Charles D. Tate Jr., 15-26. Provo, UT: Brigham Young University Religious Studies Center, 1992. Alma labored 25 years in spite of internal and external opposition to the Church. Nehor taught priestcraft and after his death his followers continued his opposition. When the Church in our day experiences opposition, Church members should continue to teach the doctrines of the Church and realize that opposition has often resulted in spiritual growth for both the individual and the Church. [N.K.Y.]

R.033 Reeve, Rex C., Jr. "Fourth Nephi." In *Encyclopedia of Mormonism*, edited by Daniel H. Ludlow, 1:155-56. 5 vols. New York: Macmillan, 1992. 4 Nephi narrates four generations of peace, a time when there could not have been a happier people (4 Nephi 1:16). It also foreshadows the later destruction of the Nephites following their gradual rejection of the gospel. [B.D.]

R.034 Reeve, Rex C., Jr. "God's Ways or Man's: The Ultimate Choice." In *Studies in Scripture: Alma 30 to Moroni*, edited by Kent P. Jackson, 107-15. Salt Lake City: Deseret Book, 1988. The Book of Mormon, particularly Helaman 7-12, clearly defines the choices of agency and the corresponding consequences, whether good or evil. Nephi, who ministered shortly before the Lord's birth, was sorrowful because of the works of darkness and secret combinations among his people. Nephi, in contrast, was stable in the midst of inconsistency. He received great blessings. [J.W.M.]

R.035 Reeve, Rex C., Jr. "The Path to Eternal Life (2 Nephi 31-33)." In *A Symposium on the Book of Mormon*, 109-12. Salt Lake City: Church of Jesus Christ of Latter-day Saints, CES, August 1986. Uses the Book of Mormon, especially Nephi's writings to answer questions such as: "Why is the doctrine of Christ of great worth?," "What is the gate leading to the straight and narrow path?," "How essential is baptism?," and "How can you endure to the end?" Concludes that Nephi's example and teachings show what is required to gain eternal life. [A.T.]

R.036 Reeve, Rex C., Jr. "We Labor Diligently to Persuade Our Children to Believe in Christ: 2 Nephi 25:21 to 26:11." In *The Book of Mormon: Second Nephi, The Doctrinal Structure*, edited by Monte S. Nyman and Charles D. Tate Jr., 259-67. Salt Lake City: Bookcraft, 1989. Believers in Christ in Lehi's group had a true knowledge of Jesus Christ. This sure knowledge rested on the testimonies of at least four prophets—Lehi, Nephi, Jacob, and Isaiah, who saw Christ and possessed the sure witness of the Holy Ghost. Their faith and understanding of him was founded in the observance of the law of Moses, which points to Christ. They endeavored to bring their children to Christ and realized that some of their seed would receive the Savior and others would reject him. [J.W.M.]

R.037 *References to the Book of Mormon.* Kirtland: Church of Jesus Christ of Latter-day Saints, 1835. The earliest known reference guide to the Book of Mormon. Items listed are in order of pagination. The references refer to the chapters of the Book of Mormon and describe the contents of the chapter. [D.M.]

R.038 Reiser, A. Hamer. "Lets Read the Book of Mormon." *Instructor* 98 (September 1963): 339. Suggests a method of study for the Book of Mormon: read to learn only the story; re-read marking every reference to Jesus Christ; read the third time looking for passages that expound doctrine, principles, ordinances, and ideas. [J.W.M.]

R.039 "A Remarkable Prediction." *Deseret Weekly* 48 (24 March 1894): 419-20. The joining of the sticks of Judah and Joseph (the Bible and the Book of Mormon) will precede the gathering of Israel. [D.M.]

R.040 "A Remarkable Vision." *MS* 70 (May 1908): 305-11. In part of his vision recorded in the Book of Mormon, Nephi saw Columbus who would discover the New World (1 Nephi 13:12-13). [B.D.]

R.041 Remy, Jules. *A Journey to the Great Salt Lake City.* 2 vols. London: Jeffs, 1861. A historical work against Mormonism. Volume 1 discusses Joseph Smith's character and the events surrounding the appearance of the Book of Mormon. The author supports the Spaulding theory. [M.R.]

R.042 Reorganized Church of Jesus Christ of Latter Day Saints. *The History of the Reorganized Church of Jesus Christ of Latter Day Saints.* Independence, MO: Herald Publishing House, 1951. Retells the events of the coming forth of the Book of Mormon as told by Joseph Smith and his associates. [J.W.M.]

R.043 Reorganized Church of Jesus Christ of Latter Day Saints. *An Invitation to Read the Book of Mormon.* N.p: n.p., n.d. An overview of the Book of Mormon. Suggests three ways of reading the book: read from start to finish, follow the historical sequence, or search specific doctrines. [J.W.M.]

R.044 Reorganized Church of Jesus Christ of Latter Day Saints. *The "Manuscript Found" or "Manuscript Story" of the Late Rev. Solomon Spaulding, from a Verbatim Copy of the Original Now in the Care of Pres. James H. Fairchild, of Oberlin College, Ohio. Including Correspondence Touching the Manuscript, Its Preservation and Transmission until It Came into the Hands of the Publisher.* Lamoni, Iowa: RLDS Church, 1885. Explains the manner in which the Spaulding Manuscript was preserved and placed in the possession of the RLDS church. Includes letters from James H. Fairchild stating that the Spaulding theory for the Book of Mormon need be relinquished and from L. L. Rice explaining how he had obtained the manuscript. Includes a reprint of the manuscript. [J.W.M.]

R.045 Reorganized Church of Jesus Christ of Latter Day Saints. *The New Testament of Ancient America.* Independence, MO: Herald Publishing House, 1955. Contains an adaptation of 3 Nephi 1-14, followed by an overview of the Book of Mormon and its coming forth. The purpose of the book is to be a witness of God's dealings with man and the messiahship of Christ. Old Testament scriptures are fulfilled by the book and archaeology testifies of its truthfulness. It does not supersede the Bible, but sustains it. [J.W.M.]

R.046 Reorganized Church of Jesus Christ of Latter Day Saints. *Pronouncing Vocabulary of the Book of Mormon.* Lamoni, IA: Herald House,

1902. Guide for standardized pronunciation of Book of Mormon names. Includes people and places and a scripture reference for each. [A.C.W.]

R.047 Reorganized Church of Jesus Christ of Latter Day Saints. *Revelation and Scripture.* Independence, MO: Herald House, 1979. Revelation is the transmitting of God's love and purposes for individuals or mankind. There are a multitude of ways in which revelation is received—through study and meditation or on an intuitive or emotional level. Thus, the honest may feel disagreement concerning interpretation of revelation and it must be judged according to the Book of Mormon and other accepted scriptures. Only one may receive revelation for the Church as a whole. [J.W.M.]

R.048 Reorganized Church of Jesus Christ of Latter Day Saints. "Why do you need the Book of Mormon? Isn't the Bible enough?" In *Reorganized Latter Day Saint Distinctives*, 12-13. Independence, MO: Herald Publishing House, n.d. The Bible holds first place in the canon of law and doctrine but is supplemented by the second witness for Christ—the Book of Mormon. It is the testimony of those who wrote it and those who brought it forth. The RLDS Church accepts the testimony of Joseph Smith and others concerning the book and its coming forth. [J.W.M.]

R.049 *Report of the Committee on American Archaeology.* Lamoni, IA: Herald Publishing House, 1902. Contains maps and an outline of Book of Mormon history as prepared by the RLDS Committee on American Archaeology. Outlines the Nephite history, Jaredite history, describes conditions discovered by early explorers and priests after Columbus, and gives archaeological evidence of extinct animals and civilizations that were mentioned in the Book of Mormon,. [J.W.M.]

R.050 *Report of the Committee on American Archaeology.* Lamoni, IA: Herald House, 1910. A work on Book of Mormon archaeology and geography. Outlines the history of the Nephites and Jaredites with the intention of creating a map of Book of Mormon events. Includes professional opinions regarding the origin of the inhabitants of ancient America. Several maps are also included. [B.D.]

R.051 Reynolds, Alice Louise. "The Book of Mormon Tested." *Relief Society Magazine* 10 (September 1923): 427-29. Faith-promoting stories of people who received a testimony of Jesus Christ after reading the Book of Mormon. [J.W.M.]

R.052 Reynolds, Arch S. *How Did Joseph Smith Translate?: A Study of the Method of his Translation of the Various Books of Scriptures.* Springville, UT: Art City Publishing, 1952. The prophet Joseph Smith translated the Book of Mormon by means of the seer stone, the Urim and Thummim. Excerpts from the journals of Joseph Smith, Oliver Cowdery, David Whitmer, Emma Smith, and Martin Harris declare his methods of translation. The characters appeared sentence by sentence and the translation below it. George Reynolds and B. H. Roberts suggest that Moroni may have assisted him. [J.W.M.]

R.053 Reynolds, Arch S. *The Urim and Thummim and Other Media Used by the Prophet Joseph Smith to Translate The Scriptures.* Springville, UT: Art City, 1950. Uses the Bible, Book of Mormon, and historical accounts from the early writers of the Church to show that the Urim and Thummim and other "media" have been used since ancient times to receive communication from God. Joseph Smith also employed such media to translate the scriptures. [J.W.M.]

R.054 Reynolds, George. "Aaron, Son of Mosiah." *Juvenile Instructor* 26 (1 November 1891): 650-53. Aaron chose missionary service over the opportunity to serve as king and suffered hardship and inhumane treatment to preach the gospel to the Lamanites. Though little is known about him, the Book of Mormon sets forth the greatness of his character. [J.W.M.]

R.055 Reynolds, George. "Agriculture among the Nephites." *Juvenile Instructor* 15 (15 March 1880): 71. Deals with aspects of agriculture in the Book of Mormon. [D.M.]

R.056 Reynolds, George. "Akish, the Jaredite." *Juvenile Instructor* 26 (15 October 1891): 631-

33. An article for youth that draws attention to the fact that the downfall of the Jaredites was due to their desire to have a king rule over them. King Akish's deeds of cruelty, treachery, and iniquity created a kingdom so filled with corruption and secret societies that civil war broke out and ended only after the destruction of the nation. [J.W.M.]

R.057 Reynolds, George. "The Alma Family." *MS* 42 (19 January–3 May 1880): 33-37, 49-52, 65-68, 81-84, 97-101, 129-31, 145-47, 160-64, 177-79, 193-95, 225-26, 241-43, 257-58, 278-79. Presents a life sketch of the Alma family, many of whom became prophets. The life of Alma the Younger is compared to the Apostle Paul—both were called upon to repent and became great missionaries for the Lord. The prophecies of Alma are among the most numerous, important, and interesting in the Book of Mormon, and his inspired advice to his sons contains many doctrinal matters. Helaman the son of Helaman, grandson of Alma, carried on the work of righteousness in spite of the Gadianton robbers. His son Nephi was a great prophet who paved the way for the visit of Christ in America. Nephi's brother Lehi and Lehi's son Nephi were also great leaders. [J.W.M.]

R.058 Reynolds, George. "Amulek." *Juvenile Instructor* 10 (6 February 1875): 35-36. Biographical sketch of Amulek who was a man "of liberal education, of great faith, of unswerving integrity, and untiring zeal for the cause of truth." Also discusses Alma, Zeezrom, and the divine justice displayed in the destruction of Ammonihah. [A.C.W.]

R.059 Reynolds, George. *Are We of Israel?* Independence, MO: Zions, August 1931. The Book of Mormon clearly shows that the promises made to Abraham, Jacob, and Joseph were fulfilled at least partially through Lehi's family, who were of the house of Manasseh. Brigham Young indicates that Latter-day Saints are of the house of Ephraim, and are being gathered by the Book of Mormon. [J.W.M.]

R.060 Reynolds, George. "The Art of War among the Nephites." *Juvenile Instructor* 15 (15 April 1880): 77, 94. Describes different aspects of warfare as found in the Book of Mormon, with emphasis on the battle techniques of Moroni. Notes that detailed accounts of warfare do not appear in the Book of Mormon until the period of the judges. [D.M.]

R.061 Reynolds, George. "The Bible and the Book of Mormon—A Parallel." *Young Woman's Journal* 9 (October 1898): 490-92. Shows parallels and commonalties between the Book of Mormon and the Bible. For example, both books were written by different men over a span of several centuries and both contain hymns or psalms. [D.M.]

R.062 Reynolds, George. "The Book of Mormon and the Three Witnesses." *Juvenile Instructor* 17 (15 September 1882): 281. Examines the authenticity of the Book of Mormon in light of the testimonies of the Eight Witnesses and the Three Witnesses, noting that although some left the Church, none ever denied that they had seen the gold plates. [A.C.W.]

R.063 Reynolds, George. "The Book of Mormon and the Three Witnesses." *MS* 44 (9 October 1882): 645-47. Testimonies of Three Witnesses are tangible evidence of the Book of Mormon's veracity. If Joseph Smith were an impostor, he would have showed the plates more widely for credence. Having but a few witnesses is further proof of its truthfulness. [A.C.W.]

R.064 Reynolds, George. *Chronological Chart of Nephite and Lamanite History.* Salt Lake City: Deseret Book, 1956. A full color chart with a historical time line dealing with the Nephites and Lamanites. [J.W.M.]

R.065 Reynolds, George. *Complete Concordance of the Book of Mormon.* Salt Lake City: Deseret Book, 1900. A concordance or alphabetical listing of all the words of the Book of Mormon (except twenty of the most common words, such as *a, the, and*) accompanied with scriptural references and a brief excerpt of the scriptural passage showing the context of each word of the concordance. [L.D.]

R.066 Reynolds, George. *Dictionary of the Book of Mormon; Comprising its Biographical Geographical, and Other Proper Names; Together with Appendices by Janne M. Sjodahl.* Salt Lake City: Juvenile Instructor Office, 1883, [R]1954. This dictionary contains all of the places and people of the Book of Mormon. Each entry comprises a thorough treatment of the subject in clear and understandable vocabulary; scriptural references are included. [J.W.M.]

R.067 Reynolds, George. "Domestic Life among the Nephites." *Juvenile Instructor* 14 (15 December 1879): 285-86. A description of certain aspects of Nephite living. Includes comments on textiles, ornamentation, architecture, gardens, interior decorations, foods, and transportation. [D.M.]

R.068 Reynolds, George. "Evidences of the Book of Mormon: Some External Proofs of its Divinity." *Contributor* 17 (1895–1896): 164-68, 231-38, 271-78, 361-68, 417-24. Also in *MS* 59 (10, 17, 24, June, 1, 8 July 1897): 353-58, 369-76, 385-93, 401-9, 417-25. A five-part series that includes a brief overview of the Book of Mormon, an account of Spanish conquerors who destroyed evidence of Hebrew influence reasoning that "Satan had counterfeited in this people the history, manners, customs, traditions, and expectations of the Hebrews," a description of artifacts containing Hebrew characters, and evidence that the religious traditions of the Indians corroborate Book of Mormon statements. [A.T.]

R.069 Reynolds, George. "He Shall Perish." *IE* 2 (September 1988): 801-6. 2 Nephi 10 prophesies that a king will never be raised up unto the gentiles upon the land. Reynolds tells of the tragic fates of Louis Napoleon and Maximilian who tried to establish an empire in Mexico (1861) after the Book of Mormon had come forth and warns all people against attempting such a thing. [B.D.]

R.070 Reynolds, George. "Historians of the Nephites." *Contributor* 1 (March 1880): 137-38. There were four families who were charged with the care of the plates that contained the records of the Nephites. Jacob's family, King Benjamin's family, Alma and his family, and Mormon and his son Moroni. The author provides a dated list of the historians. [J.W.M.]

R.071 Reynolds, George. "History of the Book of Mormon." *Contributor* 5 (October-December 1833, January-September 1884): 1-5, 41-47, 81-85, 121-25, 161-68, 201-6, 241-46, 281-86, 321-27, 361-67, 401-8, 441-47. Twelve-part series. Discussions include: the discovery, translation, and contents of the gold plates; Oliver Cowdery's description of Hill Cumorah; the Three Witnesses; loss of the 116 pages of the Book of Mormon and the substitution of the small plates of Nephi; the 1830 edition; the history of the Book of Mormon, including the abridgment work of Mormon; a synopsis of Nephite history, which is divided into 3 epochs; the history of the Jaredites. [L.D.]

R.072 Reynolds, George. "Internal Evidences of the Book of Mormon." *Juvenile Instructor* 17 (15 August 1882): 251-52. Cites historical consistency, absence of anachronisms, purity of doctrines, harmony with Bible and Indian traditions, prophecies of the Book of Mormon that have been fulfilled, and scientific truths that accord with the Book of Mormon. Refutes criticisms and polemical arguments. [A.C.W.]

R.073 Reynolds, George. "Internal Evidences of the Book of Mormon: Showing the Absurdity of the 'Spaulding Story.'" *Juvenile Instructor* 17 (1 August 1882): 235-38. Also in *MS* 44 (August 1882): 539-41, 548-51. Refutes the Spaulding manuscript as a basis for the creation of the Book of Mormon, pointing out wide differences between the two, including background, dates, characters, and content. Argues that if Joseph Smith were "too illiterate" to write the Book of Mormon, he was equally as incapable of changing the Spaulding manuscript into the Book of Mormon. [A.C.W.]

R.074 Reynolds, George. "The Lamanites (A Book of Mormon Sketch)." *MS* 42 (June-July 1880): 385-88, 401-4, 417-20, 433-36, 449-52, 465-67. Sketches out the character of the Lamanites. Also writes concerning Sariah, Lehi's wife. [B.D.]

R.075 Reynolds, George. "The Land of the Nephites." *Juvenile Instructor* 15-16 (15 November; 1, 15 December 1880; 1, 15 January; 1 February 1881): 261, 274-75, 286, 7-8, 22-

23, 26-27. A series of essays on Book of Mormon geography. To the earlier Nephites "the whole of North America was known as the land of Mulek, and South America as the land of Lehi." From the period of Mosiah until Christ South America was "divided into two grand divisions": Zarahemla and the land of Nephi. [D.M.]

R.076 Reynolds, George. "Language of the Nephites." *Juvenile Instructor* 15 (15 August 1880): 191-92. Compares two views concerning the language of the Nephites: (1) people wrote and spoke Egyptian; or (2) they wrote Hebrew words in Egyptian characters. Sees Hebrew roots in the following Book of Mormon words: Ziff, Rameumpton, Sheum, Gazelem, and Rabbanah. [D.M.]

R.077 Reynolds, George. "The Language of the Record." *Contributor* 17 (February 1896): 231–38. A listing of numerous scrolls, inscriptions, and tablets purportedly found on the American continent with Hebrew or Egyptian characters upon them, and a comparison between American Indian languages and Hebrew with similarities noted. All these are proposed as evidence of the Hebrew ancestry of American Indians and the truthfulness of the Book of Mormon record. [S.H.]

R.078 Reynolds, George. "The Laws of the Nephites." *Juvenile Instructor* 15 (1, 15 January, 1, 15 February, 1 March 1880): 5, 22-23, 27-28, 46-47, 59. Discusses the Nephite political system under the monarchy and judges. Also considers legal matters under the judges, such as procedures for being heard as the "voice of the people," various sanctions for crime, and treatment of prisoners of war. [D.M.]

R.079 Reynolds, George. "Lesser Lights of the Book of Mormon." *Contributor* 1 (April 1880): 149-51. Also in *MS* 81 (19 June 1919): 388-90. Enos rose to prominent leadership through his humility, faith, and concern for others. This is evidenced by his prayer while hunting in the forest. [J.W.M.]

R.080 Reynolds, George. "Lesser Lights of the Book of Mormon: Antipus and Muloki." *MS* 81 (31 July 1919): 481-84. A description of the life and activities of two lesser-known characters of the Book of Mormon, Antipus and Muloki. Antipus was a Nephite military leader until about 62 B.C. and Muloki was a fellow missionary of the four sons of Mosiah. [B.D.]

R.081 Reynolds, George. "Lesser Lights of the Book of Mormon: Jarom and Zoram." *MS* 81 (26 June 1919): 411-14. Reynolds describes the Nephite people of Jarom's time. Zoram was the commander of the Nephite armies around 81 B.C. He led the Nephites to free Nephite prisoners. [B.D.]

R.082 Reynolds, George. "Lesser Lights of the Book of Mormon: Samuel, the Lamanite." *MS* 81 (24 July 1919): 467-70. A synopsis of Samuel the Lamanite including his prophecies and the condition of unrighteousness among the Nephites. [B.D.]

R.083 Reynolds, George. "Lesser Lights of the Book of Mormon: Teancum." *MS* 81 (14 August 1919): 522-26. A description of the military leadership and exploits of Teancum. Teancum killed Morianton, Amalickiah, and Ammoron with his own hands. [B.D.]

R.084 Reynolds, George. "Lessons from the Life of Nephi." *Juvenile Instructor* 26 (15 April–1 October 1891): 233-35, 282-84, 297-99, 348-51, 373-76, 406-9, 437-40, 475-77, 503-4, 536-38, 574-77, 586-87. A narrative of Nephi's life and lessons that may be learned from the life of Nephi. At times it is better to suffer wrongs than to demand one's rights, and the purposes of God will not be thwarted. [J.W.M.]

R.085 Reynolds, George. "The Moneys of the Nephites." *Juvenile Instructor* 15 (1 November 1880): 249-50. Lays out the monetary measurement of the Nephites as codified by Mosiah. The coins are named after people or places. Barley seems to have been the standard of measurement, just as was the case from the races from which the English people sprang. [D.M.]

R.086 Reynolds, George. *The Myth of the "Manuscript Found" or the Absurdities of the "Spaulding Story."* Salt Lake City: Juvenile Instructor Office, 1883. Sets forth the absurdities that are connected with the Spaulding manuscript. "The upholders of [the myth of the manuscript found] are not only at variance with each other, but that all their assertions are inconsistent with the well-known facts associated with its discovery." [L.D.]

R.087 Reynolds, George. "Nephite Proper Names." *Juvenile Instructor* 15 (15 September 1880): 207-8. Lists Book of Mormon proper names that may or may not be found in the Bible, including Sariah, Nephi, Melek (or Mulek), Gershon, and Isabel. Looks for Hebrew or Egyptian roots. [D.M.]

R.088 Reynolds, George. "The Nephites under the Judges." *Contributor* 2 (February–May): 139-42, 171-74, 205-8, 235-38. Four-part series. For 120 years following the death of King Mosiah, the Nephites were under the rule of the Judges. Their rule was not always peaceful nor their government stable. There were internal as well as external enemies. Priestcrafts and corruption were introduced by Nehor, Amlici, Korihor, and others. The decline in Nephite morality led to the existence of the Gadianton robbers. Samuel the Lamanite preached repentance but few received his words. [J.W.M.]

R.089 Reynolds, George. "Objections to the Book of Mormon." *Contributor* 3-4 (December 1881–February 1882, October 1882): 81-83, 105-8, 134-37, 4-6. Discusses arguments against the Book of Mormon—objections are based on falsehoods, dishonesty, and insincerity. [L.D.]

R.090 Reynolds, George. "The Originator of the 'Spaulding Story.'" *MS* 44 (23 October 1882): 676-79. A history of the Spaulding manuscript that deals with the major characters of the story—Solomon Spaulding, P. Hurlburt, Mrs. Davidson, and E. D. Howe. [B.D.]

R.091 Reynolds, George. "Personal Appearance of the Nephites." *Juvenile Instructor* 15 (15 May 1880): 110-11. Describes the personal appearance of the Nephites as being "white and delightsome people," perhaps "well proportioned, ruddy of countenance, auburn hair and light eyed." [D.M.]

R.092 Reynolds, George. "The Repentant Lawyer." *MS* 42 (January 1880): 1-3. Zeezrom was the leading lawyer in the city of Ammonihah who sought every opportunity to win a case, especially against the servants of God. However, he soon recognized his guilt and wished to repent. [B.D.]

R.093 Reynolds, George. "Science and Literature Among the Nephites." *Juvenile Instructor* 15 (1 May 1880): 105-6. The Nephite civilization began with highly intelligent and learned leaders who were well acquainted with geography and astronomy. They had access to unpolluted scriptures, including the otherwise unknown writings of Zenos, Zenock, Neum, and Ezias. They may have been familiar with the books of Abraham and Joseph. [D.M.]

R.094 Reynolds, George. "Shiz—The Headless." *IE* 3 (June 1900): 588-89. Discusses ridicule given to the Book of Mormon concerning the death of Shiz and Coriantumr's race for the rulership of the Jaredite nation. [L.D.]

R.095 Reynolds, George. "The Skeleton in Armor." *MS* 40 (25 November 1878): 737-40. Reynolds quotes an article in the *American Magazine* of 1837 that describes the excavation of a skeleton in armor and having arrows with brass arrowheads. Reynolds discusses the possibility that this was a Jaredite, Nephite, or Lamanite and concludes that it was probably a Jaredite. [B.D.]

R.096 Reynolds, George. *Story of the Book of Mormon*. Salt Lake City: J. H. Parry, 1888. Retells the entire story of the Book of Mormon. Includes illustrations. [A.T.]

R.097 Reynolds, George. "Testimony to the Book of Mormon." *MS* 49 (14 February 1887): 104-7. Reynolds writes of David Whitmer's continued testimony of the Book of Mormon. The Spaulding theory is definitely false and the Book of Mormon is from God. The only witnesses to the authenticity of the Book of Mormon are the Three Witnesses and the Eight Witnesses. [B.D.]

R.098 Reynolds, George. "Three Prophets in Three Distant Ages Born." *Juvenile Instructor* 14 (15 October 1879): 238-39. The biblical prophets Joseph and Samuel and Book of Mormon prophet Nephi are noteworthy examples to the youth of the Church. Discusses Nephi's love of Isaiah's writings and compares the Book of

Mormon version of Isaiah with the biblical. [A.C.W.]

R.099 Reynolds, George. "Time Occupied in Translating the Book of Mormon." *Juvenile Instructor* 17 (15 October 1882): 315-17. Examines the sequence of events during the translation period of the Book of Mormon and concludes that the work must have happened as Joseph Smith claimed. The time it took to translate the book was relatively short because of divine aid and the use of Urim and Thummim. [A.C.W.]

R.100 Reynolds, George. "Time Occupied in Translating the Book of Mormon." *MS* 44 (December 1882): 791, 798-99. An analysis of how long it took to translate the Book of Mormon and how many pages were completed per day. From April 7 to May 15 Joseph Smith translated 503 pages and from May 15th to June 11th he translated 120 pages. [B.D.]

R.101 Reynolds, George. "The Zoramites." *Juvenile Instructor* 14 (1 December 1879): 272-73. Retells the story of the Zoramites, explaining their heresies, their persecution of poor people, and the resulting war. [A.C.W.]

R.102 Reynolds, George, and Janne M. Sjodahl. *Book of Mormon Geography: The Lands of the Nephites and the Jaredites.* Salt Lake City: Deseret Book, 1957. It is difficult to identify the geography of the Book of Mormon, as there is little effort made by the writers to describe physical features. The speculation of Reynolds and Sjodahl follow in five parts, considering all of the geographical entries of the Book of Mormon. Each city is considered according to the description contained within the Book of Mormon. [J.W.M.]

R.103 Reynolds, George, and Janne M. Sjodahl. *Commentary on the Book of Mormon.* 7 vols. Salt Lake City: Deseret Book, 1955, [R]1960. This multivolume work contains verse-by-verse commentary on the Book of Mormon. The text of the Book of Mormon is included. Also includes discussions of the history and missions of major personalities of the book, treatment of word meanings and usages including comparisons with biblical terms, comments and testimonies of Church leaders, discussion of doctrine, and each volume outlines the chronology of the scriptures included in its scope. [L.D.]

R.104 Reynolds, Noel B. "Book of Mormon, Government and Legal History in The." In *Encyclopedia of Mormonism*, edited by Daniel H. Ludlow, 1:160-62. 5 vols. New York: Macmillan, 1992. The three main Book of Mormon groups—Nephite, Lamanite, and Jaredite—were ruled at times by hereditary kings. The Nephites changed to a reign of judges after a period of about 400 years. Nephites based their laws on the Mosiac code. Continual warfare existed between Nephites and Lamanites except from A.D. 33 to A.D. 250 when both lived harmoniously under an ecclesiastical system without judges or kings. [N.K.Y.]

R.105 Reynolds, Noel B. "The Brass Plates Version of Genesis." In *By Study and Also by Faith*, edited by John M. Lundquist and Stephen D. Ricks, 2:136-73. Salt Lake City: Deseret Book and FARMS, 1990. A textual analysis methodology is presented for measuring dependence and independence of separate texts. This methodology is used to show that the Book of Mormon passages of Genesis, originating from the brass plates, are much more like the version of Genesis in the Pearl of Great Price, and are independent from the Genesis text in the Book of Mormon. The common phrases, as verified by computer searching, are put into the model, weighted, and scored. [A.A.]

R.106 Reynolds, Noel B. "The Gospel as Taught by Nephite Prophets." In *Reexploring the Book of Mormon*, edited by John W. Welch, 257-59. Salt Lake City: Deseret Book and FARMS, 1992. Examines a six-point formula that defines the "gospel" and "doctrine" of Jesus Christ. The formula is outlined in 2 Nephi 31:2-32, 3 Nephi 11:23-39, and 3 Nephi 27:13-21. [E.G.]

R.107 Reynolds, Noel B. "The Gospel of Jesus Christ as Taught by the Nephite Prophets." *BYU Studies* 31 (Summer 1991): 31-50. The concept of the gospel in the Book of Mormon comprises a "six-point formula" consisting of the following: repentance, baptism, the Holy Ghost, faith, endurance to the end, and eternal life. Three core texts provide a definition of the gospel (2 Nephi 31, 3 Nephi 11:31-41, and 3 Nephi 27:13-21) and other passages aid the discussion, utilizing the classical rhetorical device of merismus. [D.M.]

R.108 Reynolds, Noel B. "How to 'Come Unto Christ.'" *Ensign* (22 September 1992): 7-13. The meaning of the gospel, or the manner in which individuals come unto Christ, is set forth in the Book of Mormon (2 Nephi 31, 3 Nephi 11, and 3 Nephi 27). The gospel of Christ includes belief, repentance, baptism, Holy Ghost, and enduring to the end, with the atonement of Jesus set at its center. [A.C.W.]

R.109 Reynolds, Noel B. "Nephi$_1$." In *Encyclopedia of Mormonism*, edited by Daniel H. Ludlow, 3:1003-5. 5 vols. New York: Macmillan, 1992. An overview of Nephi's major accomplishments, and a general description of his history, visions, record keeping, and literacy. [A.T.]

R.110 Reynolds, Noel B. "Nephi's Outline." *BYU Studies* 20 (Winter 1980): 131-49. Also in *Book of Mormon Authorship: New Light on Ancient Origins*, edited by Noel B. Reynolds, 53-74. Provo, UT: Brigham Young University Religious Studies Center, 1982. References to the brass plates indicate that they contain information not found in the Bible. Examines indirect textual evidence in the Book of Mormon to prove other "distinctive contents of the plates of brass." 1 Nephi consists of two accounts, an abridgment of Lehi's writings and Nephi's own record. Eight tables reveal the parallel structure of these two records. [E.G.]

R.111 Reynolds, Noel B. "Nephi's Political Testament." In *Rediscovering the Book of Mormon*, edited by John L. Sorenson and Melvin J. Thorne, 220-29. Salt Lake City: Deseret Book and FARMS, 1991. The struggle over the right to power and rule created centuries of strife and war in the Book of Mormon. The book was written to show that those who accepted the teachings of Christ accepted Nephi as the legitimate ruler. The Lamanites contended that the eldest son/legitimate ruler had been usurped. This explains the Lamanite desire to dominate. [J.W.M.]

R.112 Reynolds, Noel B. "Nephite Uses and Interpretations of Zenos." In *The Allegory of the Olive Tree: The Olive, the Bible, and Jacob 5*, edited by Stephen D. Ricks and John W. Welch, 21-49. Salt Lake City: Deseret Book and FARMS, 1994. An examination of the language and phraseology used by Book of Mormon prophets—Lehi, Nephi, Jacob, Alma, Samuel, Mormon, and Moroni—shows the influence that the earlier prophet Zenos had upon their writings. Though centuries later the influence is faint, Benjamin's teachings reflect the teachings of Zenos. [J.W.M.]

R.113 Reynolds, Noel B. "The Political Dimension in Nephi's Small Plates." *BYU Studies* 27 (Fall 1987): 15-37. Explains Nephi's political reasons for writing the small plates. Nephi's "small plates systematically defend the Nephite tradition concerning origins and refute the competing account advanced by the Lamanites. Thus, the writings of Nephi can be read in part as a political tract or 'lineage history,' written to document the legitimacy of Nephi's rule and religious teachings." [B.D.]

R.114 Reynolds, Noel B., ed. *Book of Mormon Authorship: New Light on Ancient Origins*. Provo, UT: Brigham Young University Religious Studies Center, 1982. A collection of articles by various authors previously published in *BYU Studies* and in the *Ensign*. The object of this collection is to rigorously test the claims of antiquity of the Book of Mormon. [J.W.M.]

R.115 Rice, Moyle Q. "The Language and Style of the Book of Mormon." M.A. thesis, University of Nebraska, 1937. A literary analysis of the Book of Mormon. The author compares its language and style with the Bible attempting to determine what influence the Bible may have had on the Book of Mormon. [M.R.]

R.116 Rich, Ben E., comp. *Scrapbook of Mormon Literature*. 2 vols. Chicago: Henry C. Etten, 1912. Two-volume compilation includes tracts and articles of varying authorship. Both volumes contain early missionary tracts, instructions to missionaries as to their conduct in the mission field, doctrinal statements from Joseph Smith and other Church leaders, and statements about Mormonism from people both in and out of the Church. Includes a list of prophecies made by Joseph Smith. Includes an analysis of the Book of Mormon and discusses doctrines taught within the book. [L.M.]

R.117 Rich, Benjamin Leroy. *The Book of Mormon: a lecture given by invitation April 29, 1900 before the Ohio Liberal Society, Cincinnati, Ohio.* N.p.: n.p., 1900. Defends the Book of Mormon by giving an overview of its story as a sacred history of the early inhabitants of America and a historical account of the coming forth of the book. Tells the history of the Spaulding theory, and discusses Martin Harris's visit to Professor Anthon as a fulfillment of Isaiah 29. [J.W.M]

R.118 Rich, Edward S. *The Word of God is Truth, a Discussion of the Scriptures.* N.p., 1967. The Book of Mormon confirms the biblical account, and Rich exhorts the reader to continuously study the infallible word of God. He cites prophecies concerning the coming forth of the Book of Mormon, and discusses the words of ancient and modern prophets concerning the nature of God and Christ, the Savior's role on earth and in the eternities, and latter-day events on earth. [L.M.]

R.119 Rich, John W., comp. *The Book of Mormon on Trial, Based on the 'Trial of the Stick of Joseph' by Jack West.* Sacramento: Fritz'n Rich, 1963. Based on Jack West's "Trial of the Stick of Joseph," John Rich and illustrator Fritz Alseth use caricature illustrations to portray a mock trial of the Book of Mormon. With biblical references, archaeological evidences, and the testimonies of the Three and Eight Witnesses, the Book of Mormon is proved authentic. [A.C.W.]

R.120 Rich, Russell R. "The Dogberry Papers and the Book of Mormon." *BYU Studies* 10 (Spring 1970): 315-20. Speaks of the Dogberry Papers, a circulating paper written by Esquire Cole. The first articles concerning Joseph Smith and the Book of Mormon were very negative. Cole changed his views and started printing chapters of the Book of Mormon in his paper. When Cole discontinued printing the chapters and began to speak evil of Joseph, the popularity of the paper decreased. [G.A.]

R.121 Rich, Russell R. "Where were the Moroni Visits?" *BYU Studies* 10 (Spring 1970): 255-58. Attempts to determine the location of Moroni's visits to Joseph Smith. [G.A.]

R.122 Rich, Wendell O. *A Chronology of the Book of Mormon.* Logan: n.p., 1949. A chart that shows the chronology of events that take place in the Book of Mormon. It portrays the Nephites, Lamanites, and Mulekites on a timeline extending from 600 B.C. to A.D. 450, and shows corresponding world events in Greece, Rome, and Babylon. [A.C.W.]

R.123 Richards, A. Z., Jr. "The Star in the Western Sky." *MS* 98 (17 December 1936): 810-12. Many prophesied of the star that would appear at the Savior's birth, including Samuel the Lamanite, whose prophecy was quite detailed. [J.W.M.]

R.124 Richards, F. D. "Secret Combinations." *MS* 30 (30 May 1868): 344-48. The author points out the existence of secret organizations in the United States: the Ku Klux Klan, the Loyal League, the Grand Army of the Republic and Fenianism. The Book of Mormon shows how secret societies brought destruction. Richards quotes all of Ether 8:13-26 and Helaman 6:22-30, and urges the Saints to "keep from all secret combinations and political associations." [B.D.]

R.125 Richards, Franklin D. *Bibliography of Utah: Book of Mormon.* N.p., July 1884. In answer to questions by historian Herbert Bancroft, Richards gave a brief overview of the Book of Mormon story and how it came forth. This account contains many quotes concerning the Book of Mormon from Joseph Smith, Orson Pratt, and others. [J.W.M.]

R.126 Richards, Franklin D. "The Book of Mormon." N.p., 1884. Recounts the story of the Book of Mormon, beginning with the Jaredites departure at the time of the Tower of Babel. Includes a list of Book of Mormon translations, listing languages, dates, and the person who was in charge of the translation and publication. If the doctrinal, historical, and prophetic parts of the Book of Mormon are compared with other sources, it will be discovered there is much to substantiate its authenticity. [J.W.M.]

R.127 Richards, Franklin D. "Holding Fast To The Iron Rod." In *Collected Discourses Delivered By President Wilford Woodruff, His Two Counselors, the 12 Apostles, and Others, (1886-1889)*, edited by Brian H. Stuy, 1:103-12. Sandy, UT: B. H. S. Publishing 1987. All members of the Church need to hold to the iron rod (1 Nephi 8), which is the word of God. By staying on the straight and narrow path one can obtain eternal life and supernal joy. [J.W.M.]

R.128 Richards, Franklin D. "The Lamanites." *MS* 16 (21 October 1854): 657-61. Writes that the wild imaginations of men have blinded them to the pure and simple truth. They have imagined all sorts of theories of the Indians' descent yet they do not believe the Book of Mormon, which tells the truth plainly. The LDS policy toward the Indians is to try to educate, elevate, and convert the Indians. He quotes from Mormon 5:19-20 that the gentiles will scatter the Lamanites after which the Lord will remember the covenant he has made with Abraham and all the house of Israel. [B.D.]

R.129 Richards, Franklin D. "Origin of American Aborigines." *Contributor* 17 (May 1896): 425-28. Also in *MS* 58 (22 October 1896): 683-87. Also published as "Origin of the American Aborigines." *Liahona* 14/20 (1916-1917): 305-8; and "Ephraim and Manasseh In America." *The Utah Genealogical and Historical Magazine* 23 (April 1932): 66-71. The prophet Joseph Smith taught in the Nauvoo House concerning the stick of Joseph, Ephraim, and Manasseh. Lehi was of the family of Manasseh and Ishmael and his family were of the house of Ephraim. The one hundred sixteen lost pages of the Book of Mormon contained a clear account of Ishmael's ancestry. That is the reason, the prophet said, that no mention of Ishmael's genealogy is in the Book of Mormon. Richards discusses the marriage relationships and union of the families. Lehi's sons married Ishmael's daughters thus combining the two tribes. Richards writes that this fulfills the prophecy in Genesis 48:20 that Ephraim and Manasseh together should become a multitude of nations. [J.W.M.]

R.130 Richards Franklin D. "Revelation and Priesthood." *Deseret Weekly* 52 (4 January 1896): 65-67. Also in *Collected Discourses* 4:367-75. People have a hard time accepting the Book of Mormon because of the tradition that teaches that the heavens are sealed. The Book of Mormon and the Bible fulfill the prophecy in Ezekiel 37. "The Book of Mormon is the Bible of the American continent." [D.M.]

R.131 Richards, Franklin D., and James A. Little. "Book of Mormon Chronology." In Richards' and Little's *A Compendium of the Doctrines of the Gospel*, 289-301. Salt Lake City: Deseret News Press, 1882. A list of Book of Mormon events with their attendant dates in chronological order. [J.W.M.]

R.132 Richards, Franklin D., and James E. Little. "Book of Mormon—Evidences of Its Divine Authenticity." In *A Compendium of the Doctrines of the Gospel*, 95-101. Salt Lake City: Deseret News Co., 1882. The Book of Mormon fulfills the prophecy of Enoch, King David, Isaiah, Ezekiel, and Joseph who was sold into Egypt (see 2 Nephi 3). Orson Pratt said that there is nothing in all of the ancient ruins that conflict with the Book of Mormon. There is no contradiction in the book itself in history, prophecy, or doctrine, nor is there any conflict with the Bible. Many of the Book of Mormon's prophecies have been fulfilled. [J.W.M.]

R.133 Richards, George F. Untitled talk. *CR* (April 1912): 37-41. Jesus Christ is the noblest son of God and his redemptive mission was performed in behalf of all men. In similitude of the Savior we esteem Joseph Smith as one of noblest of the sons of God. His mission to bring forth the Book of Mormon and to restore truth to the earth is one of greatest importance to all the world. The Book of Mormon is one of the greatest evidences that Joseph Smith was a prophet of God. [J.W.M.]

R.134 Richards, George F. Untitled talk. *CR* (April 1927): 88-92. It is most important to teach all men the gospel and to give them the opportunity to have the saving ordinances. Men of the world need a tutor to understand the scriptures. Witnesses of the Book of Mormon testify that an angel laid the plates before them and a voice from heaven declared that the plates had been translated by the gift and power of God. [J.W.M.]

R.135 Richards, Joel. "A Book to Bring the World to Christ." *Instructor* 103 (October 1968): 412-13, 418. Speaks of the distribution of the Book of Mormon, and gives testimonial accounts of missionaries and converts who have felt the power of the Book of Mormon. Missionaries who use the Book of Mormon in their proselytizing efforts have great success. [G.A.]

R.136 Richards, LeGrand. "... Always Be a Missionary." *IE* 61 (December 1958): 960-64. As a part of the restoration of the gospel, the Book of Mormon became the companion volume of the Bible. No one who reads the Bible sincerely can deny that a volume of scripture is needed to record the fulfillment of the promises made to Joseph. [J.W.M.]

R.137 Richards, LeGrand. "America, A Land of Promise." In *BYUSY* (16 April 1957). Provo, UT: BYU Press. America, North and South, is a land which is choice above all others. The Book of Mormon enumerates the promises and responsibilities given to those who possess them. [J.W.M.]

R.138 Richards, LeGrand. "The Book of Mormon." *IE* 70 (June 1967): 38-42. Book of Mormon scriptures clarify perplexing biblical passages such as John 10:16, Ezekiel 38:18-19, and Isaiah 29:1-2. [B.W.J.]

R.139 Richards, LeGrand. "The Book of Mormon, An Aid to Testimony." *IE* 49 (November 1946): 709, 748, 750. There is "no motivating power in this world" comparable to the testimony of truth concerning Jesus Christ and there is no greater testimony of Jesus Christ than that of the Book of Mormon. [J.W.M.]

R.140 Richards, LeGrand. "The Book of Mormon Fulfills Bible Prophecies." In Richards's *A Marvelous Work and a Wonder*, 55-69. Salt Lake City: Deseret Book, 1950, [R] 1974. The Bible contains many prophecies that confirm the need for the Book of Mormon. [J.W.M.]

R.141 Richards, LeGrand. "Book of Mormon Fulfills Prophecy." *CR* (April 1976): 121-24. Isaiah's writings are of great importance for this time; for instance, Isaiah 29 is a powerful witness for the restoration and Book of Mormon—truly a "familiar spirit," and a "marvelous work and a wonder." [R.C.D.]

R.142 Richards, LeGrand. "The Book of Mormon Is Scripture." In *LDS Area General Conference Report, Munich #1*. Salt Lake City: Deseret Book, 1973. The Church has the most important message that the modern world has to hear: a man lived on this earth, died, and then has returned with a message from God. Moroni, an ancient American prophet, has returned with the record of his people. This record is a message from God. [J.W.M.]

R.143 Richards, LeGrand. "Book of Mormon Revelation Clarifies Scriptures." *CR* (April 1967): 18-23. "The Book of Mormon has made possible the proper interpretation and understanding of many of the holy scriptures of the Bible that no theologian could properly understand or explain until the Book of Mormon came forth." Elder Richards gave several examples: "other sheep," Joseph's fruitful bough, Ezekiel's two sticks, Isaiah 29, the mountain of the Lord's house, and the New Jerusalem. [R.C.D.]

R.144 Richards, LeGrand. "The Coming Forth of the Book of Mormon." In Richards's *A Marvelous Work and a Wonder*, 41-54. Salt Lake City: Deseret Book, 1950, 1974. Reviews the story of the coming forth of the Book of Mormon, tells how Professor Anthon fulfilled Isaiah's prophecy (Isaiah 29:11), discusses Moroni's prophecy concerning Joseph Smith, the testimony of the Three Witnesses, the Lord's promise in Moroni 10:4-5, and teaches that the Book of Mormon is a new witness for Christ. [A.C.W.]

R.145 Richards, LeGrand. "Evidences of the Divinity of the Book of Mormon." In Richards's *A

Marvelous Work and a Wonder, 71-82. Salt Lake City: Deseret Book, 1950, 1969, 1974. Discusses the testimonies of the Three and Eight Witnesses to the Book of Mormon. Using the scriptures as a guide Richards discusses the Urim and Thummim, the origin of the Indians, Nephi's testimony and the promised witness to the truthfulness of the book for seekers of the truth. [L.D.]

R.146 Richards, LeGrand. "God Moves in a Mysterious Way." *IE* 73 (December 1970): 69-71. Speaks concerning God and Christ, and teaches that Old Testament prophets foretold of the coming forth of the Book of Mormon. [J.W.M.]

R.147 Richards, LeGrand. "Isaiah and Book of Mormon Prophecies." *CR* (October 1966): 41-44. The Book of Mormon teaches that the writings of Isaiah are very important for those of the present era. Isaiah saw this day in detail. He saw the Restoration, Joseph Smith, the Book of Mormon, Salt Lake City, and many other things. [R.C.D.]

R.148 Richards, LeGrand. "The Lamanites, A People of Promise." In *BYUSY* (24 February 1970). Provo, UT: BYU Press. The promises of the Book of Mormon found in Alma and 2 Nephi are being fulfilled and the Lamanites are bearing witness of its truthfulness. [J.W.M.]

R.149 Richards, LeGrand. "A Marvelous Work." *IE* 58 (June 1955): 440-46. Describes the importance of the Book of Mormon in the Restoration, missionary work, and daily life. Author gives his witness to the truthfulness and validity of the book. [E.G.]

R.150 Richards, LeGrand. "The Most Important Message." *IE* 66 (June 1963): 518-21. The Book of Mormon is tangible evidence that the angel Moroni came to visit the earth with the greatest message possible: that Jesus is the Christ. The author states that some prophecies and statements found in the Bible can only be understood by the added information found in the Book of Mormon. [J.W.M.]

R.151 Richards, LeGrand. "A New Witness for Christ." Salt Lake City: n.p., 1957. A tract that introduces the Book of Mormon by presenting biblical scriptures that speak of the Book of Mormon. [D.W.P.]

R.152 Richards, Le Grand. "Ours . . . The Greatest Message." *IE* 62 (June 1959): 438-39. The Book of Mormon is the most tangible evidence that the message and work of Joseph Smith is true; it is a witness of Jesus Christ. The author uses stories and letters of members and non-members to verify his message that people all over the world recognize the value of the Book of Mormon. [J.W.M.]

R.153 Richards, LeGrand. "The Stick of Joseph; Joseph's Message to Judah." In Richards's *Israel! Do You Know?*, 25-72. Salt Lake City: Deseret Book, 1954, 1976. Uses the biblical prophecy recorded in Ezekiel 37 to determine that the Book of Mormon represents the stick of Joseph. The Book of Mormon shows Judah that the law of Moses has been fulfilled and that Jesus Christ is God. [A.C.W.]

R.154 Richards, LeGrand. Untitled talk. *CR* (April 1937): 62-65. The Book of Mormon is the most tangible evidence of the divine mission of the prophet Joseph Smith and a testimony of it is extremely important. It explains the origin of the early civilizations of America. [B.D.]

R.155 Richards, LeGrand. Untitled talk. *CR* (September, October 1949): 49-54. A testimony of the Book of Mormon. Mentions that there were horses in ancient America as claimed by the Book of Mormon and that its prophecies are being fulfilled. [B.D.]

R.156 Richards, LeGrand. Untitled talk. *CR* (April 1963): 115-19. A national commentator said the most important message would be discovered by a man who lived on the earth and who had died and returned with a message from God. Moroni has done just that and the tangible evidence of the visit is the Book of Mormon. It clarifies prophecies in the Bible that have puzzled men for centuries. [J.W.M.]

R.157 Richards, LeGrand. Untitled talk. In *Official Report of the First Area General Conference for Germany, Austria, Holland, Italy, Switzerland, France, Belgium and Spain*, August 1973, 34-37. Salt Lake City: Church of Jesus Christ of Latter-day Saints, 1973. Recalls the story of a news broadcaster who declared the message of greatest importance would be that a man that had lived on this earth and died had come back to give a message from God. The Church of Jesus Christ of Latter-day Saints is unique in that it was organized because of just such a message brought by Moroni. It is the companion volume to the Bible. [J.W.M.]

R.158 Richards, Samuel W. "The Aztec City in Central America—The Lost Tribes." *MS* 14 (20 November 1852): 614-16. Presents a reprint of an article from the *Boston U.S. Weekly Journal* that tells of an ancient Aztec city whose inhabitants are believed to be part of the lost ten tribes. Their record is found in a book of parchment bound by brazen clasps and containing curious heiroglyphics. Richards predicts that evidence in support of the Book of Mormon will overwhelm the skepticism regarding its origins. [J.W.M.]

R.159 Richards, Samuel W. "Discovery of Ruined Cities in California." *MS* 15 (17 December 1853): 817-20. Writes concerning an article from the *San Francisco Herald* that describes ruined cities of California. "The wonderful and magnificent ruins . . . continue to puzzle and astonish the learning and wisdom of the great men of the nineteenth century, while every fresh discovery is an increasing evidence in favor of the Book of Mormon." [D.M.]

R.160 Richardson, Ebbie L. V. "David Whitmer, a Witness to the Divine Authenticity of the Book of Mormon." M.A. thesis, Brigham Young University, 1952. A thesis that examines the life of David Whitmer, his testimony of the divinity of the Book of Mormon, and his involvement with the Mormons. As one of the witnesses who saw an angel and the gold plates, Whitmer's testimony of the Book of Mormon is valuable. [A.C.W.]

R.161 Ricks, Eldin. *Book of Mormon Commentary.* Volume 1. Salt Lake City: Deseret News, 1951. Sets forth biblical prophecies that relate to the Book of Mormon, tells the historical facts surrounding the coming forth of the Book of Mormon, and provides commentary on 1 Nephi. [A.C.W.]

R.162 Ricks, Eldin. *Book of Mormon Study Guide.* Salt Lake City: Deseret News Press, 1955. Ricks's instructional aid to Book of Mormon study consists of a series of detailed questions that follow the sequential order of the text of the Book of Mormon. The study guide is in a workbook format with space provided to answer the questions and is designed to accompany the reading of the scriptural text. [A.C.W.]

R.163 Ricks, Eldin. "Book of Mormon: Title Page from the Book of Mormon." In *The Encyclopedia of Mormonism*, edited by Daniel H. Ludlow, 1:144. 5 vols. New York: Macmillan, 1992. A brief discussion of the title page of the Book of Mormon. The title page was used as the description of the Book of Mormon for the federal copyright application. [A.T.]

R.164 Ricks, Eldin. *The Book of Mormon: Wide Margin Edition.* Provo, UT: Ricks, 1987. A loose-leaf size edition of the Book of Mormon text with wide, lined margins designed for personal study notes. [J.W.M.]

R.165 Ricks, Eldin. *The Case of the Book of Mormon Witnesses.* Salt Lake City: Olympus, 1963. A supplement to Ricks's *Book of Mormon Study Guide* that consists of testimonies by numerous witnesses to the authenticity and veracity of the Book of Mormon. Includes a background history of Joseph Smith and the gold plates and testimonies of the Three Witnesses, the Eight Witnesses, Lucy Mack Smith, Brigham Young, and others. [A.C.W.]

R.166 Ricks, Eldin. *Combination Reference: A Simple and Orderly Arrangement of Selected References to the Standard Works of the Church of Jesus Christ of Latter-day Saints.* Salt Lake City: Deseret Book, 1943, 1969. An arrangement of scriptural references to the standard works of the Church organized in dictionary format by subject. Subjects include angels, antiquity of the gospel, apostasy, baptism, Bible, confirmation, and death. [L.D.]

R.167 Ricks, Eldin. "The Formation of the Book of Mormon Plates." *IE* 63 (1960): 796-97, 852-54. Explains the different writings that comprise the plates given to Joseph Smith. They include: (1) Mormon's abridgment, (2) the small plates, (3) the plates (abridgment) of Mormon, and (4) the sealed plates. [R.C.D.]

R.168 Ricks, Eldin. "Moroni, Visitations of." In *Encyclopedia of Mormonism*, edited by Daniel H. Ludlow, 954-55. 5 vols. New York: Macmillan, 1992. Discusses the visitations of Moroni to Joseph Smith, the Three Witnesses, Mary Whitmer, W. W. Phelps, Heber C. Kimball, John Taylor, and Oliver Granger. [B.D.]

R.169 Ricks, Eldin. "Nephi." In *Know Your Religion: Our Prophets, Old and New*, 2:1-16. Provo, UT: Brigham Young University, 1960. Retells the story of Nephi. [D.M.]

R.170 Ricks, Eldin. "The Plates That Mormon Found and the Manuscript That Joseph Lost." In *The Ninth Annual Sydney B. Sperry Symposium: The Book of Mormon*, 60-82. Provo, UT: BYU Educational System, 24 January 1981. The 116 pages of lost manuscript were translated from the book of Lehi (large plates of Nephi). The small plates of Nephi that replaced them are of great value to "our day." The large plates contained secular history, genealogy, and sacred writings. The small plates covered the time period of Lehi to Mosiah with sacred writings selected for a purpose that Nephi did not know. While abridging the plates Mormon came upon the small plates. He saw their value and included them in his record, adding his own appendage. [J.W.M.]

R.171 Ricks, Eldin. "The Small Plates of Nephi and the Words of Mormon." In *The Book of Mormon: Jacob through Words of Mormon, To Learn with Joy*, edited by Monte S. Nyman and Charles D. Tate Jr., 209-19. Provo, UT: Brigham Young University Religious Studies Center, 1990. Making sense of the "Words of Mormon appendage" requires an understanding of the records that Mormon was abridging. Mormon found the small plates that contained a religious record only, added his own appendage and placed them with his abridgment. Thus, in spite of the loss of the 116 pages, the entire record of the Nephites is available. [J.W.M.]

R.172 Ricks, Eldin. *Story of the Formation of the Book of Mormon Plates, an Analysis of the Sources and Structure of the Sacred Record*. Salt Lake City: Deseret News Press, 1958. Discusses Joseph Smith's reception and translation of the gold plates. Mormon abridged the large plates of Nephi that contained a more secular record of the time from Lehi's exodus to the time of King Benjamin, who then began to write the more spiritual approach. Mormon included the small plates of Nephi with his abridged record. His only addition was a short transition piece that he placed in the record. [J.W.M.]

R.173 Ricks, Eldin. "The Words of Mormon." In *Encyclopedia of Mormonism*, edited by Daniel H. Ludlow, 1:149. 5 vols. New York: Macmillan, 1992. Describes the date and purpose of the book entitled the Words of Mormon. [A.T.]

R.174 Ricks, Joel E. "America's Ancient Inhabitants." *MS* 55 (October 1893): 672-75, 695-98, 711-14. A report of the author's explorations in Salt River Valley, Arizona, wherein he hypothesizes that the inhabitants of Salt River Valley came from Hagoth's voyages to the north country (Alma 63). The peoples had buildings and temples made of cement and probably used metal. [B.D.]

R.175 Ricks, Joel E. "The Book of Mormon a Divine Record: Witnesses Never Denied Their Testimony." *Liahona* 14 (3 April 1917): 631. A note affirming that the witnesses to the Book of Mormon were constantly true to their testimony. [D.M.]

R.176 Ricks, Joel E. "Book of Mormon Geography." *Brigham Young College Bulletin: Society Report* 3 (15 December 1904): 1-19. Believes that Book of Mormon geography is discernible. Identifies the "narrow neck of land" as the Isthmus of Panama and the "River Sidon" as the river Magdalena. Maps included. [J.W.M.]

R.177 Ricks, Joel E. *Helps to the Study of the Book of Mormon*. Independence, MO: Zion's, 1916. This instructional aid intended to increase understanding of the Book of Mormon includes a chronology, maps, photos, an account of how Joseph Smith obtained the gold plates, and a dictionary of proper names found in the Book of Mormon. Ricks also presents an explanation of the Urim and Thummim and uses geography, archaeology, ancient traditions, and biblical prophecies to demonstrate the divinity of the Book of Mormon. [A.C.W.]

R.178 Ricks, Joel E. *The Geography of the Book of Mormon.* Logan: n.p., 1939. The purpose in writing this text is to "emphasize the geographic references in the [Book of Mormon], and to ... identify those locations in the light of modern geography." Concludes that the Book of Mormon events covered both the North and South American continents, basing these ideas on the supposition that Panama is the "narrow neck of land." Several maps are included. [A.C.W.]

R.179 Ricks, Joel E. "The Land of Zarahemla." *Juvenile Instructor* 41 (1, 15 April, 15 November 1906): 193-96, 225-28, 673-77. Identifies an area in Bogata, Columbia as the Land of Zarahemla. Presents photographs and a description of the geography, climate, and vegetation of the area, drawing parallels with passages of the Book of Mormon text. [J.W.M.]

R.180 Ricks, Joel E. "Modern Research and the Book of Mormon." *MS* 72 (28 July 1910): 465-69. Writes of various external evidences of the Book of Mormon that Joseph Smith, according to Ricks, would not have been aware of. Mentions the great ruins that have been discovered in Central and South America, evidence of iron, wool, cement, elephants, and domesticated horses, ox, sheep, and swine. [B.D.]

R.181 Ricks, Joel E. *The Nephites in Story.* Logan: n.p., 1940. A a storybook version of the Nephite history for youth that sequentially covers all of the general Book of Mormon events, with the omission of the Jaredite record. Includes maps, geographical information, and archaeological data and suppositions, which the author incorporates into the story. [A.C.W.]

R.182 Ricks, Joel E. "A Study of Book of Mormon Geography." *Brigham Young College Bulletin* 3 (15 December 1904): 1-19. Suggests that the land northward is North America, the land southward is South America. The narrow neck is the Isthmus of Panama. The Hill Cumorah mentioned in the Book of Mormon is the same as the Hill Ramah of the Jaredites and is where Joseph Smith discovered the plates. Ricks continues to suggest precise locations for almost all cities mentioned in the Book of Mormon. [B.D.]

R.183 Ricks, Joel E. "Urim and Thummim." *IE* 18 (May 1915): 611-15. Gives a definition of the Urim and Thummim and discusses its history using the scriptures as a guide. [L.D.]

R.184 Ricks, Joel E. "Urim and Thummim." *MS* 86 (21 August 1924): 529. Sets forth a description and history of the Urim and Thummim. [A.T.]

R.185 Ricks, Joel E. *Whence Came the Mayas.* Salt Lake City: n.p., 1943. Uses archaeological, geographical, scriptural, and historical information to theorize that the Mayan culture was related to the cultures of the Nephites and Jaredites. Desires to prove that advanced civilizations lived on the American continent before the arrival of Columbus. [A.C.W.]

R.186 Ricks, Stephen D. "Benjamin." In *Encyclopedia of Mormonism*, edited by Daniel H. Ludlow, 1:99-100. 5 vols. New York: Macmillan, 1992. A description of King Benjamin who was also the prophet of his people and was entrusted with the small plates by Amaleki. [B.D.]

R.187 Ricks, Stephen D. "Book of Mormon Studies." In *Encyclopedia of Mormonism*, edited by Daniel H. Ludlow, 1:205-9. 5 vols. New York: Macmillan, 1992. Historical overview of analyses, criticisms, and defenses of the Book of Mormon. Notes in detail those by Alexander Campbell, Orson Pratt, George Reynolds, Janne M. Sjodahl, B. H. Roberts, Francis Kirkham, Hugh W. Nibley, John L. Sorenson. [N.K.Y.]

R.188 Ricks, Stephen D. "The Coronation of Kings." In *Reexploring the Book of Mormon*, edited by John W. Welch, 124-26. Salt Lake City: Deseret Book and FARMS, 1992. Examines Mosiah 1-6 in light of ancient Near Eastern kingship rites, including the location of the sanctuary, investiture with insignia, anointing, receipt of a regal name, and other elements. [N.K.Y.]

R.189 Ricks, Stephen D. "Deuteronomy: A Covenant of Love." *Ensign* 20 (April 1990): 55-59. The entire book of Deuteronomy appears to follow the structure of a covenant ceremony, perhaps written for the passing of the mantle of leadership from Moses to Joshua. The book of Mosiah in the Book of Mormon resembles this process. The elements of covenant making follow a suggested outline: an introduction of the covenant parties, a review of history, individual commandments, blessings and cursings, witness and oaths of acceptance, and the reading of the covenant and the deposit of the text. [J.W.M.]

R.190 Ricks, Stephen D. "Fasting in the Book of Mormon and the Bible." In *The Book of Mormon: The Keystone Scripture*, edited by Paul R. Cheesman, S. Kent Brown, and Charles D. Tate Jr., 127-36. Provo, UT: Brigham Young University Religious Studies Center, 1988. Also published as "Fasting in the Old Testament and in the Book of Mormon." Provo, UT: FARMS, 1988. Explains that fasting, an important LDS practice, was a common religious practice in the ancient worlds of the Bible and the Book of Mormon. Fasting was both an individual and communal event. Some fasts were periodic and institutionalized, such as the fast of the Day of Atonement, and others were spontaneous and were conducted following a death, as a religious exercise, or as petitionary or preparatory measure. Fasts were often accompanied by prayer, anointing, mourning, and the donning of sackcloth and ashes. [A.C.W.]

R.191 Ricks, Stephen D. " 'Holy War' in the Book of Mormon and the Ancient Near East." In *Reexploring the Book of Mormon*, edited by John W. Welch, 202-5. Salt Lake City: Deseret Book and FARMS, 1992. In this paper, Ricks sets forth the ideology of holy war in the Book of Mormon. Wars in the ancient Near East were always waged with approval and direction of the gods or God. Joshua's and Israel's soldiers were to be ritually clean when going into battle. Moroni in his battles used prophetic advice. Helaman's stripling Ammonite warriors were noted for their moral purity. [N.K.Y.]

R.192 Ricks, Stephen D. " 'Holy War': The Sacral Ideology of War in the Book of Mormon and in the Ancient Near East." In *Warfare in the Book of Mormon*, edited by Stephen D. Ricks and William J. Hamblin, 103-17. Salt Lake City: Deseret Book and FARMS, 1990. Ancient Israel had a sacral ideology of war stating God gave them the right to rule and conquer. Violations of ritual purification caused the loss of battles and wars. The Book of Mormon peoples used the Lord's guidance to know when, where, and how to meet their enemies. Apostate cities were to be destroyed and when the Nephites lost their righteous qualities, they were defeated. [N.K.Y.]

R.193 Ricks, Stephen D. "I Have a Question: Many times in prophecy, the present and past tenses are used, even though the prophecy refers to a future event. Can you explain the use of verb tenses in prophecy?" *Ensign* 18 (August 1988): 27-28. Explains that future events are so vivid in a prophet's mind that they are described as if they had already occurred; Abinadi's defense to King Noah in Mosiah 16 is a particularly good example. [E.G.]

R.194 Ricks, Stephen D. "I Have a Question: The name of one of the Lord's disciples listed in 3 Nephi 19:4—Timothy—seems to be Greek in origin. Is there an explanation for the appearance of a Greek name in the Book of Mormon?" *Ensign* 22 (October 1992): 53-54. Gives several plausible explanations for the appearance of "Timothy" and "Lachoneus" (another word of possible Greek origin) in the Book of Mormon. Discusses the possibility of Mulekite contact with Grecian influences, and evidence of ancient contacts between Israelites and Greeks. [A.C.W.]

R.195 Ricks, Stephen D. "The Ideology of Kingship in Mosiah 1-6." In *Reexploring the Book of Mormon*, edited by John W. Welch, 114-16. Salt Lake City: Deseret Book and FARMS, 1992. The rites of a new king commonly known in Egyptian and Mesopotamian societies were used in Israel and described in the

Book of Mormon. The elements of kingship found in the Book of Mormon include accession to the throne, ambivalent view of kingship, the king as a protector for the weak, and covenants with the Lord. The rich and complex ideology is most excellently portrayed in the book of Mosiah. [N.K.Y.]

R.196 Ricks, Stephen D. "Joseph's Smith's Means and Methods of Translating the Book of Mormon." Provo, UT: FARMS, 1984. In an argument against the "automatic method" of translating the Book of Mormon, Ricks points out that Joseph Smith's own statements establish that it was through the "gift and power of God" and by means of the Urim and Thummim that the Book of Mormon was translated. [J.W.M.]

R.197 Ricks, Stephen D. "King, Coronation, and Covenant in Mosiah 1-6." In *Rediscovering the Book of Mormon*, edited by John L. Sorenson and Melvin J. Thorne, 209-19. Salt Lake City: Deseret Book and FARMS, 1991 King Benjamin's farewell address and Mosiah's succession to his father's throne reflect features of ancient Israelite and near eastern culture. The coronation of the new King took place in the temple and involved a new name and an anointing. A renewal of the covenant was also important. Article contains a table of similarities and scriptural passages that show the comparisons. [J.W.M.]

R.198 Ricks, Stephen D. "Olive Culture in the Second Temple Era and Early Rabbinic Period." In *The Allegory of the Olive Tree: The Olive, the Bible, and Jacob 5,* edited by Stephen D. Ricks and John W. Welch, 460-76. Salt Lake City, Deseret Book and FARMS, 1994. Using ancient sources in the Apocrypha, Pseudepigrapha, Mishnah, and Talmud, this article explores the role of the olive in the Second Temple period and the early rabbis and shows how they relate to the themes in Jacob 5. The pruning, nourishing, dunging, and engrafting that are so much a part of Jacob 5 are also contained in the literature of the Second Temple era. [J.W.M.]

R.199 Ricks, Stephen D. "Treaty/Covenant Patterns in King Benjamin's Address." *BYU Studies* 24 (Spring 1984): 151-62. Treaty-covenant assemblies were common in the ancient Near East, one of which was the Feast of the Tabernacles. King Benjamin's address (Mosiah 1-6) was perhaps related to the Feast of the Tabernacles. It may well be related to the covenants made at Sinai. It is possible that it also reflects an even more ancient Near Eastern covenant renewal pattern. [J.W.M.]

R.200 Ricks, Stephen D., and Robert F. Smith. "New Year's Celebrations." In *Reexploring the Book of Mormon*, edited by John W. Welch, 209-11. Salt Lake City: Deseret Book and FARMS, 1992. The New Year's celebrations of the Book of Mormon and the Old Testament assume great importance for coronation of kings, covenant renewal, feast days, and other activities. The Lamanites were confused to find their king Amalickiah dead on New Year's day (Alma 62:36-39). Joseph Smith did not realize that he took the plates from Hill Cumorah on the Jewish New Year's day. [N.K.Y.]

R.201 Ricks, Stephen D., and William J. Hamblin. "Conference on Warfare in the Book of Mormon." In *Reexploring the Book of Mormon*, edited by John W. Welch, 199-201. Salt Lake City: Deseret Book and FARMS, 1992. Report of the Conference on Warfare held in 1987. Papers presented deal with weapons mentioned in the Book of Mormon, scholars' views of Mesoamerican warfare, Nephite, Jaredite, and Mayan warfare, warfare rituals in the Book of Mormon, martial law, and Gadianton robbers' counter culture. [N.K.Y.]

R.202 Ricks, Stephen D., and John W. Welch, eds. *The Allegory of the Olive Tree: The Olive, the Bible, and Jacob 5.* Salt Lake City: Deseret Book and FARMS, 1994. Articles by various authors examine Zenos's allegory in Jacob 5 as a symbol of Christ, Nephi's uses and interpretations of the allegory, textual analyses, ancient historical and religious backgrounds of the symbolism of the olive tree, the olive in early Jewish and Christian writings, and botany and horticulture of olives. [J.W.M.]

R.203 Ricks, Stephen D., and William J. Hamblin, eds. *Warfare in the Book of Mormon.* Salt Lake City: Deseret Book and FARMS, 1990. Publishes the papers presented at the FARMS

Symposium on Warfare in the Book of Mormon. See annotations under individual authors. [J.W.M.]

R.204 Ricks, Welby W. "Discoveries of Purported Ancient Hebrew Writing in Eastern United States." *UASN* 13 (25 June 1953): 3. Also in Christensen, Ross T. *Progress in Archaeology: An Anthology,* 210-11. Provo, UT: Brigham Young University, 1963. Few discoveries of the Hebrew script known by Nephite peoples have been made. However, one find in Newark, Ohio, has Hebrew-like inscriptions. [J.W.M.]

R.205 Ricks, Welby W. "A Purported Phoenician Inscription in New Mexico." In *Papers of the Fifteenth Annual Symposium on Archaeology of the Scriptures,* edited by Ross T. Christensen, 94-100. Provo, UT: Brigham Young University, 1964. A purported Phoenician inscription in New Mexico bearing an abbreviated form of the Ten Commandments in Hebrew is found to be fraudulent after a thorough investigation. Investigations must be made to insure the continued success of Book of Mormon archaeology and the reputation of the LDS Church. [J.W.M.]

R.206 Riddle, Chauncey C. *Code Language in the Book of Mormon.* Provo, UT: FARMS, 1992. Identifies four major kinds of hidden meanings or code language in the Book of Mormon: (1) obscure usages, (2) technical usages, (3) metaphorical/allegorical usages, (4) double entendres. The author explains such terms as: "looking beyond the mark," "innocent blood," the "tree of life," "prosper in the land," "the seed of Abraham," "amen," "house of Israel," and the name of God. [B.D.]

R.207 Riddle, Chauncey C. "Days of Wickedness and Vengeance: Analysis of 3 Nephi 6 and 7." In *The Book of Mormon: Helaman through 3 Nephi 8, According to Thy Word,* edited by Monte S. Nyman and Charles D. Tate Jr., 191-205. Provo, UT: Brigham Young University Religious Studies Center, 1992. Draws parallels between the period just before the cataclysm in 3 Nephi and the present age, including: (1) the main participants in both eras are of the house of Israel, (2) the fury of Satan is increased, and (3) the coming of Christ ends the destruction. [D.M.]

R.208 Riddle, Chauncey C. "Korihor: The Arguments of Apostasy." *Ensign* 7 (September 1977): 18-21. Korihor's arguments (Alma 30) are examined. He argues naturalistic empiricism (knowing all truth by the senses, which disqualifies the spiritual), humanism (success comes only by human means), and relativism (the individual judges his own actions according to his own criteria). [J.W.M.]

R.209 Riddle, Chauncey C. "Pride and Riches." In *The Book of Mormon: Jacob through Words of Mormon, To Learn with Joy*, edited by Monte S. Nyman and Charles D. Tate Jr., 221-33. Provo, UT: Brigham Young University Religious Studies Center, 1990. Jacob instructs his people concerning pride and riches in Jacob 2:12-21. It is a call to humility and proper attitudes toward wealth, faith in Christ and the attaining of a fullness of faith, which is charity. From charity grows the desire to share. That which must be shared first is the gospel of Jesus Christ, then that which is shared is done in the Lord's own way. [J.W.M.]

R.210 Ridges, David J. *Isaiah Made Easier: A Quick-Reference Manual for Bible and Book of Mormon Students.* Springville, UT: Copies Plus Printing, 1991. Includes the text of Isaiah from the Bible and the Book of Mormon with parenthetical comments to help the reader understand various Hebraisms or literary devices. [E.G.]

R.211 Rigdon, John Wickliff. "Sidney Rigdon and the Early History of the Mormon Church." In *Friendship, New York Sesqui Centennial Times, Sesqui Centennial Edition* (July, 1965): 2-3. The only living son of Sidney Rigdon tells of Sidney Rigdon's conversion to the Church. He states that soon after his joining the Church, Sidney was accused of writing the Book of Mormon. Sidney always denied this allegation and the idea that he had known Solomon Spaulding. [J.W.M.]

R.212 Riggs, Timberline W. "What is the Book of Mormon and Who Was Joseph Smith?" In Riggs's *A Skeptic Discovers Mormonism*, 96-104. Salt Lake City: Deseret Book, 1946.

Story of the coming forth of the Book of Mormon, with a testimony of its divine nature. [J.W.M.]

R.213 Riley, William L. "A Comparison of Passages from Isaiah and Other Old Testament Prophets in Ethan Smith's *'View of the Hebrews'* and the Book of Mormon." M.A. thesis, Brigham Young University, 1971. Compares the Book of Mormon and the *View of the Hebrews*. The parallels have also been studied by B. H. Roberts and Hugh Nibley, who say that any connections that may be made are also found in the Bible. The emphasis of this paper is on passages from Isaiah that are common to all three books. [J.W.M.]

R.214 Ritchie, William A. "Their Mouths Are Stopped with Dust." *Archaeology* 4 (September 1952): 136-44. Summary of the latest excavations in New York, providing the archaeological history of the state. Lists evidences supporting the movements of Book of Mormon peoples in New York. [E.G.]

R.215 Robbins, James H. "Readers' Research: The Question of Lehi's Lineage." *ZR* 5 (Summer 1979): 3-4. Suggests that Lehi's ancestors may have defected from the Northern Kingdom (2 Chronicles 11:16) and were assimilated into the tribes of the Southern Kingdom as an explanation to Book of Mormon critics that all Israelites knew their lineage and Lehi found his only by reading the brass plates. [A.T.]

R.216 Robbins, James H. "A Testimony: Scriptures of the Future." *ZR* 8 (Spring 1980): 7-8. Lists Book of Mormon passages that tell of scriptural writings that would come forth in a future day. Also includes a Three Nephite story. [A.T.]

R.217 Robe, Russell. *Persuasion and Perplexity: A Faith-Promoting Analysis of Anti-Mormon Propaganda.* Salt Lake City: Emblem Editions, 1990. Explains the motives and psychological structure of anti-Mormon communications. Offers advice to those who are troubled by faith-destroying rhetoric. [D.M.]

R.218 Roberts, B. H. "Accounting for Evident Transcriptions of Bible Passages in the Translation of the Nephite Record." In Roberts's *Defense of the Faith and the Saints,* 1:269-74. 2 vols. Salt Lake City: Deseret News, 1907, 1912. Joseph F. Smith answers the objection that some passages in the Book of Mormon follow the King James English translation verbatim and others so closely resemble it that it appears they were copied. It seems that it is of minor importance compared to the overwhelming evidence that the book is true. The Nephites did carry Old Testament records with them. Some portions were quoted by the Savior who carried the same message to both continents. When Joseph Smith recognized this fact he may have used the Bible to assist the translation process. [J.W.M.]

R.219 Roberts, B. H. "Analysis of the Book of Mormon." *Contributor* 10 (February 1889): 126-30. Reprinted in *Scrap Book of Mormon Literature*, compiled by Ben E. Rich, 1:154-61. 2 vols. Chicago, IL: Etten, 1913. Gives an analysis of the composition of the Book of Mormon, provides an explanation of Mormon's work of abridgment, identifies the contributors to the Book of Mormon text, and presents a comparison of the Book of Mormon Isaiah with the biblical Isaiah. [C.F.C.]

R.220 Roberts, B. H. *Analysis of the Book of Mormon: Suggestions to the Reader.* Salt Lake City: Deseret News Co., n.d. Examines the structure of the Book of Mormon—the first section of the Book of Mormon represents a verbatim translation of the "smaller plates" of Nephi and the remainder is an abridgment with comments, warnings, prophecies, and admonitions mixed with narrative by Mormon and his son Moroni. Compares biblical passages with similar verses quoted in the Book of Mormon. [J.W.M.]

R.221 Roberts, B. H. "Answers to Questions Respecting the Manual Theory of Translating the Book of Mormon." In Roberts's *Defense of the Faith and the Saints,* 1:275-311. 2 vols. Salt Lake City: Deseret News, 1907, 1912. In an effort to answer the rumor that the seer stones were responsible for the translation of the Book of Mormon, Roberts notes that the mechanical theory (word-for-word translation) has led to some difficulties—it often results in unintelligible jargon. The Book of Mormon is not a literal translation. Article contains additional theories with responses by Brother Roberts. [J.W.M.]

R.222 Roberts, B. H. "The Apostasy: Section IX. The Nephite Christian Church." In Roberts's *Outlines of Ecclesiastical History: A Textbook*, 215-18. Salt Lake City, UT: Church of Jesus Christ of Latter-day Saints, 1950. Concise summary of the Nephite path from righteousness after Christ's visit to utter destruction and anarchy a few centuries later. Identifies pride, wealth, class distinctions, anti-Christian church persecution, the revival of Nephite/Lamanite distinctions and secret combinations, and an attempt at church reorganization as the factors that led to apostasy on the western hemisphere. [A.C.W.]

R.223 Roberts, B. H. "The Belief Among Christians that the Bible Contains All the Revelations Given to Man by God." *MS* 50 (1888): 344-47. Bible passages are used to refute the belief that the Bible contains all the revelation God has ever given to man. [B.R.M.]

R.224 Roberts, B. H. "The Belief Among Christians that the Canon of Scripture is Closed." *MS* 50 (1888): 330-35. Bible passages are used to show that revelation from God has not ceased, that prophecy continues in modern times, and that the Book of Mormon is a new witness for Jesus Christ brought forth through this modern revelation. Bible passages that have been used to cast doubt on the Book of Mormon are explained and the arguments refuted. [B.R.M.]

R.225 Roberts, B. H. "Bible Quotations in the Book of Mormon and the Reasonableness of Nephi's Prophecies." *IE* 7 (January 1904): 179-96. See also *A Book of Mormon Treasury*, 173-89. Salt Lake City: Bookcraft, 1959, 2nd edition 1976. Discusses the close similarities between the Sermon on the Mount in Matthew 5-7 and in 3 Nephi 12-14, and suggests that Joseph Smith used the available language of the New Testament to ease the burden of translating. [J.W.W.]

R.226 Roberts, B. H. "Book of Mormon." *MS* 50 (27 August 1888): 552-54. Affirms the need for a "New Witness" to confirm the divine nature and authenticity of the Bible. The Book of Mormon is the new witness and was translated by the "gift and power of God." [J.W.M.]

R.227 Roberts, B. H. "The Book of Mormon a Witness for the Christ." *Liahona* 27 (9 July 1929): 48. The Book of Mormon gives the account of the resurrected Christ visiting and teaching the ancient inhabitants of the western world. The purpose of the Book of Mormon is to convince both Jew and gentile that Jesus is the Christ, the Eternal God. [C.F.C.]

R.228 Roberts, B. H. "Book of Mormon Controversy." *MS* 50 (20 February 1888): 113-17. Roberts responds to Mr. Bolitho, who attempts to prove the Book of Mormon false by showing that the Book of Mormon dates of Christ's birth and death do not accord with the Bible. Roberts explains the possible differences between Nephite and Jewish calendrical systems, citing scripture and chronologists. [A.C.W.]

R.229 Roberts, B. H. "The Book of Mormon Defended by B. H. Roberts." *Deseret Evening News* (5 December 1903): 21. Response to an accompanying article, "The Book of Mormon attacked by 'M.'" Roberts refutes common accusations that the Book of Mormon plagiarizes Shakespeare and the New Testament. [A.C.W.]

R.230 Roberts, B. H. *Book of Mormon Difficulties*. N.p., 1977. Collection of unpublished papers defending the Book of Mormon. Discusses linguistics, the question of the origin of the native Americans, the literature available to Joseph Smith when he translated the Book of Mormon, similarities between the Book of Mormon and Ethan Smith's *View of the Hebrews*, and the Christ figure in America. Roberts declares his faith in the Book of Mormon believing that in time God will vindicate it and all will know of its truthfulness though now they scoff. [J.W.M]

R.231 Roberts, B. H. "A Book of Mormon Study" (1922). In *Studies of the Book of Mormon*, edited by Brigham D. Madsen, 149-319. Urbana and Chicago: University of Illinois Press, 1985. A working paper raising questions for further research about possible relationships between the Book of Mormon and Ethan Smith's *View of the Hebrews* and other sources that explore the possibility that the American

Indians were descendants of the lost ten tribes. [J.W.W.]

R.232 Roberts, B. H. "Book of Mormon Translation: Interesting Correspondence on the Subject of the Manual Theory." *IE* 9 (July 1906): 706-13. A response to an inquiry made concerning the theory of translation of the Book of Mormon as presented in the Senior Manual of 1905-1906. [B.R.M.]

R.233 Roberts, B. H. "The Book of Mormon: What the Record Contains." *Liahona* 14 (1916-1917): 1-2. A brief description of the Book of Mormon and its people, and a discussion of its purpose as a witness for Jesus Christ. [B.R.M.]

R.234 Roberts, B. H. "A Call to Repentance." *IE* 25 (December 1922): 159-65. America is a choice land and all who possess it must repent and serve God or be swept off. [B.R.M.]

R.235 Roberts, B. H. "Christ in the Book of Mormon: His Appearance on the American Continent." *IE* 27 (1924): 188-92. Reprinted as Roberts, B. H. "Christ in the Book of Mormon." In *A Book of Mormon Treasury*, 241-46. Salt Lake City, Bookcraft, 1959, 2nd edition 1976. Discusses the pre-mortal spirit life of Christ; the revelation of Christ to the brother of Jared; the Nephite knowledge of Christ through visions and revelations; and the visit of the risen Christ among the Nephites. [C.F.C.]

R.236 Roberts, B. H. "Christ in the Traditions of American Native Races." *IE* 20 (May 1917): 571-97. Native American traditions and beliefs are correlated with the birth and death of Jesus Christ and the Book of Mormon account of Christ's coming to the western hemisphere. [B.R.M.]

R.237 Roberts, B. H. "Christian Argument Applied to Mormonism." *Liahona* 26 (5 February 1929): 389-93. The angel Moroni visited Joseph Smith telling him of the records that contain an abridged history of the ancient inhabitants of America and the fullness of the gospel. Joseph Smith received the plates and translated them using the Urim and Thummim. Witnesses testified of the plates. [C.F.C.]

R.238 Roberts, B. H. "Christ's Personal Appearance in the Western Hemisphere: The Supreme Message of the Book of Mormon." *IE* 20 (April 1917): 477-99. Writes of a monument of Christ erected on the border of Argentina and Chile as a sign of peace between the two nations. Another monument of Christ, the LDS temple, was built in Hawaii. "Those who believe in the Book of Mormon also believe that this group of islands was colonized by certain adventurous people from the mainland of America [Hagoth, Alma 63]." These two monuments have been erected on a land that Christ once visited. [B.D.]

R.239 Roberts, B. H. *A Comprehensive History of the Church of Jesus Christ of Latter-day Saints*. 6 vols. Salt Lake City: Deseret Book, 1930. A history of the Church, including detailed discussions of the coming forth of the Book of Mormon, Joseph obtaining the plates, Lucy Mack Smith's description of the Urim and Thummim, the translation, Professor Anthon's letter, and the loss of the 110 pages of manuscript. Examines the mode of translation as reported by those who were near the prophet. Reports the testimony of the Three Witnesses and the Eight Witnesses, discusses anti-Mormon criticism and the excommunication of the Three Witnesses. Reveals details of the publication of the Book of Mormon, the efforts to thwart its publication, and other problems concerning the copyright. Provides an analysis of the purpose and structure of the book. Considers the conflict between Book of Mormon teachings and the revelation given to the Prophet on marriage. [J.W.W.]

R.240 Roberts, B. H. "David Whitmer." *Contributor* 9 (March 1888): 169-72. Presents a history of David Whitmer's life, the circumstances of the viewing of the plates, his final testimony, the charges that he had denied his testimony, and his rebuttal. He is declared a faithful witness to his death. [J.W.M.]

R.241 Roberts, B. H. "David Whitmer." *MS* 50 (20 February 1888): 120-23. Reviews the life of David Whitmer who retained his testimony of the Book of Mormon until his death in 1888. [B.D.]

R.242 Roberts, B. H. *Defense of the Faith and the Saints*. 2 vols. Salt Lake City: Deseret News,

1907. Investigates the manner of translation of the Book of Mormon. The process seems to indicate great spiritual, mental, and physical effort had to be made on the part of the translator in connection with his use of the Urim and Thummim. A thorough examination is made of the Spaulding theory, the allegations that the Prophet Joseph had met secretly with Sidney Rigdon before the Book of Mormon's publication, and Rigdon's denials. The Book of Mormon originated as a sacred record of ancient inhabitants of America, preserved by the hand of God. [J.W.M.]

R.243 Roberts, B. H. "Destruction of Ancient Nations in America—The Book of Mormon Message to the Gentile Nations Occupying the Land." *IE* 27 (February 1924): 288-92. The Jaredite/Nephite nations were destroyed because of wickedness. America is a choice land and all who possess it must live righteously or be swept off of the land. The gentile nations who occupy America during the present era must worship God or be destroyed as were earlier inhabitants. [B.R.M.] 24

R.244 Roberts, B. H. "Doubling the Evidence of Faith." *Liahona* 28 (2 April 1931): 543. The Book of Mormon came forth at a time when there was a great need for faith. It is a record of God's personal dealings with the ancient inhabitants of America and its purpose is to convince the Jew and gentile that Jesus is the Christ, the Eternal God. [C.F.C.]

R.245 Roberts, B. H. "The Fifth Gospel." *MS* 67 (12, 19, 26 January; 2 February 1905): 17-20, 43-46, 52-55, 75-78. Defines the contributions of 3 Nephi: the appearance of the risen Christ on the American continent, his ministry was not limited to the eastern hemisphere, he also visited the lost tribes of Israel and raised up prophets in the Americas who foretold his appearance. Roberts notes the distinction made between the Savior's remarks to the twelve and those to the multitude, and points out that 3 Nephi specifies the proper mode of baptism and the sacrament. [R.H.B.]

R.246 Roberts, B. H. "Higher Criticism and the Book of Mormon." *IE* 14 (June, July 1911): 665-77, 774-86. Also found in "Book of Mormon Essays by B. H. Roberts." Provo, UT: FARMS Produces a Mormon view of the historical-critical method of biblical source analysis. "The methods . . . of higher criticism we recognize as proper; but we must disagree as to the correctness of many of the conclusions arrived at by that method." The author deals with the literary critics by delivering logic against logic, but also establishes the spiritual nature of the Book of Mormon. [D.W.P.]

R.247 Roberts, B. H. "His Final Decade: Statements about the Book of Mormon (1924-33)." Provo, UT: FARMS, 1990. A composite of Book of Mormon quotes made by Roberts in Church conferences, letters, and other works. Subjects include: understanding the implications of the "work of God," serving the Lord is a prerequisite for preserving America, the Book of Mormon is a witness of the truthfulness of the Bible, and many others. [J.W.M.]

R.248 Roberts, B. H. *History of the Church of Jesus Christ of Latter-day Saints, Volume One.* Salt Lake City: Deseret News, 1902. Contains the story of the coming forth of the Book of Mormon interspersed with journal entries, important footnote accounts, newspaper articles, accounts given to scribes, and commentary. Discusses Moroni's visit, the circumstances under which the records were delivered to the prophet, the attempts to steal them, the work of translation, Martin Harris's visit to Professor Anthon, the loss of the 116 pages of manuscript, the translation process, the restoration of the Aaronic Priesthood, the Witnesses of the Book of Mormon, copyright laws, and the publication of the book. [J.W.M.]

R.249 Roberts, B. H. "Jacob and Benjamin." In *A Scrapbook*, edited by Lynn Pulsipher, 68-71. Provo, UT: Pulsipher, 1989. Also in *MS* 50 (1888): 773-75. Short biographical sketches of Jacob and King Benjamin. Jacob saw the Redeemer in his youth and recorded the prophecy of Zenos. Benjamin was an able warrior and wise and industrious leader. [A.C.W.]

R.250 Roberts, B. H. "Jesus is the Christ—The Eternal God." *Liahona* 23 (1925): 29-31. Gives the purpose of the Book of Mormon; identifies Jesus Christ as deity and discusses the "Light of Christ." [C.F.C.]

R.251 Roberts, B. H. "The Making of the Record Pertaining to the Natives of the Americas—the Location of the Record Revealed to Joseph Smith and Its Translation." *MS* 50 (1888): 393-97. A discussion of the origin of the Book of Mormon. It is an abridgment by Mormon from many other writings of ancient prophets and was hidden by Moroni in the Hill Cumorah; its location was revealed to Joseph Smith and he translated and published the book. [B.R.M.]

R.252 Roberts, B. H. "The Manner of Translating the Book of Mormon." In Roberts's *Defense of the Faith and the Saints,* 1:255-69. 2 vols. Salt Lake City: Deseret News, 1907. Statements from Oliver Cowdery, David Whitmer, Martin Harris, and other regarding the Urim and Thummim and the manner in which the Book of Mormon was translated. [J.W.M.]

R.253 Roberts, B. H. "Mormon Views of America." In Roberts's *Defense of the Faith and the Saints,* 1:403-41. 2 vols. Salt Lake City: Deseret News, 1907. The Book of Mormon teaches that the two American continents are a promised land dedicated to the seed of Joseph and the gentile races, to be free from bondage if the inhabitants will but serve God, a sacred land where the New Jerusalem will be established. [J.W.M.]

R.254 Roberts, B. H. "Moroni: A Sketch of the Nephite Republic." *Contributor* 11 (1889-90): 15-18, 54-58, 81-85, 131-36, 164-68, 227-31, 262-66, 293-96, 335-88, 445-50. An account of the government and politics of the Nephites prior to and during the time of the Nephite republic as described in the book of Mosiah. Main emphasis is on Captain Moroni and his leadership. [B.R.M.]

R.255 Roberts, B. H. "The Mythology and Traditions of the Natives of the Americas; The Amazement of the Catholic Priests." *MS* 50 (1888): 360-63. Discusses the experiences of the Catholic priests who accompanied Cortez on his expedition to the Americas and conquest of the Aztecs. They discovered the Native American traditions and myths to be similar to their own traditions and rites of worship. [B.R.M.]

R.256 Roberts, B. H. "The Necessity of a New Witness." *MS* 50 (1888): 313-15. Describes why the Book of Mormon is needed as a new witness for God. [C.F.C.]

R.257 Roberts, B. H. "Nephi." In *A Scrapbook*, edited by Lynn Pulsipher, 65-67. Provo, UT: Pulsipher, 1989. Also in *MS* 50 (1888): 132-34. Short biographical sketch of Nephi$_1$, showing his faith in and obedience to God. Nephi labored as an "agriculturist, miner, architect, builder, engraver, warrior, ruler, instructor, prophet, seer, and revelator." [A.C.W.]

R.258 Roberts, B. H. "A Nephite's Commandments to His Three Sons." *IE* 3 (June-September 1900): 570-78, 653-57, 760-66, 835-43. Also found in "Book of Mormon Essays by B. H. Roberts." Provo, UT: FARMS. The story of Alma the Younger's conversion. Just before he died, he delivered to his sons Helaman, Shiblon, and Corianton his "commandments," a father's advice and admonitions. Each son is different, and therefore Alma's advice was different for each of his sons. [C.F.C.]

R.259 Roberts, B. H. "A New Witness for God." *Contributor* 9-10 (July 1888–January 1889): 322-38, 377-402, 413-17, 457-63, 19-22, 48-54, 90-94. Cessation of revelation is contrary to the teachings of Christ. There is a vast amount of archaeological evidence to prove there were ancient civilizations in pre-Columbian America. The Christian theme known in ancient American mythology, symbols, and traditions suggests that God dealt with the western world the same as the eastern. The Book of Mormon reveals the story of these ancient people. Book of Mormon prophecies are being fulfilled; they bear witness of the divine authenticity of the Book of Mormon. [J.W.M.]

R.260 Roberts, B. H. *New Witnesses for God.* Salt Lake City: Deseret News, 1909, [R]1951. Extensive treatise on Joseph Smith as a witness for God, the coming forth of the Book of Mormon, Book of Mormon lands, peoples, government, evidences of the truth of the Book of Mormon, the Three Witnesses, philosophical considerations, and many other subjects advanced as secondary evidences in support of the truth of the Book of Mormon. [J.W.W.]

R.261 Roberts, B. H. "An Objection to the Book of Mormon Answered." *IE* 12 (July 1909): 681-89. An answer to the criticism that certain chapters of Isaiah were written after Lehi's departure from Jerusalem and thus could not have been included in the Book of Mormon. [B.R.M.]

R.262 Roberts, B. H. "The Origin and History of the Native of the Americas—The Visitation of the Messiah." *MS* 50 (1888): 376-80. The Book of Mormon story of Lehi's flight from Jerusalem to the western hemisphere explains the origin of the native American people and their traditions and rites that are similar to Christian traditions and religious rites. [B.R.M.]

R.263 Roberts, B. H. "Origin of the Book of Mormon." *American Historical Magazine* 3-4 (1908–1909): 441-68, 551-80, 22-44, 168-96. See also Roberts's *Defense of the Faith and the Saints,* 2:95-299. 2 vols. Salt Lake City: Deseret Book, 1912. A reply to Theodore Schroeder's article contained in earlier editions of the *American Historical Magazine* that stated the theory that Spaulding's *Manuscript Found* was the source from which the Book of Mormon originated. [B.R.M.]

R.264 Roberts, B. H. "Originality of the Book of Mormon." *IE* 8 (September/October 1905): 801-15, 881-902. Also found in "Book of Mormon Essays by B. H. Roberts." Provo, UT: FARMS. Shows that the Book of Mormon is original in its thoughts and ideas and is not the thoughts or philosophy of Joseph Smith and his associates. Discusses the doctrine of truth, the doctrine of opposite existences, the agency of man, the atonement, the fall of Adam, and the purpose of man's existence. [C.F.C.]

R.265 Roberts, B. H. *A Parallel between the Book of Mormon and* A View of the Hebrews *by Ethan Smith.* N.p., c. 1922. Reprinted in *Studies of the Book of Mormon,* edited by Brigham D. Madsen, 321-344. Urbana and Chicago: University of Illinois Press, 1985. A short summary of possible relationships between the Book of Mormon and the *View of the Hebrews* presented in "A Book of Mormon Study" (1922). [J.W.W.]

R.266 Roberts, B. H. "The Probability of Joseph Smith's Story." *IE* 7 (1904): 321-31, 417-32. Also found in "Book of Mormon Essays by B. H. Roberts." Provo, UT: FARMS Events surrounding the translation of the Book of Mormon. The visitation of angels, the use of the Urim and Thummim to translate records, the giving of the gold plates back to the angel Moroni, and the loss of the 116 pages should not be looked upon as improbable. [C.F.C.]

R.267 Roberts, B. H. "The Prophecy Pertaining to There Being Three Witnesses—The Testimony of the Three Witnesses—Testimony of the Eight Witnesses." *MS* 50 (1888): 408-13. An explanation of why Joseph Smith never displayed the golden plates for public view to prove their authenticity. The Lord works by faith and establishes truth through the testimony of witnesses. Includes the testimonies and stories of the Three Witnesses and Eight Witnesses. [B.R.M.]

R.268 Roberts, B. H. "Purpose of Man's Creation." *Liahona* 28 (25 November 1930): 274. Alma says that after the resurrection there is no dissolution that takes place, but spirit and body become inseparably united into one spiritual personage, spirit predominating, and that is why the revelations say, "Man is spirit." [C.F.C.]

R.269 Roberts, B. H. *Rasha the Jew: A Message to All Jews.* Salt Lake City: Deseret News Press, 1932. First published as *The Redeemed Hebrew,* 1926. A message to all Jews that Jesus is the Christ, the Eternal God, and that a new witness to these truths has been brought forth. The Book of Mormon brings knowledge of Christ in the New World as it discusses the signs of his birth and death. The divinity of Christ is proclaimed in the Book of Mormon. The testimony of the Three Witnesses and the Eight Witnesses is given to prove that Joseph Smith had the ancient American record. [C.F.C.]

R.270 Roberts, B. H. "Recapitulation of the Foregoing Chapters—The Final Test of the Book of Mormon—the Author's Closing Testimony." *MS* 50 (1888): 456-61. A review of the prophecies concerning the Book of Mormon, the evidence of its authenticity, and the author's testimony to its truthfulness. [B.R.M.]

R.271 Roberts, B. H. "Remarks on the Foregoing Article (Mansfield's 'Jacob's Isle')." *IE* 7 (February 1904): 267-69. A discussion of the meaning of the word "isle" as contained in biblical and Book of Mormon geography. Agrees with Mansfield that Jacob's reference to the lands of the Book of Mormon as an "isle of the sea" means a body of land (however large) reached by crossing an ocean. [B.R.M.]

R.272 Roberts, B. H. *The Seventy's Course in Theology: A Survey of the Books of Holy Scripture, Vol. 1.* Dallas, TX: S. K. Taylor, 1907. Contains seven lessons on the Book of Mormon. Discusses the visitation of Moroni, and the translation and publication of the book. Includes an analysis of the contents, the purpose, and value of the Book of Mormon. [J.W.M.]

R.273 Roberts, B. H. "Some Objections to the Book of Mormon Answered." *IE* 5 (March 1902): 339-50. Uses the Bible and historical records to answer alleged contradictions contained in the Book of Mormon regarding Christ being born at Jerusalem, the date of Christ's birth, and the three days of darkness that covered the earth at his crucifixion. [B.R.M.]

R.274 Roberts, B. H. "The Spaulding Theory of the Book of Mormon—The Theory That Sidney Rigdon Wrote the Book of Mormon." *MS* 50 (1888): 424-28. Argues against the Solomon Spaulding theory for the origin of the Book of Mormon and the idea that Sidney Rigdon wrote the Book of Mormon. [B.R.M.]

R.275 Roberts, B. H. "The Spirit of the Book of Mormon." *MS* 67 (8 May 1905): 305-9. Describes the uplifting, enlightening, and inspirational aspects of the Book of Mormon. [R.H.B.]

R.276 Roberts, B. H. "Suggestions to the Reader of the Book of Mormon." *MS* 50 (27 August 1888): 534-58. Suggests that the reader remember that the Book of Mormon is an abridgment of records of a more extensive nature. The first one hundred fifty-seven pages, however, are the writings of Nephi and were inserted just as they came from the hand of Nephi and those kings who followed him. The latter part of the book was the work of Moroni, Mormon's son. The book must be read with real desire and a prayerful heart. The Holy Ghost will attend and confirm the divine origin of the book, but not in an imposing way—the reader must ask. [J.W.M.]

R.277 Roberts, B. H. "The Test of Joseph Smith Being a Prophet and of the Book of Mormon Being a Record from God." *MS* 50 (1888): 440-47. A discussion of prophecies in the Book of Mormon that have been fulfilled including those concerning the Three Witnesses, the Christian claim that there can be no more Bible, the words of Charles Anthon, and the martyrdom of some of its witnesses. [B.R.M.]

R.278 Roberts, B. H. "Testimony of the New Witness—The Book of Mormon." In *A Scrapbook*, edited by Lynn Pulsipher, 141. Provo, UT: Pulsipher, 1991. The heart of the Book of Mormon is its testimony of Christ. Prophets prophesied concerning his birth and death and their prophecies were fulfilled. Christ visited the people on the American continent after he was resurrected. [C.F.C.]

R.279 Roberts, B. H. "Translation of the Book of Mormon." *IE* 9 (April, May 1906): 425-36, 547-53. Roberts defends his theory about the role that the Urim and Thummim and Joseph Smith played in translating the Book of Mormon. He shows that literal translations are difficult or impossible in similar languages, and points out that it would be even harder from the Egyptian-like language of Mormon's plates. [K.M.]

R.280 Roberts, B. H. Untitled talk. *CR* (October 1901): 33-35. Joseph Smith had great courage in declaring that many would believe in the Book of Mormon. In the face of loneliness and persecution he dared to translate the Nephite record. The numerical count of those who believe its words is a fulfillment of this prophecy. [J.W.M.]

R.281 Roberts, B. H. Untitled talk. *CR* (4 April 1921): 120. God the Eternal Father and his son Jesus Christ appeared to Joseph Smith in a vision. The Book of Mormon, a new volume of scripture, was revealed. Three Witnesses testified that an angel showed them the original plates. [C.F.C.]

R.282 Roberts, B. H. Untitled talk. *CR* (6 October 1922): 14-20. Discusses the mission of the United States of America as a promised land, the decrees of God concerning the land of Zion, and predictions of calamities if it fails God as an instrument in the accomplishment of his high purposes. The gentile nation is to be a nursing father and mother to the remnants of Israel. [C.F.C.]

R.283 Roberts, B. H. Untitled talk. *CR* (7 April 1923): 63-65. Discusses the purpose of the Book of Mormon as stated on the title page: "to the convincing of the Jew and Gentile that Jesus is the Christ, the Eternal God." God brought forth the Book of Mormon, which is being called the American scripture. At the time it came forth, the Christian world believed in the divinity of Christ and did not need such a statement, but there are many in the Christian world who now need a testimony and witness that Jesus Christ is God. [C.F.C.]

R.284 Roberts, B. H. Untitled talk. *CR* (7 October 1923): 88-92. Discusses the messages of the Book of Mormon. The Book of Mormon tells of the visit of the Redeemer to the inhabitants of the western world. It predicts the rise of the great Gentile nation—the United States of America. The Book of Mormon is a new witness for God and Christ and the truth of the gospel. [C.F.C.]

R.285 Roberts, B. H. Untitled talk. *CR* (April 1924): 76-80. Nephi had great visions concerning the life and the mission of Christ. He saw that other books would come forth—the Book of Mormon, the Doctrine and Covenants, and the Pearl of Great Price—to establish the truth of the record of the Twelve Apostles of the Lamb of God. [C.F.C.]

R.286 Roberts, B. H. Untitled talk. *CR* (October 1925): 144-50. Reprinted in *IE* (1926): 230-37. Answers the question that a little boy asked, "Why are people?" It cannot be answered in the Old or in the New Testament The Book of Mormon (2 Nephi 2:24-25) teaches the purpose of God in the creation. [C.F.C.]

R.287 Roberts, B. H. Untitled talk. *CR* (April 1927): 33-38. The Eastern States Mission is making an attempt to take the message of the Book of Mormon to the Jews. The book is to be a witness to the Gentiles and especially to Jews that Jesus Christ is the Son of God. Many shall believe in the Book of Mormon, and they shall carry the words of that book to the remnants of the land, meaning the American Indians. The Jews shall begin to believe in Christ, and they shall begin to gather in upon their promised land, Palestine. [C.F.C.]

R.288 Roberts, B. H. Untitled talk. *CR* (October 1927): 22-23. Moroni warns that anyone who should possess the land of promise must serve God or be swept off (Ether 2:9-12). [C.F.C.]

R.289 Roberts, B. H. Untitled talk. *CR* (April 1928): 106-13. Gives examples of truths the world would have lost if the Book of Mormon had not been brought forth (Alma 41:10; 2 Nephi 2:24-25; 1 Nephi 3:7; Ether 12:26-27). The Book of Mormon corrects some errors in the philosophies and religions of men. [C.F.C.]

R.290 Roberts. B. H. Untitled talk. *CR* (April 1929): 118-21. The Book of Mormon is an important means of acquainting the world with LDS thought. [C.F.C.]

R.291 Roberts, B. H. Untitled talk. *CR* (April 1930): 41-49. Refers to the Book of Mormon as the record of Joseph in the hands of Ephraim that supplies the world with a new witness for Christ and the fullness of the gospel. [C.F.C.]

R.292 Roberts, B. H. Untitled talk. *CR* (April 1932): 97. Talks about the role of witnesses. God gave the same commission to the Book of Mormon witnesses in the new dispensation as he did to the ancient witnesses. [C.F.C.]

R.293 Roberts, B. H. Untitled talk. *CR* (April 1933): 115-20. The United States of America is a choice land. There are two great prophecies in the Book of Mormon: it is a witness of the divinity of Christ, and it gives prophecies concerning the great gentile nation. If the Gentiles sin against the gospel, it shall be taken from among them. But if they will repent, they shall be numbered among his people. [C.F.C.]

R.294 Roberts, B. H. "What the World Owes the Book of Mormon." *MS* 90 (4 October 1928): 625-30. A discussion of the value of the Book of Mormon, from its aphorisms to its powerful testimony of Jesus Christ and his resurrection. [B.R.M.]

R.295 Roberts, Bliss, and Mary Ann Roberts. *Picture Scriptures: The Book of Mormon.* Salt Lake City: Acorn, 1981. A guide for teaching children the Book of Mormon by using pictures and illustrations. [D.W.P.]

R.296 Roberts, Brian Curtis. "Stylometry and Wordprints: A Book of Mormon Reevaluation." M.A. thesis, Brigham Young University, 1983. Literary authorship analysis using stylometry and wordprints. Several contributors to the Book of Mormon were examined: Mormon, Nephi, Alma the Younger, Moroni, Jesus Christ, Jacob, and Isaiah. The 1830 edition was used. The conclusion is that the "results give every indication that there are multiple authors in the Book of Mormon." [J.W.M.]

R.297 Roberts, Dorothy S. "The Book of Mormon Was My Answer." *Ensign* 18 (October 1988): 42-43. A conversion story of a young woman who had a recurring dream similar to that of Lehi's dream of the tree of life. Puzzled by its meaning over a period of years, she found her answer in the Book of Mormon. [J.W.M.]

R.298 Roberts, Richard C. *"View of the Hebrews."* In *Encyclopedia of Mormonism*, edited by Daniel H. Ludlow, 4:1509-10. 5 vols. New York: Macmillan, 1992. Describes the content and thesis of Ethan Smith's *View of the Hebrews,* and the possibility of a relationship with it and the Book of Mormon. I. Woodbridge Riley was the first to suggest a relationship; Mr. Couch asked the Church to respond and B. H. Roberts made a study of the issue. B. H. Roberts's work was published in 1985 by B. D. Madsen suggesting that B. H. Roberts was not faithful to the Book of Mormon. [B.D.]

R.299 Robinson, C. H. "Ancient American Races." *MS* 50 (16 January 1888): 33-36. A report of Professor Chad H. Robinson's lecture on the ancient American races. At a Salt Lake City theatre he displayed five mummified Olmec people that were discovered in Arizona. These mummies are of a white race that existed in ancient America. The article describes the discovery of manuscripts and artifacts in Central and South America that support the Book of Mormon. [B.D.]

R.300 Robinson, Christine H. "And the Book of Mormon and the Holy Scriptures Are Given of Me for Your Instruction." *Relief Society Magazine* 46 (December 1959): 845-46. The Lord has preserved the scriptures for the inspiration and instruction of his children. This divine preservation is particularly evident in the Book of Mormon. The Nephite prophets tell of the importance of the brass plates and the records they kept. We show appreciation by reading their records. [J.W.M.]

R.301 Robinson, Harry A. B. "Brother Alma, the Younger." *Book of Mormon News-Letter.* 2 vols. San Antonio, TX: Bob's Printing Service, 1949. Focuses on Lehi's speech to his household—the historical setting, Lehi's covenant and prophecy. Adds some notes on archaeological evidence and the achievements of the Mayans. [J.W.M.]

R.302 Robinson, Harry A. B. *Know Your Book of Mormon.* San Antonio, TX: The Brothers Alma, 1947. Identified as a "synchronic, chronological study of the Book of Mormon." Contains historical highlights, illustrations, notes, and comments. [D.W.P.]

R.303 Robinson, Stephen E. "Early Christianity and 1 Nephi 13-14." In *The Book of Mormon: First Nephi, The Doctrinal Foundation*, edited by Monte S. Nyman and Charles D. Tate Jr., 177-91. Provo, UT: Brigham Young University Religious Studies Center, 1988 The apocalyptic vision of Nephi (1 Nephi 13-14), when combined with the vision of John the Revelator, helps to draw greater historical conclusions about the great and abominable church and the apostasy. [A.T.]

R.304 Robinson, Stephen E. "The 'Expanded' Book of Mormon?" In *The Book of Mormon: Second Nephi, The Doctrinal Structure*, edited by Monte S. Nyman and Charles D. Tate Jr., 391-413. Provo, UT: Brigham Young University

Religious Studies Center, 1989. A rebuttal to a theory proposed by Blake Ostler in "The Book of Mormon as a Modern Expansion of an Ancient Source" as well as other scholarly attacks on the Book of Mormon, including the suggestion that the Book of Mormon relies on Armenian and Anselmic theories. Ostler's claim is based on disallowance of predictive prophecy. Robinson explains how "pre-Christians" could prophecy of Christ, and points out fallacies in Blake's syllogisms. [A.C.W.]

R.305 Robinson, Stephen E. "Warring against the Saints of God." *Ensign* 18 (January 1988): 34-39. Those who war against Zion, God, and the Saints of God are those who belong to the church of the Devil or the great and abominable church. This article discusses the apostasy of Christ's church after his death and the death of the apostles, and compares the apocalyptic references (including John's Revelation) to the apostasy in 1 Nephi 13-14. Terms and identities relating to the great and abominable church both historically and topologically are defined and discussed. [A.A.]

R.306 Robison, Lindon J. "Economic Insights from the Book of Mormon." *Journal of Book of Mormon Studies* 1 (Fall 1992): 35-53. Economic systems are distinguished by their emphasis on equity and efficiency. Most countries of the world today have adopted a combination of controls and free-market incentives. The Book of Mormon teaches that only through caring can equity and efficiency be simultaneously achieved. [R.H.B.]

R.307 Robison, Pamela Kaye. *Abinadi, Man of God.* Independence, MO: Herald House, 1981. An illustrated storybook for children. Features an account of Abinadi, his preaching, and eventual martyrdom. [A.C.W.]

R.308 Robison, Stanford. *The Maya Legacy: A Sequel to the Book of Mormon.* Las Vegas: Author, 1977. Robinson wishes to tell "the tragic story of the Maya Lamanite who was forsaken by the Lord. It tells of his past, his present, his future, and [the Latter-day Saints'] obligation to this neglected branch of Lehi's family. It is a true story gleaned from historical, archaeological, and sociological facts, and is woven in and around the Book of Mormon narrative." Includes two fold-out maps. [A.C.W.]

R.309 Rodriguez De Fuentes, Carmen. "A Lamp unto My Feet." *Ensign* 23 (October 1993): 68-69. The author testifies that numerous times in her life the Book of Mormon has guided her in making decisions and given her comfort. [S.H.]

R.310 Rogers, Thomas F. "Thoughts about Joseph Smith: Upon Reading Donna Hill's *Joseph Smith: The First Mormon*." In *By Study and Also by Faith,* edited by John M. Lundquist and Stephen D. Ricks, 2:585-618. Salt Lake City: Deseret Book and FARMS, 1990. Members of the Church need to examine the historical accounts of Joseph Smith with an open view, weigh and evaluate the evidence before coming to the conclusion that he was a charlatan. The Book of Mormon contains principles that are not taught anywhere with such clarity. [J.W.M.]

R.311 Rolapp, Henry H. *Two Thousand Gospel Quotations, from the Bible, Book of Mormon, Doctrine and Covenants, and Pearl of Great Price.* Salt Lake City: Deseret Book, 1918. 2nd edition, *Gospel Quotations from the Bible, Book of Mormon, Doctrine and Covenants and Pearl of Great Price.* Salt Lake City: Deseret Book, 1923. Includes some 2000 scriptural quotations from the LDS canon arranged according to topic. Topics include the Holy Trinity, man's pre-existing relationship with God, Satan and his work, the fall of man, free agency, the atonement, apostasy from and restoration of the gospel, the Book of Mormon, continuous revelation, priesthood, missionary work, gospel principles and ordinances, the gathering of Zion, and the Second Coming of Christ. [A.C.W.]

R.312 Rolph, Daniel N. "Prophets, Kings, and Swords: The Sword of Laban and Its Possible Pre-Laban Origin." *Journal of Book of Mormon Studies* 2 (Spring 1993): 73-79. Relates Nephi's and the Three Witnesses' descriptions of the sword of Laban and swords used in the Book of Mormon, and discusses other important swords in Israelite and pre-Israelite tradition. Suggests that the sword of Laban may be one of the swords of Israelite tradition. [A.T.]

R.313 Romney, Joseph B. "Moroni, Angel." In *Encyclopedia of Mormonism*, edited by Daniel H. Ludlow, 1:953. 5 vols. New York: Macmillan, 1992. A brief description of the angel Moroni who appeared to Joseph Smith September 21, 1823, visited with him on many occasions, and committed the plates to him. [B.D.]

R.314 Romney, Joseph B. "The Savior's Ministry on 3 Nephi—A Pattern for Conversion." In *A Symposium on the Book of Mormon*, 113-15. Salt Lake City: Church of Jesus Christ of Latter-day Saints, CES, August 1986. 3 Nephi produces a six-part pattern for conversion, which includes receiving a testimony of Christ, acceptance of the first principles and ordinances of the gospel, and acceptance of the principles of the Sermon on the Mount. [A.T.]

R.315 Romney, Marion G. "America's Fate and Ultimate Destiny." In *Brigham Young University 1976 Devotional and Fireside Speeches of the Year*, 317-31. Provo, UT: Brigham Young University Press, 1977. Explains how the United States of America is a choice and favored land by the Lord, gives historical insights as to America's divine guidance in the past, and explains how the Nephites and Jaredites were not permitted to remain on the land in their wicked state. [A.C.W.]

R.316 Romney, Marion G. "And the Lamanites Shall Blossom as the Rose." *IE* 66 (June 1963): 498-501. The Lamanites are promised that the covenants made to their fathers will be fulfilled, that a remnant would receive the Book of Mormon, and would associate with other members of the house of Israel in the building of their inheritance in the land of America. [J.W.M.]

R.317 Romney, Marion G. "Atonement–Justice–Mercy." *CR* (October 1974): 52-56. The Book of Mormon teaches the doctrines of salvation, including the atonement of Christ, a literal resurrection, the judgment, and justice and mercy. [R.C.D.]

R.318 Romney, Marion G. "The Book of Mormon." *Ensign* 10 (May 1980): 65-67. Also *CR* (April 1980): 87-91. Those who read the Book of Mormon and possess its teachings will be judged according to what is written in it. The Church is under condemnation because it has taken lightly the teachings of the book. [J.W.M.]

R.319 Romney, Marion G. "The Book of Mormon." *IE* 52 (May 1949): 283, 328-30. The Book of Mormon is a witness of the truthfulness of the Bible and is a fortification against modernists who attack the Bible. [J.W.M.]

R.320 Romney, Marion G. "The Church in Mexico." *IE* 61 (June 1958): 460-64. The Book of Mormon is the promised sign that the work of the Lord has begun among all nations. "We may draw a lesson from the history of the Mexican people and their progenitors," as it is outlined in the Book of Mormon. [J.W.M.]

R.321 Romney, Marion G. "Conference Report, October 7, 1970." In *Book of Mormon Talks by General Authorities*, 187-89. Provo, UT: FARMS, 1990. Romney testifies of the truth and importance of the Book of Mormon and shows how it purely testifies of Jesus Christ, from the first to the last chapter. [B.D.]

R.322 Romney, Marion G. "Conference Report, April 6, 1975." In *Book of Mormon Talks by General Authorities*, 203-4. Provo, UT: FARMS, 1990. In this discourse Romney emphasizes the importance of the Book of Mormon. The Lord himself said it is true (D&C 19:26). It is the most correct book on the earth. If youth are familiar with the teachings of the Book of Mormon they will be able to make correct choices when pressured by their peers. [B.D]

R.323 Romney, Marion G. "Conference Report, October 4, 1975." In *Book of Mormon Talks by General Authorities*, 208-10. Provo, UT: FARMS, 1990. Romney asks, "Can we maintain our basic freedoms, peace, and prosperity for another 200 years?" Yes, he responds, and the Book of Mormon tells how. Ether 2:15 explains that the American continent is a land of promise. [B.D.]

R.324 Romney, Marion G. "Discovering the Book of Mormon." *NE* (May 1975): 23. Reprinted in *Book of Mormon Talks by General Authorities*, 205. Provo, UT: FARMS, 1990. Shows that the Book of Mormon teaches faith, courage, and how to receive a forgiveness of sins. [B.D.]

R.325 Romney, Marion G. "Drink Deeply From the Divine Fountain." *IE* 63 (June 1960): 435-36. Encourages Church members to read the Book of Mormon because the book will fill the reader's mind with "the waters of life," remind him/her of spiritual truths, bring great blessings into the home, cause children and parents to respect once another, and arm the reader against the faulty teachings of the world. [J.W.M.]

R.326 Romney, Marion G. "The Keystone of Our Religion." *IE* 73 (December 1970): 51-57. Reaffirms that the purpose of the Book of Mormon is to bear witness of Jesus Christ. [J.W.M.]

R.327 Romney, Marion G. "Look to God and Live." *IE* 65 (December 1962): 944-45. The gospel of Jesus Christ is the answer to all the world's problems. We can "look to God and live" (Alma 37:47). Alma knew the consequences of running counter to that advice. There are three requisites for looking to God: a true knowledge of God, a knowledge of his commandments, and obedience to the commandments. [J.W.M.]

R.328 Romney, Marion G. " 'Mormon' Church Nickname." *CR* (April 1979): 71-75. The name "Mormon Church" is a nickname that came from the Book of Mormon prophet called Mormon who abridged most of the materials of the Book of Mormon. [R.C.D.]

R.329 Romney, Marion G. "My Church Shall Be Called In My Name." *IE* 64 (June 1961): 432-35. Also in *CR* 131 (April 1961): 116-20. Acceptance of the Book of Mormon requires acceptance of modern revelation and Joseph Smith as a prophet of God. The Church received its name from Jesus Christ, as he said in 3 Nephi 27 and D&C 115:3-4. [J.W.M.]

R.330 Romney, Marion G. "A Pure Heart and Clean Hands." In *Look to God and Live*, edited by George J. Romney, 261-73. Salt Lake City: Deseret Book, 1971. Expounds on several verses from Alma's discourse on the gospel in Zarahemla (Alma 5). Features a mixture of doctrine and application. [D.M.]

R.331 Romney, Marion G. "Read the Book of Mormon." In *Learning For The Eternities*, edited by George J. Romney, 81-86. Salt Lake City: Deseret Book, 1977. Romney lists many reasons why individuals should read the Book of Mormon: to substitute the lusts of the world with the things of the Spirit, to anchor one's own children in Christ, to "find the plainest explanation of Christ's divine mission," and to learn the folly of putting trust in the treasures and learning of the world. [J.W.M.]

R.332 Romney, Marion G. "Remember Book of Mormon Teachings." *CR* (April 1980): 87-91. There are many reasons for Latter-day Saints to read and study the Book of Mormon: the Lord has commanded them to do so, they will be judged by its teachings, it will help them avoid evil and continually meditate upon God, and it will greatly assist youth and families to remain strong and faithful. [R.C.D.]

R.333 Romney, Marion G. "Repentance and Forgiveness." *CR* (October 1980): 69-73. True repentance, followed by baptism and laying on of hands for the gift of the Holy Ghost, with faith in Christ's atonement, always brings forgiveness. This truth is most clearly taught in the Book of Mormon. [R.C.D.]

R.334 Romney, Marion G. "The Role of the Indian." In *BYUSY* (15 February 1971). Provo, UT, 1971. Also in *Book of Mormon Talks by General Authorities*, 190-97. Provo, UT: FARMS, 1990. Discusses the establishment of Zion on the American Continent. The descendants of Joseph, through the lineage of Lehi, will be the builders of Zion with the assistance of the Gentiles. Several Book of Mormon scriptures show the role of the Lamanites in building Zion. [B.D.]

R.335 Romney, Marion G. "The Standard Works of the Church." *Relief Society Magazine* 56 (June 1969): 406-11. The Book of Mormon is one of the four standard scriptural works of the Church. It was translated by Joseph Smith, is the "keystone of our religion," and the world will be judged by its contents. [J.W.M.]

R.336 Romney, Marion G. Untitled talk. *CR* (April 1958): 125-29. One message of the Book of Mormon is that the Lamanites were once a favored people of the Lord and they will again be redeemed. Another message is that the inhabitants of all nations must repent or be destroyed. [B.D.]

R.337 Romney, Marion G. Untitled talk. In *Official Report of the First Mexico and Central America Area General Conference of the Church of Jesus Christ of Latter-day Saints*, Mexico City, Mexico, August 25-27, 1972, 133-37. Salt Lake City: Church of Jesus Christ of Latter-day Saints, 1973. Deals with the teachings of the Book of Mormon, the organization of the Church, and the prophet Moroni, and bears testimony of the Book of Mormon. The Book of Mormon clearly explains that the inhabitants of Mexico share the heritage of the House of Israel. [L.D.]

R.338 Romney, Marion G. "Using the Book of Mormon in Missionary Work." *CR* (April 1960): 110-13. The Book of Mormon is the most effective missionary tool in the Church. Those who read it daily will increase spirituality, protect their families from all types of evil, and draw closer to God. [R.C.D.]

R.339 Romney, Marion G. "A Warning to America." *CR* (October 1975): 51-55. The Book of Mormon declares America to be a choice land of freedom, peace, and prosperity, and it will remain a choice land only if its inhabitants are righteous. [R.C.D.]

R.340 Roundy, Phyllis Ann. "Mormon." In *Encyclopedia of Mormonism*, edited by Daniel H. Ludlow, 2:932-33. 5 vols. New York: Macmillan, 1992. Mormon was the abridger of the gold plates, leader of the Nephite armies, and father of Moroni. The article describes his writings in the Book of Mormon. [B.D.]

R.341 Rowland, Linda. "Chiasmus Settles the Question." *ZR* 44 (August 1989): 6-7. Testimony that chiasmus in 2 Nephi 2 validates the authenticity of the Book of Mormon. [A.C.W.]

R.342 Royall, Paul F. "That Our Children May Know." *Ensign* 1 (October 1971): 6-8. The Book of Mormon is a book of remembrance of the teachings of the fathers designed to teach the children of Lehi about Christ. This book of remembrance is to be supplemented by our own, which should record written testimonies, spiritual experiences, and genealogies of family members. [J.W.M.]

R.343 Roylance, Glen M. "When Men Seek Independence From God." In *The Sixth Annual CES Religious Educators Symposium on the Book of Mormon*, 82-85. Salt Lake City: Church of Jesus Christ of Latter-day Saints, 1982. Humility is singled out as the quality that keeps an individual most dependent on God. The author uses fictional stories, a poem, and an example of Korihor to show what happens when man trusts in the arm of flesh. [A.T.]

R.344 Royle, J. C. "Faith and Credulity." *The Earnest Worker* 6 (December 1883): n.p. The Book of Mormon has come forth to test the credulity of the world. Attempts to show that Joseph Smith is not a credible witness. Favors the Spaulding theory. Alleges that during printing parts of the Book of Mormon were lost and could not be duplicated. [J.W.M.]

R.345 "Ruins Recently Discovered in Yucatan Mexico." *TS* 4 (November 1842): 15-16. Reports of ruins of temples, castles, and pyramids adorned with reliefs and frescos. Many of the buildings were oriented eastward and possessed walls that were finished with a hard composition like concrete. It was thought that these ruins were archaeological evidences of the Book of Mormon. [J.W.M.]

R.346 "The Rule of Kings Abolished." *Relief Society Magazine* 5 (November 1918): 647-49. Mosiah sought to teach his people that great iniquity and destruction characterizes the rule of monarchs. [J.W.M.]

R.347 Rust, Richard Dilworth. "All Things Which Have Been Given of God . . . Are the Typifying of Him: Typology in the Book of Mormon." In *Literature of Belief: Sacred Scripture*, edited by Neil E. Lambert, 233-43. Provo, UT: Brigham Young University Religious Study Center, 1981. "Holds that the Book of Mormon fulfills its basic mission of testifying of Christ through a 'pervasive typology' as well as by its direct statements, prophecies, and quotations. He defines typology, discusses Book of Mormon teachings regarding it, and then shows its application to Book of Mormon individuals, groups, and objects—with the golden book itself a type of Christ, the ultimate treasure." [A.T.]

R.348 Rust, Richard Dilworth. "The Book of Ether: A Warning For the Last Days." *Ensign* 18 (December 1988): 18-19. Terming the book of Ether a parable based on actual history, this author points out six divisions in the text that begin with the phrase, "And now I, Moroni...." The preface to the Book of Ether is in the last two chapters of Mormon. It clearly instructs of faith, the danger of secret combinations, and how a nation that turns from Christ is destroyed. It is a pattern for this day. [J.W.M.]

R.349 Rust, Richard Dilworth, "The Book of Mormon, Designed for Our Day." In *Review of Books on the Book of Mormon* 2 (1990): 1-23. The literary elements in the Book of Mormon create an experience that motivates and teaches the reader. The epic structure gives the Lamanites a sense of their heritage and shows them how to achieve their greatest potential. Another literary element is Hebrew poetry that relates the covenantal relationship between God and man. Literary elements combined with the spirit are designed to teach the Lamanites of their heritage and the covenants of the Lord, and to convince the Jews and Gentiles that Jesus is the Christ. [J.W.M.]

R.350 Rust, Richard Dilworth. "Book of Mormon Imagery." In *Rediscovering The Book of Mormon*, edited by John L. Sorenson and Melvin J. Thorne, 132-39. Salt Lake City: Deseret Book and FARMS, 1991. The Book of Mormon is filled with images that appeal to the senses and paint graphic pictures in the mind. There are six main contrasting images: fire (that both purifies and destroys), light and darkness, captivity and deliverance, wilderness or wandering, water or fruitfulness, and dust. [J.W.M.]

R.351 Rust, Richard Dilworth. " 'I Know Your Doing': The Book of Mormon Speaks to Our Times." *Ensign* 18 (December 1988): 15-18. The Book of Mormon was written anciently specifically for our time with "historical realities" that are "prophetic parallels" significant to us. There are patterns and types that are "custom-made" for Lehi's seed, Jews, and Gentiles, with urgent calls to each group and with the overall message to come to Christ. [J.W.M.]

R.352 Rust, Richard Dilworth. "Poetry in the Book of Mormon." In *Rediscovering the Book of Mormon*, edited by John L. Sorenson and Melvin J. Thorne, 100-13. Salt Lake City: Deseret Book and FARMS, 1991. See a similar discussion in *NE* 13 (March 1983): 46-50. Understanding Hebrew poetry enhances the study of the Book of Mormon. There are many examples of parallelistic and chiastic structures that make the teachings and prophecies of the Lord more memorable and meaningful. Some passages of the book are reformatted to reveal their poetic structure. [J.W.M.]

R.353 Rust, Richard Dilworth. "Purpose of the War Chapters in the Book of Mormon." In *Warfare in the Book of Mormon*, edited by Stephen D. Ricks and William J. Hamblin, 29-32. Salt Lake City: Deseret and FARMS, 1990. The author notes that the largest battle in the first 570 years of Nephite history is covered in two sentences, some wars are covered in one, and others have extensive coverage. Mormon edited history to provide today's world with valuable lessons. One lesson seems to be that a small, faithful, righteous group aided by God can gain victory over large armies. Further it shows the folly of war and how iniquity brings on the destruction of peoples. [N.K.Y.]

R.354 Rust, Richard Dilworth, and Donald W. Parry. "Book of Mormon Literature." In *Encyclopedia of Mormonism*, edited by Daniel H. Ludlow, 1:181-85. 5 vols. New York: Macmillan, 1992. A wide variety of literary forms and Hebrew poetry are found in the Book of Mormon, including memorable narratives, rhetorically effective sermons, diverse letters, allegory, figurative language, imagery, symbolic types, and wisdom literature. Examples of each are given. The Book of Mormon is a spiritually and literarily powerful book that is direct yet complex, simple yet profound. [N.K.Y.]

R.355 Ruthven, Malise. "The Mormons' Progress." *Wilson Quarterly* (Spring 1991): 23-47. Discusses many aspects of the LDS religion including a section describing Joseph Smith's experiences in bringing forth the Book of Mormon. [D.M.]

R.356 Rytting, Paul. "Mosiah." In *Encyclopedia of Mormonism*, edited by Daniel H. Ludlow, 2:960-61. 5 vols. New York: Macmillan, 1992. States who Mosiah$_2$ was, how long he reigned, and what reforms he instituted. Before he died, instead of appointing a new king, he established a system of paid judges to govern the people. [B.D.]

S.

S.001 S., J. M. "Book of Mormon Evidence." *MS* 79 (24 May 1917): 328-30. Archaeological evidence that horses existed in ancient America supports the Book of Mormon. Evidence of advanced textile art confirms statement of "all manner of fine linen." [A.C.W.]

S.002 S., J. M. "Confirming the Book of Mormon." *MS* 79 (4 January 1917): 8-10. The Book of Mormon teaches of ancient connections between Asia and America. The article quotes G. Elliot Smith, who theorizes that a cultural migration took place from Egypt to ancient America, c. 900 B.C., citing archaeological evidence. [A.C.W.]

S.003 S., J. M. "Indians Becoming White and Delightsome." *MS* 79 (February 1917): 72-74. Argues that the Indians of North and South America are making spiritual and "material progress" and becoming "white and delightsome," thus fulfilling a prophecy of the Book of Mormon. [D.W.P.]

S.004 S., J. Z. "The Book of Mormon." *MS* 42 (19 April 1880): 246-47. Old Indian and Spanish histories that are preserved in Mexican libraries and museums provide evidence of the divine authenticity of the Book of Mormon. [J.W.M.]

S.005 S., L. P. "The Choice Seer—Who Is He?" *The Rod of Iron* 1 (June 1924): 22-24. Analyzes 2 Nephi 3 and finds that a choice seer will be a blessing to the descendants of Lehi. The choice seer may be Jesus Christ, whose work was the Book of Mormon. [J.W.M.]

S.006 S., L. P. "The Work of This Dispensation." *The Rod of Iron* 1 (May 1924): 17-19. The mission of the Book of Mormon and the work of this dispensation is to save souls, to gather Israel, to teach the covenants of God, and to build Zion. [J.W.M.]

S.007 "Samuel, the Lamanite Prophet." *Young Woman's Journal* 31 (December 1920): 695-705. Recreates the drama of Samuel the Lamanite's mission to the Nephites. Continues with discussions about Jesus' appearance to the Lehites. [D.M.]

S.008 Santiago. "Prehistoric Races of Arizona." *Contributor* 10 (April 1889): 204-6. There is much evidence of an ancient civilization in Arizona. The legends that surround these people closely resemble the story of the Nephites chronicled in the Book of Mormon. [J.W.M.]

S.009 "The Savior in America." *Instructor* 77 (April 1942): 185-86. An Easter message that includes an extensive quotation from 3 Nephi concerning the appearance of Jesus Christ in America. [R.H.B.]

S.010 Sawyer, John. "What Was a Mosia?" Provo, UT: FARMS, 1965. The Hebrew word *Mosia*^{a} (Savior) denotes "a champion of justice in a situation of controversy, battle, or oppression." In Old Testament usage it refers to someone who holds a specific office or position. The Book of Mosiah tells of one *Mosia*^{a} (Savior) after another—Alma, Zeniff, and King Mosiah. It is unknown whether Mosiah was always called such or he was given the title after he delivered his people from war by escaping the land of Nephi. [J.W.M.]

S.011 Scharffs, Gilbert W. *The Truth About "The God Makers."* Salt Lake City: Publishers Press, 1986. Responds to charges made against Mormonism in the book *The God Makers*. Some charges that pertain to the Book of Mormon are that Mormon doctrine is not based on the Book of Mormon or the Bible, much of the Book of Mormon is copied from the Bible, Book of Mormon prophets quoted New Testament prophets, the Book of Mormon contains many contradictions, and various others. These are refuted by LDS teachings. [J.W.M.]

S.012 Scharffs, Gilbert W. "Unique Insights on Christ from the Book of Mormon." *Ensign* 18 (December 1988): 8-12. The Book of Mormon features many unique insights concerning Jesus Christ and his gospel that are not contained in the Bible. They include specific teachings about Christ's atonement, the plan of salvation, the Lord's relationship to mankind, free agency, the necessity of grace and works, affirmation of the truthfulness of the Bible, Jesus' eminent position as Jehovah, his priesthood, and his latter-day work. The Book of Mormon witnesses that Jesus is the Christ. [A.A.]

S.013 Scharffs, Horst. "One Hundred Pounds of Potatoes." *Ensign* 19 (July 1989): 52-53. Discusses a personal testimony of a boy who used his faith in the Book of Mormon to pray for strength. [L.D.]

S.014 Schenck, Joseph. *Itzamna, the Dew of Heaven.* St. Louis, MO: Vanity, 1968. Itzamna the Dew of Heaven, the blonde, blue-eyed god of the ancient Mayan civilization, has qualities that recall the life and mission of Jesus Christ. [J.W.M.]

S.015 Schenck, Joseph. *Temples in the Sky (Archaeological Evidence Relative to the Book of Mormon).* St. Louis, MO: Vanity, 1966. Includes numerous photographs and maps, demonstrating that the archaeological ruins of Latin America have an affinity with Egyptian culture, and correlate with the Book of Mormon. [D.M.]

S.016 Schlesinger, Philip J. *Isaiah and the Book of Mormon.* N.p., 1990. A commentary on Isaiah passages in the Book of Mormon, written by a Jewish convert. [D.M.]

S.017 Schneider, Johann. "The Dream Seemed Meaningless." *Ensign* 19 (September 1989): 66. A long-forgotten dream comes true when two LDS missionaries teach Johann and Margrit Schneider about the Church and the Book of Mormon. Reading the book brought a realization that the book and the Church were true. [J.W.M.]

S.018 Schofield, K. "Missionary Book Report." *Friend* 18 (September 1988): 34. Cartoon message for children. A nine-year-old boy presents a book report on the Book of Mormon in his school, impressing his teacher to the point that she desires to read it. [J.W.M.]

S.019 "The Scholar and the Book of Mormon." *Relief Society Magazine* 10 (September 1923): 433-34. Scholarly critics of the Book of Mormon, found in large numbers on college campuses, try to discredit the divine origin of the Book of Mormon. [J.W.M.]

S.020 Schwarz, Ted. *Arnold Friberg: The Passion of a Modern Master.* Flagstaff, AZ: Northland, 1985. Schwarz's biography of Arnold Friberg includes a history of Friberg's artistic work on the Book of Mormon and reproduces many of his paintings, including the brother of Jared, discovery of the Liahona, Abinadi in Noah's court, and Christ's appearance to the Nephites. [A.C.W.]

S.021 Scott, Hazel Imrie. *Heroes of the Book of Mormon.* Independence, MO: Herald House, 1986. RLDS activity book designed for teaching the Book of Mormon to children. [D.M.]

S.022 Scott, Richard G. "The Power of the Book of Mormon in My Life." *Ensign* 14 (October 1984): 6-11. Cites several personal experiences to show that the Book of Mormon can be a source of spiritual guidance and strength to those who read it frequently, ponder its principles and teachings, and apply those principles to their lives. The Book of Mormon contains the answers to "specific problems we face in everyday life." [S.P.S.]

S.023 Scott, Richard G. "True Friends That Lift." *Ensign* 18 (November 1988): 76-77. The Book of Mormon is the most important tool used to correct the effects of false traditions and to resolve problems and challenges, but has no value if the book remains unused. It is "a precious friend provided by a loving Savior." [J.W.M.]

S.024 Scott, Richard G. "We Love You—Please Come Back." *CR* (5-6 April 1986): 11-13. Also in *Ensign* 16 (May 1986): 10-12. Studying the Book of Mormon is an important part of the repentance process. Many messages pertaining to repentance are found within its pages. Suffering does not bring repentance; rather, it is faith and the atonement of Jesus that cure the soul. The Book of Mormon teaches that selfishness is the root of all sin. [J.W.M.]

S.025 Scoville, Monte C. "Counseling With the Lord." *Instructor* 98 (March 1963): 104-5. Seeking a testimony with real intent and counseling with the Lord allows a testimony of the Book of Mormon to grow. [A.C.W.]

S.026 "Scriptures on 2,600-Year-Old Silver Scrolls Found in Jerusalem." *Ensign* 17 (June 1987): 56-57. Silver scrolls found in a burial cave just outside Jerusalem are described. Includes the inscriptions contained thereon. Author concludes that fine metalworking was known at the time Lehi left Jerusalem. [A.T.]

S.027 Searle, Don L. "Book Convinced Him." *Ensign* 20 (March 1990): 50-52. An Italian scientist/atheist put the Book of Mormon to many scientific tests, only to receive a witness of its truthfulness from the Holy Ghost. [J.W.M.]

S.028 Sears, John. *Final State of Mankind, Demonstrated by the Prophecies of the Old and New Testaments, Also the Book of Mormon and the Doctrine and Covenants.* Salt Lake City: Joseph Hyrum Parry & Co., 1886. A booklet containing commentary and scriptural quotes from the Bible, Book of Mormon, and Doctrine and Covenants that pertain to prophecies of the second coming, the new Jerusalem, judgment, and the degrees of glory. [J.A.T.]

S.029 Seastrand, James K., and Rosel Seastrand. "The Holy Bible And The Book of Mormon." In Seastrand's *Journey To Eternal Life and Distractions Along The Way: Scriptural Answers To Challenges of LDS Church Beliefs,* 137-42. Las Vegas, NV: Newmark Publishing, 1990. An argument for the need for continuous revelation and the Book of Mormon. [J.W.M.]

S.030 "Secular Proofs of the Book of Mormon." *MS* 61 (April 1899): 229-31. A reprint of an article from the *Deseret News* that gives the substance of a lecture by George Reynolds. Evidences that prove the ancient inhabitants of this continent were Nephites: Hebrew inscriptions on stone, metal and parchment and a story that a "francisco" discovered a secret "Nephite hiding place," the whereabouts of which he could not reveal under a oath of secrecy. [B.D.]

S.031 Seely, David Rolph. "The Allegory of the Olive Tree and the Use of Related Figurative Language in the Ancient Near East and the Old Testament." In *The Allegory of the Olive Tree: The Olive, The Bible, and Jacob 5,* edited by Stephen D. Ricks and John W. Welch, 290-304. Salt Lake City: Deseret Book and FARMS, 1994. Compares literary language of the Old Testament and the use of figurative language in the ancient Near East to better understand the allegory of Jacob 5. Explains that modern literary terms do not correlate exactly with ancient literary traditions, thus necessitating reader understanding of a text's historical context. [A.C.W.]

S.032 Seely, David Rolph. "Enos and the Words Concerning Eternal Life." In *The Book of Mormon: Jacob through Words of Mormon, To Learn with Joy,* edited by Monte S. Nyman and Charles D. Tate Jr., 235-50. Provo, UT: Brigham Young University Religious Studies Center, 1990. The "words . . . concerning eternal life" (Enos 1:3) provide the catalyst for repentance in the life of Enos. One of the benefits of true conversion is charity, which is a gift of the Spirit. Enos takes the admonition found in his father's teachings and applies them, with true conversion as the end result. Other examples of true conversion are cited. [J.W.M.]

S.033 Seely, David Rolph. "The Image of The Hand of God in The Book Of Mormon and The Old Testament." In *Rediscovering The Book of Mormon,* edited by John L. Sorenson and Melvin J. Thorne, 140-50. Salt Lake City: Deseret Book and FARMS, 1991. References to the hand, arm, or finger of God appears 345 times in 1,184 pages of the Old Testament and 135 times in the Book of Mormon, an average of once every 3.4 pages in each book of scripture. The references may be understood literally or symbolically. [J.W.M.]

S.034 Seely, David Rolph. "The Ten Commandments in the Book of Mormon." In *Doctrines of the Book of Mormon, 1991 Sperry Symposium,* edited by Bruce A. Van Orden and Brent L. Top, 166-81. Salt Lake City: Deseret Book, 1992. Book of Mormon theology finds its foundation in the ten commandments and the book shows the consequences of disobedience to them even leading to the destruction of a people; yet Abinadi taught that obedience to them would not bring salvation except for the atonement of Christ. Although the ten commandments are listed only once in the Book of Mormon, there are twenty-four passages where two or more of the commandments are mentioned together. The ten commandments are applicable to all. The first five commandments demonstrate man's relationship to God, while the second five are concerned with man's relationship with man. [N.K.Y.]

S.035 Seely, David Rolph, and John W. Welch. "Zenos and the Texts of the Old Testament." In *The Allegory of the Olive Tree: The Olive, The Bible and Jacob 5,* edited by Stephen D. Ricks and John W. Welch, 322-346. Salt Lake City: Deseret Book and FARMS, 1994. Compares the words of Zenos with the words of other early Israelite prophets. Old Testament literature is replete with symbols that represent the house of Israel as an olive tree or a vine. Different prophets use different aspects of the allegory, speaking of destruction and restoration, of scattering and gathering, but always of the involvement of the Lord with the house of Israel. [J.W.M.]

S.036 Seeman, Curt H. "Preparation and Precaution in Scriptural Study; Part II." In *14th Annual Symposium on Archaeology of the Scriptures,* edited by Forrest R. Hauck, 12-21. Provo, UT: Extension Publication, Brigham Young University, 13 April 1963. Warns that archaeology cannot verify scriptures; cites the Charles Anthon story to demonstrate the futility of relying upon scholarly authorities for religious beliefs. [A.C.W.]

S.037 Shapiro, R. Gary, comp. *An Exhaustive Concordance of the Book of Mormon, Doctrine and Covenants and Pearl of Great Price.* Salt Lake City: Hawkes, 1977. An alphabetical listing of nearly every word occurring in the Book of Mormon, Doctrine and Covenants, and Pearl of Great Price with context entries. Words found in the title page and the thirty original chapter headings of the Book of Mormon are also included. [J.T.]

S.038 Sharp, James P. "It Happened in Mexico." *IE* 43 (January 1940): 22, 32. In response to the accusations of three traveling Methodist preachers, the author attempts to prove through archaeology the existence in pre-Columbian Central America of horses, cement, and jewelry—things mentioned in the Book of Mormon. [J.T.]

S.039 Sharp, Loretta M. "The Mythic Machiavelli: The Prince and Mandragola. Mythic Patterns in a Portrait of the Artist as a Young Man; Archetypal Patterns in the Book of Mormon." M.A. thesis, Brigham Young University, 1971. Discusses several archetypal patterns that occur in the Book of Mormon. These include the archetypal night journey, the Cain-Abel archetype, the Oedipal statement, the Great Mother archetype, and the resulting masculinity of the book. She provides several examples of each archetype, and relates them to the scriptural context. [A.C.W.]

S.040 Sharp, W. H. H. "The Angel Moroni." *Contributor* 1 (March 1880): 142-43. Quotes Revelation 14:6-8 and explains that Moroni was the angel who held the keys of the gospel and came to earth in the latter days to commit them to Joseph Smith. Gives a biographical outline of Moroni's mortal life and discusses his latter-day work in bringing the Book of Mormon to light. [A.C.W.]

S.041 Sharp, W. H. H. "A Voice from Heaven." *Our Deseret Home* 2 (1883): 146. Discusses the wickedness of the American nation as related to the prophecies of Samuel the Lamanite. He includes numerous quotes from the Book of Mormon and information about early explorers of America, and promotes the idea that the earth is a live animal. [A.C.W.]

S.042 Shaw, Faye. "The White Man's Book of Heaven." In *Recent Book of Mormon Developments, Articles from the Zarahemla Record,* 1:99-100. Independence, MO: Zarahemla Research Foundation, 1992. 2 Nephi 12:79-80 (RLDS versification) prophesies that the gentile book will be carried forth to the Lamanites. This article describes two Nez Perce Indians who traveled to St. Louis, Missouri, from the Northwest to find a book that nobody gave them. [B.D.]

S.043 Shaw, Mary C. "Pigmy Elephants." *IE* 39 (January 1936): 19. Newly discovered fossils of elephants were found on an island off the coast of California. This discovery may indicate that the Book of Mormon contains the truth. [J.W.M.]

S.044 Sheen, Isaac. "Antiquarian Evidences of the Book of Mormon." *True L.D.S. Herald* 9-10 (May-August 1866): 130-33, 147-50, 163-65, 178-83, 3-5, 20-23, 35-36. Archaeological and historical concepts associated with the Americas and parallels between the Old and New Worlds (i.e., Hebrew and Egyptian languages and customs found among the Indians) are discussed in light of many claims made in the Book of Mormon. [J.T.]

S.045 Sheen, Isaac. "Reply to an Inquiry No. 2." *True L.D.S. Herald* 10 (15 September 1866): 82-83. Explains how the Book of Mormon contains the fullness of the gospel. [B.D.]

S.046 Sheffield, William. "Voice From the Dust." In *Encyclopedia of Mormonism,* edited by Daniel H. Ludlow, 4:1538. 5 vols. New York: Macmillan, 1992. Identifies the phrase "voice from the dust" as speaking of the coming-forth of the Book of Mormon using scriptural evidence. [B.D.]

S.047 Shields, Steven L. *Book of Mormon Study Series: Studies in 1 Nephi.* Independence, MO: Herald House, 1987. Explores themes found in 1 Nephi: the Nephite sojourn in the wilderness, the tree of life, Nephi's vision, the olive tree, and the Liahona. [J.W.M.]

S.048 Shields, Steven L. *Book of Mormon Study Series: Studies in 3 Nephi.* Independence, MO: Herald House, 1987. Studies in 3 Nephi: the birth of Christ, Jesus Christ, the son of God, Jesus visits the Nephites, the Sermon on the Mount, other sheep. [J.W.M.]

S.049 Shields, Steven L. *Studies in Alma.* 2 vols. Independence, MO: Herald House, 1989-90. A study guide with scriptural paraphrases, questions, and activities designed to aid the reader in understanding the book of Alma. [D.W.P.]

S.050 Shields, Steven L. *Studies in Helaman.* Independence, MO: Herald House, 1990. A study guide with scriptural paraphrases, questions, and activities designed to aid the reader in understanding the book of Helaman. [D.W.P.]

S.051 Shipps, Jan. *Mormonism: The Story of a New Religious Tradition.* Urbana: University of Illinois Press, 1985. The first two chapters of this book describe the history of the Mormon church until the publication of the Book of Mormon. The author stresses the importance of the Book of Mormon in converting people to Joseph Smith's cause. Only later did the First Vision begin to take prominence. [B.D.]

S.052 Shreeve, Thomas A. "A Sacred History: External Evidences of the Truth of the Book of Mormon." *Juvenile Instructor* 22-23 (February-December 1887, January-March 1888): 54-55, 76, 90-92, 107-9, 118-19, 142-43, 157-58, 162-63, 190-91, 194-95, 222, 237-38, 242-43, 258-59, 284-85, 300-301, 316-17, 324-25, 340-41, 356-57, 4-5, 34-35, 61, 76-77. Uses historical, linguistic, and archaeological evidence to prove the truthfulness of the Book of Mormon. Basing his facts on research done by noted linguists and archaeologists of the time, the author writes concerning the god Quetzalcoatl, religious customs and ruins of advanced civilizations, comparisons between the Hebrew and Mayan languages, and the Egyptian hieroglyphic writings. Shreeve also tells of similarities in biblical beliefs between early people of both the western and eastern hemispheres and explains why Joseph Smith was incapable of writing the Book of Mormon without divine aid. [A.C.W.]

S.053 Shreeve, Thomas A. "Study of the Book of Mormon." *Contributor* 9 (1887–1888): 275-80. An address encouraging Book of Mormon study. Tells of the finding of Egyptian characters by Augustus LePlongeon among the Mayans and traditions of Christ's ministration among the American Indians. [A.T.]

S.054 Shumway, Eric B. "Polynesians." In *Encyclopedia of Mormonism*, edited by Daniel H. Ludlow, 3:1110-12. 5 vols. New York: Macmillan, 1992. Identifies the Polynesians as descendants of Lehi. Quotes general authorities, including President Joseph F. Smith, who said to the Maoris in New Zealand, "you are some of Hagoth's people." [B.D.]

S.055 Shute, R. Wayne, and Wayne E. Brickey. "Prophets and Perplexity: The Book of Helaman as a Case Study." In *The Book of Mormon: Helaman through 3 Nephi 8, According to Thy Word*, edited by Monte S. Nyman and Charles D. Tate Jr., 177-90. Provo, UT: Brigham Young University Religious Studies Center, 1992. Using the model of J. T. Dillon called "moments of inquiry," the authors show how $Nephi_2$ and Samuel the Lamanite engendered perplexity in their audiences, and may do the same for modern audiences. [D.M.]

S.056 "Significance of Cumorah." *MS* 97 (12 September 1935): 596-97. Mentions the erection of the Cumorah Monument, identifies Moroni as a resurrected Nephite prophet. Stresses the doctrine of the immortality and resurrection of man. [R.H.B.]

S.057 Sill, Sterling W. "Book of Mormon." In *BYUSY* (24 March 1957). Provo, UT: BYU Press. We may not be able to walk where Jesus walked, but of greater worth is that we can think what Jesus thought. The Book of Mormon reveals the thoughts of Christ. Heroes of the Book of Mormon are worthy of emulation. Sill highlights Mormon, who possessed a celestial mind. [J.W.M.]

S.058 Sill, Sterling W. "The Book of Mormon." In Sill's *The Majesty of Books,* 38-41. Salt Lake City: Deseret Book, 1974. The Book of Mormon's express purpose is to bring men to Christ. This book also tells of God's commitment to liberty, freedom, and agency. America has a "brilliant future" when Jesus will establish his government with two capitals, one in America, and the other in Jerusalem. [J.W.M.]

S.059 Sill, Sterling W. "A Man Called Jacob." *Instructor* 102 (November 1967): 424-25. Briefly discusses some of the characteristics of Jacob, son of Lehi. Jacob is portrayed as a man to whom others look for an example of spiritual living. [J.T.]

S.060 Sill, Sterling W. "Mormon and Moroni." Salt Lake City: Salt Lake Institute of Religion, 1973. A devotional that discusses the lives of Mormon and Moroni. Identifies their greatness and faithfulness and history. [D.W.P.]

S.061 Silver, Gerald. *Lehi's Wilderness Journey: An Ensign Sponsored Trip of South Arabia*. Salt Lake City: Church of Jesus Christ of Latter-day Saints, October 1977. A filmstrip (94 frames, 16 1/2 minutes) based on a journey to the Arabian Peninsula. Arabia "portrays the geography and cultural conditions that could have existed in Lehi's day and gives the viewer a better feeling for and understanding of the journey that Lehi and his family experienced in traveling from Jerusalem to the land Bountiful." [A.C.W.]

S.062 Simmerman, Gerald M. "Nephi Confounds the Wicked Judges." *Friend* 15 (November 1985): 48-49. Nephi, son of Helaman, confronts the wicked judges (Helaman 6-9). [J.W.M.]

S.063 Simmons, Neil. "Chief Captain Moroni Remembered." In *Recent Book of Mormon Developments, Articles from the Zarahemla Record*, 2:187-88. Independence, MO: Zarahemla Research Foundation, 1992. Diego Durán describes Mexican Indians' celebration of Huitzilopochtli, a god who, when alive, was never caught, never taken prisoner in war, and always triumphant. Simmons relates Huitzilopochtli with Moroni. [B.D.]

S.064 Simmons, Neil. "Marijuana and the Book of Mormon." In *Recent Book of Mormon Developments, Articles from the Zarahemla Record*, 1:127. Independence, MO: Zarahemla Research Foundation, 1984. 2 Nephi 11:94 (RLDS versification) says that Satan leads men by the neck with a flaxen cord. No flax existed in Mesoamerica, but the ancient Americans did use *cannabis sativa* (common name marijuana), a plant that resembles flax. [B.D.]

S.065 Simmons, Neil, and Raymond C. Treat. "Maya Hieroglyphs Point to the Book of Mormon." *ZR* 19-21 (Winter, Spring, Summer 1983): 1-5, 24. Examines research into Maya glyphs and states that this research has produced two finds important to Book of Mormon believers: the glyphs are partly phonetic, and the glyphs deal mainly with history. Based upon findings from glyphs, the author proposes Yaxchilan to be Zarahemla and Palenque to be Bountiful. [A.T.]

S.066 Simmons, Rae. "The Need To Study." In *Recent Book of Mormon Developments, Articles from the Zarahemla Record*, 2:161-62. Independence, MO: Zarahemla Research Foundation, 1992. 2 Nephi 14:4 (RLDS versification) tells us to "feast upon the words of Christ." Simmons writes of her motivation to study and results that came from studying. [B.D.]

S.067 Simmons, Rae. "Zenos: One of the Major Prophets." *Witness* 70 (Fall 1990): 11. Cites the teachings and prophecies of Zenos included in the Book of Mormon to demonstrate his importance as a prophet. [A.C.W.]

S.068 Simmons, Verneil W. "Another Look at the Book of Mormon Ministry of Christ." *ZR* 29-31 (Summer, Fall 1985, Winter 1986): 1-3, 23. Suggests that Christ appeared to the Nephites on Rosh Hashanah (near September 22). The institution of the sacrament among the Nephites is compared to the last supper. Warns against the changing of ordinances. [A.T.]

S.069 Simmons, Verneil W. "Archaeology and the Book of Mormon." *Restoration Witness* 7 (June 1969): 4-5, 14. Upon arriving in Mesoamerica the Spanish destroyed the books of the Mayan people because they considered them evil. An unknown Mayan man rewrote his people's history in the 1550s, and it later resurfaced in 1700 and has come to be known as *Popol Vuh*, the Book of the people. This and other archaeological finds have many things in common with the Book of Mormon. [J.W.M.]

S.070 Simmons, Verneil W. *Peoples, Places and Prophecies: A Study of the Book of Mormon.* Independence, MO: Zarahemla Research Foundation, 1986. A discussion of three groups—Jaredites, Nephites, and Mulekites—who traveled from the Old World to the New World. Geographical, historical, and archaeological evidences are cited with the intent to prove the veracity of the Book of Mormon. Author cites the *Popul Vuh*, the Dead Sea Scrolls, the Bible, and other sources. [A.C.W.]

S.071 Simmons, Verneil W. "Why I Wrote Peoples, Places, and Prophecies." *ZR* 8 (Spring 1980): 4-6. Describes the experiences that led her to write: she believed in two Hill Cumorahs and believed the "narrow neck" to be the "Isthmus of Tehuantepec in southern Mexico." [A.T.]

S.072 Simmons, Wayne E. ". . . And they Are One God." In *Recent Book of Mormon Developments, Articles from the Zarahemla Record*, 1:136-37. Independence, MO: Zarahemla Research Foundation, 1984. The confusion among theologians and scholars about whether God and Christ are two separate beings or the same person is solved by Mosiah 8:28-31 (RLDS versification). The Book of Mormon explains that they are separate but one. Simmons explains this oneness as similar to the oneness of husband and wife. [B.D.]

S.073 Simmons, Wayne E. "It Is Written." In *Recent Book of Mormon Developments, Articles from the Zarahemla Record*, 1:138-39. Independence, MO: Zarahemla Research Foundation, 1984. An article on the importance of scripture and continuing revelation. 2 Nephi 11:40-42 (RLDS versification) says that the nations that possess the Book of Mormon shall be judged according to it. [B.D.]

S.074 Simmons, Wayne E. "A Patriarchal View of Israel, Part 1." In *Recent Book of Mormon Developments, Articles from the Zarahemla Record*, 1:130-32. Independence, MO: Zarahemla Research Foundation, 1984. Discusses how RLDS members can be considered part of the house of Israel. Lehi was of the tribe of Manasseh and the Reorganized Church of Jesus Christ of Latter Day Saints is "definitely a divine enterprise in which Ephraim and Manasseh are called together, here in the Americas which is Joseph's land." [B.D.]

S.075 Simmons, Wayne E. "A Patriarchal View of Israel, Part 2." In *Recent Book of Mormon Developments, Articles from the Zarahemla Record*, 1:133-35. Independence, MO: Zarahemla Research Foundation, 1984. Moroni, in Ether 6:7-8 (RLDS versification), explains that Joseph who was sold into Egypt was a type in that his seed should establish the New Jerusalem on the American Continent. Ezekiel 37:16-19 explains that the Bible and the Book of Mormon, the sticks of Judah and Joseph, will be united. Thus, the Book of Mormon explains the gathering of Israel in the last days especially in the allegory of the olive tree. [B.D.]

S.076 Simon, Jerry F. "Minister the Same Words Which Jesus Has Spoken." In *A Symposium on the Book of Mormon,* 116-19. Salt Lake City: Church of Jesus Christ of Latter-day Saints, August 1986. The Book of Mormon teaches individuals how to be gospel teachers. A teacher prays, searches the scriptures before teaching, and then receives the Holy Ghost who instructs. One should keep personal opinions personal; opinions should not be taught as truth. One should never teach beyond one's own comprehension, stay away from contentious subjects, and remain silent on the subjects the Lord has chosen to be silent about. Teach the words Jesus spoke. [J.W.M.]

S.077 Simpson, Robert L. "The Next Fifteen Minutes." *NE* 19 (July 1989): 4-6. Simpson as a youth gave a Book of Mormon, complete with testimony, to a friend. The friend showed him an encyclopedia that claimed Joseph Smith and the Book of Mormon to be counterfeit. Devastation turned into testimony three days later in a quorum meeting. [J.W.M.]

S.078 Sims, George. "Fulfillment of Prophecies of the Book of Mormon Concerning the Land of America." *MS* 25 (October 1863): 691-94. The Book of Mormon states that "whatsoever nation shall possess [America] shall serve God, or they shall be swept off." This promise to America, the "promised land," was fulfilled in the days of the Jaredites who allowed secret combinations to flourish. Those who remain faithful to Jesus Christ will enjoy the ministration of angels, fellowship with prophets, communion with saints, the gift of the Holy Ghost, and possession of the land of promise. [J.W.M.]

S.079 Sirota, Mark F. *Paraphrase and Commentary on the Book of Mormon: 3 Nephi.* Mesa, AZ: M. F. Sirota, 1983. A photocopied anthology of texts and commentaries on 3 Nephi 1-10, taken from 4 major sources, including volume 7 of *Commentary on the Book of Mormon,* by George Reynolds and Janne Sjodahl. [D.W.P.]

S.080 *The Sixth Annual Church Educational System Religious Educators' Symposium on the Book of Mormon.* Salt Lake City: Church of Jesus Christ of Latter-day Saints, 1982. Papers presented at the sixth annual symposium on the Book of Mormon. Articles by Church educators, including Susan Easton Black, Charles Beckert, Robert Christensen, and numerous others. [J.W.M.]

S.081 Sjodahl, J. M. "Ancient Indian Literature." *IE* 29 (September 1926): 1035-42. Refers to the record-keeping habits of the inhabitants of the Americas as discovered by European observers. An English translation of several records is given, and a kinship shown between traditions among the American pre-European peoples and the milieu from which the Book of Mormon emerged. [D.M.]

S.082 Sjodahl, J. M. "Archaeological Finds in Arizona." *IE* 28 (July 1925): 813-21. Several crosses with Latin inscriptions, a spear, and sword that were excavated near Tucson, Arizona, are discussed as possible evidence for pre-Columbian contact between the Americas and Europe. Author speculates that a reference to a "mountain" in the inscriptions may be connected to the Hill Cumorah mentioned in the Book of Mormon. [J.T.]

S.083 Sjodahl, J. M. "Archaeological Research and the Book of Mormon." *IE* 25 (October 1922): 1104-7. Takes the position that contemporary archaeology corroborates the claim that Book of Mormon peoples had Middle Eastern roots. [D.M.]

S.084 Sjodahl, J. M. "Archaeology and the Book of Mormon." *MS* 87 (26 February 1925): 132-34. The conclusions of modern research of the mound builders coincides with the Book of Mormon account of the Jaredite people. Modern archaeologists conclude that the Indians are of one race, their migrations were from south to north, the original inhabitants of America bear an unmistakable relationship to the Semitic branches of eastern culture and Egypt. [J.W.M.]

S.085 Sjodahl, J. M. *Authenticity of the Book of Mormon.* Liverpool: MS Office, 1915. Also published as Sjodahl, J. M. "Authenticity of the Book of Mormon," *MS* 77 (29 July, 5, 12, 19, August 1915): 465-70, 481-87, 497-503, 513-19. Wishes to convince the reader that the Book of Mormon is authentic by using historical, linguistic, and archaeological evidence, plus the testimonies of the eleven witnesses and examples of biblical scriptures that have been fulfilled through the Book of Mormon. The Book of Mormon is a "good book" that leads people to improve themselves and their lives. [A.C.W.]

S.086 Sjodahl, J. M. "The Book of Mormon and Modern Research." *IE* 25 (December 1921): 152-58. This defense of the Book of Mormon concludes that archaeological and anthropological data about the pre-Columbian Americas do not contradict the Book of Mormon and often coincide with it. [D.M.]

S.087 Sjodahl, J. M. "Book of Mormon Characters." *IE* 27 (December 1923): 146-48. Discusses the Anthon transcript and declares that the letter written by Anthon concerning the figures on the paper presented by Martin Harris provides an opinion that is without value. Anthon's brief examination and his finding do not correlate with the characters as preserved. [D.M.]

S.088 Sjodahl, J. M. "Book of Mormon Evidence." *MS* 76 (3 December 1914): 776-77. Illustrates similarities between the ancient Nephite and Toltec civilizations. The history of the Toltec peoples and their destruction by the Aztecs lends evidence to the historicity and truth of the Book of Mormon. [K.M.]

S.089 Sjodahl, J. M. "Book of Mormon Evidence." *MS* 79 (May 1917): 328-30. Quotes one source that mentions the discovery of horse bones in America, and another source that describes the discovery of a petroglyph in Arizona that represents dinosaurs and four-toed horses. [B.D.]

S.090 Sjodahl, J. M. "Book of Mormon Evidence." *MS* 89 (10 March 1927): 150-51, 157-58. Recent scientific research is used to establish facts mentioned in the Book of Mormon. The use of steel in the Book of Mormon is supported by recent findings of hardened tools and steel implements in ancient American ruins. [J.T.]

S.091 Sjodahl, J. M. "Book of Mormon Facts." *Juvenile Instructor* 57 (May-June 1922): 243-45, 305-9. A collection of various facts that attempt to portray the Book of Mormon as an ancient record as well as a prophetic book: World War I and the giving of Palestine to the Jews are shown to be foretold, the mentioning of steel and iron are defended, and the possible origin of the name America is discussed as coming from Book of Mormon people. [J.T.]

S.092 Sjodahl, J. M. "The Book of Mormon Plates." *IE* 26 (April 1923): 541-45. Discusses the length, width, and weight of the plates, according to witnesses or people who talked to witnesses. He also treats the possible number of words that could have been inscribed on a given leaf. [D.M.]

S.093 Sjodahl, J. M. "Confirming the Book of Mormon." *MS* 79 (January 1917): 8-10. Quotes G. Elliot Smith who argues that the ancient Americans descended from the Egyptians. His evidence for this theory are the similar practices of circumcision, mummification, tattooing, architecture, and mythology. [B.D.]

S.094 Sjodahl, J. M. "Credibility of the Witnesses." *IE* 26 (September 1923): 969-79. The author defends the reliability of both the Three and the Eight Witnesses to the Book of Mormon. The witnesses consistently adhered to their testimony and each had an unassailable reputation. [D.M.]

S.095 Sjodahl, J. M. "Credibility of the Witnesses." *MS* 85 (October 1923): 625-27, 644-47, 661-63, 676-78. A biographical summary about each of the Eleven Witnesses. Sjodahl quotes portions of published testimonies of the Three Witnesses. [B.D.]

S.096 Sjodahl, J. M. "Have the Lamanites Jaredite Blood in Their Veins?" *IE* 31 (November 1927): 56-57. Proposes that not all the Jaredites perished in the final Jaredite cataclysm. He speculates that some of them fled and joined the people of Mulek. [D.M.]

S.097 Sjodahl, J. M. "Hvitra-manna-land and Lamoni." *IE* 26 (December 1922): 190-93.

Relates names from sagas and American geography to Book of Mormon names such as "Laman" and "Lamoni," which the author suggests refers to "white." This is seen as a Book of Mormon evidence. [D.M.]

S.098 Sjodahl, J. M. *An Introduction to the Study of the Book of Mormon*. Salt Lake City: Deseret Book, 1927. An approach to the Book of Mormon through the study of ancient languages, geography, the history of the LDS Church, and the cultures of ancient civilizations in the Old and New Worlds. [J.T.]

S.099 Sjodahl, J. M. "The Jaredite Lands." *IE* 42 (June 1939): 336-37, 370-71. An analysis of the geographical statements given in the Book of Ether and possible North American correlations. [J.T.]

S.100 Sjodahl, J. M. "Language of White Indians." *IE* 28 (April 1925): 568-71. An analysis of the language of "white Indians" found by an American explorer in the mountains of Darien, in Panama, reveals a vast number of words related to old world words in both form and meaning. Some Hebrew words are found in this Indian language. [J.W.M.]

S.101 Sjodahl, J. M. "Meaning of the word 'Mormon.'" *IE* 30 (March 1927): 433-34. Quotes Joseph Smith's statement that "Mormon" means "more good," or, in other words, "better." The first syllable is English, the second is Egyptian. The "good" in the name is related to the gospel as good news. Several native American languages have superlatives that translate "more good." [D.M.]

S.102 Sjodahl, J. M. "The Name Moroni." *IE* 28 (October 1925): 1132-34. The appellation "Moroni" shows up in Asia, the Americas, and even in Paul's exclamation "maranatha" (1 Cor. 16:22). [D.M.]

S.103 Sjodahl, J. M. "New Book of Mormon Evidences." *MS* 96 (17 May 1934): 305-7. Explores geographical/historical/archaeological implications of Lehi's journey out of Jerusalem. Says hostile Arabs prevented a journey through inhabited areas. [A.C.W.]

S.104 Sjodahl, J. M. "Notes on the Book of Mormon." *IE* 30 (April, May June, July 1927): 526-31, 623-26, 696-700, 795-800. Discusses the gold plates, the burial of the plates at the Hill Cumorah, the Urim and Thummim, the characters on the plates, Joseph Smith's preparation for translation, the scribes, and manuscripts. [D.M.]

S.105 Sjodahl, J. M. "The Signs of the Times: The Book of Mormon." *Juvenile Instructor* 64 (July 1929): 385. External evidence of the Book of Mormon substantiates its validity. Scientists have tried to prove it a forgery, but after one hundred years they have not succeeded and it has stood the test of time and close examination. [J.W.M.]

S.106 Sjodahl, J. M. "A Study of Book of Mormon Texts." *IE* 26-27 (July, August, September 1923, November, January, May 1924): 825-30, 880-84, 1045-46, 18-22, 237-39, 675-76. Internal evidences of the Book of Mormon's authenticity are argued using analysis of words and names used in the book that reflect ancient Hebrew customs, and parallels between the Book of Mormon and American Indian languages. [J.T.]

S.107 Sjodahl, J. M. "Suggested Key to Book of Mormon Geography." *IE* 30 (September 1927): 974-87. Surveys theories on Book of Mormon geography, and offers his own speculation. He concludes that Lehi landed in South America just south of the Isthmus and that he died in Peru. Nephi went on to Ecuador and then Colombia. Zarahemla was located on the Atlantic side of Central America. [D.M.]

S.108 Sjodahl, J. M. *A Suggested Key to Book of Mormon Geography*. Salt Lake City: Deseret Book, 1957. A large map of the North and South American continents marked with names of cities, rivers, and locations that are found in the Book of Mormon text. [J.W.M.]

S.109 Sjodahl, J. M. "Tut-Ankh-Amen and Sun-Worship." *IE* 26 (May 1923): 638-43. Speculates that the Lamanite culture may have established the Egyptian practice of sun-worship in America, accounting for the appearance of this practice among certain Indian groups. [J.T.]

S.110 Sjodahl, J. M. "Two Outstanding Features of Book of Mormon History." *Relief Society Magazine* 14 (October, November 1927): 475-

80, 550-53. Discusses the determination of the people of Ammon not to defend themselves against the Lamanite attack. Some Indian traditions reflect this peaceful approach to war. The united order was practiced among the Nephites after the Savior's visit. Indian traditions hold to many of the principles of the united order. [J.W.M.]

S.111 Skinner, Andrew C. "Alma's 'Pure Testimony.'" In *Studies in Scripture: 1 Nephi to Alma 29*, edited by Kent P. Jackson, 294-306. Salt Lake City: Deseret Book, 1987. Using the text of Alma 5-8, this article defines "pure testimony" as that which is "deeply associated with the Savior." It is "clear, plain, and absolute" as well as "clean, cleansing, and purifying." Faith in Christ, a correct understanding of God's character, and true knowledge, which is given only by the Holy Ghost, bring about spiritual rebirth. [J.W.M.]

S.112 Skinner, Andrew C. "The Course of Peace and Apostasy." In *Studies in Scripture: Alma 30 to Moroni*, edited by Kent P. Jackson, 218-30. Salt Lake City: Deseret Book, 1988. Just 49 verses within 4 Nephi teach a stark contrast between celestial unity and the path of apostasy to deepest depravity. Mormon lived in a time of great wickedness and yet through his relationship with the Second Comforter possessed the strength to live a righteous life—a good lesson for the latter days. [J.W.M.]

S.113 Skinner, Andrew C. "Nephi's Ultimate Encounter with Deity: Some Thoughts on Helaman 10." In *The Book of Mormon: Helaman through 3 Nephi 8, According to Thy Word*, edited by Monte S. Nyman and Charles D. Tate Jr., 115-27. Provo, UT: Brigham Young University Religious Studies Center, 1992. An essay on making one's calling and election sure. Shows the perversion of this doctrine as exhibited by the Zoramites. Nephi's steadfast faithfulness allowed him to attain it, and ultimately he saw God. [D.M.] 113

S.114 Skinner, Andrew C. "Promises Fulfilled." In *Studies in Scripture: Alma 30 to Moroni*, edited by Kent P. Jackson, 259-70. Salt Lake City: Deseret Book, 1988. Discusses the law of witnesses and the Three Witnesses to the Book of Mormon, the idea of kingship in Jaredite history, and the effect of secret combinations. The exodus of Jared is likened to Noah's ark. "When the Lord makes a prophecy or promise it must surely come to pass." [J.W.M.]

S.115 Skousen, Royal. "The Book of Mormon Critical Text Project." In *Joseph Smith: The Prophet, the Man*, edited by Susan Easton Black and Charles D. Tate Jr., 65-75. Provo, UT: BYU Religious Study Center, 1993. A project intending to establish the original English text of the Book of Mormon and to understand its history and changes. Computerized versions of the original text and the printer's text were created, then comparisons made 19 subsequent editions. Findings validate the witnesses' testimony that Joseph Smith saw the words in revelation from God during the translation process. [J.W.M.]

S.116 Skousen, Royal. "Book of Mormon Editions." In *Encyclopedia of Mormonism*, edited by Daniel H. Ludlow, 1:175-76. 5 vols. New York: Macmillan, 1992. Book of Mormon editions are described and format changes noted. Editions include: 1830, 5,000 copies, E. B. Grandin, New York; 1837, 5,000 copies, P. P. Pratt, Kirtland, Ohio; 1840, 2,000 copies, E. B. Robinson & Don C. Smith, Cincinnatti, Ohio; 1841, 4,050 copies, Kimball, Young, & Pratt, Liverpool, England; 1879, Orson Pratt changed format, Salt Lake City, Utah; 1920, James Talmage more changes in format; 1981, Quorum of 12 committee made extensive format changes. RLDS have published editions in 1858, 1874, 1892, 1908, 1966, and 1987. [N.K.Y.]

S.117 Skousen, Royal. "Book of Mormon Manuscripts." In *Encyclopedia of Mormonism*, edited by Daniel H. Ludlow, 1:185-86. 5 vols. New York: Macmillan, 1992. There are two Book of Mormon manuscripts in existence—the original manuscript written by scribes from a dictated translation and a manuscript copy of the original given to the publisher. The original was placed in the cornerstone of a building and 75% of it was destroyed by moisture. The printer's manuscript has on average three differences per page from the original in the form of natural scribal errors and it is in the custody of the RLDS church with only two lines missing on page one. [N.K.Y.]

S.118 Skousen, Royal. "Jacob 4-6: Substantive Textual Variants between Manuscripts and Editions." In *The Allegory of the Olive Tree: The Olive, The Bible, and Jacob 5,* edited by Stephen D. Ricks and John W. Welch, 105-39. Salt Lake City: Deseret Book and FARMS, 1994. Published as a preliminary report in "Jacob 4-6: Substantive Textual Variants." Provo, UT: FARMS, 1992, and "Jacob 4-6: Textual Notes." Provo, UT: FARMS, 1992. Presents a computerized collation of Jacob 4-6 "based on the original manuscript, the printer's manuscript, the first three editions of the Book of Mormon (1830, 1837, and 1840), and the 1981 edition of the Book of Mormon." Shows the substantive variations between the 1981 edition and the other five sources, ignoring spelling variation, capitalization, and punctuation that makes no difference in the meaning. [J.W.M.]

S.119 Skousen, Royal. "New Fragments from the Original Manuscript of the Book of Mormon." In *DLLS Proceedings 1992: Proceedings of the Deseret Language and Linguistic Society 1992 Symposium,* 1-4. USA: Deseret Language and Linguistics Society, 1992. Brief overview of the Book of Mormon critical text project with update on recent findings concerning new fragments from the original manuscript. [A.C.W.]

S.120 Skousen, Royal. "The Original Book of Mormon Manuscript." In *Reexploring the Book of Mormon,* edited by John W. Welch, 9-12. Salt Lake City: Deseret Book and FARMS, 1992. Some 140 differences exist between the original transcript of the Book of Mormon and the copied printer's manuscript. Recent comparisons using computer techniques and access to more legible copies have shown about one correction per manuscript page, most corrections representing natural transcription errors. The original manuscript was often written under difficult circumstances with a quill pen. Changes have been reviewed and found to include corrections for atypical spellings, awkward grammar, and Hebraisms. [N.K.Y.]

S.121 Skousen, Royal. "Piecing Together the Original Manuscript." *BYU Today* 46 (May 1992): 18-24. Skousen reports on his work on a critical text of the Book of Mormon, notably his work with the Wilford Wood original manuscript fragments, which in 1937 Wood purchased from Lewis Bidamon's son, Charles. The project has illuminated Hebrew-like expressions in the original text, some errors of transmission between the original and the printer's manuscripts, and more information concerning the translation process. [B.D.]

S.122 Skousen, Royal. "Towards a Critical Edition of the Book of Mormon." *BYU Studies* 30 (Winter 1990): 41-69. Defines and shows a need for a critical edition of the Book of Mormon. Discusses translational methods of Joseph Smith. Summarizes Skousen's work on a new critical edition of the Book of Mormon. [J.W.M.]

S.123 Skousen, W. Cleon. *The Challenge of Our Times.* Salt Lake City: Bookcraft, 1953. The Book of Mormon is given to test the faith of mankind. It is a companion to the Bible and answers vital questions more now than when it was first published. The writings of ancient American prophets are found in the book and many of their prophecies pertain to this time when they are just now being fulfilled. The land of America is a land of importance to God and man. Those who are righteous will be blessed. A warning against pride and secret societies permeates the book. The most significant part of the book is Christ's visit, organizing his church and establishing his ordinances. [J.W.M.]

S.124 Skousen, W. Cleon. *Hidden Treasures from the Book of Mormon.* 4 vols. Provo and Salt Lake City: Dana Press and Publisher's Press, 1971-1972. A four-volume work designed as an instructional aid to Book of Mormon study. The workbook format proceeds verse by verse, with accompanying commentaries, maps, drawings, fill-in-the-blank questions, charts, and topics of discussion. [A.C.W.]

S.125 Skousen, W. Cleon. "The Importance of Isaiah's Ministry." In Skousen's *The Fourth Thousand Years,* 513-42. Salt Lake City: Bookcraft, 1966. Only Nephi was allowed to distribute the same amount of details concerning the last days as Isaiah did. The Book of Mormon establishes the authorship of the book of Isaiah. The important ministry of Isaiah and the unity of the text he wrote is exhibited by his writings preserved in the Book of Mormon. [J.W.M.]

S.126 Skousen, W. Cleon. "Isaiah and Nephi Write About America and Modern Times." In Skousen's *The Fourth Thousand Years,* 578-603. Salt Lake City: Bookcraft, 1966. Because of Nephi's great depth of understanding of Isaiah's writings, both culturally and spiritually, his commentary is of inestimable value concerning the prophecies that relate to America. Isaiah and Nephi both saw the coming forth of the Book of Mormon, Martin Harris's visit to professor Anthon, and the witnesses who would testify of the Book of Mormon's truthfulness. [J.W.M.]

S.127 Skousen, W. Cleon. "The Last Days of Joseph and His Remarkable Prophecies Concerning the Future." In Skousen's *The Third Thousand Years,* 143-56. Salt Lake City: Bookcraft, 1964. Genesis 50 concerns the prophecy of Joseph who was sold into Egypt, his posterity and the record they would keep—the Book of Mormon. A comparison between the text of the Inspired Version of Genesis 50 and the Book of Mormon text that correlates with it shows the integrity of Joseph Smith as a translator. The two renditions agree in content, but disagree in detail because of the different authorship of the two accounts. [J.W.M.]

S.128 Skousen, W. Cleon. "The Prophet Lehi, Contemporary of Jeremiah." In Skousen's *The Fourth Thousand Years,* 698-701. Salt Lake City, UT: Bookcraft, 1966. Though Jeremiah fails to mention his contemporary laborers by name, Lehi apparently was called to be one of the prophets to whom Jeremiah refers only collectively. Lehi's life was threatened and he was warned by the Lord to leave Jerusalem. His family and the family of Ishmael traveled eight years to safety, taking the records of the Jews with them in the form of brass plates. [J.W.M.]

S.129 Sleight, Thos. "The Book of Mormon." *MS* 48 (23, 30 August 1886): 529-32, 548-51. Uses biblical scriptures to prove the truthfulness of the Book of Mormon, gives summary of 1 Nephi, discusses plates (who wrote them, what language was used, their size and description). Explains how Joseph Smith found the plates in the Hill Cumorah, and gives a history of the founding of the LDS church. [A.C.W.]

S.130 Slivka, Scott. "The Best at Something." *NE* 19 (July 1989): 19. This high school student desired to know more about the Book of Mormon than anyone in his school, a pursuit that brought feelings of self worth and spiritual security. [J.W.M.]

S.131 Smart, Ninian, and Richard D. Hecht. *Sacred Texts of the World: A Universal Anthology.* New York: Crossroad, 1982. Contains excerpts from sacred texts and scriptures of many of the world's religions. The editors quote 3 Nephi 21 from the Book of Mormon as a representative scriptural text from Mormonism and state that it represents "the charter for Joseph's foundation of the Church of Jesus Christ of Latter-day Saints and the vision which drew the faithful in their drive to create a new society in the American West." [D.M.]

S.132 Smith, Alice Colton. "In the Service of Your Fellow Men." *Relief Society Magazine* 56 (July 1969): 546-47. Uses the teachings of the Book of Mormon to show the importance of Christian service by members of the Church. [J.W.M.]

S.133 Smith, Brent D. *The House of Israel and Native Americans.* Provo, UT: FARMS, 1984. The author proposes "first to explore the antecedents and development of the notion of Hebrew descent; next to examine this view vis-a-vis contending views in the early years of the American Republic—both in the dialogue of the learned men of the day and the popular view espoused from the pulpit and published in written form; and lastly to touch upon the relationship between the issue of Indian Origins and the ascription of Indian ancestry offered in the Book of Mormon." [B.D.]

S.134 Smith, Brian L. "Joseph Smith: Gifted Learner, Master Teacher, Prophetic Seer." In *Joseph Smith: The Prophet, the Man,* edited by Susan Easton Black and Charles D. Tate Jr., 169-81. Provo, UT: BYU Religious Study Center, 1993. Joseph Smith was a gifted learner who was taught by the ancient prophets of God. When he went to the Hill Cumorah the heavens were opened and, as Nephi, he was given a panoramic vision. As he translated the Book of Mormon, he asked questions and brought down the very powers of heaven to give him the answers. In the beginning he used the Urim and Thummim, but he became so acquainted with the spirit of revelation and prophecy that in time he no longer needed the instruments. [J.W.M.]

S.135 Smith, C. Paul. *I Will Send My Messenger: An Introduction to Mormonism.* Dawsonville, GA: Communication Production Specialists, 1988. The Book of Mormon is "Another Testament of Jesus Christ." Presents a brief history regarding the publication of the work, and an overview of its contents. [D.W.P.]

S.136 Smith, David A. Untitled talk. *CR* (April 1931): 100-106. Smith cites contemporary sources that describe ancient American culture in a way that supports the Book of Mormon. Some of the sources he cites are Prescott, *Conquest of Mexico*; Claverijo, *History of Mexico*; Holmes, *Ancient Cities of Mexico*; "New Clues to the Mayan Riddle," *Popular Science Monthly*, January, 1930. [B.D.]

S.137 Smith, David Asael. *Suggestions for Book of Mormon Lectures; with Quotations from Leading Archaeologists and Historians.* Independence, MO: Zion's, 1949. Quotes from archaeologists and historians to demonstrate the veracity of the Book of Mormon. Includes a discussion of cement, iron, and steel; shows a comparison of Indian traditions and myths with similar stories from the Bible, including Indian belief in communion, baptism, the creation and flood, and the Great White God. [A.C.W.]

S.138 Smith, D. C. "Traits of the Mosiac History Found among the Aztec Nations." *TS* 3 (15 June 1842): 818-20. Relates Aztec traditions of the flood to the book of Ether in the Book of Mormon. Aztec traditions also reflect the tower of Babel and the dove that confused the tongues of mankind, permitting a select few to speak the same language. [J.W.M.]

S.139 Smith, Don Carlos. Untitled. *TS* 2 (15 March 1841): 353-55. Response to an article from the *Upper Mississippian.* Corrects the idea that Mormon was a contemporary prophet among the Latter-day Saints. Notes that the plates Joseph Smith translated were not brass. Defends as feasible the proposition that God can speak now as well as in biblical times. The Book of Mormon title page and the testimony of the Eleven Witnesses are included. [D.M.]

S.140 Smith, Don Carlos, and Ebenezer Robinson. "American Antiquities—More Proofs of the Book of Mormon." *TS* 2 (15 June 1841): 440-42. Reprint from the (New York) *Weekly Herald.* Tells of the visit of Mr. Catherwood and Mr. Stephens to Honduras, and of their observations of ruins. They were impressed with the artwork, and the achievement of the ancient inhabitants in architecture. Similarities with Christian motifs are noted. [D.M.]

S.141 Smith, Elbert A. *The Great Restoration.* Independence, MO: Herald House, n.d. Explores the Great Apostasy and the possible ways of recovering of the Church of Jesus Christ—reform or restoration. The gospel restoration began when Moroni visited Joseph Smith, bringing the original Christian teachings—the Book of Mormon. [J.W.M.]

S.142 Smith, Frederick A. "Why Study the Book of Mormon?" *The Rod of Iron* 1 (July, August, September 1924): 26. The Book of Mormon is of great historical worth to the American Indians and to those who seek to understand a history of religion. It is a record of the Lord's dealings with his people and gives an account of his doctrine. [J.W.M.]

S.143 Smith, George Albert. "Book of Mormon Origin: Spaulding." *JD* 12:332-38. The Book of Mormon is the key to unlocking the messages of the Bible. Criticism arose that the Book of Mormon could not be true, for it is not grammatical and if it had been revealed of God it would have been grammatical. However, the Lord speaks to men in their own language. It is untrue that the Book of Mormon was written by Solomon Spaulding. [J.W.M.]

S.144 Smith, George Albert. "The Book of Mormon—The Savior in the New World." In *Sharing The Gospel with Others: Excerpts From the Sermons of President Smith*, edited by Preston Nibley, 98-103. Salt Lake City: Deseret News Press, 1948. Includes reprints of two articles. The first is a call to read the Book of Mormon and to share its precious truths with all of God's children. The second article is a conference talk in which the author announces that the Book of Mormon is printed in Braille. He recounts facts concerning the publication of the first edition of the book and the pact made by the people in the area of publication never to read the book. [J.W.M.]

S.145 Smith, George Albert. "Nephi Sees Our Day." *CR* (April 1918): 36-42. The prophet Nephi looked into the future and saw our day and described present world conditions with its prevalent evil and war. He saw in a detailed way Satan's various tactics in getting mankind to sin against God's laws. [R.C.D.]

S.146 Smith, George Albert. Untitled Talk. *CR* (April 1930): 64-69. A testimony of the Book of Mormon. Many have believed in the words of the book and the Lord's work has commenced among all nations. [B.D.]

S.147 Smith, George Albert. Untitled Talk. *CR* (April 1936): 13-16. The newly published Book of Mormon in Braille is part of the effort to distribute the book throughout the world. In fulfillment of the prophecy that many would believe the Book of Mormon (2 Nephi 30:3) the book has been published in many languages and there are more to follow. [J.W.M.]

S.148 Smith, George Albert. Untitled Talk. *CR* (April 1950): 142-46. A story of Smith's encounter with a tribe of Catawba Indians. Smith gave a man a Book of Mormon and said it explained the origin of the Indians. Smith testifies of the divinity of the Book of Mormon and how glorious it is to have the knowledge it contains. [B.D.]

S.149 Smith, Harry E. "A Book of Mormon Testimony." *The Rod of Iron* 2 (January 1925): 45. Smith, as a sixteen-year-old Methodist boy, came into contact with a man reading a book. He was invited to attend the man's church. While there he was prompted to quote wonderful scriptures that he did not recognize. He was amazed to find that these scriptures were from the Book of Mormon. [J.W.M.]

S.150 Smith, Heman C. "Book of Mormon Witnesses." *Journal of History* 4 (1911): 357-65. This work examines the reasons behind Oliver Cowdery's and David Whitmer's estrangement from the Church. [A.T.]

S.151 Smith, Heman C. *The Truth Defended, or A Reply to Elder D. H. Bay's, "Doctrines and Dogmas of Mormonism."* Lamoni, IA: Herald House, 1901. An apologetic work, written by a former Church Historian of the Reorganized church, responding to criticisms raised by Bays in his work, *Doctrines and Dogmas of Mormonism*. Bays did not accept the divine origin of the Book of Mormon. Smith defends the book, asserting that Joseph Smith was inspired of God in translating it. [M.R.]

S.152 Smith, Heman Hale. "Martin Harris." *Journal of History* 4 (1911): 214-22. A biography that relates the story of Martin Harris's loss of the 116 manuscript pages of the Book of Mormon and his experience of seeing the gold plates and signing the testimony of the Three Witnesses. Includes a letter by Martin Harris wherein he states that he never denied the truth of the Book of Mormon. [A.T.]

S.153 Smith, Hyrum M. Untitled talk. *CR* (October 1903): 67-71. The world is in ignorance of gospel truth because many plain and precious truths have been removed from the Bible (1 Nephi 13). [B.D.]

S.154 Smith, Hyrum O. *The Book of Mormon Evaluated*. Independence, MO: Herald House, n.d. The moral precepts of the Book of Mormon are faultless and the book presents its own evidence of its divine origin. The purpose of the Book is to teach of Christ and it supports the claims of the Bible. [J.W.M.]

S.155 Smith, Hyrum O. *The Book of Mormon Evaluated*. Independence, MO: Herald Publishing, 1855?. Contains a collection of previously published items, "Book of Mormon Lectures" by H. A. Stebbins, "Book of Mormon Talks" by Orion (Hyrum O. Smith), "Book of Mormon Vindicated" by I. M. Smith, and "The Book of Mormon Evaluated" by Hyrum O. Smith. [J.W.M.]

S.156 Smith, Hyrum O. *Book of Mormon Talks, Birth Offering Series #4*. Lamoni, IA: Reorganized Church of Jesus Christ of Latter Day Saints, 1902. Written in the form of a discussion between a father and his four children. Answers criticisms of the Book of Mormon. The Book of Mormon is complimentary to the Bible. [A.T.]

S.157 Smith, Isaac M. *The Book of Mormon Vindicated*. Independence, MO: Ensign House, 1898, 3rd ed. 1917. Reprinted as *Mormonism II: Pro-Mormon Writings of the Twentieth Century*, edited by Gary L. Ward, 1-119. New York: Garland, 1990. "A simple statement of facts as to what the Book of Mormon really is, and a plain presentation of the scriptural evidences in favor of its divine origin." Defines the mission of the Book of Mormon, tells of its coming forth and significance to the tribes of Israel, and of the prophecies it contains and fulfills. [A.C.W.]

S.158 Smith, Israel A., et al. *Outline Studies of the Book of Mormon Institute*. Independence, MO: Herald House, 1951. Contains outlines of sermons by RLDS church dignitaries, including I. A. Smith, D. O. Chesworth, W. Wallace Smith, Maurice L. Draper, H. E. Velt, and R. A. Cheville. Topics include Book of Mormon history and doctrine. [D.M.]

S.159 Smith, J. H. "The Last Living Witness to the Book of Mormon." *MS* 45 (20 August 1883): 536-38. Because the prophet Joseph Smith took no credit for the discovery of the ancient plates and the translation thereof, men have criticized this book more than any other. Had he claimed to have found and translated them by his own genius, people would believe the Book of Mormon and proclaim Joseph a clever and learned man. The Book of Mormon is filled with internal evidences of its divinity, and there are also the testimonies of the witnesses. [J.W.M.]

S.160 Smith, J. H. "A Marvelous Work and a Wonder." *MS* 45 (8 October 1883): 648-52. Isaiah 29 prophesies future events concerning the Book of Mormon. The history of the Church proves that the Mormon church is a marvelous work and a wonder. Most of the persecution against the Church stems from the Book of Mormon. [B.D.]

S.161 Smith, J. H. "The Unpardonable Sin and the Three Witnesses." *MS* 50 (March 1888): 177-79. Evaluates the Three Witnesses' lives in respect to Paul's words on the unpardonable sin (Hebrews 6: 4-6). Smith declares that the Three Witnesses did not commit the unpardonable sin as described by Paul. He maintains that "it surely was the purpose of God that they should go the road they had traveled." [B.D.]

S.162 Smith, J. R. "The Book of Mormon in the Light of Recent Jewish Archaeological Research." *IE* 34 (July 1931): 522-23, 559-60. A Jewish archaeologist, Isadore Lhevinne, affirms that Jews discovered America. Evidence shows that Jews reached Mexican shores on more than one occasion hundreds of years before Columbus. [J.W.M.]

S.163 Smith, Jesse N. Untitled talk. *CR* (April 1905): 50-52. As a child, the author had in his possession an old first edition of the Book of Mormon because his family was very poor. He was embarrassed and felt inferior to the other children. The Prophet Joseph Smith gave him a new Book of Mormon and encouraged him to read it at school as well as at home. When young married couples begin their lives together, the author invites them to possess their own copies of the book. [J.W.M.]

S.164 Smith, Joseph. "Correspondence." *TS* 4 (15 May 1843): 194. A letter to the editor written by Joseph Smith in rebuttal to the allegation that the word "Mormon" was translated from a Greek word. Joseph interprets the word "Mormon" to mean "more good." He attests that the language from which the plates were translated was Reformed Egyptian. He reaffirms the divine intervention of God in the translation process. [J.W.M.]

S.165 Smith, Joseph. *Joseph Smith Tells His Own Story*. Independence, MO: Price Publishing, 1985. A reprint of articles from the *Times and Seasons* vols. 3 and 4 in which Smith published his own story of family history, the First Vision, the coming forth of the Book of Mormon, and the organization of the Church. [J.W.M.]

S.166 Smith, Joseph. *The Prophet Joseph Smith Tells His Own Story; A Brief History of the Early Visions of the Prophet*. Independence, MO: Zion's, n.d. An account of Joseph Smith's history, written in 1838. A further history is added by an unknown author and includes a description of the organization of the Church, the Kirtland Temple dedication, the Saints' persecution in Missouri, the trek to Illinois, the martyrdom of Joseph and Hyrum, and the move westward. [J.W.M.]

S.167 Smith, Joseph. "Traits of the Mosaic History." *TS* 3 (15 June 1842): 818-20. Refers to the Aztec version of the flood and links it to the book of Ether. [D.M.]

S.168 Smith, Joseph. *Visions of Joseph Smith the Seer*. Plano, IL: RLDS Church, 1879. Provides the historical details of Joseph Smith's First Vision and of the coming forth of the Book of Mormon. It states the testimonies of the Eleven Witnesses, and then proceeds to give archaeological evidence of the divine authenticity of the Book of Mormon. This evidence is comprised of Hebrew inscriptions found by the mounds built near Newark, Ohio. [A.C.W.]

S.169 Smith, Joseph. *Visions of Joseph Smith the Seer; Discoveries of Ancient American Record and Relics, with the Statements of Dr. Lederer (Converted Jew) and Others*. Lamoni, IA: Reorganized Church of Jesus Christ of Latter Day Saints, 1879. Rehearses the Joseph Smith story. It contains a description of the Hill Cumorah and the visit of the angel Moroni. It gives an account of the Book of Mormon. Recounts the discovery of artifacts that had Hebrew inscriptions upon them. The testimonies of the Three Witnesses were substantiated by later affirmation. [J.W.M.]

S.170 Smith, Joseph III. "Last Testimony of Sister Emma." *SH* 26 (1 October 1879): 289-90. This interview conducted by Emma Smith's son in part concerns the Book of Mormon, its translation and publication. The question and answer format of the article declares that the prophet Joseph had not met Sidney Rigdon until after the publication of the book. Emma assisted in the translation, handled the cloth-wrapped plates, and verifies the book's divine authenticity. [J.W.M.]

S.171 Smith, Joseph F. "The Manuscript Found." *IE* 3 (February, March, April 1900): 241-49, 377-83, 451-57. This three-part essay describes in detail the author's experience in obtaining Solomon Spaulding's romance while in Honolulu. [D.M.]

S.172 Smith, Joseph F. "The Original Manuscript of the Book of Mormon." *IE* 3 (November 1899): 61-65. Challenges allegations printed in U.S. newspapers that David Whitmer had possession of the original manuscript of the Book of Mormon, and that elders from the Church visiting him in Richmond, Missouri, offered him $100,000 for it. [D.M.]

S.173 Smith, Joseph F. "Testimonies of the Witnesses to the Book of Mormon." *IE* 30 (September 1927): 948-54. Writes concerning the law of witnesses, the Three Witnesses, and other witnesses of the Book of Mormon. [J.W.M.]

S.174 Smith, Joseph F. "Where Is the Original Manuscipt of the Book of Mormon?" *IE* 2 (November 1899). Also in *A Book of Mormon Treasury*, 11-15. Salt Lake City: Bookcraft, 1959, 1976. Refutes a claim made in an article printed in the *St. Louis Republic* concerning the whereabouts of the original manuscript of the Book of Mormon by arguing that the manuscript was placed in the southwest corner of the Nauvoo house. [A.T.]

S.175 Smith, Joseph F., Jr. "The Original Manuscript of the Book of Mormon." *IE* 10 (June 1907): 572-76. The original manuscript of the Book of Mormon remained in the hands of Joseph Smith who put the pages in the cornerstone of the Nauvoo house. These were nearly destroyed by water and time. The only remnants are now in the possession of the Church. [J.W.M.]

S.176 Smith, Joseph Fielding. "Alma on the Resurrection." In *Answers to Gospel Questions*, 1:35-37. 5 vols. Salt Lake City: Deseret Book, 1957. A discussion and interpretation of Alma 40:19, or Alma's doctrine concerning the order of the resurrection among those who died before or after the time of Christ. [L.D.]

S.177 Smith, Joseph Fielding. "Archaeological Investigation and the Book of Mormon." In *Answers to Gospel Questions*, 2:195-98. 5 vols. Salt Lake City: Deseret Book, 1958. Determines that there is no evidence that non-LDS archaeologists have used the Book of Mormon as a guide for their archaeological work in the Americas. [L.D.]

S.178 Smith, Joseph Fielding. "Are there any Vital Changes in the Book of Mormon?" In *Answers to Gospel Questions*, 2:199-201. 5 vols. Salt Lake City: Deseret Book, 1958. Discusses typographical errors made in the early copies of the Book of Mormon, the preservation of parts of the original manuscript, and how having the proper spirit prevents criticism. [L.D.]

S.179 Smith, Joseph Fielding. "The Baptism of Alma." In *Answers to Gospel Questions*, 3:203-4. 5 vols. Salt Lake City: Deseret Book, 1960. Discusses the baptism and priesthood ordination of Alma and postulates that Alma held the priesthood before he fled the court of King Noah. [L.D.]

S.180 Smith, Joseph Fielding. "The Book of Mormon—A Divine Record." *IE* 64 (December 1961): 924-27. A plea to study the Book of Mormon again and again is made with the promise that the Lord has "greater things" to manifest if members of the Church will esteem the Book of Mormon. [J.W.M.]

S.181 Smith, Joseph Fielding. "The Book of Mormon," "A Divine Record," "The Three Witnesses," and "The Prophesied Future of the Indian People." In Smith's *Seek Ye Earnestly...*, 377-403. Salt Lake City: Deseret Book, 1970. These chapters provide a defense of the Book of Mormon. Smith discusses the adverse conditions under which the book was published, and he issues the warning that every member must read the Book of Mormon to know for himself/herself for no "member of the church can stand approved in the presence of God who has not seriously and carefully read the Book of Mormon." The witnesses of the Book of Mormon never denied their testimony of that book. The promises made to the Nephite prophets concerning their descendants are great. [J.W.M.]

S.182 Smith, Joseph Fielding. "Book of Mormon Critics Refuted." *IE* 65 (December 1962): 906-7. Also in *CR* 132 (October 1962): 21-22. A plea to the members of the Church to study the Book of Mormon. Critics of the Book of Mormon visit the homes of members pointing out the changes in the Book of Mormon and discrepancies with the Bible. [J.W.M.]

S.183 Smith, Joseph Fielding. "Coming Forth of the Book of Mormon and Witnesses of Book of Mormon." In *Doctrines of Salvation, Vol 2: Sermons and Writings of Joseph Fielding Smith*, edited by Bruce R. McConkie, 209-43. Salt Lake City: Bookcraft, 1956. Rehearses the events of the translation and the subsequent publication of the Book of Mormon. He discusses the Urim and Thummim, and tells of the important mission of Samuel H. Smith when he placed a Book of Mormon in the home of John P. Greene. Witnesses of the book are discussed along with the location of Cumorah in western New York. [J.W.M.]

S.184 Smith, Joseph Fielding. "Did the Nephites Have a Church Organization Before the Days of Alma?" *IE* 62 (August 1959): 584-85. Also in *Answers to Gospel Questions*, 3:38-41. 5 vols. Salt Lake City: Deseret Book, 1960. Asserts that the Nephites did indeed have a church organization before the days of Alma, and that Lehi, King Benjamin, and King Mosiah each had a church organization. Whenever and wherever there were gospel ordinances administered by a minister there was a church organization. [R.C.D.]

S.185 Smith, Joseph Fielding. *Essentials in Church History*. Salt Lake City: Deseret Book, 1979. Contains a historical account of the coming forth of the Book of Mormon—the visit of the angel Moroni, the translation, the lost manuscript, the witnesses and their testimonies. [J.W.M.]

S.186 Smith, Joseph Fielding. "For Ye Are Bought With a Price." In *BYUSY* (14 May 1957). Provo, UT: Brigham Young University. Recounts the plan of salvation from the fall of Adam to the atoning sacrifice of Jesus Christ using quotations from 1 and 2 Nephi. [J.W.M.]

S.187 Smith, Joseph Fielding. "Handling Anti-Book of Mormon Charges." *CR* (October 1961): 18-20. A strong encouragement to the members of the Church to read and study the Book of Mormon. The only reason the anti-Mormon critics are able to discourage or disturb members is either because they lack "the faith" or they do not have "the background in knowledge to resist these false teachers." [R.C.D.]

S.188 Smith, Joseph Fielding. "How Can First Nephi 3:7 and Doctrine and Covenants 84:4 be Reconciled?" *IE* 65 (September 1962): 630-31. Also in *Answers to Gospel Questions*, 4:111-15. 5 vols. Salt Lake City: Deseret Book, 1963. Discusses Matthew 12:39 to show that there are no contradictions between 1 Nephi 3:7 and D&C 84:4. He concludes that the injunction of the Lord to build a temple was hampered by such opposition that the plan of the Lord was merely postponed—"the purposes of the Lord will prevail." [J.W.M.]

S.189 Smith, Joseph Fielding. "How Was Lehi a Descendant of the Jews?" *IE* 58 (October 1955): 702. Also in *Answers to Gospel Questions*, 1:142-43. 5 vols. Salt Lake City: Deseret Book, 1957. Lehi and the Nephites are referred to as "Jews" in several Book of Mormon and Doctrine and Covenants passages (2 Nephi 30:4; D&C 19:27; D&C 57:4), even though they were literal descendants of Ephraim and Manasseh (Alma 10:3). They were Jews not so much by actual descent as by citizenship, having lived in Jerusalem in the kingdom of Judah, or through intermarriage. [R.C.D.]

S.190 Smith, Joseph Fielding. "Is There a Contradiction Between Alma 7:10 and Matthew 2:5-6?" *IE* 58 (April 1955): 222. Also in *Answers to Gospel Questions*, 1:172-75. 5 vols. Salt Lake City: Deseret Book, 1957. There is no contradiction. Joseph Smith and all of his associates knew perfectly well that Bethlehem was where Jesus was born. The expression used in Alma 7:10 was not that Jesus was born *in* Jerusalem, but *at* Jerusalem. This is a Hebrew expression and simply refers to a geographical area—Jerusalem and environs, including Bethlehem. [R.C.D.]

S.191 Smith, Joseph Fielding. "Is There a Contradiction Between Jacob 2:24-27 and Doctrine and Covenants 132:39?" In *Answers to Gospel Questions*, 4:212-15. 5 vols. Salt Lake City: Deseret Book, 1963. Concludes there is no contradiction based on Jacob 2:30 and 2 Samuel 12:7-8. [L.D.]

S.192 Smith, Joseph Fielding. "Joseph Smith's 'Translation' of the Scriptures." *IE* (1914): 589-96. Quotes the Eighth Article of Faith declaring that Latter-day Saints believe both the Bible and the Book of Mormon to be the words of God. Nephi taught that the Hebrew scriptures had "plain and precious parts" removed. For this reason Joseph Smith was called on to revise the Bible and produce an "inspired translation." [J.W.M.]

S.193 Smith, Joseph Fielding. "Keep the Commandments." *IE* 53 (December 1950): 965-66. Church members (and those in the world if they only knew) should be grateful that the Lord has given further or/and clearer light of revelation in the Book of Mormon and other modern scriptures. [R.C.D.]

S.194 Smith, Joseph Fielding. "Nephi Sees Our Day." In *Proceedings of the Manchester Area Conference*, 5-7. Salt Lake City: Church of Jesus Christ of Latter-day Saints, 1972. The prophet Nephi saw the latter days in vision, with all of their evil and all of their good. [J.W.M.]

S.195 Smith, Joseph Fielding. "Nephite Baptisms and the Gift of the Holy Ghost." *IE* 65 (June 1962): 390-91. The gift of the Holy Ghost may not be received without the laying on of hands. Book of Mormon prophets had the authority to bestow that gift. The Lord did not overlook any necessary ordinances for the Nephites when he visited with them following his resurrection. [J.W.M.]

S.196 Smith, Joseph Fielding. "Nephites and Lamanites." In Smith's *Progress of Man*, 130-43. Salt Lake City: Deseret New Press, 1940.

Jacob 5 in the Book of Mormon provides the history of the house of Israel. Today this is a record of warning to all to avoid the pitfalls and rebellions that destroyed those who formerly inhabited this continent. [J.W.M.]

S.197 Smith, Joseph Fielding. "Origin of the First Vision." *IE* 23 (April 1920): 496-505. The First Vision answered many questions prevalent in the 19th century. The account of that vision agrees with the doctrine of the Church and the Book of Mormon. Those who read the Book of Mormon will know of its truthfulness and authenticity. [J.W.M.]

S.198 Smith, Joseph Fielding. "The Original Manuscript of the Book of Mormon." In *Book of Mormon Treasury*, 16-18. Salt Lake City: Bookcraft, 1959, 1976. The original copy of the Book of Mormon manuscript was nearly destroyed while it rested in the cornerstone of the Nauvoo House. Its fragments are now in different locations. The Reorganized church has the printer's copy of the Book of Mormon. [A.T.]

S.199 Smith, Joseph Fielding. "Predictions in the Bible Concerning the Book of Mormon." *IE* 26 (September 1923): 958-62. Also in *A Book of Mormon Treasury*, 190-95. Salt Lake City: Bookcraft, 1959, 1976. Discusses Bible predictions that have been associated with the Book of Mormon—the prophetic blessings that Jacob gave Joseph and his two sons, the oracles in Micah and Isaiah, parts of Isaiah 29, Ezekiel 37, and John 10. [D.M.]

S.200 Smith, Joseph Fielding. "The Present Status of the Lamanites." In *Answers to Gospel Questions*, 3:122-23. 5 vols. Salt Lake City: Deseret Book, 1960. Discusses the curse of dark skin being placed upon the Lamanites and how their evil ways brought back the curse of dark skin after it had been removed. [L.D.]

S.201 Smith, Joseph Fielding. "The Priesthood of the Nephites." *IE* 59 (March 1956): 142-43. Also in *Answers to Gospel Questions*, 1:123-26. 5 vols. Salt Lake City: Deseret Book, 1957. Discusses whether or not the Nephites had the Aaronic priesthood, concluding that the Nephites operated under the Melchizedek priesthood from the time of Lehi to the coming of Christ. [L.D.]

S.202 Smith, Joseph Fielding. "Progression and Retrogression." *IE* 22 (April 1919): 465-73. In rebuttal to the theory of evolution, this article points out that the first man on earth was intelligent, kept records, and knew the gospel. Then the children of men rebelled and fell into a degenerate state. Ancient America and the Book of Mormon are good examples of progression and retrogression. [J.W.M.]

S.203 Smith, Joseph Fielding. "Publication of the Book of Mormon." *Relief Society Magazine* 14 (September 1927): 423-29. Quotes Samuel H. Smith's story of the coming forth of the Book of Mormon; praises the title page and the promise therein. Gives historical facts concerning the publication and sales of the book. [J.W.M.]

S.204 Smith, Joseph Fielding. "Rebaptism of Nephi III." In *Answers to Gospel Questions*, 3:205-6. 5 vols. Salt Lake City: Deseret Book, 1960. Discusses 3 Nephi 11:21, Helaman 16:3-4, and 3 Nephi 11:28, and how the people were rebaptized when Christ came because the law of Moses was done away with and they were living a new law based on 3 Nephi 9:15-22, 11:10-40, 12:18-19, and 15:4-10. [L.D.]

S.205 Smith, Joseph Fielding. *The Restoration of All Things: A Series of Radio Talks*. Salt Lake City: Deseret News, 1944. Since the day of publication of the Book of Mormon, the flood of opposition towards it has increased. The Book of Mormon answers the critics successfully, fulfills biblical prophecy, and is a testimony against the world. Since not all believe, special witnesses had to be chosen. The Three Witnesses of the Book of Mormon remained true to their testimonies. [J.W.M.]

S.206 Smith, Joseph Fielding. "Seasons of Prayer." *CR* (October 1919): 141-46. An admonition to pray, as the Book of Mormon instructs, at all times and places. If members of the LDS church are not praying it is because, as the Book of Mormon teaches, they do not have the Spirit, for if they had it, then they would be praying. [R.C.D.]

S.207 Smith, Joseph Fielding. "The Stick of Joseph in the hand of Ephraim." In *Answers to Gospel Questions*, 3:197-98. 5 vols. Salt Lake City: Deseret Book, 1960. If Lehi is of the house of Manasseh, how can the Book of Mormon claim to be the stick of Ephraim referred to in Ezekiel 37? Smith argues that Ishmael, co-founder of the Lehi colony, was of the house of Ephraim. He also analyzes the Ezekiel passage finding that the stick was of Joseph thus including both Ephraim and Manasseh. [J.W.M.]

S.208 Smith, Joseph Fielding. "Testimonies of the Witnesses to the Book of Mormon." *IE* 30 (September 1927): 948-54. Also in *Book of Mormon Treasury*, 30-38. Salt Lake City: Bookcraft, 1959. Sets forth the Lord's law of witnesses as recorded in the scriptures. The provision for witnesses to testify regarding the reality of the gold plates perfectly fits the scriptural pattern and the Book of Mormon itself predicted that there would be such witnesses. The Book of Mormon witnesses remained true to their testimonies all of their lives. [D.M.]

S.209 Smith, Joseph Fielding. "They Bear Witness." *IE* 59 (December 1956): 921-22. The Lord has always had witnesses to bear testimony of his truths—the coming forth of the Book of Mormon follows suit. All who read the Book of Mormon may read the testimony of the Three Witnesses. [J.W.M.]

S.210 Smith, Joseph Fielding. "Three Days of Darkness." *IE* 62 (October 1959): 728. Also in *Answers to Gospel Questions*, 3:44-45. 5 vols. Salt Lake City: Deseret Book, 1960. Luke 23:44 states that at Christ's crucifixion there was a period of darkness over all the earth until the ninth hour. The Book of Mormon, however, states that it was a three-day darkness on the American Continent. Both accounts are correct. The God of miracles who caused a three-hour darkness on one continent also caused a three-day darkness on the other. The greater period of darkness came because of the extreme wickedness of those in America. [R.C.D.]

S.211 Smith, Joseph Fielding. "The Three Witnesses." *IE* 69 (July 1966): 612, 652. The Three Witnesses remained faithful to their testimonies of having seen the plates. While all three fell away from the Church, Oliver Cowdery and Martin Harris returned and died faithful members. David Whitmer never returned, but reaffirmed his testimony to his dying day. [J.W.M.]

S.212 Smith, Joseph Fielding. "Translation and Publication of the Book of Mormon." *IE* 30 (September 1927): 946-48. Surveys the events leading to the publication of the Book of Mormon and discusses the length of translation time, the roles of Martin Harris, Oliver Cowdery, and the Three Witnesses, the obtaining of the copyright, and the preparation for publication. [D.M.]

S.213 Smith, Joseph Fielding. "Translation of the Book of Mormon." *MS* 89 (22 September 1927): 593-95. The translation of the Book of Mormon commenced about April 7, 1829, and the copyright is dated June 11, 1829. In this short period of just under two months the translation was completed. [J.W.M.]

S.214 Smith, Joseph Fielding. "Urim and Thummim." *IE* 57 (1954): 382-83. A brief historical sketch of what is known about the Urim and Thummim, from the brother of Jared, Abraham, Moses, Mosiah, and Joseph Smith. [R.C.D.]

S.215 Smith, Joseph Fielding. "Were the Nephite Twelve, Apostles?" In *A Book of Mormon Treasury*, 152-53. Salt Lake City: Bookcraft, 1959, 1976. Also in *Answers to Gospel Questions*, 1:121-22. Salt Lake City: Deseret Book, 1957. States that the Nephite twelve disciples were apostles, possessing powers and authority similar to that held by Peter and the twelve apostles in Jerusalem. [A.T.]

S.216 Smith, Joseph Fielding. "When Did Jesus Appear to the Nephites?" *IE* 64 (May 1961): 296-97. The appearance of Christ in America occurred shortly after his ascension from the Mount of Olives into heaven. [J.W.M.]

S.217 Smith, Joseph Fielding. "Where Are the Plates?" *IE* 30 (September 1927): 948-54. Possession of the actual golden plates is not requisite according to God's law of witnesses, which is fulfilled by the witness of the Spirit and the Three and Eight Witnesses. [S.H.]

S.218 Smith, Joseph Fielding. "Where Did Alma Get His Authority?" *IE* 66 (July 1963): 582-83. Also in *Answers to Gospel Questions*, 4:161-64. Salt Lake City: Deseret Book, 1963. Explains that since there were no members of the tribe of Levi among the Nephites, the Nephites officiated by virtue of the Melchizedek Priesthood rather than the Aaronic. Concludes that Alma received the priesthood before Noah became king and remained righteous enough to retain this authority, although he immersed himself while baptizing Helam as part of the repentance process. [A.C.W.]

S.219 Smith, Joseph Fielding. "Who Were the Prophets Zenos and Zenock?" In *Answers to Gospel Questions*, 4:138-42. Salt Lake City: Deseret Book, 1963. There are no records of the Hebrew prophets Zenos and Zenock other than the fragments attributed to them in the Book of Mormon, notably Zenos's allegory of the olive tree in Jacob 5. [A.C.W.]

S.220 Smith, Joseph Fielding. "Your Question Answered by Joseph Fielding Smith Regarding Mosiah 15." *IE* 65 (March 1962): 150, 214-15. There have been many intelligent, honest men who never heard the gospel and will not be held accountable for their sins, for their acts were done in faith and obedience to what they had been taught. [J.W.M.]

S.221 Smith, Joseph Fielding. "Your Question Answered by Joseph Fielding Smith—The Debt We Owe." *IE* 64 (November 1961): 800-801. Jacob (2 Nephi 9) taught concerning the atonement and mission of Jesus Christ, and Aryan's debt to him. Out of love members of the Church should show deep gratitude by obedience and in humble prayer. [J.W.M.]

S.222 Smith, Julina. "A Discussion of the Inter-relation of the Latter-day Saints and the American Indians." M.A. thesis, Brigham Young University, 1932. Deals with the historical relations between the Mormons and the Indians, and gives a brief overview of the Book of Mormon, explaining how that and biblical prophecies have influenced relations between the Latter-day Saints and the American Indians. [A.C.W.]

S.223 Smith, Lucy. "The Printing of the Book of Mormon." *Restoration Voice* 69 (January/February 1990): 5-8. Reprinted from *Joseph Smith the Prophet and His Progenitors*. Historical narrative concerning Joseph Smith's meetings with E. B. Grandin, Oliver Cowdery's manuscript transcriptions, securing the copyright, and other details associated with the printing of the Book of Mormon. [A.C.W.]

S.224 Smith, Lucy Mack. *Biographical Sketches of Joseph Smith the Prophet and His Progenitors for Many Generations*. Liverpool, England: S. W. Richards, 1st edition, 1853. 2nd edition, Plano, IL: RLDS Church, 1880. Deals with events in the lives of the author's family members. She discusses her son Joseph and the coming forth of the Book of Mormon, and gives in detail historical facts about the origin and early days of the Church of Jesus Christ of Latter-day Saints, including the events surrounding the translation of the Book of Mormon and the 116 pages of lost manuscript. [A.C.W.]

S.225 Smith, Lucy Mack. "History of the Prophet Joseph by his Mother, Lucy Smith: Chapters XXIV-XXVIII." *IE* 5 (April 1902): 401-21. The *Improvement Era* reprinted all of Lucy Smith's history. These chapters record that Joseph brought home the breast plate, the translation began, Mrs. Harris was opposed the work, Martin Harris lost the 116-page manuscript, the Urim and Thummim was taken from Joseph Smith, and Oliver Cowdery wrote for Joseph as a scribe. [B.D.]

S.226 Smith, Lucy Mack, and James Patrick McEwan. "The Book of Mormon—A Latter-day Missionary of the Restored Gospel." *Instructor* 94 (July 1959): 254-55. Lucy Mack Smith relates the conversion of Mrs. and Rev. John P. Greene, Phineas Young, Brigham Young, Mrs. Murray, and the wife of Heber C. Kimball through a single copy of the Book of Mormon left with Rev. Greene. [R.H.B.]

S.227 Smith, Lyle. "Chiasmus." *Witness* 65 (May 1989): 4-6. Chiasmus is a Hebrew literary style that renders words, phrases, or ideas in an intentional order then immediately repeats them.

It is prevalent in the Book of Mormon. Includes examples. [J.W.M.]

S.228 Smith, Lyle. "Diving For Underwater Ruins." *Witness* 80 (Spring 1993): 8. Reports an expedition to Lake Peten Itza where manmade mounds lay at the bottom of the lake, in keeping with the Book of Mormon, which reports that cities sank at the crucifixion of Christ. [J.W.M.]

S.229 Smith, Lyle. "Maya Language and the Book of Mormon." *Witness* 70 (Fall 1990): 12-14. Finds parallels between Maya hieroglyphs and themes in the Book of Mormon to demonstrate the validity of Mesoamerica as the setting for Book of Mormon events. [A.C.W.]

S.230 Smith, Lyle. "Mirror Images in Mesoamerica." *Witness* 66 (Fall 1989): 4-7, 10. Chiasmus is used so profusely in the Book of Mormon that this author examines the mirror image of chiasmus in other forms such as art and architecture. The article contains figures and photographs as examples. [J.W.M.]

S.231 Smith, Lyle. "Royal Fifth." *Witness* 69 (Summer 1990): 14-15. Michael Coe has noted that the books of Mayan writing were reportedly very similar in appearance to Egyptian, thus vindicating the Book of Mormon. [A.C.W.]

S.232 Smith, Lyle. "Teotihuacan: A City of Our God?" *Witness* 78 (Fall 1992): 10-14. Examines archaeological and religious history of the city of Teotihuacan between 100 B.C. and A.D. 400 to discover correlations with Book of Mormon cultural history. [A.C.W.]

S.233 Smith, Lyle, and Sherrie Kline Smith. "Palenque Tablet of 96 Glyphs." *Witness* 76 (Spring 1992): 10-14. "The Tablet of 96 Glyphs from Palenque provides a strong witness that the Maya knew about and utilized the same literary practices as Hebrew writers." The writers point out literary practices that appear in the Book of Mormon: the phrase "it came to pass," chiasmus, and paired opposites. [B.D.]

S.234 Smith, Paul Thomas. *The Story of the Joseph Smith Transcript of Characters from the Book of Mormon.* Salt Lake City: Author, 1980. Retells the story of Martin Harris's visit to Anthon with the Book of Mormon characters. Also contains some primary sources and letters dealing with the characters. [D.W.P.]

S.235 Smith, R. H. "Indian Traditions." *Juvenile Instructor* 14 (15 February 1879): 46-47. Says Indian traditions support authenticity of Book of Mormon. Encourages youth to carry gospel to these "poor, ignorant Lamanites—since they are ready to receive a record of their forefathers." [A.C.W.]

S.236 Smith, Richard Pearson. "The Nephite Monetary System." *IE* 57 (May 1954): 316-17. A scholarly analysis of the monetary system of the Nephites used around 82 B.C. and described in Alma 11. The Nephite system was a slight modification of a binary system, where each unit would have twice the value of the next smaller one. Shows parallels with similar systems in Egypt and Macedonia. [R.C.D.]

S.237 Smith, Robert F. "Book of Mormon Event Structure: Ancient Near East, with Excursus, The Arabian Nexus." Provo, UT: FARMS, 1984. Explores the events that occurred in the ancient Near East preceding the time and just following Lehi's departure for the promised land. It includes a suggested dating system for Book of Mormon peoples based upon the Mesoamerican calendar. Includes a discussion of the Southern Arabian Peninsula and Lehi's excursion in the wilderness. [J.W.M.]

S.238 Smith, Robert F. "The 'Golden Plates.'" In *Reexploring the Book of Mormon*, edited by John W. Welch, 275-78. Salt Lake City: Deseret Book and FARMS, 1992. It was a common ancient American practice to make plates of tumbaga alloy and treat them with acid to remove surface copper. This left a soft gold surface easy to engrave yet supported by a strong thin sheet. A total of 120-200 plates written on both sides with one third sealed would leave from 80-266 surfaces for the record we have. [N.K.Y.]

S.239 Smith, Robert F. " 'It Came to Pass' in the Bible and the Book of Mormon." Provo, UT: FARMS, 1984. The use of the Book of Mormon passage "it came to pass" is comparable to the use of the phrase *wayehi* in the Old Testament. The article includes tables showing the comparisons made. [J.W.M.]

S.240 Smith, Robert F. "The Land of Jerusalem: The Place of Jesus' Birth." In *Reexploring the Book of Mormon*, edited by John W. Welch, 170-72. Salt Lake City: Deseret Book and FARMS, 1992. Scholars allege the Book of Mormon was in error when it claimed that Jesus was born in the land of Jerusalem. The land of Jerusalem designation, used only once in the Bible, also included the area of Bethlehem and is confirmed by several recent studies. [N.K.Y.]

S.241 Smith, Robert F. "Lodestone and the Liahona." In *Reexploring the Book of Mormon*, edited by John W. Welch, 44-46. Salt Lake City: Deseret Book and FARMS, 1992. Laman could not explain why the Liahona worked by faith and why the writing on it was changed from time to time. The use of magnetite as a compass was well known in this time period. Use of magnetic ores for compasses was known among the Olmecs of Vera Cruz, Mexico. [N.K.Y.]

S.242 Smith, Robert F. "New Information About Mulek, Son of the King." In *Reexploring the Book of Mormon*, edited by John W. Welch, 142-44. Salt Lake City: Deseret Book and FARMS, 1992. Mulek connects the Book of Mormon with the Old Testament as it has been confirmed that he was a son of King Zedekiah. The Old Testament names him Malachiah, the son of Hammelech, or more accurately MalkiYahu, son of the king. [N.K.Y.]

S.243 Smith, Robert F. "Shakespeare and the Book of Mormon." Provo, UT: FARMS, 1981. Lehi's expression, "the cold and silent grave, from whence no traveler can return" (2 Nephi 1:14) has been the object of scorn and ridicule by Book of Mormon critics for more than a century. According to these critics Joseph Smith plagiarized a quotation of Shakespeare's Hamlet. Smith addresses the problem of Lehi's/Shakespeare's expressions by noting and discussing similar phraseology in both modern and ancient texts. Lehi's expression speaks metaphorically of death, the grave, the netherworld, and afterlife, not unlike many other ancient sources. [D.W.P.]

S.244 Smith, Robert F. "Some Neologisms from the Book of Mormon." In *Conference on the Language of the Mormons*, 64-68. Provo, UT: Language Research Center, Brigham Young University, 31 May 1973. Discusses some of the more popular neologisms found in the Mormon canon. Emphasis is placed upon word origins and pronunciation. [D.S.T.]

S.245 Smith, Robert F. "Textual Criticism of the Book of Mormon." In *Reexploring the Book of Mormon*, edited by John W. Welch, 77-79. Salt Lake City: Deseret Book and FARMS, 1992. Discusses instances of changes made in earlier and later Book of Mormon editions, and differences between the Book of Mormon and the King James Bible—i.e., Joseph Smith uses *Ramah* whereas the King James Bible uses *Ramath*, 2 Nephi 27:3 reads *Zion* instead of *Ariel*, or *City* as in Isaiah 29:7, and the 1981 Book of Mormon has replaced *fathers* with *father* in Jacob 2:27 as per the original printer's manuscript. [N.K.Y.]

S.246 Smith, Robert F., Gordon C. Thomasson, and John W. Welch. "What Did Charles Anthon Really Say?" In *Reexploring the Book of Mormon*, edited by John W. Welch, 73-76. Salt Lake City: Deseret Book and FARMS, 1992. Relates events of Martin Harris's meeting with Charles Anthon and subsequent statements by Anthon negating the experience. Shows by phraseology and contradictions that Anthon lied afterwards to protect his reputation. [A.C.W.]

S.247 Smith, R. H. "Indian Traditions." *Juvenile Instructor* 14 (15 February 1879): 46-47. Recounts missionary labors among the Pueblo and Zuni Indians, who recognized the message in the Book of Mormon as belonging to their ancestors. [D.M.]

S.248 Smith, Robert William. *Miniature Model of the Gold Plates*. Salt Lake City: Pyramid, 1938. Presents a paper and wood model of the gold plates. [D.W.P.]

S.249 Smith, Robert William, comp. *The Mystery of the Ages Containing Information Regarding the Great Pyramid of Gizeh in Egypt and the Pyramids and Peoples of Ancient America.*

Salt Lake City: Pyramid, 1931. This booklet calls attention to the wonder of the Great Pyramid of Egypt and points out that ancient Americans show archaeological similarities to the ancient Egyptians. Smith discusses astronomy and geometry as related to the construction of these ancient structures and explores how Mayan ruins and the legend of Quetzalcoatl relate to the Book of Mormon. [A.C.W.]

S.250 Smith, Sherrie D. "Chinese Civilization and the Book of Mormon." *ZR* 13-14 (Summer, Fall 1981): 1-4. Contains " 'evidences' that the Jaredites went across Asia through China"—shows parallels between the Chinese dragon and Quetzalcoatl, and between a lighted stone in Chinese tradition and the stones used in the Jaredite barges. The real name of the brother of Jared was never given, a practice that is still a tradition in China. [A.T.]

S.251 Smith, Sherrie D. "Jade: Stones of Light." *ZR* 24-26 (Fall 1984): 4-5. Examines the criteria for the substance of the 16 Jaredite stones. The author argues that jade fits each criteria of the substance that was used. [A.T.]

S.252 Smith, Sherrie D. "Sacred Stones." *ZR* 24-26 (Spring, Summer, Fall 1984): 1-3. Contains a brief description of a trip that the author took to Central America to visit possible Book of Mormon locations. The author concluded that the Pi disks (circular jade disks found in a tomb at Monte Alban) and doughnut shaped objects represented the 16 Jaredite stones used for lighting the barges. [A.T.]

S.253 Smith, Sherrie Kline. "Copán Carvings Depict Nephite/Lamanite Warfare Methods." *Witness* 69 (Summer 1990): 12-13. After viewing carvings that depicted women as victims of war in Copán, Honduras, the author better understood passages in Mormon and Moroni concerning the final destruction of the Nephites. [A.C.W.]

S.254 Smith, Sherrie Kline. "The La Mojarra Stela: Can It Be the Coriantumr Stone?" *Witness* 80 (Spring 1993): 4-8. Archaeologists consider the La Mojarra Stela, discovered in 1986, to be the most important key to understanding the spread of Mesoamerican writing and calendrical practices. Some Book of Mormon believers wonder if this is the stone of Coriantumr (Omni 1:35-40). Included are photographs of the stone. [J.W.M.]

S.255 Smith, Timothy L. "The Book of Mormon in a Biblical Culture." In *Encyclopedia of Mormonism*, edited by Daniel H. Ludlow, 1:168-69. 5 vols. New York: Macmillan, 1992. The Book of Mormon doctrines match those of early Christian Apostolic times and give clear direction on biblical ordinances such as baptism of adults and children, the sacrament, doctrines of the Holy Ghost, the nature of God, the function of priesthood, and continued life after death. The book defines very well how biblical prophecies will be fulfilled in latter days. [N.K.Y.]

S.256 Smith, Timothy L. "The Book of Mormon in a Biblical Culture." In *Journal of Mormon History* 7 (1980): 3-21. The Book of Mormon is not only consistent with biblical teachings but supplements its doctrine. With the coming of the Book of Mormon, clear direction was given on issues that had been declared essential for salvation, such as baptism by immersion, the gift of the Holy Ghost, universal redemption, the necessity of righteousness, obedience, and good works. He gives many other examples of concepts that are parallel in both the Book of Mormon and Bible. [C.W.B.]

S.257 Smith, Virgil B. "The Book of Mormon." In Smith's *How To Spark Gospel Learning*, 33-38. Salt Lake City: Inland West Distributors, 1961. A teaching guide for parents. This chapter posses pertinent questions concerning the Book of Mormon, how people know it is true, why are the plates made of gold, and others. Scriptural quotations suggest answers. [J.W.M.]

S.258 Smith, Walter Wayne "The Book of Mormon, Its Translation and Publication." *Journal of History* 14 (January 1921): 1-37. History of the manuscript of the Book of Mormon written by the Church Historian of the Reorganized church. It includes historical accounts by Oliver Cowdery, the testimony of the Three Witnesses, the Eight Witnesses, the copyright,

S.259 Smith, William. "Evidences of the Book of Mormon." *M&A* 3 (January 1837): 433-35. Defends the Book of Mormon, drawing on proof texts found in Genesis 48-49, Psalm 85:11, and Ezekiel 37. Links truth and law with the descendants of Joseph, as found in the Book of Mormon. [D.M.]

S.260 Smith, William. *William Smith on Mormonism: A True Account of the Origin of the Book of Mormon.* Lamoni, IA: n.p., 1883. Personal account of the organizations of the LDS & RLDS churches as well as the coming forth and translation of the Book of Mormon. He relates first-hand experiences from the family of Joseph Smith and gives his personal testimony of the veracity of the book. [C.W.B.]

S.261 Snell, Jim, ed. *An Open Book: The Book of Mormon.* 37 issues. Kansas City: Snell's Print Shop, 1970-1982. Snell encourages Latter-day Saints to live righteously and gives a great deal of advice in areas such as repentance, avoidance of pride, obedience to the commandments, and dependence on God for faith. [C.W.B.]

S.262 Snow, Eliza R. "History of Jesus." *Juvenile Instructor* 3 (15 March, 1 April, 15 April, 1 May, 15 May, 1 June 1868): 43, 51, 58, 67, 79-80, 82-83. Chronicles Jesus' visit to the Lehites after the cataclysm. [D.M.]

S.263 Snow, Harold L. "Ancient Pictographs of Southern Utah." *IE* 30 (December 1926): 163-65. Corresponding words in ancient near Eastern languages and those of American Indians is seen as evidence of the truthfulness of the Book of Mormon because Latter-day Saints believe the book is a sacred history of ancient inhabitants of America who came from Jerusalem. [J.W.M.]

S.264 "The Sole Surviving Witness of the Authenticity of the Book of Mormon." In *History of Ray County, MO.,* 456-61. St. Louis, MO: Missouri Historical Co., 1881. An objective discussion of David Whitmer, the last of the Three Witnesses of the Book of Mormon. Produces Whitmer's last statement in 1881, affirming his testimony of the Book of Mormon. [D.W.P.]

S.265 "Solomon Spaulding's Manuscript." *The Oberlin Review* 13 (24 October 1885): 27-28. Recounts the theory that the Book of Mormon was created from Spaulding's *Manuscript Found.* With the finding of that document by L. L. Rice the theory is weakened. [D.M.]

S.266 "Some of Mormon's Teachings." *Evening and Morning Star* 1 (January 1833): 60. Quotes extensively from Mormon's writings to teach the Saints of truth, goodness, and glory. The Saints are to be mindful of the words of the prophets, to keep them growing in grace. [E.G.]

S.267 "Some Teens Squirm Their Way Through." *IE* 68 (November 1965): 1042-51. The Book of Mormon teaches "choice lessons of life." References are cited to illuminate reasons for reading the scriptures, understanding the agency of mankind, listening to the Psalm of Nephi, seeking good counsel, and having faith. Commentary is included. [J.W.M.]

S.268 Sommerfeldt, Vern D. "A New Perspective for Stimulating Personal Study of the Book of Mormon." Ph.D. diss., Brigham Young University, 1988. Many Church members undervalue the Book of Mormon as a basis for personal and family gospel study. Members treat the book carelessly and receive condemnation or treat it respectfully and reap blessings. The purpose of the Book of Mormon is to persuade men to come to Christ. It is the key that validates and clarifies the meaning of other sacred writings. [J.W.M.]

S.269 Sondrup, Steven P. "The Psalm of Nephi: A Lyric Reading." *BYU Studies* 21 (Summer 1981): 57-72. Looks not at the acoustic features of the Psalm of Nephi (alliteration, rhythm, assonance, and the like), but at its lyric qualities. States that the psalm is "an intricately patterned system of ideational parallels" that is the "essence of lyricism." The total significance of reading 2 Nephi 4 as lyric poetry becomes evident when other lyric poems from the scriptures are read in juxtaposition. "Thematically similar Old Testament psalms" mentioned by the author include Psalms 51 and 84. [D.W.P.]

S.270 Sonne, Alma. "Book of Mormon a Great Converter." *IE* (June 1953): 424. A brief summary of the missionary journey of Samuel Smith and his usage of the Book of Mormon, which resulted in the conversion of Rev. John P. Greene and others. [R.H.B.]

S.271 Sonne, Alma. "The Book of Mormon: A Great Missionary." In *BYUSY* (4 March 1958). Provo, UT: BYU Press, 1958. A man studying to be a Catholic priest reads the Book of Mormon and becomes convinced of its truth. He finds answers in the Book of Mormon that he could not find during in his biblical studies. [A.C.W.]

S.272 Sonne, Alma. "Read the Book of Mormon." *IE* 64 (December 1961): 964-67. Writes concerning the value of reading the Book of Mormon. Adds his testimony to those of the Three Witnesses, Joseph Smith, and the book itself. [J.W.M.]

S.273 Sonne, Alma. "Truth Will Prevail." *IE* 60 (June 1957): 408-9. In spite of an "avalanche of abuse and ridicule," the Book of Mormon stands true and powerful. The Book of Mormon reveals many truths, the purposes of God, and the results of wrong doing; it also emphasizes the sanctity of the commandments, proclaims the deity of Christ, and confirms the teachings of the Holy Ghost. [J.W.M.]

S.274 Sonne, Alma. "Urim and Thummim." *MS* 111 (April 1949): 101, 127. Prophets of old used the Urim and Thummim. The claims made by Joseph Smith were not illogical. King Saul used the devices as well as Moses and others. Joseph Smith's account of using them is not out of harmony with these accounts. They are defined as "lights" and "perfections." [J.W.M.]

S.275 Sorensen, Parry D. "Light Out of Darkness." *MS* 98 (18 February 1937): 103. The Book of Mormon is published in Braille, fulfilling the prophecy in Isaiah that "the blind shall see out of obscurity and out of darkness." [J.W.M.]

S.276 Sorenson, A. D. "Lehi on God's Law and an Opposition in All Things." In *The Book of Mormon: Second Nephi, The Doctrinal Structure*, edited by Monte S. Nyman and Charles D. Tate Jr., 107-32. Provo, UT: Brigham Young University Religious Studies Center, 1989. Analyzes Lehi's teachings in 2 Nephi 2:11, exploring opposition and "ethical opposites." The implications are far-reaching: God's laws make existence possible. [A.C.W.]

S.277 Sorenson, Donna D. "America—A Choice Land." *Relief Society Magazine* 27 (May 1940): 343-44. The Book of Mormon prophesied of Christopher Columbus and declares America to be "a choice land," "a land of liberty." The fulfillment of this promise rests upon obedience to Jesus Christ by those who occupy the land. [J.W.M.]

S.278 Sorenson, Elaine Shaw. "Seeds of Faith: A Follower's View of Alma 32." In *The Book of Mormon: Alma, The Testimony of the Word*, edited by Monte S. Nyman and Charles D. Tate Jr., 129-40. Provo, UT: Brigham Young University Religious Studies Center, 1992. Alma defines faith as hope for things not seen which are true. He compares faith to planting and growth of a seed that if nourished would bring forth the fruit of eternal life. The author says the fruit is most precious and sweet and those who eat it will be filled and never hunger or thirst. [N.K.Y.]

S.279 Sorenson, John L. "Ancient America and the Book of Mormon Revisited." *Dialogue* 4 (Summer 1969): 80-94. Notes shared patterns between ancient Mesoamerica and the Near East in the following areas: architecture, astronomy, calendrical systems, writing, burial practices, use of incense, figurines, sacrifice, ritual washing, sanek symbolism, tees, and kingship complex. These connections indicate that the Book of Mormon is an ancient text. [A.C.W.]

S.280 Sorenson, John L. *An Ancient American Setting for the Book of Mormon*. Salt Lake City: Deseret Book and FARMS, 1985. A treatment of geography that settles on a "plausible" scene in Mesoamerica (the Grijalva River as the Sidon), treats the nature of "history" in the scripture, and discusses how scholars learn about the ancient world. Specific data from external studies are then used to shed light on the Nephite record book by book. [J.L.S.]

S.281 Sorenson, John L. "Ancient Europeans in America?" In *Reexploring the Book of Mormon*, edited by John W. Welch, 108-10. Salt Lake City: Deseret Book and FARMS, 1992. Inscriptions thought to have been made by ancient Celts have been found in caves and rock shelters near Springfield, Colorado. Ogam writing known in Ireland was found in caves in Colorado. [N.K.Y.]

S.282 Sorenson, John L. *Animals in the Book of Mormon: An Annotated Bibliography.* Provo, UT: FARMS, 1992. Annotated bibliography facilitating inquiry concerning Book of Mormon uses of animals, the presence and significance of animals in ancient Mesoamerica, and the usage of animal terms in Semitic languages. Includes comprehensive listing of all significant Book of Mormon statements about animals. [A.C.W.]

S.283 Sorenson, John L. "Anthropological Approaches to the Book of Mormon." In *Book of Mormon Institute*, 25-36. Provo, UT: Brigham Young University Extension Publications, 5 December 1959. Calls for contextual study of the scripture in all its human dimensions—biological, linguistic, cultural, social—which can provide broad confirmation, rather than seeking anecdotal "proofs," as has been typical. [J.L.S.]

S.284 Sorenson, John L. "Bible Prophecies of the Mulekites." In *A Book of Mormon Treasury*, 229-37. Salt Lake City: Bookcraft, 1959. Speculating that Mulek was a pre-adolescent, possibly an infant, the author suggests that many elements in the Book of Mormon might lead one to think that Mulek was brought to the New World by Phoenicians. It is further suggested that Ezekiel 7:22 clearly tells of a child of Zedekiah who was a "tender twig" to be "cropped" and "planted" in another land. [J.W.M.]

S.285 Sorenson, John L. "The Book of Mormon as a Mesoamerican Codex." *SEHA* 139 (December 1976): 1-9. Reprinted, Provo, UT: FARMS, 1981. Referring to Anthon's statements that what he saw had a codex format, this piece discusses points that are compatible with an interpretation of the Book of Mormon as a Mesoamerican codex. [J.L.S.]

S.286 Sorenson, John L. "Book of Mormon Geography in the Light of Ceramic Distributions." *UASN* 8 (November 1952). The sequence of pottery distribution around Guatemala City is suggested as alignable with Nephite culture history in that area. [J.L.S.]

S.287 Sorenson, John L. "Book of Mormon Peoples." In *Encyclopedia of Mormonism*, edited by Daniel H. Ludlow, 1:191-95. 5 vols. New York: Macmillan, 1992. The Book of Mormon describes fifteen distinct groups of people: Nephites, Lamanites, Mulekites, Jaredites, Jacobites, Josephites, Zoramites, Ishmaelites, people of Zeniff, people of Alma, Amulonites, Amlicites, Amalekites, Anti-Nephi-Lehies, Ammonites, and minor groups such as people of Nehor and the Gadianton robbers. Includes a description of each group. [N.K.Y.]

S.288 Sorenson, John L. "The 'Brass Plates' and Biblical Scholarship." *Dialogue* 10 (Autumn 1977): 31-39. Reprinted, Provo, UT: FARMS, 1977. A detailed statement of what is known of the content, form, and history of the brass plates. The ways in which its contents differ from the Masoretic version are consistently parallel to those distinguishing the Elohist (E) version of "the Old Testament." [J.L.S.]

S.289 Sorenson, John L. "The Chronological Discrepancy between Alma 53:22 and Alma 56:9." Provo, UT: FARMS, 1990. Alma 53:22 and Alma 56:9 give dates for the same event two years apart. Examines how this chronological discrepancy may be explained. [J.L.S.]

S.290 Sorenson, John L. "Comparison of Fundamental Traits of the Book of Mormon and Ancient American Civilizations." *UASN* 4 (20 January 1952). Also in *Progress in Archaeology: An Anthology*, edited by R. T. Christensen, 108. Provo, UT: University Archaeological Society, Special Publications, No. 4. A list of 23 traits considered by Steward as characteristic of early "formative" culture common to both Mesoamerica and the Andean region is compared with Book of Mormon culture. None of

Steward's elements are contrary to the Book of Mormon. [J.L.S.]

S.291 Sorenson, John L. "The Composition of Lehi's Family." In *By Study and Also by Faith*, edited by John M. Lundquist and Stephen D. Ricks, 2:174-96. Salt Lake City: Deseret Book and FARMS, 1990. By investigating references in the Book of Mormon to those who came to the new land with Lehi, an educated speculation is made with respect to the ages, occupations, and number of people. A list is presented according to the assumptions made, showing the make up of the intermarrying Lehi and Ishmael families. [A.A.]

S.292 Sorenson, John L. "A Day and A Half's Journey for a Nephite." In *Reexploring the Book of Mormon*, edited by John W. Welch, 187-88. Salt Lake City: Deseret Book and FARMS, 1992. The location of the narrow neck of land has been a puzzle. The Isthmus of Tehuantepec measures 120 miles and is now thought by many to be the 'narrow neck of land' and is within the range of a Nephite journey of a day and a half. [N.K.Y.]

S.293 Sorenson, John L. "Digging into the Book of Mormon: Our Changing Understanding of Ancient America and Its Scripture." *Ensign* 14 (September-October 1984): 26-37, 12-23. Reprinted, Provo, UT: FARMS, 1984. Locates Book of Mormon lands in Mesoamerica and discusses problems of method in comparing the scripture to "scientific findings," then summarizes some recent findings about Mesoamerican civilization (e.g., warfare, writing, roads, metals, population) particularly relevant to the Book of Mormon. [J.L.S.]

S.294 Sorenson, John L. "Early Archaeological Sequences in Highland Guatemala, A Review." *UASN* 17 (January 1954). New details on archaeology of the area around Guatemala City in Book of Mormon times are given. Some features can be compared with the ancient Near East. [J.L.S.]

S.295 Sorenson, John L. "The Elephant in Ancient America." *UASN* 4 (January 1952). Radiocarbon dating indicates early culture in Arizona was contemporaneous with mastodons in the vicinity of 4000 B.C. This may be the first serious evidence supporting the survival of this animal as late as the Jaredites. The book of Ether has "elephants" less than two millennia later. [J.L.S.]

S.296 Sorenson, John L. "An Evaluation of the Smithsonian Institute, 'Statement Regarding the Book of Mormon'." Provo, UT: FARMS, 1982. The form letter passed out by the Smithsonian in response to inquiries about the Book of Mormon contains considerable irrelevant or erroneous information that is critically analyzed here. [J.L.S.]

S.297 Sorenson, John L. "Evidences of Culture Contacts between Polynesia and the Americas." M.A. thesis, Brigham Young University, 1952. Language and cultural traits of Polynesia and the Americas are compared under scores of headings. The abundant parallels indicate voyages as explanations but lack of geographical and chronological clustering leaves the picture unclear, and provides no good evidence for the LDS Hagoth-Polynesian supposition. [J.L.S.]

S.298 Sorenson, John L. "Fortifications in the Book of Mormon Account Compared with Mesoamerican Fortifications." In *Warfare in the Book of Mormon*, edited by Stephen D. Ricks and William J. Hamblin, 425-44. Salt Lake City: Deseret Book and FARMS, 1990. Archaeological discoveries have found 262 Mesoamerican sites with extensive defensive fortifications. Sorenson provides tables of sites, and types of fortification, and compares them with Book of Mormon descriptions. [N.K.Y.]

S.299 Sorenson, John L. "Further on Authentication and Elucidation of the Book of Mormon." *UASN* 6 (May 1952). Also in *Progress in Archaeology: An Anthology*, edited by R. T. Christensen, 147-48. Provo, UT: University Archaeological Society, Special Publications, No. 4. Comparison of Book of Mormon cultures with known New or Old World cultures can be directed toward authentication or elucidation. Little has been done toward shedding light on the scriptures. Almost all necessary work has only begun. [J.L.S.]

S.300 Sorenson, John L. "The Gates of God." *NE* 5 (March 1975): 18-25. The architecture of towers in the Book of Mormon may have been influenced by Old World structures such as the Tower of Babel. The idea that elevation was sacred is seen in the towers of Nephi, King Benjamin, and the Zoramites, but the towers may also have had political significance. Includes photos of Mesoamerican structures that could be interpreted as towers. [A.C.W.]

S.301 Sorenson, John L. *The Geography of Book of Mormon Events: A Source Book.* Provo, UT: FARMS, 1992. A comprehensive analysis of Book of Mormon geography. Sorenson gives a history and summary of all Latter-day Saints who have written on geography. He indicates what the text says, verse by verse, on geography and presents a trial map based on the text. Also presents problems of establishing distances and deciphering directional statements in the Book of Mormon. [B.D.]

S.302 Sorenson, John L. "I Have A Question? I have heard that the sizes of the Nephite and Lamanite populations indicated in the Book of Mormon do not make sense. What do we know about their numbers?" *Ensign* 22 (September 1992): 27-28. Discusses population growth among Lehi's colony, both natural and through assimilation of resident groups. Mentions Sherem as proof of "outsiders," but concludes that information in the Book of Mormon record is too limited for a clear picture to be constructed. [A.C.W.]

S.303 Sorenson, John L. "Incense-Burning and 'Seer' Stones in Ancient Mesoamerica: New Evidence of Migrations of Biblical Peoples to the New World." *UASN* 21 (July 1954). Also in *Progress in Archaeology: An Anthology*, edited by R. T. Christensen, 118-19. Provo, UT: University Archaeological Society, Special Publications, No. 4. Summary of an unpublished, lengthy paper that emphasizes certain parallels in ideas and practices between the ancient Near East and Mesoamerica. [J.L.S.]

S.304 Sorenson, John L. "Indications of Early Metal in Mesoamerica." *UASN* 5 (1954): 1-5. The first seriously documented challenge to the orthodox view that metals in Mesoamerica were only late. Cites a score of possible exceptions. [J.L.S.]

S.305 Sorenson, John L. "Instant Expertise on Book of Mormon Archaeology, A Review Article." *BYU Studies* 16 (Spring 1976): 429-32. Books by Farnsworth, West, Priddis, and Cheesman display defective scholarship despite the zeal of the writers. Gullible LDS book-buyers are blamed for encouraging such poor products. [J.L.S.]

S.306 Sorenson, John L. "The Land of Promise." *NE* 5 (January 1975): 20-29. A collection of photographs by James Christensen and Book of Mormon scriptures suggest possible Book of Mormon sites to help readers visualize the scriptures more fully. [J.W.M.]

S.307 Sorenson, John L. "Latest Discoveries." In *Reexploring the Book of Mormon*, edited by John W. Welch, 111-13. Salt Lake City: Deseret Book and FARMS, 1992. Large stone carvings found in many places continue to baffle archaeologists and linguists. Press releases of "latest discoveries" have not been seasoned by time or studies and are often not accurately reported by the press. It may take years of study to assess the stones' import and meaning. [N.K.Y.]

S.308 Sorenson, John L. "Mesoamericans in Pre-Columbian North America." In *Reexploring the Book of Mormon*, edited by John W. Welch, 218-20. Salt Lake City: Deseret Book and FARMS, 1992. Book of Mormon records conflict with the view that American civilization moved from the Bering Sea southward. Archaeological, linguistic, and historical evidence now confirms the Book of Mormon description of movement from south to north. [N.K.Y.]

S.309 Sorenson, John L. "Mesoamericans in Pre-Spanish South America." In *Reexploring the Book of Mormon*, edited by John W. Welch, 215-17. Salt Lake City: Deseret Book and FARMS, 1992. Current research has shown that for 4,000 years people, materials, and ideas have moved fluidly between both American continents even though Book of Mormon histories cover just Mesoamerica. Linguistic studies, material trading, biological studies, and other information confirm cultural interplay as Alma 63:4 and Helaman 3:8 indicate. [N.K.Y.]

S.310 Sorenson, John L. *Metals and Metallurgy Relating to the Book of Mormon Text.* Provo, UT: FARMS, 1992. Contains an annotated bibliography of sources on the Old World metallurgical background of peoples who may have emigrated to America from southwest Asia and some related methodological issues, and an annotated bibliography on aspects of the history of pre-Columbian metalworking in the New World, with emphasis on Mesoamerica. Includes an index and commentary regarding probable and possible pre-A.D. 900 Mesoamerican metal specimens, and a summary of statements in the Book of Mormon text about metals, ores, and metal processing, with notes on Hebrew usage of metal-related terms. [B.D.]

S.311 Sorenson, John L. "The Mulekites." *BYU Studies* 30 (Summer 1990): 6-22. Reprinted, Provo, UT: FARMS, 1990. An attempt to synthesize all that is known from the Book of Mormon and collateral biblical records about the Mulekites. [J.L.S.]

S.312 Sorenson, John L. "Nephi Speaks to Our Day with Plain and Precious Prophecy." *Instructor* 97 (September 1962): 309, 319. Nephi concentrated on the hopeful future—our day, when his family's descendants are beginning to flourish—rather than ugly details of intervening history. [J.L.S.]

S.313 Sorenson, John L. "Nephi's Garden and Chief Market." In *Reexploring the Book of Mormon*, edited by John W. Welch, 236-38. Salt Lake City: Deseret Book and FARMS, 1992. Nephi$_2$'s garden near a highway leading to the chief Zarahemla market seemed incompatible with ancient urban settlements. For decades the existence of large urban cities in Mesoamerica was disputed but has since been proved, as well as the existence of chief markets in pre-Columbian Mexico. [N.K.Y.]

S.314 Sorenson, John L. "The Nephite Calendar in Mosiah, Alma, and Helaman." In *Reexploring the Book of Mormon*, edited by John W. Welch, 173-75. Salt Lake City: Deseret Book and FARMS, 1992. The Book of Mormon refers to dates in the Nephite time reckoning system, but there is no method of correlating the dates to our own calendar. Research has shown that major battles coincided with the end of the Nephite year. [N.K.Y.]

S.315 Sorenson, John L. "Once More: The Horse." In *Reexploring the Book of Mormon*, edited by John W. Welch, 98-100. Salt Lake City: Deseret Book and FARMS, 1992. Book of Mormon references to horses have little supporting evidence prior to A.D. 1500. True horses are documented into the late glacial age in America and might well have existed as late as 2000 B.C. Argentine scientists maintain their horses were native and not of Spanish origin. Horse remains have been found in Mayapan and other Yucatan sites where the dating is yet to be done. [N.K.Y.]

S.316 Sorenson, John L. "Plain and Precious Prophecy." *Instructor* 97 (September 1962): 309-19. Nephi's prophecies focused on people and principles, as he viewed the "sweep of history and God's plan." Almost half of Nephi's discourse about his vision was related to the influence of a book of scripture. [A.C.W.]

S.317 Sorenson, John L. "Possible 'Silk' and 'Linen' in the Book of Mormon." In *Reexploring the Book of Mormon*, edited by John W. Welch, 162-64. Salt Lake City: Deseret Book and FARMS, 1992. The Book of Mormon reference to silk and linen in Alma 1:29 is questioned by scholars. Cloth fiber made from cocoons of insect larva is known in the wilds of Mexico. Kapok from the silk cotton tree in Yucatan, and rabbit fur garments made by Aztecs exist, and items inventoried by the Spaniards included linen. Linen-like fibers made from yucca and other plants and bark cloth from the fig tree sustain Book of Mormon claims. [N.K.Y.]

S.318 Sorenson, John L. "Prophecy Among the Maya." In *Reexploring the Book of Mormon*, edited by John W. Welch, 263-65. Salt Lake City: Deseret Book and FARMS, 1992. Maya *bobatil* foretold specific events and these were written in books. The coming of the Spaniards was predicted to the day and year. They saw history repeated in cycles and governed their lives by prophetic outlook. Such practices continued Book of Mormon prophetic tradition. [N.K.Y.]

S.319 Sorenson, John L. "A Reconsideration of Early Metal in Mesoamerica." *Katunob* 9 (March 1976): 1-8. Reprinted in *Metallurgy in Ancient Mexico*, by W. Bray, J. L. Sorenson, and J. R. Moriarty, III. University of Northern Colorado, Museum of Anthropology, Miscellaneous Series, No. 45, 1982. Reprinted, Provo, UT: FARMS, 1982. Metals technology was present in Mesoamerica during Book of Mormon times, contrary to received opinion. [J.L.S.]

S.320 Sorenson, John L. "Seasonality of Warfare in the Book of Mormon and in Mesoamerica." In *Warfare in the Book of Mormon*, edited by Stephen D. Ricks and William J. Hamblin, 445-78. Salt Lake City: Deseret Book and FARMS, 1990. Reviews possible calendars used by the Nephites and notes in extensive tables the time of year when battles and preparations for battles were made. The records show that most occurred during the end of dry season in Mesoamerica. [N.K.Y.]

S.321 Sorenson, John L. "Seasons of War, Seasons of Peace in the Book of Mormon." In *Rediscovering the Book of Mormon*, edited by John L. Sorenson and Melvin J. Thorne, 249-55. Salt Lake City: Deseret Book and FARMS, 1991. A popular version of "Seasonality of Warfare in the Book of Mormon and in Mesoamerica," in *Warfare in the Book of Mormon*, edited by Stephen D. Ricks and William J. Hamblin, 445-78. [J.L.S.]

S.322 Sorenson, John L. "Silk and Linen in the Book of Mormon." *Ensign* 22 (April 1992): 62. Excerpt from Sorenson's *An Ancient American Setting for the Book of Mormon* giving archaeological support for the mention of silk and linen in the Book of Mormon. Native American plants and fibers were used to make cloth similar to silk from the Far East and European linen. [A.C.W.]

S.323 Sorenson, John L. "Social Structure and Cult among the Nephites." Paper presented to the Annual Symposium of the Society for Early Historic Archaeology, October 1974, Provo, UT. An expanded version of "Nephite Social Structure." [J.L.S.]

S.324 Sorenson, John L. "Some Mesoamerican Traditions of Immigration by Sea." Provo, UT: FARMS, 1955. Quotes pre-Columbian and early Spanish records of traditions from various sources indicating that the ancestors of the Indians made oceanic voyages to the Americas. [D.M.]

S.325 Sorenson, John L. "Some Voices from the Dust: A Review of Papers of the Fifteenth Annual Symposium on the Archaeology of the Scriptures." *Dialogue* 1 (Spring 1966): 144-49. Puts the Society for Historical Archaeology in context in the history of LDS thought about archaeology then evaluates papers by Jakeman, Tucker, Norman, Putnam, and others as sometimes displaying lack of currency and narrow range of methodology. [J.L.S.]

S.326 Sorenson, John L. "Study Maps of the Book of Mormon." Provo, UT: FARMS, 1985. Packet of maps excerpted from *An Ancient American Setting for the Book of Mormon*. [J.L.S.]

S.327 Sorenson, John L. "The Twig of the Cedar." *IE* 60 (May 1957): 330-31. Also "Bible Prophecies of the Mulekites." In *A Book of Mormon Treasury*, 229-37. Salt Lake City: Bookcraft, 1959. Reprinted, Provo, UT: FARMS, 1981. Relates Ezekiel 17:22-24 to Mulek's transplantation to America. A Mexican tradition of the arrival of an immigrant group by sea may also be related to Mulek. [J.L.S.]

S.328 Sorenson, John L. "Traditions of Immigration by Sea in the Peopling of Meso-America." *El México Antiguo* 8 (1955): 425-39. Also in "Traditions of Immigration by Sea in the Peopling of Meso-America." Provo, UT: FARMS, 1955. Documents a variety of traditions that show that the idea that ancestors had arrived by sea was widespread. [J.L.S.]

S.329 Sorenson, John L. "Transoceanic Crossings." In *The Book of Mormon: First Nephi, The Doctrinal Foundation*, edited by Monte S. Nyman and Charles D. Tate Jr., 251-70. Provo, UT: Brigham Young University Religious Studies Center, 1988. The text of 1 Nephi 17-18 is

S.330 Sorenson, John L. "Wheeled Figurines in the Ancient World." Provo, UT: FARMS, 1981. A substantial though unpolished survey of the literature under four headings: Mesoamerican wheeled figurines, function, wheels and movement in Mesoamerican belief, and wheeled figurines in the Old World. A brief appendix relates the material to the few statements in the Book of Mormon about "chariots." [J.L.S.]

S.331 Sorenson, John L. "When Lehi's Party Arrived in the Land, Did They Find Others There?" *Journal of Book of Mormon Studies* 1 (Fall 1992): 1-34. Numerous Book of Mormon references infer the presence of other population groups present in America when Lehi's group landed. The presence of multiple languages among population groups in Mesoamerica strongly implies that ancestral people were in America for thousands of years. When Amulek met Alma in the city of Ammonihah he promptly identified himself as a Nephite, an indication that he lived among a non-Nephite population. The crew(s) of the ship(s) that brought Mulek's party were probably Phoenician, as all Mediterranean ports were then in Babylonian hands. [R.H.B.]

S.332 Sorenson, John L. "Winds and Currents: A Look at Nephi's Ocean Crossing." In *Reexploring the Book of Mormon*, edited by John W. Welch, 53-56. Salt Lake City: Deseret Book and FARMS, 1992. Discusses Nephi's route and ocean crossing. Departure from Arabia is best from April 1-15 to avoid dangerous swells near India. The great storm Nephi describes could have been in the Bay of Bengal, where such are common. Eastern travel across the Pacific has been confirmed by studies of the El Niño phenomenon. Such a Pacific Ocean crossing is estimated to have taken less than a year. Liahona guidance would have optimized the time. [N.K.Y.]

S.333 Sorenson, John L. "The World of the Book of Mormon." Provo, UT: Brigham Young University, Extension Division, Leadership Week Publications, 1955. Transcripts of five lectures pertaining to the world of the Book of Mormon: the physical world, the cultural world (in two parts), the world of ideas, and the transmission of ideas. The aim is to provide context in order to aid understanding of the scripture. Includes question-and-answer sessions. (Many ideas in Sorenson's 1985 book were first introduced in these lectures.) [J.L.S.]

S.334 Sorenson, John L. "Writing Systems Among the Book of Mormon Peoples." *NE* 7 (November 1977): 48-50. A popular-level discussion of how Mesoamerican writing systems worked and points of similarity to what the Book of Mormon says about Nephite writing. [J.L.S.]

S.335 Sorenson, John L., Angela Crowell, and Allen J. Christensen. "Parallelism, Merismus, and Difrasismo." In *Reexploring the Book of Mormon*, edited by John W. Welch, 80-82. Salt Lake City: Deseret Book and FARMS, 1992. A discussion of poetic devices common to the Book of Mormon and Old Testament and Mesoamerican texts, including chiasmus, parallelistic couplets, merismus, and difrasismo. [N.K.Y.]

S.336 Sorenson, John L., Gordon C. Thomasson, and Robert F. Smith. "Old World Languages in the New World." In *Reexploring the Book of Mormon*, edited by John W. Welch, 29-31. Salt Lake City: Deseret Book and FARMS, 1992. Reports cognates in American Indian and Ob-Ugarian languages. Linguistic developments support the theory that Old and New World languages are related, thus strengthening the case for the Book of Mormon. [E.G]

S.337 Sorenson, John L., and John W. Welch. "Seven Tribes: An Aspect of Lehi's Legacy." In *Reexploring the Book of Mormon*, edited by John W. Welch, 93-95. Salt Lake City: Deseret Book and FARMS, 1992. Examines the division of Lehi's descendants into seven tribes: Nephites, Jacobites, Josephites, Zoramites, Lamanites, Lemuelites, and Ishmaelites. Observes that this tribal structure was established at Lehi's final blessing and endured until the collapse of Nephite society almost one thousand years later. It served important religious, military, political, and legal functions. [A.C.W.]

S.338 Sorenson, John L., and Martin H. Raish. *Pre-Columbian Contact with America across the Oceans: An Annotated Bibliography.* 2 vols. Provo, UT: Research Press, 1990. More than 5,600 literature items in many languages are listed covering pro- and anti- positions, theory, and methodology. Detailed bibliographical data and annotations, some very detailed, are provided for most items, reporting how they relate to the topic. [J.L.S.]

S.339 Sorenson, John L., and Paul Y. Hoskisson. "Lost Arts." In *Reexploring the Book of Mormon,* edited by John W. Welch, 101-4. Salt Lake City: Deseret Book and FARMS, 1992. Arts and technology once known, lost, and rediscovered in Central and South American civilizations include concrete arches found Guatemala and Peru, potter's wheels and a lathe discovered in burial sites at Pashash in Peru, and ceramics found among early Polynesian cultures. [N.K.Y.]

S.340 Sorenson, John L., and Robert F. Smith. "Barley in Ancient America." In *Reexploring the Book of Mormon,* edited by John W. Welch, 130-32. Salt Lake City: Deseret Book and FARMS, 1992. In recent times pre-Columbian barley has been discovered at Phoenix, Arizona, and in caves of Oklahoma, recalling the mention of barley in the Book of Mormon. Further studies need to be made to establish how and when such barley discovered was grown. [N.K.Y.]

S.341 Sorenson, John L., and Robert F. Smith. "Two Figurines From the Belleza & Sanchez Collection." In *Reexploring the Book of Mormon,* edited by John W. Welch, 18-19. Salt Lake City: Deseret Book and FARMS, 1992. The figurines found on the Pacific Coast beach of Acajutla, Sonsonate, El Salvador, clearly belong to a class of ancient Egyptian funerary statuettes known as *ushabti.* Both figurines, incised with hieroglyphic Egyptian texts, were popular for much of Egyptian history. [N.K.Y.]

S.342 Sorenson, John L., and Melvin J. Thorne, eds. *Rediscovering the Book of Mormon.* Salt Lake City: Deseret Book and FARMS, 1991. New discoveries about the Book of Mormon made by LDS scholars. The essays show meaningful and complex patterns in the Book of Mormon—patterns of style, ideas, history, and actions. They also provide considerable evidence for the authenticity of the Book of Mormon. [J.L.S.]

S.343 Sorensen, Parry D. "A Witness of Divine Truth." *MS* 99 (July 1937): 426-28. Martin Harris acted as Joseph's scribe during the translation of the Book of Mormon. He became convinced of the authenticity of the translation upon showing a translation and copies of the original characters to two well-known experts. He was one of the Three Witnesses and never denied his testimony of the Book of Mormon. [K.M.]

S.344 Sowers, Kenneth. "The Mystery and History of the Urim and Thummim." In *Restoration Studies II,* edited by M. Draper and A. Lindgren, 75-79. Independence, MO: Temple School, 1983. Examines the historical accounts concerning the Urim and Thummim. It appears that the interpreters of the Book of Mormon are separate items from the Urim and Thummim described in the Bible. [J.W.M.]

S.345 Spain, Carolyn Y., and Eldred F. Spain. *Studies in Mosiah.* Independence, MO: Herald House, 1989. A study aid designed to assist individuals in their study of the book of Mosiah. Contains commentary and discussion questions. [D.W.P.]

S.346 Spaulding, Solomon. *The "Manuscript Found"—The Solomon Spaulding Manuscript.* Oberlin College Library, 1908. A fictional account of a Roman citizen who made his way to the American continent and there set up a colony among the natives. Includes an introductory letter by L. L. Rice, who found the manuscript, in which he concludes that this story was not the basis for the Book of Mormon. [A.C.W.]

S.347 Spence, Robert S. "Signs of Christ's Coming." *Contributor* 4 (June 1883): 356-57. Using the text of Ezekiel concerning the "stick of Joseph," the author examines Old Testament scriptures and Indian legends to establish that the coming forth of the "stick of Joseph," the Book of Mormon, was a sign of Christ's second coming. [J.W.M.]

S.348 Spencer, Marjorie M. "My Book of Mormon Sisters." *Ensign* 7 (September 1977): 66-71. This author made extensive notes about women in the scriptures. She expounds upon their characteristics and examples for others to follow (or not follow). She explores the adjectives used to describe them, the tribulations they endured, and the doctrine that is presented to both male and female. [J.W.M.]

S.349 Spencer, Orson. "Letter of Orson Spencer." *TS* 4 (2 January 1843): 49-59. Thoughtful description of the dynamics of the author's conversion. After hearing negative things about the Book of Mormon, Spencer studied the book and was converted to Jesus Christ. [D.M.]

S.350 Spencer, Orson. "Seventh Letter of Orson Spencer to the Rev. W. Crowel A. M." *MS* 9 (1 September 1847): 258-62. Discusses the Book of Mormon within the context of the establishment of the Latter-day kingdom of God, citing Isaiah 29 as a prooftext. Responds to perceived weaknesses in language by writing that "an uninspired man might as well attempt to originally compose the Old and New Testament" as the Book of Mormon. [D.M.]

S.351 Spencer, Pearl. "The Peace Pipe and the Book of Mormon." *IE* 35 (July 1932): 545. The Indian legend concerning the peace pipe is one of great significance to the Book of Mormon. The pipe was a symbol of Jesus, the Prince of Peace. The account of Jesus' visit to the Americas might help to explain this legend more fully. [J.W.M.]

S.352 Sperry, Sidney B. *Answers to Book of Mormon Questions*. Salt Lake City: Bookcraft, 1967. Resolves diverse questions about the Book of Mormon text as it relates to the Pentateuch, the writings of Isaiah, Shakespearean quotations, New Testament citations, domesticated animals, and others. [D.L.L.]

S.353 Sperry, Sidney B. "The Book of Mormon and Textual Criticism," In *Book of Mormon Institute*, 1-8. Provo, UT: Brigham Young University Extension Publications, 5 December 1959. Argues against multiple authorship of the book of Isaiah and the first five books of Moses (the Pentateuch), with evidence from the Book of Mormon. Proposes that some textual variants in Isaiah as quoted in the Book of Mormon have an ancient source; argues that the Book of Mormon text can help determine the text of the Bible; and proposes that "Son of Righteousness" in the Book of Mormon should actually be "Sun of Righteousness." [R. S.]

S.354 Sperry, Sidney B. "The Book of Mormon as Translation English." *IE* 38 (March 1935, October 1954): 140-41, 187-88, 703. Response to the argument that the Book of Mormon is an "imitation of biblical dictation." Sperry demonstrates that the Book of Mormon is an inspired translation, not simply an anthology of quotations, thoughts, or sayings of Joseph Smith, by examining various Isaianic passages in the Book of Mormon and comparing them with the Isaiah of the Septuagint, the Authorized Version, and the Hebrew text. [D.W.P.]

S.355 Sperry, Sidney B. *Book of Mormon Chronology*. Salt Lake City: Deseret Book, 1970. Written to correct minor errors in the chronology of the 1920 edition of the Book of Mormon. Book-by-book discussion of the given chronology, suppositions, and variant interpretations. [A.C.W.]

S.356 Sperry, Sidney B. *Book of Mormon Compendium*. Salt Lake City: Bookcraft, 1968. Thorough commentary on many aspects of the Book of Mormon. At least one chapter is devoted to each book of the Book of Mormon, plus chapters on the origin and translation, language and script, title page, witnesses, the Isaiah problem, the concept of God, teachings concerning death and the hereafter, and personal religion and brotherhood in the Book of Mormon. [A.C.W.]

S.357 Sperry, Sidney B. "Book of Mormon Contributions to the Archaeology of the Old Testament." In Sperry's *Ancient Records Testify in Papyrus and Stone*, 229-40. Salt Lake City: General Boards of M.I.A. of the Church of Jesus Christ of Latter-day Saints, 1938. Deals directly with how the Book of Mormon contributes to the authenticity of the Bible. Sperry uses Book of Mormon references to argue that

Moses wrote the Pentateuch, and that Isaiah wrote the works that bear his name. The Book of Mormon is a companion to the Bible. [G.A.]

S.358 Sperry, Sidney B. "Book of Mormon Essays by Sidney B. Sperry." Provo, UT: FARMS, n.d. A series of essays published under one title. The articles included are "The Book of Mormon and Textual Criticism," "The Book of Mormon's Message on Brotherhood," "Some Universals in the Book of Mormon," "Did Father Lehi Have Daughters Who Married the Sons of Ishmael?," "The Lamanites Portrayed in the Book of Mormon," "Moroni the Lonely," and "Some Problems of Interest Relating to the Brass Plates." [J.W.M.]

S.359 Sperry, Sidney B. *Book of Mormon Testifies.* Salt Lake City: Bookcraft, 1952. The author analyzes each book in the Book of Mormon by giving its literary structure, purposes for writing, and content. The Book of Mormon is summarized in three main messages: a warning to the inhabitants of the American continent, the testimonies of Christ, and the Lord's promises to Israel. [G.A.]

S.360 Sperry, Sidney B. "The Book of Mormon's Message on Brotherhood." *Ensign* 3 (March 1973): 57-59. Cites various incidents from the Book of Mormon to show the teaching and practices of the Nephites concerning brotherhood and social justice. It particularly deals with the relations between family members, neighbors, workers, and enemies. [B.T.]

S.361 Sperry, Sidney B. "Did Father Lehi Have Daughters Who Married the Sons of Ishmael?" *IE* 55 (September 1952): 642. Also in *A Book of Mormon Treasury*, 154-56. Salt Lake City: Bookcraft, 1959, 1976. Lehi had at least two "daughters who married the sons of Ishmael." According to Erastus Snow, the sons of Ishmael "married into Lehi's family" and 2 Nephi 5:6 indicates that Nephi had sisters. [A.T.]

S.362 Sperry, Sidney B. "Hebrew Idioms in the Book of Mormon." *IE* 57 (October 1954): 703, 728-29. Technical study of Hebrew grammar and idioms found profusely throughout the Book of Mormon. Compound Hebrew prepositions, plural compounds, and over three dozen examples of Hebrew idioms are given in the article. These studies support the idea that the Book of Mormon was originally written in Hebrew. [R.C.D.]

S.363 Sperry, Sidney B. "The Isaiah Problem in the Book of Mormon." *IE* 42 (September 1939): 524-25, 564-69. The Book of Mormon quotes twenty-one whole chapters and parts of other chapters of Isaiah. The authorship of Isaiah has been questioned by prominent scholars, and this "higher criticism" brought about the disintegration of belief in the unity of Isaiah. Some have faithfully held to the belief of unity and Sperry gives their reasoning. [J.W.M.]

S.364 Sperry, Sidney B. "The Isaiah Quotation: 2 Nephi 12-24." Provo, UT: FARMS, 198?. Analyzes the Lord's words to Israel through Isaiah the prophet and concludes that these teachings tell of (1) the coming of Christ and the power of his atonement, (2) the prophecies of the latter days of interest to Nephi's people and the house of Israel, (3) the Lord who will redeem his people in the last days and remain in their midst, and (4) the judgments of God concerning the nations of the earth. [J.W.M.]

S.365 Sperry, Sidney B. *Knowledge is Power.* Salt Lake City: Bookcraft, 1958. Chapters 12-20 deal with the Book of Mormon. Discusses the last years of Moroni's life, Hebrew idioms in the Book of Mormon, the meaning of the Urim and Thummim, Lehi's daughters, and the parallelistic features found in Isaiah and in the Book of Mormon. [G.A.]

S.366 Sperry, Sidney B. "The Lamanites Portrayed in the Book of Mormon." *IE* 51 (December 1948): 792-93, 826-27. Also in *A Book of Mormon Treasury*, 114-21. Salt Lake City: Bookcraft, 1959, 1976. Sets forth Book of Mormon characteristics and prophecies regarding the Lamanites. The Lamanites were used as a scourge to the Nephites; often the Lamanites were more righteous than the Nephites; the American Indians are descendants of Book of Mormon peoples; and the Lamanites will yet "receive the gospel" and become a "white and delightsome people." [A.T.]

S.367 Sperry, Sidney B. "Moroni the Lonely, The Story of the Writing of the Title-Page to the Book of Mormon." *IE* 47 (February 1944): 83, 116, 118. Also in *IE* 73 (November 1970): 110-11, and in *A Book of Mormon Treasury*, 122-26. Salt Lake City: Bookcraft, 1959, 1976. Moroni was alone for thirty-six years. He finished the Book of Mormon, abridged the book of Ether, and wrote the title page. [J.W.M.]

S.368 Sperry, Sidney B. "Moroni's Mission and the Bible." *MS* 97 (12, 19 September 1935): 594-95, 604-5. Describes the first visitation of the angel Moroni to Joseph Smith, Joseph's call to the ministry, and scriptures quoted and interpreted by Moroni. Emphasis is placed on prophecies of key events in the latter days. [R.H.B.]

S.369 Sperry, Sidney B. "Omni and the Words of Mormon." Provo, UT: FARMS, 1984. Analyzes Omni 1:16-30, written by Amaleki, son of Abinadom, which explains the relationship of the descendants of Mosiah to the Mulekites in Zarahemla. "Book of Mormon history from Omni 12 is a history of the Mulekite people who adopted Nephite Leadership and Nephite Culture." Also, the Book of Omni gives an account of King Benjamin's life. [B.D.]

S.370 Sperry, Sidney B. *Our Book of Mormon*. Salt Lake City: Bookcraft, 1950. Simplifies the complex structure of the Book of Mormon by providing an overall synopsis of the text. He orders the fifteen books of the Book of Mormon into four divisions: (1) the small plates of Nephi, (2) Mormon's explanatory notes, (3) the literary labors of Mormon, and (4) the literary labors of Moroni; he follows with a literary synopsis of each of the fifteen books. Several types of literature are identified, including "the American Gospel" (3 Nephi 1:4-21; 8-28, Jesus' Nephite ministry), pastoral, prophetic, and war epistles, one psalm, one lamentation, memoir, prophetic discourse, oratory, patriarchal blessings, symbolic prophecy, prophetic narrative, prophetic dialogue, allegories, prayers, songs, and genealogies. More than fifty percent of the book is "historical narrative." Deals with the problem of biblical texts (Isaiah, the Sermon on the Mount, 1 Corinthians chapters 12 and 13) found in the Book of Mormon. [D.W.P.]

S.371 Sperry, Sidney B. *The Problems of the Book of Mormon*. Salt Lake City: Bookcraft, 1964. Divides the "problems" of the Book of Mormon into two categories. The first are technical, doctrinal, and interpretive problems for members of the Church. The second relates to those raised by critics of the book and the Church. He addresses the nature of man, the problem of history, the use of the Urim and Thummim, the "Gentiles" of the Book of Mormon, the brass plates, Jesus as the Father and the Son, the Pentateuch, Isaiah, Sermon on the Mount, and more. The last five chapters answer criticism raised by apostate Arthur Budvarson. [J.W.M.]

S.372 Sperry, Sidney B. *Science, Tradition and the Book of Mormon*. Salt Lake City: Church of Jesus Christ of Latter-day Saints, MIA, 1973. A reference manual for the youth. Sperry talks of the migration of the Jaredites and Nephites, suggesting also some possible landing sites. He gives archaeological evidence that relics found in ancient China resemble those found in the ancient Americas. Many Indian legends tell of a sacred book that was taken away that would return to the earth, and Sperry compares this legend with the Book of Mormon. [G.A.]

S.373 Sperry, Sidney B. "Some Problems of Interest Relating to the Brass Plates." *IE* 54 (September 1951): 638-39, 670-71. Raises numerous unanswered questions about brass plates. How did current writings of Jeremiah get recorded on the plates when they were guarded exclusively by Laban? What merit does Old Testament criticism about the origin of the Pentateuch and Deuteronomy have in light of what is known about the brass plates? How did Laban, a descendant of Joseph, come to be the custodian of the plates in Jerusalem, the capitol of the southern kingdom of Judah? [R.C.D.]

S.374 Sperry, Sidney B. "Some Universals in the Book of Mormon." *IE* 49 (April 1946): 212-13, 240-42. Also in *DN* (15 February 1947):

10, 12. Universal teachings in the Book of Mormon include the truth that all men are equal before God (1 Nephi 17:33-35, 2 Nephi 26:33); certain truths are found in all the world (Alma 29:8); spiritual truths may be tested and faith increased (Alma 32); men are that they might have joy (2 Nephi 2:30); when you serve men, you serve God (Mosiah 2:16-18). [B.D.]

S.375 Sperry, Sidney B. "The Text of Isaiah in the Book of Mormon." M.A. thesis, University of Chicago Divinity School, 1926. A detailed study of the parallels in Isaiah texts in the Bible and Book of Mormon. This study includes tables in both English and Hebrew showing the textual differences. The conclusions are that the text of Isaiah considered Deutero-Isaiah dates earlier than 600 B.C. when Lehi brought the plates of Laban to the American continent and that Joseph Smith worked independently from the King James Version. [J.W.M.]

S.376 Sperry, Sidney B. *Themes of the Restored Gospel*. Salt Lake City: Bookcraft, 1950. The majority of the book is devoted to "the spirit of modern scripture," in which Sperry discusses modern scriptural doctrine, including teachings found in the Book of Mormon. He explores the concept of God, great personalities of the Book of Mormon, personal religion, brotherhood, the hereafter, judgment, and universal aspects of the Book of Mormon. [C.W.B.]

S.377 Sperry, Sidney B. "Three Outstanding Messages of The Book of Mormon to This Generation." *MS* 113 (September-November 1951): 202-3, 222, 226-27, 239, 245, 256-58, 265. The Book of Mormon is first a warning voice to our day and time. We must serve God or perish, and beware of secret combinations. Second, it is a testimony that Jesus is the Christ. The third outstanding message shows the Lord's concern toward the house of Israel. [J.W.M.]

S.378 Sperry, Sidney B. "Were There Two Cumorahs?" Provo, UT: FARMS, 1964. A careful study of the passages of scripture found in the Book of Mormon concerning the hill in which the sacred records were hidden by Mormon seems to indicate that it was located in Middle America. The theory that the records were first deposited in the hill Cumorah in New York state seems to fall apart when the text of the Book of Mormon is closely examined. The conclusion is that the records must have been transported. [J.W.M.]

S.379 Sperry, Sidney B. "What is the Meaning of Urim and Thummim?" *IE* 43 (November 1940): 657, 690, 692-93. Sperry analyzes the Assyrian and Babylonian similarities to the Hebrew Urim and Thummim to find a better translation than the unsatisfactory "lights and perfection." He concludes that a better translation is "revelations and visions" or "revelations and manifestations." He speculates on the manner in which the instrument functioned. [B.D.]

S.380 Stafford, Harry Errald. *The Early Inhabitants of the Americas*. New York: Vantage Press, 1959. Uses archaeological evidence, legends, traditions, and myths of the native inhabitants, as well as historical accounts to show that the Book of Mormon coincides with ancient evidence and thus it must surely be the record of the ancient inhabitants of the Americas. Ties Book of Mormon migrations with specific locations and civilizations according to Book of Mormon texts. [J.W.M.]

S.381 Stallings, Sandra. "Cham Nap." *NE* 16 (May 1986): 38-39. A 14-year-old Cambodian boy struggled to read the Book of Mormon to strengthen his testimony and to learn English. [J.W.M.]

S.382 Stapley, Delbert L. "Christ's Visit to the Western Hemisphere Following His Resurrection." *Relief Society Magazine* 40 (March 1953): 211-15. Christ's visit to the American continent brought hope and assurance of eternal life. There had been ample evidence of his crucifixion and death as foretold by Samuel the Lamanite. Mormon considered this story of great importance to Jews and Gentiles of the latter days. The witnesses of the New World testified and supported the New Testament's account of the Savior's crucifixion and resurrection. [J.W.M.]

S.383 Stapley, Delbert L. "The Glorious Standard." *IE* 66 (December 1963): 1103-6. Recalls Book of Mormon prophecies that foretold the discovery and establishment of the promised land of America. There are blessings for those who keep God's commandments and cursings for those who do not. The constitution was divinely inspired. [J.W.M.]

S.384 Stapley, Delbert L. "Overcoming Evil Designs: Nephi's Counsel." *CR* (October 1961): 20-24. Notes Nephi's teaching that Satan will try to deceive in the last days, and reviews schemes used by Satan today. We cannot with safety say "all is well in Zion." [R.C.D.]

S.385 Stapely, Delbert L. Untitled talk. *CR* (April 1963): 33-38. Jacob gave important counsel that was designed to protect homes and families from immoral behavior. Yielding to the temptation that leads to immoral behavior will lead to broken homes and innocent victims who are affected both psychologically and spiritually. [J.W.M.]

S.386 Stapley, Delbert L. "The Vision of Lehi." *IE* 69 (June 1966): 504-6. Also in *CR* (April 1966): 23-27. Lessons can be learned from the record of Lehi's vision of the tree of life. Prayer and humility are important to learning the truth by the power of the Holy Ghost. Temptation may come in attractive attire that blurs perception and weakens sensibility. [J.W.M.]

S.387 Stapley, Orley S. Untitled talk. *CR* (October 1916); 111-13. A woman who was very ill accepted the Book of Mormon as true, desired baptism, and believed she would be made whole. She had to be carried into the waters of baptism, but was able to walk out. Evidence of ancient fortifications and cities lie all around and are memorials to the people who lived anciently in the Americas. [J.W.M.]

S.388 Starks, Arthur E. *Combined Concordances for the Scriptures*. Independence, MO: Herald House, 1962, 1975. This volume comprises *A Concordance Supplement for the Inspired Version of the Holy Scriptures*, *A Complete Concordance to the Book of Mormon*, and *A Complete Concordance to the Doctrine and Covenants*. These concordances are based on the RLDS scriptures and use their chapter-verse divisions. Formatted alphabetically by words and key phrases. [A.C.W.]

S.389 Stathis, Stephen W., and Charles H. Whittier. "The Enigma of Solomon Spaulding." *Dialogue* 10 (1977): 70-73. Brief biography of Solomon Spaulding, deploring the fact that he is only remembered today for his connection to the Book of Mormon manuscript when his life consisted of so many other noteworthy accomplishments. [A.C.W.]

S.390 Stayton, Linda L. "I Felt Drawn To That Book." *Ensign* 7 (September 1977): 73-74. A long search for a religion that could be accepted led this guilt-ridden lady to investigate many churches. A visit to Nauvoo and a gift of the Book of Mormon was the answer to prayers. [J.W.M.]

S.391 Stebbins, Henry A. *The Book of Mormon Lectures: Claims of the Book of Mormon Examined in the Light of History, Archaeology, Antiquity, and Science*. Independence, MO: Ensign House, 1894, [R]1901. A series of nine lectures that begins with Stebbins's testimony of the Book of Mormon followed by an overview of its history. Lectures deal with archaeology, geography, linguistics, the Biblical scriptures, and other items. [A.C.W.]

S.392 Stebbins, Henry A. *Modern Knowledge of the Antiquities of America*. Independence, MO: Ensign Publishing, March 1897. American antiquities support the claims of the Book of Mormon. Prior to the publication of the book extensive facts about the ancient Americans' language, ancestry, and works were unknown to the world. Gives information about publication dates for works about American antiquities and when their use began in America. [J.W.M.]

S.393 Stebbins, Henry A. "Prehistoric America and the Book of Mormon." *Journal of History* 6 (1913): 2-19. Archaeologists have uncovered great civilizations in America. The scattering from the tower of Babel led people "everywhere" on the earth and the Book of Mormon bears witness of that fact. The book supports the Bible both in history and doctrine. It teaches of Christ and the historians have recorded that American natives had knowledge of Christianity before the Spanish came. [J.W.M.]

S.394 Steed, A. Merlin. "The Dawning Day For The Lamanites." *MS* 95 (1 June 1933): 353-59, 363. Describes a time when Indian students visited the Alberta, Canada Temple. They saw wall paintings that depicted Lehi offering a sacrifice after landing on American soil, and a picture of Christ administering the sacrament to a Lamanite at his coming after his resurrection. [B.D.]

S.395 Stendahl, Krister. "The Sermon on the Mount and Third Nephi." In *Reflections on Mormonism: Judaeo-Christian Parallel,* 139-54. Provo, UT: Brigham Young University Religious Studies Center, 1978. 3 Nephi 11-26 is the New Testament part of the Book of Mormon, the teachings and ministry of the Savior. It is apocryphal in nature. The Book of Mormon text is significantly different from the New Testament, baptism being the central feature. 3 Nephi introduces a Johannine Jesus rather than a Matthean portrayal, and proclaims Jesus as the Mosiah, the Redeemer. [J.W.M.]

S.396 Stevens, Thelona D. *An Introduction to the Book of Mormon.* Independence, MO: Foundation for Research on Ancient America, 1984. A booklet briefly setting forth a number of topics dealing with the Book of Mormon, including the language, translation, title page, manuscripts, archaeology, geography, witnesses, composition of the plates, and other items. [D.W.P.]

S.397 Stevens, Thelona D. *Nephi, Son of Lehi.* Independence, MO: Foundation for Research on Ancient America, 1986. Booklet has short essays about Nephi, addressing his role as a shipbuilder, his leadership qualities, his priesthood, and his interest in educating his people. [D.M.]

S.398 Stevens, Thelona D. *A Summary of the Book of Mormon: Book by Book.* Independence, MO: Foundation for Research on Ancient America, 1984. A booklet that provides a concise historical summary of each of the fifteen books of the Book of Mormon. [D.W.P.]

S.399 Stevenson, Bertha S. "The Third Witness." *IE* 37 (August 1934): 458-59. Chronicles the final years of Martin Harris's life and his journey to Utah. Harris spoke to congregations bearing his witness of the Book of Mormon. He died in July 1870 and was buried with a Book of Mormon in one hand and a Doctrine and Covenants in the other. [J.W.M.]

S.400 Stevenson, E. "A Visit to David Whitmer." *Juvenile Instructor* 22 (February 1887): 55. David Whitmer, the final surviving witness for the Book of Mormon, bore an undimmed testimony of the Book of Mormon and told of the visit of one of the three Nephites. [J.W.M.]

S.401 Stevenson, Edward. "Historical Scenes Around Cumorah Hill." *Utah Monthly Magazine* 8 (April-May 1892): 242-46, 289-91. Describes the location and appearance of the Hill Cumorah, and then tells of the Jaredite and Nephite destructions that had occurred there. Stevenson then discusses America as a land of liberty and Moroni's final act of burying the plates in the Hill Cumorah. [A.C.W.]

S.402 Stevenson, Edward. *Reminiscences of Joseph, the Prophet, and the Coming Forth of the Book of Mormon.* Salt Lake City: Edward Stevenson, 1893. The author presents his own and others' eyewitness accounts of events in the life of Joseph Smith. This book gives the history of Joseph's childhood through his martyrdom. Includes a description of Cumorah, speaks of its history, and gives descriptions of the things Joseph received with the golden plates. [L.M.]

S.403 Stevenson, Edward. "The Three Witnesses To The Book of Mormon." *MS* (May 1886): 341-43. As a witness who sat in the presence of the prophet Joseph and the Three Witnesses, this author presents his accounts of some of the occasions when testimonies were born. The author states that he was "deeply inspired" as he heard them many times testify of being in the presence of a heavenly messenger who talked with them and showed them the plates. They were shown the Urim and Thummim and told these seer stones were used by ancient prophets. [J.W.M.]

S.404 Stewart, F. L. *Exploding The Myth About Joseph Smith, The Mormon Prophet.* New York: House of Stewart Publications, 1967. Written in rebuttal to *No Man Knows My History,* by Fawn Brodie. Finds numerous discrepancies, erroneous claims and associations. Brodie's claim that Joseph Smith's family was irreligious is an error. The Kentucky revivals had no connections with the New York religious controversies. Investigates the "Dogberry articles" that ran in the Palmyra *Reflector* and finds that evidence was overlooked by Brodie. Joseph Smith could not have written the Book of Mormon with his limited access to education and written materials. [J.W.M.]

S.405 Stewart, Ora Pate. "Article of Faith Eight: We believe the Bible . . ." In Stewart's *We Believe: A Simplified Treatment of the Articles of Faith,* 85-90. Salt Lake City: Bookcraft, 1954. Stewart points out that the "Bible is not the complete history of God's dealings with man; neither is the Book of Mormon." However, it is the word of God. The Bible has mistakes of omission that took place during the time of copying and multiple translations. This is not so for the Book of Mormon, which was translated under divine supervision only once. The "Stick of Judah" and the "Stick of Joseph" are "one in the testimony they bear." [J.W.M.]

S.406 Stewart, Ora Pate. *Branches Over the Wall.* Salt Lake City: Bookcraft, 1950. Retelling of the Book of Mormon in simplified language. [A.C.W.]

S.407 Stewart, Ora Pate. *Treasures Unearthed.* Salt Lake City: Bookcraft, 1953. Stewart discusses various Book of Mormon topics such as the Lamanite curse, the issue of white Indians, Nephi's sisters, calendars, shipbuilding, organized crime, arts, industry, and prophecies concerning our day. The topics are in random order, and are written in the form of short articles. [A.C.W.]

S.408 "The Stick of Ephraim." *IE* 8 (August 1905): 781-82. Lehi was a descendant of Manasseh and Ishmael was a descendant of Ephraim. Hence, the Book of Mormon is the stick of Joseph, which comprises descendants of Manasseh and Ephraim. [D.M.]

S.409 "The Stick of Ephraim." *MS* 68 (22 March 1906): 189-91. Addresses the question, "Why is the Book of Mormon called the stick of Ephraim when Lehi descended from Manasseh?" It recounts Ezekiel's prophecy that the sticks of Judah and Joseph would come together. The blessings given to Joseph and Ephraim by the Patriarch Jacob show that as the birthright tribe, Ephraim is nearly always referred to in the Bible instead of Manasseh. Zoram and Ishmael were descendants of Ephraim, and in the latter days the Book of Mormon is being used primarily by descendants of Ephraim. For all of these reasons the Book of Mormon is referred to as the stick of Ephraim. [K.M.]

S.410 "Stick of Joseph." In *Encyclopedia of Mormonism,* edited by Daniel H. Ludlow, 3:1418. 5 vols. New York: Macmillan, 1992. Latter-day Saints consider the Book of Mormon to be the "Stick of Joseph." It has also been called the "Stick of Ephraim" (Ezekiel 37). [J.W.M.]

S.411 Stiles, Kendall. "Democratic Government in Ancient America." *Ensign* 22 (April 1992): 62. Discusses Mosiah$_2$'s democratic system of government as described in Mosiah, Alma, Helaman, and 3 Nephi. The political structure was based on a system of judges, the people were the ultimate authority, and honesty and accountability were emphasized. [A.C.W.]

S.412 Stocks, Hugh G. *The Book of Mormon in English, 1870-1920: A Publishing History and Analytical Bibliography.* Los Angeles: University of California Press, 1986. Examines the production and distribution of the Book of Mormon from 1870-1920. This article contains a description of each printing that took place during this period and the factors that determined the format, location of publication, and cost. A comparison is made between publication of the Book of Mormon and publications of the Seventh-day Adventists and Christian Scientists. [J.W.M.]

S.413 Stocks, Hugh G. "Book of Mormon Translations." In *Encyclopedia of Mormonism,* edited by Daniel H. Ludlow, 1:213-14. 5 vols. New York: Macmillan, 1992. Book of Mormon translations began with the Danish translation in 1851, 36 complete book translations into other languages by 1990, and selections from the book into 44 additional languages. These selections will be replaced by complete book translations in the near future. [N.K.Y.]

S.414 Storrer, A. A. "A Dream Come True." *Ensign* 14 (August 1984): 55. Through prayer and the Book of Mormon a period of indecision about whether this author should join the Church came to an end. [J.W.M.]

S.415 *Stories from the Book of Mormon.* Salt Lake City: Department of Seminaries and Institutes of Religion, 1967. Booklet illustrates the sacred history of the brother of Jared and his associates. [D.M.]

S.416 *Stories from the Book of Mormon: How We Got the Book of Mormon.* Salt Lake City: Department of Seminaries and Institutes of Religion, 1967. A pictorial book for children that tells the story of the coming forth of the Book of Mormon. [D.W.P.]

S.417 *Stories from the Book of Mormon: Lehi Obeys the Lord.* Salt Lake City: Department of Seminaries and Institutes of Religion, 1967. Black and white picture book detailing Lehi's and his family's initial departure into the wilderness. [D.M.]

S.418 *Stories from the Book of Mormon: The Book of Mormon.* Salt Lake City: Department of Seminaries and Institutes, 1967. A pictorial overview of the Book of Mormon. Illustrations have explanatory subscripts. [D.M.]

S.419 *Stories from the Book of Mormon: The Building of a Ship.* Salt Lake City: Department of Seminaries and Institutes of Religion, 1967. Retells, through illustration, the story of how Nephi built a ship by divine mandate. [D.M.]

S.420 *Stories from the Book of Mormon: The Precious Record.* Salt Lake City: Department of Seminaries and Institutes of Religion, 1967. A black-and-white book of drawings with captions that deal with the acquisition of the plates of brass. [D.M.]

S.421 *Stories from the Book of Mormon: The Prophet Abinadi.* Salt Lake City: Department of Seminaries and Institutes of Religion, 1967. A picture book containing the story of Abinadi's encounter with King Noah. [D.M.]

S.422 "The Story Behind Stela 5." *SEHA* 110 (2 December 1968): 1-7. Contains a chronological summary of significant events relative to the discovery and interpretive studies of Stela 5. Three photographs are supplied. [D.M.]

S.423 "Story of Faith: The Brother of Jared." *Friend* 18 (January 1988): 16-17. Brief illustrated story for children about the brother of Jared. [D.M.]

S.424 "The Story of the Origin of the World's Strangest Book." *MS* 98 (17 September 1936): 602-4. Recounts the stories of Joseph Smith's vision, of his receiving the plates, of the translation process of the Book of Mormon, and of the witnesses that testified of seeing the Book of Mormon. [M.D.P.]

S.425 Story, Ruth P. "The Book of Mormon and a Feather." *Restoration Witness* 164 (August 1976): 11-14. The parents of a new convert accepted his conversion and received a Book of Mormon. Reading the book brought warm and wonderful experiences that bear witness of the book's spiritual nature. [J.W.M.]

S.426 Stott, Douglas W. *An Analysis of Possible Prophetic Techniques Employed by Mormon in Abridging the Nephite Record for Latter-day Readers.* N.p., 1982. Delineates the parts of the Book of Mormon worked on by Mormon. Discusses the lost 116 pages. Refers to the "types" or "situation symbols" from the Old World carried through the Book of Mormon. Points out relevant passages for today's world. [D.M.]

S.427 Stout, Walter M. *The Book of Mormon Practical Geography.* Upland, CA: n.p., 1970. Contains maps of Book of Mormon geography that favor the Mesoamerican theory. Book of Mormon scriptural passages provide the criteria for this theory. [J.W.M.]

S.428 Stout, Walter M. *Landing Places of Book of Mormon Colonies.* N.p., 196?. Provides hypothetical maps and tries to establish Book of Mormon geographical connections. [D.M.]

S.429 Stowell, Earl. "The Book of Mormon." In Stowell's *The Magic of Mormonism*, 203-11. Salt Lake City: Bookcraft, 1965. The Book of Mormon is the second witness of Christ offered by the "other sheep" (John 10:16). The miraculous events surrounding its coming forth, its purpose, statistics about the book, and its story are all included. [J.W.M.]

S.430 Stubbs, Brian D. "Book of Mormon Language." In *Encyclopedia of Mormonism*, edited by Daniel H. Ludlow, 1:179-81. 5 vols. New York: Macmillan, 1992. The features of Book of Mormon language are typical of a translated work from ancient Near Eastern texts. Nephite historians claimed that they wrote in reformed Egyptian with a Jewish/Hebrew background after being isolated for their thousand-year history. The book's extensive use of Hebrew language patterns, name roots, names with Egyptian and Hebrew backgrounds, and Hebrew poetic types make it clear that Joseph Smith did not imitate the King James Bible to write the Book of Mormon. [N.K.Y.]

S.431 Stubbs, Brian D. "Elements of Hebrew in Uto-Aztecan: A Summary of the Data." Provo, UT: FARMS, 1988. Compares the Uto-Aztecan language with Hebrew. The similarities in the lexical, morphological, and root-specific semantics may point to a connection between the Aztec peoples and the Hebrews of the Old World. [J.W.M.]

S.432 Stubbs, Brian D. "Hebrew and Uto-Aztecan: Possible Linguistic Connections." In *Reexploring the Book of Mormon*, edited by John W. Welch, 279-81. Salt Lake City: Deseret Book and FARMS, 1992. Compares Hebrew with the Uto-Aztecan tongues (which include N. Paiute, Shoshoni, Hopi, Papago, Tarahumara, Yaqui, and Nahuatl) with sound correspondence, vocabulary, semantic patterns, fossilized verb forms, and other morphological aspects of the languages. He presents 203 equivalences between Semitic and Uto-Aztecan reflecting many Hebrew roots but shows that developed languages indicate absorption of several languages into a new mixed language over time. [N.K.Y.]

S.433 Stucki, J. U. *Some Religious Literature and Prophetic History of America*. New York: Vantage Press, 1981. Reprints the title page, lists (in order) the books of the Book of Mormon, and gives the account of Moroni's visit that is also found in the Pearl of Great Price. Contains many excerpts from the book itself, with writings from Nephi, Isaiah, Jacob, King Benjamin, King Mosiah, Alma, Helaman, Captain Moroni, Pahoran, Mormon, and Moroni. [J.W.M.]

S.434 *Study Book of Mormon: First Nephi*. Independence, MO: Zarahemla Research Foundation, 1988. Text of 1 Nephi is arranged according to parallelistic and poetic style. Includes notes and comparisons of different editions of the Book of Mormon. [D.W.P.]

S.435 Sturgess, Gary. "The Book of Mormon As Literature." Provo, UT: FARMS, 1982. Judging the Book of Mormon by the standards of ancient literature helps to understand its value. It is not a history. It testified that Jesus Christ is the Eternal God and that the people of Lehi are the chosen of Israel. Chiasmus is found in the Book of Mormon. There is also much typology found in it, reminiscent of Near Eastern literature. [J.W.M.]

S.436 Sukys, Renata W. "Abinadi's Teaching Style." *Ensign* 22 (April 1992): 28-29. Focuses on the teaching style and doctrines taught by Abinadi to the priests of Noah. [A.C.W.]

S.437 Sumsion, J. Bert. "The Book of Mormon: The Light of the Western Hemisphere." *Liahona* 14 (1916-1917): 517-19. Touches on the attempts of "learned men" to account for the origins of the American natives, but suggests that the answer to their origin is found in the Book of Mormon. [D.S.T.]

S.438 *A Sure Foundation: Answers to Difficult Gospel Questions*. Salt Lake City: Deseret Book, 1988. Consists of commonly asked questions on various issues and answers by Latter-day Saint writers, some of which deal with the Book of Mormon. See entries under individual authors. [D.M.]

S.439 Swiss, Ralph E. "The Tame and Wild Olive Trees: An Allegory of Our Savior's Love." *Ensign* 18 (August 1988): 50-52. The chapters preceding the allegory of the olive tree in Jacob 5 provide important insights into why the allegory was included in the Book of Mormon. Zenos's allegory tells of the love of the Master (Jesus) of the vineyard, which love is

S.440 Sykes, Egerton. "The Origins of the Book of Mormon." *New World Antiquity* 24 (March-April 1977): 32-33. In response to a paper read by John Sorenson at the SEHA 23rd Symposium in 1973 the author notes that the LDS tradition in the Book of Mormon is the only perspective that has "reasonable historical background" that explains Mesoamerica and agrees with his own diffusion theory. [J.W.M.]

S.441 Symes, Joseph. "The Best Attested of All Bibles." *Deseret Weekly* 53 (25 July 1896): 180-81. Also in *MS* 58 (August 1896): 529-32. While not accepting the supernatural, Symes argues that the Book of Mormon is the best attested, or has the greatest evidences attached to it, of all Bibles (sacred books) in the world. Refers to Joseph Smith's account of the first vision and of the gold plates, as well as the testimonies of the Three and Eight Witnesses. [D.M.]

S.442 Szink, Terrence L. "A Just and a True Record." In *Studies in Scripture: Alma 30 to Moroni*, edited by Kent P. Jackson, 125-38. Salt Lake City: Deseret Book, 1988. 3 Nephi 1-5 is an example of the cycle of apostasy to righteousness and back to apostasy. It was a time of great peril as society ripened in iniquity and secret oaths held it together. Lachoneus taught that the only safety from this great threat was to obtain strength through personal righteousness. The Nephites were besieged by the Gadianton robbers. [J.W.M.]

S.443 Szink, Terrence L. "Nephi and the Exodus." In *Rediscovering the Book of Mormon*, edited by John L. Sorenson and Melvin J. Thorne, 38-51. Salt Lake City: Deseret Book and FARMS, 1991. When Nephi authored the account of his family's exodus from the land of Jerusalem, he wrote it in such a way as to pattern it after the exodus from Egypt by the children of Israel. [J.W.M.]

S.444 Szink, Terrence L. "An Oath of Allegiance in the Book of Mormon." In *Warfare in the Book of Mormon*, edited by Stephen D. Ricks and William J. Hamblin, 35-45. Salt Lake City: portrayed as the Master cares for, grieves over, and rejoices in the condition of his vineyard. [J.W.M.] Deseret Book and FARMS, 1990. Oaths are important in Book of Mormon history. Moroni's use of the title of liberty is an excellent example. Such a ritual is described in the history of oaths taken by the Hittite soldiers and those in the Kingdom of Mari. In the Old Testament animals were cut in pieces to communicate "come to arms or you will be killed," and in fact, some were killed who did not come. The same threats were used in the Book of Mormon where the choice was support the war or die. [N.K.Y.]

S.445 Szink, Terrence L. "To a Land of Promise." In *Studies in Scripture: 1 Nephi to Alma 29*, edited by Kent P. Jackson, 60-72. Salt Lake City: Deseret Book, 1987. Nephi recorded 1 Nephi 16-18 thirty years after the time it happened. Since Nephi was unable to write all of the experiences, what he did record must have been of great worth. He told of the Liahona, the broken bow incident and the death of Ishmael. A comparison of similarities and significant differences is made between the text of the Bible concerning the Exodus of the children of Israel and the Book of Mormon exodus of the colony of Lehi. [J.W.M.]

T.

T.001 Talbot, Leo P. "Bless Those Elders." *Ensign* 23 (March 1993): 65. The author's story of conversion to the LDS Church as a result of reading the Book of Mormon given to him by missionaries. [S.H.]

T.002 Talbot, Leo B. "A Mailbox, Indecision, and Prayer." *NE* 11 (October 1981): 28-29. A Book of Mormon left in the author's mailbox lay unread for several years. Prayer seemed to be the way to find the truthfulness of the book and dispel fearful and doubtful feelings. Assurance and conversion followed a simple prayer. [J.W.M.]

T.003 Talmage, James E. "The American Nation in Prophecy." In *Sunday Night Talks*, 298-305. Salt Lake City: Church of Jesus Christ of Latter-day Saints, 1931. A radio address commenting on how the Book of Mormon foresaw the founding events of the United States. Presentiments of the U.S. government were indicated in the book of Mosiah. [D.M.]

T.004 Talmage, James E. "The Bible and Other Scriptures." *MS* 87 (15 January 1925): 37-39. The LDS Church accepts both the Bible and the Book of Mormon to be the word of God. The Book of Mormon, however, has received a more correct translation than has the Bible. [D.W.P.]

T.005 Talmage, James E. "The Book of Mormon: Scriptures of the American Continent: Origin of the American Indians." *MS* 79 (22 February 1917): 113-15. Brief summary of Book of Mormon story, and Joseph Smith's translation. Modern revelation is not improbable. The Book of Mormon is "parallel volume" to the Bible, not a substitute; the two are not contradictory. [A.C.W.]

T.006 Talmage, James E. "The Destiny of the American Nation Declared by Prophecy." *MS* 79 (25 January 1917): 49-53. A paper that argues that "the commanding position of the United States among the world powers, and the prominent place of the American nation is to maintain as the exponent and champion of human rights were foreseen and predicted centuries before the beginning of the Christian era" by prophets of the Book of Mormon. [D.W.P.]

T.007 Talmage, James E. "How the 'Mormons' Got Their Name." *MS* 78 (5 October 1916): 625-626. The term "Mormon," a nickname given to members of the Church of Jesus Christ of Latter-day Saints, was derived from the scripture called the Book of Mormon. Members of the Church, however, are quick to point out that the proper name of their Church is the Church of Jesus Christ of Latter-day Saints. [D.W.P.]

T.008 Talmage, James E. "How We Got the Book of Mormon." *Instructor* 72 (December 1937): 525-26. Under the direction of Moroni, Joseph Smith obtained the plates and translated them according to the gift and power of God. He was an unschooled boy and an instrument in the hands of the Lord who confounded the mighty with his work. [J.W.M.]

T.009 Talmage, James E. "Inspiration the Cause of Popular Opposition." *IE* 26 (September 1923): 1032. Some reject the Book of Mormon on account of its supernatural origin. Joseph Smith claimed that an angel revealed to him where to find the plates and that God inspired him in translating them. However, the Book of Mormon is harmonious with the Bible, and the story of its origin should not surprise anyone. [B.D.]

T.010 Talmage, James E. "Is the Bible Sufficient?" *MS* 98 (16 September 1937): 597. Calls attention to the many difficulties that occurred during the translation and publication of the Bible. Although many people reject the Book of Mormon, it is yet the word of God and was translated correctly by a prophet of God. [J.W.M.]

T.011 Talmage, James E. "Isaiah and the Book of Mormon." *CR* (April 1929): 44-49. Bears witness of the truth of the Book of Mormon, emphasizes that it is the best literature for missionary work, and recommends that we pursue all possible investigation, comparison, research, and scholarship (even for Book of Mormon geography) in Book of Mormon studies. Warns scholars to let the Book of Mormon speak for itself. The Book of Mormon clearly confirms a unity of authorship in Isaiah. [R.C.D.]

T.012 Talmage, James E. "Jesus Is the Christ." *IE* 66 (December 1963): 1051, 1112. Reprint from *MS* 80 (1918): 705. Unites the Bible and the Book of Mormon in bearing witness that Jesus is the Christ. An examination of the two texts reveals sixteen important facts concerning Christ's mission, including his premortal and antemortal Godhood, his foreordination as the Redeemer, and the predictions of his birth to Mary. The testimony of two witnesses—the Bible and the Book of Mormon—establishes the truth. [J.W.M.]

T.013 Talmage, James E. *Journal Abstracts and Letters 1876-1933.* N.p.: n.p., n.d. A collection of papers from letters and journals kept by Talmage. Two letters report Talmage's work on revision of the Book of Mormon, suggesting to the First Presidency a list of minor revisions. [J.W.M.]

T.014 Talmage, James E. "A Messenger from the Presence of God." *MS* 80 (19 September 1918): 593-95. A testimony of the Book of Mormon and explanation of how it came into existence through the appearance of an angel. [B.D.]

T.015 Talmage, James E. "A New Witness for Christ." *Liahona* 21 (June 1924): 494-95. Although the Book of Mormon is an invaluable history, its priceless character lies in its role as a second testimony of Jesus Christ. [L.M.]

T.016 Talmage, James E. "A New Witness of the Christ." *MS* 80 (October 1918): 689-91. The Book of Mormon would be nothing more than an "important contribution to the common find of human knowledge" if all it were no more than a history of the ancient Americans, but it is a new witness for Jesus Christ's mission and ministry. [B.D.]

T.017 Talmage, James E. "A Night of Light." *MS* 86 (18 December 1924): 801-4. For centuries members of the Nephite and Lamanite communities looked forward to the time when Jesus would be born into the world. Such an occasion would be "a night of light" unto the world. [D.W.P.]

T.018 Talmage, James E. "Olden Scriptures and New." In *Sunday Night Talks*, 288-97. Salt Lake City: Church of Jesus Christ of Latter-day Saints, 1931. Two books of scripture, from both sides of the world, bear witness of Christ. The Book of Mormon is an "independent witness of the Christ." [D.M.]

T.019 Talmage, James E. "One Hundred Years Ago Today." *MS* 89 (22 September 1927): 600-603. Recalls the coming forth of the Book of Mormon through Moroni, the Nephite prophet who appeared as an angel to Joseph Smith. Emphasizes that the Book of Mormon "stands as an independent witness of Jesus the Christ as the Son of the Eternal Father, and as the Redeemer." [D.W.P.]

T.020 Talmage, James E. "Scriptures of the American Continent." *Liahona* 14 (1917): 611-12. Summarizes the Book of Mormon and the story of its coming forth, and explains that much of the opposition to the book was due to Joseph's claim that he had been visited by an angel and received divine help in its translation. This claim was an affront to the dogma that miracles had ceased. [L.M.]

T.021 Talmage, James E. "Scriptures of the American Continent." *MS* 82 (29 July 1920): 491-93. The Book of Mormon is a record written on gold plates of the ancient people of the New World, taken from the Hill Cumorah and translated from Reformed Egyptian and published in 1830. It includes the history of Lehi's people from 600 B.C. to 420 A.D. Joseph Smith claimed it was done through the power of God and revelation, and that brought much persecution. The idea of supernatural intervention opposed all the theological theories of his day. The Book of Mormon in no way replaces the Bible nor contradicts it. [J.W.M.]

T.022 Talmage, James E. "Sheep of Another Fold." *MS* 80 (10 October 1918): 641-43. Talmage describes the eloquence and beauty of the parable of the shepherd in John 10. No one understood John 10:16 until the Book of Mormon taught that the other sheep were the scattered remnants of the house of Israel, some of whom were the Nephites and Lamanites. [B.D.]

T.023 Talmage, James E. "The Stick of Joseph." *MS* 88 (June 1926): 376-78. The Book of Mormon is the stick of Joseph identified in Ezekiel 37:15-20. Lehi is a descendant of Joseph through Manasseh and Ishmael is the descendant of Ephraim, thus completing the house of Joseph. [J.W.M.]

T.024 Talmage, James E. *The Story and the Philosophy of 'Mormonism.'* Salt Lake City: Deseret News Press, 1920. Gives a narrative of the coming forth of the Book of Mormon, Moroni's visit and instructions to Joseph Smith. The Book of Mormon does not take the place of the Bible. The Bible foretold of the coming forth of the Book of Mormon. The Spaulding theory regarding the origin of the Book of Mormon has been disproved. [J.W.M.]

T.025 Talmage, James E. "The Story of 'Mormonism'." In Talmage's *The Story of Mormonism*, 5-26. Salt Lake City: Deseret Book, 1930. Gives the story of Joseph Smith, the first vision, and the coming forth of the Book of Mormon. The Book of Mormon is a companion to the Bible, not a replacement. Latter-day saints believe that the Bible foretold of the Book of Mormon. The Spaulding theory has been disproved. [J.W.M.]

T.026 Talmage, James E. "A Testimony from the Dust." *MS* 87 (5 February 1925): 92-93. The coming forth of the Book of Mormon fulfills the prophecy of Isaiah that a testimony or speech would come forth "out of the dust" (Isaiah 29: 4). [D.W.P.]

T.027 Talmage, James E. "Unique Character of Contents of the Book of Mormon." *IE* 26 (September 1923): 1015-18. While the historical and ethnological information in the Book of Mormon is invaluable, the theological themes are far more important. The theological aspects in the Book of Mormon harmonize with those of the Bible. [D.M.]

T.028 Talmage, James E. Untitled talk. *CR* (October 1917): 138-44. Doctrines of the Bible are clarified by the Book of Mormon such as heaven and hell, baptism of infants, and the plan of salvation. [J.W.M.]

T.029 Talmage, James E. *The Vitality of Mormonism: Brief Essays on Distinctive Doctrines of the Church of Jesus Christ of Latter-day Saints.* Salt Lake City: Deseret Book, 1948. Chapters 33-41, dedicated to the Book of Mormon, set forth the importance of the Book of Mormon in relation to the Bible, the account of Moroni's visit to deliver the plates, the story of the Book of Mormon, the witnesses of the book, Ezekiel's prophecy of the sticks of Joseph and Judah, the Book of Mormon as a witness for Christ, Jesus' organization of the church in the Americas with all of the ordinances essential for salvation, Christ's visit to his "other sheep" in America, and related items. [J.W.M.]

T.030 Talmage, James E. "A Voice from the Dust." In *Sunday Night Talks,* 278-87. Salt Lake City: Church of Jesus Christ of Latter-day Saints, 1931. Cites Isaiah 29 and Ezekiel 37 as prophecies about the Book of Mormon. Gives an overview of the Book of Mormon and discusses its translation. [D.M.]

T.031 Talmage, James E. *Voices of the Dead, a Testimony from the Dust.* N.p., n.d. Internal evidence testifies that the Book of Mormon fulfills both Old Testament prophecies as well as prophecies that are found within the pages of the Book of Mormon itself. [J.W.M.]

T.032 Talmage, James E. "What is Mormonism?" *MS* 87 (22 January 1925): 58-64. Presents an overview of the contents of the Book of Mormon, emphasizing the fact that Jesus Christ is the central character of the book, and that the LDS church is clearly distinguished from other Christian sects by the manner in which it believes in modern revelation. The Book of Mormon is an example of such revelation. [D.W.P.]

T.033 Talmage, James E. "Whence Came the American Indians?" *MS* 87 (29 January 1925): 74-76. Briefly presents the history of Lehi and his family, including the separation between the Nephites and Lamanites. Descendants of the Lamanites became the American Indians. [D.W.P.]

T.034 Tanner, David S. *Heaven and Earth: Past, Present and Future. A Correlation of LDS Scripture and Other Writings.* Volume II. San Jose, CA: Davis S. Tanner, 1976. Covers the period of time from Solomon to Christ. Shows a comparative chronologically of the Bible, the Book of Mormon, the Doctrine and Covenants and the Pearl of Great Price, as well as early Church writings and writings of Joseph Fielding Smith. [J.W.M.]

T.035 Tanner, John S. "Jacob and His Descendants As Authors." In *Rediscovering The Book of Mormon,* edited by John L. Sorenson and Melvin J. Thorne, 52-66. Salt Lake City: Deseret Book and FARMS, 1991. The writings of Jacob and his descendants display a "stylistic diversity." The style change from the small plates of Nephi to Mormon's abridgment of the large plates of Nephi is rough, providing evidence of the splice of one record into another. [J.W.M.]

T.036 Tanner, John S. "Jacob, Son of Lehi." In *Encyclopedia of Mormonism,* edited by Daniel H. Ludlow. 2:713-14. 5 vols. New York:

Macmillan, 1992. Jacob, son of Lehi, was born in the wilderness and suffered tribulation much of his life. He was the successor to Nephi as the spiritual leader of the Nephites. His writings teach of the coming of Christ and the scattering and subsequent gathering of Israel. [B.D.]

T.037 Tanner, John S. "Literary Reflections on Jacob and His Descendants." In *The Book of Mormon: Jacob through Words of Mormon, To Learn with Joy*, edited by Monte S. Nyman and Charles D. Tate Jr., 251-70. Provo, UT: Brigham Young University Religious Studies Center, 1990. The portion of the small plates of Nephi recorded by Jacob and his descendants are first person documents that best reveal the man through the style of writing that he uses. Jacob was a sensitive man who endured great hardship in his youth. He was visited by Christ. His words are pleading and mournful, reflecting his quiet nature. [J.W.M.]

T.038 Tanner, Morgan W. "Book of Ether." In *Encyclopedia of Mormonism*, edited by Daniel H. Ludlow, 1:156-57. 5 vols. New York: Macmillan, 1992. The book of Ether is an edited version of the twenty-four gold plates found by Limhi and translated by Mosiah. Its themes include secret combinations, the importance of following prophets, and wickedness brings destruction. It teaches of Christ's premortal spirit body, that Three Witnesses would testify of the Book of Mormon, and that a New Jerusalem will be built in the western hemisphere. [B.D]

T.039 Tanner, Morgan W. "Jaredites." In *Encyclopedia of Mormonism*, edited by Daniel H. Ludlow, 2:717-20. 5 vols. New York: Macmillan, 1992. The Jaredites, named after their leader Jared, left the Old World at the time of the Tower of Babel, about the third millennium B.C. Their record appears in the book of Ether in the Book of Mormon, and is comparable to Near Eastern epics. They were annihilated sometime between 600 and 300 B.C. [J.W.M.]

T.040 Tanner, N. Eldon. "Book of Mormon and America's History and Destiny." *CR* (April 1976): 73-78. All the major events that shaped the destiny of the Americas have been recorded or prophesied in the Book of Mormon. Includes the historical events related to the Jaredites, Lehi, Columbus, the Pilgrims, the United States, the U.S. Constitution, the Restoration, and America's future. [R.C.D.]

T.041 Tanner, N. Eldon. "Christ in America." *Ensign* 5 (May 1975): 34-36; see also *CR* 145 (April 1975): 51-55. Retells the story of Christ's visit to America after his resurrection, with mention of Old Testament prophecies of the Book of Mormon. [B.T.]

T.042 Tanner, N. Eldon. "I Will Go And Do The Things . . ." *IE* 66 (December 1963): 1060-61. In response to his calling as a member of the First Presidency, Tanner quotes Nephi who said "I will go and do the things which the Lord hath commanded" (1 Nephi 3:7). [J.W.M]

T.043 Tanner, N. Eldon. "The Inevitable Choice." *Ensign* 7 (September 1977): 2-5. The Book of Mormon is a study of the nature of man. The extremes of both good and bad behavior are exhibited as well as those who fit into the gray area. The inevitable choice must be made—righteousness and great blessings or wickedness and destruction. [J.W.M.]

T.044 Tanner, N. Eldon. "Savior's Teachings Needed Today." *CR* (April 1975): 51-55. An address having four main points: (1) the great countries of South America are part of the Book of Mormon lands; (2) the Bible predicts the coming forth of the Book of Mormon in several places, including Ezekiel 37:16-17; John 10:16; Revelation 14:6-7; (3) 3 Nephi, known as the "fifth gospel," provides greater detailed information about Christ's ministry than do the four gospels in the New Testament; (4) Christ ministered to the Nephites in the New World. [R.C.D.]

T.045 Tanner, N. Eldon. "The Two Great Commandments." *IE* 68 (June 1965): 527-28. Also in *CR* (April 1965): 93-96. Tells of his challenge to the Saints to read the Book of Mormon, and gives examples of people whose lives benefited from it. Keeping the two great commandments, first to love God with all your whole soul and the second to love your neighbor, begins within the walls of your own home. [J.W.M.]

T.046 Tate, Charles D. "Book of Mormon References to Deity." *Ensign* 22 (April 1992): 63. "In keeping with its declared purpose as a witness of Jesus Christ, the Book of Mormon contains 476 references to Him by name in its 531 pages," almost one reference per page. Only 30 pages contain no specific name reference to deity, excluding pronouns. [A.C.W.]

T.047 Tate, George S. "The Typology of the Exodus Pattern in the Book of Mormon." In *Literature of Belief: Sacred Scriptures*, edited by N. Lambert, 245-62. Provo, UT: Brigham Young University Religious Study Center, 1981. A condensed version of the same article is found in "Nephi and the Exodus." *Ensign* 17 (April 1987): 64-65. By establishing through literary analysis that the biblical Exodus theme finds typological fulfillment in historical events and occurrences of the Book of Mormon, Tate demonstrates that "typological unity" exists in the Book of Mormon. This theme plays a prominent role, and finds actual and figural usage in the Book of Mormon. It is a recurring theme built upon by many inspired writers—Nephi, Jacob, and Alma the Younger. [D.W.P.]

T.048 Taylor, Debbie. *Lehi Obeys God's Command*. Independence, MO: Foundation for Research on Ancient America, 1987. An illustrated storybook about Lehi, paraphrased and told in first person from the perspective of Nephi. [D.M.]

T.049 Taylor, Hal L. "A Man May Know For Himself." In *Ninth Annual Sydney B. Sperry Symposium: The Book of Mormon*, 96-102. Provo, UT: Brigham Young University, 1981. The promise given in Moroni 10:4-5 is of great importance to members of the Church. Each individual must know the truth and receive a testimony for himself/herself. Author presents details on how this may be accomplished. [J.W.M.]

T.050 Taylor, J. "Ancient Ruins." *TS* 5 (December 1844): 744-48. The immense ruins in Central America should dispel any doubts that the Book of Mormon records the history of ancient civilizations of America. [J.W.M.]

T.051 Taylor, J. "Stephens' Works on Central America." *TS* 4 (1 October 1843): 346-47. It is helpful to compare Stephens's writings on Central America with the Book of Mormon, for his works help to verify the Book of Mormon. [J.W.M.]

T.052 Taylor, John. *Answer to Some False Statements and Misrepresentations Made by the Rev. Robert Heys, Wesleyan Minister, in an Address to History Society in Douglas and its Vicinity, on the Subject of Mormonism*. Nauvoo: Penrice and Wallace, 1840. Argues against false statements made regarding the coming forth of the Book of Mormon and the idea that Sidney Rigdon had altered the Spaulding manuscript to produce the Book of Mormon. [J.W.M.]

T.053 Taylor, John. "The Book of Mormon and the Atonement." In Taylor's *Mediation and Atonement*, 40-54. Salt Lake City, UT: Deseret News Co., 1882. Extracts from the books of Ether, 1 and 2 Nephi, Mosiah, Alma, Helaman, and Mormon that speak of Christ's atonement. No commentary on these scriptures, simply direct quotes from the Book of Mormon. [A.C.W.]

T.054 Taylor, John. *Calumny Refuted and the Truth Defended, Being a Reply to the Second Address of the Rev. Robert Heys, Wesleyan Minister the Wesleyan Methodist Societies in Douglas and its Vicinity*. Nauvoo: Penrice and Wallace, 184?. Through the employment of biblical scriptures, Taylor answers Rev. Heys's complaints about "Mormonism." Heys argues against Mormon doctrines: the Book of Mormon does not possess equal authority with the Bible; little children are incapable of sin; all without the law are alive in Christ; immersion is the proper mode of baptism; it is a mockery before God to baptize little children. [J.W.M.]

T.055 Taylor, John. *An Examination into and an Elucidation of the Great Principle of the Mediation and Atonement of our Lord and Savior Jesus Christ*. Salt Lake City: Deseret News, 1892. Chapter 14 points out many references to Christ's atonement in the Book of Mormon. The law of Moses was a shadow and type of the atonement, which was fulfilled by Jesus who gave his own life. [J.W.M.]

T.056 Taylor, John. "God Is Cognizant of All Things." *JD* 26 (14 December 1884): 30-39. A commission of professors and scientists are meeting to examine the manuscript of the Book of Mormon to determine its validity. Whatever they decide does not affect the Book of Mormon, for it is true. The Book of Mormon and other scriptures outline the purpose of the creation of man. [J.W.M.]

T.057 Taylor, John H. Untitled talk. *CR* (April 1941): 39-40. Taylor points out some lessons learned from Lehi's dream. The tree of life is the love of God. [B.D.]

T.058 Taylor, M. Henry. "Paul Henning, Early Latter-day Saint Archaeologist." In *Papers of the Fifteenth Annual Symposium on Archaeology of the Scriptures,* edited by Ross T. Christensen, 90-93. Provo, UT: Brigham Young University, 1964. Paul August E. Henning devoted his life to Book of Mormon archaeology in Mexico uncovering the external evidences that would prove the authenticity of the book. [J.W.M.]

T.059 Taylor, Robert. "The Most Unusual Book in the World." *Restoration Witness* 164 (September 1976): 26-30. The final editors of the Book of Mormon, Mormon and Moroni, selected the message of the Book of Mormon under the inspiration of God. It was their intent to present a clear message by relating the events of their era to those who would live in the present era. The book is also a testimony of Christ. [J.W.M.]

T.060 "Teachings of the Book of Mormon on Priesthood." *Rod of Iron* 1 (October 1924): 37-39. The Book of Mormon teaches that men were ordained to the priesthood before they came to earth. God gives the priesthood to men, and then they are born to the priesthood in the patriarchal lineage. The priesthood is an eternal institution and the calling of men to it can only come through God. [J.W.M.]

T.061 Terry, Keith C. *Out of Darkness.* U.S.A.: J. B. Media International, 1991. A long story book incorporating information that has recently been disclosed from Book of Mormon studies. [D.M.]

T.062 Terry, Keith, and Ann Terry. "Emma . . . Her Beginnings." In Terry's *Emma: The Dramatic Biography of Emma Smith,* 3-13. Santa Barbara, CA: Butterfly publishing, 1979. Emma Smith was the courageous woman, wife of the prophet. She helped her husband go to the Hill Cumorah and waited until he returned with the heavy load of plates. Emma assisted in the translation and defended her husband to the skeptics. She carried the original manuscripts of the Book of Mormon under her skirts through the freezing wilderness of Missouri into Illinois. [J.W.M.]

T.063 "Testimonies of Four Witnesses of the Book of Mormon." *IE* 71 (September 1968): 14. Transcriptions of the testimonies of Emma Smith, Martin Harris, Oliver Cowdery, and David Whitmer testifying of the truthfulness of the Book of Mormon. [L.D.]

T.064 "Testimonies of the Book of Mormon." *Ensign* 13 (December 1983): 6-9. A collection of testimonies on the Book of Mormon by LDS Church presidents from Joseph Smith to Spencer W. Kimball. [D.M.]

T.065 "The Testimony of Three Witnesses and The Testimony of Eight Witnesses." *Evening and Morning Star* 1 (January 1833): n.p. Gives the Testimonies of the Three and Eight Witnesses and a hymn rejoicing in their testimony of the Book of Mormon. [M.D.P.]

T.066 "That They May Know." *NE* 7 (October 1977): 35-37. A new proselytizing method is to put your testimony in the front cover of the Book of Mormon along with your picture. Examples are given. [M.D.P.]

T.067 Thatcher, Moses. "Ancient American Civilizations and Their lessons." In *Collected Discourses Delivered by President Wilford Woodruff, His Two Counselors, The 12 Apostles, and Others, Vol. 1. (1886-1889),* edited by Brian H. Stuy, 171-77. Sandy, UT: B. H. S. Publishing, 1987. The ruins of the people of Nephi that are found in Central America and Mexico show that they were not barbarians, but intelligent, civilized people. The record of their civilization has come forth in the Book of Mormon. There is much evidence left to

T.068 Thatcher, Moses. "Divine Origin of the Book of Mormon." *MS* 43 (6, 13, 27 June 1881): 353-56, 369-72, 385-87, 401-2. Presents historical evidences to prove the divine authenticity of the Book of Mormon. He quotes from the Popol Vuh to show that the Quiche's creation account is similar to that of the Bible; he also refers to Ixtlelxochitl to argue that the accounts of the flood are similar. [B.D.]

T.069 Thatcher, Moses. "An Interesting Lecture: Delivered by Apostle Moses Thatcher in Ogden, Utah." *MS* 50 (17-24 December 1888): 801-4, 817-20. A two-part series reprinted from the *Deseret News*—a transcript of a lecture given by Moses Thatcher. The people who constructed the pyramids of the sun and the moon were white. There was a high quality of cement found and the interior of the rooms were beautifully painted. These people taught traditions of a white man who taught them to cultivate their ground, and would some day return to be their king. [J.W.M.]

T.070 Thomas, Albert H. "External Evidences of the Book of Mormon." *MS* 67 (27 April 1905): 269-72. Quotes contemporary historians and ancient authors whose writings confirm or support historical elements of the Book of Mormon. Among these are Lord Kingsborough who was impressed by the knowledge of Genesis possessed by the American Indians; Rosales who relates a Chilean tradition of a visitation by a wonderful personage who taught them of the creator; Prescott who tells of astonished Catholics who found the sign of the cross and a ceremony of partaking of the body and blood of deity. [R.H.B.]

T.071 Thomas, Brett P. "They Did Remember His Works." In *The Book of Mormon: Helaman through 3 Nephi 8, According To Thy Word*, edited by Monte S. Nyman and Charles D. Tate Jr., 93-113. Provo, UT: Brigham Young University Religious Studies Center, 1992. Shows a connection between the instructions given by Helaman to his sons Nephi and Lehi and the spiritual outpouring that occurred when the two sons were imprisoned by a group of Lamanites. [D.M.]

T.072 Thomas, Darwin L. "Being Parents, Being Children." *Ensign* 7 (September 1977): 12-17. At a time when families are in crisis the Book of Mormon gives great comfort. Parents' responsibility is to teach their children. Children have the responsibility to believe their parents and then to desire to know for themselves. [J.W.M.]

T.073 Thomas, Darwin L., and Kim Thomas. "Youth and the Book of Mormon." *NE* 7 (September 1977): 8-12, 14. The Book of Mormon has a message for our day. The responsibility of parents to teach is equaled by the responsibility of youth to learn from their parents, to know for themselves through the witness of the Holy Ghost, and to prepare for the future by studying the Book of Mormon. [J.W.M.]

T.074 Thomas, Gordon K. "The Book of Mormon in the English Literary Context of 1837." *BYU Studies* 27 (Winter 1987): 37-45. Poets in England in the early nineteenth century believed they would play an important role in a "restoration" of what they believed was imminent. A vast amount of ancient writings were discovered at this time. Some were revealed as counterfeits, so though the world was ready for ancient writings suspicion clouded every claim. The mixed atmosphere of excitement and distrust met early Mormon missionaries in England. [J.W.M.]

T.075 Thomas, H. Richard. "Song of Nephi." *Instructor* 102 (October 1967): 409-11. 2 Nephi 4:16-35 shares much of the character and attitude of Nephi. The Song of Nephi begins with a feeling of despair and ends with an inspiring prayer of commitment to a better way of life. It is a pattern to follow on the road to repentance. [J.W.M.]

T.076 Thomas, Janet. "How Rare a Possession." *NE* 17 (November 1987): 28-33. Reports on the making of the film *How Rare A Possession*. The film recreates the life of Vincenzo D. Francesca and many Book of Mormon scenes. [J.W.M.]

T.077 Thomas, Janet. "New Summer Friends." *NE* 23 (June 1993): 32-35. High school "Students Trying Out Moroni's Promise" (S.T.O.M.P.) read the Book of Mormon during the summer to gain a testimony. [S.H.]

T.078 Thomas, M. Catherine. "A Great Deliverance." In *Studies in Scripture: 1 Nephi to Alma 29*, edited by Kent P. Jackson, 103-14. Salt Lake City: Deseret Book, 1987. 2 Nephi 3-5 contains three main ideas: Joseph in Egypt, Nephi's psalm, and the mark of the dark skin. These chapters are replete with the Savior's commitment and love for his children. Nephi's account records important promises to the descendants who carry the mark upon them. [J.W.M.]

T.079 Thomas, M. Catherine. "Jacob's Allegory: The Mystery of Christ." In *The Allegory of the Olive Tree: the Olive, The Bible, and Jacob 5*, edited by Stephen D. Ricks and John W. Welch, 11-20. Salt Lake City: Deseret Book and FARMS, 1994. The symbolism of the olive tree in Jacob 5 is layered. The tree seems to reflect Christ on one level, the branches represent Israel on another, and the individual on still another. The greatest value of the allegory lies in Jacob's explanation of the constant awareness of the Lord and the Spirit's unceasing work in behalf of the individual. [J.W.M.]

T.080 Thomas, M. Catherine. "A More Excellent Way." In *Studies in Scripture: Alma 30 to Moroni*, edited by Kent P. Jackson, 271-81. Salt Lake City: Deseret Book, 1988. Ether 9-15 outlines only two ways of living, "each antithetical to the other." Either one must choose God and his will or Satan and his evil doings. The choices individuals make set the course of their lives. Deliverance comes from a reversal of choices. Faith is an important element in the reversal process and implies the need for healthy desire. [J.W.M.]

T.081 Thomas, M. Catherine. "Theophany." In *Studies in Scripture: Alma 30 to Moroni*, edited by Kent P. Jackson, 172-83. Salt Lake City: Deseret Book, 1988. Theophany, or the appearance of God to man, teaches more in a few minutes than centuries of man's reasoning can produce. 3 Nephi 17-19 displays the Savior's great empathy for the people and his love of children. So profound was the appearance of the Savior among the Nephites that much could not be written. [J.W.M.]

T.082 Thomas, M. Catherine. "Types and Shadows of Deliverance in the Book of Mormon." In *Doctrines of the Book of Mormon, 1991 Sperry Symposium*, edited by Bruce A. Van Orden and Brent L. Top, 182-93. Salt Lake City: Deseret Book, 1992. There are many examples in the Book of Mormon of deliverance of individuals from sin, groups from bondage, and armies from harm. Accounts of journeys help one to understand deliverance. Ultimately the greatest deliverance is from sin. [N.K.Y.]

T.083 Thomas, Mark. "Listening to the Voice from the Dust: Moroni 8 As Rhetoric." *Sunstone* 4 (January/February 1979): 22-24. Rhetoric is a tool to understanding; it is an approach to literature that attempts to discover how the writer presents his vision to the reader. There are three types of letters in the Book of Mormon—war epistles, narratives, and doctrinal. This article focuses on a letter Mormon wrote to his son Moroni on infant baptism. [J.W.M.]

T.084 Thomas, Mark. "The Meaning of the Revival Language in the Book of Mormon." *Sunstone* 8 (May/June 1983): 19-25. Shows certain similarities between activities and language in the Book of Mormon and those found in religious revivals of the early nineteenth century. Includes some interesting comparisons, such as being saved from our sins, not in them. [M.R.]

T.085 Thomas, Mark. "Scholarship and the Future of the Book of Mormon." *Sunstone* 5 (May/June 1980): 24-29. The Book of Mormon has features common to any literary work. It has historical background, literary forms, symbols, and grammar. Mormon scholars should use textual criticism, historical criticism, and literary criticism to interpret the Book of Mormon as scholars of other literary works have used. This method is invaluable to expose the message. [J.W.M.]

T.086 Thomas, Robert K. "A Literary Analysis of the Book of Mormon." M.A. thesis, Reed College, 1947. A literary analysis of the Book of Mormon. After briefly examining theories regarding its origin, the author examines several historical and philosophical claims and contributions of the book. Also contains a short discussion of the allegation that the Book of Mormon quotes Shakespeare. Thomas concludes that the Book of Mormon represents a significant literary achievement. [M.R.]

T.087 Thomas, Robert K. "A Literary Critic Looks at the Book of Mormon." In *A Believing People,* 213-19. Provo, UT: Brigham Young University Press, 1974. Through a critical evaluation and literary analysis, the author examines the extent to which Joseph Smith as a translator is responsible for the language and style of the Book of Mormon. New England influences such as "the more part" and "hefted" are only superficial. Joseph Smith was more than inspired of God, he surely partook of the gift and power of God. [J.W.M.]

T.088 Thomas, Robert K. "A Literary Critic Looks at the Book of Mormon." In *To the Glory of God,* edited by Charles D. Tate and Truman G. Madsen, 149-61. Salt Lake City: Deseret Book, 1972. Introduces the idea that the Book of Mormon itself "claims to be Hebraic history." That is, it is a book of "God's dealings with his chosen people—no more, no less." Thomas writes concerning a few Book of Mormon characters—Nephi, Abinadi, Enos, Jarom, Omni, Amaron, Chemish, Abinadom, Amaleki—personalities who fit the "Hebraic pattern" of history, a pattern which is constant throughout the Book of Mormon. [D.W.P.]

T.089 Thomasson, Gordon C. "Choosing Our Language after We Choose a 'Language of the Church': or, Who Do We Want to Talk to and Will They Hear Us?" In *Conference on the Language of the Mormons,* 35-42. Provo, UT: BYU Language Research Center, 1974. Choosing a language for a given area involves decisions of a social and political nature beyond the linguistic issues. Using a particular language may mark a person in a political sense. It may suggest values not consistent with the gospel. It is an extremely hard task. Finding the right language in which to translate the Book of Mormon is critical. [J.W.M.]

T.090 Thomasson, Gordon C. " 'Daddy, What's a Frontier?': Second Thoughts on the Environment that Supposedly Produced the Book of Mormon." N.p., 25 April 1970. Address delivered at a Brigham Young University Book of Mormon Symposium. Questions the assumptions of those who claim that the Book of Mormon is merely a reflection of Joseph Smith's environment. Critiques theses that have associated early Mormon history with aspects of the American frontier. [D.M.]

T.091 Thomasson, Gordon C. "Lamanites." In *Encyclopedia of Mormonism,* edited by Daniel H. Ludlow, 2:804-5. 5 vols. New York: Macmillan, 1992. For a similar discussion see "I Have a Question: What exactly does the word 'Lamanite' mean?" *Ensign* 7 (September 1977): 39-40. Describes the Lamanites as descendants of Laman and Lemuel, sons of Lehi. However, generally the Lamanites were those who were not Nephites. [B.D.]

T.092 Thomasson, Gordon C. "Mormon Symbols: Structures of Mormon Consciousness and the Basis of Mormon Communication Activities, Mormon Language, and Mormon Arts." In *Conference on the Language of the Mormons,* edited by Harold Madsen and John L. Sorenson, 75. Provo, UT: Brigham Young University Language Research Center, 1973. Mormon logic and thinking are based symbols, rituals, and temple iconography that had their roots in the Book of Mormon. The worldview that has grown out of this book has attached new symbols to English words that carry specific and unique implications. [J.W.M.]

T.093 Thomasson, Gordon C. "Mosiah: The Complex Symbolism and the Symbolic Complex of Kingship in the Book of Mormon." Provo, UT: FARMS, 1982. Also in *Journal of Book of Mormon Studies* 2 (Spring 1993): 21-38. With the purpose of bringing people to Christ, Mormon included more material from the reign of Mosiah in his abridgment than any other king except for Nephi, son of Lehi. The responsibility of Mosiah's kingship to his subjects is likened to God's responsibility for his children. Noah is likened to Satan and his usurping of power and the potential destruction of those who allow such rule. Photographs of symbols of kingship are included. [J.W.M.]

T.094 Thomasson, Gordon C. "Righteousness As a Counterculture." *NE* 2 (April 1973): 46-49. Most pre-Columbian cultures that archaeologists have discovered have been civilizations based on warfare, aggressive and competitive in nature. They are cultures familiar to Book of Mormon readers as having roots in societies which rejected the gospel. They result in blood sacrifice instead of the individual's need for the personal sacrifice of a broken heart and contrite spirit. [J.W.M.]

T.095 Thomasson, Gordon C. "The Survivor and the Will to Bear Witness." In *Reexploring the Book of Mormon*, edited by John W. Welch, 266-68. Salt Lake City: Deseret Book and FARMS, 1992. Mormon, Moroni, Alma and many others were witnesses of the destruction of large numbers of people. Their reactions can be compared to those of survivors of Hitler's and Stalin's death camps. As survivors they documented the atrocities. Their records bear distinctive and unexpected similarities to other descriptions of similar experiences. [N.K.Y.]

T.096 Thompson, Anita. "Please Read It to Me." *NE* 20 (July 1990): 8-10. Personal story. Author tells of the Book of Mormon's influence in her son's life. [E.G.]

T.097 Thompson, Charles B. *Evidences in Proof of the Book of Mormon Being a Divinely Inspired Record*. Batavia, NY: D. D. Waite, 1841. Three parts. Excerpts from this work in "Evidences in Proof of the Book of Mormon." *TS* 3 (1 January 1842): 640-44. Sets forth evidences to prove the Book of Mormon's truthfulness to benefit those embarking on missionary work, for the encouragement of those who had just joined the Church, and to correct false doctrine concerning the Book of Mormon's "real intent and character." Discusses scriptural accounts of the scattering and gathering of Israel, the sign of the record of Joseph, and America as a land of promise. Refutes allegations made against the Book of Mormon and issues a warning to the inhabitants of America. [J.W.M.]

T.098 Thompson, G. Forrest. *Greetings between Judah and Joseph*. Idaho Falls, ID: Vanity, 1990. A 49-chapter commentary on Zenos's parable of the olive tree in Jacob 5. [D.M.]

T.099 Thorgeivson, J. "The Nine Bibles of the World." *MS* 83 (27 January 1921): 60-61. Lists nine books that serve as foundations for different religions, or the nine bibles of the world, in which is included the Book of Mormon. [M.D.P.]

T.100 Thorne, Melvin J. "Ezias." In *Encyclopedia of Mormonism*, edited by Daniel H. Ludlow, 2:481. 5 vols. New York: Macmillan, 1992. Ezias was a prophet of Old Testament times mentioned by Nephi in Helaman 8:13-20. [B.D.]

T.101 Thorne, Melvin J. "Helaman$_1$." In *Encyclopedia of Mormonism*, edited by Daniel H. Ludlow, 2:584. 5 vols. New York: Macmillan, 1992. Helaman, the son of King Benjamin, became a king of the Nephites. [J.W.M.]

T.102 Thorne, Melvin J. "Moroni$_1$." In *Encyclopedia of Mormonism*, edited by Daniel H. Ludlow, 2:955-56. 5 vols. New York: Macmillan, 1992. The first Moroni mentioned in the Book of Mormon lived prior to Christ's birth and was but twenty-five years old when he commanded the Nephite armies. He raised the title of liberty to rally his people to the defense of their freedom. [J.W.M.]

T.103 Thorne, Melvin J. "Mosiah$_1$." In *Encyclopedia of Mormonism*, edited by Daniel H. Ludlow, 2:959. 5 vols. New York: Macmillan, 1992. King Mosiah, father of Benjamin, led his people away to protect them from the Lamanites about 200 B.C. and discovered and settled with the people of Zarahemla. He interpreted the writings of the Jaredites. [J.W.M.]

T.104 Thorne, Melvin J. "Nephi$_2$." In *Encyclopedia of Mormonism*, edited by Daniel H. Ludlow, 3:1005. 5 vols. New York: Macmillan, 1992. Nephi$_2$ was the Nephite chief judge in 39 B.C., served a mission to the Lamanites, and ruled during the great famine recorded in the book of Helaman. [A.T.]

T.105 Thorne, Melvin J. "Nephi$_3$." In *Encyclopedia of Mormonism*, edited by Daniel H. Ludlow, 3:1006. 5 vols. New York: Macmillan, 1992.

Nephi$_3$, the son of Nephi$_2$, was a man of great faith who heard the voice of Jesus Christ declaring that he would be born on the morrow; he was the leading disciple of the American Church following the resurrection of Christ. [A.T.]

T.106 Thorne, Melvin J. "Nephi$_4$." In *Encyclopedia of Mormonism*, edited by Daniel H. Ludlow, 3:1006. 5 vols. New York: Macmillan, 1992. Nephi$_4$ was the record keeper during the time when the descendants of Lehi lived the law of consecration. His death took place after A.D. 110. [J.W.M.]

T.107 Thornock, A. LaVar, Mervin L. Gifford, Vernon W. Mattson Jr., John Child, and Duane H. Marchant. "The Book of Mormon." In *Is There An Answer?* edited by A. LaVar Thornock, 41-47. Pocatello, ID: Carter's Printing, 1968. Prepared to answer many common objections to LDS theology. Objections include: the Bible does not speak of the Book of Mormon; since the Bible is complete there should be no need for additional scripture; Mormons use a different Bible; much is copied from the Bible; Joseph Smith wrote the book; Lehi is not mentioned in the Bible; and the gold plates are not available to view. [J.W.M.]

T.108 Thornton, H. Newton. "A Record of the Mighty Deed on this Continent to be Preserved." *IE* 24 (October 1921): 1084-85. "External evidence of the historical credibility and truth of the Book of Mormon" is found in the reconstruction of ruins in Mexico and Central America. Two pyramids found in Mexico and the ruins of a great city that existed three to four thousand years ago bear witness of a great civilization. [J.W.M.]

T.109 "The Three Witnesses." *Historical Record* 7 (1888): 609-24. Contains the testimony of the Eight Witnesses and a biographical sketch of each. [J.W.M.]

T.110 Tice, Richard. "How Rare a Possession." *Ensign* 18 (January 1988): 14-17. Discusses the making of a film, "How Rare a Possession." The film's purpose is to create a deeper appreciation and awareness of the Book of Mormon, to strengthen testimonies of the scripture, and to encourage people in and out of the Church to read and study the book. [A.A.]

T.111 Tiffin, Dalton A. *Some Important Reminders: The Divine Origin of the Book of Mormon*. Weston, Ontario: Dalton A. Tiffin, n.d. Pamphlet attempting to prove the validity of the Book of Mormon. Includes the testimony of the Three and Eight Witnesses, an account of the finding of the Spaulding manuscript, a reprint of a letter from the president of Oberlin College where the Spaulding manuscript is kept. [J.W.M.]

T.112 "Time for the Feast." *NE* 16 (May 1986): 28-29. An instructional aid for young people. A program is presented whereby a person may read the entire standard works in four-and-one-half years by reading one chapter a day. [B.D.]

T.113 Tobin, Tammy L. "Truly the Word of God." *Ensign* 13 (December 1983): 20-21. Author recounts her conversion to the gospel through the Book of Mormon. As a Catholic nun, she encountered two missionaries who gave her a copy of the Book of Mormon and challenged her to read the account of the Jesus Christ's visit to the Americas. As she did she knew the story was true and was baptized the following Sunday. [S.P.S.]

T.114 Top, Brent L. "Faith Unto Repentance." In *Doctrines of the Book of Mormon, 1991 Sperry Symposium*, edited by Bruce A. Van Orden and Brent L. Top, 194-211. Salt Lake City: Deseret Book, 1992. Prophets have always been told to teach repentance and faith on the Lord. Faith is clearly identified in the Book of Mormon as the foundation of repentance. Enos and Ether were told their sins were forgiven through their faith in Christ. The book cites the importance of broken hearts and contrite spirits that lead to confession of guilt and submission to God's will. Confession is cited as being effective if sins are forsaken. Alma discusses the "mighty change of heart." [J.W.M.]

T.115 *A Topical Guide to the Scriptures of the Church of Jesus Christ of Latter-day Saints*. Salt Lake City: Deseret Book, 1977. Six hundred forty topics are alphabetically listed, including Book of Mormon references. References include a line of the scripture for easier identification. [J.W.M.]

T.116 Totten, Norman. "Categories of Evidence for Old World Contacts with Ancient America." In *The Book of Mormon: The Keystone Scripture*, edited by Paul R. Cheesman, S. Kent Brown, and Charles D. Tate Jr., 187-205. Salt Lake City: Bookcraft, 1988. Early explorers found the peoples of the Americas to be widely varied in culture and physical appearance. It is argued that the diffusion theory allows for greater understanding than the isolation theory. There are considerable amounts of evidence indicating there were many cultures present in America prior to Columbus in 1492. [J.W.M.]

T.117 "Transatlantic Antiquities." *MS* 6 (1 August 1845): 56-57. Briefly tells of the research of Josiah Priest, Stephens, and Catherwood and their discoveries of the remains of mighty cities on the American continent that testify of the Book of Mormon. [M.D.P.]

T.118 "Traveling in the Wilderness." *Friend* 19 (August 1989): 8-10. Cartoon depiction for children of Lehi's family traveling in the wilderness. [J.W.M.]

T.119 Treat, Mary Lee. "Another 'Wise Purpose' for the Small Plates." *ZR* 11 (Winter 1981): 1-2. Discusses a possible "wise purpose" for the small plates. Since Nephi and Lehi experienced Jerusalem and the Old World their writings have a more distinct Jewish flavor to them. This is essential for a witness to Jews that Jesus is the Messiah and that the Book of Mormon is true. [A.T.]

T.120 Treat, Mary Lee. "A Call to Repentance." In *Recent Book of Mormon Development, Articles from the Zarahemla Record*, 2:214. Independence, MO: Zarahemla Research Foundation, 1992. As Treat was examining pottery in Guatemala, she thought how shameful it was that only pottery was left from a once-great nation. She realized that she must repent and the whole nation must repent or it will die as the Nephites died. [B.D.]

T.121 Treat, Mary Lee. "The Consistency of Satan's Tactics." *ZR* 62 (July/August 1992): 2-4. Summarizes the tactics and pitfalls of the three great anti-Christs, Sherem, Nehor, and Korihor. The blandishments resorted to by these three are recognizable today, both in and out of the church. [D.M.]

T.122 Treat, Mary Lee. "The Faith of Christ." *ZR* 64 (November/December 1992): 1, 4. Points out that the Book of Mormon prophets before Christ believed in and testified of Christ. Suggests that those who live at the current time follow their example. [D.M.]

T.123 Treat, Mary Lee. "The Lamb Chapter." *ZR* 41 (February 1989): 3. Nephi uses the word *lamb* 59 times. The term is found just a few other times in the Book of Mormon. John the Revelator uses *lamb* much more than other New Testament writers. Perhaps the frequent use of *lamb* by John and Nephi was due to their being shown the same vision. [A.T.]

T.124 Treat, Mary Lee. "The Learning of the Jews. The Purpose Principle in Action: Why Heads." *ZR* 42 (April 1989): 3. Also in *Recent Book of Mormon Development, Articles from the Zarahemla Record*, 2:42-43. Independence, MO: Zarahemla Research Foundation, 1992. According to the "purpose principle," everything in the Book of Mormon is there for a purpose. In Jacob 1:4 Jacob writes that he should engraven the heads of preaching, revelation, or prophesying on the plates. As used here, "heads" is a Hebraism meaning the most important or best of such teachings. [B.D.]

T.125 Treat, Mary Lee. "Maya Hieroglyphs for Cardinal Directions Found—Or North is North." *ZR* 32-33 (1986): 14. People deciphering Book of Mormon geography have argued about whether the Nephite "north" is true north. This article reports hieroglyphs found in Rio Azul that were oriented correctly to the cardinal directions. [A.T.]

T.126 Treat, Mary Lee. "No Erasers." *ZR* 13-14 (Fall 1981): 5. Lists verses where mistakes were made by the engraver of gold plates and the way in which the engraver corrected them. These include 1 Nephi 2:41, 1 Nephi 3:245, and Alma 14:112 (RLDS versification). [A.T.]

T.127 Treat, Mary Lee. "O House of Israel." *ZR* 47 (February 1990): 3-4. This article presents the results of a word-by-word comparison of Isaiah passages used in the Book of Mormon. Entire verses and phrases are lost from the book of Isaiah in the Bible, and the biblical Isaiah had lost the concept of the restoration of the entire House of Israel. [A.T.]

T.128 Treat, Raymond C. "1980 and the Book of Mormon." *ZR* 12 (Spring 1981): 3. 1980 was a Jubilee year according to Jewish tradition. It was also a special year for the Book of Mormon. Three important events were "(1) the discovery of the original Anthon Transcript, (2) the presentation of a portion of the Book of Mormon in Hebrew to some Jews in Israel, and (3) the publication of Ralph Lesh's map of Book of Mormon geography." [A.T.]

T.129 Treat, Raymond, C. "Another Ancient Pattern: Chiastic Structure in the Book of Mormon." *ZR* 17, 18 (Summer/Fall 1982): 8-12. A brief review of an ancient literary form known as chiasmus. The material presented offers insight into the structure and history of chiasmus and its occurrence in the Book of Mormon as additional evidence to the book's historical authenticity. [D.S.T.]

T.130 Treat, Raymond C. "Approaches to Studying the Book of Mormon." *ZR* 19, 20, 21 (Winter/Spring/Summer 1983): 10-13. The Book of Mormon is important and relevant today. The article outlines several different methods of Book of Mormon study and the merits of each: "the straight through method," "reading the research of others," "the topical method," examining definitions and synonyms, and pondering. [A.T.]

T.131 Treat, Raymond C. "Are You Listless? A New Revelation about the Book of Mormon." *ZR* 60 (March/April 1992): 2-4. Refers to a study by J. M. Cascione showing that the Bible contains lists of items in combinations of twos, threes, fours, fives, sixes, sevens, tens, and twelves, each of which is associated with a particular category, as in Hebrew poetry. Gives examples from the Bible and Book of Mormon. [D.M.]

T.132 Treat, Raymond C. "Are You Really a Book of Mormon Believer?" In *Recent Book of Mormon Development, Articles from the Zarahemla Record*, 2:221. Independence, MO: Zarahemla Research Foundation, 1992. According to God, in order to be a true believer in the Book of Mormon one must evidence five elements. The true believer must feast on the words of Christ, ponder, know about types, know the story line, and do the things in verse 103 of Alma 14 (RLDS versification). [B.D.]

T.133 Treat, Raymond C. "Becan: A Dramatic Validation of a Book of Mormon Warfare Pattern." *ZR* 8 (Spring 1980): 1-3. Contains a map, restoration drawing, cross section and artist's reconstruction of the walls of Becan. This city, located in Guatemala, is perhaps one of the cities fortified by general Moroni as it has trenches dug outside the walls that correspond to the information found in the book of Alma. [A.T.]

T.134 Treat, Raymond C. "Benefits of In-Depth Study." *ZR* 22-23 (Fall 1983 and Winter 1984): 8-10, 13. This is a continuation of "Approaches to Studying the Book of Mormon" (*ZR* 19-21). Studying chiasmus, charting scriptures, defining words and phrases, identifying types, pondering and topical study, are all suggested as methods for understanding the Book of Mormon. The author gives examples of each. [A.T.]

T.135 Treat, Raymond C. "The Book of Mormon and Mesoamerican Outlines Compared: Beginning, Highpoints, and Endings." *ZR* 2 (September 1978): 1-2, 6. Compares the Jaredites to the Olmec people and states that the archaeological evidence shows that the Olmec civilization began, had its high point, and ended at times that match the Jaredite civilization. Also compares the Mulekites, Nephites, and Lamanites with the Classic Maya. [A.T.]

T.136 Treat, Raymond C. "The Book of Mormon is Our Key to the Future." *ZR* 27-28 (Winter, Spring 1985): 8-13. Encourages readers to study and ponder the Book of Mormon to learn how the Book of Mormon is the "key to the future." The author has found five topics in which it helps us understand the future: "the gospel," "additional scripture," "zion," "the restoration of the house of Israel," and "more of Jesus Christ." [A.T.]

T.137 Treat, Raymond C. "A Book of Mormon Tour Guide: Chichen Itza." *ZR* 9 (Summer 1980): 5-8. Contains maps and photographs of Chichen Itza, a summary of the archaeological work, and "site description and culture history," as well as Book of Mormon correlations suggesting that this possibly was a Lamanite city. [A.T.]

T.138 Treat, Raymond C. "A Book of Mormon Tour Guide: Monte Alban." *ZR* 6 (Fall 1979): 2-7. Contains pictures, maps, site description, and Book of Mormon connections to of the ruins at Monte Alban. Author concludes that Monte Alban was possibly a Jaredite city as well as a possible Lamanite, Mulekite, or Nephite city. [A.T.]

T.139 Treat, Raymond C. "Book of Mormon Tour Guide: Palenque." *ZR* 19-21 (Winter, Spring, Summer 1983): 16-18, 24. Contains photographs, maps, drawings, site description, and archaeological notes of the temples at Palenque and proposes that Palenque is the city Bountiful. [A.T.]

T.140 Treat, Raymond C. "Book of Mormon Tour Guide—Part 4: Yaxchilan." *ZR* 19-21 (Winter, Spring, and Summer 1983): 6-9, 20. Contains maps, a topographical drawing, site description, and photographs of Yaxhilan and suggests that Yaxchilan was Zarahemla. [A.T.]

T.141 Treat, Raymond C. "Book of Mormon Tour Guide: Teotihuacan—City of the Gods." *ZR* 4 (Spring 1979): 5-8. Gives a history of archaeological work and Book of Mormon correlations. Suggests that Teotihuacan is a city of the "land northward" spoken of in Alma and Helaman. [A.T.]

T.142 Treat, Raymond C. "Book of Mormon Warfare: More Than Meets the Eye." *ZR* 65 (January/February 1993): 1-4. Book of Mormon warfare is a type for spiritual warfare. The 3 Nephi story of Lachoneus as an illustration of this principle. [A.T.]

T.143 Treat, Raymond C. "The Chinese Language and the Book of Mormon." *ZR* 12 (Spring 1981): 1-3. Examines work done by C. H. Kang who has shown biblical influence in the make-up of Chinese characters. The author suggests that there is evidence of the "Jaredite Pattern" in the characters. [A.T.]

T.144 Treat, Raymond C. "Classic Maya Population: An Example of Convergence." *ZR* 1 (February 1978): 5. Considers archaeological evidence that shows Classic Maya population levels to be concurrent with those found in the Book of Mormon. [A.T.]

T.145 Treat, Raymond C. "Classic Maya Subsistence: Another Example of Convergence." *ZR* 1 (December 1978): 5, 8. Examines Classic Maya food to show a convergence between Mesoamerican archaeology and the Book of Mormon. Archaeologists are learning that population levels were too high to be supported by slash-and-burn agriculture. [A.T.]

T.146 Treat, Raymond C. "The Convergence Pace Quickens: Barley Found in the New World." *ZR* 22-23 (Fall 1983 and Winter 1984): 1-3, 14-15. Also in *Recent Book of Mormon Development, Articles from the Zarahemla Record*, 1:15-17. Independence, MO: Zarahemla Research Foundation, 1992. According to a scientific report, barley has been excavated from an ancient Indian site in Arizona. Such a discovery appears to be significant evidence of the authenticity of the Book of Mormon. [B.D.]

T.147 Treat, Raymond C. "Editorial Comment: Chiasmus in the News." *ZR* 47 (February 1990): 1. Comments on recent negative publicity given the Book of Mormon when Jefferey Lundgren convinced his followers that chiasmus was the only way God speaks in scripture. [A.C.W.]

T.148 Treat, Raymond C. "El Mirador: Massive Guatemala Site Shows Great Promise." In *Recent Book of Mormon Development, Articles from the Zarahemla Record*, 1:27-29. Independence, MO: Zarahemla Research Foundation, 1992. Describes some of the discoveries of the preliminary work done in El Mirador and concludes that it "promises to be one of the more interesting sites to believers in the Book of Mormon." [B.D.]

T.149 Treat, Raymond C. "The Four Levels." In *Recent Book of Mormon Development, Articles from the Zarahemla Record*, 1:148-53. Independence, MO: Zarahemla Research Foundation, 1992. The four levels in which God classifies individuals are the celestial, terrestrial, telestial, and no glory. In order to understand the life styles of each level, Treat uses the four responses to the word of God as found in Lehi's vision of the rod of iron, the parable of the sower, and Alma's parable of the seed. [B.D.]

T.150 Treat, Raymond C. "The Growing Together of the Bible and the Book of Mormon." In *Recent Book of Mormon Development, Articles from the Zarahemla Record*, 2:215. Independence, MO: Zarahemla Research Foundation, 1992. The ancient Hebrew nature of both texts is revealed as the Bible and the Book of Mormon "grow together" as prophesied in 2 Nephi 2:20-23 (RLDS versification). [B.D.]

T.151 Treat, Raymond C. "The Hidden Principle: Come unto Christ." ZR 65 (January/February 1993): 2-3. The phrase "come unto Christ" (or similar phraseology) is found 43 times in the Book of Mormon. This phrase "describes a covenant relationship," a spiritual covenant made before baptism (see Mosiah 18:10; 21:32-33). "To become as a little child" (3 Nephi 9:22) is synonymous with coming unto Christ. [A.T.]

T.152 Treat, Raymond C. "The Importance of Covenant in the Restoration of the House of Israel." ZR 50 (August 1990): 3-4. The Book of Mormon begins and ends with the concept of covenant. It is found in the opening and closing verses. This article encourages Book of Mormon readers to study the covenants found in the Book of Mormon in order to gain understanding and to be "used by God to assist" in his work. [A.T.]

T.153 Treat, Raymond C. "Massive Guatemala Site Shows Great Promise." ZR 7 (Winter 1979-1980): 1-2, 7-8. Documents the history of archaeological work at El Mirador in Guatemala and suggests that this was a city abandoned by the Nephites about A.D. 300 (concurrent with the archaeological record). [A.T.]

T.154 Treat, Raymond C. "Mesoamerican Archaeology and the Book of Mormon." ZR 5 (Summer 1979): 1-2, 6-8. Through illustrated outlines, the article compares the major points of the Mesoamerican and Book of Mormon cultural histories. The evidence and correlations presented support the authenticity of Book of Mormon cultural history. [D.S.T.]

T.155 Treat, Raymond C. "Mesoamerican Linguistics." ZR 34 (1986): 4-6. Discusses the development of the Mayan language based upon the research of Cambell and Kaufman and proposes that the Mayan language is descended from that of the Nephites. Briefly discusses the relationship of the Olmec-Jaredite languages. [A.T.]

T.156 Treat, Raymond C. "More to Come: Six Steps to Spiritual Power." ZR 13-14 (Summer and Fall 1981): 8-9, 12-14, 16. Suggests a six step approach using the Book of Mormon to develop spiritual power—study, fast, pray, humility, faith in Christ, joy and consultation, yielding to God, sanctification, purification, spiritual power. Follow these steps to prepare to receive the remaining portions of the Book of Mormon and to bring forth Zion. [A.T.]

T.157 Treat, Raymond C. "Mormon's Hidden Message." ZR 10 (Fall 1980): 1-2, 4. Perhaps Mormon included so much information about geography in the Book of Mormon for the following reasons: to aid the gentiles in locating the remnant, to locate the Hill Cumorah, to provide a historical base similar to the Bible, and to enrich the understanding of the reader. [A.T.]

T.158 Treat, Raymond C. "Needed: A Revelation about Types." ZR 59 (January/February 1992): 2-4. Types in the scriptures are important for us to understand in order to get all we can from the scriptures. The Lehite's journey in the wilderness is a type of our spiritual journey, Nephite warfare descriptions are types, and the 158 years between Mosiah$_2$ and the coming of Christ is a type of the period of restoration and the second coming. [B.D.]

T.159 Treat, Raymond C. "Never Murmur." In *Recent Book of Mormon Development, Articles from the Zarahemla Record*, 2:220. Independence, MO: Zarahemla Research Foundation, 1992. "The opening story of the Book of Mormon—the journey of Lehi and his group from Jerusalem to the Land of Promise—is a classic story of the contrast between murmuring and not murmuring." Murmuring or complaining is the result of unbelief. This is constantly shown in the examples of Laman and Lemuel. [B.D.]

T.160 Treat, Raymond C. "A New Insight: Why Joseph?" *ZR* 58 (December 1991): 1, 4. The writers of the Book of Mormon emphasized that Lehi was a descendant of Joseph because they knew that the tribe of Joseph would be the means of saving the rest of the house of Israel in the last days. Those of the lineage of Ephraim and Manasseh will work together as the tribe of Joseph in the last days. [J.W.M.]

T.161 Treat, Raymond C. "The Primary Purpose of the Book of Mormon." *ZR* 61 (May/June 1992): 1-2, 4. Proposes that the primary purpose of the Book of Mormon is to inform the Lamanites concerning the covenants made to their fathers. The secondary purpose is to convince the Jews and Gentiles of Jesus' Christological mission. Suggests that we be more diligent in bringing the Book of Mormon to the attention of the Lamanites. [D.M.]

T.162 Treat, Raymond C. *Recent Developments in Belize*. Independence, MO: Foundation for Research on Ancient America, 1984. According to some Book of Mormon scholars, Belize is the most likely location of the Jaredite civilization. Archaeologists have found evidence to validate Book of Mormon historical references there. [J.W.M]

T.163 Treat, Raymond C. "The Significance of the Dead Sea Scrolls." *ZR* 66 (March/April 1993): 4. The author sees the publication of the Dead Sea Scrolls to be a catalyst for bringing the Bible and Book of Mormon together (2 Nephi 3:12). [A.T.]

T.164 Treat, Raymond C. "The Significance of Understanding the Difficult Words of Jesus." In *Recent Book of Mormon Development, Articles from the Zarahemla Record*, 2:49. Independence, MO: Zarahemla Research Foundation, 1992. The book, *Understanding the Difficult Words of Jesus*, by Biven and Blizzard argues that the thought patterns and idioms in the New Testament are Hebrew. Treat writes that "non-restoration Christian's . . . interest in the Hebrew nature of both the Old and New Testament is . . . a necessary prelude to their recognition of the Hebrew nature—and consequently, the divinity—of the Book of Mormon." [B.D.]

T.165 Treat, Raymond C. "A Simplified Look at Mesoamerica." *ZR* 13-14 (Summer and Fall 1981): 7, 10-11, 15. Examines the archaeological finds from the Pre-Classic period (2000 B.C.–A.D. 100), and Classic (A.D. 100–900) in Mesoamerica. The author relates these finds to the Jaredite, Mulekite, Lamanite, and Nephite civilizations. Parallels are drawn between the Olmecs and the Jaredites as well as the Nephites/Lamanites and the Maya. [A.T.]

T.166 Treat, Raymond C. "Toward a Better Understanding of Science." In *Recent Book of Mormon Development, Articles from the Zarahemla Record*, 1:3. Independence, MO: Zarahemla Research Foundation, 1984. Scientists do not gradually accumulate knowledge in a continuous upward movement, but progress by jumping from one paradigm to another. Studying American archaeology can be rewarding as long as we realize which paradigm the archaeologists are using. If we realize this our testimonies of the Book of Mormon will not be affected by seemingly contradictory archaeological evidence. [B.D.]

T.167 Treat, Raymond C. "Transoceanic Contact: Another Example of Convergence." *ZR* 2 (Spring 1979): 1-2, 12. Mesoamerican archaeology is gradually converging with the pattern presented by the Book of Mormon. Article discusses recent evidence of ancient transoceanic contacts between the New and Old Worlds. [A.T.]

T.168 Treat, Raymond C. "Understanding Our Covenant." In *Recent Book of Mormon Development, Articles from the Zarahemla Record*, 2:34-39. Independence, MO: Zarahemla Research Foundation, 1992. Explains the steps in a Hebrew covenant as written by Richard Booker in *The Miracle of the Scarlet Thread*. If we understand the covenant that we have made with God we will not harm anyone, doubt will be dispelled, and we will receive power.

The purpose of the Book of Mormon is to establish the covenant. [B.D.]

T.169 Treat, Raymond C. "Volcanoes, Archaeology and the Book of Mormon." *ZR* 16 (Spring 1982): 1-2, 8. "This article discusses two ancient volcanic eruptions in El Salvador and their significance to the Book of Mormon." The eruptions were ca. A.D. 600 and ca. A.C.W. 260. The author predicts that further digs in these areas will uncover tremendous finds relating to the Book of Mormon. [A.T.]

T.170 Treat, Raymond C. "What is in the Book of Mormon is There for a Purpose." *ZR* 24/25/26 (Spring/Summer/Fall 1984): 12-15, 21-22. The Book of Mormon was written for today. The article contains three charts—one showing how the Book of Mormon contents were divinely controlled, one illustrating that we have less than one percent of what was written, and a chart of the eight tribes of Nephites. [A.T.]

T.171 Treat, Raymond C. "Wheat and Barley: Problem or Opportunity." *ZR* 1 (September 1978): 7-8. Because of scarcity of evidence, lack of interest, and faulty research design evidence of wheat and barley in the New World prior to the 1500s has not been located. With new technology, phytoliths (fossilized plant cells) will show the presence of these grains during Book of Mormon time periods. [A.T.]

T.172 Treat, Raymond C. "Wordprints: Further Evidence for Book of Mormon Authorship." *ZR* 22-23 (Fall 1983 and Winter 1984): 4-5, 15. Contains a brief review of *Book of Mormon Authorship,* by the Brigham Young University Religious Studies Center. The article contains a description of Manovia, Cluster Analysis, and Discriminant Analysis. These studies support the Book of Mormon claim that it was written by a number of ancient authors. [A.T.]

T.173 Treat, Ray, and Mary Lee Treat. "158 Years: A Type for Our Day." *ZR* 46 (December 1989): 1-4. Examines the possibility that the 158 years covered from the "Reign of King Mosiah II in 124 B.C. to the coming of Christ in A.D. 34" is a type of the Second Coming of Christ. [A.T.]

T.174 Tuckett, Madge Harris, and Belle Harris Wilson. *The Martin Harris Story.* Provo, UT: Press Publishing, 1983. A biographical treatise of Martin Harris that includes a discussion of his willingness to sacrifice much of his own property and personal life, in spite of his own doubts and apprehensions, to assist with the publication of the Book of Mormon. [J.T.]

T.175 Tullidge, Edward W. "The Coming Forth of the Book of Mormon." In Tullidge's *Life of Joseph the Prophet,* 6-93. Plano, IL: RLDS Church, 1880. Provides a detailed narrative of the coming forth of the Book of Mormon from Moroni's first visit to the publication of the book and organization of the Church. Uses Joseph Smith's own descriptions of events interspersed with accounts from Oliver Cowdery, Lucy Mack Smith, and the three witnesses. [J.W.M.]

T.176 Turnbull, John S. *A Dictionary of the Book of Mormon.* Salt Lake City: n.p., 1946? Defines proper names in the Book of Mormon. [D.M.]

T.177 Turley, Reid Pinegar, and Linda D. Turley. "The Book of Mormon." In Turley's *And Ye Shall Teach*, 25-38. N.p.: n.p., 1978. A collection of imaginative object lessons, as well as scriptural passages and quotes from leaders of the Church to aid teachers and speakers. [J.W.M.]

T.178 Turley, Richard E., Jr. "Seer Stones." In *Encyclopedia of Mormonism*, edited by Daniel H. Ludlow, 3:1293. 5 vols. New York: Macmillan, 1992. Joseph Smith records that the angel Moroni gave him the Urim and Thummim to translate the Book of Mormon. He used these and other seer stones in a variety of ways, but primarily to receive revelation. [J.W.M.]

T.179 Turner, Denise. "Anna's Book of Mormon Christmas." *Ensign* 20 (December 1990): 20-21. Anna, a new convert to the Church, received a Book of Mormon for Christmas. Her joy in the gospel was an inspiration to all who knew her. [J.W.M.]

T.180 Turner, Floy L., comp. *Prophecies and Sermons from the Book of Mormon.* Provo, UT: J. Grant Stevenson, 1965. Book of Mormon texts that focus primarily on visions, prophetic utterances, and sermons. [J.A.T.]

T.181 Turner, Floy L., comp. *Readings from the Book of Mormon*. Provo, UT: J. Grant Stevenson, 1965. An abridgment of the Book of Mormon for the purpose of introduction or review. [J.A.T.]

T.182 Turner, Jule Ann Bishop. "Costumes of Ancient Meso-America: An Art and Research Project." Closure Project (B.I.S.), Brigham Young University, Dept. of Independent Studies, 1990. Investigates the use of silk and cotton in Mesoamerica, considering a Book of Mormon time frame and geographical context. Discusses weaving and dyeing processes and symbols incorporated in costumes and clothing. [E.G.]

T.183 Turner, Rodney. "A Faith unto Salvation." In *Studies in Scripture: Alma 30 to Moroni*, edited by Kent P. Jackson, 16-27. Salt Lake City: Deseret Book, 1988. The false teachings of Korihor and the Zoramites contained in Alma 31-33 are indicative of latter-day false doctrines. To combat these heresies Alma presented the "virtue of the word of God." Faith in the Lord Jesus Christ and hope in him provides the antidote to the false teachings of the world. Prayer is an essential part of faith. [J.W.M.]

T.184 Turner, Rodney. "The Great Conversion." In *Studies In Scripture: Vol. 7, 1 Nephi to Alma 29*, edited by Kent P. Jackson, 205-29. Salt Lake City: Deseret Book, 1987. The mission of the Holy Ghost is most clearly defined in Mosiah 1-6. King Benjamin must have made an intense study of Nephi and the brass plates, applied their teachings in his life and taught others the same. Quickened by the Holy Spirit, King Benjamin was well aware of the Savior's teachings and the role of the Holy Ghost. [J.W.M.]

T.185 Turner, Rodney. *Great Families of the Book of Mormon*. Provo, UT: Brigham Young University, 1957. A series of five lectures dealing with five Book of Mormon families. The Lehite family featured two opposite characters—Nephi and Laman. The family of Mosiah included Mosiah$_1$, Benjamin, Mosiah$_2$, and his four sons. The house of Alma represents "the greatest of the ruling houses in the Book of Mormon." This family included Alma$_1$ and Alma$_2$, Helaman$_1$, Helaman$_2$, Nephi, Lehi, and others. The family of Mormon (Mormon and Moroni) witnessed the decline and fall of the Nephite nation. The family of Christ is represented by those who become his spiritual sons and daughters. [D.W.P.]

T.186 Turner, Rodney. "The Infinite Atonement of God." In *Studies In Scripture: Vol. 8, Alma 30 to Moroni*, edited by Kent P. Jackson, 28-40. Salt Lake City: Deseret Book, 1988. Amulek's teachings to the Zoramites constitute chapters 34-55 of Alma. Contrary to the doctrine of Augustine, Amulek teaches that man is "carnal, sensual, and devilish by nature," but he is not doomed to stay that way. Through the atonement of Christ men may rise above that nature to be given a kingdom in the Lord's eternal worlds. This life is a probationary state and whatever spirit that a man possesses in this life will rise with him in the resurrection. [J.W.M.]

T.187 Turner, Rodney. "The Lamanite Mark." In *The Book of Mormon: Second Nephi, The Doctrinal Structure*, edited by Monte S. Nyman and Charles D. Tate Jr., 133-57. Salt Lake City: Bookcraft, 1989. God is not racist, but it is not by chance that the color of one's skin differs from another's. God judges by looking upon the heart. The Lord blesses and curses according to an individual's righteousness or wickedness. "Marks" are symbolic of the withdrawal of the Spirit and are related to natural consequences of adopting negative characteristics. Dark skins were for the identifying process and can and will be lifted for the righteous. [J.W.M.]

T.188 Turner, Rodney. "Morality and Marriage in the Book of Mormon." In *The Book of Mormon: Jacob through Words of Mormon, To Learn with Joy*, edited by Monte S. Nyman and Charles D. Tate Jr., 271-85. Salt Lake City: Bookcraft, 1990. Stresses the plague that sexual sin has become. In the Book of Mormon immorality is listed as a sin. Nephites at certain times were considered more unrighteous than the Lamanites because of their immoral practices. The three great sins that plagued Book of Mormon peoples were denying the Holy Ghost, murder, and sexual immorality. [J.W.M.]

T.189 Turner, Rodney. "The Personal Message of the Book of Mormon." In *Know Your Religion: Our Standard Works*, 13-26. Provo, UT: Brigham Young University, 1958. Messages of the Book of Mormon include: free agency—the opportunity to make choices, faith—the key to perfect knowledge and eternal life; doing the right things for the right reason constitutes religion; our personal fellowship with Jesus Christ depends on our doing righteous things because we want to. [J.W.M.]

T.190 Turner, Rodney. "The Prophet Nephi." In *The Book of Mormon First Nephi: The Doctrinal Foundation*, edited by Monte S. Nyman and Charles D. Tate Jr., 79-97. Provo, UT: Brigham Young University Religious Studies Center, 1988. Briefly describes the lineage of Lehi, then examines the portion of the Book of Mormon dealing with Nephi, specifically focusing on Nephi's relationship with his brothers, the confrontation with Laban, Nephi's vision, the kingdom set up by Nephi in the Americas, and the Psalm of Nephi [A.T.]

T.191 Turner, Rodney. "The Three Nephite Churches of Christ." In *The Book of Mormon: The Keystone Scripture*, edited by Paul R. Cheesman, S. Kent Brown, and Charles D. Tate Jr., 100-126. Provo, UT: Brigham Young University Religious Studies Center, 1988. The three churches of "organized bod[ies] of believers in Christ or God" established in the Book of Mormon by Nephi, Alma, and Jesus Christ are discussed. The rise and decline of each are outlined with modern-day applications. [J.A.T.]

T.192 Turner, Rodney. "Two Prophets: Abinadi and Alma." In *Studies in Scripture: 1 Nephi to Alma 29*, edited by Kent P. Jackson, 240-59. Salt Lake City: Deseret Book, 1987. Discusses Mosiah 14-18. Likening Abinadi to John the Baptist, the author points out that both were prophets of the law of Moses. They preached repentance, warned of the judgments of God, and testified of Christ. Both were victims of priestcrafts and both died violent deaths. They were preparatory prophets who paved the way of transition from old covenants under the law of Moses to the new covenants in Christ. Alma assumed the critical role of carrying on the message of salvation that Abinadi had presented and created a Zion society. [J.W.M.]

T.193 Tuttle, A. Theodore. "Field White to Harvest—South America." *IE* 68 (June 1965): 501-2. The South American people are descendants of Israelites who built great civilizations and walked and talked with the risen Lord. The Book of Mormon is a record of their departure from their homeland, their wars, and their destruction. Their legends still contain fragments of their Book of Mormon heritage. [J.W.M.]

T.194 Tuttle, A. Theodore. *South America, Land of Promise*. Provo, UT: Brigham Young University Press, 1964. "A land choice above all other lands" as declared in the Book of Mormon includes South America as well as North America. South America is a land of great potential. The call to students of BYU is to missionary work among the loving but underprivileged people of South America. [J.W.M.]

T.195 Tuttle, Carol Wagner. "I'm Afraid to Talk to My Neighbor about the Church Because . . ." *Ensign* 18 (March 1988): 30-32. Analyzing our feelings is one way to understand our fear concerning giving away a Book of Mormon to nonmember friends, sharing a testimony, or inviting someone to meet the missionaries. [J.W.M.]

T.196 Tvedtnes, John A. "Book of Mormon Tribal Affiliation and Military Caste." In *Warfare in the Book of Mormon*, edited by Stephen D. Ricks and William J. Hamblin, 296-326. Salt Lake City: Deseret Book and FARMS, 1990. Examines evidence that tribal affiliation remained important in Nephite/Lamanite society throughout the entire Book of Mormon period and that military leaders tended to come from certain lineage groups. The author suggests that this is why such Nephite military leaders as Mormon, Moronihah and the two Moronis began their careers at such a young age. [J.A.T.]

T.197 Tvedtnes, John A. "Borrowings from the Parable of Zenos." In *The Allegory of the Olive Tree: The Olive, The Bible, and Jacob 5,* edited by Stephen D. Ricks and John W. Welch, 373-462. Salt Lake City, Deseret Book and FARMS, 1994. Many of the biblical and pseudepigraphic writers had access to the parable of Zenos and they each borrowed elements from it. The task of combining these many elements in order to write Jacob 5 would have been far beyond the capabilities of Joseph Smith. [J.W.M.]

T.198 Tvedtnes, John A. "Burial as a Return to the Womb in Ancient Near Eastern Belief." *SEHA* 152 (March 1983): 5-7. A textual and etymological study of evidence that the tomb was, in the ancient Near East, considered to be like the mother's womb. One of the words examined is the Hebrew *maqôm*, normally rendered "place" in English. Author cites examples of the use of the word in the Bible and Phoenician texts that mean "tomb." Examples from the Book of Mormon of the English word "place" are similarly used. [J.A.T.]

T.199 Tvedtnes, John A. "Colophons in the Book of Mormon." In *Rediscovering the Book of Mormon*, edited by John L. Sorenson and Melvin J. Thorne, 32-37. Salt Lake City: Deseret Book and FARMS, 1991. Defines colophons as signposts that most often appear following a text to recap, explain, or mark the end. Nephi and editors that followed him included many prefaces to the materials they abridged as well as summaries to conclude. These important highlights show the amount of editorial judgment required by the editors. [J.W.M.]

T.200 Tvedtnes, John A. "Composition and History of the Book of Mormon." *NE* 4 (September 1974): 41-43. A brief explanation of the origin and transmission of the various records compiled by Mormon into the book that bears his name. Accompanied by a flow chart. [J.A.T.]

T.201 Tvedtnes, John A. "Hebraisms in the Book of Mormon: A Preliminary Survey." *BYU Studies* 11 (Autumn 1970): 50-60. A condensed version also found in "The Hebrew Background of the Book of Mormon." In *Rediscovering the Book of Mormon*, edited by John L. Sorenson and Melvin J. Thorne, 77-91. Salt Lake City: Deseret Book and FARMS, 1991; and in "I Have a Question: Since the Book of Mormon is largely the record of a Hebrew people, is the writing characteristic of the Hebrew language." *Ensign* 16 (October 1986), 64-66. Modified for publication in *A Sure Foundation: Answers to Difficult Gospel Questions* 21-26. Salt Lake City: Deseret Book. A survey of Hebraisms—Hebrew words, idioms, and expressions—contained in the Book of Mormon. The Hebraisms anciently endured the language alterations of the Nephites (see Mormon 9:33) and in the nineteenth century survived the translation of the gold plates from "reformed Egyptian" (Mormon 9:32) to English. Several Hebrew types found in the Book of Mormon are identified, including Hebrew plurals, idiomatic words and expressions, the repetition of the conjunction "and," pronominal suffixes, the construct state, adverbs, the cognate accusative, and the employment of the Hebrew prepositional phrase *bo*. [D.W.P.]

T.202 Tvedtnes, John A. "I Have A Question: What were the ages of Helaman's 'stripling warriors'?" *Ensign* 22 (September 1992): 28. Using the law of Moses' stipulation that Israelite soldiers be at least twenty years old, Tvedtnes examines the circumstances and time frame surrounding the people of Ammon, their oath, and their sons' appearance as valiant soldiers. Concludes that it is highly probable that the stripling warriors were between 21 and 26. [A.C.W.]

T.203 Tvcdtness, John A. "Identification." *NE* 5 (May 1975): 50. A quiz to identify characters from the Book of Mormon and the Bible. [J.W.M.]

T.204 Tvedtnes, John A. "Isaiah Variants in the Book of Mormon." In *Isaiah and the Prophets*, edited by Monte Nyman, 165-77. Salt Lake City: Bookcraft, 1984. See a similar discussion in "The Isaiah Variants in The Book of Mormon." Provo, UT: FARMS, 1983. Originally presented at the "Isaiah and the Prophets" symposium held at Brigham Young University on March 19-20, 1982, this paper is a much abbreviated version of the longer study of the same name. Author selects various types of variants from the original study, with emphasis on those supporting the Book of Mormon version of Isaiah. [J.A.T.]

T.205 Tvedtnes, John A. "King Benjamin and the Feast of Tabernacles." In *By Study and Also by Faith*, edited by John M. Lundquist and Stephen D. Ricks, 2:197-237. Salt Lake City: Deseret Book and FARMS, 1990. A considerably expanded version of the author's 1978 article, "The Nephite Feast of Tabernacles." The revision presents additional evidence to support the idea that the Nephite gathering in Zarahemla under King Benjamin was in celebration of the Israelite Feast of Tabernacles. [J.A.T.]

T.206 Tvedtnes, John A. "The Language of my Father." *NE* 1 (May 1971): 19. A combination Hebrew/Egyptian text was found at Arad, which may contain language similar to the "reformed Egyptian" in which the original Book of Mormon was written. [J.A.T.]

T.207 Tvedtnes, John A. "Linguistic Implications of the Tel-Arad Ostraca." *SEHA* 127 (October 1971). Originally presented as a paper at the 20th annual Symposium on the Archaeology of the Scriptures & Allied Fields, the article examines some of the sixth century Hebrew ostraca uncovered at Arad, with emphasis on a combination Hebrew/Egyptian text that may be similar to the "reformed Egyptian" in which the original Book of Mormon was written. [J.A.T.]

T.208 Tvedtnes, John A. "Mormon's Editorial Promises." In *Rediscovering the Book of Mormon*, edited by John L. Sorenson and Melvin J. Thorne, 29-31. Salt Lake City: Deseret Book and FARMS, 1991. The consistency in Mormon's work as an editor is illustrated by the promises he made to return to specific topics and the fulfillment of those promises. In some cases, it was Mormon's son who accomplished what his father had set out to do. The author concludes that Mormon planned and executed his work. [J.A.T.]

T.209 Tvedtnes, John A. "The Nephite Feast of Tabernacles." Provo, UT: FARMS, 1978. Also in *Tinkling Cymbals: Essays in Honor of Hugh Nibley*, edited by John W. Welch, 145-77. Provo, UT: John W. Welch, 1978. An examination of textual evidence that the Nephite assembly conducted by King Benjamin in the city of Zarahemla (Mosiah 2-6) was a celebration of the Israelite Feast of Tabernacles. The author elicits evidence from the Bible and the Mishnah. [J.A.T.]

T.210 Tvedtnes, John A. "A Phonemic Analysis of Nephite and Jaredite Proper Names." *SEHA* 141 (December 1977): 1-8. Originally presented as a paper at the 22nd annual Symposium on the Archaeology of the Scriptures & Allied Fields, the article analyzes the sound system of the Nephite and Jaredite languages, using transliterations of names from these languages found in the English Book of Mormon. The author concludes that the Nephite names reflect the phonology of the Hebrew language, while the Jaredite names have a different origin. [J.A.T.]

T.211 Tvedtnes, John A. "The Sons of Mosiah: Emissaries of Peace." In *Warfare in the Book of Mormon*, edited by Stephen D. Ricks and William J. Hamblin, 118-24. Salt Lake City: Deseret Book and FARMS, 1990. Presents evidence from the Book of Mormon that the primary impetus for the Lamanite mission of the sons of Mosiah was to establish peaceful relations between the Nephites and the Lamanites. [J.A.T.]

T.212 Tvedtnes, John A. "The Timing of Christ's Appearance to the Nephites." In *When Did Jesus Appear to the Nephites in Bountiful*. Provo, UT: FARMS, 1989. Originally presented as a paper at the annual Symposium on the Archaeology of the Scriptures & Allied Fields, October 1988, the article challenges proposals by Kent Brown and Jerome Horowitz that Christ's appearance to the Nephites in the city Bountiful took place several months after his resurrection. [J.A.T.]

T.213 Tvedtnes, John A. "Vineyard or Olive Orchard?" In *The Allegory of the Olive Tree: The Olive, The Bible, and Jacob 5*, edited by

Stephen D. Ricks and John W. Welch, 477-83. Salt Lake City, Deseret Book and FARMS, 1994. Also published as a preliminary report as "Vineyard or Olive Orchard?" Provo, UT: FARMS, 1992. Discusses the term *vineyard* and the term *orchard* as used in Jacob 5 and in the King James Bible. Semitic languages may imply a more general meaning to the word translated as vineyard. The broader sense of the word means "generous, good, fertile land," and may include both orchard and vineyard in Egyptian. In Coptic it may mean garden. The use of the word in Jacob 5 follows ancient tradition. [J.W.M.]

T.214 Tvedtnes, John A. "Was Lehi a Caravaneer?" Provo, UT: FARMS, 1984. Challenges Nibley's suggestion (in *Lehi in the Desert*) that Lehi was involved in the caravan trade. He provides evidence that this was not the case and elicits evidence that Lehi's family may have been involved in metallurgy. [J.A.T.]

T.215 Tvedtnes, John A. "Was Mormon a Member of a Military Class?" *SEHA* 163 (April 1988): 3-5. Suggests that Mormon became a military leader because he belonged to a military caste whose responsibility it was to lead the Nephite armies. [J.A.T.]

T.216 "Twenty-Second Day of September." *MS* 98 (16 September 1937): 600-601. Discusses the translation Joseph Smith made of the golden plates, the conclusion scholars have made, the Three Witnesses, and the Eight Witnesses. [L.D.]

T.217 Tyler, Daniel. "The Book of Mormon." *Juvenile Instructor* 12 (1 July 1877, 15 July 1877, 1 August 1877, 15 August 1877, 15 September 1877): 147-48, 159-60, 170-71, 182-83, 212-13. Series on Book of Mormon evidences taken from Isaiah 29, Ezekiel 37, and Genesis 48 and 49. Accepts as valid the testimonies of the Book of Mormon witnesses. [D.M.]

U.

U.001 Ultican, Helen. "Joy Comes in Witnessing about the Book of Mormon." In *Recent Book of Mormon Development, Articles from the Zarahemla Record*, 2:165. Independence, MO: Zarahemla Research Foundation, 1992. A testimony of the joy of sharing and witnessing of the Book of Mormon. [B.D.]

U.002 Ultican, Helen. "Lifted up in Pride." *ZR* 29-31 (Summer/Fall 1985/Winter 1986): 11, 21-22. A topical study of teaching about pride in the Book of Mormon. The author has found 61 references and reprints several of these passages with a commentary on each. The author cautions readers to avoid the snare of pride. [A.T.]

U.003 Underwood, Grant. "Book of Mormon Usage in Early LDS Theology." *Dialogue* 17 (Autumn 1984): 35-74. Doctrinal history or historical theology must be founded in scripture. This study explores the pre-Utah period of the use of Book of Mormon scriptures and identifies scriptures that were used most frequently and how they were understood. A comprehensive study is made with tables, graphs, and index references. [J.W.M.]

U.004 Underwood, Grant. "The Earliest Reference Guides to the Book of Mormon." *Journal of Mormon History* 12 (1985): 69-89. The study of the interpretations of the Book of Mormon text in the early days of the Church is helped by three documents called "reference guides." One is thought to have been printed in Kirtland in 1835, another in 1841 as part of the first European edition of the Book of Mormon, and the third a year later in Philadelphia, about which little is known. [J.W.M.]

U.005 Underwood, Grant. "Insights from the Early Years: 2 Nephi 28-30." In *The Book of Mormon: Second Nephi, The Doctrinal Structure*, edited by Monte S. Nyman and Charles D. Tate Jr., 323-39. Salt Lake City: Bookcraft, 1989. Life's experience was a great testimony to early Saints of the validity of the Book of Mormon because 2 Nephi 28-30 described the religious beliefs that prevailed in their day. Some early Mormon writers drew parallels between the

U.006 Underwood, Grant. "Jacob 5 in the Nineteenth Century." In *The Allegory of the Olive Tree: The Olive, the Bible, and Jacob 5,* edited by Stephen D. Ricks and John W. Welch, 50-69. Salt Lake City: Deseret Book and FARMS, 1994. Early leaders of the Church understood the allegory of the olive tree and saw their roles as servants of the Lord to assist in the final pruning and grafting in of the Master's vineyard. They saw themselves as a true branch of the olive tree planted in the poorest spot of ground, and used passages of Jacob 5 in their sermons to encourage members to do good works and promote the building of Zion. [J.W.M.]

U.007 Underwood, Grant R. "The Millenarian World of Early Mormonism." Ph.D. diss., University of California, Los Angeles, 1988. Includes a chapter entitled, "The Book of Mormon and the Millenarian mind." Deals with the relationship between the Book of Mormon and early LDS concepts of the New Jerusalem, the role of the Lamanites as descendants of Joseph, and the gathering of Israel. Includes tables on early Book of Mormon citations in Church publications. [D.M.]

U.008 "Update: Translation of the Book of Mormon." *Ensign* 21 (April 1991): 75. For twenty years after publication the Book of Mormon was printed only in English, but during the next 127 years, 31 translations were completed, and in the past 11 years, 64 new translations have been made. [J.W.M.]

U.009 Urrutia, Benjamin. "The Name Connection." *NE* 13 (June 1983): 38-41. A brief report on the possible origins and meaning of select Book of Mormon proper names—i.e., Mormon, Cumorah, Shiblon, and Mosiah. [J.A.T.]

U.010 Urrutia, Benjamin. "Shiblon, Coriantumr, and the Jade Jaguars." *SEHA* 150 (August 1982): 1-3. The names "Shiblon" and "Corianton" relate to the lion cub. In ancient America the jaguar, which is in the same family as the lion, was prominent, as found in several artifacts. These relationships may go back to the Jaredites. [D.M.]

U.011 "Use Book of Mormon to Counter Error, President Benson Teaches." *Ensign* 19 (January 1989): 75-76. Ezra Taft Benson told members to "use the Book of Mormon in handling objections to the Church." He gave a four-step method on how to do so and said that the Book of Mormon "exposes the enemies of Christ, confounds false doctrine, lays down contentions, and fortifies the humble followers of Christ." [M.D.P.]

V.

V.001 Valletta, Thomas R. "The Captain and the Covenant." In *The Book of Mormon: Alma, The Testimony of the Word*, edited by Monte S. Nyman and Charles D. Tate Jr., 223-48. Provo, UT: Brigham Young University Religious Studies Center, 1992. A tribute to Moroni, a great man and general who used the covenant-making process to bring about peace between the Nephites and their enemies. Moroni defended his people's liberty and Mormon added this to his record for us to use in our times. [N.K.Y.]

V.002 Van Allsburg, Phillip W., Jr. *The Book of Mormon Dictionary: A Reference Guide for Young People.* Monongahela, PA: n.p., 1983. Simplified for young people, this dictionary booklet provides definitions and illustrations of Book of Mormon words. [J.W.M.]

V.003 Van Den Berghe, Elizabeth S. "His Faith Began with Physics." *Ensign* 23 (August 1993): 70-73. Narrates the conversion of Tom Ngo to the LDS Church. A physics student, Tom gained a testimony of the Book of Mormon by studying its philosophical chapters first and by praying about its truthfulness. [S.H.]

V.004 Van Orden, Bruce A. "An Examination of the Strategies of Instruction Employed by Prophets and Teachers in the Book of Mormon and Their Potential Application to Current LDS Instructional Settings." M.A. thesis, Brigham

Young University, 1975. A report on general philosophical principles of teaching and learning found in the Book of Mormon. Analysis of prominent figures such as Lehi, Nephi, Mormon, Alma, and Jesus Christ reveals their teaching preparation, purposes, and style, providing examples and principles of applications for current teachers in the LDS education system. [J.T.]

V.005 Van Orden, Bruce A. "The Indispensable Role and Activities of Unnamed Teachers in the Book of Mormon." In *A Symposium on the Book of Mormon*, 102-5. Salt Lake City: Church of Jesus Christ of Latter-day Saints, 1979. Little is said about those appointed to be priests and teachers under Jacob, Mosiah, King Benjamin, Alma, Alma the younger, and other leaders. The teachers are not named, but their work was vital to the success of the Church in those times. The same is true in the Church today. [N.K.Y.]

V.006 Van Orden, Bruce A. "George Reynolds: Loyal Friend of the Book of Mormon." *Ensign* 16 (August 1986): 48-51. This article traces the life of George Reynolds, emphasizing his love of the Book of Mormon and his work in studying and writing about it—especially for the purpose of training the youth of the Church in the Book of Mormon's history and doctrine. [S.P.S.]

V.007 Van Orden, Bruce A. "The Law of Witnesses in 2 Nephi." In *The Book of Mormon: Second Nephi, The Doctrinal Structure*, edited by Monte S. Nyman and Charles D. Tate Jr., 307-21. Salt Lake City: Bookcraft, 1989. When revealing any new information to men, the Lord has always followed the law of witnesses. When a new dispensation is inaugurated there is more than one witness. Second Nephi is consistent with this law. In 2 Nephi 11, Nephi explicitly applies this law and connects the testimonies of Jacob, Nephi, and Isaiah with his own. His purpose is to prove to mankind of the mission and reality of Christ and that all men must come to him or perish. [J.W.M.]

V.008 Van Orden, Bruce A. "Sanctification by the Holy Ghost." In *Doctrines of the Book of Mormon, 1991 Sperry Symposium*, edited by Bruce A. Van Orden and Brent L. Top, 212-22. Salt Lake City: Deseret Book, 1992. The Book of Mormon speaks of sanctification by the Holy Ghost and by the blood of Christ. Alma teaches no one can be saved except his garments are cleansed from sin by the blood of Christ. The author lists 14 steps of sanctification given by Nephi and 27 teachings in Alma 5 that lead to sanctification. Alma concludes when we can not look on sin save it is with abhorrence, the process of sanctification is working. We must practice faith, repentance, develop humility, and yield our hearts unto God. [N. K. Y.]

V.009 Van Orden, Bruce A. " 'We Prophesy of Christ.' " *Ensign* 20 (February 1990): 22-25. 2 Nephi is a record of four witnesses of Christ: Lehi, Jacob, Isaiah and Nephi. Each bear testimony of the restoration of Israel and of the importance of the atonement in the lives of individuals. [J.W.M.]

V.010 Van Orden, Dell, and Malan Heslop. "Book of Mormon—Place in Time." *CN* 53 (27 November 1983, 4 December 1983): 8-9, 8-9. Chart synchronizing Book of Mormon events with biblical and secular history, beginning with the Jaredites and continuing until the Nephite destruction. [A.C.W.]

V.011 Van Wagenen, Genevieve. "Get Out of That Rocking Chair." *IE* 67 (September 1964): 741. Author visited the grave of Oliver Cowdery, whose testimony of the Book of Mormon is found on the headstone. She desired to tell the Church membership to read the Book of Mormon, it contains hidden treasures. [J.W.M.]

V.012 Vance, Joseph A. "Book of Mormon Readings." *MS* 72 (7 April 1910): 212-15. Advances two explanations of how Joseph Smith was provided with duplicate texts covering the material in the lost 116 pages of translation. [R.H.B.]

V.013 Vandenberg, John H. "The Book of Mormon Restores Truth." *CR* (April 1974): 14-17. Members of the Church of Jesus Christ of Latter-day Saints are sometimes called "Mormons" because of the great prophet Mormon whose magnificent work was to write and compose most of the Book of Mormon. The book restores or expands upon many precious true doctrines, such as the nature of the godhead, corporeal individuality, revelation, and man's purpose and destiny. [R.C.D.]

V.014 Vandenberg, John H. "Touchstone of Truth." *Ensign* 4 (May 1974): 11-13. Also in *CR* 144 (April 1974): 14-17. As a result of the apostasy numerous truths have been lost from the Bible. Many of the truths have been restored in the Book of Mormon. [B.T.]

V.015 Vellinga, M. C. *Mormon Mysteries Revealed*. Los Angeles, CA: West Coast Publishing, 1927. Writes on a variety of Book of Mormon related subjects to show how the Mormon use of the Bible is incorrect. Discusses the restoration of the gospel by Joseph Smith, the coming forth of the Book of Mormon, the cessation of revelation, the antiquity of the Book of Mormon, "other sheep," and other items. Attempts to dispel the myths by using correct interpretations of the Bible. Finds that Joseph Smith is the author of the Book of Mormon. [J.W.M.]

V.016 Velt, Harold Iven. *America's Lost Civilizations*. Independence, MO: Herald House, 1948-1949. The high culture and notable achievements found in the archaeology of early American civilizations are outlined and shown to be consistent with the description of civilization found in the Book of Mormon. Christian influence in America before Columbus and Hebrew/Egyptian origins of American aborigines are also discussed in relation to the Book of Mormon. [J.T.]

V.017 Velt, Harold Iven. *The Riddle of American Origins*. Independence, MO: Herald House, 1941. Uses the Book of Mormon to answer some archaeological riddles, primarily the sudden appearance of great civilizations and subsequent degeneration in ancient America when an evolutionary process would normally be expected. [J.T.]

V.018 Velt, Harold Iven. *The Sacred Book of Ancient America*. Independence, MO: Herald House, 1952. Biblical prophecies fulfilled by the Book of Mormon and the lives and testimonies of the witnesses of the golden plates are reported and shown to support the authenticity of the Book of Mormon. The physical attributes, theological contents, and prophecies of the golden plates (Book of Mormon) are also discussed. [J.T.]

V.019 Vernon, Gregory G. "The Lord Finds a Scripture." In *Stories of Insight and Inspiration,* edited by Margie Calhoun Jensen, 32-34. Salt Lake City, UT: Bookcraft, 1976. Missionaries working in Alaska were prompted to let the Book of Mormon fall open to any scripture and the book opened to the story of Hagoth. The lady they were teaching was touched by the similarities to her own tribal traditions and indicated that the name Hagoth was familiar to her. [J.W.M.]

V.020 Vessels, Rodney J. *The Book of Mormon Speaks*. Minneapolis, MN: University of Minnesota Press, 1973. Analyzes the "rhetorical vision" in the Book of Mormon by looking at examples of discourse in the record, such as King Benjamin's address and the missionary discussions given by the sons of Mosiah. Demonstrates how salvation is proclaimed through the spoken word. [A.C.W.]

V.021 Vessels, Rodney J. "I Want to Be a Book of Mormon Missionary." *NE* 6 (April 1976): 6-8. Vessels tells of his experiences reading the Book of Mormon and lists five ways to become a Book of Mormon missionary. [M.D.P.]

V.022 Vest, H. Grant. "The Problem of Isaiah in the Book of Mormon." M.S. thesis, Brigham Young University, 1938. A textual analysis of the Isaiah scriptures found in the Book of Mormon compared with the King James Version. The similarities, often word for word, between the two texts are explained, but greater emphasis is given to the many differences found in the comparison. Where differences are noted, the Book of Mormon agrees with other versions of Isaiah texts—i.e. the Syriac, Septuagint, and Latin versions. Other differences are found to be Joseph Smith's own word choice while translating. [J.T.]

V.023 Vestal, Kirk H., and Arthur Wallace. *The Firm Foundation of Mormonism*. Los Angeles: LL Co., 1981. An apologetic work attempting to demonstrate evidence supporting Mormon beliefs. The authors provide a review of some of the evidence tending to support the Book of Mormon's complexity and authenticity. Among the topics discussed pertaining to the Book of Mormon are the Eleven Witnesses, archaeology, linguistic complexities, proper names, the allegory in Jacob 5, the Nephite monetary system, modern philosophies predicted by Book of Mormon writers, and others. [M.R.]

V.024 Vincent, Joseph E. "Some Views on Book of Mormon Geography." In *14th Symposium on Archaeology of the Scriptures*, 61-69. Provo, UT: Brigham Young University Press, 1963. See a similar discussion in *Book of Mormon Lands*. Mentone, CA: GEMAC, 1960?. Problems and methodology in defining Book of Mormon boundaries and geographic locations of cities, rivers, etc. are outlined. A map is included giving the author's version of Book of Mormon geography. [J.T.]

W.

W.001 W., H. L. "The Question Box." *Christian Century* (30 June 1937): 841. Deuteronomy 5:22 records that the Lord wrote the Ten Commandments on stone tablets and Joseph Smith claims that the Lord gave him a record engraved on plates of gold. The question is what became of these plates? There are many ancient accounts of deities who delivered the law to an intermediary. This book holds a place of honor in the Mormon Church because of its supposed divine origin. [J.W.M.]

W.002 W., J. F. "On Proving the Book of Mormon." *MS* 81 (16 October 1919): 664-66. The manner in which individuals prove the Book of Mormon to be true is by applying Moroni's promise (Moroni 10:3-5)—by praying to God in the name of Jesus, having faith and a sincere heart. [D.W.P.]

W.003 W., R. C. "Egyptology and the Book of Mormon." *IE* 26 (February 1923, March 1923, April 1923): 311-27, 437-47, 546-54. Attempts to demonstrate the philological plausibility of the Book of Mormon. The author describes the reliability of Mormon 9:32-33, which says that to save space on the plates the authors wrote in a reformed or shorthand Egyptian, but that if they could have written in Hebrew the record would have been more precise. [D.M.]

W.004 Waddoups, William. "Martin Harris and the Book of Mormon." *IE* 26 (September 1923): 980-81. A presentation of two recorded testimonies of Martin Harris concerning his vision as one of the Three Witnesses. [D.M.]

W.005 Wadsworth, Richard. "I Have a Question: Does the Book of Mormon prophesy of the prophet Joseph Smith?" *Ensign* 19 (April 1989): 52-53. Rarely is a prophet named by name in prophesy; however his mission is often foretold. The Book of Mormon has ten references to Joseph Smith's mission. [J.W.M.]

W.006 Wakefield, Chris. *The Book of Mormon Chart of Men in Office*. Idaho Falls, ID: C. L. Wakefield, 1984. A chronological chart of every man mentioned in the Book of Mormon and the offices held by each—i.e., prophet, king, military personality. [J.T.]

W.007 Waldman, Nahum, Alan Goff, and John W. Welch. "The Breaking of the Bow." Provo, UT: FARMS, 1983. The breaking of the bow symbolism of Near Eastern culture is present in the Book of Mormon. The symbolism has four parts: It represents military power, symbolizes the establishment of political mastery, exalts the power of God in the Old Testament, and symbolizes sexual vigor. Nephi's brothers accuse him of usurping power; while the bow was broken there was no peace. [J.W.M.]

W.008 Walker, Gary Lee. "The Downfall of the Nephite Nation: Lessons for Our Time." In *Studies in Scripture: Alma 30 to Moroni*, edited by Kent P. Jackson, 139-48. Salt Lake City: Deseret Book, 1988. So murderous had the Gadianton robbers become in 3 Nephi 6-10, that the Lamanites and Nephites banded together and through their repentance they were delivered. Three short years found them prosperous and proud. Secret combinations arose to destroy the people of God and chaos reigned; tribal organization prevailed. Studying these chapters and applying the lessons found therein to our day is essential. [J.W.M.]

W.009 Walker, Steven C. "More Than Meets the Eye: Concentration of the Book of Mormon." *BYU Studies* 20 (1980): 199-205. The Book of Mormon is a literary concentrated book, with few excess words, rare verbal superfluity, and little prolix. Its density compares to that of the King James Version of the Bible. Speaking of Book of Mormon history Walker states, "The Book of Mormon manages to cram over three thousand years' worth of complex migrations and wars and political upheavals and cultural evolutions and intimately detailed religious chronicles of several peoples into its 522 pages." Not only is the history concentrated, with selections and wording carefully chosen by inspired writers and editors, but the Book of Mormon contains many figures of speech that demonstrate stylistic brevity—such as aphorisms, parallelisms, humor, questions, and chiasmus. [D.W.P.]

W.010 Walker, Steven C., and Richard S. Van Wagoner. "Joseph Smith: 'The Gift of Seeing'." In *A Book of Mormons*, 287-94. Salt Lake City: Signature, 1982. Joseph Smith was the recipient of the plates at the hands of Moroni, and the subsequent translation was through the gift and power of God. [J.W.M.]

W.011 Wallace, Arthur. "The Allegory of the Tame and the Wild Olive Trees Horticulturally Considered." In *Scriptures for the Modern World*, edited by Paul R. Cheesman and C. Wilfred Griggs, 113-20. Provo, UT: Brigham Young University Religious Studies Center, 1984. The horticultural preciseness in the allegory of the olive tree recorded in Jacob 5-6 helps to show that Joseph Smith did not write the Book of Mormon, but translated it. Whoever wrote the allegory had a profound knowledge of the science of olive tree cultivation. [B.D.]

W.012 Wallace, Arthur. *Can Mormonism be Proved Experimentally?* Ann Arbor, MI: Edward Brothers, 1973. Argues that science and religion cannot "prove" or "disprove" the existence of God; however, reason and faith each have their role to play in the pursuit of truth. Modern scientific methods along with modern revelation (i.e. Joseph Smith and the Book of Mormon) are outlined as means for drawing conclusions concerning the reality of God. [J.T.]

W.013 Wallace, Arthur, compl. *America's Witness for Jesus Christ: The Book of Mormon*. Salt Lake City: Utah Publishers Press, 1978. An abridged version of the Book of Mormon with an emphasis on Christ-related material. Also includes an index of name-titles used in the Book of Mormon to describe Christ. [J.T.]

W.014 Wallace, Henry A. "Wallace Extols Power of Great Books As National Fair Is Opened by Publishers." *New York Times* (5 November 1937): 3. Many books, including the Bible, are cited for their powerful influence, and the Book of Mormon is extolled as "the most powerful" American religious book to come forth in the nineteenth century. Though it has affected only one percent of the people, that percentage was affected in such a profound way as to affect the whole of the United States. [J.W.M.]

W.015 Wallis, James H. "A Fascinating Story." *MS* 95 (6 April 1933): 225-29. Book of Mormon gives world new light on ancient history. Archaeology confirms its truth. Quetzalcoatl stems from Christ's visit. Hagoth's expeditions possibly settled South Pacific islands. Politics and war are highly developed in Book of Mormon, which is a divine record. [A.C.W.]

W.016 Walton, Veva (Fike). "A Review of the Book of Mormon." *An Album of Reviews* 9 (1966): 1-6. A straightforward description of the Book of Mormon. Concludes that the Book of Mormon will provide interesting reading for those who are interested in the gospel as taught in the Bible. [D.M.]

W.017 Wandell, Charles W. "Letter." *TS* 2 (15 September 1841): 544-45. Missionary letter sent to the *Times and Seasons*. Includes an excerpt of a statement by Charles Anthon, who describes the characters given to him by Martin Harris, with the intention of discrediting the LDS story about him. The author then cites works by Humboldt, Raffinesque, and Stephens to argue that Anthon's description unwittingly coincides with inscriptions found in Latin America. [D.M.]

W.018 "War and the Art of War among Book of Mormon Peoples." *Relief Society Magazine* 5 (October 1918): 592-96. Methods of warfare in the Book of Mormon were elementary in the beginning but became more sophisticated with time and under Moroni grew to an art. Still the weapons were crude and the armaments were fairly ineffective and many people were killed, ravaged, and raped. [J.W.M.]

W.019 Ward, John H. "Ancient American Civilization." *Juvenile Instructor* 18 (1 January 1883): 4-7. Relates the Book of Mormon to archaeological finds throughout the Americas. Discusses marriage customs, baptism, and legends. Adds information about the Mexican calendar, textiles, and landscaping. [D.M.]

W.020 Ward, John H. *The Hand of Providence: As Shown in the History of Nations and Individuals, From the Great Apostasy to the Restoration of the Gospel.* Salt Lake City: Juvenile Instructor's Office, 1883. Relics have been discovered in almost every part of the western continent which testify of ancient civilizations. Ancient civilizations of America were highly developed. The Book of Mormon is their record. There are many evidences that indicate this is true: breast plates, elephant remains, architecture, bronze, fine cloth, and many others. [J.W.M.]

W.021 Ward, Thomas. "American Antiquities." *MS* 7 (1 March 1846, 15 March 1846): 67-71, 85-87. *Millennial Star* editor quotes writings by Josiah Priest and others concerning mounds found in the U.S., and then quotes excerpts from the book of Alma dealing with Moroni and his fortifications. [D.M.]

W.022 Ward, Thomas. "The Book of Mormon." *MS* 6 (15 August 1845): 65-70. Sacred works other than those contained in the Bible exist, as biblical authors have recorded—the Book of Jasher, Book of the Acts of Solomon, Book of Nathan, Book of Gad, and others. Using Old Testament references, the author claims that the seed of Abraham occupied the American Continent as well as the Old World. The stick of Joseph and the stick of Judah are combined in the Book of Mormon and the Bible. [J.W.M.]

W.023 Warner, C. Terry. "Jacob." *Ensign* 6 (October 1976): 24-30. Jacob was a powerful teacher who had seen Christ face to face and enjoyed the ministrations of angels. Jacob was born in the wilderness, listened to Laman and Lemuel contend with his father and brother, and was not deceived. He faced Sherem, the anti-Christ, and also recorded the allegory of Zenos. [J.W.M.]

W.024 Warner, C. Terry. "An Open Letter to Students: On Having Faith and Thinking for Yourself." *NE* 1 (November 1971): 14-19. Uses the story of Alma and Korihor to teach about faith and reasoning. [M.D.P.]

W.025 Warner, Elisha. *Old Testament Patriarchs.* Salt Lake City: Max Warner, 1966. Contains many teachings of the Book of Mormon concerning the Old Testament patriarchs and a talk on the Book of Mormon. The author gives his view of what the Book of Mormon is and why Mormon wrote the book. [J.W.M.]

W.026 Warner, Ross W. *The Fulfillment of Book of Mormon Prophecies.* Salt Lake City: Hawkes, 1975. Believes that the Holy Ghost is the primary witness of the Book of Mormon but suggests that the reader's testimony of the book will also be enhanced by understanding the fulfillment of Book of Mormon prophecies. Prophecies discussed pertain to the coming forth of the Book of Mormon, Joseph the seer, America, the land of promise, the Gentiles, the Lamanites, the Jews, and the idea that there would be two churches only. [R.J.L.]

W.027 Warner, Ross W. "Prophecies in the Book of Mormon Relating to Our Times." In *A Symposium on the Book of Mormon*, 106-8. Salt Lake City: Church of Jesus Christ of Latter-day Saints, 1979. Provides a list of 54 prophecies given in the Book of Mormon and supplies a reference to where they have been discussed in Church literature. [N.K.Y.]

W.028 Warner, Ross W. "A Study of Problems Relative to the Fulfillment of Selected Prophecies in the Book of Mormon, with Particular Reference to the Prophetic View from 1830 Onward." M.S. thesis, Brigham Young University, 1961. "The purpose of this study is to classify under appropriate headings the prophecies of the Book of Mormon relating to the period 1830 to 1961, to see what evidence exists regarding the fulfillment of such prophecies and to summarize the findings. These prophecies have been classified under the following chapter headings: the Book of Mormon, Joseph the seer, America—land of promise, the Gentiles, the Lamanites, the Jews, and two churches only." [A.T.]

W.029 Warren, Bruce W. "A Cautious Interpretation of Mesoamerican Myth: Reflections Upon Olmec-Jaredite Roots." *SEHA* 154 (July 1983): 1-8. Suggests that some of the legends of the Popol Vuh have affinities with the book of Ether. Notes the meaning of "Shiblon" (lion cub) and a possible connection with Ixbalan (little jaguar). [D.M.]

W.030 Warren, Bruce W. "Secret Combinations, Warfare, and Captive Sacrifice in Mesoamerica and the Book of Mormon." In *Warfare in the Book of Mormon*, edited by Stephen D. Ricks and William J. Hamblin, 225-36. Salt Lake City: Deseret Book and FARMS, 1990. Writes concerning secret combinations and human sacrifice among Jaredite, Nephite, and later Mesoamerican societies, and sets forth their cruelty and depravity. [N.K.Y.]

W.031 Warren, Bruce W., and Thomas Stuart Ferguson. *The Messiah In Ancient America*. Provo, UT: Book of Mormon Research Foundation, 1987. New archaeological discoveries in Mesoamerica confirm the validity of the Book of Mormon. The authors discuss historical accounts, traditions, and myths and display photographs of ancient pictographs concerning Quetzalcoatl as the Christ figure in America who taught Christian values and ordinances. The Book of Mormon is another testament of Jesus Christ. [J.W.M.]

W.032 Washburn, Jesse A. *Chronology Chart: Bible and Book of Mormon Events*. Provo, UT: n.p., 1928. Contains four maps and a long fold-out chronological chart showing sacred and secular events from both the Bible and the Book of Mormon. [D.M.]

W.033 Washburn, Jesse A. "A Study of the Geography of the Book of Mormon as Found within the Record Itself." M.S. thesis, Brigham Young University, 1940. Examines the travel and geographical locations of the Jaredites, Mulekites, Nephites, and Lamanites. The issue of birth and death rates in relation to population size is also discussed. [R.J.L.]

W.034 Washburn, Jesse A., and Jesse N. Washburn. *An Approach to the Study of Book of Mormon Geography*. Provo, UT: NE, 1939. The author believes the geographical background of Book of Mormon events influences other aspects of the record, such as doctrinal interpretations. Scriptural references of the travel and place locations of the Jaredites, Mulekites, Nephites, and Lamanites are enhanced by discussion of population sizes, simple maps, and other illustrations. [R.J.L.]

W.035 Washburn, Jesse A., and Jesse N. Washburn. *From Babel to Cumorah*. Provo, UT: New Era Publishing, 1937, [R]1958. This book conveys in narrative form the journeys of the Book of Mormon people, beginning with the Jaredites and concluding with Moroni. Provides a chronological sequence of events contained in the sacred record. [J.W.M.]

W.036 Washburn, Jesse N. *Book of Mormon Guidebook and Certain Problems in the Book of Mormon*. Orem: Washburn, 1968. A student manual that discusses the geographical setting, organizational structure, and narrative storyline of the Book of Mormon. To a lesser extent, doctrinal teachings are also examined. These areas of study are divided into three parts involving the Jaredites, Mulekites, and Nephites. [R.J.L.]

W.037 Washburn, Jesse N. *Book of Mormon Lands and Times*. Bountiful: Horizon, 1974. Exploring the commentary, narrative, and setting of the Book of Mormon, Washburn applies scholarly and geographical theory to point out the consistency of detail. Such consistency helps establish its divine origin. [J.W.M.]

W.038 Washburn, Jesse N. *The Contents, Structure and Authorship of the Book of Mormon*. Salt Lake City: Bookcraft, 1954. Analyzes the complex nature of the Book of Mormon, chapter by chapter, and looks at poetry, message, historical narrative, parables, and language. The Book of Mormon will stand any test for authenticity. [J.W.M.]

W.039 Washburn, Jesse N. *The Miracle of the Book of Mormon.* Orem, UT: Book Production Services, 1984. Divides the Book of Mormon into elements of doctrine, narrative, geography, structure, and miscellany. Correlates Book of Mormon scriptures with biblical chronological events, divides the geography into four lands (maps are included), the way in which the book is presented, and miscellaneous items of poetry and chiasmus. [J.W.M.]

W.040 Watson, Wingfield. *The Book of Mormon. An Essay on Its Claims and Prophecies.* Boyne, MI: n.p., 1884. In defense of the Book of Mormon, this author briefly explains the contents of the book, then gives twelve truths about it, some of which are: no man can prove that it is not true; there is no ground to reject it as revelation from God; it is supported by witnesses; is not opposed in any way to science; it does not oppose the teachings of the Bible; its teachings improve lives. [J.W.M.]

W.041 Watson, Wingfield. *Latter-day Signs, The Book of Mormon.* Lyons: n.p., 1897. The Book of Mormon fulfills the promise that the gospel would be preached in all the world (Matthew 24:14). In spite of the "army of sectarian preachers" who combine against it, the Book of Mormon will spread throughout the earth. Signs and wonders will follow those who believe. The gospel is the same in the Book of Mormon as in the New Testament, but the Book of Mormon clarifies passages that are difficult to understand. It is also warning voice. [J.W.M.]

W.042 Watt, Ronald G. " 'Had You Stood in the Presence of Peter,' A Letter From Oliver Cowdery to Phineas Young, 1846." *Ensign* 7 (February 1977): 78-79. As one of the three witnesses to the Book of Mormon, Oliver Cowdery had been an important asset to the Restoration. He assisted in the translation of the Book of Mormon and stood in the presence of angels, including Peter. This letter includes his petition to be allowed to return to the Church. [J.W.M.]

W.043 Wauchope, Robert. *Lost Tribes and Sunken Continents: Myth and Method in the Study of American Indians.* Chicago: University of Chicago Press, 1962. Chapter 4 is titled "Lost Tribes and the Mormons." Edward King and others of his time held to the theory that the Mesoamerican people were descendants of the "Lost Tribes of Israel." The Church of Jesus Christ of Latter-day Saints denies the Book of Mormon is about the Lost Ten Tribes but asserts that Hebrews of Jerusalem came to America. Parallels between the Book of Mormon and accounts of Ixtilxochitl and Popol Vuh seem to support the Book of Mormon. [J.W.M.]

W.044 " 'We Add Our Witness': Living Prophets Share Their Feelings about the Book of Mormon." *Ensign* 19 (March 1989): 5-9. Testimonies about the Book of Mormon from living prophets and apostles, including Ezra Taft Benson, Gordon B. Hinckley, and Thomas S. Monson. [L.D.]

W.045 Weaver, Gregg. "Finding the Word of God." In *Stories of Insight and Inspiration,* edited by Margie Calhoun Jensen, 41-43. Salt Lake City: Bookcraft, 1976. In his search for a religious philosophy this man had neglected Christianity. He was impressed to read about Jesus Christ. In spite of intentions to read the Bible to learn about the Son of God, he found himself reading the Book of Mormon and received a testimony of the Savior. [J.W.M.]

W.046 Webb, Robert C. (James Edward Homans). *The Case Against Mormonism.* New York: L. L. Walton, 1915. A response to criticisms raised by various critics of Mormonism, written by a non-Mormon under the pseudonym of Robert C. Webb. Provides a discussion of prominent criticisms of the Book of Mormon including the Anthon denials, reformed Egyptian, Solomon Spaulding, Shakespeare, and modern phrases. [M.R.]

W.047 Webb, Robert C. (James Edward Homans). "Egyptology and the Book of Mormon." *IE* 26 (February-April 1923): 311-27, 437-47,

546-54. Essay that proposes that the characters on the gold plates were derived from Hieratic or Demotic Egyptian (Mormon 9:32-33). Analysis of other major written languages available ca. 600 B. C.—i.e. Phoenician-Hebrew, Egyptian hieroglyphs, cuneiform—reveals that they do not meet the writing requirements outlined in the Book of Mormon itself. The nature of the gold plates as an alloy is also discussed. [J.T.]

W.048 Webb, Robert C. (James Edward Homans). *Joseph Smith as Translator, A Candid Examination of His Claims to Have Translated the Book of Mormon.* Salt Lake City: Deseret News Press, 1936. A non-Mormon writing under the pseudonym of Robert C. Webb discusses issues related to the Book of Mormon and the Book of Abraham. Little knowledge of the Egyptian language, especially reformed Egyptian, was available to Joseph Smith. The author discusses ancient linguistic possibilities for various words and proper names in the Book of Mormon. [M.R.]

W.049 Webb, Robert C. (James Edward Homans). *The Real Mormonism: A Candid Analysis of an Interesting But Much Misunderstood Subject in History, Life and Thought.* New York: Sturgis and Walton, 1916. A response to various anti-Mormon criticisms, written by a non-Mormon under the pseudonym of Robert C. Webb. Discusses the coming forth of the Book of Mormon and the numerous theories of Book of Mormon origins raised by unbelievers. [M.R.]

W.050 Webb, Robert C. (James Edward Homans). "Truth Seeking: Its Symptoms and After Effects." *IE* 16 (13 September 1913): 1075-91. Also in *DN* (5 July 1913): 8-9. A response to Reverend F. S. Spalding's pamphlet *Joseph Smith, Jr., as a Translator.* Spalding attacks the Book of Mormon by testing the translation of the book of Abraham, saying that the validity of the Book of Mormon rests upon the correct translation of the book of Abraham. Webb warns that the opinions of the scholars contacted are merely opinions and premature as well. [J.W.M.]

W.051 Weed, Grant B. *Speeches Given As a Part of a Series on Sunday Evening on Temple Square.* N.p., 22 June 1958. The Book of Mormon is a history of God's dealings with his people as is the Bible. It teaches gospel principles with clarity. [J.W.M.]

W.052 Weeks, Marvin E. *Consolidated Concordance: Book of Mormon, Doctrine and Covenants, Inspired Version of the Bible.* Independence, MO: School of Saints, 1984. Contains hundreds of topics with scriptural cross-references from the Book of Mormon, Doctrine and Covenants, and the Inspired Version of the Bible. [J.W.M.]

W.053 Weight, G. Dale. "A Great Guide in Solving Problems." *Instructor* 105 (October 1970): 362-63. Demonstrates Book of Mormon's influence on youth. Stories of Alma the Younger, Enos, Ammon, Joseph Smith, and Jesus Christ are especially applicable; the Book of Mormon gives youth a "cause" with which to identify. [A.C.W.]

W.054 Weiner, George. "America's Jewish Braves." *Mankind* 4 (n.d.): 56-64. In 1644 Antonio de Montezinos, a Jewish adventurer, declared he had found the lost Ten Tribes in America. The Spanish, who in the Inquisition tried to eliminate Jewish influence, continued to do so in America. They destroyed artifacts and architecture that made the link. The belief that the Lost Ten Tribes were in America has had a profound influence on the history of the world. Among the books written supporting this theory, the Book of Mormon is a significant work. [J.W.M.]

W.055 Weisman, Howard. "The Lord Is with Us." *Ensign* 20 (April 1990): 30-32. The Holy Ghost bore witness to this Jewish convert of the truthfulness of the Book of Mormon. He was able to understand his Jewish religion and the purpose of the temple better, and to unite his family in death as they had been in life. [J.W.M.]

W.056 Welch, John W. "Alma 36: A Masterpiece." In *Rediscovering the Book of Mormon*, edited by John L. Sorenson and Melvin J. Thorne, 114-131. Salt Lake City: Deseret Book and

FARMS, 1991. A popular condensation of Welch's "Chiasmus in Alma 36." Provo, UT: FARMS, 1989. Alma 36 is an excellent example of chiasmus in the Book of Mormon. [J.W.W.]

W.057 Welch, John W. "Ammon and the Cutting Off the Arms of Enemies." In *Reexploring the Book of Mormon*, edited by John W. Welch, 180-82. Salt Lake City: Deseret Book and FARMS, 1992. In the ancient Near East, it was a common practice for conquering soldiers to remove victim's body parts as a sign of victory, or perhaps also to obtain an accurate accounting of the dead. Cutting off arms became a customary punishment for thieves in the Moslem world. It may have been symbolic. The story of Ammon fits these ancient Near Eastern traditions. [J.W.M.]

W.058 Welch, John W. "Ancient Near Eastern Law and the Book of Mormon." Provo, UT: FARMS, 1981. Displays five ways the study of biblical law can enhance Book of Mormon understanding and five cases where the Book of Mormon can shed light on biblical legal studies. [J.W.W.]

W.059 Welch, John W. "B. H. Roberts: Seeker after Truth." *Ensign* 16 (March 1986): 56-62. Reprinted in *A Sure Foundation: Answers to Difficult Gospel Questions*, 60-74. Salt Lake City: Deseret Book, 1988. Historical explanation of why B. H. Roberts wrote a Book of Mormon study forcefully pointing out problems that defenders of the faith should address, especially regarding the *View of the Hebrews* and American antiquities; gives evidence that Roberts did not lose faith in the Book of Mormon. [J.W.W.]

W.060 Welch, John W. "Benjamin's Speech: A Classic Ancient Farewell Address." In *Reexploring the Book of Mormon*, edited by John W. Welch, 120-23. Salt Lake City: Deseret Book and FARMS, 1992. Certain themes appear consistently in farewell addresses of many ancient religious and political leaders, as if the speakers were following a pattern. Recent research finds Benjamin's speech to be the most complete example of this speech topology yet found anywhere in world literature. [R.H.B.]

W.061 Welch, John W. "Book of Mormon Religious Teachings and Practices." In *Encyclopedia of Mormonism*, edited by Daniel H. Ludlow, 1:201-5. 5 vols. New York: Macmillan, 1992. Describes basic doctrines as taught by Jesus: repentance, baptism, priesthood authority, sacrament prayers, church worship, covenants, the church name, manner of worship, rich versus poor, and excommunication. Verification of belief in Christ before his advent is offered in covenants, worship, miracles, prayer, fasting, and other teachings from the Book of Mormon. [N.K.Y.]

W.062 Welch, John W. "A Book You Can Respect." *Ensign* 7 (September 1977): 45-48. Personal experiences with scholars, involving chiasmus, ancient history, philosophy, and textual studies, showing how scholarship can help enhance respect for the Book of Mormon, while leaving proof of the book's truthfulness in the sphere of testimony. [J.W.W.]

W.063 Welch, John W. "The Calling of a Prophet." In *The Book of Mormon: First Nephi, The Doctrinal Foundation*, edited by Monte S. Nyman and Charles D. Tate Jr., 35-54. Provo, UT: Brigham Young University Religious Studies Center, 1988. Analyzes the call of Lehi in light of ancient Israelite prophetic literature, showing that the elements of Lehi's throne vision and prophetic commission in 1 Nephi 1 compares closely with the cultural and religious experiences and expectations in Israel and neighboring civilizations in Lehi's day. [J.W.W.]

W.064 Welch, John W. "The Case of an Unobserved Murder." In *Reexploring the Book of Mormon*, edited by John W. Welch, 242-44. Salt Lake City: Deseret Book and FARMS, 1992. The trial of Seantum for his murder of the chief judge is analyzed. Cases of unwitnessed murders presented special problems under the law of Moses. Seantum's self-incriminating confession satisfies all three special requirements needed to override the normal two-witness rule. [R.H.B.]

W.065 Welch, John W. "Chiasmus Bibliography." Provo, UT: FARMS, 1987. A listing of about 400 books, articles, and papers dealing with chiasmus in the Bible, Book of Mormon, and elsewhere in world literature. [J.W.W.]

W.066 Welch, John W., ed. *Chiasmus in Antiquity.* Hildesheim: Gerstenberg Verlag, 1981. A team of scholars analyze chiasmus in Akkadian, Ugaritic, Hebrew, Aramaic, Greek, Latin, and the Book of Mormon. Includes extensive bibliography and register of chiastic passages in many literatures. [J.W.W.]

W.067 Welch, John W. "Chiasmus in Biblical Law: An Approach to the Structure of Legal Texts in the Hebrew Bible." In *Jewish Law Association Studies IV*, edited by Bernard Jackson, 5-22. Atlanta, GA: Scholars, 1990. Demonstrates the existence and explores the function of chiasmus and parallelism in Biblical legal texts. In connection with Leviticus 24:13-23, discusses the chiastic structure of Alma 41:13-15. Also provides literary analysis of Exodus 21:2-23:19. [A.C.W.]

W.068 Welch, John W. "Chiasmus in Helaman 6:7-13." In *Reexploring the Book of Mormon*, edited by John W. Welch, 230-32. Salt Lake City: Deseret Book and FARMS, 1992. Another example of chiasmus has been discerned in Helaman 6:7-13. Chiasmus encompasses the entire report for the year, suggesting that the account was written as a single literary unit that Mormon copied verbatim from the large plates of Nephi. The literary structure of the chiasmus is analyzed. [R.H.B.]

W.069 Welch, John W. "Chiasmus in Helaman 6:7-13." Provo, UT: FARMS, 1987. Analysis of the chiastic structure of the complete text of Helaman 6:7-13, a Nephite annal recording an unusual period of unity and peace between Nephites and Lamanites. [J.W.W.]

W.070 Welch, John W. "Chiasmus in the Book of Mormon." *BYU Studies* 10 (Autumn 1969): 69-84. Also in *Book of Mormon Authorship: New Light on Ancient Origins*, edited by Noel B. Reynolds, 33-52. Provo, UT: Brigham Young University Religious Studies Center, 1982. The first article published about chiasmus in the Book of Mormon. Gives examples of extended inverted parallelisms from the Old Testament and Book of Mormon. [J.W.W.]

W.071 Welch, John W. "Chiasmus in the Book of Mormon." *NE* 2 (February 1972): 6. Popular presentation of the discovery and significance of chiasmus in the Book of Mormon, building on conclusions generally accepted by biblical scholars. [J.W.W.]

W.072 Welch, John W. "Criteria for Identifying the Presence of Chiasmus." Provo, UT: FARMS, 1989. Sets forth a series of criteria to be employed in calculating the degree to which a text manifests chiasmus, and discusses the extent to which modern readers can determine if the presence of chiasmus in a text was intentionally created by the ancient author. [J.W.W.]

W.073 Welch, John W. "Decorative Iron in Early Israel." In *Reexploring the Book of Mormon*, edited by John W. Welch, 133-34. Salt Lake City: Deseret Book and FARMS, 1992. Mosiah 11:8 mentions "all manners of precious things, of gold, and of silver, and of iron." Although a person today would not normally consider using iron as a precious decoration, evidence is presented to show that this was done in antiquity. [R.H.B.]

W.074 Welch, John W. "The Destruction of Ammonihah and Law of Apostate Cities." In *Reexploring the Book of Mormon*, edited by John W. Welch, 176-79. Salt Lake City: Deseret Book and FARMS, 1992. The law of Moses contains instructions to utterly destroy apostate cities and to gather and burn all their spoil (Deut. 13:12-16). Recent research has uncovered several striking affinities between the account of the destruction of the wicked city of Ammonihah and this ancient Israelite law (Alma 16:9). [R.H.B.]

W.075 Welch, John W. "The Execution of Zemnarihah." In *Reexploring the Book of Mormon*, edited by John W. Welch. 250-52. Salt Lake City: Deseret Book and FARMS, 1992. Zemnarihah, the captured leader of the Gadianton robbers, was hanged upon the top of a tree, the tree was then felled and the people sang out "all as one" in praise of God (3 Nephi 4:30-33). Several evidences are presented that suggest that some kind of ancient ritual was being observed. [R.H.B.]

W.076 Welch, John W. "Exemption From Military Duty." In *Reexploring the Book of Mormon*, edited by John W. Welch, 189-92. Salt Lake

City: Deseret Book and FARMS, 1992. The people of Ammon, having taken an oath never again to take up arms, were the only Book of Mormon group given an exemption from military service. This privilege was consistent with ancient Israelite law. [R.H.B.]

W.077 Welch, John W. "The Father's Command to Keep Records in the Small Plates of Nephi." Provo, UT: FARMS, 1984. Nephi's instructions to Jacob consistently determined the character and contents of the books of Jacob, Enos, Jarom, and Omni. Nephi instructed that only prophecy, preaching, and little history be included. [J.W.W.]

W.078 Welch, John W. "Finding Answers to B. H. Roberts's Questions." Provo, UT: FARMS, 1985. Recent data and scholarly work provide plausible answers to questions asked by Mr. Couch in 1921 and about which Roberts prepared a working paper, regarding Native American origins, languages, horses, and archaeology. [J.W.W.]

W.079 Welch, John W. "Getting Things Strai[gh]t." In *Reexploring the Book of Mormon*, edited by John W. Welch, 260-62. Salt Lake City: Deseret Book and FARMS, 1992. In contemporary English *straight* usually means "not crooked," while the word *strait* means "narrow." In the 1829 manuscripts of the Book of Mormon the spelling *straight* was never used; Oliver Cowdery always spelled these homonyms as *strait*. The 1828 *American Dictionary of the English Language* shows both spellings as interchangeable. The words *straight* and *strait* are both used in the King James Version of the Old Testament. Understanding their range of meaning in Hebrew may shed light on ideas intended by Isaiah, Lehi, and Nephi. [R.H.B.]

W.080 Welch, John W. "Hugh Nibley and the Book of Mormon." *Ensign* 15 (April 1985): 50-56. An account of Hugh Nibley's favorite discoveries and monumental contribution to Book of Mormon scholarship. [J.W.W.]

W.081 Welch, John W. "I Have a Question: How long did it take Joseph Smith to translate the Book of Mormon?" *Ensign* 18 (January 1988): 46-47. Historical records show that it took only sixty-five or less working days to translate the Book of Mormon. Welch discusses the order of probable translation—Mosiah to Moroni in April-May, and the small plates of Nephi in June. [J.W.W.]

W.082 Welch, John W. "If a man . . . The Casuistic Law Form in the Book of Mormon." Provo, UT: FARMS, 1987. Explores the evidence that Nephite law continued to use the casuistic law form prevalent in biblical law. [J.W.W.]

W.083 Welch, John W. "Jacob's Ten Commandments." In *Reexploring the Book of Mormon*, edited by John W. Welch, 69-72. Salt Lake City: Deseret Book and FARMS, 1992. An analysis is provided of the ten essential principles and rules of Nephite religion in 2 Nephi 27-38. [R.H.B.]

W.084 Welch, John W. "Jesus Christ in the Book of Mormon." In *Encyclopedia of Mormonism*, edited by Daniel H. Ludlow, 2:748-50. 5 vols. New York: Macmillan, 1992. Summary of the main teachings of the prophets in the Book of Mormon about Jesus Christ, his atonement, his resurrection, his role in the Plan of Salvation, the judgment, and individual prophecies about his mortal mission and Godhood. [B.D.]

W.085 Welch, John W. "Joseph Smith: 'Author and Proprietor.'" In *Reexploring the Book of Mormon*, edited by John W. Welch, 154-57. Salt Lake City: Deseret Book and FARMS, 1992. Discusses copyright laws and explains that the terms "author" and "proprietor" were legally correct descriptions of Joseph Smith's relationship with the Book of Mormon and not inconsistent with his role as translator. [A.C.W.]

W.086 Welch, John W. "Judicial Process in the Trial of Abinadi." Provo, UT: FARMS, 1981. The trial of Abinadi, as recorded by Alma, who was a priest in the court of Noah, is shown to have followed ancient Israelite legal practices and is interpreted accordingly. [J.W.W.]

W.087 Welch, John W. "King Benjamin's Speech in the Context of Ancient Israelite Festivals." Provo, UT: FARMS, 1985. A report on Mosiah 1-6 in light of ancient Israelite and Jewish rituals and practices associated with the celebration of New Year, Day of Atonement, and Feast of Tabernacles, particularly on Sabbatical Years. [J.W.W.]

W.088 Welch, John W. "The Last Words of Cenez and the Book of Mormon." In *The Allegory of the Olive Tree: The Olive, The Bible, and Jacob 5,* edited by Stephen D. Ricks and John W. Welch, 305-21. Salt Lake City: Deseret Book and FARMS, 1994. In the late nineteenth century a work called *Biblical Antiquities* or *Liber Antiquitatum Biblicarum* surfaced. It includes the history of a great prophet-warrior-leader named Kenaz. Spelling variants are Cenez, Zenec, and Zenez. He is mentioned by Josephus as Keniazos. These writings concerning him closely resemble Jacob 4-6. It is unlikely that Cenez is either Zenos or Zenoch found in the Book of Mormon. These writings were published in Latin in 1893 and were not translated into English until 1917. [J.W.M.]

W.089 Welch, John W. "Law and War in the Book of Mormon." In *Warfare in the Book of Mormon,* edited by Stephen D. Ricks and William J. Hamblin, 46-102. Salt Lake City: Deseret Book and FARMS, 1990. Customary Jewish law and ancient Israelite attitudes toward war seem to have persisted among Book of Mormon peoples. This article explores the effect of martial law on government, politics, political offices, and freedom of travel, as well as the legal obligation to fight, exemptions from military duty, treatment of captives, and other legal duties of soldiers and citizens. [J.W.W.]

W.090 Welch, John W. "The Law of Mosiah." In *Reexploring the Book of Mormon,* edited by John W. Welch, 158-61. Salt Lake City: Deseret Book and FARMS, 1992. Subtle and sometimes technical information concerning the changes in Nephite law and society that accompanied the introduction of the law of Mosiah in 92 B.C. are faithfully preserved in the Book of Mormon. [R.H.B.]

W.091 Welch, John W. "Legal Perspectives on the Slaying of Laban." *Journal of Book of Mormon Studies* 1 (Fall 1992): 119-41. This article marshals ancient legal evidence to show that Nephi's slaying of Laban should be understood as a protected manslaughter rather than a criminal homicide. Exodus 21:13 protected more than accidental slayings or unconscious acts, particularly where God was seen as having delivered the victim into the slayer's hand. Nephi did not commit the equivalent of a first-degree murder under the laws of his day. [R.H.B.]

W.092 Welch, John W. "Lehi's Counsel Vision and Mysteries of God." In *Reexploring the Book of Mormon,* edited by John W. Welch, 24-25. Salt Lake City: Deseret Book and FARMS, 1992. The vision of the council of God's heavenly hosts, as seen by Lehi and other prophets, made them privy to the secret decrees of the council. These secret decrees are believed to be what constituted the "mysteries" of God. [R.H.B.]

W.093 Welch, John W. "Lehi's Last Will and Testament: A Legal Approach." In *The Book of Mormon: Second Nephi, The Doctrinal Structure,* edited by Monte S. Nyman and Charles D. Tate Jr., 61-82. Provo, UT: Brigham Young University Religious Studies Center, 1989. Near Eastern family law explains Lehi's position over his sons, their marriages, their family organization, and the rights of the firstborn sons. [J.W.W.]

W.094 Welch, John W. "Longevity of Book of Mormon People and The 'Age of Man.'" *The Journal of Collegium Aesculapium* 3 (1985): 34-45. Plausible birth- and death-dates are developed for the lineages of Lehi, Mosiah$_1$, Alma the Elder, and Jared, with resulting insights into the lives of Book of Mormon prophets. The article includes a chart of comparative life spans of Book of Mormon characters. [J.W.W.]

W.095 Welch, John W. "The Lord's Prayers." *Ensign* 6 (January 1976): 14-17. New Testament prayers of Jesus are discussed in the context of Jewish prayer practices and are related to the prayers of Jesus preserved in 3 Nephi. Jesus gave thanks to God especially for revelation, asked for forgiveness, and asked that God's will be done and temptation resisted. [J.W.W.]

W.096 Welch, John W. "A Masterpiece: Alma 36." In *Rediscovering the Book of Mormon,* edited by John L. Sorenson and Melvin J. Thorne, 114-31. Salt Lake City: Deseret Book and FARMS, 1991. Chiasmus is a phenomena that occurs in ancient poetry. Alma 36 follows the same pattern. The chapter is reformatted and six levels of complexity are pointed out. [J.W.M.]

W.097 Welch, John W. "The Melchizedek Material in Alma 13:13-19." In *By Study and Also by Faith,* edited by John M. Lundquist and Stephen D. Ricks, 2:238-72. Salt Lake City: Deseret Book and FARMS, 1990. Compares references to Melchizedek, including Alma 13:13-19, other Book of Mormon references, biblical references, traditions of Jewish writers and early Christians, references in the Old and New Testaments, and insights by Joseph Smith in his Inspired Version of the Bible. Alma clarifies much of the mystery surrounding Melchizedek. [A.A.]

W.098 Welch, John W. "The Narrative of Zosimus and the Book of Mormon." *BYU Studies* 22 (Summer 1982): 311-32. Examines parallels between 1 Nephi and a little-known but early pseudepigraphon about a man who has a vision similar to Lehi's and meets a group in this vision that escaped the Babylonian destruction of Jerusalem and were taken across the ocean by God. [J.W.W.]

W.099 Welch, John W. "The Nephite Sacrament Prayers: From King Benjamin's Speech to Moroni 4-5." Provo, UT: FARMS, 1986. Also in abbreviated form in "Our Nephite Sacrament Prayers." In *Reexploring the Book of Mormon,* edited by John W. Welch, 286-89. Salt Lake City: Deseret Book and FARMS, 1992. Shows how the LDS sacrament prayers come from Moroni 4-5, not originally from D&C 20, and that the Nephite prayers are a liturgical reenactment of the precise words of Jesus in 3 Nephi 18. The sacramental prayer language extends back at least to the words of King Benjamin in Mosiah 5. [J.W.W.]

W.100 Welch, John W. "New Testament Word Studies." Provo, UT: FARMS, 1991. An analysis of word meanings in the New Testament shows a consistency between the original usage of words in the New Testament and their usage in the Book of Mormon. [J.W.M.]

W.101 Welch, John W. "No, Sir, That's Not History!" In *Reexploring the Book of Mormon,* edited by John W. Welch, 88-92. Salt Lake City: Deseret Book and FARMS, 1992. Presents an analysis of B. H. Roberts's writing of *Studies of the Book of Mormon* and Ethan Smith's *View of the Hebrews.* Roberts began the study in January 1922 and completed it May 29, 1922 before leaving to preside over the Eastern States mission. Roberts's subsequent labors and testimonies concerning the Book of Mormon show his belief in this scripture. [R.H.B.]

W.102 Welch, John W. "Number 24." In *Reexploring the Book of Mormon,* edited by John W. Welch, 272-74. Salt Lake City: Deseret Book and FARMS, 1992. Certain numbers were meaningful in antiquity. Seven was the number of spiritual perfection, twelve was a governmental number. The number twenty-four was associated with heavenly government, especially priestly judgment and temple service. Eight occurrences of the number twenty-four in the Book of Mormon are analyzed. [R.H.B.]

W.103 Welch, John W. "The Plain and Precious Parts." In *Reexploring the Book of Mormon,* edited by John W. Welch, 37-40. Salt Lake City: Deseret Book and FARMS, 1992. The loss of many plain and precious parts of the gospel is seen as consisting of three stages: (1) the meaning or understanding of the Savior's teachings is altered; (2) covenants are lost through neglect of their performance; and (3) eventually things are physically lost from the Bible, a consequence of the first two actions. [R.H.B.]

W.104 Welch, John W. "Preliminary Comments on the Sources behind the Book of Ether." Provo, UT: FARMS, 1986. Discusses records and sources used by Ether and Moroni to produce the book of Ether, including an archaic king list, the record of the brother of Jared, and the prophecies of Ether—recognizable as separate text fragments appended together by Moroni's abridging. [J.W.W.]

W.105 Welch, John W. "Recent Developments in Book of Mormon Research." Provo, UT: FARMS, 1986. Gives teachers practical suggestions about the use of current Book of Mormon research in the classroom. [J.W.W.]

W.106 Welch, John W. "Series of Laws in the Book of Mormon." Provo, UT: FARMS, 1987. Discussion of texts in the Book of Mormon that list laws and compares them with law lists and codes from the Old Testament and the ancient Near East. Shows internal logical development in Nephite legal history. [J.W.W.]

W.107 Welch, John W. "The Sermon at the Temple." In *Reexploring the Book of Mormon*, edited by John W. Welch, 253-56. Salt Lake City: Deseret Book and FARMS, 1992. Jesus' Sermon on the Mount (Matthew 5-7) presents serious challenges to scholars. The Savior's Sermon at the Temple (3 Nephi 11-18) provides a context for understanding the Sermon on the Mount. [R.H.B.]

W.108 Welch, John W. *The Sermon at the Temple and the Sermon on the Mount: A Latter-day Saint Approach*. Salt Lake City: Deseret Book and FARMS, 1990. A thorough LDS interpretation of the Sermon on the Mount in Matthew 5-7 and analysis of the words of Jesus at the temple in Bountiful in 3 Nephi 11-18. The Book of Mormon provides keys to unlock the mystery of the Sermon on the Mount. 3 Nephi is a covenantal temple text, giving instructions and commandments relevant to covenant making. A table compares the texts of Matthew 5-7, 3 Nephi 12-14, and the Joseph Smith Translation of Matthew 5-7. [J.W.W.]

W.109 Welch, John W. "Some Old World Perspectives on the Book of Mormon; A Book You Can Respect." *Ensign* (September 1976): 27-30, 45-48. Welch gives a summary of the history of Judah during Lehi's lifetime in order to understand the setting of the quest for a promised land, and shows the many ways the Book of Mormon can be respected as a literary masterpiece. [B.D.]

W.110 Welch, John W. "Statutes, Judgments, Ordinances, and Commandments." In *Reexploring the Book of Mormon*, edited by John W. Welch, 62-65. Salt Lake City: Deseret Book and FARMS, 1992. 2 Nephi 5:10 mentions that the people observed the "judgments, and the statutes, and the commandments . . . according to the law of Moses." An analysis of the associated Hebrew terms is provided. [R.H.B.]

W.111 Welch, John W. "Study, Faith, and the Book of Mormon." In *Brigham Young University 1987-88 Devotional and Fireside Speeches*, 139-49 Provo, UT: Brigham Young University, 1988. Reprinted as "Study and Faith in the Book of Mormon." *BYU Today* 42 (September 1988): 18-24 Discusses scholarly studies that can increase appreciation for the Book of Mormon. The Book of Mormon will remain a sealed book to all those who do not approach it with both spiritual faith and academic rigor. [J.W.W.]

W.112 Welch, John W. "A Study Relating Chiasmus in the Book of Mormon to Chiasmus in the Old Testament." M.A. thesis, Brigham Young University, 1970. Defines simple, compound, and complex chiasmus, surveys the use of chiasmus in Ugaritic epics, the Old Testament, Homer, and later Greek and Latin authors, and compares the appearance of chiasmus in those literatures with chiasmus in the Book of Mormon. The degree of use of chiasmus in the Book of Mormon is similar to that in the Old Testament. [J.W.W.]

W.113 Welch, John W. "Synagogues in the Book of Mormon." In *Reexploring the Book of Mormon*, edited by John W. Welch, 193-95. Salt Lake City: Deseret Book and FARMS, 1992. The Book of Mormon describes a considerable diversity in synagogues. Some were built after the manner of the Jews, some after the manner of the Nehors, and one in Antionum after a manner that amazed Alma and his companions. Similarly, ancient Israelite communal worship appears to have begun as a flexible practice and was known in several developmental stages. [R.H.B.]

W.114 Welch, John W. "Ten Testimonies of Jesus Christ from the Book of Mormon." In *Doctrines of the Book of Mormon, 1991 Sperry Symposium*, edited by Bruce A. Van Orden and Brent L. Top, 223-42. Salt Lake City: Deseret Book, 1992. Analyzes the names, descriptions, and testimonies of Jesus Christ used by Lehi, Nephi, Jacob, Benjamin, Abinadi, Alma, Amulek, Samuel the Lamanite, Mormon, and Moroni, to show that each prophet used a different and often unique set of theological terms and concepts, christologically significant and also strongly connected to the personal experiences and perceptions of each prophet. [J.W.W.]

W.115 Welch, John W. "Theft and Robbery in the Book of Mormon and Ancient Near Eastern Law." Provo, UT: FARMS, 1985. Ancient law distinguished between the crimes of theft and robbery, a distinction also consistently evident in the Book of Mormon. [J.W.W.]

W.116 Welch, John W. "They Came from Jerusalem: Some Old World Perspectives on the Book of Mormon." *Ensign* 6 (September 1976): 26-31. Reprinted in *The Book of Mormon, It Begins with a Family*, 14-22. Salt Lake City: Deseret Book, 1983. Overview of Jerusalem during Lehi's lifetime and the probable impact of the reforms of Josiah on Book of Mormon thought. Deals with conditions in Jerusalem and surrounding nations about 600 B.C., the urgency of record-keeping in that era, the state of turmoil and flux, and the role of prophets like Jeremiah. [J.W.W.]

W.117 Welch, John W. "Thieves and Robbers." In *Reexploring the Book of Mormon*, edited by John W. Welch, 248-49. Salt Lake City: Deseret Book and FARMS, 1992. Under ancient Near Eastern law there were significant differences between a thief and a robber. The former was usually a local person who was tried and punished under civil law by fellow townspeople. The latter was treated as an outsider, was dealt with under military law, and could be executed. These ancient legal and linguistic distinctions are observable in the Book of Mormon. [R.H.B.]

W.118 Welch, John W. "Three Accounts of Alma's Conversion." In *Reexploring the Book of Mormon*, edited by John W. Welch, 150-53. Salt Lake City: Deseret Book and FARMS, 1992. The Book of Mormon provides three accounts of Alma's conversion. Numerous phrases used in parallel throughout all three accounts show that a single person was the author of all three. [R.H.B.]

W.119 Welch, John W. "View of the Hebrews: 'An Unparallel.'" In *Reexploring the Book of Mormon*, edited by John W. Welch, 83-87. Salt Lake City: Deseret Book and FARMS, 1992. Presents an analysis of the parallels and of the lack of them between the Book of Mormon and Ethan Smith's 1823 *View of the Hebrews*. The differences far outweigh the similarities between these two texts. [R.H.B.]

W.120 Welch, John W. "Was Helaman 7-8 an Allegorical Funeral Sermon?" In *Reexploring the Book of Mormon*, edited by John W. Welch, 239-41. Salt Lake City: Deseret Book and FARMS, 1992. It was not uncommon for early Israelite prophets to use striking conduct to emphasize the import of their warnings (Jeremiah 13:1-11; Jeremiah 19:1-13; 1 Kings 11:29-39; 2 Kings 11:29-39; 2 Kings 13:15-19; Isaiah 20:2-6). It is suggested that Nephi's sermon from a tower in his yard employed similar imagery to draw a crowd and to emphasize his warning message. [R.H.B.]

W.121 Welch, John W. "What Is B. H. Roberts' 'Study of the Book of Mormon' and How Have Critics Used It to Discredit the Book of Mormon?" In *A Sure Foundation: Answers to Difficult Gospel Questions*, 60-74. Salt Lake City: Deseret Book, 1988. Papers written in 1922 by B. H. Roberts bluntly state problems and arguments that could be used against the Book of Mormon, but he was firm in his faith in the Church and the Book of Mormon. His contention was that the power of the Holy Ghost was the source for finding the truth of the Book of Mormon and external evidence was not reliable. [J.W.M.]

W.122 Welch, John W. "What Was a 'Mosiah?'" In *Reexploring the Book of Mormon*, edited by John W. Welch, 105-7. Salt Lake City: Deseret Book and FARMS, 1992. Although the exact derivation of the Book of Mormon name *Mosiah* is unknown, it appears that the term is identical to the Hebrew *moshiah,* whose key meaning is "savior." Interestingly, this term applies perfectly to the Mosiahs in the Book of Mormon. [R.H.B.]

W.123 Welch, John W., S. Kent Brown, and John A. Tvedtnes. "When Did Jesus Appear to the Nephites in Bountiful?" Provo, UT: FARMS, 1989. Three theories about the timing of Jesus' appearance in Bountiful are set forth: shortly after the crucifixion, about 50 days after the crucifixion, and about 11 months after the crucifixion. Given the ambiguous reference in 3 Nephi 10, no definite conclusion can be reached. [J.W.W.]

W.124 Welch, John W. "Why Study Warfare in the Book of Mormon?" In *Warfare in the Book of Mormon*, edited by Stephen D. Ricks and William J. Hamblin, 3-24. Salt Lake City: Deseret and FARMS, 1990. Essay explaining the importance of war in the religious world view of the Nephites, listing and naming the main Nephite conflicts, and discussing methodological problems that must be observed in studying the war chapters in the Book of Mormon. Concludes that no study of the Book of Mormon, either as an ancient document or as it speaks to the modern world, can be well-grounded without an understanding of the book's perception and ideology of war. [J.W.W.]

W.125 Welch, John W. "Words and Phrases in Jacob 5." In *The Allegory of the Olive Tree: The Olive, The Bible, and Jacob 5,* edited by Stephen D. Ricks and John W. Welch, 174-85. Salt Lake City: Deseret Book and FARMS, 1994. Report of a computer count of the words in Jacob 5. There is a great deal of repetition of words in the allegory, and the vocabulary more closely resembles the Hebrew vocabulary of the Old Testament than the New. Some exact phrases may be reminiscent of the theophany of Mt. Sinai; others relate to early anti-pagan language. [J.W.M.]

W.126 Welch, John W., ed. *Reexploring the Book of Mormon*. Salt Lake City: Deseret Book and FARMS, 1992. A series of updates on current book of Mormon research, edited to make them useful to scholars and general readers. Introductions place each update in context, giving the questions and problems that stimulated the original research and the direction of subsequent research. [J.W.W.]

W.127 Welch, John W., David Fox, Roger Keeler, Paul Hoskisson, Deloy Pack, Robert Smith, and Bruce Warren. "Words and Phrases." In *Reexploring the Book of Mormon*, edited by John W. Welch. 282-85. Salt Lake City: Deseret Book and FARMS, 1992. The occurrences and significance of several words and phrases are examined. These include: Lord God Omnipotent, Holy One of Israel, island and isles of the sea, great and abominable church, heart, from whence no traveler can return, second death, and it came to pass. [R.H.B.]

W.128 Welch, John W., and David J. Whittaker. "Mormonism's Open Canon: Some Historical Perspectives on Its Religious Limits and Potentials." Provo, UT: FARMS, 1987. Explores historically the balance in Mormonism between its acceptance of an open canon and its strict adherence to scripture as the word of God. Traces the LDS experience with the continuous revelation of God's will "line upon line." [J.W.W.]

W.129 Welch, John W., David R. Benard, and Daniel C. Peterson. "Secret Combinations." In *Reexploring the Book of Mormon*, edited by John W. Welch, 227-29. Salt Lake City: Deseret Book and FARMS, 1992. Points out flaws in the argument that Joseph Smith borrowed the term *secret combinations* from a term used to refer to a "supposed conspiracy among the Freemasons" in New York in the 1820s. This is unlikely since the phrase was not used until much later. [J.W.M.]

W.130 Welch, John W., Donald W. Parry, and Stephen D. Ricks. " 'This Day.' " In *Reexploring the Book of Mormon*, edited by John W. Welch, 117-19. Salt Lake City: Deseret Book and FARMS, 1992. The words "this day" appear eighteen times in the Book of Mormon. The legal and religious implication of the term indicates high holy days, which in and of themselves produced a binding legal effect on holy religious status. [R.H.B.]

W.131 Welch, John W., Gary Gillum, and DeeAnn Hofer. *Comprehensive Bibliography of the Book of Mormon Arranged Alphabetically by Author*. Provo, UT: FARMS, 1987. Book of Mormon bibliography arranged alphabetically by author. [J.W.M.]

W.132 Welch, John W., Gary Gillum, and DeeAnn Hofer. *Comprehensive Bibliography of the Book of Mormon Arranged Chronologically*. Provo, UT: FARMS, 1987. This one hundred page bibliography of books and articles written about the Book of Mormon is listed according to their date of publication. [J.W.M.]

W.133 Welch, John W., Gary Gillum and DeeAnn Hofer. *Comprehensive Bibliography of the Book of Mormon Arranged by Subject*. Provo, UT: FARMS, 1987. Bibliography of books and articles about the Book of Mormon arranged according to subjects. [J.W.M.]

W.134 Welch, John W., and Gordon C. Thomasson. "The Sons of the Passover." In *Reexploring the Book of Mormon*, edited by John W. Welch, 196-98. Salt Lake City: Deseret Book and FARMS, 1992. The similarities of Alma's instructions to his sons with the Jewish holiday of Passover are striking. The pattern in Alma's instructions follow Passover traditions found at the time of Christ (perhaps earlier). [J.W.M.]

W.135 Welch, John W., Gordon C. Thomasson, and Robert F. Smith "Abinadi and Pentecost." In *Reexploring the Book of Mormon*, edited by John W. Welch, 135-38. Salt Lake City: Deseret Book and FARMS, 1992. Moses received the Ten Commandments at about the same time as the celebration of Pentecost. With this association the story of Abinadi in Mosiah 11-17 comes vividly to life. [R.H.B.]

W.136 Welch, John W., and Matthew G. Wells. "Concrete Evidence for the Book of Mormon." In *Reexploring the Book of Mormon*, edited by John W. Welch, 212-14. Salt Lake City: Deseret Book and FARMS, 1992. Originally published in May 1991. The superior quality of cement found in many archaeological sites is consistent with the Book of Mormon account in Helaman 3:7-11 that dates the technology at approximately 46 B.C. These finds are also helpful in locating Book of Mormon lands. [J.W.M.]

W.137 Welch, John W., Robert F. Smith, and Gordon C. Thomasson. "Dancing Maidens and the Fifteenth of Av." In *Reexploring the Book of Mormon*, edited by John W. Welch, 139-41. Salt Lake City: Deseret Book and FARMS, 1992. In ancient Israel maidens would gather to dance on the 15th day of the month of Av. Lehi and his people would have known of this tradition and perhaps the Lamanite daughters had gathered in celebration of a vestige of this event. [R.H.B.]

W.138 Welch, John W., and Tim Rathbone. "Book of Mormon Translation by Joseph Smith." In *Encyclopedia of Mormonism*, edited by Daniel H. Ludlow, 1: 210-12. 5 vols. New York: Macmillan, 1992. Few details of the translation process are known except that Joseph Smith used the "Nephite interpreters." Joseph Smith knew no foreign languages but dictated the Book of Mormon page by page to scribes without reviewing what was previously written. [N.K.Y.]

W.139 Welch, John W., and Tim Rathbone. "How Long Did It Take Joseph Smith to Translate the Book of Mormon? In *Reexploring the Book of Mormon*, edited by John W. Welch, 1-8. Salt Lake City: Deseret Book and FARMS, 1992. Cf. *Ensign* 18 (January 1988): 46-47. Sets forth the time it took Joseph Smith to translate the Book of Mormon, pointing out that it was a phenomenal achievement. [N.K.Y.]

W.140 Welch, John W. and Tim Rathbone. "Textual Consistency." In *Reexploring the Book of Mormon*, edited by John W. Welch. 21-23. Salt Lake City: Deseret Book, and FARMS, 1992. The miraculous nature of the task of dictating the Book of Mormon is revealed in several ways—the first copy was the final copy; it was remarkably free of strikeovers; only minor changes have been made in spelling, punctuation, capitalization, and grammar. The greatest miracle is the consistency within the text. Cites examples of material used with consistency—Alma's conversion accounts, King Benjamin's address, the prophecy of Zenos, King Benjamin's legal teachings. [J.W.M.]

W.141 Welch, John W., and Tim Rathbone. "The Translation of the Book of Mormon: Preliminary Report on the Basic Historical Information." Provo, UT: FARMS, 1986. Summarizes basic historical information pertaining to the translation of the Book of Mormon by Joseph Smith. Section I gives an annotated chronology of events from 1827 through 1830. Section II examines two theories about the order in which the texts of the Book of Mormon were translated. Section III shows that the 590 pages printed in the 1830 edition of the Book of Mormon were translated, dictated, and written all within an extremely short and intensely busy period of time. [B.D.]

W.142 Weldon, Clair. *The Book of Mormon.* Independence, MO: RLDS Church, 1976. Deals with Book of Mormon origins and context, including Nephite culture, Jaredite history, and the ministry of Jesus Christ. [J.W.M.]

W.143 Weldon, Clair E. "The Divine Authenticity of the Book of Mormon." *Courage: Journal of History, Thought & Action* 1 (December 1970): 102-6. Written to tell readers that the Book of Mormon is an authentic and divine work. Readers can determine its authenticity trough personal study and prayer. [J.W.M.]

W.144 Weldon, Roy E. *The Bible Points to the Book of Mormon and the New World.* Independence, MO: Herald House, 1969. Pamphlet filled with pictures, archaeological evidence, legends, and traditions designed to persuade one to believe that the Book of Mormon fulfills biblical prophecies. The Book of Mormon is related to the "Popul Vuh"—the Mayan book of God. [J.W.M.]

W.145 Weldon, Roy E. *Book of Mormon Evidences Joseph Smith a Prophet.* Independence, MO: Herald House, 1970. This pamphlet contains photographs of artifacts and archaeological evidence that the Book of Mormon described long before their discovery. Joseph Smith passes the biblical test of what makes a true prophet of God. [J.W.M.]

W.146 Weldon, Roy E. *The Book of Mormon Story in Pictures.* Independence, MO: Herald House, 1968. Architecture that resembles Egyptian types and carved reliefs that are unmistakably Hebrew help to explain the "bearded white god" idea found in ancient America. The Book of Mormon records the visit of Christ in America and archaeology verifies the truthfulness of the record. This pamphlet includes photographs, histories, myths, and traditions of ancient America. [J.W.M.]

W.147 Weldon, Roy E. "Emergence of the Nephite Record." *Witness* 65 (May 1989): 14-15. Mayan traditions state that two migrations of ancestors came to America, one from the east, the other from the west. The Book of Mormon witnesses of a New Jerusalem in America. The Book of Mormon will be used with the Bible to witness for Christ to silence unbelievers. [J.W.M.]

W.148 Weldon, Roy E. *The Nephite Prophets Speak to Our Day.* Independence, MO: Herald House, 1975. Book of Mormon prophets wrote to those who live in the New World and their prophecies are being fulfilled. Prophets, from Nephi to Moroni, saw the gulf of separation that divides the wicked and the righteous in our day. The last days are here with false prophets, anti-Christs, hysteria, irresponsibility, and rationalization. The Book of Mormon confounds false doctrine. [J.W.M.]

W.149 Weldon, Roy E. *Nephite Proverbs: Maxims and Truisms.* North Kansas City, MO: Color Press, 1989. A listing of scriptures under topic headings. Each scripture is followed by quotations from modern authors that testify of the truthfulness of the scripture. [J.W.M.]

W.150 Weldon, Roy E. "A New Star Did Appear." *Witness* 71 (Winter 1990): 5-7. Discusses the sophistication of Mayan astronomy to show that the ancient inhabitants of the Americas would have noticed the appearance of a new star at Christ's birth. [A.C.W.]

W.151 Weldon, Roy E. *Other Sheep: An Examination of the Rich and Convincing Evidences in the Bible.* Independence, MO: Price, 1986. The Book of Mormon is defended through analysis of early Spanish Colonial writings regarding the histories of the Aztecs, Toltecs, and Maya, and the author draws parallels between the archaeology of South America and the Book of Mormon. [J.T.]

W.152 Weldon, Roy E. *Restoration Witnesses.* Independence, MO: Herald House, 1966. A reproduction of fifteen articles found in *The Saint's Herald* beginning in July 1957. The Book of Mormon's ability to predict future happenings as well as provide information that was later proven by science lend credibility to its authenticity. The Book of Mormon's teachings on evolution and other "philosophies of men" are discussed, as well as anachronisms, and authorship. Weldon compares the philosophies of men with the philosophy of the Book of Mormon. [J.T.]

W.153 Weldon, Roy E. "When God Moves, Satan Moves." *Witness* 66 (Fall 1989): 14-15. The Book of Mormons tells of the struggle between God's servants and Satan's servants. Every time the Lord gives revelation and prophecy, Satan tries to intervene. [J.W.M.]

W.154 Weldon, Roy E., and F. Edward Butterworth. *Book of Mormon Claims and Evidences: A Cyclopedic Text of Information Pro & Con Relative to the Book of Mormon.* 4 vols. Independence, MO: Buckeye, 1979-1981. Volume one investigates external evidences of the Book of Mormon: agriculture, archaeology, architecture, astronomy, and Indian traditions. Volume two deals with Christ's visit to America and the evidence found to substantiate the Christian influence in America. Volume three explores the Mayan Calendar, Indian legends, evolution vs. divine creation, word origin, and hierogryphs. Volume four continues with metallurgy, migrations, mythology, and symbolism. [J.W.M.]

W.155 Weldon, Roy E., and F. Edward Butterworth. *Book of Mormon Deeps; a Comprehensive Text of Known Information Relative to the Internal Evidences of the Book of Mormon.* 4 vols. Weldon and Butterworth, 1977-1979. Designed for group study, this philosophical approach shows that Book of Mormon statements of concepts and beliefs are consistent with a high degree of civilization with modern philosophies and life styles. Its moral values apply to our day. Faith is noted as properly coming under the heading of philosophy. The parallels in ancient America and modern America are striking concerning rebellion, politics, and the sexual revolution. The prophetic role of the Book of Mormon transcends the role of science. The Book of Mormon adds those plain and precious things that have been taken from the Bible and bears witness of its truthfulness. Includes testimonies that go beyond intellectual reasoning. It is a book of fine literature. [J.W.M.]

W.156 Weldon, Roy, and F. E. Butterworth. *Criticisms of the Book of Mormon Answered.* Independence, MO: Herald House, 1973. A response to "honest objections and sincere criticisms" against the Book of Mormon, including its origins (i.e., the Spaulding manuscript), the problem of biblical passages quoted verbatim, seeming literary errors, anachronisms, and changes in the Book of Mormon. [J.T.]

W.157 Weldon, Walter. *The Purpose of the Book of Mormon.* Winner, SD: Walter Weldon, 1976. The roles and identities of Gentiles, Lamanites, and the promised land as outlined in the Book of Mormon are discussed. [J.T.]

W.158 Wells, J. F. "On Proving the Book of Mormon." *MS* 81 (October 1919): 664-66. Moroni is very clear on how to prove the truthfulness of the Book of Mormon. All who seek to properly know the truth will have it revealed to them by the Lord. Thousands have done it. The Bible and the Book of Mormon testify of each other. [B.D.]

W.159 Wells, J. F. "The Three Witnesses." *Utah Genealogical and Historical Magazine* 18-20 (October 1927–October 1929): 158-63, 34-38, 69-73, 172-78, 187-90. Includes testimonies and histories of Oliver Cowdery, David Whitmer, and Martin Harris. [J.W.M.]

W.160 Wells, Janette V. "Sharing the Book of Mormon." *Friend* 22 (April 1992): 2-4. A story of a young girl who shared the message of the Book of Mormon with her friends through her charitable actions. [M.D.P.]

W.161 Wells, Junius F. "The Engraving of the Three Witnesses." *IE* 30 (September 1927): 1022-25. Discusses the process of making a duplication of the engravings of the Three Witnesses of the Book of Mormon. [L.D.]

W.162 Wells, Junius F. "Oliver Cowdery." *IE* 14 (March 1911): 377-94. Documents the connection of Oliver Cowdery with the Prophet Joseph Smith and the translation of the Book of Mormon. [J.W.M.]

W.163 Wells, Junius F. "Oliver Cowdery." *MS* 73 (6-20 April 1911): 209-15, 225-29, 241-43. Presents a sketch of the life of Oliver Cowdery, in an attempt to dispel inaccuracies previously published. Though he faltered and fell, he should be honored, for he never joined the Church's enemies nor did he deny his testimony of the Book of Mormon as the work of the Lord. Cowdery was the scribe for most of the Book of Mormon and was one of the Three Witnesses. [J.W.M.]

W.164 Wells, R. S. "The Book of Mormon Confirmed." *MS* 60 (January, February 1898): 24-28, 33-39, 56-63, 72-77, 81-87. Series of five articles with evidence of the authenticity of the Book of Mormon—there were two races of ancient Americans, the Jaredites in North America and the Nephites in South America (Omni 1:23 and Alma 22:30-34); American Indians are of Hebrew origin; there is evidence of ancient metal engraving on tablets in book form; the Peruvians believe they originated from a people led by four brothers; there is evidence of advanced civilizations, ancient coins, and ancient implements on the American continent; there is evidence of great destruction at the crucifixion of Christ and that the Messiah was known to ancient Americans. [B.D.]

W.165 Wells, Robert E. "The Liahona Triad." In *Doctrines of the Book of Mormon, 1991 Sperry Symposium*, edited by Bruce A. Van Orden and Brent L. Top, 1-15. Salt Lake City: Deseret Book, 1992. The triad of faith, diligence, and heed were required to make the Liahona function for Lehi and his family. Nephi demonstrated faith in getting the brass plates and in building a boat. Mormon and others exemplify diligence and perseverance. The word *heed* was used much by Nephi in his writing. These things can lead individuals to Christ. There are many different kinds of modern Liahonas: conscience, patriarchal blessings, even the Book of Mormon. [N.K.Y.]

W.166 Wells, Robert E. *The Mount and the Master*. Salt Lake City: Deseret Book, 1991. Analyzing the Sermon on the Mount, this author compares the account in 3 Nephi with three translations of the Bible. He defines of key words, gives scriptural and personal examples of the concept, explores the state of happiness that is promised in each of the beatitudes, and discusses the required acts and thoughts of achieving such a state. [J.W.M.]

W.167 Wells, Robert E. Untitled talk. In *Proceedings of the Santiago, Chile Area Conference*, 8-9. Salt Lake City: Church of Jesus Christ of Latter-day Saints, March 1977. The Book of Mormon testifies of Jesus Christ, his doctrine, the power of his name, the reality of his life, and the scope of his priesthood. It contains more information about Christ than does the Bible. He is the creator and is a distinct individual from the Father. He is Jehovah of the Old Testament. [J.W.M.]

W.168 Wells, Rulon S. Untitled talk. *CR* (October 1934): 108-11. Focuses on the mission of angel Moroni (Revelation 14:6-7) to bring the gospel message to the world through the Book of Mormon. Each nation must have the privilege of hearing the gospel in their own language in order to fulfill the scripture in the book of Revelation. Members of the Church must learn the languages of the world and declare that Jesus Christ has restored his truths again upon the earth. [J.W.M.]

W.169 Wendel, Eileen Chabot. *The Book of Mormon Illustrated*. Ogden, UT: Brigham Young Publishers, 1982. Selected passages from the Book of Mormon are arranged along with illustrations to provide a "comic book" style of narrative. [J. T.]

W.170 Wendel, Eileen Chabot. *Nephi the Valiant*. Book 2 of *Stories from the Golden Records*. Salt Lake City: Deseret Book, 1960. A cartoon-style book for children that tells the story of the Book of Mormon from 1 Nephi to the book of Enos. [J.W.M.]

W.171 Wendel, Eileen Chabot. *Stories from the Golden Records*. Salt Lake City: Deseret Book, 1960. A series of books in cartoon format for children that relate stories from the Book of Mormon. [J.W.M.]

W.172 "Were All the Unsealed Records of the Book of Mormon Translated?" *IE* 5 (March 1902): 393-95. Claims that Joseph Smith translated all of the unsealed portions of the Book of Mormon. [L.D.]

W.173 West, Camille G. "Antonio's Book." *Ensign* 21 (March 1991): 28-30. Antonio de Jesus

Salazar received his father's Book of Mormon, which had been given to him by a member of the Mormon Battalion in the 1840s in northern New Mexico. Reading the Book of Mormon changed Antonio's life. [J.W.M.]

W.174 West, Franklin L. *Fruits of Religion.* Salt Lake City: Deseret Book, 1946. The Bible is the main book of scripture for the Church of Jesus Christ of Latter-day Saints; the Book of Mormon is the companion volume of scripture that guides practice, doctrine, and conduct of the Church and clarifies doctrines such as the Lord's interest in all people of the earth, the nature of the soul of man, baptism of little children, democracy, mode of baptism, and the fall of Adam. [J.W.M.]

W.175 West, Jack H. *Trial of the Stick of Joseph: A Lecture Series.* Salt Lake City: Sounds of Zion, 1981. Also, in Spanish, *Juicio del Palo de Jose: Testigos Personales.* Peru: n.p., 1967. A three-part lecture that recounts the events surrounding a mock trial of the Book of Mormon. Analyzes the testimonies of witnesses who claimed to have seen the gold plates, and discusses internal and external evidences of the Book of Mormon. [J.T.]

W.176 West, Roy A. *An Introduction to the Book of Mormon: A Religious-Literary Study.* Salt Lake City: Church of Jesus Christ of Latter-day Saints Department of Education, 1940. A study aid for reading the Book of Mormon. Emphasizes a literary approach while also discussing the purpose, origin, and evidences of the Book of Mormon. [J.T.]

W.177 West, Sandee Gladden. "The Ad." *Ensign* 20 (August 1990): 48-49. A high school student answered an ad in the *Reader's Digest* and received a Book of Mormon. After reading passages in the book of Mosiah explaining death and resurrection, this young woman learned of her own father's death. The Spirit bore witness of the truthfulness of the teachings. [J.W.M.]

W.178 Westenskow, Melvin. *Treasures to Share.* Salt Lake City: Deseret Book, 1948. The explanation of the relationship between the Book of Mormon and the Bible is found within the pages of the Book of Mormon itself. Latter-day Saints do not replace the Bible with the Book of Mormon, they are companions, one complimenting the other. The Bible does prophesy of the Book of Mormon in many places, just as it foretells of Christ without revealing his name. The use of metal and cement in the Book of Mormon was once ridiculed, but is now verified by archaeology. The Book of Mormon adds credence to the Bible. It is a second witness to the divinity of Christ. [J.W.M.]

W.179 "What Happens in the Book of Mormon." *Friend* 14 (January 1984): 28-29. Eleven pictures for children depicting events of the Book of Mormon. [A.T.]

W.180 *What Shall We Believe?* Phoenix, AZ: Visual Arts Co., n.d. Shows the organization of the Church, the coming forth of the Book of Mormon as the stick of Joseph, the plan of salvation, and the first principles of the gospel. Contains charts of the chronology of the Book of Mormon. [J.W.M.]

W.181 "When a Book of Mormon Witness Passed On." *MS* 98 (27 February 1936): 138-39. Brief life story of Oliver Cowdery. He was a special witness for the Book of Mormon and never denied the Book of Mormon even though he was once excommunicated but later rebaptized. [M.D.P.]

W.182 "Where Are the Hills of Ramah and Cumorah?" *Instructor* 75 (January 1940): 8. In an article published by the *Messenger and Advocate* in Kirtland, Ohio, July, 1835, a quote attributed to Joseph Smith appeared. It described the Hill Ramah as being about one mile west of the Hill Cumorah (in New York). Between these two hills was the final battleground of both the Nephite and Jaredite nations. [J.W.M.]

W.183 "Where the Book of Mormon Went to Press." *Ensign* 19 (February 1989): 43-47. Presents color photographs and explanations of people, places, and artifacts associated with the first printing of the Book of Mormon. [J.W.M.]

W.184 Whitehead, Earnest L. *A Concise Reference to the Book of Mormon.* Utah: Bookcraft, 1920. This pamphlet contains scriptural references to many LDS doctrinal subjects found in the

Book of Mormon: authority, America as the promised land, baptism and salvation, baptism of infants, Christ as a personal being, faith and works, an unchangeable gospel, and others. [J.W.M.]

W.185 Whitehead, Earnest L. *The House of Israel; a Treatise on the Destiny, History and Identification of Israel in All the Five Branches.* Salt Lake City: E. L. Whitehead, 1947. A treatise that discusses the history and prophetic future of the tribes of Israel (including the Book of Mormon people) with particular emphasis on their divine mission and role among the nations of the earth. [J.T.]

W.186 Whiting, Gary R. *The Book of Mormon Is Christian: A Study of the Major Christian Doctrines Comparing the Bible and Book of Mormon.* Wichita, KS: Zion's Outpost, 1988. The 1908 edition of the Book of Mormon is used for all referencing in this lesson plan that compares the Book of Mormon with the Bible. Patterns in the Book of Mormon are the same as biblical patterns. Biblical evidences for the Book of Mormon are brought to the attention of the student as well as the purpose of the book and Christ's teachings that are contained within its pages. [J.W.M.]

W.187 Whiting, Gary R. "The Testimony of Amaleki." In *The Book of Mormon: Jacob through Words of Mormon, To Learn with Joy*, edited by Monte S. Nyman and Charles D. Tate Jr., 295-306. Provo, UT: Brigham Young University Religious Studies Center, 1990. Although Amaleki wrote only seventeen verses, he contributed substantially to the Book of Mormon. His writing contains historical information, bears witness of Christ, describes the migration of a Nephite group to Zarahemla, tells of Mulek, gives the Jaredite link, and mentions the people of Zeniff. [J.W.M.]

W.188 Whitmer, David. "An Interview with David Whitmer." *DN* (16 August 1878). In a question/answer interview Whitmer described the plates, the Urim and Thummim, and affirmed his testimony of the Book of Mormon. [J.W.M.]

W.189 Whitmer, David. *The Last Witness Dead.* Monongahela, PA: Ladies' Uplift Circle of the Church of Jesus Christ, 1936. Reprints obituaries on David Whitmer from Missouri newspapers. Stresses his tenacious testimony as one of the Three Witnesses. States some details of his vision, including the handling of the Urim and Thummim and sword of Laban. [D.M.]

W.190 Whitmer, David. *The Solution of The Mormon Problem: What Is It?* N.p.: n.p., 1926. Reprint of pamphlet written by David Whitmer entitled "An Address to All Believers in the Book of Mormon," with a preface by John J. Snyder. [J.W.M.]

W.191 Whitmer, John. "Address." *MA* 2 (March 1836): 285-88. Reiterates his testimony as one of the Eight Witnesses of the Book of Mormon. Testimony is borne with conviction. [D.M.]

W.192 Whitney, Orson F. "The Book of Mormon, Historical and Prophetic Phases." *IE* 30 (September 1927): 941-48. Reports of his visit to Palmyra, Manchester, and the Hill Cumorah, outlines many of the features of the Book of Mormon: the history and prophecy in the book, reference to Zion, America as a land of liberty, the relationship of Joseph and Judah, and Jesus Christ in America. [D.M.]

W.193 Whitney, Orson F. "The Land of Zion." In Whitney's *Saturday Night Thoughts*, 31-35. Salt Lake City, UT: Deseret News, 1921. Contains an overview of the Book of Mormon, and a discussion of Book of Mormon prophecies related to the responsibilities and position of America. Both Nephite and Jaredite prophets understood that America is the land of Zion. Its destiny is linked closely with Jerusalem. [J.W.M.]

W.194 Whittaker, A. C. *The Challenge "The Book of Mormon" Makes to the World.* Salt Lake City: 196?. Challenging others to duplicate the Book of Mormon, the author has published this list of conditions under which the book was translated. [J.W.M.]

W.195 Whittaker, David J. "Orson Pratt: Early Advocate of the Book of Mormon." *Ensign* 14 (April 1984): 54-57. Traces Orson Pratt's work as a "student, advocate, and editor" of the Book of Mormon. Recounts how he drew heavily on the work of his brother, Parley P. Pratt, and on his own scientific background to defend the Book of Mormon. Tells of his work in making extensive format changes to the 1879 edition of the Book of Mormon to make it more accessible to students. [S.P.S.]

W.196 "Who Am I? A Book of Mormon Quiz." *Friend* 4 (March 1974): 38-39. A quiz for children on different characters in the Book of Mormon. [M.D.P.]

W.197 *Why I Believe the Book of Mormon*. Lamoni, IA: Board of Publication of the RLDS Church, 1909. An apologetic tract using common prooftexts as well as unusual ones, such as Ezekiel 17 and Hosea 8:11-12. [D.M.]

W.198 "Why Not Investigate?" *MS* 50 (March 1888): 161-62. The author suggests that some scientific body endeavor to prove or disprove whether archaeological discoveries validate the Book of Mormon. [B.D.]

W.199 Widtsoe, John A. "Alma Speaks to the Twentieth Century." *IE* 31 (November 1927): 20-31. Reprinted in *A Book of Mormon Treasury*. Salt Lake City: Bookcraft, 1976, 83-98. Alma the Younger taught principles that are relevant in our day. The combined teachings of Alma connect the premortal life, present day, and future life. Alma's teachings deal with such concepts as the fall and redemption, the nature of the priesthood, the final judgment, humility, faith, and prayer. [D.M.]

W.200 Widtsoe, John A. *The Book of Mormon*. Independence, MO: Zion Printing, 1934. This tract explains briefly the contents, origin, authenticity, witnesses, consistency, archaeological discovery in modern times, and the Bible prophecies concerning the Book of Mormon. [J.W.M.]

W.201 Widtsoe, John A. *The Book of Mormon*. London: LDS British Mission Office, 1932. Also in *DN Church Section* (7 January 1933): 6, 7. This small leaflet was written to nonmembers to explain what the Book of Mormon is, its origin, and the authenticity of the book. The author observes that the book is consistent in its textual content. Modern archaeology has corroborated the truthfulness of the book. It supports and fulfills the teachings of the Bible and it is an inspired book. He offers a challenge to test its validity. [J.W.M.]

W.202 Widtsoe, John A. "The Book of Mormon." Number Fifteen in the Centennial Series. In Widtsoe's *The Handbook of the Restoration*, 237-42. Independence, MO: Zion's Printing, 1944. The Book of Mormon is a historical record of the ancient inhabitants of America, Christ's "other sheep." It reinforces the Bible and sets high moral standards for living. There are many evidences of its authenticity: witnesses, the book's consistency, modern scientific discoveries, Bible prophecies, its inspired contents, and the witness of the Holy Ghost. [J.W.M.]

W.203 Widtsoe, John A. "Can We Believe the Witnesses to the Book of Mormon?" *IE* 49 (June 1946): 385, 414-15. Also in *A Book of Mormon Treasury*, 39-43. Salt Lake City: Bookcraft, 1959, 1976. And in *Gospel Interpretations*. 3 vols. Salt Lake City: Bookcraft, 1947, 2:133-138. Provides several reasons to believe the testimony of the witnesses of the Book of Mormon. [J.W.M.]

W.204 Widtsoe, John A. "Did the Nephites Have the Higher Priesthood before the Coming of Christ?" *IE* 45 (June 1942): 385, 413, 415. Also in *Evidences and Reconciliation*, edited by G. Homer Durham, 240-42. Salt Lake City: Bookcraft, 1987. Argues that the Nephites possessed the higher priesthood during the era before the resurrected Jesus visited the Nephites (citing 1 Nephi 5:14-16, Alma 10:3, Mosiah 25:21, and others). [L.D.]

W.205 Widtsoe, John A. "Does the Book of Mormon Forbid Polygamy?" *MS* 95 (4 May 1933): 296-97. In Jacob's sermon on immorality (Jacob 2) polygamy is not forbidden. What is forbidden is the taking of wives and concubines without the sanction of God. [J.W.M.]

W.206 Widtsoe, John A. "Does the Kon-Tiki Voyage Confirm the Book of Mormon?" *IE* 54 (May 1951): 318-19. Also published in *Evidences and Reconciliations,* edited by G. Homer Durham, 3:99-102. 3 vols. Salt Lake City: Bookcraft, 1951. Thor Heyerdahl, a Norwegian explorer, successfully accomplished a

4000-mile sea voyage from the coast of Peru to the Tuamotu Islands across the Pacific. The balsa raft named Kon-Tiki sailed only by wind and ocean currents. The Kon-Tiki voyage clearly demonstrates that such voyages could certainly have been made, similar to the claims made in the Book of Mormon. [R.C.D.]

W.207 Widtsoe, John A. "Evidences for the Book of Mormon." *MS* 90 (January 1928): 57-58. Writes that growing evidence has confirmed the Book of Mormon. Widtsoe praises J. M. Sjodahl's *An Introduction to the Study of the Book of Mormon*, and quotes Sjodahl's testimony of the Book of Mormon. [B.D.]

W.208 Widtsoe, John A. "His Other Sheep." *MS* 92 (27 March 1930): 200-1. Perhaps the greatest message of the Book of Mormon is that God speaks to all his children, "on one continent or another, in one land or another," all will be taught the gospel of Jesus Christ. [D.W.P.]

W.209 Widtsoe, John A. "Is Book of Mormon Geography Known?" *IE* 53 (July 1950): 547, 596-97. Also published in *Evidences and Reconciliations*, edited by G. Homer Durham, 3:93-98. 3 vols. Salt Lake City: Bookcraft, 1951. Also in *A Book of Mormon Treasury*, 127-30. Salt Lake City: Bookcraft, 1959, 1976. Although there is little definite evidence or data with which to clearly identify Book of Mormon geographical sites, continued earnest, honest, and scholarly studies should not be discouraged. "All such studies are legitimate," but dogmatic conclusions made without actual verifiable data "must at the best be held as intelligent conjectures." [R.C.D.]

W.210 Widtsoe, John A. "Notes on Moroni's Message." *Young Woman's Journal* 34 (September 1823): 461-65. Lists fourteen specific points related to Moroni's visit, including the value of repentance, prayer as a catalyst, the promise of universal salvation, and warnings concerning covetousness. [D.M.]

W.211 Widtsoe, John A. "The Power of Moroni's Message." *MS* 96 (November 1934): 721-27. Concentrates on the work of salvation for the dead as introduced when Moroni quoted Malachi to Joseph Smith. [B.D.]

W.212 Widtsoe, John A. "Scholarship and the Book of Mormon." *MS* 90 (8 November 1928): 712-13. Although scientific research may substantiate items discussed in the Book of Mormon, there is no need for a scientific explanation for the book. [A.T.]

W.213 Widtsoe, John A. "Was Iron Known in Ancient America?" *IE* 53 (March 1950): 175, 231. Also published in *Evidences and Reconciliations*, edited by G. Homer Durham, 3:89-92. 3 vols. Salt Lake City: Bookcraft, 1951. The view of scholars in the field of American archaeology holds that the pre-Columbian inhabitants of America did not know of or use iron. However, this article, citing the *Science Newsletter* of November 12, 1949, recommends that this view may have to be reevaluated on the basis of new findings of iron in ancient America. [R.C.D.]

W.214 Widtsoe, John A. "Was Steel Known When Lehi Left Jerusalem?" *IE* 50 (May 1947): 304. Argues that steel existed around the time Lehi left Jerusalem, about 600 B.C. [L.D.]

W.215 Widtsoe, John A. "What Was the Vocabulary of Joseph Smith?" *IE* 54 (June 1951): 399, 476. Any translation will reflect the vocabulary of the translator. Such was the case with Joseph Smith and the Book of Mormon. An average "fairly well-educated" person possesses an 8,000 word vocabulary. Joseph Smith as a youth would have had a substantially smaller vocabulary. Interestingly, the Book of Mormon has a total vocabulary (including person and place names) of 3,307 words. [R.C.D.]

W.216 Widtsoe, John A. "Why Did Joseph Smith, the Prophet, Need the Help of the Urim and Thummim?" *IE* 43 (January 1940): 33, 37. The Urim and Thummim were used in connection with priestly functions of the Old Testament and later were important in the translation process of the Book of Mormon. Historically they served to facilitate communication with the Lord. [J.W.M.]

W.217 Widtsoe, John A., and Franklin S. Harris. *Seven Claims of the Book of Mormon: A Collection of Evidences*. Independence, MO: Press of Zion's Printing and Publishing, n.d. A missionary manual that presents seven Book of Mormon claims and gives supporting evidence. The claims include: the Book of Mormon is of divine origin, it consists of writings by successive historians, it was written in reformed Egyptian on metal plates, the native Americans are partly of Hebrew descent, and there were great civilizations in ancient America that Christ visited. [C.C.]

W.218 Widtsoe, Osborne. "The Test of Section Sixty-seven." *IE* 10 (January 1907): 161-65. Examines the idea that Joseph Smith could not have been an impostor who wrote the Book of Mormon. His limited education and young age at the time make the idea absurd, as does the fact that the educated William E. M'Lellin tried unsuccessfully to create a revelation from the Lord (D&C 67) similar to the many revelations received by Joseph Smith. [J.W.M.]

W.219 Widtsoe, Osborne J. P. "Other Sheep." In Widtsoe's *What Jesus Taught*, 291-98. Salt Lake City: Deseret Sunday School Union, 1918. Jesus appeared among the Nephites and declared that they were his "other sheep" who were identified in the book of John. [J.W.M.]

W.220 Widtsoe, Osborne J. P. *The Restoration of the Gospel*. Salt Lake City: Deseret Book, 1912. Chapter 20 deals with the eleven witnesses who viewed the gold plates of the Book of Mormon. The Three Witnesses reconfirmed their testimonies in their last days of mortality and though three of the Eight Witnesses left the Church, none of the eight denied their testimonies. [J.W.M.]

W.221 Widtsoe, Osborn J. P. "The Unfair Fairness of Rev. Spaulding." *IE* (April 1913): 593-603. Reprint from *DN* (15 February 1913). Explains why Reverent Spaulding's testing of the Book of Mormon by examining the authenticity of the book of Abraham as an ancient Egyptian text is unfair. Latter-day Saints do not value the Bible less than the Book of Mormon. The belief of the Church is that both were divinely inspired of God and are placed on the same plane, though it is recognized that the Bible may have copyists' errors. [J.W.M.]

W.222 Wight, La Preal. "I Am Brought Forth to Meet You." *IE* 53 (October 1950): 781, 810. The Book of Mormon prophet and writer Moroni prophesied that he would come forth "triumphant through the air" at a future date (Moroni 10:34). Wight sees a quite literal fulfillment in this prophecy in the statues of Moroni on the top of the Salt Lake Temple and the Hill Cumorah. Moroni now stands triumphant in the air. [R.C.D.]

W.223 Wilcox, S. Michael. "Book of Moroni." In *Encyclopedia of Mormonism*, edited by Daniel H. Ludlow, 1:157-58. 5 vols. New York: Macmillan, 1992. Explains the contents and organization of the book of Moroni. Discusses the loosely related but important items that Moroni brought together including ordinances, Mormon's sermons and letters, Moroni's exhortation and farewell including his final testimony of Jesus Christ. [B.D.]

W.224 Wilcox, S. Michael. *Choosing the Fullness: Wickedness or Righteousness*. Salt Lake City: Bookcraft, 1988. A meditation on the "two ways" theme, which contrasts fruits leading to happiness or misery. Includes a chapter on "the Nephites' rejection of the good." Discusses scriptural warnings and extols the Zion society described in 4 Nephi. [D.M.]

W.225 Wilcox, S. Michael. "I Have a Question: I am confused by the gospel principle of justification by faith. Can you explain it to me?" *Ensign* 21 (June 1991): 51-53. The Book of Mormon defines this principle particularly well by the words it substitutes in place of justification, such as blameless and guiltless. Justification then is the process through which guilt is removed through faith. [J.W.M.]

W.226 Wilcox, S. Michael. "Nephi's Message to the 'Gentiles.'" In *The Book of Mormon: Second Nephi, The Doctrinal Structure*, edited by Monte S. Nyman and Charles D. Tate Jr., 269-86. Provo, UT: Brigham Young University Religious Studies Center, 1989. 2 Nephi 25-33 represents Nephi's final discourse having the purpose of bringing gentile, Jew, and "the remnant of his seed" to Christ. The expression "gentile nation" may be used interchangeably with "Christian nations." Nephi outlines the Messiahship of Christ: He is the eternal God who manifests himself to every nation through signs, miracles, wonders, and through the Holy Ghost. Pride, learning, and the precepts of men stand in opposition to God's work. [J.W.M.]

W.227 Wilcox, S. Michael. "Samuel the Lamanite." In *Encyclopedia of Mormonism*, edited by Daniel H. Ludlow, 3:1259. 5 vols. New York: Macmillan, 1992. Approximately 5 B.C. Samuel, a Lamanite, preached repentance in Zarahemla. He prophesied of Christ's birth and crucifixion. No other evidence of his life and ministry is recorded. [J.W.M.]

W.228 Wilcox, S. Michael. "Spiritual Rebirth." In *The Book of Mormon: Mosiah, Salvation Only through Christ*, edited by Monte S. Nyman and Charles D. Tate Jr., 247-60. Provo, UT: Brigham Young University Religious Studies Center, 1991. Distinguishing between natural man and the physical body is important in understanding how overcoming the natural man becomes a rebirth through the atonement of Jesus Christ. The natural man yields to carnal and untamed desires. The physical body, however, is essential to a fullness of joy. Transforming our natural tendencies to Christ-like qualities brings about a death of the old self and brings a "mighty change" or new birth that occurs through the atonement of Christ, loving him, faith in him, and hope in his mercy. [J.W.M.]

W.229 Wilde, Orrin G. *Landmarks of Ancient America*. N.p., 1947. A 26-page non-dogmatic pamphlet on Book of Mormon geography. Guesses where locations are in relation to the American continent. [D.M.]

W.230 Wilkinson, Barbara Smith. "Understanding the Nephite Monetary System." In *Recent Book of Mormon Developments, Articles from the Zarahemla Record*, 2:222-23. 2 vols. Independence, MO: Zarahemla Research Foundation, 1992. An evaluation of the Nephite monetary system as explained in Alma 8 that establishes current American dollar values for Nephite money. [B.D.]

W.231 Wilkinson, LaVern. "Waters of Sebus." *IE* 30 (February 1927): 346-47. Ammon received the miraculous power of God as the result of obedience to God. Individuals qualify for the Lord's work by diligent study. Power is invested in them by prayer and fasting, and there must be a desire to serve. [J.W.M.]

W.232 Willes, Joseph S. "Could Joseph Smith Have Written the Book of Mormon?" *IE* 32 (June 1929): 673-77. Briefly reviews the publication history of the Book of Mormon. Argues that Joseph Smith did not have the means, the proper conditions, nor the time to have written the Book of Mormon. Rather, the book was a translation, as per the claim of Joseph Smith. [D.M.]

W.233 "William Smith's Story Concerning the Plates of the Book of Mormon." *Instructor* 75 (January 1940): 6. An interview that took place two weeks before the death of William Smith, wherein Smith avows that he did indeed lift the gold plates from which the Book of Mormon was translated. [J.W.M.]

W.234 Williams, Camille S., and Donna Lee Bowen. "Ordinary People in the Book of Mormon." *Ensign* 22 (January 1992): 36-39. Provides examples of "ordinary faithful people" in the Book of Mormon. For instance, Abish demonstrated a strong belief in the Lord, Saria showed a willingness to be obedient, and the story of the daughter of Jared teaches that position and beauty have little connection to faith or to one's ability to serve the Lord. [A.C.W.]

W.235 Williams, Clyde J. "Book of Jacob." In *Encyclopedia of Mormonism*, edited by Daniel H. Ludlow, 1:147-48. 5 vols. New York: Macmillan, 1992. A description of the book of Jacob, its organization and content. It seems to have three parts: a discourse by Jacob at the temple calling his people to repentance; prophecies of the atonement of Christ, his rejection by the Jews, and the scattering and gathering of Israel; and the confrontation with the antichrist, Sherem. [B.D.]

W.236 Williams, Clyde J. "The Book of Mormon and Overcoming Satan." In *Doctrines of the Book of Mormon, 1991 Sperry Symposium*, edited by Bruce A. Van Orden and Brent L. Top, 243-56. Salt Lake City: Deseret Book, 1992. The Book of Mormon conveys the Lord's messages concerning Satan's role, characteristics, and purpose, and places emphasis on how to identify and overcome Satan's tactics. Twelve tactics are noted and seven principles of overcoming these tactics are listed. [J.W.M.]

W.237 Williams, Clyde J. "Deliverance from Bondage." In *The Book of Mormon: Mosiah, Salvation Only through Christ*, edited by Monte S. Nyman and Charles D. Tate Jr., 261-74. Provo, UT: Brigham Young University Religious Studies Center, 1991. Relating Mosiah 7-24 to our day, this article identifies the steps that lead to bondage, what must be done to be delivered from it, and to what degree the Lord will help. There are many ways in which modern man brings bondage upon himself, but deliverance always comes by turning to Jesus Christ. [J.W.M.]

W.238 Williams, Clyde J. "An Examination of Influential Factors Affecting Students in Applying Book of Mormon Principles toward the Resolution of Personal Problems." Ph.D. diss, Brigham Young University, 1989. Members of the Church are under the condemnation of the Lord because they have failed to apply the teachings of the Book of Mormon in their lives. The practice of putting oneself into the place of individuals in the Book of Mormon is invaluable; it leads to understanding deity. The Book of Mormon carries a solution to every problem in its pages. [J.W.M.]

W.239 Williams, Clyde J. "The Godhead and Godhood As Taught in the Book of Mormon." In *A Symposium on the Book of Mormon*, 120-24. Salt Lake City: Church of Jesus Christ of Latter-day Saints, CES, August 1986. Outlines the modern Christian concept of God using the Nicean and Athanasian creeds and states that this concept is based on a misunderstanding of the scriptures. The Book of Mormon defines the following doctrines: (1) there are three distinct beings in the Godhead, (2) the Father and Son possess physical bodies, (3) there is a doctrine of the Fatherhood of Christ, and (4) man can become like God. [A.T.]

W.240 Williams, Clyde J. "Instruments in the Hands of God: The Message of Alma." In *The Book of Mormon: Alma, The Testimony of the Word*, edited by Monte S. Nyman and Charles D. Tate Jr., 89-106. Provo, UT: Brigham Young University Religious Studies Center, 1992. The sons of Mosiah were instruments in the hand of the Lord to accomplish their missionary labors. To be missionaries, they needed to possess scriptural knowledge, fast and pray, possess patience, serve as examples to the people, and remain faithful in the gospel. In turn, the Lord directed them and their joy in the harvest was great. Their missionary experiences provide us with a model for missionary work today. [N.K.Y.]

W.241 Williams, David M. *Let Us Go Back to Christ: Looking unto Jesus, the Author and Finisher of Our Faith*. Salt Lake City, 1900. Members of the Church must return to the Book of Mormon, for they have begun to stray from the basic principles and doctrines. [J.W.M.]

W.242 Williams, Frederick G., III. "Did Lehi Land in Chile." Provo, UT: FARMS, 1988. See also *Reexploring the Book of Mormon*, edited by John W. Welch, 57-61. Salt Lake City: Deseret Book and FARMS, 1992. A quote attributed to Frederick G. Williams, I, concerning the landing of Lehi and his group in Chile may not reflect the truth. Three handwritten copies of this statement exist, none of which provides evidence as to their source. [J.W.M.]

W.243 Williams, L. E. "The New Witness." *MS* 73 (23 November 1911): 737-39. Since the Christian world is filled with unbelief, there was a need for a second witness. The Book of Mormon fulfills the prophecies of Ezekiel and Isaiah. Using the "old" (the Bible) and the "new" (the Book of Mormon) to support one another, the searcher for the truth may weigh the evidence favorably. [J.W.M.]

W.244 Willis, Bertram T. "Keynote of a Prophet's Life." *MS* 98 (8 July 1937): 437-38. Alma$_2$ and the sons of Mosiah were miraculously converted to Jesus and his gospel. Alma's missionary experiences may be compared to the ministry of Jesus Christ who also accepted a lower station in life to serve his fellowmen and was subject to mockery and humiliation. [J.W.M.]

W.245 Wilson, David J. "Book of Mormon Witnesses and Their Testimony Meet Legal Standards." *Relief Society Magazine* 38 (August 1951): 512-15. The Old Testament law of witnesses was approved by Paul the Apostle, Hammurabi, and Utah code: by the mouth of two or three witnesses shall the matter be established. The Three Witnesses and Eight Witnesses of the Book of Mormon fulfill this criteria. The most important witness for which there is no substitute is the Holy Ghost who witnesses to the very soul of man. [J.W.M.]

W.246 Wilson, Douglas. "Prospects for the Study of the Book of Mormon as a Work of American Literature." *Dialogue* 3 (Spring 1968): 29-41. A non-Mormon, the author suggests that since the Book of Mormon has affected millions of Americans and their history, it ought to be seriously counted in the canon of American literature. Reasons why the Book of Mormon has not been studied as such, and logical approaches to its study are explored. [B.D.]

W.247 Wilson, Garth A. "The Mulekites." *Ensign* 17 (March 1987): 60-64. Traces the history of the Mulekite people, from the events leading up to the destruction of Jerusalem and the flight of one of King Zedekiah's sons with a group of his people, to their discovery by King Mosiah and union with the Nephites. Recounts their involvement in the record of the Book of Mormon and reminds us that they made up the major portion of the Nephite people. [S.P.S.]

W.248 Wilson, L. A. "Bearing on the Book of Mormon." *IE* 30 (February 1927): 314. Discusses the Chinese account of their first settlement in China. Relates their experiences with the migration of the Jaredites from the Tower of Babel to the great sea. [L.D.]

W.249 Wilson, Thomas P. "Odds and Ends: The Book of Mormon Bulletin." *Minnequa Historical Society* 29 (Fall 1940): 25-26. Gives brief assessment of the Book of Mormon. Says that anthropologists agree on some points with the Book of Mormon. [D.M.]

W.250 Wilson, Timothy B. *Mormon's Story: An Adaptation Based on the Book of Mormon*. U.S.A.: n.p., 1993. Book of Mormon text reformatted with the actual text in the right-hand column, and a summarized explanation for younger readers in the left-hand column. [A.C.W.]

W.251 Wilson, William A. "Three Nephites." In *Encyclopedia of Mormonism*, edited by Daniel H. Ludlow, 4:1477-78. 5 vols. New York: Macmillan, 1992. The Three Nephites (3 Nephi 28:4-9) wished to stay upon the earth until the Lord's Second Coming. Discusses legends and folklore concerning them. [B.D.]

W.252 Winchester, Benjamin. "The Claims of the Book of Mormon Established—It Also Defended." *The Gospel Reflector* 1 (15 March 1841): 105-23. The American continent was once inhabited by an enlightened people as ancient relics and archaeologists have testified. The author quotes Priest, Davis, Boudinot, and others who believe the aborigines of America belong to the house of Israel. The Book of Mormon gives an account of the destruction of the once enlightened people of the American continent. Its purpose is to clarify false doctrine, to bring people to the Holy One of Israel, to gather the lost ones of Israel, and restore the truth to the earth. [J.W.M.]

W.253 Winchester, Benjamin. "History of the Ancients of America and Also of the Book of Mormon." *The Gospel Reflector* 1 (15 March 1841): 124-37. Recounts the Book of Mormon story and tells of the coming forth of the plates with the Urim and Thummim. It is not new to find sacred instruments deposited in the earth—in the apocrypha Jeremiah hid the ark of the covenant in Mt. Nebo. The plates were hidden from view just as Moses was not allowed to show the tablets of stone to everyone. [J.W.M.]

W.254 Winchester, Benjamin. *History of the Priesthood: In Defense of the Doctrine and Position of Latter-day Saints*. Philadelphia, PA: n.p., 1843. Analyzes the history of the priesthood from the "beginning of the world to the present time." Chapter seven provides evidence for the authenticity of the Book of Mormon by presenting a brief summary of its content, its purpose, the biblical prophecies that pertain to it, and the positive results that come from reading it. [J.W.M.]

W.255 Winchester, Benjamin. "Introduction to the Subject of the Book of Mormon." *The Gospel Reflector* 1 (1 March 1841): 98-105. An examination of the prominent objections to revelation and the Book of Mormon. The Book of Mormon is the work of God and has overcome opposition, and those who are earnest seekers of truth have embraced it as an instrument in the hand of God. [J.W.M.]

W.256 Wirth, Diane E. *The Challenge to the Critics: Scholarly Evidences of the Book of Mormon.* Bountiful: Horizon, 1986. Responds to anti-Mormon comments regarding the authenticity of the Book of Mormon, and sets forth evidence to support Latter-day Saint claims. Addresses the Smithsonian statement, metal plates, stone boxes, wordprints, chiasmus, Hebraisms, reformed Egyptian, Nephite monetary system, the wheel, the tree of life theme on Stela 5 at Izapa, and Christ in America. [B.D.]

W.257 Wirth, Diane E. *Discoveries of the Truth.* Santa Clara, CA: Vanguard Graphics, 1978. Gives evidence to support her theory that the white and bearded god Quetzalcoatl is Jesus Christ. Issues discussed include Phoenician seafarers, cranial deformations, trepanning, cement, cotton, the wheel, arch, the horse, star of David, and the tree of life. [B.D.]

W.258 Wirth, Diane E. "The Tree of Life Offers Evidence of Pre-Columbian Contact." *Pursuit* (Fourth Quarter 1981): 168-71. Compares New World examples of the tree of life symbol with examples from Assyria and finds that the basic elements are similar, if not identical. Points out that the Book of Mormon, as the Church of Jesus Christ of Latter-day Saints claims, was written by early inhabitants of America. There is unmistakable evidence of trans-oceanic crossings prior to Columbus. [J.W.M.]

W.259 Wirth, Diane E., and Steven L. Olsen. "Four Quarters." In *Reexploring the Book of Mormon*, edited by John W. Welch, 145-49. Salt Lake City: Deseret Book and FARMS, 1992. Book of Mormon writers use the land division term *four quarters* in many places. This is a common practice in the Bible (Joshua 15:5, Isaiah 47:15 and 56:11, Mark 1:45, and Acts 9:32), Mayan and Indian writings, and in Ixtilxochitl's documentation. The same usage is common to Ebla and Egyptian records in the Old World. [N.K.Y.]

W.260 Wirthlin, Joseph B. "The Straight and Narrow Way." *Ensign* 20 (November 1990): 64-66. A serious and constant study of the scriptures, especially the Book of Mormon, will aid our quest through the straight and narrow way. The word of God is the rod to help avoid temptations that will lead out of the straight and narrow path. [J.W.M.]

W.261 "The Witness and the Gold Plates." *Friend* 14 (August-September 1984): 28-29. A children's story of the Three Witnesses and gold plates. [A.T.]

W.262 *Witnesses of the Book of Mormon.* Salt Lake City: Church of Jesus Christ of Latter-day Saints, 1975. A tract addressed to those who do not belong to the LDS church dealing with the biblical law of witnesses, the Three Witnesses and Eight Witnesses of the Book of Mormon. Includes the statements of the witnesses. [D.W.P.]

W.263 Wittorf, John H., ed. "Joseph Smith and the Prehistoric Mound-Builders of Eastern North America." *SEHA* 123 (October 1970): 1-9. Shows that Joseph Smith never made a conclusive statement supporting the belief that mounds and the mound builders of Northeastern America represent the remains of Book of Mormon lands or peoples. Discusses the Enon mound, Zelph mound, Adena and Hopwell cultures, and the Kinderhook plates. [B.D.]

W.264 Wolf, Teresa. "A Book for Eveline." *Ensign* 21 (September 1991): 57-58. A gift of a Book of Mormon, daily study of the book, and visits from the missionaries began to change this lady's life. [J.W.M.]

W.265 Wolfe, Walter M. "The Book of Mormon from a Bible Standpoint." *MS* 65 (4 June 1903): 353-57. Refutes arguments against the Book of Mormon that use the Bible as evidence, e.g., Revelations 22:18-19. Says Isaiah prophesied of Book of Mormon, as did Ezekiel. [A.C.W.]

W.266 Wolfe, Walter M. "Exploring American Ruins." *MS* 65 (25 February–19 March 1903): 132-34, 161-64, 176-80. This three-part series presents some legends and traditions of the American Indian in association with ruins, especially of Central America. They seem to prove that the Book of Mormon is historically correct. Throughout the Americas, the Indians believed in a Messiah who came a long time ago and promised to return. The high priest of the Quiche Indians wore a breastplate with seven precious stones. It was a Urim and Thummim used to decide the innocence or guilt of those accused of crimes. It would reveal both past and future events. [J.W.M.]

W.267 Wolfe, Walter M. "Legends Prove Truth of Scripture." *MS* 65 (April 1903): 241-44. Focuses on the origin of mankind, history, tradition, legends and mythology, and the manner in which the Book of Mormon proves the common source of religious belief. The world will someday understand "the common origin" theory and will believe the Bible and the Book of Mormon. [J.W.M.]

W.268 Wolfe, Walter M. "Modern Research and the Book of Mormon." *MS* 65 (6 August 1903): 501-3, 507-9. Cites various sources to argue the authenticity of the Book of Mormon. Writes concerning the confusion of tongues at the tower of Babel when God led people over the sea in ships to the islands. With the discoveries of ruins on the American continent the Jewish origin of American natives is being increasingly recognized. [B.D.]

W.269 "Women of the Book of Mormon." *Relief Society Magazine* 5 (January 1918): 47-50. In the ancient world Hebrew women had more status than in other cultures. Their chastity was imperative under the Mosaic law. Book of Mormon women inherited this culture. Though only three women are named in the book, references to women, mothers, and daughters are numerous. [J.W.M.]

W.270 Wood, Edward J. "An Interesting Occurrence in Canada." *Relief Society Magazine* 4 (1917): 135-37. Testimony of Kree Indians in Canada who found "their book" through a vision of their head chief. He visited the spirit world and was told of a book of sacred Indian history, which turned out to be the Book of Mormon. [J.W.M.]

W.271 Wood, Edward J. Untitled talk. *CR* (October 1915): 65-68. A Mormon bishop was invited to visit with a gathering of Kree Indians, and was asked by the chief to teach them the gospel. He taught them about the Book of Mormon. Upon completion of his teaching he was told about a vision that the chief had in which he was told of this important book that contained their history. The chief bore witness that this history was the Book of Mormon. [J.W.M.]

W.272 Wood, John Karl. *An Approach to the Book of Mormon.* Logan, UT: n.p., 1949. Notes that relatively few people read the entire Book of Mormon. Suggests that readers might dispel this problem by learning about Mormon and his interests, which the author explains in summary form. [D.M.]

W.273 Wood, Kathryn. "Hope in Christ." *Ensign* 22 (December 1992): 17. The power of hope through Christ is shown in the Book of Mormon and can be applied to an individual's personal life. Even though Mormon and Moroni lived in a "hopeless time," they continued to call their people to repentance, and left a record to give hope in our day. [A.C.W.]

W.274 Wood, Wilford C., comp. *Joseph Smith Begins His Work.* Salt Lake City: Deseret News Press, 1958. An official reproduction of the first edition of the Book of Mormon, printed from the first uncut sheets of the 1830 edition of the Book of Mormon. [L.D.]

W.275 Woodbury, Naomi. "On the Origin of the Jaredites." In *15th Symposium on Archaeology of the Scriptures.* 67-72. Provo, UT: Brigham Young University, 1964. The religious and cultural elements in the book of Ether should be compared with those of Mesopotamia prior to 2000 B.C. A comparison of the religious teachings of the book of Ether and known Sumerian historical facts is made. Jaredite names are found to be similar to many names belonging to the Sargonid period. [J.W.M.]

W.276 Woodford, Irene Briggs. "The 'Tree of Life' in Ancient America; Its Representations and Significance." M.A. thesis, Brigham Young University, 1950. Offers an interpretation of the Mesoamerican "cross-shaped tree" as being a representation of the tree of life and several important symbolic figures, including the bird, serpent, monster, and the two personages. [B.D.]

W.277 Woodford, Irene Briggs. "The 'Tree of Life' in Ancient America; Its Representations and Significance." *UASN Bulletin* 4 (March 1953): 1-18. A condensed form of her M.A. thesis, Woodford interprets the Mesoamerican tree of life and its attendant elements. [B.D.]

W.278 Woodford, Robert J., "The Articles and Covenants of the Church of Christ and the Book of Mormon." In *Doctrines for Exaltation: The 1989 Sperry Symposium on the Doctrine and Covenants*, edited by H. Dean Garrett and Rex C. Reeve Jr., 262-73. Salt Lake City: Deseret Book, 1989. The Book of Mormon contains "all things concerning the foundation of the [Lord's] Church." The influence of the doctrines in the Book of Mormon upon D&C 20 is shown. [B.D.]

W.279 Woodford, Robert J. "Book of Mormon Personalities Known by Joseph Smith." *Ensign* 8 (August 1978): 12-15. Cites accounts of visits to Joseph Smith by such Book of Mormon personalities as, Moroni, Alma, Nephi, Mormon, and the Nephite twelve disciples. [B.D.]

W.280 Woodford, Robert J. "The Chains of Hell." Salt Lake City: University of Utah Institute of Religion, 1978. Transcript of a devotional address in which the speaker discusses the devil's chains, the chains of hell, and a number of other Book of Mormon motifs that lead to spiritual well-being. [D.M.]

W.281 Woodford, Robert J. "I Have A Question: How much do we know about baptism before Christ's time?" *Ensign* 21 (July 1991): 74-75. The Book of Mormon records contain more than fifty references to baptism prior to the birth of Jesus Christ. Other scriptural passages confirm that baptism was known from the beginning when Adam and Eve were baptized. [J.W.M.]

W.282 Woodruff, Elia S. Untitled talk. *CR* (October 1928): 54-57. Relates the experience of a Lamanite woman whose house had burned to ashes. As she went back to view the damage the Spirit told her to look for her book, and she found the Book of Mormon, the only book unscorched. This important witness of the value of the book led this woman to become a member of the Church. [J.W.M.]

W.283 Woodruff, Wilford. "The Book of Mormon." *MS* 6 (15 August 1845): 65-70. Missionary-oriented essay. Justifies the existence of extra-biblical scripture. Explains the roles of the descendants of Joseph in America, using Genesis 48. Shows similarities between Israelite and Indian sacrificial customs. Refers to the "sticks" of Ezekiel 37; also discusses the relevance of Isaiah 29 and Psalm 85. Bears testimony of the part the Book of Mormon plays in the Restoration. [D.M.]

W.284 Woodruff, Wilford. "Discourse (delivered by President Woodruff at General Conference April 14, 1890)." In *Collected Discourses Delivered by President Wilford Woodruff, His Two Counselors, the 12 Apostles, and Others, Vol. 1. (1886-1889)*, edited by Brian H. Stuy, 29. Sandy, UT: B. H. S. Publishing, 1988. The need for revelation is great in the past, present, and future. We have the stick of Judah (Bible), the stick of Joseph (Book of Mormon), and the Doctrine and Covenants. Revelation need not end with these. [J.W.M.]

W.285 Woodruff, Wilford. "Nephites Found in New Mexico." *IE* 60 (April 1957): 242-43, 267-69. Also in *A Book of Mormon Treasury*, 222-28. Salt Lake City: Bookcraft, 1959, 1976. Author declares he found several tribes that he classified as Nephite (because of their beauty, cleanliness, industry, virtues, and purity of national blood) among the American Indians, including the Zunio, Lagumas, and Isletas. [A.T.]

W.286 Woodruff, Wilford. "Transatlantic Antiquities." *MS* 6 (1 August 1845): 56-57. A testimony that the Book of Mormon's divine truth will one day overwhelm the learned of the world with the Lord's power. [A.C.W.]

W.287 Woods, Fred E. "The Record of Alma: A Prophetic Pattern of the Principles Governing Testimony." In *The Book of Mormon: Alma, the Testimony of the Word*, edited by Monte S. Nyman and Charles D. Tate Jr., 305-19. Provo, UT: Brigham Young University Religious Studies Center, 1992. The book of Alma represents only 1.76 percent of the time period covered in the Book of Mormon but comprises 22.6 percent of the Book of Mormon. Mormon recognized that it was an important work. Alma always bore his witness of the truths he taught. He spent all his days from the time of his conversion trying to lift others to Jesus Christ. We can use his approach to bearing testimony in our work in the Church today. [N.K.Y.]

W.288 Wright, Dennis A. "Helping Students to Read the Book of Mormon." In *A Symposium on the Book of Mormon*, 109-10. Salt Lake City: Church of Jesus Christ of Latter-day Saints, 1979. Provides suggestions for the beginning Book of Mormon student. He suggests having students read from 3-5 minutes at a session. A mini-drama will help to acquaint students with the characters. Visual aids, small group studies, and creativity help the learner. [N.K.Y.]

W.289 Wright, G. Frederick. "The Recently Discovered 'Solomon Spaulding' Manuscript and the Book of Mormon." *Oberlin Review* 13 (20 February 1886): 133. Rejects as unfounded the claim of Professor Samuel S. Partello that he had located the Spaulding manuscript, recounting the story of the manuscript's discovery in Honolulu. Holds, nevertheless, that the question of Book of Mormon authorship is irrelevant. [D.M.]

W.290 Wright, H. Curtis. "Ancient Burials of Metal Documents in Stone Boxes." In *By Study and Also by Faith*, edited by John M. Lundquist and Stephen D. Ricks, 2:273-34. Salt Lake City: Deseret Book and FARMS, 1990. Gives a summary of numerous burials of metallic documents by a multitude of cultures. Many of these records were encased in stone boxes or other containers. Discoveries of metal documents in Alexandria have established an archaeological connection between practices of the Ptolemies and Mesopotamian kings. Various methods of preserving ancient records and writings in antiquity are researched and presented. [A.A.]

W.291 Wright, H. Curtis. "Metallic Documents of Antiquity." *BYU Studies* 10 (Summer 1970): 457-77. Discusses records of antiquity prepared on metal. Cites several metallic documents that exist today, including religious metallic documents and a metallic epigraphy. [L.D.]

W.292 Wright, H. Curtis. "Mulek." In *Encyclopedia of Mormonism*, edited by Daniel H. Ludlow, 2:969-70. 5 vols. New York: Macmillan, 1992. Describes Mulek and his people. The Book of Mormon asserts that Mulek was a son of Zedekiah who escaped from Jerusalem. Jeremiah 38:6 mentions "Malchiah the son of Hammelech," which may be a reference to Mulek. [B.D.]

W.293 Wright, Ruth B. "Draw Strength from the Book of Mormon." *Ensign* 20 (November 1990): 78-79. All individuals should gain truth and strength from the Book of Mormon. Correlates Book of Mormon principles to today's world. [L.D.]

W.294 Wunderlich, Jean. "Some Thoughts on the Social Message of the Book of Mormon." *IE* 41 (April 1938): 222-23, 234-36. Also in *A Book of Mormon Treasury*, 268-74. Salt Lake City: Bookcraft, 1959, 1976. Uses the discourses of Alma and Amulek to the Zoramites as a partial guide to determine what the Book of Mormon teaches about social action. The work teaches that violence is not a recommended "principle of social action" and "the solution of social difficulties must be sought on the spiritual plane." Also discusses what the Book of Mormon teaches about government. [A.T.]

Y.

Y.001 Yarn, David H. Jr. "The Coming of Moroni, the Mission of Moroni, Bible Prophecies and the Book of Mormon, Witnesses to the Book of Mormon." In Yarn's *Faith in a Day of Unbelief,* 5-38. Salt Lake City: Deseret Book, 1960. Moroni appeared to Joseph Smith to reveal a record engraved on gold plates. Joseph was instructed by the angel over a period of four years before receiving the plates and translating them. Many witnesses provide their testimonies of the Book of Mormon, three of whom are discussed briefly. [J.W.M.]

Y.002 Yates, Thomas J. "Succession of Book of Mormon Authors." *IE* 37 (March 1934): 162. A listing of Book of Mormon authors, the number of years each composed his writings, and their order of succession. Includes scriptural references. [J.W.M.]

Y.003 Yorgason, Blaine, and Brenton G. Yorgason. *To Mothers from the Book of Mormon: A Letter to Missionaries and Other Students of the Gospel.* Orem, UT: Keepsake Book Cards, 1989. Discusses the positive impact of Sariah, Mary the mother of Jesus, and the mothers of the "sons of Helaman." [D.M.]

Y.004 Yorgason, Brenton G. *Little Known Evidences of the Book of Mormon.* Salt Lake City: Covenant, 1989. Gives a religious history of Joseph Smith's acquisition and translation of the gold plates by divine assistance, including the use of the Urim and Thummim and the seer stone; discusses word print studies that confirm the authenticity of the Book of Mormon; relates a linguistic analysis explained by a scholar of Arabic; summarizes the contents of the Book of Mormon. [B.D.]

Y.005 Young, Biloine. *Exploring the Book of Mormon.* 4 parts. Independence, MO: Herald House, 1960. A work designed for youth that discusses the history of the acquisition and translation of the plates, the history of the Jaredites, and Lehi's voyage into the desert. [B.D.]

Y.006 Young, Brigham. "Faithfulness and Apostasy." *JD* 2:257-58. Refers to the testimonies of Martin Harris and Oliver Cowdery in relation to the Book of Mormon. Notes that Cowdery bore an aggressive testimony while practicing law in Michigan. [D.M.]

Y.007 Young, Brigham. Untitled talk. *CR* (October 1901): 66-67. It is the responsibility of the twelve to take the gospel to every nation of the earth, while those of us who stay home must read the scriptures, especially the Book of Mormon. It is a "pure translation from the original." [J.W.M.]

Y.008 Young, Clifford E. Untitled talk. *CR* (April 1946): 85-89. The motives and intentions of many of history's greatest men were called into question—Abraham Lincoln, Joseph Smith, Oliver Cowdery, and David Whitmer. Cowdery and Whitmer were witnesses of the Book of Mormon who were true to their testimonies. In an interview with James H. Moyle, David Whitmer testified after fifty-two years that the Book of Mormon was a divine book. [J.W.M.]

Y.009 Young, Levi Edgar. "Christopher Columbus: Was His Work Designed by God?" *MS* 64 (November 1902): 705-8. A testimony that Columbus was inspired by God, to support 1 Nephi 13:10-12. Includes a brief summary of Columbus's life, highlighting points that show he was inspired, and quotes Columbus's words that God made him the messenger of the new heaven and the new earth, which is spoken of in the book of Revelation, and showed him the spot where to find it. [B.D.]

Y.010 Young, Levi Edgar. "Goldsmiths of Ancient Times." *IE* 52 (April 1949): 206-8. Spanish libraries contain historical accounts that describe a chamber in which gold plates were found. Ancient American goldsmiths made plates of gold that were thin like paper and on which ancient hieroglyphs were engraved. [J.W.M.]

Y.011 Young, Levi Edgar. "Records of the Lamanites." *MS* 91 (18 April 1979): 241-43. Summarizes the Book of Mormon story concerning the Hebrew origin of the American Indians. [R.H.B.]

Y.012 Young, Levi Edgar. Untitled talk. *CR* (October 1928): 102-6. Archaeologist Max Uhle believes the ancient Americans descended from the Asians, via immigration across the Bering Strait. However, other groups may have sailed to America. The Book of Mormon teaches Hebrew doctrine influenced by Christian beliefs and proves that Christianity is a continuation of Judaism. [B.D.]

Y.013 Young, Levi Edgar. Untitled talk. *CR* (October 1935): 77-79. The Book of Mormon, like the Bible, was written over a period of time by inspired men of God and later translated at great expense to the translators. The two books present a divine message that Jesus is the Christ. Only through prayer and revelation as Moroni promises can the knowledge of God come. [J.W.M.]

Y.014 "Young Men Can See Further." *IE* 64 (October 1961): 758-59, 767. A message to young men comparing the Book of Mormon to binoculars, which allow you to see ahead in order to avoid pitfalls and traps. Uses the story of Nephi and his brothers returning to obtain the brass plates to show that young men should fulfill all of their assignments even if they think they cannot. [M.D.P.]

Y.015 Young, R. W., Jr., and Martin W. Roylance. "Concerning American Antiquities." *MS* 72 (2 June 1910): 337-41. This article contains two works, both based on an article by Alice le Plongeon who argues that there is a connection between ancient Americans and ancient Egyptians, the latter originating from ancient America: "New Light Upon the Prophets Divinity" by R. W. Young, which proposes that America is the "old world" where Adam and Eve resided; and "Evidence In Support of The Book of Mormon" by Martin W. Roylance, which adds that the connection between these ancient peoples is explained by the Book of Mormon. He identifies Valparaiso, Chili, as the landing place for the Jaredites. [J.W.M.]

Y.016 Young, S. Dilworth. "The Book of Mormon: Its Own Silent Witness." *IE* 68 (June 1965): 508-9. Claims that the Book of Mormon and restoration of the gospel fulfill the prophecies in Isaiah 29:13-14 and Daniel 2:35. The Book of Mormon is its own best witness. The Lord only asks the reader to honestly and prayerfully desire to know its truthfulness. [A.T.]

Y.017 Young, S. Dilworth. "The Seed of Faith." In *BYUSY* (10 December 1968). Provo, UT: BYU Press. Uses Alma 32 to discuss planting the "seed of faith" concerning the witnesses of the Book of Mormon plates. Includes the testimonies of the Three Witnesses. [J.W.M.]

Y.018 Young, Seymour B. "The Book of Mormon and the Spaulding Manuscript." *IE* 1 (July 1898): 648-53. Presents a concise historical overview of Solomon Spaulding's *Manuscript Found* and its purported connection to the Book of Mormon, and concludes that the two writings are so different that they bear no relationship. [D.M.]

Y.019 Young, Seymour B. "The Book of Mormon and the Spaulding Manuscript." *MS* 60 (21 July 1898): 460-64. Presents a brief historical summary of the events surrounding the origin of the Book of Mormon and the Spaulding manuscript and argues that the Book of Mormon was not taken from the Spaulding manuscript. [A.C.W.]

Y.020 Young, Seymour B. Untitled talk. *CR* (October 1914): 105-7. Samuel the Lamanite's prophecy of the signs of the Jesus' birth touched the lives of those Nephites who accepted the gospel. When a babe was born across the ocean in the Old World many in the New World were inspired by the sign of "a day and a night and a day without darkness." [J.W.M.]

Y.021 Young, W. Ernest. *A Curriculum of Readings in the Field of Religious Education from Spanish American Sources Designed for Seminary Students.* M.A. thesis, Brigham Young University, 1935. States that many archaeological, historical, and traditional evidences of ancient inhabitants of Mexico and Central America are linked with the Book of Mormon. Many items mentioned in the book have been found such as fine linen, elephants, horses, and temples. [J.W.M.]

Y.022 Youngreen, Buddy. "And Yet Another Copy of the Anthon Manuscript." *BYU Studies* 20 (Summer 1980): 346-47. Discusses the differences found in the Warnky's art studio print of the Anthon Manuscript and the prints Danel W. Bachman used in his article: "Sealed in a

Book: Preliminary Observations on the Newly Found 'Anthon Transcript.' " [L.D.]

Y.023 Youngreen, Buddy. "The Sacred Record." In Youngreen's *Reflections of Emma, Joseph Smith's Wife,* 7-9. Orem, UT: Grandin Book, 1982. Cites Emma Smith, wife of Joseph, as a witness to the authenticity of the Book of Mormon. Emma was a scribe for a time, her devotion to the work put her in peril many times, and she risked her life to warn the Prophet of any danger to the plates. [J.W.M.]

Z.

Z.001 "Zarahemla." *TS* 3 (1 October 1842): 927-28. Identifies Guatemala as the area where Zarahemla was situated. [D.M.]

Z.002 Zarahemla Research Foundation Staff. "Mayan Glyphs Translated 'It Came to Pass.' " In *Recent Book of Mormon Developments, Articles from the Zarahemla Record,* 2:32. Independence, MO: Zarahemla Research Foundation, 1992. A short report on recent translations of Mayan glyphs that mean "it came to pass." [B.D.]

Z.003 Zarahemla Research Foundation Staff. "Why Bountiful? Why Desolation?" In *Recent Book of Mormon Developments, Articles from the Zarahemla Record,* 2:148. Independence, MO: Zarahemla Research Foundation, 1992. See also *ZR* 52 (December 1990): 1. According to Alma 6:8 (RLDS versification), the Nephites usually named places after the founder. However, bountiful in Hebrew is *tob* and is a name given to a region in Palestine that was very fertile, and the word for desolation is *samem,* which means a land wasted by war or natural disaster. Perhaps these names are given because the places were not cities but large areas. [B.D.]

Z.004 "Zeniff." *Friend* 20 (October 1990): 8-9. Children's illustrated story of Zeniff and his people. [M.R.]

Z.005 Zentgraf, Rochelle. "Acting Out Can Cure Acting Up." *Ensign* 18 (February 1988): 23. A family teaches their children about Lehi's dream by having them act out the dream in a family play. [L.D.]

Z.006 Zimmerman, Dean R. *Book of Mormon Geography.* N.p., 1972?. Counts and lists 119 geographical sites in the Book of Mormon, 103 of which the author believes are identifiable. [D.M.]

Z.007 Zinser, Raymond D. "Experiment upon My Words." In *Recent Book of Mormon Developments, Articles from the Zarahemla Record,* 2:157-60. Independence, MO: Zarahemla Research Foundation, 1992. Zinser describes what he experienced while reading the Book of Mormon. He received a profound testimony after reading the Book of Mormon in one month. [B.D.]

Z.008 Zobell, Albert L. "Some Facts Concerning the Book of Mormon." *IE* 44 (September 1941): 520. Discusses the first printing and subsequent editions of the Book of Mormon and identifies different formats the Book of Mormon has taken since its first publication. [L.D.]

Z.009 Zobell, Albert L. "Where Are the Original Manuscripts?" *IE* 63 (November 1960): 802-3, 826, 828. Traces the history of two Book of Mormon manuscripts—the original manuscript and the printer's manuscript. Joseph Smith deposited the original manuscripts in the cornerstone of the Nauvoo House October 2, 1841. It was recovered in 1882. The printer's manuscript is now in the possession of the RLDS church. [R.C.D.]

Z.010 Zobell, Albert L. "Writing Paper for the Book of Mormon Manuscript." *IE* 72 (February 1969): 54-55. Recounts the contributions of R. Joseph Knight Sr. to Joseph Smith Jr. during the translation of the Book of Mormon. Mr. Knight's aid was instrumental in the process by providing food and the paper that the translation was written on. [B.W.J.]

Z.011 Zobell, Albert L., Sr. "Jaredite Barges." *IE* 44 (April 1941): 211, 252. Also in *A Book of Mormon Treasury,* 167-69. Salt Lake City: Bookcraft, 1959, 1976. Passages relating to the Jaredites are used as a basis for examining different aspects of the Jaredite journey including the design of the barges, a possible route of their journey, and their qualifications as ship builders. [A.T.]

Z.012 Zobell, Albert L., Sr. "Romance of the Third Edition of the Book of Mormon." *IE* 49 (September 1946): 548-49. Also in *A Book of Mormon Treasury*, 63-66. Salt Lake City: Bookcraft, 1959, 1976. An account of the efforts of Ebenezer Robinson to arrange the printing of the third edition of the Book of Mormon. Also mentions changes made since the second edition. [A.T.]

Z.013 Zobell, Levi A. *Alma, Son of Alma: A Story of a Prophet Statesman among the Aboriginese of the Americas*. Salt Lake City: Vanity, 1937. A biography of Alma the Younger, employing paraphrases from the Book of Mormon. Includes a section containing the sayings of Alma. [D.M.]

Z.014 Zohner, Marivene. "Home Evening in Lehi's Tent (Almost)." *Ensign* 19 (July 1989): 66-67. In their family tent in their backyard, a family reenacts the story of Lehi's discovery of the Liahona in the desert. [L.D.]

Z.015 "The Zoramites and the Rameumptum." *Friend* 23 (September 1993): 8–10. A series of pictures for children illustrating the mission of Alma and Amulek to the Zoramites. [S.H.]

Addendum
1994–1995 Book of Mormon Bibliography

Adams, William J., Jr. "Lehi's Jerusalem and Writing on Metal Plates." *Journal of Book of Mormon Studies* 3 (Spring 1994): 204-6.

Adams, William J., Jr. "More on the Silver Plates from Lehi's Jerusalem." *Journal of Book of Mormon Studies* 4 (Fall 1995): 136-37.

Andersen, Verlan H. *The Book of Mormon and the Constitution.* Compiled by Hans V. Andersen, Jr. Orem, UT: Sunrise Publishing, 1995.

Anderson, Kenneth W. "The Knowledge Hid Up Because of Unbelief." In *The Book of Mormon: Fourth Nephi through Moroni, from Zion to Destruction,* edited by Monte S. Nyman and Charles D. Tate, Jr., 31-44. Provo, UT: Religious Studies Center, 1995.

Anderson, Lynn Matthews. "Toward a Feminist Interpretation of Latter-day Scripture." *Dialogue* 27 (Summer 1994): 185-203.

Asay, Carlos E. "Golden Threads of the Book of Mormon." In *Heros from the Book of Mormon,* 201-12. Salt Lake City: Bookcraft, 1995.

Aston, Warren P. *In the Footsteps of Lehi: New Evidence for Lehi's Journey across Arabia to Bountiful,* Salt Lake City: Deseret Book, 1994.

Bagley, Pat. *Norman the Nephite's and Larry the Lamanite's Book of Mormon Time Line.* Salt Lake City: Deseret Book, 1995.

Barney, Kevin L. "Enallage in the Book of Mormon." *Journal of Book of Mormon Studies* 3 (Spring 1994): 113-47.

Barney, Kevin L. "Poetic Diction and Parallel Word Pairs in the Book of Mormon." *Journal of Book of Mormon Studies* 4 (Fall 1995): 15-81.

Baron, Ross David. Review of "Book of Mormon Christology," by Melodie Moench Charles. *Review of Books on the Book of Mormon* 7/1 (1995): 91-119.

Bateman, Merrill J. "Lehi's Tree and Alma's Seed." In *Heros from the Book of Mormon,* 16-31. Salt Lake City: Bookcraft, 1995.

Barrus, Ezra McClain. *Centered in God.* Sacramento, CA: the author, 1994.

Benson, Ezra Taft. "Joseph Smith: Prophet to Our Generation." *Ensign* 24 (March 1994): 2-5.

"Bibliography of the Writings of Sidney B. Sperry." *Journal of Book of Mormon Studies* 4 (Spring 1995): 287-96.

Boehm, Bruce J. "Wanderers in the Promised Land: A Study of the Exodus Motif in the Book of Mormon and Holy Bible." *Journal of Book of Mormon Studies* 3 (Spring 1994): 187-203.

Brewerton, Ted E. "The Book of Mormon: A Sacred Ancient Record." *Ensign* 25 (November 1995): 30-31.

Bringhurst, Newell G. "Joseph Smith, the Mormons, and Antebellum Reform—A Closer Look." *John Whitmer Historical Association Journal* 14 (1994): 73-91.

Brinley, Douglas E. "The Jaredites—A Case Study in Following the Brethren." In *The Book of Mormon: Fourth Nephi through Moroni, from Zion to Destruction,* edited by Monte S. Nyman and Charles D. Tate, Jr., 45-59. Provo, UT: Religious Studies Center, 1995.

Brough, Monte J. "The Prophet Ether: Man of the More Excellent Hope." In *Heros from the Book of Mormon,* 189-94. Salt Lake City: Bookcraft, 1995.

Bunker, Robert L. "The Design of the Liahona and the Purpose of the Second Spindle." *Journal of Book of Mormon Studies* 3 (Fall 1994): 1-11.

Burgess, Allan K. *Timely Truths from the Book of Mormon.* Salt Lake City: Bookcraft, 1995.

Bushman, Richard L. Review of *Inventing Mormonism: Tradition and the Historical Record,* by H. Michael Marquardt and Wesley P. Walters. *Review of Books on the Book of Mormon* 6/2 (1994): 122-33.

Butler, John M. "The 'Author' and the 'Finisher' of the Book of Mormon." In *The Book of Mormon: Fourth Nephi through Moroni, from Zion to Destruction,* edited by Monte S. Nyman and Charles D. Tate, Jr., 61-68. Provo, UT: Religious Studies Center, 1995.

Campbell, Les. Review of *The Lands of Zarahemla,* by E. L. Peay. *Review of Books on the Book of Mormon* 6/2 (1994): 139-45.

Carmack, John K. "Pahoran: Wartime Statesman, Defender of Freedom." In *Heros from the Book of Mormon,* 134-44. Salt Lake City: Bookcraft, 1995.

Carter, K. Codell, and Christopher B Isaac. Review of *Refuting the Critics: Evidences of the Book of Mormon's Authenticity,* by Michael T. Griffith. *Review of Books on the Book of Mormon* 6/2 (1994): 114-17.

Christensen, Joe J. "Captain Moroni, an Authentic Hero." In *Heros from the Book of Mormon,* 128-33. Salt Lake City: Bookcraft, 1995.

Christensen, Kevin. "A Response to David Wright on Historical Criticism." *Journal of Book of Mormon Studies* 3 (Spring 1994): 79-93.

Christensen, Kevin. Review of *New Approaches to the Book of Mormon: Explorations in Critical Methodology*, edited by Brent Lee Metcalfe. *Review of Books on the Book of Mormon* 7/2 (1995): 144-218.

Christiansen, Jack R. "Why We Need the Book of Mormon." In Christiansen's *Be Strong and of Good Courage,* 89-99. Salt Lake City: Bookcraft, 1994.

Clark, John. Review of *Christ in North America,* by Delbert W. Curtis. *Review of Books on the Book of Mormon* 6/2 (1994): 79-113.

Cobabe, Douglas L. "The Books of Daniel." *NE* 25 (June 1995): 48-52.

Condie, Spencer J. "Mormon: Historian, General, Man of God." In *Heros from the Book of Mormon,* 168-79. Salt Lake City: Bookcraft, 1995.

Cook, Gene R. "Moroni's Promise." *Ensign* 24 (April 1994): 12-16.

Cook, Lyndon W. "David Whitmer: Faithful Dissenter." *This People* 15 (Fall 1994): 10, 12, 15.

Coutts, Alison V. P. Review of *Recent Book of Mormon Developments: Articles from the Zarahemla Record*, vol. 2, edited by Raymond C. Treat. *Review of Books on the Book of Mormon* 7/2 (1995): 253-55.

Cracroft, Richard H. Review of *Daniel and Nephi,* by Chris Heimerdinger; and *Samuel, Moroni's Young Warrior,* by Clair Poulson. *Review of Books on the Book of Mormon* 6/2 (1994): 118-21.

Crowell, Angela M. "The Hebrew Literary Structure of the Book of Mormon." In *Restoration Studies,* edited by Paul M. Edwards and Darlene Caswell, 5:156-69. Independence, MO: Herald Publishing House, 1993.

Davis, Garold N. Review of *The Legacy of the Brass Plates of Laban: A Comparison of Biblical and Book of Mormon Isaiah Texts*, by Clay H. Gorton. *Review of Books on the Book of Mormon* 7/1 (1995): 123-29.

Dellenbach, Robert K. "The Translation Miracle of the Book of Mormon." *Ensign* 25 (May 1995): 9-11.

Donaldson, Lee L. "The Plates of Ether and the Covenant of the Book of Mormon." In *The Book of Mormon: Fourth Nephi through Moroni, from Zion to Destruction,* edited by Monte S. Nyman and Charles D. Tate, Jr., 69-79. Provo, UT: Religious Studies Center, 1995.

Draper, Richard D. "*Hubris* and *Ate*: A Latter-day Warning from the Book of Mormon." *Journal of Book of Mormon Studies* 3 (Fall 1994): 12-33.

Eaton, Melanie. "The Reward is Worth the Effort." *Ensign* 25 (May 1995): 93.

England, Eugene. Review of *Homecoming*, vols. 1-5; *A Storyteller in Zion: Essays and Speeches*; and "An Open Letter to those who are concerned about 'plagiarism' in *The Memory of Earth*," by Orson Scott Card. *Review of Books on the Book of Mormon* 6/2 (1994): 59-78.

Eyring, Henry B. "Amulek: The Blessings of Obedience." In *Heros from the Book of Mormon*, 106-11. Salt Lake City: Bookcraft, 1995.

Faulconer, James E. "The Olive Tree and the Work of God: Jacob 5 and Romans 11." In *The Allegory of the Olive Tree: The Olive, the Bible, and Jacob 5*, edited by Stephen D. Ricks and John W. Welch, 347-66. Salt Lake City: Deseret Book and FARMS, 1994.

Folsom, Marvin. Review of *The Easy-to-Read Book of Mormon: A Learning Companion*, by Lynn Matthews Anderson. *Review of Books on the Book of Mormon* 7/1 (1995): 13-18.

Fowles, John L. "The Jewish Lectionary and Book of Mormon Prophecy." *Journal of Book of Mormon Studies* 3 (Fall 1994): 118-22.

Garrett H. Dean. "Light in Our Vessels: Faith, Hope, and Charity." In *The Book of Mormon: Fourth Nephi through Moroni, from Zion to Destruction*, edited by Monte S. Nyman and Charles D. Tate, Jr., 81-93. Provo, UT: Religious Studies Center, 1995.

Gee, John. Review of "The Use of Egyptian Magical Papyri to Authenticate the Book of Abraham: A Critical Review," by Edward H. Ashment. *Review of Books on the Book of Mormon* 7/1 (1995): 19-84.

Gee, John. Review of *Written by the Finger of God: Testimony of Joseph Smith's Translations*, by Joe Sampson. *Review of Books on the Book of Mormon* 7/1 (1995): 219-28.

Gee, John, and Daniel C. Peterson. "Graft and Corruption: On Olives and Olive Culture in the Pre-Modern Mediterranean." In *The Allegory of the Olive Tree: The Olive, the Bible, and Jacob 5*, edited by Stephen D. Ricks and John W. Welch, 186-247. Salt Lake City: Deseret Book and FARMS, 1994.

Godard, Linda F. *Society and the Law: Comparing the Legal Environment in the Book of Mormon with the Litigious Trend of Today's Society*. B.A. thesis, Brigham Young University, 1994.

Goff, Alan. Review of "Apologetic and Critical Assumptions about Book of Mormon Historicity," by Brent Lee Metcalfe. *Review of Books on the Book of Mormon* 7/1 (1995): 170-207.

Gorton, H. Clay. *The Legacy of the Brass Plates of Laban: A Comparison of Biblical & Book of Mormon Isaiah Texts*. Bountiful, UT: Horizon, 1994.

Griffith, Michael T. *Refuting the Critics: Evidences of the Book of Mormon's Authenticity*. Bountiful: Horizon Publishers, 1993.

Groberg, John H. "Enos." In *Heros from the Book of Mormon*, 47-58. Salt Lake City: Bookcraft, 1995.

Grover, Lisa M. "Rising to the Challenge." *NE* 25 (June 1995): 44-45.

"Hagoth." *Friend* 25 (Jan. 1995): 27.

Hamblin, William J. "The Latest Straw Man." *Journal of Book of Mormon Studies* 4 (Fall 1995): 82-91.

Hamblin, William J. Review of *Explorers of Pre-Columbian America?: The Diffusionist-Inventionist Controversy*, by Eugene R. Fingerhut; and *Legend and Lore of the Americas before 1492: An Encyclopedia of visitors, Explorers, and Immigrants*, by Ronald H. Fritze. *Review of Books on the Book of Mormon* 7/1 (1995): 120-22.

Hamblin, Willam J. Review of *The Sanctity of Dissent*, by Paul Toscano. *Review of Books on the Book of Mormon* 7/1 (1995): 298-316.

Hamblin, William J. *Sacred Writings on Bronze Plates in the Ancient Mediterranean*. Provo, UT: FARMS, 1994.

Hamblin, William J., Daniel C. Peterson, and George L. Mitton. Review of *The Refiner's Fire: The Making of Mormon Cosmology, 1644-1844*, by John L. Brooke. *Review of Books on the Book of Mormon* 6/2 (1994): 3-58.

Hansen, Gerald Jr. "Preparing for the Judgment." In *The Book of Mormon: Fourth Nephi through Moroni, from Zion to Destruction*, edited by Monte S. Nyman and Charles D. Tate, Jr., 95-104. Provo, UT: Religious Studies Center, 1995.

Hatch, Gary Lynn. "Mormon and Moroni: Father and Son." In *The Book of Mormon: Fourth Nephi through Moroni, from Zion to Destruction,* edited by Monte S. Nyman and Charles D. Tate, Jr., 105-15. Provo, UT: Religious Studies Center, 1995.

Hauck, F. Richard. "Ancient Fortifications and the Land of Manti." *This People* 15 (Summer 1994): 46-47, 49-52, 54-55.

Hauck, F. Richard. "Archaeology and the Setting of the Book of Mormon." *This People* 15 (Spring 1994): 70-83.

Hauck, F. Richard. "In Search of the Land of Nephi." *This People* 15 (Fall 1994): 52-56, 58-60, 63.

Hauck, F. Richard. "The Trail to Zarahemla." *This People* 15 (Holiday 1994): 64-65, 67, 69-70.

Hauglid, Brian M. Review of *Strangers in Paradox: Exploration in Mormon Theology,* by Margaret and Paul Toscano. *Review of Books on the Book of Mormon* 6/2 (1994): 250-82.

Hawley, Judith A. *Nephi and Lehi, Mighty Men of God: Adapted from the Book of Mormon, Helaman 2, 37, 79-120.* Independence, MO: OM Resource Center, 1994.

Heimerdinger, Chris. *Daniel and Nephi.* Salt Lake City: Covenant, 1993.

Heimerdinger, Chris. *Tennis Shoes and the Feathered Serpent.* American Fork, UT: Covenant, 1995.

Hess, Wilford M., Daniel J. Fairbanks, John W. Welch, and Jonathan K. Driggs. "Botanical Aspects to Olive Culture Relevant to Jacob 5." In *The Allegory of the Olive Tree: The Olive, the Bible, and Jacob 5,* edited by Stephen D. Ricks and John W. Welch, 484-562. Salt Lake City: Deseret Book and FARMS, 1994.

Hinckley, Gordon B. "Moroni." In *Heros from the Book of Mormon,* 195-200. Salt Lake City: Bookcraft, 1995.

Holland, Jeffrey R. "Jacob the Unshakable." In *Heros from the Book of Mormon,* 32-46. Salt Lake City: Bookcraft, 1995.

Holland, Jeffrey R. "True or False." *NE* 25 (June 1995): 64-66.

Holmes, David I. "Vocabulary Richness and the Book of Mormon: A Stylometric Analysis of Mormon Scripture." *Research in Humanities Computing* 3 (1994): 18-31.

Holzapfel, Richard N. "Golden Bible Hill." *Mormon Heritage* 2 (July-August 1995): 44-46.

Holzapfel, Richard N. "Mormon, the Man and the Message." In *The Book of Mormon: Fourth Nephi through Moroni, from Zion to Destruction,* edited by Monte S. Nyman and Charles D. Tate, Jr., 117-31. Provo, UT: Religious Studies Center, 1995.

Honey, David B. Review of *The Allegory of the Olive Tree: The Olive, the Bible, and Jacob 5,* edited by Stephen D. Ricks and John W. Welch. *BYU Studies* 35 (1995): 238-46.

Honey, David B. "The Secular as Sacred: The Historiography of the Title Page." *Journal of Book of Mormon Studies* 3 (Spring 1994): 94-103.

Hoskisson, Paul Y. "The Allegory of the Olive Tree in Jacob." In *The Allegory of the Olive Tree: The Olive, the Bible, and Jacob 5,* edited by Stephen D. Ricks and John W. Welch, 70-104. Salt Lake City: Deseret Book and FARMS, 1994.

Howard, F. Burton. "Ammon: Reflections on Faith and Testimony." In *Heros from the Book of Mormon,* 120-27. Salt Lake City: Bookcraft, 1995.

Hoskisson, Paul Y. "By What Authority Did Lehi, a Non-Levite Priest, Offer Sacrifices?" *Ensign* 24 (March 1994): 54.

Huchel, Frederick M. Review of *Written by the finger of God,* by Joe Samson. *Review of Books on the Book of Mormon* 6/2 (1994): 150-55.

Hunt, Wallace E., Jr. "The Marketplace." *Journal of Book of Mormon Studies* 4 (Fall 1995): 138-41.

Hunter, Howard W. "The Pillars of Our Faith." *Ensign* 24 (September 1994): 54-55.

Jacobson, LeIsle. Review of *Questions to Ask Your Mormon Friend: Effective Ways to Challenge a Mormon's Arguments without Being Offensive,* by Bill McKeever and Eric Johnson. *Review of Books on the Book of Mormon* 7/1 (1995): 155-69.

Jensen, Clint. "Why Me?" *NE* 25 (June 1995): 25.

Johnson, D. Lynn. The Missing Scripture." *Journal of Book of Mormon Studies* 3 (Fall 1994): 84-93.

Johnson, Mark J. "The Exodus of Lehi Revisited." *Journal of Book of Mormon Studies* 3 (Fall 1994): 123-26.

Johnson, Mark J. *The Legacy of the Brass Plates of Laban: A Comparison of Biblical and Book of Mormon Isaiah Texts*, by Clay H. Gorton. *Review of Books on the Book of Mormon* 7/2 (1995): 130-38.

Johnson, Matthew Ty. *The Development of a Computer-based Book of Mormon Reading Program for the MTC Classroom.* Salt Lake City: Deseret Book, 1994.

Johnson, Sherrie. *Abinadi.* Salt Lake City: Deseret Book, 1994.

Johnson, Sherrie. *Alma at the Waters of Mormon.* Salt Lake City: Deseret Book, 1994.

Johnson, Sherrie. *Ammon and the King.* Salt Lake City: Deseret Book, 1994.

Johnson, Sherrie. *The Broken Bow.* Salt Lake City: Deseret Book, 1994.

Johnson, Sherrie. *Captain Moroni's Title of Liberty.* Salt Lake City: Deseret Book, 1994.

Johnson, Sherrie. *The Gadianton Robbers.* Salt Lake City: Deseret Book, 1994.

Johnson, Sherrie. *Jesus is Born.* Salt Lake City: Deseret Book, 1994.

Johnson, Sherrie. *Nephi and Lehi in Prison.* Salt Lake City: Deseret Book, 1994.

Judd, Daniel K. "The Spirit of Christ: A Light Amidst the Darkness." In *The Book of Mormon: Fourth Nephi through Moroni, from Zion to Destruction,* edited by Monte S. Nyman and Charles D. Tate, Jr., 133-46. Provo, UT: Religious Studies Center, 1995.

Judd, Frank F., Jr. "Jaredite Zion Societies: Hope for a Better World." In *The Book of Mormon: Fourth Nephi through Moroni, from Zion to Destruction,* edited by Monte S. Nyman and Charles D. Tate, Jr., 147-52. Provo, UT: Religious Studies Center, 1995.

Judd, Frank F., Jr., and Terrence L. Szink. Review of *Mormons and Jews: Early Mormon Theologies of Israel,* by Steven Epperson. *Review of Books on the Book of Mormon* 7/2 (1995): 106-22.

Killgore, Mark. "Book of Mormon Summer." *Ensign* 25 (August 1995): 28-29.

King, Arthur Henry. "Language Themes in Jacob 5: 'The Vineyard of the Lord of Hosts is the House of Israel' (Isaiah 5:7)." In *The Allegory of the Olive Tree: The Olive, the Bible, and Jacob 5,* edited by Stephen D. Ricks and John W. Welch, 140-73. Salt Lake City: Deseret Book and FARMS, 1994.

Klafkowski, Piotr. "Twenty-two Years with the Book of Mormon." In *Restoration Studies,* edited by Paul M. Edwards and Darlene Caswell, 5:170-85. Independence, MO: Herald Publishing House, 1993.

Kofford, Cree-L. "Abinadi." In *Heros from the Book of Mormon,* 68-78. Salt Lake City: Bookcraft, 1995.

Lambert, Neal E. " 'And There Was . . . a New Writing': The Book of Mormon as a Never-Ending Text." *Association for Mormon Letters Annual* 2 (1994): 196-200.

Lane, Jennifer Clark. Review of *The Book of Mormon: 3 Nephi 9-30, This Is My Gospel,* edited by Monte S. Nyman and Charles D. Tate. *Review of Books on the Book of Mormon* 6/2 (1994): 134-38.

Lane, Keith H. "The Persuasive Book of Mormon." *Latter-Day Digest* 3 (January 1994): 35-42.

Larsen, Dean L. "Zeezrom." In *Heros from the Book of Mormon,* 112-19. Salt Lake City: Bookcraft, 1995.

LeBaron, E. Dale. "Ether and Mormon: Parallel Prophets of Warning and Witness." In *The Book of Mormon: Fourth Nephi through Moroni, from Zion to Destruction,* edited by Monte S. Nyman and Charles D. Tate, Jr., 153-65. Provo, UT: Religious Studies Center, 1995.

Matthews, Robert J. "The Mission of Jesus Christ—Ether 3 and 4." In *The Book of Mormon: Fourth Nephi through Moroni, from Zion to Destruction,* edited by Monte S. Nyman and Charles D. Tate, Jr., 19-29. Provo, UT: Religious Studies Center, 1995.

Maxwell, Neal A. "King Benjamin." In *Heros from the Book of Mormon,* 59-67. Salt Lake City: Bookcraft, 1995.

McConkie, Joseph Fielding. *Here We Stand.* Salt Lake City: Deseret Book, 1995.

Merrill, Byron R. "There Was No Contention." In *The Book of Mormon: Fourth Nephi through Moroni, from Zion to Destruction,* edited by Monte S. Nyman and Charles D. Tate, Jr., 167-83. Provo, UT: Religious Studies Center, 1995.

Middleton, Michael W. "Gatherings in the Last Days: Saved in Sheaves, Burned in Bundles." In *The Book of Mormon: Fourth Nephi through Moroni, from Zion to Destruction,* edited by Monte S. Nyman and Charles D. Tate, Jr., 185-97. Provo, UT: Religious Studies Center, 1995.

Midgley, Louis. Review of *Mormon Neo-Orthodoxy: A Crisis Theology,* by O. Kendall White, Jr. *Review of Books on the Book of Mormon* 6/2 (1994): 283-334.

Midgley, Louis. Review of *Mormonism: The Story of a New Religious Tradition,* by Jan Shipps. *Review of Books on the Book of Mormon* 7/2 (1995): 219-52.

Midgley, Louis. Review of *Religion, Feminism, and Freedom of Conscience: A Mormon/Humanist Dialogue,* edited by George D. Smith. *Review of Books on the Book of Mormon* 7/1 (1995): 229-97.

Millet, Robert L. "Alive in Christ: The Salvation of Little Children." In *The Book of Mormon: Fourth Nephi through Moroni, from Zion to Destruction,* edited by Monte S. Nyman and Charles D. Tate, Jr., 1-17. Provo, UT: Religious Studies Center, 1995.

Millet, Robert L. *The Power of the Word: Saving Doctrines from the Book of Mormon.* Salt Lake City: Deseret Book, 1994.

Miner, Alan C. "A Chronological Setting for the epistles of Mormon to Moroni." *Journal of Book of Mormon Studies* 3 (Fall 1994): 94-113.

Nelson, Fred W. Review of *Light from the Dust: A Photographic Exploration into the Ancient World of the Book of Mormon,* by Scot Facer Proctor and Maurine Jensen Proctor. *Review of Books on the Book of Mormon* 6/2 (1994): 146-49.

Nelson, Russell, M. "Nephi, Son of Lehi." In *Heros from the Book of Mormon,* 1-15. Salt Lake City: Bookcraft, 1995.

"Nephi and Lehi in Prison." *Friend* 25 (March 1995): 16-19.

"Nephi Receives Great Power." *Friend* 25 (August 1995): 16-18.

Nibley, Hugh W. "Promised Lands." *Latter-day Digest* 3 (February 1994): 4-14, 16.

Norwood, L. Ara. Review of *In the Footsteps of Lehi: New Evidence for Lehi's Journey across Arabia to Bountiful,* by Warren P. and Michaela Knoth Aston. *Review of Books on the Book of Mormon* 7/1 (1995): 85-92.

Novak, Gary F. Review of *Joseph Smith's Response to Skepticism,* by Robert N. Hullinger. *Review of Books on the Book of Mormon* 7/1 (1995): 139-54.

Nyman, Monte S. "I Have a Question: What is the meaning or known fulfillment of the prophecy, 'kings shall be thy nursing fathers, and their queens thy nursing mothers'?" *Ensign* 24 (August 1994): 61-62.

Nyman, Monte S. "The Judgment Seat of Christ." In *The Book of Mormon: Fourth Nephi through Moroni, from Zion to Destruction,* edited by Monte S. Nyman and Charles D. Tate, Jr., 199-213. Provo, UT: Religious Studies Center, 1995.

Nyman, Monte S., and Charles D. Tate, Jr., eds. *The Book of Mormon: Fourth Nephi through Moroni, from Zion to Destruction.* Provo, UT: Religious Studies Center, 1995.

O'Driscoll, Jeff. "Zion Zion Zion: Keys to Understanding Ether 13." In *The Book of Mormon: Fourth Nephi through Moroni, from Zion to Destruction,* edited by Monte S. Nyman and Charles D. Tate, Jr., 215-34. Provo, UT: Religious Studies Center, 1995.

Oaks, Dallin H. "Another Testament of Jesus Christ." *Ensign* 24 (March 1994): 60-67.

Oaks, Dallin H. "The Historicity of the Book of Mormon." Provo, UT: FARMS, 1994.

Oman, Richard G. "Sacred Connections: LDS Pottery in the Native American Southwest." *BYU Studies* 35 (1995): 107-28.

Parry, Donald W. "1993 Book of Mormon Bibliography." *Review of Books on the Book of Mormon* 6/2 (1994): 335-48.

Paulson, Clair. *Samuel, Gadianton's Foe.* American Fork: Covenant Communications, 1994.

Pearson, Glenn L. *Moroni's Promise: The Converting Power of the Book of Mormon.* Salt Lake City: Bookcraft, 1995.

Peay, E. L. *The Lands of Zarahemla.* Salt Lake City: Northwest Publishing, 1993.

Peay, E. L. *The Lands of Zarahemla: Nephi's Promised Land in Central America: A Book of Mormon Commentary*, vol. 2. Provo, UT: the author, 1994.

Perry, L. Tom. "Alma, the Son of Alma." In *Heros from the Book of Mormon*, 98-105. Salt Lake City: Bookcraft, 1995.

Peterson, Andrew W. "Samuel the Lamanite." In *Heros from the Book of Mormon*, 157-67. Salt Lake City: Bookcraft, 1995.

Peterson, Daniel C. "LDS Scholars Refute Attacks on the Book of Mormon." *This People* 15 (Summer 1994): 28-33.

Peterson, Daniel C. Review of *Decker's Complete Handbook on Mormonism*, by Ed Decker. *Review of Books on the Book of Mormon* 7/1 (1995): 38-105.

Peterson, H. Donl. "Moroni, the Last of the Nephite Prophets." In *The Book of Mormon: Fourth Nephi through Moroni, from Zion to Destruction,* edited by Monte S. Nyman and Charles D. Tate, Jr., 235-49. Provo, UT: Religious Studies Center, 1995.

Pinegar, Rex D. "The Simple Things." *Ensign* 24 (November 1994): 80-82.

Porter, Larry C. Review of *Inventing Mormonism: Tradition and the Historical Record*, by Michael H. Marquardt and Wesley P. Walters. *Review of Books on the Book of Mormon* 7/2 (1995): 123-43.

Poulson, Clair. *Samuel, Moroni's Young Warrior.* Salt Lake City: Covenant, 1993.

Price, Lynn F. *Every Person in the Book of Mormon: A Chronological Reference and Synopsis.* Bountiful, UT: Horizon Publishers, 1995.

Prince, James R. "Proving the Prophet's Promise." *Ensign* 24 (January 1994): 64-65.

Pritchett, Bruce M., Jr. "Lehi's Theology of the Fall in Its Preexilic/Exile Context." *Journal of Book of Mormon Studies* 3 (Fall 1994): 49-83.

Proctor, Scot Facer, and Maurine Jensen Proctor. *Light from the Dust: A Photographic Exploration into the Ancient World of the Book of Mormon.* Salt Lake City: Deseret Book, 1993.

"Questions and Answers: I've been studying the Book of Mormon, but the Bible seems boring. Should I read and study the Bible just as much as the Book of Mormon?" *NE* 25 (June 1995): 16-18.

Rasmus, Carolyn J. "Weak Things Made Strong." In *The Book of Mormon: Fourth Nephi through Moroni, from Zion to Destruction,* edited by Monte S. Nyman and Charles D. Tate, Jr., 251-62. Provo, UT: Religious Studies Center, 1995.

Rencher, Alvin C. "Unity through the Power of Charity." In *The Book of Mormon: Fourth Nephi through Moroni, from Zion to Destruction,* edited by Monte S. Nyman and Charles D. Tate, Jr., 263-75. Provo, UT: Religious Studies, 1995.

Reynolds, Noel B. "Nephite Uses and Interpretations of Zenos." In *The Allegory of the Olive Tree: The Olive, the Bible, and Jacob 5,* edited by Stephen D. Ricks and John W. Welch, 21-49. Salt Lake City: Deseret Book and FARMS, 1994.

Rhett, James. "The Legacy of Martin Harris: Printing the Book of Mormon." *Mormon Heritage* 2 (July-August 1995): 14-20.

Ricks, Stephen D., and John W. Welch, eds. *The Allegory of the Olive Tree: The Olive, the Bible, and Jacob 5.* Salt Lake City: Deseret Book and FARMS, 1994.

Roberts, B. H. *The Truth, The Way, The Life.* Edited by John W. Welch. Provo, UT: BYU Studies, 1994.

Robinson, Hazel Jean D. "My Lesson from Pahoran." *Ensign* 24 (February 1994): 40.

Roper, Matthew. "Noah Webster and the Book of Mormon." *Journal of Book of Mormon Studies* 4 (Fall 1995): 142-46.

Roper, Matthew. Review of *Answering Mormon Scholars: A Response to Criticism of the Book "Covering Up the Black Hole in the Book of Mormon,"* vol. 1, by Jerald and Sandra Tanner. *Review of Books on the Book of Mormon* 6/2 (1994): 156-203.

Rust, Richard Dilworth. "Liminality in the Book of Mormon." *Association for Mormon Letters Annual* 2 (1994): 207-11.

Rust, Richard Dilworth. "Recurrence in Book of Mormon Narratives." *Journal of Book of Mormon Studies* 3 (Spring 1994): 39-52.

Sampson, Joe. *Written by the Finger of God.* Salt Lake City: Wellspring Publishing and Distributing, 1993.

"Samuel the Lamanite Tells about Jesus Christ." *Friend* 25 (October 1995): 16-18.

Samuelson, Cecil O., Jr. "The Brother of Jared." In *Heros from the Book of Mormon*, 180-88. Salt Lake City: Bookcraft, 1995.

Satterfield, Bruce K. "Moroni 9-10: Remembering How Merciful the Lord Hath Been." In *The Book of Mormon: Fourth Nephi through Moroni, from Zion to Destruction,* edited by Monte S. Nyman and Charles D. Tate, Jr., 277-88. Provo, UT: Religious Studies Center, 1995.

Saunders, Iain. "I Knew Nephi." *NE* 25 (June 1995): 12-14.

Scott, Ricard G. "Nephi, Son of Helaman." In *Heros from the Book of Mormon*, 145-56. Salt Lake City: Bookcraft, 1995.

Seely, David Rolph. "The Allegory of the Olive Tree and the Use of Related Figurative Language in the Ancient Near East and the Old Testament." In *The Allegory of the Olive Tree: The Olive, the Bible, and Jacob 5*, edited by Stephen D. Ricks and John W. Welch, 290-304. Salt Lake City: Deseret Book and FARMS, 1994.

Seely, David Rolph, and John W. Welch. "Zenos and the Texts of the Old Testament." In *The Allegory of the Olive Tree: The Olive, the Bible, and Jacob 5*, edited by Stephen D. Ricks and John W. Welch, 322-46. Salt Lake City: Deseret Book and FARMS, 1994.

Shipps, Jan, and John W. Welch, eds., *The William E. McLellin Journals (1831-1836)*. Urbana, IL and Provo, UT: University of Illinois Press and BYU Studies, 1994.

Skinner, Andrew C. "Zion Gained and Lost: Fourth Nephi as the Quintessential Model." In *The Book of Mormon: Fourth Nephi through Moroni, from Zion to Destruction,* edited by Monte S. Nyman and Charles D. Tate, Jr., 289-302. Provo, UT: Religious Studies Center, 1995.

Skousen, Royal. "Jacob 4-6: Substantive Textual Variants between Manscripts and Editions." In *The Allegory of the Olive Tree: The Olive, the Bible, and Jacob 5*, edited by Stephen D. Ricks and John W. Welch, 105-39. Salt Lake City: Deseret Book and FARMS, 1994.

Skousen, Royal. "The Original Language of the Book of Mormon: Upstate New York Dialect, King James English, or Hebrew." *Journal of Book of Mormon Studies* 3 (Spring 1994): 28-38.

Skousen, Royal. Review of *Bible II. Review of Books on the Book of Mormon* 6/2 (1994):1-2.

Smith, Larry K. Review of *First Nephi: Study Book of Mormon. Review of Books on the Book of Mormon* 7/2 (1995): 3-5.

Smith, Larry K. Review of *LDS Collectors Edition CD-ROM. Review of Books on the Book of Mormon* 7/2 (1995): 256-64.

Smith, Larry K. Review of *Overview of the Book of Mormon. Review of Books on the Book of Mormon* 7/2 (1995): 1-2.

Snow, Edgar C., Jr. "Narrative Criticism and the Book of Mormon." *Journal of Book of Mormon Studies* 4 (Fall 1995): 93-106.

Snow, Edgar C., Jr. "One Face of the Hero: In Search of the Mythological Joseph Smith." *Dialogue* 27 (Fall 1994): 233-47.

Sperry, Sidney B. "Were there Two Comorahs?" *Journal of Book of Mormon Studies* 4 (Spring 1995): 260-68.

Sperry, Sidney B. "Moroni Expounds Old Testament Scriptures." *Journal of Book of Mormon Studies* 4 (Spring 1995): 269-86.

Stirling, Mack C. Review of *The Book of Mormon: Helaman through 3 Nephi 8, According to Thy Word,* by Monte S. Nyman and Charles D. Tate, Jr. *Review of Books on the Book of Mormon* 7/1 (1995): 208-18.

Sturgess, Gary L. "The Book of Mosiah: Thoughts about Its Structure, Purposes, Themes, and Authorship." *Journal of Book of Mormon Studies* 4 (Fall 1995): 107-35.

" 'Take One'—Book of Mormon Movie Magic." *This People* 15 (Fall 1994): 36-39.

Tanner, Martin S. Review of "Book of Mormon Christology," by Melodie Moench Charles. *Review of Books on the Book of Mormon* 7/2 (1995): 6-37.

Terry, Keith. *Out of Darkness: A Novel.* American Fork, UT: Covenant Communications, 1995.

"The Murder of the Chief Judge." *Friend* 25 (June 1995): 15-19.

Thomas, Janet. "A Great Book." *NE* 25 (June 1995): 40-41.

Thomas, M. Catherine. "The Brother of Jared at the Veil." In *Temples of the Ancient World: Ritual and Symbolism*, edited by Donald W. Parry, 388-98. Salt Lake City: Deseret Book and FARMS, 1994.

Thomas, M. Catherine. "Jacob's Allegory: The Mystery of Christ." In *The Allegory of the Olive Tree: The Olive, the Bible, and Jacob 5*, edited by Stephen D. Ricks and John W. Welch, 11-20. Salt Lake City: Deseret Book and FARMS, 1994.

Thomas, M. Catherine. "Using the Book of Mormon to Face the Tests Ahead." In *Watch and Be Ready: Preparing for the Second Coming of the Lord*, 16-38. Salt Lake City: Deseret Book, 1994.

Thomasson, Gordon C. "What's in a Name? Book of Mormon Language, Names, and [Metonymic] Naming." *Journal of Book of Mormon Studies* 3 (Spring 1994): 1-27.

Thompson, John S. "The Jaredite Exodus: A Literary Perspective of a Historical Narrative." *Journal of Book of Mormon Studies* 3 (Spring 1994): 94-103.

Thorne, Melvin J. "What Is FARMS?" *This People* 16 (Spring 1995): 42-46.

Trimble, Brenda. "The Feathered Serpent." *Witness* 85 (Summer 1994): 7-9.

Tvedtnes, John A. "Borrowings from the Parable of Zenos." In *The Allegory of the Olive Tree: The Olive, the Bible, and Jacob 5*, edited by Stephen D. Ricks and John W. Welch, 373-426. Salt Lake City: Deseret Book and FARMS, 1994.

Tvedtnes, John A. "Cities and Lands in the Book of Mormon." *Journal of Book of Mormon Studies* 4 (Fall 1995): 147-50.

Tvedtnes, John A. "Faith and Truth." *Journal of Book of Mormon Studies* 3 (Fall 1994): 114-17.

Tvedtnes, John A. "Historical Parallels to the Destruction at the Time of the Crucifixion." *Journal of Book of Mormon Studies* 3 (Spring 1994): 170-86.

Tvedtnes, John A. "The Influence of Lehi's Admonitions on the Teachings of His Son Jacob." *Journal of Book of Mormon Studies* 3 (Fall 1994): 34-48.

Tvedtnes, John A. "My First-Born in the Wilderness." *Journal of Book of Mormon Studies* 3 (Spring 1994): 207-9.

Tvedtnes, John A. Review of *Answering Mormon Scholars: A Response to Criticism of the Book "Covering Up the Black Hole in the Book of Mormon,"* vol. 1, by Jerald and Sandra Tanner. *Review of Books on the Book of Mormon* 6/2 (1994): 204-49.

Tvedtnes, John A. "Vineyard or Olive Orchard?" In *The Allegory of the Olive Tree: The Olive, the Bible, and Jacob 5*, edited by Stephen D. Ricks and John W. Welch, 477-83. Salt Lake City: Deseret Book and FARMS, 1994.

Underwood, Grant. "Jacob 5 in the Nineteenth Century." In *The Allegory of the Olive Tree: The Olive, the Bible, and Jacob 5*, edited by Stephen D. Ricks and John W. Welch, 50-69. Salt Lake City: Deseret Book and FARMS, 1994.

Valletta, Thomas R. "The Book of Mormon As a Testimony of Jesus Christ." In *Serving with Strength throughout the World: Favorite Talks from Especially for Youth*, 251-61. Salt Lake City: Deseret Book, 1994.

Valletta, Thomas R. "Jared and His Brother." In *The Book of Mormon: Fourth Nephi through Moroni, from Zion to Destruction*, edited by Monte S. Nyman and Charles D. Tate, Jr., 303-22. Provo, UT: Religious Studies Center, 1995.

Van Orden, Bruce A. "Preach the Gospel to Every Creature." In *The Book of Mormon: Fourth Nephi through Moroni, from Zion to Destruction*, edited by Monte S. Nyman and Charles D. Tate, Jr., 323-36. Provo, UT: Religious Studies Center, 1995.

Volluz, Corbin T. "Cry Redemption: The Plan of Redemption as Taught in the Book of Mormon." *Journal of Book of Mormon Studies* 3 (Spring 1994): 148-69.

Von Harrison, Grant. *Use the Book of Mormon to Teach Reading.* Provo, UT: n.p., 1994.

Wardle, Lynn D. "Dissent: Perspectives from the Book of Mormon." *Journal of Book of Mormon Studies* 3 (Spring 1994): 53-73.

Welch, John W. "Criteria for Identifying and Evaluating the Presence of Chiasmus." *Journal of Book of Mormon Studies* 4 (Fall 1995): 1-14.

Welch, John W. "The Last Words of Cenez and the Book of Mormon." In *The Allegory of the Olive Tree: The Olive, the Bible, and Jacob 5*, edited by Stephen D. Ricks and John W. Welch, 305-21. Salt Lake City: Deseret Book and FARMS, 1994.

Welch, John W. "Powerful Personal Testimonies of Christ from the Book of Mormon." *Witness* Part 1: 85-86 (Summer-Fall 1994): 4-7, 10, 6, 11, 14-15.

Welch, John W. "A Study Relating Chiasmus in the Book of Mormon to Chiasmus in the Old Testament, Ugaritic Epics, Homer, and Selceted Greek and Latin Authors." M.A. thesis, Brigham Young University, 1970.

Welch, John W. "The Temple in the Book of Mormon: The Temples at the Cities of Nephi, Zarahemla, and Bountiful." In *Temples of the Ancient World: Ritual and Symbolism*, edited by Donald W. Parry, 297-387. Salt Lake City: Deseret Book and FARMS, 1994.

Welch, John W. "Words and Phrases in Jacob 5." In *The Allegory of the Olive Tree: The Olive, the Bible, and Jacob 5*, edited by Stephen D. Ricks and John W. Welch, 174-85. Salt Lake City: Deseret Book and FARMS, 1994.

Welch, John W. "Zenos: Hearing Mercy." *BYU Studies* 33 (1993): 172-73.

Williams, Camille S. Review of *The Easy-to-Read Book of Mormon: A Learning Companion,* by Lynn Matthews Anderson, and *Mormon's Story,* by Timothy B. Wilson. *Review of Books on the Book of Mormon* 7/1 (1995): 3-12.

Wirthlin, Joseph B. "Alma the Elder: A Role Model for Today." In *Heros from the Book of Mormon*, 79-97. Salt Lake City: Bookcraft, 1995.

Woodworth, Warner P. "The Socio-Economics of Zion." In *The Book of Mormon: Fourth Nephi through Moroni, from Zion to Destruction,* edited by Monte S. Nyman and Charles D. Tate, Jr., 337-52. Provo, UT: Religious Studies Center, 1995.

Ziebarth, Christian M. "Examining a Nephite/Latter-day Apostolic Parallel." *Journal of Book of Mormon Studies* 4 (Fall 1995): 151-54.

Appendix

Book of Mormon Editions Translated and Published by Year

English, 1830
Danish, 1851
German, 1852
French, 1852
Italian, 1852
Welsh, 1852
Hawaiian, 1855
English (Deseret Alphabet), 1869
Spanish, 1875, selections
Swedish, 1878
Spanish, 1886
Maori, 1889
Dutch, 1890
Samoan, 1903
Tahitian, 1904
Turkish, 1906
Japanese, 1909
Hebrew, 1927 (?)
Czech, 1933
Armenian-Western, 1937, selections
English (Braille), 1939
Portuguese, 1940
Tongan, 1946
Norwegian, 1950
Finnish, 1954
Rarotongan, 1965
Chinese, 1965
Korean, 1967
Afrikaans, 1972
Thai, 1976
Indonesian, 1977

Aymara, 1977, selections
Cakchiquel, 1978, selections
Croatian, 1979
Quechua-Peru, 1979, selections
Greek, 1979, selections
Hungarian, 1979, selections
Kekchi, 1979, selections
Quiche, 1979, selections
Bulgarian, 1980, selections
Navajo, 1980, selections
Quichua-Otavalo, 1980, selections
Arabic, 1980, selections
Czech, 1980, selections
Vietnamese, 1980, selections
Fijian, 1980
Russian, 1980
Catalan, 1981
Icelandic, 1981
Niuean, 1981, selections
Quechua-Bolivia, 1981, selections
Kuna, 1981, selections
Romanian, 1981, selections
Polish, 1981
Hindi, 1982
Telugu, 1982, selections
Tamil, 1982, selections
Cambodian, 1982, selections
Laotian, 1982, selections
Vietnamese, 1982
Swahili, 1982, selections
Guarani, 1982, selections

Note: The information for these tables is adapted from *Deseret News 1993-94 Church Almanac* (Salt Lake City: Deseret News, 1992), 401-402.

Maya, 1983, selections
Sinhala, 1983, selections
Kekchi, 1983
Mam, 1983, selections
Armenian, 1983, selections
Turkish, 1983, selections
Efik, 1983, selections
Chinese, 1983, selections
Kisii, 1983, selections
Greek (Demotike), 1983, selections
Hmong, 1983, selections
Persian, 1983, selections
Haitian Creole, 1983, selections
Marshallese, 1984, selections
Bengali, 1985, selections
Bislama, 1985, selections
Arabic 1986
Aymara, 1986
Malagasy, 1986, selections

Akan-Fante, 1987, selections
Greek (Demotike), 1987
Zulu, 1987, selections
Pohnpeian, 1987, selections
Papiamento, 1987, selections
Trukese, 1987, selections
Tagalog, 1987, selections
Lingala, 1988, selections
Shona, 1988, selections
Urdu, 1988, selections
Palauan, 1988, selections
Gilbertese, 1988, selections
Chamorro, 1989, selections
English-Braille, 1989, revision
Ilokano, 1991, selections
Hungarian, 1991
Cebuano, 1992, selections
Hiligaynon, 1994, selections

Translations from English by Language

Afrikaans, 1972
Akan-Fante, 1987, selections
Arabic 1986
Arabic, 1980, selections
Armenian, 1983, selections
Armenian-Western, 1937, selections
Aymara, 1977, selections
Aymara, 1986
Bengali, 1985, selections
Bislama, 1985, selections
Bulgarian, 1980, selections
Cakchiquel, 1978, selections
Cambodian, 1982, selections
Catalan, 1981
Cebuano, 1992, selections
Chamorro, 1989, selections
Chinese, 1983, selections
Chinese, 1965
Croatian, 1979
Czech, 1933
Czech, 1980, selections
Danish, 1851

Dutch, 1890
Efik, 1983, selections
English (Braille), 1939
English (Deseret Alphabet), 1869
English, 1830
English-Braille, 1989, revision
Fijian, 1980
Finnish, 1954
French, 1852
German, 1852
Gilbertese, 1988, selections
Greek (Demotike), 1983, selections
Greek (Demotike), 1987
Greek, 1979, selections
Guarani, 1982, selections
Haitian Creole, 1983, selections
Hawaiian, 1855
Hiligaynon, 1994, selections
Hindi, 1982
Hmong, 1983, selections
Hungarian, 1979, selections
Hungarian, 1991

Icelandic, 1981
Ilokano, 1991, selections
Indonesian, 1977
Italian, 1852
Japanese, 1909
Kekchi, 1979, selections
Kekchi, 1983
Kisii, 1983, selections
Korean, 1967
Kuna, 1981, selections
Laotian, 1982, selections
Lingala, 1988, selections
Malagasy, 1986, selections
Mam, 1983, selections
Maori, 1889
Marshallese, 1984, selections
Maya, 1983, selections
Navajo, 1980, selections
Niuean, 1981, selections
Norwegian, 1950
Palauan, 1988, selections
Papiamento, 1987, selections
Persian, 1983, selections
Pohnpeian, 1987, selections
Polish, 1981
Portuguese, 1940
Quechua-Bolivia, 1981, selections
Quechua-Peru, 1979, selections
Quiche, 1979, selections
Quichua-Otavalo, 1980, selections
Rarotongan, 1965
Romanian, 1981, selections
Russian, 1980
Samoan, 1903
Shona, 1988, selections
Sinhala, 1983, selections
Spanish, 1875, selections
Spanish, 1886
Swahili, 1982, selections
Swedish, 1878
Tagalog, 1987, selections
Tahitian, 1904
Tamil, 1982, selections
Telugu, 1982, selections
Thai, 1976
Tongan, 1946
Trukese, 1987, selections
Turkish, 1906
Turkish, 1983, selections
Urdu, 1988, selections
Vietnamese, 1980, selections
Vietnamese, 1982
Welsh, 1852
Zulu, 1987, selections

Index

Aaron
    A.001   R.054

Abinadi
    A.003   C.228   G.002   J.017
    J.089   M.019   M.051   M.052
    M.194   N.105   P.079   P.110
    R.193   R.307   S.034   S.421
    S.436   T.192   W.086   W.135

Abish
    J.080

Abraham, book of
    P.006   W.050   W.221

Abrahamic covenant
    N.011   R.059

activity books for children
    B.007   B.008   B.138   B.170
    B.241   B.268   C.168   C.255
    D.031   G.090   G.091   G.092
    H.010   J.101   J.102   L.079
    M.161   O.018   P.058   S.021
    W.196

Adam, fall of
    E.021   G.032   G.033   L.116
    M.053   M.203   M.209   N.110
    P.252   P.299   S.186   W.174
    W.199

Adam and Eve
    B.274   P.216   Y.015

adieu
    B.204   C.232   C.237

adultery
    P.054

afterlife
    C.201   H.081

agriculture
    D.005   P.146   R.055   S.064
    S.340   T.069   T.146   T.171
    W.011

allegory, Jacob's. *See* Jacob, book of, chapter 5; olive

Alma, book of
    B.244   C.043   H.035   H.121
    J.070   K.030   M.070   P.034
    R.330   S.049   S.278   W.056
    W.096   W.287

Alma$_1$
    B.041   F.020   G.003   J.083
    L.013   P.110   R.027   R.057
    S.179   S.218   T.192

Alma$_2$
    B.251   G.004   H.171   J.070
    J.081   M.195   P.100   P.104
    P.110   R.027   R.057   R.258
    R.327   S.111   S.176   W.024
    W.118   W.199   W.244   Z.013

Amaleki
    W.187

American Indian
    B.260   B.261   C.012   C.025
    C.030   C.031   E.059   J.001
    K.002   K.020   K.054   L.033
    L.076   L.127   P.001   P.176
    P.272   P.273   S.222   S.247
    W.270   W.285. *See also* Aztec; Inca; Maya; mound builders
    customs
        C.083   C.099   E.013   R.262
        S.044

Great Spirit
    B.060   C.083
Hebrew origin
    A.021   A.067   B.036   B.176
    C.020   C.042   C.057   E.055
    E.056   F.005   H.040   H.124
    H.161   H.197   I.017   M.170
    P.173   P.235   P.257   P.284
    R.005   V.016   W.054   W.164
    W.217   W.252   W.268   Y.011
language
    C.244   P.251   R.077   S.263
    S.281   S.334   S.336   S.431
    S.432
legends
    B.133   C.083   C.091   C.097
    D.046   E.018   E.054   F.030
    H.037   H.055   H.056   H.119
    H.135   H.215   H.219   I.017
    L.068   M.027   M.140   O.001
    P.029   P.117   P.129   P.139
    P.188   P.213   R.236   R.255
    S.014   S.063   S.137   S.138
    S.235   S.327   S.328   S.347
    S.351   S.372   S.393   T.193
    W.019   W.031   W.147   W.154
    W.164   W.266   W.267
origin
    C.063   C.076   C.089   C.099
    C.148   C.170   D.046   F.001
    F.039   H.136   H.218   J.097
    M.026   M.097   M.219   N.089
    P.030   R.128   R.129   R.145
    R.174   R.230   R.231   R.262
    S.084   S.093   S.133   S.437
    S.440   T.033   W.043   Y.012
ruins
    C.057   C.092   C.094   C.099
    C.136   C.141   E.038   H.066
    L.069   L.089   M.047   M.163
    N.005   N.013   N.018   N.031
    P.027   P.051   P.052   P.172
    P.298   R.158   R.159   R.180
    R.345   S.008   S.015   S.082
    S.140   S.228   S.232   S.286
    S.294   S.298   S.313   S.339
    S.393   T.050   T.067   T.108
    T.137   T.138   T.139   T.140
    T.141   T.148   T.153   T.165
    W.019   W.266   W.268
Ammaron
    M.224
Ammon
    A.016   C.258   G.005   L.122
    M.021   R.026   W.057   W.231
Ammonihah
    B.064
Amulek
    D.053   G.006   R.058   T.186
anachronisms
    A.017   B.204   C.153   C.188
    C.232   C.237   L.011   M.148
    M.204   M.231   M.254   W.046
    W.156. *See also* adieu; elelphant;
    horse; iron; King James language;
    steel
ancient writings in the Americas
    C.072   C.095   H.056   H.065
    H.070   H.135   H.213   H.220
    H.227   H.228   J.021   J.022
    J.045   J.074   J.092   N.214
    O.033   P.248   R.204   R.205
    R.299   S.004   S.069   S.070
    S.081   S.281   S.307   S.318
    T.067   T.068   W.171   W.029
    W.043   W.144   W.151   W.276
    W.277   Y.010. *See also* metal plates
animals
    A.013   S.282. *See also* elephant;
    horse; mastodon
anteantiosis
    C.004
Anthon transcript
    A.080   B.001   C.240   C.241
    C.242   F.003   H.071   J.092
    N.007   S.234   S.285   T.128
    W.017   Y.022
Anthon, Charles
    C.040   C.171   C.240   D.011
    E.001   F.003   K.027   K.028
    K.029   M.252   N.007   N.089
    P.091   R.144   R.248   S.036
    S.087   S.126   S.234   S.246
    W.017

anthropology
 G.105 H.124 H.135 O.032
 R.067 R.093 S.086 S.283
 S.323 W.249

anti-Christ
 A.078 B.197 C.022 C.064
 F.050 G.034 L.112 M.215
 N.121 R.208 T.121 T.183
 W.148

Anti-Nephi-Lehies
 C.264 E.026 G.023 S.110
 T.202 W.076

apocryphal writings
 A.047

apostasy
 C.249 E.015 H.003 H.204
 L.084 M.069 M.117 R.208
 R.222 R.303 R.305 S.112
 S.141 S.442 V.014

archaeology
 A.067 A.068 B.019 B.020
 B.021 B.161 B.176 C.008
 C.074 C.075 C.076 C.088
 C.091 C.094 C.101 C.125
 C.128 C.131 C.132 C.136
 C.138 C.139 C.141 D.026
 D.057 D.067 E.037 E.057
 F.012 F.028 F.029 F.033
 G.084 G.085 G.104 G.105
 H.013 H.052 H.053 H.112
 H.124 H.136 H.137 H.211
 H.212 I.008 J.024 J.027
 J.031 J.034 J.035 J.038
 J.050 K.007 K.035 K.049
 L.089 M.163 M.261 N.013
 N.019 N.028 N.030 N.100
 O.032 P.024 P.027 P.185
 P.186 P.265 P.278 R.006
 R.049 R.050 R.095 R.205
 R.299 S.036 S.086 S.137
 S.177 S.249 S.305 S.307
 S.322 S.325 S.357 S.391
 T.051 T.058 T.137 T.138
 T.139 T.140 T.141 T.165
 T.166 T.167 T.169 V.023
 W.031 W.144 W.145 W.151
 W.198

archetypal patterns
 P.142 S.039

architecture
 S.140 S.230 S.300

ascension motif
 N.052

Assyria
 C.193 W.258

Atonement
 B.029 E.021 E.023 E.024
 G.032 H.004 M.015 M.051
 M.054 M.074 M.087 M.113
 M.209 M.212 M.214 N.029
 N.110 O.006 P.011 P.252
 R.108 R.317 S.024 S.034
 S.186 S.221 T.053 T.055
 T.186 V.009 W.228 W.237

authorship of Book of Mormon
 B.250 C.197 L.035 W.289.
 See also wordprint

 divine
  A.018 B.078

 Joseph Smith
  J.095 L.035

 multiple
  B.269 H.022 H.139 H.140
  H.142 L.036 R.296 S.353
  T.035 T.172 W.114 Y.002

Aztec
 C.196 D.027

baptism
 A.073 B.069 B.222 C.118
 F.008 H.058 R.107 R.245
 S.179 S.204 T.054 W.174
 W.281

 for the dead
  H.058 M.214 W.211

 infant
  H.058 M.255 T.054 T.083
  W.174

barley
 R.085 S.340 T.146 T.171

Beit Lei. *See* Lehi Cave

Benjamin, King
- B.136, B.150, B.274, C.259
- D.035, E.019, I.002, K.031
- K.032, M.209, N.061, P.169
- R.022, R.186, R.199, R.249
- T.205, T.209, W.060, W.087

Bethlehem
- S.190

Bible
- B.034, B.159, B.166, M.056
- M.118, M.247, N.120, N.127
- P.011, R.223, R.225, S.255
- T.010, W.112

Book of Mormon, companion of and consistent with
- A.031, B.028, B.243, C.001
- C.050, C.051, C.052, C.102
- C.174, C.175, D.042, D.055
- E.053, H.079, H.116, H.154
- J.005, L.020, L.021, L.024
- L.111, M.039, M.055, M.057
- M.061, M.077, M.113, M.116
- M.237, N.089, N.128, N.130
- N.138, P.030, P.076, P.118
- P.135, P.225, P.229, P.245
- P.258, P.269, R.048, R.061
- R.118, R.136, R.138, R.143
- R.157, R.319, S.123, S.154
- S.156, S.192, S.256, S.357
- T.005, T.009, T.012, T.018
- T.021, T.024, T.025, T.027
- T.028, T.029, T.054, T.150
- W.016, W.040, W.061, W.158
- W.174, W.178, W.186, W.201
- W.202, W.243

loss of plain and precious parts
- A.006, C.036, M.204, N.122
- P.251, R.001, S.153, S.192
- S.405, T.004, T.127, V.014
- W.103, W.155

prophesies of the Book of Mormon
- C.221, C.249, M.002, M.166
- M.176, M.220, M.243, M.249
- M.255, N.024, P.116, P.171
- P.220, P.244, R.132, R.140
- R.146, R.151, R.161, S.129
- S.199, S.205, S.259, T.024
- T.026, T.030, T.031, T.041
- T.044, T.217, V.018, W.144
- W.178, W.197, W.200, W.243
- W.265, W.283, Y.016

translated correctly
- A.004, B.125, M.058, M.098
- T.004, W.221

biblical law
- W.058, W.064, W.067, W.074
- W.082, W.091, W.106, W.115
- W.117

bibliography
- C.152, D.067, F.040, G.061
- G.065, G.066, L.017, S.282
- S.310, W.065, W.066, W.131
- W.132, W.133

blood vengeance
- R.013

boasting
- A.083

Book of Mormon studies
- A.074, B.027, B.054, B.147
- B.197, B.287, C.060, C.061
- C.079, C.102, C.119, C.132
- G.049, G.051, G.104, H.017
- H.087, H.095, H.111, J.030
- K.049, K.051, L.124, N.019
- N.045, N.075, N.131, N.132
- N.133, N.134, N.135, N.136
- N.137, R.022, R.187, R.201
- R.202, R.203, S.080, S.158
- S.342, S.358, S.391, S.438
- W.105, W.111, W.126

Bountiful
- A.085, A.087, J.025, J.033
- T.139, Z.003

bow
- G.079, H.015, W.007

brass plates
- B.115, B.128, B.209, B.226
- B.237, C.109, C.260, G.021
- I.005, J.057, M.036, M.197
- M.201, M.210, M.213, P.105
- R.105, R.110, S.288, S.358
- S.373, S.420. *See also* metal plates

breastplate
    B.128   B.142   S.225   W.266

brother of Jared
    A.034   B.207   B.240   C.112
    E.062   J.003   J.008   N.023
    N.073   N.074   R.031   R.235
    S.250   S.415   S.423

calendar
    B.162   H.094   J.023   M.030
    S.314   S.320

calling and election
    S.113

Campbell, Alexander
    K.041   N.057

Campbell, Joseph
    C.064

canon, open
    W.128

cardinal directions
    H.016   L.066   S.301   T.125
    W.259

Cave of Khirbet Beit Lei. *See* Lehi cave

cement
    B.175   G.098   G.099   I.017
    M.047   S.038   S.137   T.069
    W.136   W.178   W.257

charity
    B.045   D.002   M.207   N.062
    N.114   R.209

chiasmus
    A.066   C.051   C.143   C.144
    C.147   C.223   C.237   H.099
    H.106   R.341   R.352   S.227
    S.230   S.233   S.335   S.435
    T.129   T.147   W.056   W.065
    W.066   W.067   W.068   W.069
    W.070   W.071   W.072   W.096
    W.112. *See also* Hebraisms

choice seer
    M.088   N.113   S.005. *See also* seer

Christ
  baptism of
    M.122

  birth of
    B.157   B.162   B.177   C.077
    C.218   D.037   H.062   J.023
    L.117   M.033   M.040   O.013
    O.020   P.250   R.123   R.228
    R.236   R.273   S.190   S.240
    T.017   W.150   W.227   Y.020

  character of
    A.047   B.092   B.095   B.148
    N.123   S.395   T.078   T.081

  death of
    B.162   D.037   L.098   M.033
    P.227   P.250   R.228   R.236
    W.227

  knowledge of
    B.093   J.002   J.008   R.036
    R.327   T.038   T.122   W.013
    W.061   W.084   W.164   W.287

  mission of
    B.181   C.067   C.102   C.118
    C.165   D.048   D.064   E.045
    F.055   F.059   H.068   H.179
    H.184   J.047   L.001   L.117
    M.012   M.053   M.076   M.087
    M.114   M.194   M.211   O.006
    P.077   P.166   R.023   R.118
    R.235   S.005   S.221   S.395
    S.439   T.019   T.036   W.226
    W.235

  name of
    B.147   B.148   B.152   B.206
    C.067   M.053   N.010   P.155
    T.046   W.013   W.114   W.127
    W.167

  Second Coming of
    L.053   L.054   M.102   M.104
    M.105   M.120   N.094   P.133
    S.347

  teachings of
    A.079   B.042   B.044   B.046
    B.094   B.239   C.036   C.161
    C.172   C.236   D.048   F.008
    F.055   H.008   H.022   J.071
    M.103   N.039   N.040   P.057
    P.166   R.106   S.395   T.044
    T.164   W.061   W.095   W.103
    W.142   W.166

visit to the Nephites
F.008   F.013. *See also* Christ's appearance in America; testify of Jesus Christ

Christ's appearance in America
A.029   B.028   B.042   B.105
B.257   C.009   C.162   C.195
C.204   C.218   D.037   D.054
E.045   H.215   K.023   M.017
M.040   M.165   M.192   N.039
P.139   P.216   P.263   Q.003
R.235   R.236   R.238   R.284
S.007   S.009   S.068   S.216
S.262   S.351   S.382   T.041
T.044   T.081   T.212   W.123
W.146   W.154   W.256

chronology
B.138   B.174   B.257   B.265
C.002   C.125   C.132   D.062
J.023   J.098   L.042   M.042
M.158   P.079   P.210   P.214
P.227   R.064   R.103   R.122
R.131   R.228   R.302   S.068
S.216   S.237   S.289   S.314
S.355   T.034   T.135   T.153
T.212   V.010   W.006   W.032
W.035   W.039   W.123   W.180

Civil War
B.083

climactic forms
P.041. *See also* hebraisms

codex
S.285

colophons
T.199

Columbus
C.150   C.195   E.059   F.041
G.031   H.045   H.160   L.076
M.142   M.172   N.042   P.075
P.139   R.040   S.277   T.040
Y.009

"come unto Christ"
B.087   F.009   R.108   T.151

coming forth of the Book of Mormon
A.009   A.045   A.060   A.061
B.002   B.051   B.071   B.122
B.124   B.128   B.142   B.211
B.238   B.284   C.005   C.054
C.085   C.104   C.163   C.178
C.180   C.206   C.210   C.216
C.263   D.011   E.048   E.049
E.051   F.021   F.044   F.056
G.069   G.070   G.094   H.128
H.158   H.202   I.006   J.066
J.084   K.041   L.084   M.006
M.192   N.026   N.102   N.112
P.202   P.203   P.218   P.226
P.233   P.234   P.261   R.010
R.042   R.117   R.125   R.144
R.212   R.239   R.248   R.260
R.355   S.051   S.165   S.168
S.183   S.185   S.224   S.260
S.402   S.416   S.424   S.429
T.008   T.020   T.021   T.024
T.025   T.052   T.175   W.180
W.253   Y.005

commentaries
H.085   K.050   L.092   M.125
M.126   M.127   M.128   P.156
R.103   R.161   S.079   S.124
S.356

Communism
B.099

concordances
C.002   R.065   S.037   S.388
W.052

constitution, United States
A.024   S.383

conversion stories
A.084   B.009   B.032   B.055
B.145   B.153   B.277   C.052
C.056   C.058   C.115   C.189
D.028   D.029   D.045   D.052
D.054   E.020   E.042   E.046
E.052   E.061   G.028   G.053
G.055   G.067   H.002   H.042
H.069   H.072   H.117   H.126
H.147   H.154   H.183   H.231
K.048   K.056   L.129   M.132
M.135   M.154   M.157   M.188

    M.189   M.190   M.246   N.009
    N.017   P.190   P.289   R.051
    R.297   S.017   S.027   S.077
    S.149   S.226   S.349   S.387
    S.390   S.414   S.425   T.001
    T.002   T.113   T.179   V.003
    W.045   W.055   W.177   W.264
    W.282   Z.007

copyright
    R.163   S.212   S.213   W.085

Corianton
    I.020   M.223

Coriantumr
    S.254

costumes
    B.242   T.182

cotton
    D.004   T.182   W.257

covenants
    B.216   F.048   L.003   L.104
    L.105   L.107   L.123   M.187
    O.028   P.171   P.216   P.246
    R.189   R.197   R.199   T.151
    T.152   T.168   W.103   W.108

Cowdery, Oliver
    A.040   A.043   A.046   A.052
    A.055   A.056   A.057   C.206
    G.121   J.077   N.093   S.150
    S.225   T.063   V.011   W.042
    W.159   W.162   W.163   W.181
    Y.006   Y.008

creation
    G.032   G.073   R.286   T.068

critical text
    F.002   S.115   S.119   S.122. *See also* textual variants

darkness
    P.240   S.210

Davidson, Matilda
    P.269   R.090. *See also* Spaulding manuscript

Dead Sea Scrolls
    H.011   M.062   M.081   N.027
    N.070   T.163

deception, avoiding
    B.082   B.109

Del Rio
    B.229

destruction
    B.005   B.017   B.029   B.176
    C.041   C.194   C.250   J.037
    M.007   M.244   N.002   P.029
    P.051   P.124   R.033   R.207
    R.243   S.034   S.096   S.228
    S.253   S.401   T.095   W.074
    W.164   W.252

Deuteronomy
    R.189

discipleship
    M.090

dispensations
    H.216

divorce
    C.065

doctrine
    B.198   C.152   C.154   C.178
    C.251   C.254   D.001   D.036
    D.039   E.052   F.038   H.007
    H.173   H.204   J.047   L.024
    L.078   M.056   M.117   M.118
    N.052   N.110   N.111   P.081
    R.106   R.116   T.027   T.028
    V.013   W.036   W.039   W.184

    use of the Book of Mormon in early LDS doctrine
        U.003   U.004   U.006   U.007

Doctrine and Covenants
    E.006   N.110   W.218   W.278

Dogberry, Obediah
    K.041   R.120   S.404

drama
    P.262

economic systems
    R.306   S.313

editions of the Book of Mormon
    B.159   D.018   F.002   F.015
    H.051   H.096   H.097   H.110
    H.172   H.188   H.201   I.021
    J.019   K.034   L.039   M.043

M.063 M.067 M.079 M.106
M.247 N.022 P.016 P.017
P.018 P.253 P.260 R.028
R.071 R.164 S.116 S.144
S.275 S.412 W.195 W.274
Z.008 Z.012. *See also* translation from English

  RLDS
    H.103 H.107 H.114 J.019
    M.043 P.071 S.116

Egypt
  A.066 J.061 S.015 S.093
  S.109 S.249

Egyptian
  artifacts
    E.038 S.341 W.146 Y.015
  language
    A.080 B.021 B.033 B.133
    B.223 B.235 B.237 C.171
    C.193 C.241 F.003 G.082
    G.086 H.063 I.011 I.019
    K.028 N.032 P.088 P.242
    P.247 R.076 R.077 S.044
    S.053 S.101 S.164 S.231
    S.430 T.206 T.207 W.003
    W.046 W.047 W.048 W.256

elephant
  G.001 H.061 M.163 N.048
  P.240 P.241 R.180 S.043
  S.295

encyclopedia
  B.139

endless punishment
  B.154 P.159

Enos
  E.027 E.028 E.029 J.085
  M.016 R.079

Enos, book of
  A.069 L.029 L.067 S.032

epanalepsis
  C.111

Ephraim, tribe of
  R.129 R.291 S.189 S.207
  S.408 S.409 T.160

eternal life
  R.035 R.107

Ether, book of
  B.163 D.025 R.348 S.099
  S.167 T.038 T.039 T.080
  W.104

everlasting
  B.154

evolution
  P.015 P.144 S.202

exaltation
  C.178

exodus
  B.252 B.253 N.015 O.011
  S.114 S.443 S.445 T.047

evidences of the Book of Mormon
  external
    A.014 A.015 A.026 A.068
    B.161 B.169 B.176 C.049
    C.075 C.076 C.083 C.091
    C.094 C.101 C.103 C.160
    C.193 C.196 C.221 C.257
    D.067 E.038 E.039 E.058
    F.053 G.100 H.057 H.211
    H.213 I.012 I.014 I.023
    K.005 K.035 L.058 L.089
    M.166 M.183 N.018 N.059
    N.070 N.100 P.020 P.050
    P.052 P.056 P.112 P.225
    P.242 P.286 P.288 R.008
    R.049 R.158 R.180 R.214
    R.260 R.345 S.002 S.030
    S.038 S.044 S.052 S.070
    S.085 S.088 S.089 S.105
    S.136 S.137 S.168 S.372
    S.392 T.050 T.058 T.067
    T.069 T.070 T.097 T.108
    T.117 T.141 T.146 T.148
    V.023 W.020 W.121 W.145
    W.152 W.154 W.164 W.175
    W.198 W.201 W.207 W.212
    Y.021
  internal
    B.016 B.229 C.039 C.105
    E.024 E.036 E.058 G.104
    G.108 H.057 H.214 I.025

J.052	K.011	K.035	M.004
M.252	N.059	N.079	P.118
P.238	R.008	R.011	R.072
R.073	R.126	R.260	R.341
S.085	S.106	S.159	T.031
T.097	V.023	W.140	W.155
W.175	W.202	W.254	

Ezekiel, book of,
    chapter 17
        S.327
    chapter 37

A.030	M.179	N.071	N.127
P.254	R.130	R.153	S.075
S.207	T.023	T.030	

Ezias
    T.100

faith

B.041	B.045	B.069	D.042
H.032	H.042	K.012	K.030
L.032	L.115	M.257	N.114
N.117	P.080	P.105	R.107
R.244	R.324	R.348	S.278
T.080	T.114	T.183	T.189
W.024	W.155	W.225	

faithful history
    B.283. *See also* historicity of the Book of Mormon

family

B.054	B.114	B.200	B.215
C.159	S.360		

Family Home Evening

B.267	B.278	M.038	Z.014

fasting
    L.121   R.190

fathers
    B.043   C.159   H.025

Feast of Tabernacles
    T.205   T.209. *See also* Jewish festivals

fiction
    N.037

figures of speech. *See* colophons; epanalepsis; neologisms

films
    C.080   P.143   T.076   T.110

first edition of the Book of Mormon
    J.060   W.274

1 Nephi, book of

A.090	I.005	L.118	P.215
S.047	S.434	S.445	

First Vision
    P.087   P.207   S.168   S.197. *See also* Smith, Joseph, heavenly visitations

flax
    S.064

foreordination
    M.200

forgiveness
    I.020   P.169   R.324   R.333

"four quarters"
    W.259

4 Nephi, book of
    R.033   W.224

Francesca, Vincenzo D.
    T.076

free agency

C.090	O.003	P.011	R.034
T.043	T.080	T.186	T.189

freedom

B.048	B.081	B.085	B.126
C.045	C.090	F.018	O.003
P.136	R.323		

Freemasonry

B.057	H.168	I.018	P.148
P.150	W.129		

Friberg, Arnold
    B.187   S.020

fulness of the gospel

G.056	L.095	M.117	P.244
S.045			

Gadianton robbers

B.080	C.077	H.043	H.132
M.047	P.147	P.148	P.150
R.088	S.442	W.008	

gathering of Israel. *See* Israel, gathering

genealogy
 B.058 G.048 J.057 P.210
 R.215 R.342 S.337 T.160

Genesis
 R.105 W.283

gentiles
 B.216 D.041 M.059 M.119
 N.113 R.243 R.284 R.293
 W.028 W.157 W.226

geography
 A.011 A.085 A.086 B.006
 C.013 C.014 C.097 C.098
 C.114 C.124 C.125 C.127
 C.132 C.134 C.136 C.164
 C.262 D.030 D.050 G.085
 H.013 H.016 H.021 H.031
 H.038 H.086 H.099 H.111
 H.134 H.141 H.165 H.166
 H.167 H.205 H.230 I.023
 J.025 J.037 J.094 L.048
 L.049 L.064 L.065 L.088
 M.150 M.151 M.158 N.030
 N.053 N.095 O.032 O.033
 P.023 P.024 P.025 P.027
 P.185 P.186 P.191 P.212
 P.235 P.243 P.255 P.296
 P.300 R.049 R.050 R.075
 R.102 R.176 R.178 R.179
 R.182 R.271 R.308 S.065
 S.070 S.071 S.082 S.097
 S.099 S.107 S.108 S.280
 S.292 S.293 S.301 S.306
 S.326 S.391 S.396 S.427
 S.428 T.044 T.125 T.128
 T.133 T.141 T.157 T.162
 V.024 W.032 W.033 W.034
 W.036 W.037 W.039 W.136
 W.209 W.229 Z.001 Z.006

Gideon
 G.010 J.086

Gidgiddoni
 J.087

Godhead
 D.039 H.184 J.011 L.131
 M.194 M.203 M.204 M.208
 P.155 P.252 S.033 S.072
 T.081 W.239

gold plates
 A.044 A.053 A.058 B.067
 B.142 B.218 C.054 C.109
 C.212 C.216 C.217 C.222
 D.040 F.027 G.080 G.096
 H.046 H.059 H.127 J.054
 K.040 M.050 M.081 M.257
 N.116 P.002 P.094 P.113
 P.125 P.134 P.183 P.306
 R.071 R.267 S.092 S.104
 S.129 S.170 S.208 S.217
 S.238 S.248 T.107 T.126
 V.018 W.001 W.047 W.188
 W.233 W.261 Y.010. *See also*
metal plates; stone box; tumbaga

hiding place
 C.217 L.049

government
 B.127 B.156 B.281 C.061
 C.062 C.146 D.012 D.065
 E.005 G.079 G.106 K.008
 M.164 M.169 M.242 M.244
 M.258 N.046 N.063 P.145
 Q.001 R.056 R.078 R.104
 R.111 R.113 R.254 S.337
 S.411 W.106 W.174 W.294

grace
 L.116 M.198 N.110 O.029
 P.057 P.170

grammar
 B.194 F.047 H.097 H.198
 L.011 S.143

Grandin, E. B.
 O.021 P.207 S.223

gratitude
 L.114

Great and Abominable Church
 A.023 C.029 P.059 P.090
 P.267 R.303 R.305 W.127

Great White God
 B.020 M.028 P.117 P.121
 P.129 P.131 P.139 P.140. *See also* American Indian, legends

Hagoth
    A.020   B.289   C.116   G.048
    K.024   L.085   M.230   P.060
    P.068   P.186   P.247   R.174
    V.019

hand of God
    S.033

happiness
    W.224

Harris, Lucy
    P.094

Harris, Martin
    A.038   A.049   C.040   G.122
    H.078   H.180   H.181   J.041
    J.063   M.143   O.007   S.152
    S.343   S.399   T.063   T.174
    W.004   W.159   Y.006   Y.008

"heads" (Jacob 1:4)
    T.124

Hebraisms
    B.202   B.203   B.229   B.231
    B.236   B.238   C.223   C.233
    C.234   C.235   F.047   H.063
    K.038   L.001   L.006   N.012
    N.015   P.009   P.043   R.210
    S.121   S.362   T.124   T.201
    W.256. *See also* chiasmus; climactic forms; parallelism

Hebrew language
    P.247   P.251   R.068   R.076
    R.077   R.204   S.030   S.044
    S.100   S.430   S.431   S.432
    T.164   Z.003

Helaman, book of
    C.077   C.090   H.036   N.122
    S.050   T.100   W.068   W.069

Helaman₁
    T.101

Helaman₂
    C.084

Helaman₃
    A.083   B.013   M.211   R.057
    T.071

hell
    D.001

Hill Cumorah
    C.009   C.041   C.054   C.114
    C.208   C.211   C.212   D.020
    D.030   F.026   G.094   G.119
    H.021   H.127   I.015   I.016
    L.087   M.150   M.151   P.022
    P.177   P.186   P.207   P.232
    P.240   R.182   S.056   S.183
    S.378   S.401   S.402   W.182

Hill Ramah
    M.151   R.182   W.182

historians of the Book of Mormon
    B.201   C.197   D.023   G.041
    G.109   H.044   H.162   K.004
    M.078   M.139   M.202   M.228
    R.070   R.219   W.006   Y.002

historicity of the Book of Mormon
    G.076   J.028   L.074   M.083
    M.185   M.203   N.103   O.004
    P.151   T.129. *See also* faithful history

Holy Ghost
    B.082   C.184   H.026   P.170
    R.107   S.195   S.386   T.184
    V.008. *See also* witness of the Holy Ghost

hope
    B.045   D.002   N.114   W.273

horse
    C.021   C.097   H.186   P.004
    P.288   R.180   S.001   S.038
    S.089   S.315   W.257

Howe, E. D. *(Mormonism Unvailed)*
    C.069   F.006   R.090

humility
    M.171   R.343   S.386

Hurlbut, Philastus
    J.065   L.080   R.090

illustrations
    A.001   A.012   B.187   B.188
    D.037   E.004   E.034   F.007
    G.044   J.075   J.076   J.093
    L.061   N.004   O.019   P.108
    P.294   R.096   R.295   S.020
    S.416   S.418   S.419   S.421
    T.048   W.169   W.179   Z.004
    Z.015

immorality
> S.385

incense
> S.303

indexes to the Book of Mormon. *See* topical indexes

Indian. *See* American Indian

infant baptism. *See* baptism, infant

internal contradictions
> R.132 R.273

iron rod
> L.056 P.197 R.127 T.149
> W.260

iron
> I.009 M.183 O.008 W.073
> W.213. *See also* steel

Isaiah
> J.006 N.105 R.147

Isaiah, book of
> A.005 B.143 D.010 G.050
> G.052 G.057 G.058 H.011
> J.051 J.068 L.008 L.103
> M.062 N.096 N.106 N.109
> N.129 P.062 P.116 P.228
> P.254 P.264 R.098 R.141
> R.210 R.213 R.219 R.261
> S.016 S.125 S.126 S.160
> S.350 S.353 S.354 S.363
> S.364 S.375 T.011 T.026
> T.030 T.127 T.204 V.022

Ishmael
> B.014 G.077 R.129 S.207

isles
> M.034 R.271 W.127

Israel
> gathering
> > B.261 D.007 D.047 E.012
> > F.024 J.009 M.104 M.109
> > M.120 M.179 M.199 M.210
> > P.001 P.077 R.039 R.059
> > S.035 T.036 T.097 T.127
> > U.007 V.009 W.235
>
> house of
> > M.217 P.212 R.269 W.185

"it came to pass"
> S.239 W.127

Ixtililxochitl
> F.034

Izapa. *See* Stela 5, Izapa

Jacob
> B.136 C.187 G.013 J.073
> M.022 M.054 M.064 R.209
> R.249 S.059 S.221 S.385
> T.036 T.037 W.023

Jacob, book of
> B.164 C.202 L.032 M.091
> M.123 S.191 T.124 W.088
> W.235
>
> chapter 5
> > F.014 F.049 G.047 G.059
> > H.009 H.189 H.192 K.034
> > L.012 P.176 P.179 R.016
> > R.202 S.031 S.196 S.219
> > S.439 T.079 T.098 T.197
> > T.213 U.006 V.023 W.011
> > W.125. *See also* olive

Jaredites
> B.289 F.022 H.101 I.011
> J.003 J.043 L.077 L.083
> N.076 N.081 N.100 O.001
> P.123 P.255 S.096 S.114
> S.250 T.039 T.162 W.248
> W.275
>
> barge
> > H.100 N.073 N.074 N.076
> > Z.011
>
> language
> > T.155
>
> records
> > C.109
>
> stones
> > S.251 S.252

Jarom, book of
> A.070 R.081

Jeremiah
> L.007 M.180 W.116 W.253

Jerusalem
    C.207   M.180   N.002   N.027
    N.078   O.013   P.174   S.240
    W.116

Jesus Christ. *See* Christ

Jewish festivals
    R.199   T.205   T.209   W.087
    W.134   W.135   W.137. *See also* Feast of Tabernacles; Passover

John the Baptist
    A.057

John the Revelator
    A.023   M.044   R.303   T.123

John, revelations of
    M.044

Johnston's army
    H.129

Joseph, tribe of
    L.081   P.180   P.264   R.291
    R.334   T.160

Joseph of Egypt
    L.007   M.011   R.098   R.136
    S.075   S.127   T.078

Joseph Smith Translation
    C.172   C.238   D.066   M.056
    M.197   M.213   S.192

joy
    H.104

Judah, tribe of
    L.096   P.212   R.269   S.189
    W.109

judges
    B.156   M.164   M.205   M.258
    Q.001   R.078   S.411   W.090

judgment
    M.214   N.108   P.077   P.159
    P.230   R.088   S.028   S.220
    W.199

justice and mercy
    G.032   P.160   R.317. *See also* mercy

justification
    L.119   M.198   W.225

keystone
    B.076   B.079   B.091   B.096
    B.110   F.017   M.080   M.098
    M.108   M.112   N.118   N.119
    R.326   R.335

Kinderhook plates
    C.072

King James language
    M.056   N.056   R.218   R.225

kingship
    K.008   L.123   N.035   R.056
    R.069   R.078   R.104   R.188
    R.195   R.197   R.346   S.114
    T.093

Kishkumen
    B.013

Knight, Joseph, Jr.
    P.203

Knight, Joseph, Sr.
    H.082   Z.010

Knight, Newell
    P.203

Korihor
    C.022   G.034   K.053   L.113
    P.054   R.208   T.121   T.183
    W.024. *See also* anti-Christ

La Mojarra Stela
    S.254

Laban
    E.026   E.035   H.020   H.175
    W.091

    sword of
        B.115   B.142   H.169   I.009
        R.312   W.189

Lachish letters
    N.044   N.051   N.078

Laman
    P.035   T.159

Lamanites
    B.012   C.025   C.032   C.047
    C.135   C.155   C.199   C.205
    D.016   E.023   F.023   F.051
    F.058   F.061   G.029   G.060
    H.170   H.224   I.025   J.004

J.031	J.099	K.010	K.013				
K.014	K.016	K.017	K.020				
K.026	L.128	L.130	M.025				
M.026	M.141	M.170	N.001				
N.086	N.092	N.098	P.020				
P.137	P.281	P.282	P.285				
R.074	R.128	R.148	R.316				
R.334	R.336	S.358	S.366				
S.394	T.091	U.007	W.157				

dark skin
   F.023   N.087   S.003   S.200
   S.366   T.078   T.187

view of Book of Mormon history
   B.286   K.010   L.124   R.111

"lamb"
   T.123

lament
   B.256

Lamoni's father
   A.001   A.016

Lamoni, King
   R.017

language
   A.011   C.027   C.171   F.043
   H.190   K.006   R.076   R.206
   S.350   S.430   W.168

19th century
   T.084   T.087

of the Mormons
   T.092

large plates of Nephi
   C.109   M.236   O.017   R.170
   W.068. *See also* records that became the Book of Mormon

last days
   N.068

law of consecration
   T.106

law of Moses
   A.073   B.062   B.205   H.164
   H.216   M.051   M.072   M.194
   P.165   R.104   R.153   R.205
   S.204   T.055   T.192   W.064
   W.110

Lehi
   B.136   B.258   C.225   E.008
   G.014   H.130   J.088   L.059
   L.060   M.037   M.046   N.027
   N.053   N.054   N.078   N.117
   N.121   O.011   P.036   P.100
   P.158   R.215   S.128   S.291
   S.417   T.033   T.048   T.107
   T.160   T.214   W.063   W.093

600-year prophecy
   H.207

counsel vision
   W.092

daughters
   S.358   S.361   S.365

dream of
   B.146   B.155   C.121   C.161
   G.092   H.041   J.011   L.046
   L.061   L.108   M.010   M.136
   M.196   N.101   P.197   S.386
   T.057   T.149   Z.005

record of
   B.254   B.255   C.230   G.082
   K.046   M.239   P.198   P.299
   R.110   R.170. *See also* records that became the Book of Mormon

Lehi cave
   B.118

Lehi's route
   A.087   A.088   B.035   B.208
   B.289   C.013   C.087   C.126
   C.129   C.157   C.245   D.030
   E.002   E.025   H.138   H.143
   H.144   M.068   P.005   P.199
   P.247   S.061   S.103   S.237
   S.329   S.332   S.443   T.158
   W.242

Leitworter
   A.059

Liahona
   A.079   D.051   G.088   J.070
   K.012   K.019   L.072   L.102
   N.055   P.197   S.241   S.445
   W.165   Z.014

Limhi
   G.045   K.033

linen
    S.001   S.317   S.322

linguistics
    K.034   K.050   L.003   L.009
    L.125   M.124   O.012   R.230
    S.391   T.198   V.023   W.079
    W.100   W.127   W.130   Y.004

literary devices
    C.111   E.024   G.059   G.073
    H.095   J.100   L.022   P.041
    P.049   P.141   R.206   R.210
    R.349   S.031   S.335   T.047
    T.083. *See also* anteantiosis; chiasmus; climactic forms

literary styles
    B.269   E.007   H.104   H.142
    S.031   S.269

literary value of the Book of Mormon
    B.172   B.235   C.085   C.220
    E.052   G.076   M.010   M.149
    N.085   P.141   R.115   R.354
    S.359   S.370   S.435   T.074
    T.085   T.086   T.087   W.009
    W.109   W.155   W.176   W.246

longevity
    W.094. *See also* population

Lord's prayer
    C.236   C.238. *See also* Sermon on the Mount

lost pages
    116   A.060   C.230   H.173
    H.182   K.046   L.106   M.143
    M.236   M.239   P.032   P.095
    P.164   P.198   R.071   R.129
    R.170   R.248   S.152   S.224
    S.426   V.012

lost ten tribes
    L.016

love
    B.246

Macpherson, James
    C.044

magic
    B.282

Malachi
    J.010   W.211

Manasseh, tribe of
    R.129   S.074   S.189   S.408
    S.409   T.160

manuscripts
    H.182   K.046   T.056. *See also* critical text; original manuscript; printer's manuscript

Mary
    C.218

Masonry. *See* Freemasonry

Maya
    A.065   C.143   C.144   C.145
    C.147   C.242   D.026   H.019
    H.218   H.221   I.008   I.011
    I.019   J.039   N.014   P.020
    R.185   R.308   S.014   S.053
    S.065   S.229   S.249   W.147

  astronomy
    W.150

  calendar
    J.022   M.030   W.154

  language
    S.231   S.233   T.125   T.155
    Z.002

  prophecy
    S.318

McLellin, William E.
    A.064   P.208   W.218

mercy
    B.069   C.173   E.023   I.020
    M.205   P.160

metal plates
    B.176   C.051   C.072   C.073
    C.074   C.151   C.246   C.247
    E.001   H.053   H.064   H.065
    H.067   H.151   M.139   P.119
    P.122   P.192   W.164   W.217
    W.290   W.291. *See also* ancient writings in the Americas; brass plates; gold plates; Kinderhook plates; large plates of Nephi; Padilla gold plates; small plates of Nephi

metals
    A.013 B.230 C.075 C.095
    N.048 P.297 Q.002 R.022
    S.026 S.090 S.304 S.310
    S.319 T.214 W.154 W.178
    Y.010. *See also* iron; metal plates; steel; tumbaga

Mexico
    D.026 P.281 R.320 T.108
    W.019

midrash
    C.239

missionary tool, Book of Mormon as
    B.031 B.101 B.171 B.173
    B.220 C.056 D.028 D.038
    F.063 G.071 H.002 H.074
    H.075 H.083 H.088 H.185
    L.110 M.082 M.099 M.100
    P.012 P.063 P.078 P.083
    P.102 P.106 P.115 P.196
    P.204 P.205 P.290 P.291
    P.295 R.135 R.290 R.338
    S.270 S.271 T.011 T.066
    T.195 U.001 V.019 V.021
    W.160 W.177 Y.007

Mitchell, Dr.
    K.029

monetary systems
    V.023 J.061 S.236 W.230

Monroe Doctrine
    M.243 M.244

Mormon
    G.015 H.029 H.120 H.152
    L.005 L.054 M.007 M.224
    P.099 P.100 R.340 S.060
    S.164 T.215 V.013 W.272.
    See also nickname "Mormon"
  as editor
    B.245 H.029 H.047 H.048
    H.095 H.176 K.004 L.054
    M.008 O.015 P.126 P.152
    R.071 R.172 R.219 R.353
    S.426 T.059 T.093 T.157
    T.170 T.208 V.001 W.068
  teachings
    S.266

Moroni
  angel
    C.208 C.210 G.119 L.015
    R.142 R.156 R.157 R.168
    R.313 W.168 W.222 Y.001
  visit to Joseph Smith
    A.039 A.060 C.005 C.086
    C.248 G.096 I.012 P.085
    P.164 R.121 R.272 S.368
    S.433 T.019 T.029 W.210
    Y.001. *See also* Smith, Joseph, heavenly visitations

Moroni's promise
    B.072 B.248 B.271 E.017
    E.060 F.009 H.034 H.072
    I.026 L.094 M.113 M.225
    P.112 T.049 W.158

Moroni, book of
    A.063 N.114 P.061 W.223

Moroni$_1$
    B.037 F.018 L.004 M.145
    M.240 N.046 R.060 R.254
    S.063 S.444 T.102 T.133
    V.001

Moroni$_2$
    D.013 D.068 F.019 K.004
    L.015 L.054 M.007 M.225
    P.124 P.127 P.161 P.162
    P.163 S.040 S.060 S.358
    S.367 W.210 W.222 W.279
    Y.001

Mosiah, book of
    B.084 G.067 G.075 G.078
    L.030 L.114 M.021 P.079
    P.149 P.157 S.220 S.345
    T.003 T.184

Mosiah, sons of
    P.132 T.211 W.240 W.244

Mosiah$_1$
    S.010 T.093 T.103

Mosiah$_2$
    B.156 R.356 S.411

most correct book
    B.096 L.071 N.115 N.118
    N.119 N.138 P.251 R.322

mothers
& B.043 & B.136 & Y.003

mound builders
& F.001 & I.019 & P.069 & P.186
& P.223 & P.297 & S.084 & W.021
& W.263

Mulek
& C.130 & C.133 & C.139 & C.142
& C.243 & E.032 & J.040 & J.069
& N.051 & P.209 & S.242 & S.284
& S.327 & W.292

Mulekites
& S.311 & S.369 & W.247

murmuring
& A.082 & T.159

mysteries of God
& B.150

Nag Hammadi
& N.069

Nahom
& A.086 & A.087 & A.088 & C.129
& G.077

names from the Book of Mormon
& B.183 & B.236 & B.238 & C.244
& E.041 & G.046 & H.152 & H.191
& H.193 & K.057 & L.005 & L.125
& M.218 & N.032 & N.034 & N.048
& N.055 & N.067 & P.066 & P.193
& R.046 & R.076 & R.087 & R.194
& S.097 & S.101 & S.102 & S.164
& T.176 & T.210 & U.009 & U.010
& V.023 & W.048 & W.122 & W.275
& Z.003

natural man
& B.274 & C.108 & M.209 & R.024
& T.043 & T.186 & W.228

Near Eastern influences
& C.051 & H.195 & K.038 & M.156
& N.035 & N.061 & N.069 & N.072
& N.075 & O.028 & P.052 & R.068
& R.188 & R.191 & R.197 & R.199
& R.312 & S.031 & S.263 & S.279
& S.294 & S.303 & T.164 & T.198
& T.205 & T.209 & W.007 & W.057
& W.058 & W.087 & W.093 & W.146
& W.259 & Y.004. *See also* Hebraisms; Jewish festivals

Nehor
& T.121

Nehum
& P.062

neologisms
& S.244

Nephi's psalm
& S.269 & T.075 & T.078 & T.190

Nephi's vision
& C.227 & L.118 & M.044 & M.196
& R.303 & S.194 & S.316

Nephi$_1$
& B.117 & B.232 & C.019 & C.033
& C.035 & C.260 & G.018 & G.019
& G.037 & G.079 & G.095 & H.084
& J.042 & J.090 & M.003 & M.023
& N.117 & P.074 & P.100 & P.101
& P.103 & P.292 & R.098 & R.109
& R.257 & S.397 & S.419 & T.042
& T.075 & T.190 & W.170 & W.279

Nephi$_2$
& B.132 & C.077 & G.017 & S.055
& S.062 & S.113 & T.104

Nephi$_3$
& A.072 & G.020 & P.211 & R.057
& T.105

Nephi$_4$
& R.057 & T.106

Nephite Twelve
& P.253 & S.215 & W.279

Nephites
& R.091 & R.093 & W.285

Neum
& J.007

New Jerusalem
& F.023 & F.044 & M.119 & S.028
& S.075 & T.038 & U.007 & W.147

Nibley, Hugh
& W.080

nickname "Mormon"
& L.005 & R.328 & T.007 & V.013

Noah, King
    A.003   D.035   J.017   S.421

numerology
    L.010   M.134   W.102

oaths
    C.185   J.079   M.245   P.049
    S.444

obedience
    C.019   J.072   M.171   P.105
    R.327   T.042   T.048   W.231

olive
    C.103   C.202   F.014   F.049
    G.047   G.065   H.009   H.122
    H.123   H.189   H.192   J.009
    L.012   L.016   N.066   N.113
    P.176   P.179   R.016   R.198
    R.202   S.031   S.035   S.075
    S.439   T.079   T.098   T.213
    U.006   W.011. *See also* Jacob, book of, chapter 5

Omni, book of
    A.071   D.032   S.254   S.369

opposition
    M.015   S.276

oral tradition
    E.007   J.074

ordinances
    M.117   M.122   P.061   S.068
    S.184   S.195   S.255   W.110
    W.223. *See also* Priesthood, ordinances

origin of the Book of Mormon
    B.224   C.054   C.068   J.027
    K.036   K.037   M.256   O.009
    O.016   R.263   R.304   T.086
    W.049   W.142. *See also* Smith, Ethan (*View of the Hebrews*); Spaulding theory

    divine
        B.149   C.015   C.209   F.037
        H.217   J.052   K.045   M.133
        N.008   P.014   P.221   P.228
        R.097   R.251   S.151   S.154
        S.157   S.170   S.342   T.009
        T.020   T.068   T.111   W.002
        W.037   W.143   W.217

    historical document
        E.047   G.115   N.036   O.017
        P.212   R.114   R.251   S.091
        S.380   T.070   T.129   W.217.
    See also historicity

    written by Joseph Smith
        B.234   G.115   H.031   H.076
        R.264   V.015   W.232

original manuscript
    B.165   B.211   F.047   H.103
    H.105   H.113   H.201   J.064
    K.039   L.041   L.043   L.044
    M.238   N.082   O.023   O.024
    S.117   S.119   S.120   S.121
    S.172   S.174   S.175   S.178
    S.198   T.062   Z.009

other sheep
    C.204   C.249   H.209   M.048
    M.059   P.091   P.179   P.222
    S.429   T.022   T.029   W.202
    W.208   W.219

Ottinger, George M.
    J.093

overview of Book of Mormon
    B.248   C.063   C.107   C.226
    D.011   F.007   F.056   G.074
    H.125   H.163   L.058   L.075
    M.241   N.058   N.095   N.138
    O.009   O.016   O.034   P.185
    P.243   P.261   R.019   R.020
    R.029   R.068   R.096   R.117
    R.126   R.233   R.239   S.135
    S.370   S.398   S.418   S.433
    T.020   T.030   W.193   W.200
    W.253   Y.005

Padilla gold plates
    M.050

Palmyra
    B.051

parable
    B.239   T.149

parallelisms
    B.259   C.223   C.235   F.016
    L.103   M.124   P.040   P.042
    P.044   P.045   P.046   R.352
    S.335   S.365   S.434   W.067.
See also Hebraisms

antithetical
    P.039   P.048
parenting
    B.217   H.130   R.025
parents teach children
    A.022   A.033   H.007   H.025
    H.027   R.036   S.257   T.072
Passover
    W.134. *See also* Jewish festivals
peace
    C.264   H.178   M.138   R.033
    T.211
People of Ammon. *See* Anti-Nephi-Lehies
perplexity
    S.055
Phelps, William W.
    J.063
Phoenicians
    C.133   C.140   J.040   J.069
    S.331
plagiarism
    B.227   L.011   R.229   T.107
poetry
    B.256   B.259
    ancient
        F.016   H.104   P.042   P.046
        R.349   S.434   T.131. *See also*
        Hebraisms; Nephi's psalm
polygamy
    M.134   R.239   W.205
Polynesians, origin
    A.020   B.035   B.289   C.100
    C.116   C.169   D.005   H.233
    J.046   K.024   K.025   L.085
    M.230   P.060   P.128   P.131
    P.138   R.238   S.054   S.297
Popul Vuh. *See* ancient writings in the Americas
population
    C.120   D.033   S.287   S.302
    S.331   S.337   T.116   T.145
    W.033   W.034   W.094. *See also*
    longevity

Pratt, Orson
    A.076   P.203   W.195
Pratt, Parley
    H.147   H.154   W.195
prayer
    A.069   B.103   B.219   C.166
    C.257   D.059   D.061   E.027
    E.030   H.032   H.125   K.003
    L.106   L.121   M.005   M.016
    M.122   O.015   P.072   S.206
    S.386   T.183   W.095   W.210
pride
    B.047   B.075   B.151   F.048
    H.036   J.073   L.073   M.171
    P.127   P.293   R.209   S.123
    U.002   W.226
priestcraft
    N.121
Priesthood
    M.193   M.200   P.149   W.199
    W.254
    Aaronic
        S.201
    among the Nephites
        C.207   M.200   N.121   P.145
        P.165   S.179   S.195   S.201
        S.218   S.397   W.204
    Christ's teachings concerning
        S.195
    Melchizedek
        S.201   S.218   W.097   W.204
    offices
        B.144   P.145   P.149
    ordinances
        P.061   S.179
    restoration
        A.057   B.168   C.214   M.175
        R.248
printer
    G.070   K.039
printer's manuscript
    D.008   H.103   H.105   H.113
    L.039   L.044   M.067   S.117
    S.120   S.198   Z.009. *See also*
    manuscript

promised land
    C.176   C.207   E.012   F.041
    L.019   M.242   M.243   N.011
    N.021   N.094   P.036   P.130
    P.182   P.217   P.254   R.137
    R.234   R.243   R.253   R.281
    R.288   R.323   R.339   S.078
    S.277   S.383   T.040   T.097
    T.194   W.028   W.109   W.157
    W.193

pronunciation guide
    M.218   P.066   R.046

prophecies
    A.031   C.005   C.012   C.015
    C.018   C.031   C.047   C.195
    C.220   C.250   C.252   C.253
    D.041   E.014   F.010   F.054
    F.059   F.061   G.108   G.118
    H.129   H.224   J.068   K.013
    L.002   L.076   L.084   N.086
    N.122   P.218   P.302   R.259
    R.270   R.277   S.028   S.127
    S.312   S.318   T.031   T.180
    W.005   W.026   W.027   W.028
    W.040   W.148   W.152

prophecy
    M.002   N.064   N.065   N.090
    P.100   P.301   R.001   R.193
    R.304   S.426

prophetic curse
    P.047

prosperity
    B.066   B.123   B.151

publication of the Book of Mormon
    B.129   B.238   C.048   G.049
    G.101   H.182   J.062   J.068
    J.097   K.039   K.041   M.147
    O.021   P.201   R.344   S.135
    S.144   S.181   S.203   S.212
    S.223   S.258   T.174   W.183
    W.232

purpose of the Book of Mormon
    B.022   B.023   B.024   B.025
    B.026   B.076   B.077   B.095
    B.100   B.111   B.112   B.119
    B.120   C.005   C.104   C.256
    F.063   H.108   K.043   L.104
    M.101   M.103   M.111   M.248
    N.058   N.109   N.113   P.099
    P.219   P.267   R.233   R.244
    R.250   R.272   R.283   R.349
    S.006   S.058   S.154   S.157
    T.046   T.161   W.226   W.252

Quetzalcoatl
    A.010   B.021   C.094   H.039
    H.179   H.215   M.162   P.187
    P.188   S.249   S.250   W.031
    W.257

Qumran
    N.069

racial beliefs
    J.099   R.005

Rafinesque
    C. S.   N.057

read the book, advice to
    A.019   B.053   B.086   B.102
    B.104   B.107   B.191   B.213
    B.272   C.219   C.229   C.254
    D.025   F.035   G.043   G.097
    H.174   J.091   K.001   K.042
    M.009   M.038   M.111   M.115
    M.189   M.221   O.010   P.010
    P.033   P.073   P.124   P.168
    P.195   P.200   P.305   R.004
    R.014   R.018   R.038   R.043
    R.276   R.318   R.325   R.331
    R.332   S.022   S.144   S.163
    S.180   S.181   S.182   S.187
    S.267   S.272   S.381   T.045
    T.073   T.077   T.096   T.110
    T.112   V.011   W.173   W.272
    W.288   Y.007

record keeping
    B.282   P.031   P.055   P.152
    P.237   R.342   W.116

records that became the Book of Mormon
    C.182   H.049   H.203   I.015
    J.048   L.106   M.078   M.228
    R.030   R.167   R.172   R.220
    T.035   T.036   T.037   T.170
    T.200   V.017. *See also* large plates of Nephi; Lehi's record; small plates of Nephi

reference books
    B.116   B.139   B.141   B.154
    B.210   B.212   C.254   E.040
    F.002   G.063   G.066   H.085
    H.103   H.127   I.001   L.044
    L.092   M.078   M.158   R.037
    R.066   R.116   R.165   R.166
    S.352   S.372   S.438   T.115
    T.176   U.004   V.002

remember
    C.066   M.186   M.187

repentance
    B.098   C.084   C.090   D.003
    G.064   H.200   I.020   L.009
    M.212   M.229   N.034   N.068
    P.092   P.095   R.026   R.107
    R.333   R.336   S.024   S.032
    T.114   T.120   W.210   W.235

responses to Book of Mormon critics
    A.018   B.194   B.235   C.001
    F.042   G.113   H.031   H.115
    H.156   I.014   I.017   I.022
    L.011   L.080   M.159   M.184
    M.254   N.038   N.047   N.050
    N.057   N.077   P.151   P.177
    P.246   P.270   P.271   P.276
    P.277   P.280   Q.004   R.032
    R.072   R.089   R.217   R.228
    R.229   R.230   S.011   S.019
    S.139   S.156   S.182   S.187
    S.205   S.371   S.404   T.052
    T.054   T.090   T.097   T.107
    U.011   W.041   W.046   W.049
    W.050   W.156   W.256

Restoration
    E.015   F.010   F.059   H.003
    H.204   L.084   M.205   P.098
    P.120   S.141

resurrection
    H.209   L.098   M.060   M.071
    M.205   N.110   N.125   P.084
    P.178   R.268   S.056   S.176

revelation
    N.048   P.236   R.047   R.235

revelation, continuing
    B.029   B.091   B.222   L.080
    M.066   N.033   P.002   P.077
    P.135   P.237   P.239   P.262
    P.268   P.271   R.223   R.224
    R.259   R.277   R.329   S.029
    S.073   T.005   T.032   W.255
    W.283   W.284

Revelation, book of
    C.227   M.044

Reynolds, George
    V.006

Rigdon, Sidney
    C.068   M.155   R.211

righteousness
    B.216   B.276   T.094

River of Nephi
    C.134

Roberts, B. H.
    M.013   M.014   M.015   M.018
    W.059   W.078   W.101   W.121

rod of iron
    H.041

sacrament
    A.054   B.029   G.117   H.004
    L.124   R.245   S.068   W.099

salvation
    C.178   C.251   D.002   D.042
    H.069   L.116   M.113   M.118
    M.198   N.065   N.125   P.061
    S.186   T.082   T.183   V.020
    W.180   W.210   W.211

Samuel the Lamanite
    B.132   B.157   B.256   C.077
    G.024   P.303   R.082   R.088
    R.123   S.007   S.041   S.055
    W.227

sanctification
    L.119   M.198   M.206   P.170
    V.008

Sariah
    A.032   D.022   R.074   Y.003

Satan
    A.078   C.022   D.043   M.053
    M.075   M.105   S.145   S.384
    T.121   W.153   W.236   W.280

scimitar
    H.019   H.194. *See also* warfare
sealed portion
    I.016   M.098   M.102   P.236
sealing powers
    J.010
Second Coming
    A.073   B.105   S.028   T.173
2 Nephi, book of
    A.090   B.018   L.096   L.116
    L.117   M.089   M.121   M.201
    N.111   P.180   S.005   U.005
    V.007   V.009   W.226
secret combinations
    B.057   C.024   C.026   C.038
    C.253   D.055   H.133   L.107
    N.086   P.147   P.150   R.124
    R.348   S.114   S.123   T.038
    W.008   W.030   W.129
seer
    G.107. *See also* choice seer
seer stone
    L.018   R.221   S.303   T.178
    Y.004
Sermon on the Mount
    B.221   J.071   M.049   M.059
    M.072   N.120   R.225   R.314
    S.395   W.095   W.107   W.108
    W.166. *See also* Lord's prayer
service
    B.150   S.132
sexual morality
    T.188
Shakespeare
    C.037   S.243   T.086
sheep. *See* other sheep
Sherem
    T.121   W.235
sign seeking
    P.054
silk
    C.188   S.317   S.322   T.182
simile curses
    M.245

simplified or modernized versions of the Book of Mormon
    F.038   H.089   H.131   I.004
    P.038   R.181   S.406   T.181
    W.013   W.250
sin
    G.039   G.068   L.073   M.211
    M.229   T.082   T.084
small plates of Nephi
    C.109   G.030   M.236   N.126
    O.017   P.031   R.113   R.170
    R.171   T.119   W.077. *See also* records that became the Book of Mormon
Smith, Emma
    A.053   H.092   K.040   P.094
    P.271   S.170   T.062   T.063
    Y.023
Smith, Ethan *(View of the Hebrews)*
    B.160   C.153   N.043   P.028
    R.213   R.230   R.231   R.265
    R.298   W.059   W.119
Smith, Joseph
    A.060   B.003   C.215   C.263
    D.063   E.051   H.148   H.153
    H.156   J.062   J.063   M.011
    M.065   M.121   M.202   M.203
    M.204   N.026   N.091   P.052
    P.122   R.041   R.116   R.133
    R.144   R.260   R.277   R.280
    R.310   R.329   R.344   S.051
    S.134   S.159   S.402   S.404
    W.005   W.028
    heavenly visitations
        C.086   G.093   M.156   M.175
        P.087   R.168   W.279
    interest in antiquities
        A.035   C.139
    responded to provincial opinions of his time
        B.281   G.115   M.264   N.036
        N.049   N.080   P.206   T.084
        T.090
    treasure searching
        A.050

Smith, William
    P.167   W.233

Smithsonian
    S.296   W.256

Spaulding manuscript
B.004	B.160	C.068	C.069
F.006	H.093	L.109	M.035
M.235	O.034	P.086	R.044
R.086	R.090	S.171	S.265
T.111	W.289	Y.018	Y.019

Spaulding theory
A.055	B.195	B.250	B.280
C.153	C.218	F.006	H.073
H.093	H.140	H.153	J.065
L.109	M.155	M.235	M.255
N.006	O.022	P.021	P.086
P.089	P.255	P.269	P.277
R.041	R.073	R.086	R.211
R.242	R.263	R.274	R.344
S.143	T.024	T.052	W.046
W.156	Y.019		

Spaulding, Solomon
    B.158   J.050   S.389

spirit world
    N.125

steel
B.021	B.230	I.009	I.012
I.023	N.048	O.008	Q.002
S.090	S.091	S.137	W.214. *See*

also iron; metals

Stela 5, Izapa
C.137	G.040	G.114	J.026
J.029	N.099	P.037	R.007
S.422	W.256. *See also* tree of life		

sticks of Judah and Ephraim
A.030	A.063	B.036	B.243
H.157	M.177	M.178	M.181
P.017	P.018	P.091	P.180
P.234	P.249	R.021	R.039
S.207	S.347	S.405	S.408
S.409	S.410	T.023	W.022
W.180	W.283		

stone box
B.128	C.083	C.093	C.094
C.097	C.212	C.213	H.076
P.113	P.261	W.290	

stories from the Book of Mormon for children
A.001	A.003	A.012	A.016
A.025	A.034	B.038	B.039
B.040	B.134	B.135	B.209
B.240	B.262	B.263	B.267
C.016	C.231	C.258	C.259
D.024	E.011	E.027	E.028
E.029	F.013	F.019	F.020
F.021	F.022	F.052	G.002
G.003	G.004	G.005	G.006
G.007	G.008	G.009	G.010
G.011	G.012	G.013	G.014
G.015	G.016	G.017	G.018
G.019	G.020	G.021	G.022
G.023	G.024	G.025	G.026
G.087	G.088	G.089	H.084
H.090	H.118	H.199	I.003
J.018	J.043	J.044	J.067
J.076	J.080	J.081	J.082
J.083	J.084	J.085	J.086
J.087	J.088	J.089	J.090
K.031	K.032	K.033	K.053
L.038	L.052	L.059	L.060
L.061	L.062	L.072	L.075
L.083	M.036	M.037	M.233
M.240	M.253	N.003	N.004
N.020	N.021	P.074	P.092
P.108	P.109	P.126	P.211
P.303	R.307	S.062	S.416
S.423	T.118	W.169	W.170
W.171	W.179		

Stowell, Josiah
    J.063

straight/strait
    W.079

study guide
A.074	B.030	B.070	B.131
B.138	B.182	B.184	B.278
B.288	C.071	C.152	C.254
E.003	H.028	H.089	H.090
J.013	J.014	J.096	K.009
L.092	L.093	L.097	M.221
M.234	M.263	P.010	P.081
P.082	P.189	P.301	R.020
R.038	R.162	S.049	S.050
S.098	S.124	S.345	T.130
T.134	W.036	W.155	W.176

subtitle
A.062   M.196

Sumerians
F.004

survivors
T.095

sword of Laban. *See* Laban, sword of

symbols
M.010   N.066   O.012   O.014
P.047   P.197   R.202   R.350
S.033   S.035   T.092   T.093
W.007   W.154

synagogues
W.113

teaching aids
B.121   B.140   B.141   B.177
C.123   G.081   N.124   O.026
R.177   R.295   S.076   S.257
T.112   T.177   T.203   V.004
V.005   W.105   W.288

Teancum
C.113   R.083

Teichert, Minerva Kohlhepp
E.004   J.075

temple worship
L.123   M.191

ten commandments
C.193   C.228   I.019   P.223
P.248   R.205   S.034

testify of Jesus Christ
B.024   B.079   B.087   B.147
B.148   B.152   B.171   B.214
B.222   B.244   B.247   B.249
C.198   D.055   D.060   D.064
E.045   F.017   F.060   G.112
H.008   H.116   H.149   H.150
H.177   H.208   H.223   I.013
I.022   K.022   K.038   K.044
L.031   L.058   M.032   M.033
M.055   M.086   M.092   M.100
M.107   M.123   M.182   M.192
M.196   M.222   N.012   N.052
N.109   O.005   P.012   P.016
P.102   P.106   P.111   R.045
R.048   R.139   R.150   R.152
R.227   R.233   R.250   R.269
R.283   R.291   R.294   R.321
R.326   R.347   S.012   S.377
T.012   T.015   T.016   T.018
T.019   T.029   T.032   T.046
T.059   T.119   T.122   V.009
W.013   W.114   W.147   W.167
W.178

testimonies of the Book of Mormon
A.027   B.010   B.053   B.063
B.113   B.167   B.169   B.273
C.006   C.034   C.048   C.110
C.122   C.149   C.170   C.177
C.181   C.190   C.191   C.192
C.219   C.256   D.009   D.014
D.017   D.019   E.017   E.018
E.036   F.025   G.042   G.098
G.101   H.034   H.050   H.159
I.007   J.049   J.078   J.095
K.002   K.003   K.043   L.078
L.082   L.086   L.101   M.006
M.031   M.094   M.160   M.251
M.256   N.060   O.031   P.003
P.050   P.064   P.093   P.224
P.231   P.275   P.287   P.304
R.018   R.125   R.149   R.155
R.212   R.270   R.278   R.309
S.013   S.022   S.023   S.146
S.260   S.391   T.011   T.014
T.056   T.063   T.064   T.065
T.088   T.132   W.038   W.044
W.051   W.062   W.188   W.207
W.286

testimony
D.058   D.059   H.006   L.097
M.115   S.025   S.111   T.049
T.132

textual changes
H.113

theophany
T.081   W.125

thieves and robbers
W.115   W.117

Three Nephites
    B.052   B.062   G.027   H.023
    H.129   H.170   J.015   K.055
    L.057   N.087   N.088   R.216
    S.400   W.251

throne theophany
    O.030

Title of Liberty
    B.099   F.018   L.004   S.444
    T.102

title page
    B.273   H.108   I.022   K.038
    L.099   M.186   R.163   R.283
    S.203   S.433

topical indexes
    B.279   B.288   C.010   G.120
    L.050   M.041   M.101   M.250
    O.026   P.071   P.080   P.081
    P.184   R.166   R.311   S.388
    S.407   T.115   U.002   W.149
    W.184

Tower of Babel
    B.207   I.011   L.081   L.087
    O.001   S.138   S.300   T.039
    W.268

tract
    R.116   W.200   W.262

translation
    A.037   A.041   A.056   A.081
    B.033   B.129   B.202   B.203
    B.284   C.044   C.086   C.161
    C.209   C.213   C.214   C.215
    C.236   C.248   E.051   F.043
    G.093   H.001   H.071   H.092
    H.198   H.203   H.206   J.098
    K.040   K.041   K.046   L.018
    M.065   M.088   M.239   N.008
    N.012   N.024   N.091   P.006
    P.007   P.070   P.122   P.201
    Q.004   R.052   R.099   R.100
    R.196   R.218   R.221   R.232
    R.242   R.252   R.266   R.272
    R.279   S.104   S.115   S.121
    S.122   S.134   S.164   S.170
    S.212   S.213   S.225   S.244
    S.343   S.354   S.396   T.005
    T.030   T.062   T.178   V.022
    W.048   W.050   W.081   W.138
    W.139   W.141   W.162   W.172
    W.194   W.215   W.216   W.221
    Y.004   Z.010

translation from English
    C.186   E.033   F.045   J.019
    J.054   K.052   L.023   L.109
    M.096   N.104   P.016   R.126
    S.147   S.413   T.089   T.128
    U.008

transoceanic crossings
    B.015   C.055   C.081   C.095
    C.132   C.140   C.141   C.142
    C.148   D.004   G.083   G.084
    G.103   H.055   H.061   J.040
    J.094   N.048   P.181   S.002
    S.083   S.162   S.250   S.297
    S.324   S.338   T.116   T.167
    W.206   W.258   W.268   Y.012

tree of life
    B.146   B.155   B.208   B.270
    C.083   C.137   C.145   C.200
    G.040   G.114   G.116   H.041
    J.011   J.021   J.026   J.029
    J.036   J.100   M.010   M.191
    N.066   N.099   N.101   O.019
    P.037   R.007   R.297   T.057
    W.257   W.258   W.276   W.277.
    See also Lehi, dream of

tribal structure
    S.337   T.170   T.196

tumbaga
    P.306   S.238. *See also* gold plates; metals

Twain, Mark
    C.224

two thousand stripling warriors
    B.048   B.108   C.023   G.011
    G.089   H.118   N.097   T.202

types
    J.100   M.129   M.191   R.347
    R.351   S.426   S.435   T.047
    T.055   T.082   T.142   T.158
    T.173

United States
    A.027   B.074   B.081   B.083
    B.090   B.281   C.024   C.253
    E.012   M.242   P.130   P.136
    P.217   P.272   R.281   R.293
    R.315   T.003   T.006   T.040
    W.193. *See also* constitution, United States

Urim and Thummim
    B.142   B.228   C.086   C.222
    H.066   H.082   H.196   H.198
    K.040   L.018   N.024   P.053
    P.167   Q.004   R.053   R.145
    R.183   R.184   R.242   R.252
    R.279   S.183   S.214   S.225
    S.274   S.344   S.365   S.379
    S.403   T.178   W.188   W.189
    W.216   W.253   W.266   Y.004

"vineyard"
    T.213

wandering Jew
    G.027

war
    B.126   C.060   E.022   F.036
    G.035   G.036   G.081   H.132
    H.145   H.146   M.127   M.138
    M.145   N.046   N.066   N.068
    P.013   P.026   P.146   P.182
    Q.005   R.191   R.353   S.253
    S.444   W.089

warfare
    B.115   B.137   D.012   G.036
    G.038   H.012   H.014   H.017
    H.018   H.019   H.020   H.047
    H.145   H.146   H.165   H.194
    I.009   K.007   L.122   M.129
    M.167   N.027   N.072   N.079
    P.297   R.060   R.095   R.201
    R.203   R.312   S.298   S.320
    S.321   T.094   T.133   T.142
    T.158   T.196   W.018   W.021
    W.030   W.057   W.076   W.124

weights and measurements
    F.004   H.115   J.061   P.146
    R.085. *See also* monetary systems

welfare
    A.008

wheel
    C.096   C.097   F.032   S.330
    W.256   W.257

Whitmer family
    M.146   O.024   P.096

Whitmer, David
    A.042   A.051   B.158   B.165
    B.193   C.040   C.070   C.191
    D.008   D.009   H.206   J.055
    L.047   M.238   M.239   M.259
    M.260   M.262   P.097   R.097
    R.160   R.240   R.241   S.150
    S.264   S.400   T.063   W.159

wickedness
    C.194

witness of the Holy Ghost
    B.061   B.271   E.058   H.026
    H.080   H.226   L.109   M.048
    M.099   M.132   M.153   N.017
    R.145   R.276   S.027   S.111
    T.184   W.026   W.121   W.245.
    See also Holy Ghost

witnesses
    A.007   A.036   A.044   A.048
    A.049   B.130   B.149   B.195
    B.218   B.225   C.012   C.017
    C.048   C.053   C.167   C.174
    C.221   D.044   E.009   F.044
    H.071   H.077   H.080   H.226
    I.010   J.056   J.059   J.068
    K.039   L.063   L.080   L.098
    L.120   M.131   M.152   M.153
    M.173   M.251   M.256   M.260
    N.006   N.083   N.084   N.091
    O.022   O.027   P.008   P.089
    P.094   P.134   P.164   P.221
    P.230   P.239   P.240   P.254
    R.062   R.063   R.097   R.134
    R.144   R.145   R.165   R.175
    R.239   R.256   R.267   R.269
    R.277   R.292   S.094   S.095
    S.114   S.126   S.161   S.168
    S.173   S.181   S.205   S.208
    S.209   S.211   S.212   S.217
    S.396   S.403   T.038   T.065
    T.109   T.111   T.217   V.007
    V.023   W.159   W.161   W.175

    W.189   W.191   W.203   W.220
    W.245   W.261   W.262   Y.001
    Y.017

women
    B.065   B.196   B.287   C.187
    D.022   D.034   E.043   G.078
    H.229   S.348   W.269   Y.003

wordprint
    H.022   H.139   K.004   L.034
    L.035   L.036   N.034   R.296
    T.172   W.125   W.256   Y.004

Words of Mormon
    R.171   R.173

"written for our day"
    B.075   B.096   B.266   D.056
    J.016   L.053   L.090   M.083
    M.085   M.206   M.216   M.226
    R.009   R.170   R.349   S.145
    S.194   S.312   S.377   T.073
    T.170   T.173   V.001   W.008
    W.027   W.148   W.155   W.199
    W.237   W.273   W.293

Young, Brigham
    A.075   R.059

Zarahemla
    C.059   R.179   T.140   Z.001

Zedekiah
    E.032   N.002   S.242   S.284

Zeezrom
    R.092

Zelph
    B.208   G.072   M.025

Zeniff
    J.017   N.107   Z.004

Zenock
    J.012   P.062   S.219

Zenos
    C.202   H.122   L.100   P.062
    R.112   S.035   S.067   S.219
    T.098   T.197   W.088

Zion
    B.050   N.094   P.222   R.334
    W.193

Zion's Camp
    G.072

Zoram
    B.014   R.081

Zoramites
    H.032   R.101   S.113   W.294
    Z.015

Zosimus
    W.098